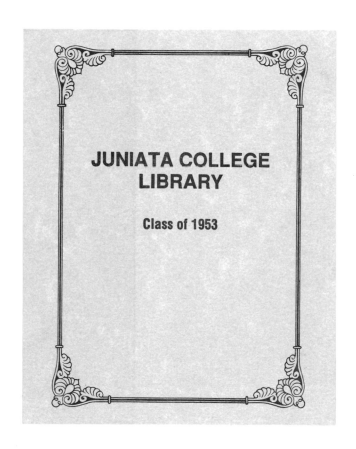

W i l h e l m   I I

Kaiser Wilhelm II, 1891

Lamar Cecil

WILHELM II

Prince and Emperor, 1859–1900

The University of North Carolina Press

Chapel Hill and London

The paper in this book meets the guidelines for permanence and
durability of the Committee on Production Guidelines for
Book Longevity of the Council on Library Resources.

98 97 96 95 94   6 5 4 3 2

This book was published with the assistance of
the H. Eugene and Lillian Lehman Fund
of the University of North Carolina Press.

Library of Congress Cataloging-in-Publication Data

Cecil, Lamar.
Wilhelm II, prince and emperor, 1859–1900.

Bibliography: v. , p.
Includes index.
1. William II, German Emperor, 1859–1941.
2. Germany—Kings and rulers—Biography. 3. Germany—
History—William II, 1888–1918. I. Title.
DD229.C4 1989   943.08′4′0924 [B]   88-27798
ISBN 0-8078-1828-3 (alk. paper)

For
M a r y   a n d   E m m a

Contents

viii | *Contents*

Illustrations

The photograph inscribed "I bide my time" is from Gen. Leopold V. Swaine, *Camp and Chancery in a Soldier's Life* (London, 1926), and is reproduced by permission of John Murray, Ltd. All other photographs are from the collection in the Royal Archives, Windsor Castle, copyright reserved, and are reproduced by gracious permission of Her Majesty, Queen Elizabeth II.

Preface

KAISER WILHELM II, in death no less than in life, manages to confound and annoy those who must deal with him. For a biographer, the last German Kaiser and King of Prussia poses three difficulties as a subject. A sovereign of autocratic pretensions, his imprint on imperial Germany was substantial, and the record for such a ruler is consequently staggering in its enormity. I can assert no claim to have examined more than a part of either the archival or, especially, the printed record. Wilhelm II was, moreover, an exceedingly foolish man, so that to explain—and sometimes merely to relate—what he did or said reduces a biographer to the greatest perplexity. Finally, he lived to a great, though hardly serene, old age. Born well before Bismarck became his grandfather's minister-president in 1862, he died early in June 1941, only days before Adolf Hitler ordered the Wehrmacht's ill-fated invasion of Russia.

Wilhelm II occupied the German throne for more than thirty years, but his connection with his subjects was tenuous indeed and only in a rarefied sense was he a part of the Germany at large over which he ruled so maladroitly. In all his long life, Wilhelm knew perhaps no more than several hundred Germans, and perhaps only ten or twenty men (and no women other than his wife) could be fairly described as being either his intimate friends or persons with whom he had a steady association. Almost all of these people were great figures drawn from the government, the military, or society. This coterie, grouped around the throne and dependent on it for their offices and other rewards, successfully insulated their sovereign against any influences that might try to penetrate its defenses, and as a result the Kaiser lived behind what one of Bismarck's successors referred to as a "Chinese wall." Wilhelm II, besides, was only spasmodically at the heart of the action in Berlin. He much preferred moving about with his handful of adjutants and advisors to regimental exercises in Potsdam or more distant and obscure garrisons, to aristocratic hunting preserves in Silesia and the mark of Brandenburg, or cruising in his yacht to the blue fiords of Norway, where he lingered for weeks on end every summer. This meant that the responsibility for the day-to-day conduct of affairs rested with the statesmen he appointed, but, even so, they had to be wary of the Kaiser. Wilhelm ruled Germany, in that nothing, whether in the governmental personnel of Prussia and the empire or in the policies these servants devised, could happen without his approval. Those who surrounded the throne therefore learned that a courtier's most prized asset was to be able to divine how to manipulate Wilhelm II's many prejudices.

Even when in Berlin, coaxed to his desk to attend to the matters which he alone could formally decide, the last Kaiser was phlegmatic and easily bored. He did not at all enjoy work, rejoicing instead in pageantry and the superficial trappings of authority. He found entire bodies of documents intolerable to read, or at least to finish. Newspapers had to be reduced to clippings in order to guarantee his attention, and when he said that he had not once read the German constitution he surely meant it. He never learned to listen, to reason, or to understand that sound decisions required a thorough scrutiny of the material bearing on the problem at hand. The last Kaiser's most pronounced—and most fatal—characteristic was his habitual inclination to act almost entirely on the basis of his personal feelings. The most momentous decisions in his early life—his renunciation of his English mother and her country, his embracing the life and ethos of a Prussian lieutenant, his implementation in the mid-1890s of a reactionary domestic regime, and the campaign a few years later to construct a gigantic navy—can be traced to vanity or to pique. This ineffable tendency to personalize everything stands revealed in the Kaiser's correspondence, which seldom amounts to more than a page or two of inconsequential froth, or in his marginal comments, littered with innumerable exclamation points, on countless documents, which display passion but rarely judgment.

If the last Kaiser was particular about what he did or what he read, eliminating anything that was unpleasant, difficult, or tedious, he was equally fastidious about people. Wilhelm trusted in his intuition, for he believed that his mind (with some assistance from the divine intelligence specially imparted to kings) would suffice to determine the proper course of action and his personality to win over anyone who might try to resist him. The Kaiser considered diplomacy his speciality, and it always attracted his attention more easily than internal affairs, which were relatively unglamorous. Diplomacy was to Wilhelm II not a profession managed by experts but rather an art reserved for himself and his royal "colleagues" in other European palaces, especially those in London and

St. Petersburg. But Wilhelm's diplomacy was hardly anything more than spontaneous talk on great ceremonial occasions, a flood of bombast that betrayed no serious preparation for such encounters. Everything had to center squarely on the monarch. His officials were to be composed only of those who agreed with him, and the criterion by which Wilhelm II valued them was not their ability but their loyalty to the crown. The same was true of the citizenry at large. Entire bodies of quite respectable subjects, such as diplomats and parliamentary deputies, could seldom achieve access to the throne simply because the Kaiser had contempt for their professions. There were other groups, notably the two out of every five Germans who were Catholics, of whom he was highly suspicious, and socialists or radicals by the hundreds of thousands, whom he considered to be criminals unworthy of his grace and favor. As for other nations, most were too contemptible for his attention. Wilhelm II despised the weak, the inconsequential, or the decaying, and consequently within Germany Prussia alone counted. Among the European powers, he believed that only Russia and Great Britain, the two nations who were Germany's equals, deserved to be objects of his highly personalized and utterly disastrous diplomacy.

A life of the last Kaiser, a man so strongly narcissistic in personality and so removed from the realities of life in imperial Germany, is therefore not an appropriate subject for displaying the nation's history. Even making allowance for the remoteness that is inevitably a sovereign's lot, Wilhelm II was uncommonly immune to the concerns and ambitions of his subjects. A history of Wilhelmine Germany would require delving into many areas of which his knowledge was at best superficial and his interest only spasmodic and uninformed. The last Kaiser's biography should be a portrait of this self-centered and isolated man who towered over his subjects but who was very distant from them, and it should reflect the narrowness of his perspective and the exclusivity of the society ranged about his throne. Such a book—a life rather than a times, a biography rather than a work of history—is what I have attempted to write. It may tell less than some will want to know about imperial Germany but not, I hope, less than may suggest how and why Wilhelm II developed into a man so singularly unsuited for the great role he was to play.

In this first volume I take Wilhelm II from his birth in 1859 to the end of 1900, the midpoint in his long life and a year that concluded with the arrival as chancellor of the wily and unprincipled Bernhard von Bülow, who would serve the Kaiser in that office for almost all of the next decade. The second and concluding volume will deal with the anxious twilight of imperial Germany, its ignominious military defeat in 1918, and the former Kaiser's long years of exile on the small estate in Holland that became his final refuge. Even in so long a study I have undoubtedly omitted much that might contribute to making Wilhelm II more intelligible. I have done so unwittingly, but there will be other imperial biographers in my wake who will try their hand at the Kaiser and perhaps succeed where I have failed. They, too, will have to wrestle with this disturbing, enigmatic sovereign and find their explanations for the problems he presents.

In my pursuit of Wilhelm II, which has now extended over two decades, I have acquired a great indebtedness to many people in many places that cannot be easily discharged. I am especially beholden to Her Majesty Queen Elizabeth II, who graciously permitted me to make use of the priceless documents and photographs gathered at the Royal Archives in Windsor Castle. There I encountered not only the formidable expertise but also the kind hospitality of the former Registrar of the Archives, Miss Jane Langton, and her successor, Miss Elizabeth H. Cuthbert. Miss Frances Dimond, the curator of photographs at the Archives, was most helpful in assembling the illustrations. The Marquess of Salisbury allowed me to examine at Hatfield House the papers of his ancestor, the third marquess, Queen Victoria's prime minister, and the late Prince Otto von Bismarck-Schönhausen extended a similar favor in Germany. Prince Friedrich-Ferdinand zu Schleswig-Holstein was a most genial and knowledgeable host at Glücksburg, and Count Rüdiger Schlitz genannt von Görtz and Baroness Anne-Katrin von Ledebur kindly made available their family papers. Hans Fleischer of Koblenz provided a useful introduction, while Hannelore Langner, Reed H. Cecil, and David Dickinson always were ready to offer me shelter while on research missions on opposite sides of the Atlantic. Mr. J. T. Coen expedited my use of the large store of materials in the Rijksarchief in Utrecht. Cambridge University Press, the University of Oklahoma Press, and John Murray, Ltd. kindly permitted the reproduction of copyrighted materials.

A number of my fellow historians of imperial Germany, men and women whose knowledge of Wilhelm II is very intimidating indeed, were generous in answering questions and attempted to set me straight on matters I had misconceived. I am especially indebted, and in many ways, to the late Hans W. Gatzke, John C. G. Röhl, and to Paul M. Kennedy, and also to the late Frederic B. M. Hollyday, Isabel V. Hull, Thomas A. Kohut, Otto Pflanze, Norman Rich, and Gerhard L. Weinberg. My colleagues, Robert W. McAhren and J. David Parker, on many occasions generously interrupted their own work to help me unravel problems generated by balky word processors or printers, and the exemplary staff of the Washington and Lee Undergraduate Library cheerfully responded more times than they would care to remember to my calls for assistance. Lewis Bateman, Executive Editor of the University of North Carolina Press, and Ron Maner, once my student at Chapel Hill and now my editor there, were both resourceful in shepherding the manuscript through to publication. The American Council of Learned Societies, the Social Science Research Council, the Virginia Association for Independent Colleges, the Research Board of the University of North Carolina at Chapel Hill, the Murphy Fund of the Department of History, and the Glenn Fund at Washington and Lee University all provided most welcome financial underwriting during a decade in which the value of the dollar was steadily worth fewer and fewer marks or pounds or guilders. Finally I wish to record the sense of indebtedness I feel to Washington and Lee University, which sustained me as I wrote, and especially to the President, John D. Wilson, to John W. Elrod, Vice-President and Dean of the College, and to the successive heads of the Department of History, William A. Jenks, H. Marshall Jarrett, and Robert W. McAhren, for their steadfast encouragement in my long enterprise. For all generosity and all wisdom that has come my way from others I am profoundly grateful.

Lamar Cecil
Lexington, Virginia
25 July 1988

Names Appearing in Text and Notes

Bigge	Sir Arthur Bigge, private secretary to Queen Victoria (1895–1901).
Bismarck	Prince Otto von Bismarck-Schönhausen, imperial chancellor (1871–1890) and minister-president of Prussia (1862–72, 1873–90).
Brauer	Arthur von Brauer, representative of Baden to the Federal Council in Berlin (1890–93), Baden minister of foreign affairs (1893–1905).
Bülow	Bernhard von Bülow (count 1899, prince 1905) state secretary of the Foreign Office (1897–1900), chancellor (1900–1909).
Caroline Mathilda	Princess of Schleswig-Holstein-Sonderburg-Glücksburg, sister of Wilhelm II's consort, the Kaiserin Augusta Victoria.
Charlotte	Princess of Prussia, sister of Wilhelm II.
Dönhoff	Countess Marie von Dönhoff, married (1886) to Bernhard von Bülow.
Dona	Princess Augusta Victoria of Schleswig-Holstein-Sonderburg-Augustenburg, married (1881) to Wilhelm.
Eissenstein	Baron von Eissenstein, Austro-Hungarian chargé, Berlin.
Empress Frederick	Victoria, Princess Royal of Great Britain, Wilhelm's mother.
Eulenburg	Count Philipp zu Eulenburg (1900 Prince zu Eulenburg-Hertefeld), diplomat and friend of Wilhelm II.
Botho Eulenburg	Count Botho zu Eulenburg, cousin of Philipp, minister-president of Prussia (1892–94).

Federal Council | The Federal Council (*Bundesrat*) was the upper house of the imperial parliament, to which all the German states contributed representatives in proportion to their population.

Fritz | Friedrich, Crown Prince of Prussia (1861–88) and Kaiser (1888).

Gelzer | Heinrich Gelzer, professor of Classical Philology and History, Jena.

Goblet | René Goblet, French foreign minister (1888–89).

Görtz | Countess Anna Görtz zu Schlitz, her husband Count Carl, and their son Count Emil, friends of Wilhelm and his parents.

Goluchowski | Count Agenor von Goluchowski, Austro-Hungarian foreign minister (1895–1906).

Grand Duke | Friedrich I, Grand Duke of Baden (1856–1907), uncle of Wilhelm II.

Grierson | Col. J. M. Grierson, British military attaché in Berlin, (1896–1901).

Hanotaux | Gabriel Hanotaux, French foreign minister (1894–95, 1896–98).

Hatzfeldt | Count Paul von Hatzfeldt-Wildenburg, German ambassador in London (1885–1901).

Heinrich | Prince Heinrich of Prussia, brother of Wilhelm II.

Herbert | Count Herbert von Bismarck, son of Chancellor Bismarck, state secretary of the Foreign Office (1885–90).

Herbette | Jules Herbette, French ambassador in Berlin (1886–96).

Hinzpeter | Dr. George Hinzpeter, Wilhelm's tutor (1866–77).

Hohenlohe | Prince Chlodwig zu Hohenlohe-Schillingsfürst, imperial chancellor (1894–1900).

Hollmann | Admiral Friedrich Hollmann, state secretary of the imperial Naval Office (1890–97).

Holstein | Friedrich von Holstein, counsellor in the Foreign Office (1880–1906).

Jagemann | Eugen von Jagemann, Baden minister of justice and the royal house (1881–93), representative to the Federal Council (1893–1903).

Kaiserin   Empress, referring either to Victoria, consort of Friedrich III, or Augusta Victoria, consort of Wilhelm II.

Kaiserin Friedrich   See Empress Friedrich above.

Kálnoky   Count Gustav Kálnoky von Köröspatak, Austro-Hungarian foreign minister (1881–95).

Kiderlen-Wächter   Alfred von Kiderlen-Wächter, German diplomat.

Knollys   Sir Francis Knollys, private secretary to the Prince of Wales (1870–1901).

Lascelles   Sir Frank Lascelles, British ambassador in Berlin (1896–1908).

Loebell   Friedrich Wilhelm von Loebell, imperial chancellery official and confidant of Bernhard von Bülow.

Malet   Sir Edward Malet, British ambassador in Berlin (1885–94).

Marschall   Baron Adolf Marschall von Bieberstein, state secretary of the Foreign Office (1890–97).

Münster   Count George zu Münster (1899 Prince Münster von Derneburg) German ambassador in Paris (1885–1900).

Noailles   Marquis Emmanuel de Noailles, French ambassador in Berlin (1896–1902).

Ponsonby   Sir Henry Ponsonby, private secretary to Queen Victoria (1870–95).

Radolin/Radolinski   Count Hugo von Radolinski (1888 Prince von Radolin), friend of Wilhelm's parents.

Rantzau   Count Kuno von Rantzau, German diplomat and son-in-law of Chancellor Bismarck.

Reichstag   The lower house of the imperial legislature, elected by universal, male franchise.

Ribot   Alexandre Ribot, French foreign minister (1890–92), premier (1892–93, 1895).

Russell   Col. Frank Russell, British military attaché, Berlin (1890–91).

Salisbury   Robert Arthur Talbot Gascoyne-Cecil, Third Marquess of Salisbury, Conservative prime minister, (1885–86, 1886–92, 1895–1902).

Schweinitz   Lothar v. Schweinitz, German ambassador in St. Petersburg (1876–92).

Senden Admiral Baron Gustav von Senden und Bibran, chief of the Naval Cabinet (1889–1906).

Spuller Eugène Spuller, French foreign minister (1889–90).

Swaine Col. Leopold V. Swaine, British military attaché in Berlin. (1882–89, 1891–96).

Széchenyi Count Imre Széchenyi, Austro-Hungarian ambassador in Berlin (1878–92).

Szögyényi Count Ladislaus von Szögyényi-Marich, Austro-Hungarian ambassador in Berlin (1892–1914).

Turban Ludwig Turban, president of the Baden State Ministry (1876–93), minister of the interior (1881–90).

Vicky Kaiserin Friedrich, see above.

Waddington William Waddington, French ambassador to Great Britain (1883–93).

Wilhelmstrasse Street in central Berlin on which many government officers were located, notably the Foreign Office at Number 76.

Wilhelm II

O n e

THE HEIR

WITH THE POSSIBLE exception of the Habsburgs, no royal family ever demonstrated so formidable a talent for marrying to advantage as the Protestant house of Saxe-Coburg. If the Catholic Habsburg emperors in Vienna steadily extended their domain by engaging their archducal sons to heiresses of equal birth, the Coburgs, an impoverished line whose isolated principality in central Germany never rose above the dignity of a grand duchy, began in the nineteenth century to marry above themselves. The Thuringian arrivistes—the "stud farm of Europe," as the Prussian statesman Otto von Bismarck described Coburg—chose their victims with discrimination and pursued them with tenacity. Occasionally misfortune dogged their ambitions, especially when Leopold of Coburg, married in 1816 to the heiress to the British throne, a year later suddenly found himself a childless widower. Consolation eventually appeared in a daughter of the French king, Louis Philippe, and Leopold lived to see one of their children become Empress of Mexico. In 1831, the Belgians elected Leopold as their ruler, and later one of his numerous nephews secured the hand of the Queen of Portugal. By the middle of the century the Coburgs' genealogical tentacles embraced parts of continental Europe over which the wizened Habsburgs had once held sway. The family's greatest nuptial triumph was the marriage King Leopold of the Belgians arranged in 1840 between another nephew, Prince Albert, and Queen Victoria of England. The Queen's mother had also begun her ascent from Coburg, for she was Leopold's sister. With typical Coburg strategy, years before she had married one of the dissipated sons of King George III of England. Victoria and Albert, destined to become man and wife, were thus first cousins.

The two children had been born within three months of one another in 1819, and Leopold soon began to plot their eventual marriage. Many obstacles, including Victoria's reluctance to marry anyone at all and the distaste of her uncle, King William IV, for the ambitious Coburgs, had to be overcome. The King conveniently died in 1837, advancing Victoria to the throne. Albert's kind and solemn manner and what the young Queen described as his "so excessively handsome" appearance, with his dark coloring and wonderfully brilliant blue eyes, won her over completely.

Prussia and Holland, the two leading Protestant monarchies in northern Europe, had resisted the Coburg nuptial tide, however, and throughout the eighteenth century and into the nineteenth the Hohenzollerns and Oranges either married their own kin or found their brides in a succession of German houses, whose dynastic mediocrity was underlined by the occasional more brilliant marriages both families contracted with the Romanovs in St. Petersburg. The house of Orange never passed into the Coburg orbit, but Prince Albert, with the encouragement of his uncle, King Leopold, eventually ensnared the Hohenzollerns. As early as 1844, he resolved to see his tiny daughter Victoria, who was called Vicky and who was then not yet four years old, one day occupy the Prussian throne.[1] In 1851, Princess Augusta, the wife of Prince Wilhelm, who was destined to succeed his childless brother King Friedrich Wilhelm IV, traveled to London to inspect the exhibition Prince Albert had organized at the Crystal Palace. Her son, Friedrich Wilhelm—known in the family as Fritz—accompanied her. She was on the lookout for a princess to whom he might some day be married. While in England, Augusta established a cordial friendship with Queen Victoria that would persist for almost forty years.

Among royalty, visions of marriage projects often began as the subjects of such maneuvers lay in their cradles, and these schemes were thereafter fervently pursued. Fritz was almost twenty when he first arrived in London in 1851 and thus was quite eligible for the altar. While little Princess Victoria, the eldest of the nine children Victoria and Albert would produce, was only ten, this did not seem to either mother grounds for postponing their preliminary soundings. The dynastic advantages were obvious, even though neither Victoria nor Albert, as Coburg descendants, had any great affection for the more powerful and aggressive Prussian Hohenzollerns. The prospect of forging an Anglo-Prussian marriage alliance was happily furthered when, during Fritz's second trip to England in 1855, he and Vicky quite spontaneously fell in love. Even though Vicky was not, strictly speaking, the German princess Augusta had sought for her only son, Fritz's mother nevertheless felt that she "possessed all the qualities needed to make a man happy." Queen Victoria in response assured Augusta that her child was "the right wife for the Prussian throne. She will not feel that in Germany she is 'on a foreign planet' but instead will quickly make herself at home."[2] Vicky and Fritz became engaged in September 1855, two months before the prospective bride's fifteenth birthday.

It is not difficult to appreciate the young couple's rapture. Fritz was a tall and handsome cavalier, and he had not yet developed the morosity that later would darken his outlook on life. Vicky possessed the beauty that had eluded her diminutive mother. Queen Victoria's chin was minimal and her eyes too prominent, but the Princess's features, like her figure, were well proportioned, and she had inherited her father's piercing blue eyes. The effect was certainly not electrifying—as it was in the case of Vicky's future sister-in-law, the exquisite Alexandra of Denmark—but very appealing. Vicky had a good mind, learning quickly and expressing herself well, but her active temperament needed a steadying hand. Prince Albert, who employed his eldest child as a sort of private secretary and who also served as her principal teacher, provided such an influence as long as he lived. She was the favorite of his many children, and Vicky adored him. "What a man that was, or rather what an angel," she reflected years after her father's death, "as good, as wise as he was clever and beautiful. How I did love him."[3] But Prince Albert died when Vicky was barely twenty-one, and thereafter she never had a counsellor capable of restraining her willfulness. Vicky had an uncurbable tendency, one that experience failed to alter, to do exactly as she pleased and to speak her mind with arresting bluntness, indifferent if not oblivious to the consequences of her behavior. She was charming and impressive but tryingly difficult.

Prince Albert not only had the power to make his daughter more temperate but also succeeded in instilling in her a respect for constitutional monarchy. He impressed upon Vicky the strong sense of duty and responsibility which, in his opinion, royal figures in the nineteenth century would be prudent to cultivate if they wished to retain their crowns. This lesson Vicky learned well, and such wisdom as she possessed was by and large a paternal inheritance. Her father's injunctions became for her articles of faith, fixidly held and blindly insisted upon no matter what barriers of history or what redoubtable personalities might rise up against them. Prince Albert's legacy, virtuous and enlightened in content, unhappily proved to be a liability when exported from England as a dogma designed to raise the Prussians from their reactionary backwardness. Vicky's inheritance from her mother was no happier. From Queen Victoria she derived some skill as a watercolorist and an astounding energy as a letter writer. But unfortunately her vehemence of expression as well as a predilection to instantaneous and sometimes incorrect judgment, a pride of place, and a belief that women of royal descent were not to be treated as the pliant handmaidens of men were also traits derived from her mother that in Berlin would prove highly unsuitable.

The prospect of the Anglo-Prussian dynastic connection that would result from a marriage between Vicky and Fritz encountered no serious objections in London, and indeed the prime minister, Viscount Palmerston, viewed the match as a strategic coup. "It will be of momentous significance for England and Europe," he assured Queen Victoria.[4] Prussian reactionaries, on the other hand, regarded the heir-apparent's marriage to an Englishwoman with considerable suspicion, if not actual hostility. Bismarck, then a prominent Prussian diplomat, was a leader of the opposition. "I don't like the English aspect of this marriage," he wrote to a friend in April 1856, "but it may be quite a good thing, for the Princess is praised as a woman of spirit and heart. . . . If she succeeds in leaving the Englishwoman at home and becomes a Prussian it will be a victory for our country. However, princely marriages usually give the house from which the bride comes influence in the one into which she weds, not the reverse. That is even more the case when the country of the wife is more powerful and more mature in its national development than that of her husband."[5]

After an engagement that lasted almost two and a half years, the couple were married on 25 January 1858 in the Chapel Royal, St. James Palace, and left shortly thereafter for Vicky's new home in Germany. Both Queen Victoria and Prince Albert admonished their daughter not to forget that she was an English princess, a distinction that in their opinion transcended the honors and titles she would acquire through marriage to a Prussian Hohenzollern. "While you must in every way avoid giving any appearance that you find your new fatherland wanting," Prince Albert wrote to Vicky a month after her marriage, "so must you certainly not create the impression as though you wish to lay aside or cast off your origins."[6] The advice was dutifully accepted. "What you say about my position is so right and is often a matter of reflection with me," Vicky replied. "If I was to lose sight of my English title and dignity I should do myself and my husband much harm, besides be forgetting my duty to you and England."[7] Vicky never questioned her father, and to a young girl without experience his advice seemed admirable. She would later admit, however, that the education devised by Prince Albert made it inevitable that she would come into conflict with the Prussian court.[8]

While the marriage initially proved very popular with the Prussian people, Vicky, who was barely seventeen, found soon after her arrival in

Berlin that Fritz's relatives regarded her with suspicion. The Hohenzollerns, generation after generation, were a cantankerous family, narrow-minded, self-centered, and quite humorless. They did not much like one another, and they certainly did not welcome outsiders. None of the dynasty, and especially Queen Elizabeth, the Bavarian-born consort of King Friedrich Wilhelm IV, had cared much for England. So great was the distaste of Fritz's aunt, the unpleasant dowager Grand Duchess Alexandrine of Mecklenburg-Schwerin, the sister and confidante of her brother Wilhelm, that she refused even to set foot in Vicky's palace. From the beginning of her marriage, Vicky felt alienated from the Hohenzollerns, whose stormy family relationships contrasted so poorly with the amicable and supportive household in which she had grown up.

Fritz's parents, the members of the clan to whom Vicky was most beholden, were especially taxing. Her father-in-law, Prince Wilhelm, who one day would become King, was a courtly man in his early sixties who was tireless in supervising every detail of his family's affairs. Conservative by nature, he was insistent on the maintenance of tradition and on the punctilious execution of court rituals. Wilhelm's enthusiasm for public spectacles was perhaps a reflection of the fact that he found little refuge in his private life. As a young man he had wanted to marry a Polish noblewoman, and only when his father had prevented this match had he turned to seek the hand of a suitable royal princess. Wilhelm took as his bride Augusta of Saxe-Weimar, who, not the passion of his youth, did not prove to be the solace of his old age. An intelligent if strong-willed and frenetic woman, Augusta talked and gesticulated constantly, entertained virtually without cessation, and wore out everyone in her entourage. She had an instinctive gift for upsetting her consort, who called her his "firebrand" (*Feuerkopf*). They lived apart for much of the year, since Augusta preferred the Hohenzollern palace at Coblenz or her own native Weimar to Berlin. Her absences did not disturb Wilhelm, who, Vicky once observed, enjoyed his freedom like a schoolboy on vacation.[9]

When Prince Wilhelm, who ascended the Prussian throne as King Wilhelm I early in 1861, was in an indulgent mood, Vicky could manage some affection for him. But most of the time she found her father-in-law's conservatism benighted, his fears about assaults on royal prerogative paranoic, and his endless interference in her family life very aggravating. King Wilhelm, who was notorious for his parsimony, prescribed when and where Vicky might travel, how many rooms she was to be allowed in the royal palaces, and how soon after she gave birth to her children she could appear in public. Like the other Hohenzollerns, Wilhelm I had no great admiration for England, a fact that understandably irritated Vicky.

It was all so exasperatingly un-British to Vicky. Writing of her father-in-law's opposition to making the Prussian ministry responsible to the parliament, as it was in London, rather than to the crown, she declared that "for anyone that has the priviledge [*sic*] (one cannot be thankful enough for) of being born in England *it is impossible* to think otherwise, but even if one was not born there common sense, I think, would tell one which side to take in this question."[10] King Wilhelm for his part never much liked Vicky, resenting the unfortunate liberal influence she exercised on the entirely too malleable Crown Prince.[11] This was no eccentric judgment, promoted by the King's lack of enthusiasm for his daughter-in-law. Grand Duke Friedrich I of Baden admired Fritz, whose sister he had married, but he agreed with Wilhelm I that Vicky played too dominating a role at home, so much so that the Grand Duke found it impossible to convey a sense of what an "almost inert tool" of his wife Fritz eventually became.[12]

Queen Augusta was even more a problem than the King. Vicky admired her mother-in-law's mental powers, which she admitted were greater than those of either Wilhelm I or Fritz. But it was this very intelligence that made the Queen so opinionated and peremptory.[13] Vicky found Augusta's petulant and unpredictable moods irksome and her incessant meddling a great annoyance. She particularly deplored the Queen's marked lack of appreciation for Fritz, whom Augusta regarded without much interest or even affection.[14] Fritz resented his mother's constant interference in family matters and sided with his father, whom he much preferred, in the frequent skirmishes between his parents. In politics, there was little sympathy between Vicky and Fritz on the one hand and the conservative King and Queen on the other, and this divergence, Vicky noted, was what drove the two households apart.[15]

No Englishwoman would have had an easy time of it at the Hohenzollern court, but Vicky fatally undermined her attempt to establish a place for herself in Berlin by insisting that she was her husband's partner, not his servant. The position of nuptial equality which she demanded, and got, outraged the Prussian aristocracy's conception of marriage, according to which the wife was expected to be the compliant mate of an omnipotent husband. Prussian nobles, Vicky complained to Queen Victoria, did not treat their wives with the consideration found in English society.[16] Furthermore, Vicky intended to make her views public. She drew a fine line between a woman who, like herself, freely stated her opinions and one who inappropriately became involved in political intrigues.[17] Vicky soon found, however, that her forthrightness of speech, even if it did not lead to actual political activity, was a distinct liability in Berlin society. It did not weigh in her favor that she was more clever than the aristocratic women who thronged the court, most of whom had little education but vast reaches of conventional piety.[18] Vicky's religious ideas, which held Christianity to be a liberal social value rather than a theological certainty, not surprisingly produced consternation in Wilhelm I's strictly orthodox retinue.[19] Her vigorous intellectual and artistic interests, in themselves a distinctly foreign element at the philistine court, were socially offensive to the Prussian aristocracy, for Hohenzollern etiquette could not accept the Princess's habit of seeking out artists in their ateliers, doctors in their clinics, and—what was worse—their being invited to receptions in her palace.[20] Vicky was also a snob. How poorly, in her opinion, did the Hohenzollerns' female courtiers compare with the glamor of aristocratic women in London society. The Prussian ladies in attendance, unlike those who served her mother, were poor, ill-dressed, thinly bejeweled, and aged in appearance. How modest was the palace china, how frugal the food.[21] Vicky never overcame her feeling that for all their accomplishments and power, the Hohenzollerns and their courtiers were parvenu in comparison to her own house, which she claimed was devoid of the spirit of caste-ridden "petitesse" that afflicted the Berlin court.[22]

The fall from grace of the English princess was rapid, and within only a few years Vicky found that she was regarded not only as different but as dangerous. The opprobrium that gathered around her coincided with the rise to power of Otto von Bismarck, a figure destined to play an unhappy role in Vicky's life. In September 1862, in the midst of a constitutional crisis between the King and the lower house of parliament, Wilhelm I summoned Bismarck, then the Prussian envoy in Paris, to become minister-president. Bismarck had assured the nervous sovereign that he was prepared to rule by royal decree until such time as the legislature bowed to the King's will. Once installed in office, he followed exactly that course until eventually the parliament surrendered. To Vicky, Bismarck's appointment was the ultimate capitulation by Wilhelm I to the forces of reaction. As early as 1859 she had described him as a "false and dangerous man," and two months before he became minister-president she wrote pessimistically to Queen Victoria that Bismarck was an unprincipled, unreliable, Anglophobic troublemaker.[23] Once Bismarck took office, matters became worse. Vicky redoubled her determination to lead Fritz into the ranks of the liberal opposition, even though this would create still more hostility between her husband and his conservative parents. In the summer of 1863, Fritz, at his wife's urging, publicly accused Bismarck of having violated the constitution. The result was a bitter outburst by Wilhelm I against his son and a barrage of hostile articles in the reactionary press against both the Crown Prince and his wife. Vicky did not flinch. "Fritz *adores* his Father," she wrote, "and till now in his eyes obedience and subordination was the first duty. Now I see myself in duty bound as a good wife and as a really devoted and enthusiastic *Prussian* (which I feel every day more that I am) of using all the influence I possess in making Fritz place his opinions and his political conscience above his filial feelings. I don't like meddling in politics—it's not a ladies' 'calling' (*Beruf*). I could have many friends if I said nothing but I wouldn't be a free born English woman in that case."[24] To Bismarck criticism was intolerable, even if it came from royalty, and he marked the Crown Princess as an enemy. Like Vicky, Fritz gradually settled into a life-long antipathy to the chancellor, whom he considered to be ruthless, devious, and too narrowly German in his outlook. On the day in 1862 that Bismarck assumed office, Fritz predicted with some accuracy that "poor Papa will have many a difficult moment at the hands of this false character!"[25]

For all her loathing for Bismarck and Prussian militarism and for the stiffness and provinciality of Berlin society, the Crown Princess recognized the great accomplishments of the Prussian people. "You know what a 'John Bull' I am," Vicky wrote to her mother in 1866, "and how enthusiastic about my [English] home. I must say the Prussians are a superior race, as regards intelligence and humanity, education and kind-heartedness, and *therefore* I hate the people all the more who by their ill government and mismanagement etc. rob the nation of the sympathies it *ought* to have. My affection to it is not blind but sincere, for I respect and admire their valuable and sterling good qualities."[26]

Vicky's protestations of Prussian virtues, although sincere, were superficial, and she was always thoroughly English at heart even if she did not always act so while in London. Returning to Berlin from a trip to England in 1863, she wrote to her mother, "Attached as I am to this country [Prussia] and anxious to serve it with might and main, the other [England] will ever remain the land of my heart and I shall ever feel the same pride of being home there, a child and subject of yours."[27] Vicky, unfor-

tunately, believed that her affection for her adopted land required bringing about its Anglicization insofar as politics was concerned, for this was
where her distaste for Prussia centered. Being headstrong and ignorant of
the complex political realities that then prevailed in Germany, she was
incapable of questioning the appropriateness of such a course. Nor was
she able to appreciate the difficulties this ambition presented and consequently the deftness with which it had to be pursued. The Crown Princess was remarkably insensitive in the way in which she trumpeted her
British viewpoint. In her speech, the word "our"—as in "our navy"—
meant England, not Germany. "Of course," she wrote to Queen Victoria
in 1866, "in Germany I *always* take the part of the *English*man, and in
England I try to stick up for the German."[28] This was pure perversity
and illustrates Vicky's irrepressible delight in provoking argument. Fritz
tended to be laconic, but his wife was passionate in expressing her views.
"I take great delight in a good argument," she once told a friend. Vicky
welcomed opposition, for she was convinced that she could persuade
those who disagreed with her that they were in error. Being certain that
she was right, Vicky in fact paid little attention to other people's opinions.[29] She was incapable of, or uninterested in, concealing her relish for
stirring up trouble, especially by making offensive comparisons. Her
niece, Princess Marie Louise of Schleswig-Holstein, like Vicky the offspring of an Anglo-German marriage, wrote in dismay about her aunt
that "when she was in Berlin, everything in England was perfect; when
she was in England, everything German was equally perfect."[30] Other
sympathetic observers were similarly alarmed, and it is hard not to agree
with one of Vicky's few close friends, Marie von Bunsen, that she was her
own worst enemy, refusing to realize how ill-suited her behavior was to
the exalted position she occupied in Germany.[31]

If Vicky's life in her new surroundings was often contentious and torn
between her English heritage and her Prussian future, Fritz more than
made up for his difficult family and Bismarck's iron regime. The bridal
couple were a well-suited pair. They loved one another without reserva-
tion, and there were no complications proceeding from family differences, disparity of rank, or religious incompatibility. Moreover, it was
endlessly gratifying to Vicky that Fritz fully shared her veneration of
Prince Albert. Later in life Fritz would declare that he had become the
man he was because of the influence his father-in-law and Vicky had
exercised, transforming him from a narrow German youth into a man of
the European west.[32] This was true enough, but it did not occur to Fritz

that as a result of having been appropriated by his wife and her family he would forfeit much of the popularity in Prussia that otherwise might have come his way.

Both husband and wife, like Prince Albert, believed that life was a thoroughly serious business, an earthly pilgrimage beset by dangers and temptations through which kings, no less than ordinary mortals, had to negotiate their way. But in personality husband and wife were utterly unalike, and of the two Vicky was considerably the more interesting. Although almost a decade younger than her groom, from the beginning Vicky presided over their household, just as Queen Augusta dominated King Wilhelm I. "A remarkable woman, so smart and with a charm that wins every heart," an admirer once wrote. "Everything must happen as she wishes and she gets what she wants."[33] Beware to those who crossed her, for Vicky, according to a friend, was "hardhearted and strong in her hatreds," a deficit of character she would pass on to her eldest son.[34] To those who saw her only casually, Vicky radiated self-confidence, energy, and intelligence—"all life and spirit, full of frolic and fun, with an excellent head, and *'a heart as big as a mountain,'* " the American plenipotentiary in Berlin reported two years before Vicky married.[35] She matured into a very attractive woman, but one who was opinionated, headstrong, and highly emotional.

Fritz, by contrast, was taciturn, undemanding, and malleable. His worldly English brothers-in-law found him rather dull.[36] A man of heightened religious feeling who rather morbidly kept his mind on the specter of premature death, Fritz was intensely proud of his ancestry, very entranced by the splendors of royal pomp, and insistent on being accorded the perquisites of his high station.[37] Fritz was extraordinarily handsome—"a German like Tacitus described them," according to the French Empress Eugénie—and was referred to throughout Germany as "Siegfried" or "the knight." Aware of the heroic impression he created, Fritz was fussy about his clothes and anxious that the enraptured public have no opportunity to realize that he was only five feet eight inches tall.[38] He delighted in sagas of the medieval German emperors and never developed an entirely realistic picture of the nation over which he one day would rule. Fritz inclined instead to idealistic visions, such as his entirely fatuous view, expressed in 1878 at the height of socialist agitation against the Hohenzollern monarchy, that "ruler and people now, God be praised, always work hand in hand in all matters rather than in conflict with one another."[39] Not long after his son made this observation, Wilhelm I was twice the victim of assassination attempts. Fritz had few intellectual interests and little taste for the arts, while Vicky was well read and an enthusiastic patron of painters and sculptors. Although absolutely fearless in battle, Fritz was neither assertive nor energetic. His admirer, the novelist Gustav Freytag, observed in 1870 that Fritz was "so kindhearted and pure in thought, and yet in many ways, so washed out (*fertig*) and in others like a child."[40] Even Vicky admitted that her otherwise perfect husband did not place a sufficient value on independence, a deficiency she typically attributed to his unfortunately not being an Englishman.[41]

The Crown Prince's parents had done little to promote any feeling of personal worth in their heir. Fritz had grown to manhood overshadowed by his father and unloved by his mother. The King was distant and uncommunicative, and he regarded his son, not without reason, as the creature first of his mother and then of his wife.[42] Although Fritz admired his father, their relationship was unsatisfactory. The King's proprietary overbearance often made Fritz angry, and he complained that it was a hard lot to be the heir of a man who was both a popular and successful monarch.[43] As a mature man, Fritz had little to do with the Empress Augusta, who thought her son immature. Fritz had no brothers and only one sister, who was seven years younger and to whom he was not very attached. His neglected and loveless childhood, so different from the sunny youth Vicky had enjoyed with her numerous siblings, made Fritz hesitant and lacking in confidence.[44] Consequently, Vicky's adoration and her unabashed self-esteem appealed greatly to him. Fritz's essentially suppressed character made him an excellent foil for his more spirited wife. Countess Walburga von Hohenthal, one of Vicky's ladies-in-waiting at the time of her marriage, declared that the bride "certainly was a little tyrant, and with a less chivalrous and devoted husband there might have been difficulties."[45] With Fritz there were none. He was always ready with sympathy, indulgence, and inexhaustible patience, though he complained on occasion that Vicky always had to be right. It was a role of which he never tired, even when his wife's intensity turned to hysteria, her positive exuberance to habitual petulance. His love sustained her in an increasingly alien world, while her encouragement instilled in Fritz a sense of worth denied him by his parents. Fritz's gratitude was as profound as his infatuation, and after more than twenty years of marriage he could declare that Vicky was "perfection itself as a woman."[46]

Early in the summer of 1858 Vicky discovered that she was pregnant. Although she had badly sprained her ankle just as her confinement began and then, at five months, tripped and fell on a chair, her health gave her physicians no cause for alarm.[47] Vicky's letters to Queen Victoria in the summer and fall of 1858 show no anxiety, and she appeared regularly at court functions and accompanied her husband on maneuvers. Shortly before the baby was due, however, Vicky's obstetricians began to suspect that the infant would not descend headfirst. Queen Victoria responded to this disturbing news by sending her own physician, Sir James Clark, to Berlin, where the approaching delivery was to take place, and a battery of German doctors was also stationed in readiness.

On 26 January 1859, just before midnight, Vicky went into labor, and the physicians summoned Dr. Eduard Martin, professor of obstetrics at the university in Berlin. He decided that Vicky's condition called for a sedative, after which he administered chloroform to the patient, whose accouchement was to take place in the same room in which King Friedrich Wilhelm IV and his brother, King Wilhelm I had been born at the end of the eighteenth century. Finally, at 2:45 on the afternoon of 27 January, the baby's rump appeared, then its legs, which were pressed up against the stomach and chest. At this point Martin gave the Crown Princess more choloroform and surgically extended the uterus. Using considerable force, he freed the baby's left arm, which was folded behind the head, after which the right arm and finally the head descended. The male child, for whose life Martin feared, momentarily appeared to the doctor to be dead, but after being slapped and doused in cold water he began to breathe and opened his eyes. Martin assumed that the infant, who was bruised on the left shoulder and elsewhere, was miraculously unimpaired by the prolonged and dangerous delivery.[48] Sir James Clark, who had witnessed the birth, at once assured Queen Victoria that her first grandchild was "in all respects a perfect child."[49] The baby was put out to a wet nurse, Fräulein Hage from Westphalia, who suckled him for the next eight months, while an English nanny, Miss Innocent, presided over the nursery. "Quite between ourselves," Vicky wrote to her mother, "I would not have had a German nurse come close to him for all the world."[50]

Three days after the baby's birth, his nurses noticed that his left arm was almost totally paralyzed. The physicians in attendance now discovered that in the course of delivery the shoulder had become dislocated and several ligaments torn. Moreover, the left shoulder was malformed, being abnormally thick between the top and the arm pit. The result was that the infant later had great difficulty sitting upright, for his head drooped to the left and his right shoulder was hunched upward. The child's arm and shoulder defect did not at first alarm Vicky and Fritz, for they believed that in time it would disappear. The infant's Prussian grandparents were less optimistic, however, and Prince Wilhelm heartlessly remarked to Fritz that he was not sure whether congratulations to the father of a defective prince were in order.[51] The ordeal had so exhausted Vicky that she was bedfast for a month, and the baby's christening therefore did not take place until 4 March. He was given an amalgamation of his father's and grandfathers' names: Friedrich Wilhelm Viktor Albert. But from birth the baby was known formally as Wilhelm and intimately as Willy in order, as his father explained, "to relax somewhat the babylonian entanglement of the legions of Fritzes" in the Hohenzollern family tree.[52]

Willy's infancy was unremarkable except for the periodic attempts to vivify his lifeless arm. When only a few days old, his right arm was tied to his side to encourage the use of the other, which was about one-third of an inch shorter. The left hand, which was capable of very little movement, was only half as large as its counterpart. A variety of spirit baths and exercises begun soon after birth resulted in some strengthening of the arm. When Willy was six months old, another of Fritz and Vicky's physicians, Dr. August Wegner, who had a wide practice among the Potsdam aristocracy, prescribed a twice-weekly series of "animal baths," in the course of which the child's arm was wrapped in the carcass of a freshly slaughtered rabbit. Wegner hoped, in vain, that the heat exuded by the dead hare would stimulate the baby's arm. The treatment repelled Vicky, but Willy enjoyed it enormously. At fourteen months, Dr. Wegner "magnetized" the child's arm, a process that apparently consisted of applying both lodestones and electrical shocks. This caused the patient no great discomfort since he had little feeling in the arm, but it did nothing to improve its condition. A succession of German and English doctors followed Wegner in the first years of Willy's life, and all of them unrealistically assured the hopeful parents of a favorable prognosis.

When the boy was four, a specialist prescribed his encasement for an hour every day in a cumbersome and humiliating "machine" that prevented Willy's turning his head, designed to prevent its tendency to loll to the left.[53] In 1865, at the age of six, the electrical shock and galvanic treatments were resumed, again with no real improvement of the arm. At the same time, Willy underwent an operation on his shoulder that resulted in a strengthening of the neck muscles and thereby corrected the abnormal inclination of his head. The following year, Vicky and Fritz engaged an infantry officer to determine if a gymnastic regimen would produce the miracle that had eluded the medical arts. When this last resort also proved barren, all further treatment was abandoned. The atrophied arm developed more slowly than the right, and in maturity it was about three inches shorter. The Prince could move it laboriously from the shoulder but not at the elbow, and the fingers, which were normally formed, had no tactile power. Willy learned to keep his lifeless member stuffed in pockets or let it rest on his sword hilt or saddle pommel.

The young prince found his useless arm very frustrating, and the medical treatments to which he was subjected, some of which were quite painful, aggravated him considerably.[54] Once the doctors and gymnasts vanished, Willy learned to accept his handicap with remarkably good grace, though it was often annoying or mortifying not to be able to do things as well as other boys, if at all. In a long life notorious for its theatrical exaggeration, Kaiser Wilhelm II treated his defect with uncharacteristic modesty and aplomb. While he was always at pains to conceal his arm's lifelessness from his subjects, a concern understandable in a figure whose every act was a public spectacle, he tried hard to ensure that his physical deficiency caused no embarrassment to his immediate entourage, who had to watch him wrestle with difficult tasks and on whom he had from time to time to call for help. On such occasions the Kaiser would simply declare that his arm made this or that undertaking impossible to perform.[55]

There is little evidence that the boy harbored any resentment against his parents for having subjected him to much needless suffering in their attempt to make him ablebodied.[56] But he surely cannot have failed to be wounded by Vicky's frequent expressions of disappointment that he was crippled and by the consequent reserve in her affection for him. As a mature man, Wilhelm II would declare that his mother's withholding of affection had shaped his character.[57] Vicky could not bring herself to accept Wilhelm's misfortune with equanimity. She repeatedly referred to the arm in letters to her parents, believing that its malformation had resulted from her fall four months before the baby's birth. Vicky was clearly repelled by the fact that her firstborn was a puny, afflicted child, promising so little of the handsome, manly figure possessed by her beloved father and by her husband. Vicky was proud of her own handsome appearance, which she typically attributed to the benefits of being from England, "the country of white teeth and rosy children."[58] That she should have a deformed son therefore seemed to her particularly cruel, an evil legacy of the Hohenzollerns. She was enraged that her husband's kin treated the boy either with pity or contempt, and she was insistent that Queen Victoria not tell her brothers and sisters in England about Willy's defective arm. She gave orders that no one, neither servants nor relatives, should see her child while he was imprisoned in his "machine."

"The *arm* makes hardly any progress," Vicky wrote to Prince Albert on Willy's first birthday in 1860. "It is a great, great distress to me. . . . It cuts me to the heart when I see all other children with the use of all their limbs, and that mine is denied that. The idea of his remaining a cripple haunts me. . . . I long to have a child with everything perfect about it like *every body else*, for I am sick of being teazed and tormented with questions, which are very kindly meant but which always seem to me like a reproach."[59] Vicky's anxiety sometimes led her to despair that Willy could ever develop into a normal man. She believed that his education would be hindered, his character warped, his manliness and sense of independence inhibited.[60] The extent of Vicky's disappointment was revealed when, in July 1860, she gave birth to a pretty and entirely normal daughter, whom she and Fritz named Charlotte. She assured Queen Victoria that this child, unlike Willy, was completely to her satisfaction. "She is 1000 times nicer because she is always good and a great deal prettier than he ever was and takes twice as much notice now, as he did when he was twice the age she is. . . . I am so proud of her and like to show her off, which I never did with him as he was so thin and pale and fretful at her age."[61] Fritz, however, did not share Vicky's resentment that their son was physically imperfect. Willy's handicap certainly distressed him, but he seldom mentioned it except to express the hope that with time it might disappear.[62]

In the course of Willy's youth, it was not his father, whose military responsibilities removed him from his family for long stretches, but his mother who had the full charge of his upbringing. "I watch over him myself," she chided her husband when Willy was twelve, "over each detail, even the minutest, of his education, as his Papa *never* has the time to occupy himself with the children."[63] Vicky had very certain ideas as to how her children were to be reared. She acknowledged rather ruefully that they were "public property," and she was determined that they become patriotic Prussians. Vicky confided to Queen Victoria that she hoped that her son would one day become a second Frederick the Great, "but one," she quickly added, "of *another* kind."[64] "His *education*," she wrote to her mother just before Willy's sixth birthday, "will indeed be an important task. I shall endeavor to make him feel that pride and devotion for his country and ambition to serve it that will make sacrifices and difficulties seem easy to him. And may I be able to instill our British feeling of independence into him, together with our brand [of] English common sense, so rare on this side of the water. The Prussians will not hate me for *that* in the end, however jealous they may now be of my 'foreign influence' over him and Fritz at present. I am as good a patriot as any one of them and all the better perhaps for not being a blind one."[65] Vicky hoped that Willy's education, although British in inspiration, would have a more beneficial effect than the rigorous training Prince Albert had designed for her brother Bertie, the Prince of Wales, who would succeed Queen Victoria in 1901 as King Edward VII. Bertie had been a lackluster student, and once released from the overly stringent grasp of his parents and tutors, he embarked upon a life devoted almost exclusively to pleasure. Vicky admired her brother's charm but deplored his morals. Her *beau idéal* for Willy was her husband or her father, but if he could not measure up to such olympian standards, perhaps he could manage to resemble her estimable but rather bland brother Arthur, Duke of Connaught.[66]

Although Vicky was very concerned throughout Willy's youth with his education, the strain of superintending a growing family sometimes told on her—Willy and Charlotte were followed by Heinrich in 1862, Sigismund in 1864, Victoria in 1866, Waldemar in 1868, Sophie in 1870, and Margaret in 1872—and she did not always have enough time to devote to the older children because of her concern for the infants. Sigismund died in 1866, which had the effect of creating two sets of children separated by a gap of four years in birth. The three older children thought of themselves as a separate faction raised with special strictness, while the three younger daughters grew up to be inseparable. What attention Vicky could devote to the elder children fell to Willy, who had, of course, a singular, kingly future. Although Willy's arm remained a great disappointment, Vicky gradually came to recognize that he was a bright little boy and in fact considerably more interesting than either Charlotte or Heinrich. She repeatedly bemoaned Charlotte's dull wits and pleasure-loving disposition, while Heinrich she found unattractively plain and not very intelligent. Neither child ever satisfied Vicky, in whose defense it should be noted that Charlotte grew up to be a frivolous scatterbrain, while Heinrich became a ponderous dullard. Vicky wrote to Queen Victoria when Willy was almost three that he would come up to her and say, "Nice little Mama, you have a nice little face and I want to kiss you."[67] His infantile lapses from good behavior, such as biting his Uncle Arthur Connaught at the Prince of Wales's wedding in England in 1863 or calling a great-aunt an "ugly monkey" on the trip back to Germany, were

Willy, aged five, and his dog, 1864

usually treated with amusement. From the cradle he was an active, noisy child—"I never saw such a bit of quicksilver," Vicky wrote of her son when he was not one year old.[68] As Willy matured, he became a likable little boy, full of jokes and confidence.[69]

Although Fritz was away for months on military duty or at the front fighting in Bismarck's wars, when at home he was an affectionate father, delighting in his infant son, who called him "Fritz, my treasure" or "Fritz, my angel." To Vicky it seemed that the child preferred his father, and she fretted that Willy did not appear to care much for her.[70] During Fritz's absences, Willy slept in Vicky's room, an arrangement in which he took great pride. He worried that she might die and wondered who then would be his mother.[71] As Willy grew older, Fritz accompanied him on hikes, took him swimming and sailing, and introduced his son to the theater. But there was also a more somber side to family life. From early childhood, Willy and Heinrich were required to accompany their mother and father when they made their periodic visits to the poor of Berlin and Potsdam, in order that the boys might develop a realistic awareness of the hard side of life. Both parents were firm in discipline and insistent on dutiful manners in their children, all of which Willy would later recall with annoyance. But it was nonetheless a happy household of loving parents and boisterous children, relaxed in their relationship with one another.[72]

Until he was six, Willy's education was in the hands of a number of governesses. Fräulein Sophie von Dobeneck, whose brother had been one of Fritz's childhood friends, was engaged as Willy's nurse when he turned two. "Dokka" was a possessive and pious woman who specialized, to Vicky's distress, in treating her charges to fearful descriptions of the fires of hell rather than teaching them useful things. She was strict, and Willy did not like her.[73] Miss Archer and Mlle. Octavie Darcourt, who taught the children English and French, enjoyed more popularity in the nursery. According to his mother, Willy's progress did not measure up to his capabilities, since on her orders he was permitted to play outdoors as much as he liked in the hope that this would improve his pale complexion, poor appetite, and sleeplessness. When Willy turned six, a male tutor began to come twice a week to teach him to read and write German. The boy enjoyed his lessons, even though holding papers with his left hand was very difficult, and he took great pride in his accomplishments.[74] Shortly before his seventh birthday in January 1866, Gustav von Schrötter, an agreeable young artillery captain, was appointed "military governor" (*Militärgouverneur*) to the young Prince and began to instruct his charge in the organization, uniforms, and weaponry of the Prussian army. Schrötter and Willy got on well, although Vicky, who did not like the idea of her son's having a military instructor, mistrusted his political views and was worried that he gave way too easily to his royal pupil.[75] Willy was a good student, for he had already developed the phenomenal memory for which he would later be justly celebrated. His ability to recite poetry was extraordinary, and a Scottish duke visiting Berlin in 1867 declared that the eight-year-old Willy was "likely to be the cleverest king that Prussia has had since Frederick the Great."[76] By the time the boy was seven, he had the rudiments of education in hand and was ready for a more intensive course of study.

Shortly after Willy's seventh birthday, his parents decided that his education should be entrusted to a tutor who would provide instruction in various special subjects. Although Vicky realized that it was time for her son's training to pass into other hands, she was unhappy that Willy would in the future be deprived of much of her salutary English outlook. Fritz, who had had a distinguished classicist as his tutor, consulted an old friend, Robert Morier, an attaché to the British legation to the North German Confederation at Frankfurt, about finding someone suitable to direct the next stage of Willy's education. Morier in turn discussed the matter with Baron Ernst von Stockmar, Vicky's private secretary, and the two men soon settled on Dr. Georg Hinzpeter as the most promising candidate.[77]

Hinzpeter was thirty-nine, angular and ascetic in appearance, taciturn, pious, and somewhat unpolished in manners.[78] Utterly bereft of a sense of humor, Hinzpeter was a joyless, icy pedant, and his interminable letters reveal a man of suffocating aridity and lugubriousness. It would be hard to imagine a man less well suited to appeal to a spirited boy such as Willy. The son of a teacher at the *Gymnasium*, or secondary school, in Bielefeld, Hinzpeter had taken a doctoral degree in history and philology at Berlin and had then found employment as a tutor in a succession of aristocratic households. In 1866 Hinzpeter's service in the family of Count Carl Schlitz genannt von Görtz in Hesse as a tutor to the count's fifteen-year-old son Emil was coming to an end. The count considered Hinzpeter to have been an exemplary teacher, and this opinion probably reached Morier through his wife, a friend of Countess Görtz. Fritz knew the family and had met Hinzpeter in the course of a visit to Schlitz in 1865. Morier hoped that Hinzpeter would be compatible with the liberal, anti-Bismarck set grouped around Vicky and Fritz, but his identification of Hinzpeter as a liberal was entirely incorrect. Although an advocate of government sponsorship of social welfare programs, Hinzpeter was a man of pronounced political conservatism and an enthusiastic advocate of the wars of unification then being waged by Bismarck.[79] He despised democracy and entertained a particular contempt for the United States—a republic, Hinzpeter liked to declare, that had produced only one truly great man. His nominee, oddly enough, was Henry Charles Carey, an eclectic writer well known in Germany for his tracts on protectionism.[80] A pious Calvinist, Hinzpeter believed that the "need for salvation" (*Erlösungsbedürftigkeit*) should be the foundation of education. There was no mirth in the celibate Hinzpeter, and he was rigorously insistent on regularity, correctness, and exactitude—"a Prussian noncommissioned officer," as one of Willy's other teachers characterized him.[81] Hinzpeter demanded that if he were to receive the appointment he be left free to shape his pupil according to his "ideal" of what a prince should be.[82]

In August 1866 Hinzpeter assumed his position with the virtual carte blanche he had demanded but, even so, not without misgivings. Instructing a royal princeling would, he feared, be far more taxing than the comfortable life he had led in rural Hesse with the Görtz family.[83] The schedule which Hinzpeter designed for Willy reflected his austerity and zealous sense of duty as well as his concern that the boy needed academic discipline. He believed that because kings led solitary lives young men who would one day rule should be brought up in seclusion. To fritter their time away in music lessons or other pastimes that would not prove useful once they assumed their crowns Hinzpeter thought entirely undesirable.[84] In summer the Prince's day began at 6 A.M. and continued, with a pause for lunch and exercise, until 6 P.M. The only concession in winter was to move the timetable forward by an hour. Hinzpeter himself taught Willy Latin, history, religion, and mathematics. For the last the boy had neither interest nor ability, but he developed a life-long enthusiasm for classical Greece by translating Latin accounts of the Olympian pantheon. Among the Romans, Caesar was the boy's favorite author, although he admitted that the endless catalog of Roman triumphs in Gaul in the *Commentaries* made him thrill to the occasional victories of the German barbarians.

Religion was not accorded any emphasis in Willy's program of study, and this was probably due to Vicky's desultory attitude toward theology. According to her son, she either repressed talk of religion or derided the subject.[85] Vicky believed that the essential value of Christian precepts was to ensure the development of rationality, liberalism, and moral probity. For Willy's edification in virtue Vicky always referred to Prince Albert, who, as the boy wrote to Queen Victoria, was "held up as a bright example almost every day."[86] Children, the Crown Princess once declared, would do well to begin their discovery of religion in beauty and charity rather than in the sanguinary narrative of the crucifixion. Hinzpeter, on the other hand, was a doctrinaire Calvinist and believed that the Bible and the Geneva hymnal were all that any regenerate Christian required. He held that confessional dogmatics should be scrupulously avoided lest they obscure the true lines of Christian belief.[87] Willy eventually rejected his mother's theistic views in favor of Hinzpeter's unquestioning orthodoxy, to which he would cling for the remainder of his long life.

Mlle. Darcourt, who married Hinzpeter in 1875, continued Willy's instruction in French. She had him copy in tiny exercise books the maxims of de la Rochefoucauld as well as pertinent quotations from Louis XIV ("Mon fils, la place d'un roi est là où est le danger.") and other great figures from the past.[88] Mr. Thomas Dealtry joined the staff in about 1869 to introduce both Willy and Heinrich to English literature. Willy was already an avid reader of Cooper, Defoe, and stories in *Harper's Weekly*, to which he subscribed, and Dealtry saw that he became familiar with Scott, Macaulay, Tennyson, and other authors. Willy delighted in the American Indian tales of Karl May, whose books were immensely popular, but for years *Ivanhoe* was his most treasured possession. Dealtry reported to the Crown Princess that the boy not only showed a commendable interest in his reading but that he also had agreeable manners and good character.[89]

Willy's schedule also provided for training in various sports. His lame arm made some exercises quite difficult to master, but he applied himself without complaint and quickly learned to be a competent swimmer and sailor. He even managed tennis and billiards. Riding presented complications, and mounting a horse made the boy very anxious, since his deformity impaired his sense of balance. As a result Willy resorted to tears and protests, but Hinzpeter forced the weeping Prince back upon his mount and relentlessly put him through his paces until finally the boy's fear was conquered. Hinzpeter thereupon returned Willy to his riding attendants, and his pupil eventually became a sound and indeed passionate rider.

With a taskmaster such as Hinzpeter in charge of his education, Willy's program did not allow much time for diversion. Hinzpeter regarded holidays and vacations not as relaxation from work but as opportunities to develop additional areas of instruction. Like Vicky and Fritz, the tutor had a great interest in the "social question" and agreed with them that education should familiarize children with everyday life.[90] The concern of Willy's parents for the poor proceeded from charity, but for Hinzpeter there was also a political ingredient. His reasoning was similar to that of Bismarck and other conservatives, who expected that the extension by the state of material aid to the impoverished working class would be reciprocated by political allegiance. Socialism would be killed by kindness. Every Wednesday and Saturday afternoon, when Willy and Heinrich had no regular classes, Hinzpeter took his charges to visit workshops, factories, and proletarian dwellings, in order that the boys might see the way in which laboring men and women lived. The visitations were continued when the two princes left Berlin on vacation trips to Bad Rehme—today's Oeynhausen—or to Coblenz, where Willy's didactic grandmother, Queen Augusta, often lectured her grandson on the virtue of using his youth to lay the moral foundations of adulthood.[91]

Although Hinzpeter would have liked to keep Willy at a distance from other children in order better to prepare him for his singular career, Vicky insisted that her son should have friends who would be chosen without respect to rank or station. Willy's brother Heinrich was his constant companion; together they acted out the events of the French Revolution, both princes attired in Jacobin caps.[92] The sons and daughters of visiting royalty, aristocratic court officials, and foreign diplomats completed Willy's circle of friends. The boy's favorite playmates were Eugen von Roeder and Mortimer von Rausch, both sons of army officers. Poultney Bigelow, son of the American minister in Paris, had been sent to Potsdam to be educated and served Willy as a specialist in Apache warfare. Willy and Bigelow constituted the exclusive membership of the "Ancient and Honorable Order of Red Men," which decreed that the young barons and counts of the Prussian aristocracy were palefaces who were to be massacred in the palace woods. Bigelow recalled that as far as Willy was concerned "no game interested him much that did not suggest war."[93] Two sons of the liberal Prussian statesman, Baron Georg von Bunsen, were also frequently summoned to join Willy in play, an invitation of which Hinzpeter disapproved because the Bunsen boys, he believed, were poorly disciplined and also had imbibed liberal political ideas from their English mother.[94]

Hinzpeter supervised the boys' games and expressed alarm if the play became too rough, but from his comrades Willy neither sought nor received special treatment because he was a royal prince or because he had a withered arm.[95] He did expect, however, to be acknowledged as a leader not a follower, and as a result his playmates found Willy somewhat tiresome. Willy was unpopular with his Hessian cousins, whom he occasionally visited, and sometimes with other children, because they felt he was too insistent on having his way.[96] John William Lowther, the son of an aristocratic British diplomat accredited to Berlin, recalled that Willy "didn't readily brook contradiction, was masterful in our children's games, insisted upon always commanding our toy armies, and always claimed, though he had not always achieved, the victory." The Prince's imperious behavior toward Lowther in martial contests was per-

Willy at eight, 1867

haps only impatience in the presence of someone not equal to the competition, for when barely three Willy could differentiate between the various regiments of the Prussian army.[97] Even the Crown Princess, who found much to praise in her small son, admitted that Willy had a willful and domineering streak.[98]

When Willy turned eleven, it was time to plan for his future attendance at a *Gymnasium*, after which he would present himself for the examination (*Abiturexamen*) that would qualify him for matriculation in a university. This meant a more intensive program of instruction, and as a result Greek and geography were introduced into the curriculum. Willy's instruction in the arts was not neglected. He heard lectures on archaeology from an expert at the Altes Museum, and along with his parents he visited the ateliers of the capital's foremost painters and sculptors. Cultural expeditions with Hinzpeter, who had little knowledge of art, were less pleasant, for the tutor insisted that masterpieces were to be viewed programmatically. One trip would be devoted exclusively to Greek antiquities, another to those of classical Rome, still others to paintings of this or that school. As far as Hinzpeter was concerned, these museum missions were successful if Willy managed to memorize the requisite factual information concerning the artists and their creations.[99] In this respect Willy did not disappoint his demanding tutor, and Hinzpeter's expectations strengthened the boy's prodigious talent for factual recall. This diffuse training conformed to Vicky's view of the eclectic education royal children should receive. The aim of her offspring's academic training, so a friend reported, was to see that they were "superior in knowledge of all sorts, to those over whom they may be placed, in order that superiority of education may add to the respect entertained for superiority of position."[100]

Vicky's ambition was perhaps sound, but the results proved dismal. An education that managed, in Hinzpeter's hands, to be both exacting and superficial meant that as an adult Willy would command an astounding number of facts but fail to possess a thorough understanding of even a single area of learning. The rigor and cheerlessness with which Hinzpeter—a man who could readily criticize but seldom compliment—carried out his pedagogical scheme also ensured that the boy would develop no real love of learning and would resent being lectured to. It will therefore hardly be surprising to find that once his years of academic training were safely ended, Willy would dedicate himself to pleasure, to insist on having his own way, and to relish being praised. But as long as Hinzpeter was in charge, Willy had to endure in silence the humiliations and demands imposed by his teacher, all of which he disliked. His friend Bigelow described Willy as "much bored" by Hinzpeter's "henpecking," and later in life the Kaiser would complain how mistaken his education had been.[101]

In spite of the constant interest Vicky took in her son's instruction, she did not grasp that Hinzpeter's tutelage was too severe. In the beginning, Vicky had some doubts that Hinzpeter had been the right choice, but before long she declared that she was very pleased with her son's progress, which she attributed entirely to his tutor. She wrote to Fritz, who was with the victorious German armies in France, on January 28, 1871, that Hinzpeter was *"an excellent* tutor, I never saw or knew a better."[102] It never occurred to her that Hinzpeter's astringent program resembled the joyless education Prince Albert had prescribed with such unfortunate results for Willy's uncle, the Prince of Wales, a man of singular charm who always preferred amusement to any kind of intellectual activity. Queen Victoria, who had belatedly recognized the consequences that an excess of discipline had had on her eldest son, repeatedly warned Vicky not to let Willy be driven into the ground by his resolute tutor.[103] It was sensible advice but it went unheeded.

Although Vicky approved of Hinzpeter's teaching methods, she could not bear his dictatorial insistence on exercising the right he had demanded before assuming his position of having sole control over Wilhelm's education. She was Hinzpeter's admirer but also his rival. Writing to Queen Victoria early in 1877, just as Hinzpeter's service came to a close, she declared that "I bore with Dr. Hinzpeter for these many years because I respected him and thought him in *many* ways a *great*, great blessing for Willy, tho' I knew all the while Dr. Hinzpeter detested me, and it often took *superhuman* patience to stand his crochets and caprices and to smooth the quarrels his violent temper got him into with almost everyone he came near."[104]

Hinzpeter never reciprocated the Crown Princess's respect, and he admitted that his relationship with her, as well as with Fritz, eventually became embittered. To Hinzpeter it was a question of whether it was to be he or Willy's parents who would direct the boy's education. Was Willy, he asked, to have an education fit for a prince or for a mere courtier?[105] The undercurrent of Hinzpeter's competition might have disturbed Vicky more had it been possible for her to detect any attenuation in Willy's affectionate relationship with her or with his father. Willy took an obvious pleasure in Fritz's company and was proud of his mother's artistic and domestic accomplishments. When Willy was almost eight, Vicky admitted that while he was a little spoiled and inclined to be bossy and prideful, he was really a "dear, interesting, charming boy, clever, amusing and engaging."[106] Vicky's satisfaction in her firstborn would not last long, and she did not fail to realize that he had faults as well as virtues. The day after Willy's twelfth birthday, she wrote to her husband, "I am sure you would be pleased with William if you were to see him—he has Bertie's [the Prince of Wales] pleasant, amiable ways—and can be very winning. He is *not* possessed of brilliant abilities, nor of any strength of character or talents, but he is a dear boy, and I hope and trust will grow up a useful man. . . . I am happy to say that between him and me there is a bond of love and confidence, which I feel sure nothing can destroy."[107] Only the day before Fritz had written in his diary, "Thank God there is between him and us, his parents, a simple, natural, cordial relation, which it is our constant endeavour to preserve, that he may always look upon us as his true, his best friends."[108]

The favorable, if somewhat qualified, estimation of her eldest child by Willy's mother as he came into young manhood was one that other observers generally shared. "Everyone who has had the gratification of speaking to Prince William," Lady Emily Russell, the wife of the British envoy in Berlin, wrote to Queen Victoria in 1873, "is struck by his naturally charming and amiable qualities, his great intelligence and his admirable education."[109] Lady Emily's positive report was perhaps exaggerated in order to please Willy's grandmother, but there are similar judgments by contemporaries who were not compromised by any ties to the Queen.[110] Although Willy won praise for his intelligence, no one could manage to describe him as handsome. Marie von Bunsen, whose brothers had been his playmates, declared in 1876 that Willy "promised to turn out to be very nice, like his father, but unfortunately not so good-looking [as Fritz], the most imposing and handsome man I have ever seen."[111]

In spite of Vicky's careful attention to her son's upbringing, she continued to be alarmed by influences that competed for Willy's attention and threatened, in her opinion, to have an injurious effect on his character and personality. She was fearful that since Willy would inevitably grow up in Berlin or Potsdam he would gradually acquire the ramrod, unlettered manner of the Prussian military aristocracy. She liked to dress her boy in civilian clothes rather than in uniform, but from early childhood Willy was impressed by the soldiers who thronged his grandfather's court. "A soldier is a splendid man," he informed his mother when he was only two.[112] On Willy's tenth birthday, 27 January 1869, he was gazetted to the First Foot Guards regiment and awarded Prussia's highest order, the Black Eagle. Vicky was not impressed. "Poor Willy in his uniform looks like some unfortunate little monkey dressed up standing on the top of an organ," she wrote to Queen Victoria.[113] She worried that as a soldier her son would be exposed to the sort of retrograde ideas she had always tried to keep at a distance.[114] While it was true that mingling with the rank and file of the army would sharpen Willy's awareness of the lower classes, military life would intensify in him those shortcomings of pride and willfulness she had already detected and, besides, cause him to neglect his studies.[115] Once Willy became a soldier he would, alas, belong to the Hohenzollerns, and indeed Wilhelm I began to assert a proprietary interest in his grandson, requiring his presence at parades so repeatedly that the boy's education was being imperiled. If Willy's academic development was to be fulfilled, his mother believed that he would have to be removed from Berlin.[116]

To distract Willy's attention from the military trappings of the Prussian court, Vicky tried to buy a farm in Silesia. Although this plan failed, she did secure for her family's use a small house with a garden and animals in the royal domain at Potsdam. As an antidote to the baleful, militarist influences at court, the Crown Princess wanted Willy to spend as much time in England as possible. She sent him to visit Queen Victoria as often as Wilhelm I would allow his grandson to travel abroad. Wilhelm especially liked London and told his sister Charlotte that when his school days were over he would like to return there for a long stay.[117] Vicky did what she could to encourage her son's interest in ships and the sea, since this inclination, if assiduously promoted, would eventually remove him from the passionately military character of Potsdam and Berlin. The masts and rigging of an English man-of-war were erected on the palace lawn in Potsdam, and an outline of the deck of the ship traced on the ground so that Willy could learn something about the sea even while on land. Although the boy developed a keen interest in ships, soldiers continued to enthrall him. He followed with great enthusiasm the course of the Franco-Prussian war of 1870–71, in which his father served with conspicuous distinction, and joined his mother in visiting the wounded in military hospitals. The prospect that a Prussian victory would result in his grandfather's becoming the German Kaiser struck the boy as very welcome. On the day in January 1871 that the empire was proclaimed in Louis XIV's great palace at Versailles, Wilhelm wrote to Queen Victoria, "I am sure you were pleased dear Grandmama that Germany is united and our dear Grandpapa its Emperor."[118]

In 1873, when Willy was fourteen, he passed the qualifying examination for admission to the upper level of a *Gymnasium*. Hinzpeter, who had abandoned his earlier view that royal princes should be educated in seclusion, resented the distractions to Willy's studies caused by the demands of the Prussian court. In this, if little else, he and Vicky were in agreement. Hinzpeter was convinced that a *Gymnasium* education would have the happy effect of concentrating the young prince's attention on his studies and also of familiarizing him with classes of people other than the aristocratic nexus that surrounded the Prussian throne and that would one day constitute his own retinue.[119]

Although Vicky had declared when Willy was only a small child that she wanted him to go away to school, now that the time had arrived she, as well as Fritz, was reluctant to see him leave. Vicky knew, however, that unless her son left Berlin, the education thus far achieved would be undone by Wilhelm I's constant demands that his grandson take part in military affairs. Fritz concurred, although he regretted how seldom he would now be able to see his son. Exposure to other boys of Willy's age, Fritz hoped, would help rid him of those undesirable characteristics that he believed tutorial training inevitably produced.[120] As for Willy, the news that he was destined for a distant school full of strangers came as an unpleasant surprise, but he soon got used to the idea and looked forward to leaving Berlin.

With Hinzpeter and Willy's parents thus united in their plan for the boy's future education, it would next be necessary to find a suitable institution. Since Prussian princes had historically been trained only by private tutors and had not attended boarding schools, there was no precedent to guide Vicky and Fritz. Nor was there a specific school with an exclusive claim to the education of young German noblemen that would therefore be the obvious choice for Willy. Hinzpeter was assigned the task of finding the proper academy, but this proved to be difficult, for many headmasters quailed at the thought of having a Hohenzollern prince among their students.[121] After some investigation, Hinzpeter recommended the Lyceum Fridericianum at Cassel in Prussian Hesse, a bourgeois school situated in a city noted for its healthy climate and political liberality. Here Willy could absorb sturdy middle-class virtues that would serve as an antidote to the aristocratic, military character of the Prussian court.

The Crown Prince and Princess approved Hinzpeter's choice, but they encountered formidable opposition when they informed Wilhelm I of their plans for Willy's future education. Throughout the years of Willy's childhood, the Kaiser had only with greatest reluctance granted the requisite permission for the boy to travel beyond Berlin and its environs. He had grown quite fond of his grandson, inviting him frequently to dinner when Vicky and Fritz were away. When Willy turned fifteen, he began to send reports on military affairs to his grandfather, a subject of more interest to Wilhelm I than the boy's academic pursuits.[122] The Kaiser's opinion was that Prussian princes were soldiers, not scholars, and he wanted the boy to remain in the capital in order that he might take an increasingly active part in public and military affairs. Wilhelm I's resistance merely increased Vicky's determination to remove her son from Berlin. She believed that Willy's education was a matter for his parents, and not Wilhelm I, to determine, and the difference of opinion among the Hohenzollerns grew into a tempestuous quarrel.[123] Eventually, however, the Kaiser, perhaps influenced by the Kaiserin Augusta, backed down and decreed that Willy might go to Cassel for two and a half years and then enter the army. He ordered General Walter von Gottberg, the boy's "military governor" since 1871, to assume charge of the household in Cassel, but he refused a request by Hinzpeter, undoubtedly in the sovereign's opinion the person responsible for the unfortunate educational experiment about to begin, for the award of the title of Secret Privy Counsellor (*Geheimrat*).[124] On 12 September 1874, Willy, along with his brother Heinrich, Hinzpeter, and General von Gottberg, arrived in Cassel. It marked, Willy later recalled, the end of his childhood.

THE EDUCATION

OF A PRINCE

T HE ARRIVAL of the royal party at the palace in Cassel was complicated by a suspicious porter, who was reluctant to believe that the two simply dressed boys who descended with Hinzpeter from a public conveyance were in fact princes of Prussia. Once this misunderstanding had been cleared up, General von Gottberg set about establishing the household, which alternated between the town palace (*Fürstenhof*) and Wilhelmshöhe, a castle set in an elegant park on the hills overlooking the city. Although Gottberg was very efficient, he had a relaxed and amiable manner that ingratiated him with Wilhelm, Heinrich, and the rest of the staff. Hinzpeter, however, disliked Gottberg intensely, for he mistrusted any other person, and especially a military figure, who might have an influence on his royal pupils.[1] Hinzpeter succeeded in asserting his dominance over Gottberg, and there was never any question that the tutor was the ultimate authority in all matters pertaining to the princes. In addition to Hinzpeter and Gottberg, the staff included a teacher to continue Wilhelm's instruction in English and French. Initially a Swiss gentleman filled the position, but in October 1875 he was replaced by François Ayme, a twenty-five-year-old Frenchman who had been recommended to Wilhelm's parents by the distinguished French statesman, Adolphe Thiers. Ayme seems to have been a sensible young man, and he fortunately got on well not only with his students but also managed to become a friend of both Gottberg and Hinzpeter.

The *Gymnasium* at Cassel was a private school attended primarily by children of townspeople. The headmaster was Gideon Vogt, who taught Latin and Greek and whom Wilhelm remembered fifty years later as strict but unpedantic and quite affable outside the classroom. Vogt was an energetic and judicious man who was equal to dealing with the problems created by the enrollment of so august a pupil as the eventual heir to the Hohenzollern crown.[2] Before Wilhelm's admission, Vogt had forthrightly informed the boy's parents that he would undertake the education of the young Prince only if they were prepared to have their son be treated as any ordinary student. Only on one point did Vogt yield, and that was to accommodate the Kaiser's insistence that his grandson's class have no more than twenty-one students.[3] In addition to the head-master, there were four or five other teachers, all of whom Wilhelm liked except for a rather dry history master.

Within a week of his arrival, Wilhelm felt entirely at home. According to Hinzpeter, Wilhelm at first had some trouble adjusting to his new surroundings and treated the boys in his class with a mixture of conceit and arrogance. The news that a Prussian prince would become their schoolmate had understandably filled Vogt's students with alarm, but they nevertheless accepted Wilhelm, and he eventually made a number of friends.[4] The Prince's fellow pupils were by and large boys from bour-geois backgrounds, including one who was Jewish, and his teachers were gratified that Wilhelm chose as his friends a group of well-mannered and responsible students. Wilhelm's favorite was Adolf Wild, who was an inseparable companion in charade games and outings to the municipal theater. As Kaiser, many years later Wilhelm would ennoble his old friend, by then a general, as Wild von Hohenborn.

Among Wilhelm's classmates, the only one who left a record of his experience at Cassel was Friedrich Schmidt, the son of a Berlin bureau-crat. Schmidt's brief description of his royal friend indicates that there was nothing unusual about Wilhelm other than his exalted rank. Accord-ing to his tutor Ayme, Wilhelm was among the best students in his class and one who, although manly and robust, never incurred demerits be-cause of lapses in good behavior. Ayme found his charge like other boys of his age except for the fact that Wilhelm spoke frequently of religious matters, a tendency for which the tutor could detect no cause but proba-bly reflected Wilhelm's absorption of Hinzpeter's Calvinism. He was, in Ayme's opinion, "polite and friendly as well as very civil in social mat-ters, not in the least affected and always concerned to make himself agreeable." At the same time, Ayme noted the tendency to pridefulness that the boy's mother had earlier deplored. Wilhelm's otherwise uncom-plicated manner was spoiled, although apparently not seriously, by his love of pomp and rhetoric, and on occasion he could assume a sedate manner that served to remind the other boys of his regal descent.[5]

The regimen that Hinzpeter designed for his pupil at Cassel was hardly less demanding than the system he had imposed for years in Berlin.[6]

Wilhelm was up before the sun and worked steadily through the morning. He took lunch at noon, bolting it down so that he could then have an hour and a half for sports. Classes resumed at two, and at the end of the instruction period Wilhelm had to present himself before Hinzpeter to report what he had learned during the day. At five the boys had an hour for dinner, after which they worked until eight and then had coaching sessions on subjects in which they were weak. Bedtime was at 9 or 9:30. One evening every week Hinzpeter forced General von Gottberg to hold what the tutor labeled "reconciliation dinners" (*Versöhnungsdiner*), to which local citizens from various gradations of society were invited. When Hinzpeter took his charges walking he let no opportunity for instruction go unused. He encouraged Wilhelm to express an instantaneous opinion on every passerby, in the curious expectation that this exercise would strengthen his pupil's self-confidence.[7] Sunday afternoons the boys had to themselves, and they sometimes organized lectures on subjects of general interest, with Wilhelm enlightening his classmates on Alexander the Great's campaigns in Persia and India. Occasionally the boys held debates in which they represented contemporary politicians. Wilhelm's Jewish friend, Siegfried Sommer, assumed the role of Eduard Lasker, his coreligionist and a leader of the National Liberal party. Wilhelm, whose casting was a matter of some delicacy, portrayed Hermann Schulze-Delitzsch, a pioneer in the working class cooperative movement.

The curriculum at the *Gymnasium* placed a heavy emphasis on classical languages. Wilhelm continued his reading of Greek and Roman masters, delighting in the deeds of bravery depicted in the *Iliad* but finding Cicero to be a rhetorical bore. He took a lively interest in antique sculpture, especially statues that represented military heroes. Medieval German history, with its chronicle of the great Hohenstaufen emperors, was the boy's favorite subject. In addition to the regular program that all students took, Wilhelm had to continue his instruction in French and English and also perfect his horsemanship. For pleasure he read German history of the middle ages and historical novels of various periods, especially the Egyptian tales of Georg Ebers, for whose work his mother had a great enthusiasm. He continued to devour Scott's novels, and Hinzpeter introduced him to Dickens, who became a favorite. Wilhelm also read Count Arthur de Gobineau's study of the Renaissance, which was recommended by his grandmother Augusta and his Aunt Louise, the Grand Duchess of Baden. Queen Victoria sent her grandson books, including a life of Prince Albert, which Wilhelm praised for providing him with an exemplary account of devotion to work and moral purity.[8] Hinz-

Prince Wilhelm of Prussia at sixteen, 1875

peter also took Wilhelm and Heinrich on trips, but he typically designed these for educational value as well as for pleasure. One frequent destination was the small Hessian town of Schlitz, where Hinzpeter's former employer Count Schlitz von Görtz lived. Here the princes, who according to their tutor had formerly known only relatives or officials, became acquainted with the rural citizenry, who enlightened the boys by treating them as ordinary mortals.[9]

During his three years at Cassel, Wilhelm stayed in close contact with his family. He wrote frequently to his mother on mundane affairs as well as politics. "Dear Mama," he scribbled in 1876 when seventeen, "I must write you a line because I know you will be so delighted that England has bought the Suez Canal. How jolly."[10] He occasionally returned to Berlin, and for several summers the Crown Prince took his wife and children, along with Hinzpeter, to the Dutch coast for holidays. While there is no evidence of any diminution in Wilhelm's affectionate regard for his parents in this period of his life, it was during the boy's stay at Cassel that the first traces of the eventual alienation between mother and son can be faintly detected. While a *Gymnasium* student, Wilhelm parroted his mother and father's view that magnanimous reforms from above were the most effective response to working class agitation, but Ayme suspected that these liberal protestations were in fact superficial.[11] His interests as a young man were in fact strongly military and religious, subjects that were either alien to the Crown Princess or that did not much concern her. Perhaps Wilhelm already realized that he and his mother did not share the same outlook on life. That, at least, is what late in life he would declare to have been the case.[12]

The Crown Princess found her eldest child to be increasingly foreign and feared that he was turning against his parents. Not long after Wilhelm went to Cassel she began to realize, to her dismay, that, not only in intellect but in character and disposition as well, her firstborn was not very British but was instead unfortunately emerging as "a regular Hohenzollern," a development she had predicted from the moment Wilhelm first entered the Prussian army on his tenth birthday in 1869.[13] Although Ayme found that Wilhelm was bright though not brilliant and regularly among the leading scholars of his class, the Crown Princess took a more somber view of his progress. She feared that her son's intellectual gifts, as well as his academic energy, were not very pronounced and that with respect to mental development he unfortunately took after his father's side of the family. This inheritance, coupled with the negative effect she had long believed Wilhelm's arm would have on his education, now seemed to be taking its toll.[14] He was "very awkward and uncouth," she declared, and unnaturally sensitive about criticism, something which she, no less than Dr. Hinzpeter, had always been ready to supply in abundance. Even Wilhelm's looks did not please his mother, for he had thick features and pimples rather than the "fresh and rosy" faces of English boys at Eton.[15] Fritz, on the other hand, had only praise for his son. When, in January 1877, Wilhelm passed his university admission examination with a mark of *gut*, his father declared that nothing in years had pleased him more. It indicated that the boy's scholarship was sound and that at eighteen Wilhelm was more mature than the Crown Prince himself had been at the same age.[16]

With Wilhelm's completion of the program at Cassel in the winter of 1877, Hinzpeter's work was at an end. He surrendered his position with a feeling that his long association with Wilhelm had not been a success. From the beginning the tutor considered what he called the Cassel "experiment" a failure and on Wilhelm's graduation in 1877 confessed that his expectations had not been attained.[17] Moreover, Hinzpeter had come to dislike his pupil's personality, which was in some respects not unlike his own. Wilhelm, for eleven years under Hinzpeter's iron hand, gradually developed the same coldness that was such a prominent feature of his teacher's disposition. Hinzpeter declared that the Prince's steeliness was so pronounced that he loved no one, not even his mother and father. That being the case, the tutor felt that he was fortunate at least to enjoy his pupil's respect.[18] An additional consolation for Hinzpeter lay in his reflection that "children often develop wonderfully and quite other than one expects or indeed often fears, and even in those cases where they are burdened with physical handicaps. Caesar and Nelson are certainly to be regarded as heroes . . . and yet both were proven epileptics."[19] Hinzpeter retired to Bielefeld, where he resided until his death in 1907. Wilhelm kept up with his old tutor, who provided him with letters of advice and visited him frequently. Wilhelm never lost his reliance on Hinzpeter's judgment, and for many years he was the only person outside of the royal family who was allowed to address Wilhelm with the familiar "*du*." In his old age Hinzpeter was contradictory if not hypocritical about his former student, publicly testifying to Wilhelm's virtues as a sovereign while at the same time privately maintaining that he had matured into a man of very limited ability, one who unfortunately somehow combined Hohenzollern stupidity with English debauchery. But then, as Hinzpeter had observed when Willy was only fifteen, the boy had a soul like that of no other human being.[20]

Wilhelm reciprocated Hinzpeter's criticism by frequently expressing dissatisfaction with the way his tutor had ordained his education. At first, to be sure, the boy had found his new school quite pleasant. "I like my life at Cassel very much," he wrote to his English grandmother three months after his arrival, "and going to school gives me great pleasure, as I like my masters, my studies and schoolmates." After a term or two in residence he was still favorably disposed.[21] But as he matured at Cassel, Wilhelm grew increasingly restive at his tutor's marmoreal grip. The effect on Wilhelm of his long tutelage under such a repressive, humorless, and hypercritical man was an urge one day to be his own master, to give free rein to a natural exuberance forcibly contained by a relentless taskmaster. Years later Wilhelm was frank in declaring that it was Hinzpeter's regimen that had formed his personality, but by a process of rejection rather than emulation. Hinzpeter's motives, he admitted, had been noble, but Wilhelm knew all the same that something had gone fatally amiss in his education. In constantly forcing Wilhelm to excel, Hinzpeter had totally disregarded his individuality and succeeded only in intensifying his determination to do things his own way. Moreover, Hinzpeter never complimented him no matter how hard he worked, and the result was a strangulation of his feelings. Hinzpeter could dispense nothing but discipline, and Wilhelm was forced ostensibly to follow the dictates of his teacher. Within, however, he had developed a hardness of heart and a resolve one day to have his own way.[22]

Even if Hinzpeter had been a warmer personality, there was something lifeless and mechanical about the way in which he taught, a deficiency Wilhelm discovered in his other instructors as well. Eight years after leaving Cassel he raged against the educational "crimes" he had endured there. "War to the knife against such teaching!" he declared.[23] In his memoirs written a half-century later, Wilhelm described his disappointment that his courses in history had been only chronicles of events rather than an investigation of the leading personalities and the customs of their subjects. Even more deplorable was the fact that the concentration on Greeks and Romans resulted in a neglect of German history, which at Cassel did not go beyond the middle of the seventeenth century and which consequently entirely avoided the stirring accomplishments of Wilhelm's two heroes in his Prussian genealogy, Frederick the Great and his grandfather, Wilhelm I.[24] Not too many years after departing from Cassel, Wilhelm petulantly recalled the arid chores inflicted on him by the classicists on the staff. "Under the scapel of the grammarian [and] the fanatical philologist," he wrote in 1885, "every brief sentence was divided [and] quartered, until the skeleton had been found with joy and had been triumphantly exhibited to the admiration of all in order to demonstrate in how many ways ἐπί or ἄν any other trivial thing may be prefixed or affixed. It was enough to shed tears."[25] As Kaiser, Wilhelm II was very critical of the excessive burden of work piled upon him at Cassel. *Gymnasia*, he declared in 1890, were suitable only for classicists, and German youths who wanted an education that corresponded to modern times would do better to attend the cadet academies that trained future army officers.[26] Wilhelm would see to it that his own sons would later be enrolled at such institutions.

A week after Wilhelm's graduation, the Kaiser decided that it was time for his grandson to embark on his military career and on 9 February 1877 gazetted him to the First Foot Guards—the "First Regiment of Christianity"—quartered at Potsdam. Wilhelm was delighted, for, as Hinzpeter had noted with disappointment not long before Wilhelm left Cassel, he was enthralled by Potsdam and its military allure.[27] He got on well with his commanding officer and found that his childhood familiarity with the landscape was a valuable asset during regimental exercises. Army duty was entirely to Wilhelm's taste, and he fell in quickly with his brother officers.

Wilhelm's conversion into a professional soldier alarmed his mother, for his military life made few demands on her son's mind. A note of really serious irritation about Wilhelm now began to creep into the Crown Princess's correspondence with Queen Victoria. She bewailed the fact that she could not get Wilhelm to "read a book or write a line, or do anything except *enjoying* having *nothing to do*."[28] "Master Willie talks great nonsense," she informed Queen Victoria à propos of Wilhelm's support for Russia in the Tsar's war in 1877–78 against the Turks, with whom she and her husband were strongly sympathetic.[29] A change of scene seemed imperative, and Wilhelm's parents resolved to remove their son from Potsdam as quickly as possible and enroll him in a German university where his time might be more gainfully applied. The Kaiser, who had had no formal education whatsoever, was very opposed to this idea, and only after very considerable effort did the Crown Prince persuade his father to allow Wilhelm to suspend his tour of duty at Potsdam in order to enter the university at Bonn. This was a natural choice, for the Crown Prince had studied there as had Wilhelm's grandfather, Prince Albert of Saxe-Coburg and Gotha. It was, besides, the institution preferred by the Prussian nobility for its sons. Wilhelm probably would have chosen to stay with his regiment but he did not protest his parents' insistence that he continue his education.

In June 1877 Wilhelm moved to Bonn and took up residence on the ground floor of the Villa Frank, a comfortable house overlooking the Rhine. In charge of his household staff was Major Wilhelm von Liebenau, a strict and rather boorish man with inelegant manners.[30] Liebenau was well acquainted with the Crown Prince and Princess, who had instructed him to keep Wilhelm tightly in hand, a charge which Liebenau, like Hinzpeter a strict and ceremonious pedant, tried in vain to fulfill. The major and his tyrannized family lived above Wilhelm, who took most of his meals with them. Liebenau's assistant was Albano von Jacobi, a huge, homely army captain who had been an adjutant of the Crown Prince and who soon became Wilhelm's good friend. Liebenau and Jacobi were both loyal soldiers but entirely devoid of any intellectual attainments.

Wilhelm remained at Bonn for four semesters, hearing a variety of lectures, some at the university, others privately at home. He found a number of his professors as dreary as some he had had at Cassel. Hugo Haelschner's lectures on the law and those delivered by Wilhelm Wilmanns on German literature struck him as tedious, and he abandoned Jürgen Meyer, a philosopher whose classes the Crown Princess had urged her son to attend, because he discovered that he had no taste for the subject. As at Cassel, Wilhelm's favorite subject was history, and a professor whom he remembered with great admiration was Wilhelm Maurenbrecher, from whom he could at last learn something of the development of modern Germany. Maurenbrecher, whose flamboyant lecturing style later reminded Wilhelm of the great Heinrich von Treitschke, shared his pupil's enthusiasm for historical personalities, and Wilhelm delighted in the professor's pungent descriptions, especially his characterization of Jérôme Bonaparte as an "inflated, conceited jerk" (*aufgeblasener, eingebildeter Hanswurst*).[31] He enjoyed lectures on German political and legal history delivered by Hugo Loersch, in whose hospitable house Wilhelm spent many pleasant evenings. Other instructors who won his favor were Adolf Held, an economist, Karl Justi, whose specialty was modern art, and the distinguished physicist, Rudolf Clausius.

The teacher who made the most lasting impression on Wilhelm was Reinhard Kekule, a young authority on Greek art. It was from Kekule that Wilhelm deepened the appreciation he had already acquired for Hellenic antiquities, a subject for which he maintained a vast enthusiasm until his death over sixty years later. Three days a week at noon, Kekule accompanied Wilhelm to the local museum, where he gave his pupil an hour's introductory lecture on Greek statuary. Wilhelm and his teacher became friends, and he often visited the professor and his family, who lived just down the street. Kekule found his student a very likable young man and was sorry when Wilhelm left Bonn in 1879. On his departure, Wilhelm composed a short poem on Pallas Athena in which he paid tribute to his "master" for bringing him, "a passionate museum-child," into the orbit of this most sublime goddess. After leaving Bonn, Wilhelm occasionally corresponded with Kekule and as Kaiser granted him a title of nobility and took him along on a voyage to Greece.[32]

The faculty at Bonn found their royal pupil an agreeable youth but not an exceptional intellect. While the curator of the university, who did not have Wilhelm in class, was pleased with the young Prince, those who provided him with instruction found his personality pleasant but his academic accomplishments quite modest.[33] According to Ernst von Dryander, the pastor of the church in Bonn which Wilhelm attended regularly, his teachers felt that he had a clear, intelligent head but was rather childish in the way in which he thought and expressed himself.[34] Professor Maurenbrecher, for one, did not reciprocate Wilhelm's enthusiasm and expressed reservations about the Prince's academic ability as well as the way in which he lived.[35] Karl Justi provided what is probably a balanced portrait of the twenty-year-old student in a letter written on 3 August 1879, the day before Wilhelm concluded his studies at Bonn. "He is a very lively person, also in the way in which he grasps things," Justi declared, "but by no means possessed of exceptional gifts. . . . Moreover, in his likes and dislikes he seems to be just as opinionated (*dezidiert*) as he is hasty, and he refuses to have anything to do with contrary opinions."[36]

Wilhelm might have made a better impression on his teachers had he worked harder. It seems doubtful that his claim, made in his second year at Bonn to a friend of his mother's, that he was "working away as hard as I can" is at all valid.[37] Wilhelm's uncle, the Grand Duke of Baden, feared that his nephew's indolence and lack of proper guidance (*richtiger Leitung*) would have a deleterious influence on Prince Friedrich Wilhelm, the Grand Duke's son and heir who was also a student at Bonn. The Prince had been sent there so that he could become better acquainted with his first cousin, the future Kaiser. "Prince Wilhelm," the Grand Duke wrote to an advisor, "is exclusively devoted to pursuing his own pleasure, paying so little attention to public lectures that it was impossi-

Prince Wilhelm in his Borussen fraternity uniform, ca. 1878

ble to discuss them with him afterward."[38] This was undoubtedly the sort of attitude that led Franz von Roggenbach, a friend of Wilhelm's parents, later to characterize the Prince's career at Bonn as a "fiasco." Hinzpeter, who occasionally visited Wilhelm in Bonn, was similarly unimpressed.[39]

Professor Justi noted with regret that what Wilhelm enjoyed most about the university was its fraternity life.[40] In his second year at Bonn, Wilhelm and his Baden cousin joined the Borussen, the most socially exclusive of all German fraternities. Its membership was composed almost entirely of wealthy and well-connected East Elbian noblemen together with a sprinkling of Hohenzollern and other royal princes. The Borussen were a highly ingrown social caste, intensely loyal to one another throughout life and always ready to help fraternity brothers succeed in careers in the army or the bureaucracy. The fraternity took itself very seriously and expected its members to be treated with deference. The behavior of the Borussen oscillated between rough, drunken dissipation and the most fastidious elegance, but in either state, they tended to be peremptory and condescending to more ordinary persons.[41]

Long before arriving in Bonn, Wilhelm had developed a willful streak that had alarmed both his mother and Dr. Hinzpeter. Wilhelm's experience as a fraternity man in Bonn, where he was at long last beyond the reach of the two possessive figures who had dominated his youth, reinforced the assertive, domineering side of his personality. Many Borussen (like Wilhelm himself) would move on from the university to the Prussian army and make their own contribution to its authoritarian, snobbish ethos. Among the Borussen, and among his lieutenant friends at Potsdam, Wilhelm encountered examples of behavior he successfully emulated, and by the time he had reached his early twenties he had matured into a typical aristocratic soldier—hard, self-satisfied and ready to yield to no man. Even among the Borussen and young officers Wilhelm's heartlessness was remarkable. "Cold as a block of ice," the chancellor's son, Herbert von Bismarck (himself a Borussen and army reservist), noted with alarm, an opinion reiterated by acquaintances and relatives who knew the young Prince.[42]

Carousing in Bonn and hunting on neighboring estates was the order of the day for the Borussen, and Wilhelm plunged with delight into these distractions. Other than his cousin he had no intimates—"I have very few real friends," he wrote while at Bonn—and among his fraternity brothers he made few contacts he would keep up for life.[43] He and his cousin eventually drifted apart, and only Count Franz von Tiele

Winckler, whose great Silesian estate became one of Wilhelm's perennial hunting grounds, remained a favorite. Long after Wilhelm had left Bonn he liked to wear his colorful Borussen jacket and attend its annual dinners in Berlin. He valued the patriotic sentiments promoted by the fraternities and believed that they provided a beneficial experience for statesmen of the future. He would declare not long after becoming Kaiser, "it is my firm conviction that every young man who joins a corps finds his true direction in life through the spirit that prevails there. It is the best education that a young man can receive for his life in the years ahead."[44] Wilhelm arranged later for several of his sons to go to Bonn, where they joined the Borussen and followed an academic regimen identical to that of their father, with the same negligible results.[45]

Unburdened of Hinzpeter's habit of using his free time to sharpen his awareness of the "social question," Wilhelm played croquet with his neighbors on the Koblenzerstrasse, went rowing on the Rhine, and developed a considerable talent for fencing. The commander of a detachment of hussars quartered in Bonn frequently entertained Wilhelm, who also regularly attended concerts, especially looking forward to seeing "*il maestro*" Wagner conduct his operas in Cologne.[46] Some of Wilhelm's weekends were spent visiting relatives in the vicinity. He often made the short trip down the Rhine to Koblenz to stay with his grandmother, Kaiserin Augusta, who spent most of every summer in her monumental palace that stretched along the river. Augusta saw to it that her grandson met army officers stationed in the area and gave Wilhelm religious books that he assured her he found very stimulating.[47] He also frequently went to Darmstadt to see his aunt, the attractive and lively Grand Duchess Alice of Hesse, his mother's sister. She, too, was full of religious advice, warning her nephew against theological radicalism and enumerating the virtues of "the real religion and practical Christianity."[48] Wilhelm felt like one of the family, and he would arrive in Darmstadt on Friday and not return to Bonn until Monday, a relaxation that would have been inconceivable under the inflexible Hinzpeter.

While a university student, Wilhelm also began to travel abroad by himself. His earlier trips outside Germany had been family affairs, taking him only to England or the Dutch coast. Wilhelm was anxious to be on his own and therefore welcomed the opportunity to represent his grandfather in Brussels on the occasion of King Leopold II's twenty-fifth wedding anniversary in 1878. He then proceeded to Paris, which he disliked because of its feverish bustle. He never returned. On the other hand, Wilhelm found Oxford, which he visited in the spring of 1879, quite delightful and would have liked to matriculate there after leaving Bonn. His interest in Oxford rested, however, not on the opportunities for study it afforded but rather on the pleasure of boating along the Thames.[49] Later in the same year he vacationed on the rugged Devon coast at Ilfracombe. Wilhelm found the area pleasing, but the German tutor who accompanied him declared that the Prince was ever ready to air his own views but unwilling to listen to anyone else's.[50]

Wilhelm's life at Bonn was markedly more pleasant than the long years in Berlin and Cassel under Hinzpeter's demanding tutelage. He seems to have thoroughly enjoyed himself, free now at last to say and do as he pleased. While Wilhelm let his schoolwork slip and spent more time than he should chasing deer and other game, he did not plunge into the excessive drinking for which his Borussen brothers were notorious. Nor did he display much interest in the young women of Bonn who mingled with his fellow university students.[51] Wilhelm's unwillingness to surrender to intoxication may have struck his bibulous fraternity brothers as prudish, and his interest in religion, which occasionally caused comment, was unusual in one so young, but on the other hand he was positive and enthusiastic and shared his friends' love of sports and society.

Although the faculty declared Wilhelm's intellectual gifts to be disappointing, those who casually met the young Prince found him pleasant and attractive, and some even saw in him indications of great promise.[52] Throughout life Wilhelm II could make a pleasing impression, but those who knew the Prince best as he emerged from Cassel into a world that allowed him finally to give free rein to his feelings—notably his mother, his military retinue, and his university instructors—saw that behind the amiable facade was a man determined to have his own way. Even the unrefined Colonel von Liebenau, who served in Wilhelm's household both at Cassel and Bonn for a number of years, recognized that his young charge needed to be encouraged to be more modest and less prideful.[53] Wilhelm's rather bland uncle, the ever-diplomatic Duke of Connaught, whom the Crown Princess hoped her son might grow up to resemble, struck a carefully equivocal note in a letter to Queen Victoria written in 1878, when Wilhelm was nineteen. "He is a nice boy," the Duke wanly assured his mother, "although a little proud and selfish, but that will wear off I think."[54]

The Crown Princess, always ready to dilute her protestations of love for her son with criticism of his personality and character, was increasingly less impressed. On Wilhelm's graduation from Cassel in January 1877, she had described him as a "dear good boy" but nonetheless one whose immaturity and ignorance made her apprehensive about the future.[55] Wilhelm's zeal for his brief army service in 1877 was not at all to his mother's taste, for she was convinced that army life would only increase the harshness and the insularity of outlook that were already becoming prominent in his character. Wilhelm's subsequent experience at Bonn disillusioned her entirely. He had hardly arrived there when the Crown Princess began to complain that Wilhelm was affecting a sort of "mystery" and independence, and at the end of the summer of 1877, when Wilhelm had been in Bonn for only three months, she was in despair at the cold and distant manner her son had adopted.[56] By 1879, when Wilhelm turned twenty, the Crown Princess had to admit that he lacked industry and intellectual curiosity. There was also his hardness of heart and his lack of spontaneous affection, failings the Crown Princess identified as unfortunate Hohenzollern traits and a legacy from the austere Dr. Hinzpeter. She could not grasp that her own overly assertive character lay at the root of her son's coldness. By the summer of 1880, the disappointment of the Crown Princess in her son was complete. She felt that he neglected her, which was bad, but his political views were even worse than his behavior. Prince Albert had been concerned that, given the boy's paternal lineage, he might mature into a "conceited Prussian"; and that, the Crown Princess feared, was exactly what had happened. "Willy is *chauvinistic* and *ultra* Prussian to a degree and with a violence which is often very painful to me," she wrote to Queen Victoria in August 1880. "I avoid all discussions, always turn off the subject or remain silent! . . . With my own children I often feel like a hen that has hatched ducklings."[57]

The Crown Princess's disappointment in her son is understandable, for he had not developed into the handsome, liberal Anglophile she had hoped he would. But there is an excessive, carping tone in her incessant complaints. Surely few mothers can have been as relentless in criticizing their children for not having measured up to exalted expectations. The Crown Princess was impossibly demanding and therefore inevitably disappointed. Like Dr. Hinzpeter, she was an inveterate critic, seldom satisfied with anyone or anything. Her letters inveigh without remission against Bismarck, the German government and its politics, the obscurantism of the house of Hohenzollern, the philistinism of German society, and the blemishes of character and lack of accomplishment of her three eldest children. Only England, her late father, the Crown Prince, her two dead sons, and her three young daughters qualified as objects worthy of the Crown Princess's affection.

By the late 1870s, the Crown Princess, always willful and opinionated (like her son Wilhelm), had become sour and self-pitying. Her letters testify to an increasing emotional and physical malaise. Fate had not treated her kindly, for blow after blow had rained on her family and household. First there was the death of her beloved sister Alice of Hesse in December 1878, followed closely by the fatal illness of her favorite child, the ten-year-old Waldemar, who died in March 1879. Wilhelm, alas, was not the equal of his dead brother. "So many pretty and charming traits of Waldie's character come back to me!" the Crown Princess wrote in anguish to her mother a few weeks after Waldemar's death. "Oh that Willy had his warm and affectionate, spontaneous nature, his industry and activity and interest in everything. . . . To everything that one used to have to *urge* the elder brother one had almost to restrain Waldie from. . . . His being strong and handsome made me so proud!"[58] She admitted that the boy's death, so close after Alice's, had damaged her health and that both Fritz and her doctors believed she needed "to do something serious" to regain her strength. But over a year later she could only cry, "When I look at my other children round the Christmas tree I bitterly miss the two dear boys that were my pride and joy."[59] Then in 1881, diphtheria, which had carried off Waldemar, struck down, though it did not kill, one of her younger daughters. At about the same time the children's English governess, Miss Byng, who was the Crown Princess's household confidante, had to return to England, fatally stricken with cancer. All this told on Vicky's health, and she suffered constantly from headaches and rheumatism. Strained to the breaking point by her disappointments and tragedies, she seems to have taken out her wretchedness on Wilhelm, thereby magnifying what she felt was amiss in him. It became impossible for the Crown Princess to see anything positive in her eldest child or even to try to achieve some sort of sympathetic understanding of his personality and character.

The Crown Prince, watching his son and heir grow older, felt much the same disenchantment. The pride he had taken in Wilhelm's encouraging performance on his examinations at Cassel early in 1877 evaporated after his son moved on to Bonn. The man did not, alas, resemble the boy, and the Crown Prince, like his wife and probably for the same reason, was quickly and deeply disappointed. Wilhelm had unfortunately become a quintessential Prussian lieutenant, brusque and brittle. In spite of the pains lavished on Wilhelm's education and training, he seemed to his father to have become more immature than ever.[60] The Crown Prince, besides, was jealous of Wilhelm, who had succeeded in establishing the sort of close relationship with the old Kaiser that had never been possible for Fritz. With such a firm alliance between his father and his son, the Crown Prince took to wondering if his own life had any real purpose.[61]

To Kaiser Wilhelm I, who had had no university education, four semesters at Bonn was quite enough for his grandson, just as thirty years earlier he had decreed that it would do for his son. He insisted that Wilhelm return to Potsdam and resume his army career, declaring that military service was "much more important than traveling."[62] So in the fall of 1879, a few months short of his twenty-first birthday, Wilhelm joined his regiment. His mother, who had long known that this move was inevitable, was dismayed that her son would for the rest of his life belong to the Hohenzollern army. Wilhelm's education unhappily had not succeeded in imparting to him the traits of character the Crown Princess might have wished, and she could now only wistfully express the hope that "*life* must now bring out what there is to develop."[63]

Wilhelm took his military duties very seriously, but one of his adjutants, Captain Adolf von Bülow, described him as "still rather young but even so a quite ordinary youth." Bülow was unable to note any improvement with the passage of time and believed that what the Prince required was a period of exile in the provinces under the command of a stern military or bureaucratic official.[64] Wilhelm lived in the New Palace in Potsdam, where he was attended by his body servant, Wilhelm Schulze, a Prussian who entered the Prince's service in October 1879 and served him faithfully for over forty years.[65] Like most young unmarried officers Wilhelm spent almost all of his free time in the mess of the First Foot Guards, taking his lunch and dinner there and concluding the day by playing cards or billiards with his comrades, some of whom had been Borussen at Bonn. His life was contained in the regiment, and there is no indication that he sought any diversions in Berlin. Neither culture nor vice attracted Wilhelm, and his trips to the capital were restricted to calls on his parents and grandparents or devoted to ceremonial affairs. Wilhelm did not like Berlin, which he found "dreadful" and where, he wrote in English to a friend living in Vienna, "I never feel happy, really happy. Only Potsdam, that is my 'eldorado' & where one feels free with the beautiful nature around you & soldiers as much as you like, for I love my dear Regiment very much, there [are] such nice young men in it."[66]

The reason for Wilhelm's regularity of life probably lay in his dislike of alcohol and in the narrowness of the society in which he moved. The company he kept at this time was singularly devoid of women, and the few whom he did know were either princesses from other royal houses who were circumspectly behaved and protectively chaperoned or married noblewomen whom he had met at court. He abhorred the frivolous women who composed a part of Berlin society and who, according to his indictment, talked of nothing but clothes and spent their time flirting. This sort of thing, he wrote to Countess Marie von Dönhoff, an Italian-born aristocrat who was a good friend of his mother's, "is something beneath a real man & gentleman, especially I think it beneath myself."[67] His only female friends in society, both intimates of the Crown Princess, were Countess Dönhoff, who was often away with her diplomat husband, and Countess Marie ("Mimi") von Schleinitz, a prominent hostess who had much charm and learning.

In 1878, when Wilhelm was nineteen, he fell in love, and early in the following year he became engaged. Wilhelm's betrothed was Princess Augusta Victoria, the daughter of Duke Friedrich of Schleswig-Holstein-Sonderburg-Augustenburg, a branch of the Danish royal family. Her mother, the Duchess Adelheid, was a princess of the prominent and well-connected noble house of Hohenlohe and a first cousin, once removed, of Wilhelm's grandfather, Prince Albert. The Hohenlohes had lost their sovereign rights during Napoleon's invasion of Germany at the beginning of the nineteenth century, but they continued to be officially recognized as "mediatized" nobles and as such eligible as royal marriage partners. "Dona," the family nickname which Wilhelm called his fiancée, also bore the name Feodora, after her maternal grandmother, a half-sister of Queen Victoria. The connection between the bride-to-be and the English crown was reinforced by the fact that Duke Friedrich's younger brother, Prince Christian, had married Princess Helena, one of the Crown Princess's younger sisters.

In spite of Duke Friedrich's impeccable genealogical background, his position was in fact unenviable. He possessed no principality over which to rule, he had only a small fortune, a modest estate at Primkenau in Silesia, and no expectations of a bountiful inheritance. A more serious problem was a shadow that obscured his right to the sovereign privileges that were necessary to enable his heirs to marry royalty on an equal basis. Many years earlier Duke Friedrich's father had renounced his claim to the duchies of Schleswig and Holstein, which were then the crown properties of his childless cousin, King Frederick VII of Denmark. This renunciation led to considerable discussion as to whether the Sonderburg-Augustenburg line was any longer to be reckoned as being of the blood royal. In any case, after 1866 there was nothing for him to rule, for in that year Bismarck seized the two duchies and incorporated them into Prussia, an appropriation that created great enmity between the Augustenburgs and the Hohenzollerns.

The Duke's declining fortunes and his questionable claim to royal status tarnished but did not automatically eliminate his three daughters from consideration as bridal candidates for Prussian royalty. The Augustenburgs could offer certain nuptial advantages. The family was staunchly Protestant, its connections widespread, and its very weakness as a nonsovereign line would ensure that its princesses would be compliant rather than assertive consorts, a factor which must surely have appealed to the henpecked Wilhelm I. A Hohenzollern-Augustenburg marriage would have the further benefit of reconciling a German princely house to the new empire and its Prussian sovereign, a consideration that had some importance in a period when particularist feelings were strong and Bismarck found himself confronted by a number of resourceful enemies among the German rulers. Moreover, there was throughout the Augustenburg family tree ample evidence of effortless fecundity.

The notion of a marriage between Dona and Wilhelm had existed for some time, and indeed Wilhelm believed that his mother and Queen Victoria had decided on the match while he was still a child.[68] Not only were the two families kin in numerous ways, but Duke Friedrich had been a close friend of Wilhelm's father when both were students at Bonn, and he had later served with distinction on Fritz's staff during the Franco-Prussian war. The Augustenburgs had asked the Crown Prince and Princess to serve as godparents to Dona, their firstborn child. Her suitability as an eventual bride for Wilhelm may have occurred to the four parents as early as 1868, when neither child was yet ten years old. The Crown Princess assembled a collection of pictures of Dona in the early 1870s that Wilhelm claimed for himself in 1873 at the age of fourteen. By the time Dona and Wilhelm had reached their middle teens, Queen Victoria was beginning to consider the diplomatic advantages of a union between her grandson and her great-niece. In 1875, in the course of a visit to Germany, the Queen had broached to Duke Friedrich the subject of a nuptial alliance. The Crown Princess was simultaneously at work on arranging an Augustenburg marriage, although at this point she was undecided on which of Duke Friedrich's three daughters the eventual choice should fall.

Wilhelm was kept ignorant of these maneuvers, but in the course of a visit to the Augustenburgs he resolved the question of which daughter should be the future Queen of Prussia and German Empress by taking a decided interest in Dona. During the late 1870s the two families visited back and forth, and in April 1879, en route to a hunt in Silesia, Wilhelm stopped off at Primkenau, proposed, and was accepted.[69] The engagement was not publicly announced, since the formal marriage settlement had to be arranged. In the midst of these negotiations Duke Friedrich died suddenly, in January 1880, a development that delayed the betrothal until the following June.

The bride-to-be won the unreserved praise of the Crown Prince, who was pleased that this was a match, like his own, dictated by love rather than diplomacy. Wilhelm had shown excellent judgment, for Dona was, her future father-in-law declared, "a Princess distinguished by gifts of mind, heart and temperament as well as by dignified grace."[70] The attitude of the Crown Princess toward her son's future bride was ambivalent. She felt that Wilhelm was too immature for marriage and would have preferred to see him broaden his mind by travel. But since Wilhelm, to his mother's regret, had little interest in anything other than his military career, a path not conducive to good morals any more than it was to intellectual achievement, the best course was for him to marry at once. She did not care which of Duke Friedrich's daughters became Wilhelm's wife. The Crown Princess found Dona's mind commonplace and unlikely to promote her son's straggling mental development, but the bride-to-be had character and goodness, which were important qualifications. The Crown Princess therefore actively promoted the match.[71]

Not all of the Hohenzollerns took such a positive view of their prospective relation, and the reservations of some of the court found a response in Berlin's aristocratic society.[72] Dona came from a nonregnant house, her mother was only of marginal royal rank, and her father's family was distinguished neither by historical accomplishment nor wealth. The Princess, moreover, was a few months older than her groom-to-be and, whatever her charms, she was not notably beautiful. One aristocratic diarist wrote disparagingly to her sister that Wilhelm's parents seemed "to be trying to make the worst possible match for their child with the greatest possible speed."[73]

Wilhelm I and Kaiserin Augusta, in particular, were obstacles. Wilhelm's grandmother thought he was rushing too quickly to the altar, while the King, although he liked Dona, found her origins too ordinary for the great role she would eventually have to play as Wilhelm's consort.[74] But Wilhelm I, although in his eighties, had not lost his appreciative eye for feminine attractiveness. Dona, he declared, and the rather plain but svelte Princess Stéphanie of the Belgians, the fiancée of the Habsburg Crown Prince Rudolf, would make an admirable matched pair, for their figures were similar, although Dona had the prettier face.[75] Bismarck, who was soon consulted, had nothing against the union, but he was insistent that for so important a marriage the Princess's royal status had to be formally ratified. After some difficulty, the chancellor succeeded in wringing an appropriate certification from Professor Schulze of Heidelberg, an authority on such *arcana imperii*.[76] Thanks to Bismarck's persuasive intervention, the Kaiser's opposition dissipated, although he continued to lament the fact that Dona came from "so *small* a dynasty." However, Wilhelm I eventually declared to the Empress Augusta that their grandson could not have selected a more suitable bride.[77] Augusta, always ready to challenge her husband, was convinced neither by the Kaiser's assurances nor by the flattering descriptions of Dona forwarded by Queen Victoria. Wilhelm's German grandmother felt that he had moved too quickly, and she shared the Crown Princess's opinion that the bride's intellectual powers were somewhat deficient. But Dona had a powerful ally in the Crown Prince, who assured his son that he would do everything in his power to secure approval of the marriage.[78] Wilhelm also set to work to overcome the Empress's objections, and he could soon inform his mother of a "glorious victory" in winning his grandmother's approval.[79]

In May 1880, a little over a year after the couple had become engaged, the Crown Princess reported to Queen Victoria that the public objections to the marriage, as well as her own private reservations, had been overcome. "I must say I think people have come around wonderfully," she wrote. "Everyone seems disposed to like Dona, and what feeling there was against the marriage has almost disappeared."[80] No one but the bride was responsible for this change of heart. Dona's primary virtue was her modest bearing and natural manner. While her figure and carriage were excellent, she was not a pretty nor even a handsome young woman, for her features were somewhat heavy and irregular. But Dona possessed a kind heart as well as an even temper, and she expressed by her every word and gesture a determination to embrace without question her husband's family and future subjects. Dona undoubtedly had been warned of the reservations expressed in Berlin about her fiancé's choice, but she met the challenge presented by her critics with tact and good judgment.[81]

Wilhelm's choice of Dona had nothing to do with the political considerations that recommended her to Bismarck. Dona was Wilhelm's good

Prince Wilhelm on the eve of his marriage, 1880

friend before she became his fiancée, and her position was strengthened by the fact that she had almost no competition. At the time that Wilhelm became ready for marriage there was a dearth of suitable bridal candidates. The German royalty available was limited in number, and some candidates had to be excluded by considerations of consanguinity, religion, or political hostility. The assortment of grand duchesses from Hesse or Baden, who otherwise might have been suitable, were too young or too closely kin. The same objections applied to Queen Victoria's English granddaughters.[82] Nuptial prospects in St. Petersburg, where one earlier Hohenzollern had found his bride, were in equally short supply. Nevertheless, Wilhelm did not choose Dona because she was the *only* princess available or because diplomatic exigencies pointed to a match with the house of Augustenburg, but because he fell head over heels in love with her.

While Dona was physically not unattractive, it does not seem likely that Wilhelm decided on her because he was ravished by her beauty or enticed by a flirtatiousness that he disliked in women. What he admired were dignity and virtue, both of which Dona could richly supply. He assured his fiancée's uncle (to whom Wilhelm had the same relationship by marriage), Prince Christian of Schleswig-Holstein, that Dona "has such a winning expression in her eyes, such a reassuring manner, and in addition her whole appearance makes such a noble and wonderful impression." Wilhelm declared that he was so "enraptured" (*entzücht*) that "my decision to do everything to make her mine was immediate, clear, and unshakable."[83] As for Dona, she cannot have failed to be dazzled by the brilliant prospects of a marriage to a future sovereign. She liked Wilhelm, to be sure, but she was not swept off her feet. Her love developed gradually, but it became absolute and enduring.[84]

Dona was a woman of character, and Wilhelm approved of her serious sense of purpose. She shared his firm, if conventional, morality and was as prim an opponent of luxury, vice, drink, and coquettishness as was her future husband. As Wilhelm's mother realized, Dona had a prosaic mind that seldom ventured beyond domestic concerns, but this did not seem a problem since Wilhelm took no sustained pleasure in intellectual pursuits. Like Wilhelm, Dona was punctilious in matters of etiquette and dress, and over the years she would develop, as would he, a rather heavy-handed devotion to ceremonial ritual. Dona had no discernible interest in politics, and it may be that Wilhelm saw in her a consort who would not become involved in affairs of state but instead be content to be a docile and obedient wife. Wilhelm did not like for women to aspire to too prominent a role.[85] He had, after all, long observed the difficulties that the Empress Augusta had made for his grandfather and probably had already begun to resent the domination that his own mother exercised over his father, a factor that would eventually contribute heavily to Wilhelm's alienation from the Crown Princess. He may even have decided to marry such a conservative woman as a protest against his English mother's modern views.[86] Dona, unlike the Crown Princess, was entirely traditional, thoroughly German, and throughout her life devoid of any traces of cosmopolitanism. A friend correctly described her as "from start to finish . . . a German wife of the good old type."[87]

Wilhelm's tutors at Cassel had noted his unusual interest in religion, and this was an attribute of character which Dona fully shared. Like Wilhelm she was pious and faithful in worship, although she never developed any interest in the theological disputations that her future husband would find so invigorating as a mature man. Her belief was simple and unquestioning, and she was prepared to capitulate fully to Wilhelm's strong religious convictions. "Dona and I share the same principles," Wilhelm reported with satisfaction to his grandmother Augusta. "Thy God is my God."[88] Dona likewise rejoiced that Wilhelm, so unlike most of their generation, was a devout Christian.[89] He wrote to his Aunt Louise of Baden that he hoped to create with Dona "a good Christian home." The example he aspired to imitate was, revealingly, not his own parents' sunny though theologically free-minded household but the rigidly orthodox and ever-quarrelsome home of his grandparents, Kaiser Wilhelm I and his unhappy consort.[90]

Dona arrived in Berlin on 26 February 1881 and was escorted through the city in a festive parade, the solemnity of which was disturbed by the intrusion of a float sponsored by the Singer Sewing Machine Company featuring a seamstress busily plying her trade. Wilhelm confessed to his sister Victoria that he was nervous, but, supported by the bodyguard company of his First Foot Guards lined up behind him, he welcomed Dona to his capital.[91] The groom, according to one observer, "behaved so zealously that it appeared as though he were oblivious to the fact that he was greeting the arrival [of his bride]. He presented himself rigidly before his future wife. Truly Prussian!"[92] The civil service took place on the evening of 27 February, followed on the next morning by the religious rites. Tradition required that for the next two days Wilhelm and his wife participate in an endless round of public ceremonies. On 1 March they travelled to Potsdam, where still more social rituals claimed them. To the bride's regret, Wilhelm did not want to have any sort of honeymoon, and they never had one. Life in Potsdam, he unromantically told Dona, was so comfortable that it was not worth seeking anything better.[93] It was an inauspicious beginning to a marriage that would endure, for better or for worse, until Dona's death forty years later.

Three

A POTSDAM LIEUTENANT

ONA AND WILHELM resided in the royal palace in the center of Potsdam until the renovations of the small but elegant "Marble Palace" on the outskirts of the town could be completed. This work was accomplished by the beginning of the summer, and in mid-June 1881 the relocation of the household took place. A considerable retinue of ladies-in-waiting and adjutants accompanied the bridal couple. The marshal of the court was Colonel von Liebenau, who had managed Wilhelm's household both at Cassel and at Bonn. The arrogant Liebenau was an unfortunate choice, for he was lacking in polish and governed Wilhelm's entourage in an authoritarian and parsimonious manner that soon annoyed everyone, including Wilhelm and Dona.[1] Captain Adolf von Bülow, Wilhelm's adjutant since 1879, offered no counterbalance to Liebenau's strict, martial airs. The son of Bernhard Ernst von Bülow, Bismarck's trusted state secretary of the Foreign Office until his death in 1879, Bülow had been a schoolmate of Chancellor Bismarck's son Herbert.[2] Wilhelm had an unreserved trust in his adjutant, to whom he would remain very attached until Bülow's death in 1897. Bülow was a redoubtable horseman but ill suited to be a courtier, for, like Liebenau, he had a rather brusque and coarse manner, which eventually rubbed off on his royal master. Even his brother Bernhard, a rising young diplomat who would eventually become imperial chancellor, admitted that Adolf's disposition had too heavy a dose of Potsdam.[3] He also affected a sort of omniscience that Dona found very aggravating, and he was obstinate to a degree that Wilhelm's friend Count Philipp zu Eulenburg declared to be truly frightening.[4] Neither Bülow nor Liebenau were the sort of men who could, or would, inculcate in Wilhelm modesty, reflection, or an appreciation of the world beyond the parade ground at Potsdam.

In Dona's suite from the first year of her marriage were three pious, aristocratic ladies destined to remain in service for almost forty years. Countess Theresa von Brockdorff, who assumed the position of chief mistress of the robes, was a handsome widow of thirty-five and a cousin of Captain von Bülow's. The countess had a quick tongue and some sense of humor, but she was also a snob with a fanatical attachment to court ritual and etiquette. Countess Brockdorff's two assistants, Countess Mathilda von Keller and Claire von Gersdorff, were not endowed with much in the way of charm or beauty. Countess Keller was faithful and utterly vacuous, a "female Prussian, with all the virtues and disadvantages thereof," as one friend labeled her.[5] Fräulein von Gersdorff, whose intelligence was restricted to artistic matters and not formidable even in that area, had a number of irritating mannerisms, including a sing-song voice, that occasionally unnerved the rest of the entourage. The three courtiers, whose evangelical piety equaled that of their royal mistress, were called behind their backs the "Hallelujah Aunts," and, whatever their admirable qualities, they provided very little in the way of diversion or interest. Like Dona, they were conventional aristocratic women, dutiful, religious, rigidly moral, and hostile to foreign influences. None except Countess Brockdorff had a trace of wit. On his hearth, Wilhelm would always be afforded dignity and virtue, but throughout his married life he would have to look elsewhere for intellectual stimulation or amusement.[6]

During the first year of their marriage, Dona and Wilhelm hardly left Potsdam. Their lives quickly settled into a pattern that endured for decades. Wilhelm departed after breakfast for duty with his regiment, leaving Dona to ride horseback or write letters. She corresponded occasionally on matters of social welfare with Hinzpeter, who bombarded her with letters full of such sententious injunctions as "in a very special sense you two must live for one another and in one another," and who suggested that a woman's place was at home with her family and not in politics.[7] It was advice that Dona faithfully followed. If Wilhelm returned home for lunch, he and his wife would afterwards ride. On evenings that he did not dine with his fellow officers, dinner was at five, with the entire retinue in attendance, after which the group read or talked, but sometimes instead Wilhelm and Dona played croquet or painted. In the late summer of 1881, Dona found that she was pregnant, and her first child, Prince Wilhelm, was born early in May of the following year. Five brothers followed in swift succession—Eitel Friedrich (1883), Adalbert (1884), August Wilhelm (always known as "Auwi") in 1887, Oskar (1888), and Joachim (1890)—and then finally the only daughter, Victoria Louise (1892). Dona took an active part in managing the royal nursery, and, with such a numerous and closely spaced brood, family responsibilities absorbed almost all of her time.

Those who observed the young couple assumed that the marriage was happy, and there was in fact always a fundamental appreciation by both partners of the virtues of the other. At the same time, neither Dona nor Wilhelm was fully satisfied. In the early years of her marriage, Dona felt an intense admiration for her husband, hanging upon his every word and anxious never to be separated from him. She realized, however, that she did not have exclusive possession of Wilhelm, who was affectionate but never tender and who seemed to prefer the company of political friends or regimental comrades to the cozy home she tried to establish for him in Potsdam.[8] But when he was with her, Wilhelm was certainly attentive and considerate, and Dona grew to love him deeply. A month after her marriage she wrote to her sister, "For a long time at first I did not love him so much as I do now. [My love] grew ever more and more and more, and I could not possibly describe to you how much I love him now."[9] Recognizing very early that the army was her husband's true passion, not long after her marriage Dona prudently began to learn to recognize the insignia of his various batallions and regiments.[10]

From Wilhelm's perspective, married life threatened at times to be a return to the crushingly dutiful life ordained by his parents and Hinzpeter, from which he had been liberated when he entered the university at Bonn in 1877.[11] He had a genuine affection for children, but, like his own father, Wilhelm had little interest in the daily chores of child rearing. He was proud of his growing family, especially because there were so many princes. Girls, according to his mother, Wilhelm considered to be of "no use."[12] The Crown Princess also claimed, with her usual critical exaggeration, that her son found all women to be either "dolts or idiots," but it is true that Wilhelm, who had had very little female company in his youth, never developed much interest in women.[13] In maturity, he criticized nations he did not like, notably France, as having unfortunate characteristics that were in his opinion distinctly feminine.[14] Wilhelm was cavalier and on occasion charming but also somewhat distant, being visibly more relaxed when no women were present. Marriage brought into his household a number of female courtiers who made Wilhelm uncomfortable, and he reacted by putting up a front of reserve, a defense that distressed both his wife and his mother. As Wilhelm grew older he found the pious "Hallelujah Aunts" (as he, too, called them), who constituted almost exclusively the society that Dona kept throughout her life, tiresome and too much underfoot.[15] He could also hardly have escaped realizing early on in his marriage what others saw quite clearly. Dona was very virtuous, an exemplary wife and mother, but she was at best rather lusterless, at worst a dull-witted bore.[16]

Wilhelm soon found that married life was more tolerable if he spent less time at home. He often went hunting with friends in Brandenburg and Silesia, and when in Potsdam, Wilhelm lunched and supped frequently with his regiment. These separations disturbed Dona, and she worried about the effect such a restless life might eventually have on her husband.[17] There were rumors of flirtations and affairs, but most of the Prince's acquaintances thought the likelihood of such boudoir adventures very remote, and even those who believed that Wilhelm perhaps had lovers were unable to point to any specific courtesan as the recipient of his favors.[18] Wilhelm did in fact engage in a number of affairs from 1882, the year after his marriage, until he ascended the throne in 1888, most of them conducted while on shooting expeditions in Austria. These liaisons were messy, for the Prince was indiscreet, and Chancellor Bismarck had some difficulty in covering their traces.[19] The only woman involved with Wilhelm who left a trail was Countess Elizabeth von Wedel-Bérard, an international adventuress about whom little is known.[20] Wilhelm met the countess in 1884 through the intervention of an Austrian archduke who had been her lover. She had recently acquired a "housekeeping" position in the Persian legation in Berlin and there received a number of letters from Wilhelm, one of which concluded with the endearment "Adieu chère adorée, je vous [sic] embrasse avec votre permission et je baise les belles mains de mon ange, ange [aux] cheveux rouges." Wilhelm's letters refer to parts of a repeating firearm that he had entrusted to the countess for delivery in Vienna, where she was to attempt to obtain a patent for an Austrian gun that the German General Staff was anxious to examine. She failed in this undertaking, and, when shortly thereafter gossip began to spread about the royal romance, Wilhelm terminated the relationship.

Once Wilhelm became Kaiser in 1888 his love affairs apparently ceased altogether, and he in fact found an escape from his marriage not in mistresses but in the First Foot Guards Regiment. Dona's veiled complaints about her husband in the early years following their marriage were not that she had been jilted by another woman but rather that she had become an army widow.[21] Dona's experience in this respect was identical to that of countless other wives of young guards officers. Bismarck once declared that "the First Guard Regiment is military monasticism, esprit de corps to the point of insanity. These men must not be allowed to marry."[22] Wilhelm was away from home more and more, leaving Dona alone to cope with her numerous pregnancies and to endure the embarrassment she felt in having to appear in society by herself. Even when Wilhelm joined his family for lunch or supper, he insisted on having his adjutants eat with him. He was always merry on these occasions, but Dona's reserved manner clearly indicated to her guests that she would have much preferred to have had her husband to herself.[23] To Wilhelm the regiment became the refuge, sought but not found in his marriage, from the oppression of his domineering English mother and his acquiescent father. "Here [in the regiment]," he declared, "I found my family, my friends, my interests—everything of which I had up to that time had to miss."[24] Fifty years later, Wilhelm's memory of these early army days, in which he said he had learned the meaning of "old-Prussian spirit and of old-Prussian comradeship," was still bright.[25] It was thus not his family, either his own or his parents', nor the process of his education but the army that provided Wilhelm his real love and supplied him not only with a code of behavior but also with a stock of conservative, Prussian ideas. Wilhelm never questioned the virtue of this heritage, and he died sixty years later, a true and devoted Prussian lieutenant to the end—"*Ub' immer Treu' und Redlichkeit, bis in dein kühles Grab*" (Be ever true and upright, unto thy cold, cold grave), as the clock of the garrison church in Potsdam chimed.

The enthusiasm with which Wilhelm threw himself into his military duties resulted in his being cut off from almost any society save that of his fellow officers in Potsdam. He rode with them, dined frequently in their mess, participated in regimental exercises and maneuvers, and lectured with enthusiasm, as well as to good effect, on famous battles of antiquity.[26] Wilhelm became identified with a group of younger guard officers—men resembling Adjutant Bülow and the marshal of the court Liebenau—who were conservative in their views, fixidly attached to the Prussian military tradition, and who, the Austro-Hungarian envoy reported to Vienna, unfortunately promoted the strain of "boisterous Junkerism" (*burschikoses Junkerthum*) in their future ruler.[27] Wilhelm's friend Count Philipp zu Eulenburg noted to his dismay that to the Prince "every Prussian officer was not only the quintessence of all that was honorable but also of all good morals, all education and intellectual gifts."[28] This idolatry of the officer corps inevitably led to an excessively narrow perspective along with a sort of self-satisfaction with pretensions of omniscience.[29]

Wilhelm's delight in the army gratified the corps, but they soon realized that the man who would one day be their supreme commander had only a limited military talent and an annoying supply of arrogance. As a child Wilhelm had been bossy at playing war games, and now years later his fellow officers would have the same experience. Gen. Walther von Loë, who as a close friend of the Crown Prince had every reason to want to find what talent he could in Wilhelm, took a dim view of the Prince's military abilities and hoped that Wilhelm's adjutant, Captain von Bülow, could salvage something. Loë complained that Wilhelm paid no attention to senior officers but insisted instead on implementing his own inferior ideas.[30] Loë's friend, General Emil von Albedyll, the chief of the Military Cabinet, had much the same view, noting in 1883 that the young Hohenzollern Prince had the reputation of being a "little teapot" (*kleiner Theetopf*). To Bülow would have to fall the task of making what could be made out of such unpromising material.[31]

Bülow, on whom both Albedyll and Loë had pinned their hopes, labored hard in his five years (1879–1884) as Wilhelm's adjutant to turn him into a real soldier. Bülow found this to be a virtually impossible task, since Wilhelm, though replete with superficial gestures, basically had not a trace of the traditional earnestness of either a Prussian officer or of a Hohenzollern prince. This, Bülow was certain, was because he had received an unsuitable education from teachers who had failed to curb his opinionated mind. In spite of all his exertions to make something of his charge, Bülow declared that he had failed in most respects, for Wilhelm's mental level was that of an immature teenager. Furthermore, Bülow considered that his pupil's mushy (*brei*) ideas revealed his lamentable English ancestry. But at least *some* progress had been made, and Wilhelm, he declared, was aware that he needed help.[32]

What could be done to prevent the eventual heir to the throne from developing into nothing more than an ordinary, if eager, soldier? The British ambassador, detecting in the Prince a "certain narrowness of views," prescribed a trip to England as an antidote.[33] Wilhelm's military isolation also concerned Chancellor Bismarck as well as his son Herbert, and they therefore wanted to relocate the Prince to Berlin, where he could be afforded a more broadminded society. But Wilhelm's military companions argued that in the capital he would be exposed to unfortunate "democratic" influences. Bülow declared that what the Prince was required to know of politics he could quite satisfactorily learn without leaving Potsdam.[34] Wilhelm I, whose sympathies always lay with the military, decided to let his grandson remain there with his regiment.

So, during the mid-1880s, Wilhelm continued to pursue his duties with fervor and seldom went to Berlin, where he was regarded in government circles as well as in public opinion at large—in the description of a British diplomat of the same mind—as a person "of small importance."[35] Even Wilhelm's future intimate, Philipp zu Eulenburg, found him unimpressive on their first encounter in 1883.[36] Indeed, prominent German officials knew little of the Prince other than that he was said to be happily married and enraptured by his military career.[37]

When Wilhelm did appear in Berlin it was usually to call upon his grandfather at tea time, when the old Kaiser did not like to be alone. From the time Wilhelm returned to Potsdam in 1879, following the completion of his studies in Bonn, Prussian courtiers had noted the increasing closeness of the octogenarian Emperor and his young and adoring grandson, who often accompanied Wilhelm I on his vacations at Bad Ems. Wilhelm was genuinely fond of the aging monarch, whom he regarded as his sole protector within the Hohenzollern family and who was, as he put it, "the only one who understands me."[38] Even his signature faithfully copied the Kaiser's decorative flourishes. The old sovereign took an obvious pleasure in his grandson, who helped him with his correspondence and often dined with him when the Empress was away. Wilhelm's devotion to the army impressed the Kaiser, although he wished his grandson would spend less time hunting and more attending to his regiment.[39] The Kaiser delighted in his namesake's conservative political views and his energetic and alert personality, so unlike the liberal ideas and taciturnity of the Crown Prince. Wilhelm I was relieved that, contrary to his expectations, Wilhelm had not become an "English democrat," a conversion that had unfortunately been all too successful with the Crown Prince.[40]

In September 1881, the Kaiser, without consulting the Crown Prince, decided to promote his grandson to major and transfer him from the First Foot Guards to the command of the famous Guard Hussars. This was an unprecedented step and caused considerable comment, since young Hohenzollern princes had traditionally served only in the Foot Guards during their military apprenticeship. The Kaiser's order undoubtedly annoyed the Crown Prince, always self-conscious about his dignity, especially in military matters, for his father had given him the prized hussar's uniform only when he was well into middle age.[41] Like the Foot Guards, the hussars were a very aristocratic corps, and among the lieutenants and captains were a number of princes from ruling houses. In the ranks of his new command, Wilhelm's closest friends were not his fellow royals but Major Walter ("Moses") Mossner, a baptized Jew whom Wilhelm would later ennoble, and Oskar von Chelius, a nouveau riche who had considerable musical talents. Chelius led the regimental band and shared the Prince's taste for Wagner's operas.[42]

The hussars were notable for their ribaldry and addiction to unrestrained banter and horseplay, in all of which Wilhelm indulged with relish.[43] From his hussar comrades Wilhelm also acquired a taste for coarse language and gestures, which complimented the martial brusqueness he had already picked up from Liebenau, Bülow, and his friends in the Foot Guards. Wilhelm's sharp, soldierly manner endeared him to many of the younger officers with whom he associated. He could talk about nothing besides the army and had an amazing fund of information about his fellow officers.[44] But Wilhelm was also a notorious stickler in matters pertaining to discipline, dress, and military etiquette. His grandfather had told him on entering the army that "in the service nothing is trivial," and Wilhelm took this injunction completely to heart.[45] There was no question but that in the regiment things were to be done his way. The British military attaché, whose judgment was similar to that of other observers, reported in 1887 that Wilhelm was "inclined to be obstinate and self-willed, and is rather disposed to affirm that a Prince of Prussia can do no wrong."[46] Some experienced military figures found the young Prince's martial pedanticism exasperating. Gen. Leo von Caprivi, who would succeed Bismarck as chancellor in 1890, had confided to a friend a few years earlier that Wilhelm "thinks he understands *everything* . . . he's as obstinate as a mule."[47] In his mid-twenties Wilhelm was already in every respect exactly the man he would later be as Kaiser or still later as an aging exile in Holland—rankly opinionated, blind to his errors, and utterly self-centered. In spite of his evident faults, few dared to challenge or criticize Wilhelm, although his divisional commander frequently did warn him not to be so egotistical. Most officers were silent or took advantage of the Prince's susceptibility to flattery, a weakness that gradually developed to alarming proportions.[48]

If Wilhelm's eagerness to excel as a soldier could sometimes be aggravating, so could his insistence that the hussars abide by his strict moral code. Wilhelm drank sparingly and even so mixed his wine with water, and, while he did not insist that his modest consumption be followed, he did prescribe that the mess serve German rather than French champagne. Wilhelm had a particular dislike for gambling, which, like drinking, was prevalent among the hussars, and he was very suspicious of the deleterious influence exercised by Berlin society on his troops. Wilhelm ordered that one aristocratic salon, where games were played for stakes and flirting abounded, be put off-limits to the hussars, but his outrage concentrated on the Union Club, which acted as a magnet for aristocratic officers anxious to escape the tedium of Potsdam and other garrison towns.[49] Wilhelm I was the club's official patron, and its membership consisted of a number of royal princes (including Wilhelm), the jeunesse dorée of the Prussian aristocracy, and a handful of wealthy Jews. Wilhelm was alarmed by the financial ruin suffered by impecunious officers who had played without success at stakes set by wealthier members, and he forbade his hussars to relax at the club.

Wilhelm's battle against vice was less important for its effect on the army, or on the Union Club, than it was in firmly enlisting as a close friend a man who was destined to play a leading role in his life during the next few years. This was Gen. Count Alfred von Waldersee, a distant relative of the Hohenzollerns, punctiliously aristocratic in deportment and rigidly conservative in his political ideas. Waldersee, who served as quartermaster general and vice chief of the General Staff from 1882 to 1888, possessed military talent of a high order, but he was also a schemer who aspired not only to succeed the aged Field Marshal Helmuth von Moltke as chief of the General Staff but also eventually to displace Bismarck from the chancellorship. These ambitions were not likely to be realized under either Wilhelm I or the Crown Prince, for neither liked Waldersee. The general, moreover, had a formidable opponent in the Crown Princess, who correctly believed that he exercised an unhealthy influence on her son.[50]

Waldersee had a thorough appreciation of the advantages to be derived from a close association with the old Kaiser's grandson. He was ever ready with a soothing word, a moral injunction, or a cleverly constructed insinuation, all of which were calculated to appeal to Wilhelm's feelings and to advance Waldersee's position. Wilhelm fell victim to these blandishments, and in 1882 he began to call regularly on Waldersee, sometimes at the discommoding hour of 7 A.M. He discovered in the general a fellow conservative, a staunch Protestant, and a foe of all forms of vice. In his battle against the Union Club Wilhelm had Waldersee's full support. The general introduced the Prince to his teetotaler wife, a New England grocer's daughter who had previously been married to one of Dona's great uncles. The witheringly pious Countess Waldersee, a woman of unrelieved monotony, soon established herself firmly in

Dona's graces, teaching her how to dress *à la mode américaine.*[51] The "Hallelujah Aunts" quickly allied with the countess, whose astringent piety resembled their own.

In 1884, two years after forming his friendship with Waldersee, Wilhelm acquired another new confidant in Count Herbert von Bismarck, the chancellor's elder son. In the course of a trip Wilhelm made to St. Petersburg in the spring of that year, Bismarck, the first secretary of the German embassy, took him under his wing. After the Prince's return to Germany the two men began a lively correspondence that continued even after Herbert's return to Berlin in 1885 to become state secretary of the Foreign Office. Few of his fellow diplomats were able to measure up to Herbert's exacting professional standards or to be equal partners in his caustic repartee or notorious debauchery. Wilhelm certainly could not, and it is hardly surprising that Herbert never became genuinely attached to him. In general, Herbert regarded the Prince as a tinsel soldier without much substance, seeking only amusement in his military duties.[52] At the same time, the chancellor's son could neatly calculate the advantages that might accrue to a close relationship with an eventual heir to the throne, and he therefore was careful to cultivate Wilhelm by writing him frequently in a respectful, and occasionally worshipful, tone. Herbert, like his father, was no liberal, but he found Wilhelm excessively conservative, a deviation he attributed to Waldersee's reactionary counsel. Nevertheless, the Prince's apparent willingness to follow Chancellor Bismarck's lead in diplomatic affairs was very gratifying. And while Wilhelm disapproved of the flagrant bacchanalia to which Herbert regularly succumbed, he seems to have taken a vicarious pleasure in associating with such an earthy and dissolute figure and gradually allowed the chancellor's son to exercise considerable influence over him.[53]

Just before coming under Herbert von Bismarck's spell, Wilhelm met Count Philipp zu Eulenburg, who quickly became the most intimate friend he was ever to make.[54] Eulenburg had originally intended to have a career in the army, but in 1877, owing to the entreaties of his good friend Herbert Bismarck, he had become a diplomat and a protégé of the Bismarcks, father and son. Although a member of a distinguished noble family, Eulenburg's aesthetic sensitivity set him apart from the rest of the Prussian aristocracy. He had some talent as a composer and lyricist of romantic ballads based on Teutonic themes, and he took extraordinary delight in matters of household decoration and entertainment. Eulenburg was essentially a dilettante, and as a diplomat his forte lay as much in retailing gossip or analyzing personal relationships as in a solemn

presentation of political intelligence. Although Eulenburg affected a resigned world-weariness, he had a lively interest in advancing his own
career and extending his influence. He knew how to adorn his courtly
airs with sycophantic touches, and his vast correspondence with Wilhelm—and with others from whom he had something to gain—exudes a
gushy, self-serving extravagance.

Eulenburg's first diplomatic assignment was as secretary of legation in
Munich, where he met Wilhelm in 1883, when the Prince stopped in the
Bavarian capital.[55] In May 1886 Count Richard Dohna-Schlobitten and
his brother Eberhard invited Wilhelm to a hunt on their vast estate at
Prökelwitz in Silesia. It was on this occasion, which extended over several days, that he and Eulenburg became favorably acquainted with one
another.[56] Herbert Bismarck noted with satisfaction the growing friendship between his friend Eulenburg and Wilhelm and urged Eulenburg to
exploit this relationship.[57] Eulenburg was a polished courtier who had
no need of Herbert's advice on how to ingratiate himself. There was no
duplicity at work here, for Eulenburg was an ardent monarchist, conservative to the core, and genuinely fond of Wilhelm. He charmed not only
Wilhelm but also Dona, who found her husband's new friend "*very* nice"
and who eventually came to trust Eulenburg no less than did Wilhelm.[58]
Eulenburg soon began to accompany Wilhelm to hear Wagner's operas,
and under Eulenburg's tutelage the Prince's enthusiasm for "the master's" music increased, for his friend was a Wagnerite and an intimate of
the composer's widow. Thereafter, when Eulenburg was in Berlin on
diplomatic missions he dined regularly with Wilhelm and on his return
to Munich kept in touch through letters, in which he provided the latest
tittletattle from the bizarre court of the demented Wittelsbach king, Ludwig II.

The atmosphere that enveloped Wilhelm at his grandfather's court
and the political attitudes to which he was exposed by friends such
as Waldersee, Adolf von Bülow, Herbert Bismarck, Liebenau, and Eulenburg were profoundly conservative. This group, with a few variations
such as Waldersee's mistrust of Russia, believed that the crown must
remain the ultimate authority, the army the guarantor of order, and that
German diplomacy should strive to maintain the traditional close relations between Berlin and the two bastions of East European reaction, the
Habsburg Empire and Russia. To these men, England figured neither as a
diplomatic partner nor as a model for the sort of reform that should

ensue in Germany when Wilhelm I died and the Crown Prince and Princess mounted the Hohenzollern throne. Wilhelm adopted his friends' ideas, and by his mid-twenties he had developed a profound hatred of parliaments, a conviction that the crown had the right to set aside the imperial constitution, and a veneration for the Prussian army.[59] German liberals, identifying the young Prince as a satrap of the reactionary camp, were disturbed; to Wilhelm's parents their son's drift to the right was a deep disappointment and indeed a personal affront.

Throughout the 1880s Wilhelm was thus locked between two opposing groups, both of which hoped to win his allegiance. On the one hand there were his mother, father, and their handful of disciples, who expected some day to lead Germany, with Prince Wilhelm in train, into a more progressive future. They feared anyone, such as Waldersee or the Bismarcks, who tried to sow ill will between Wilhelm and his father.[60] On the other side were the conservative forces, who wrote off the Crown Prince as hopelessly liberal and felt that his much-feared ascension would have to be endured but not supported. In Wilhelm the conservatives saw their cause reborn, and to them the greatest danger was that he might somehow be hoodwinked into adopting his parents' English views. He therefore had to be separated from the Crown Prince and Princess, whom the chancellor as well as Herbert Bismarck mistrusted and whose influence both worked hard to counter. The Bismarcks had a strong ally in Captain von Bülow, whose thralldom over Wilhelm was so great that in 1885 Herbert described the Prince as Bülow's "creation."[61] Wilhelm's closest confederate in the ranks of German diplomats, other than Eulenburg, was the captain's engaging but vacuous brother, Bernhard, who had succeeded Herbert as first secretary in St. Petersburg. Wilhelm had met Bernhard in 1884, and thereafter the two had entered into a correspondence. Bernhard, like his brother, had no great love for England or for Wilhelm's parents, and the result of the Bismarck-Bülow-Eulenburg-Waldersee ascendancy—according to Friedrich von Holstein, a friend of all the men involved except Waldersee—was Wilhelm's "systematic alienation" from his mother and father.[62] In the battle for possession of Wilhelm's loyalties, the victory went to the rightist clique, and by the mid-1880s he was widely regarded as a firm adherent of the "old Prussian" group in Berlin.[63]

Wilhelm was aware that to the conservatives he was the hope of the future. For the moment, he might be without power (although not without allies), but his hour would strike. Hence the ominous inscription the Prince wrote on an 1883 photograph depicting him in tartan dress for a

William Prince of Prussia, "I bide my time," 1884

costume ball honoring his parents on their silver wedding anniversary: "I bide my time."[64] From Wilhelm's conservative point of view, the Crown Prince was the less dangerous of his parents, for his liberalism was not so deep and his personality lacked Vicky's forcefulness. In the end Wilhelm fell out with both of his parents, but for his father, unlike his mother, he always felt a residual but highly qualified affection. The Crown Prince's relationship with his heir was a repetition of Hohenzollern history. Wilhelm I had been a stern and distant parent, and, as the Crown Prince matured, his father had pointedly neglected him and excluded him from many affairs of state. Perhaps the Kaiser was jealous of his son, for the Crown Prince had acquired a heroic stature as the result of his victorious commands in the wars of unification, while the aged sovereign had not been an active participant on the battlefield since he had witnessed the defeat of Napoleon at Waterloo as a youth in 1815.[65] In any case, father and son got on poorly and carefully avoided one another.

The Crown Prince had had a cordial relationship with his son when Willy was a boy, but this began to fall apart when Wilhelm turned eighteen and entered the university at Bonn in 1877. The Crown Prince was dismayed that Wilhelm seemed juvenile, and he complained, with good cause, that his son was wanting in tact and too inclined to be didactic in conversation.[66] Wilhelm's transformation from a guileless boy to an indifferent university student had alarmed his father, but his son's subsequent deterioration into a guards martinet was truly irksome. The Crown Prince was an authentic military hero and therefore found his son's martial posturing to be despicable, ersatz soldiery. Fritz deplored the narrow insularity of the guards' mentality, especially its dislike for England, that Wilhelm had adopted from his fellow army officers.[67] He consequently took what appears to have been spiteful pleasure in belittling Wilhelm's minimal military accomplishments in the presence of his brother officers, and he sarcastically referred to him as "my son, the compleat Guards lieutenant."[68]

The Crown Prince, whose jealousy was easily inflamed, resented the close and affectionate ties between his father and his son, and he expressed his bitterness openly. If the Kaiser wanted his grandson to do something, the Crown Prince invariably objected; he was suspicious of the traffic between the old ruler and Wilhelm and resentful that his son received more favors from the throne than he did, or indeed ever had.[69] There was little pressure that the Crown Prince could bring to bear on Wilhelm, for he had neither honors nor military promotions to distribute, and even his son's allowance was paid by his grandfather, thus making the Prince financially independent of his parents. "I can't endure it!" the Crown Prince once declared to Wilhelm's old tutor Hinzpeter. "My father and my son clasp hands on top of my head and press me down."[70] The Crown Prince's morbid disposition led him to have still another resentment against his son. This derived from Fritz's fear that he would not long outlive his father or might even predecease him, and that it consequently would be Wilhelm who would enjoy the real glory of the throne for which he and Vicky had waited so long.[71] Moreover, the Crown Prince mistrusted his son's attachment to the Bismarcks, to General Waldersee, and to the army, fearing that Wilhelm was trying to build up a conservative fronde that would be directed against the liberal element surrounding his parents.[72]

As the years went by, Wilhelm I seemed to be indestructible, and the Crown Prince abandoned any hope of an early ascent to the throne. He feared that if he ever became Kaiser he would be too decrepit with age to be an effective ruler. The Crown Prince, frustrated at being disregarded, became increasingly derisory and negative. He retreated more and more into a dreamworld of medieval splendor, dwelling there in a state of apathetic self-pity, from which even his far more energetic wife could not rouse him. Protesting that he was never told anything or paid any attention and used only as a "parade horse" for receiving foreign dignitaries, the Crown Prince refused to pay much attention to affairs of state and let others attend to his responsibilities.[73] It peeved him no end that Bismarck, on the other hand, was not only the center of attention but got private railroad cars and decorations studded with diamonds, none of which had come his way. The Crown Prince would on one occasion describe the pomp the crown would assume when he became Kaiser but on the next enter into dark speculation that perhaps it would be for the best if he died or abdicated in Wilhelm's favor.[74] Fritz's most pronounced characteristic was lethargy, and in idleness his unhappiness became profound. Some of the Crown Prince's exasperated friends began to refer to their future sovereign as a "mollusk," while a more charitable observer, his old admirer Gen. Albrecht von Stosch, lamented the fate of this "poor weak soul." "The prince is helpless, and one feels completely helpless toward him."[75]

The Crown Prince's deepening inertia resulted in his being almost totally dominated by his wife. He adopted her love of English art, interior decoration, and domestic life, and expressed regret that Germany would never be like *mein liebes England.*[76] Although the Crown Prince never wholly endorsed British parliamentary institutions or the notion of constitutional monarchy, he realized that the regal absolutism behind which Bismarck operated was anachronistic and would have eventually to give way to a less personal regime.[77] In matters of diplomatic gravity the Crown Prince unswervingly upheld Germany's interest, but in lesser difficulties involving Anglo-German relations he sometimes served as his wife's accomplice. The royal couple, for example, conspired to keep fine paintings in English collections from being sold to German museums, and the Crown Princess did not hesitate to supply the British press with material that put Bismarck in a compromising light.[78] Gradually, she succeeded in withdrawing her husband from the military milieu in which he had spent his career and enveloped him in her world of political liberals, artists, intellectuals, and foreigners. The contrast between the resentful and reclusive Crown Prince and his energetic, sociable son was not lost on the public or on the army, both of which were more and more drawn to Wilhelm.[79] Besides, the identification of the Crown Prince with anti-Bismarckian liberals led those who were either careful or ambitious to avoid him in order to give no offense to the all-powerful chancellor. Fritz acutely resented the lack of attention paid him, and he responded with a rude insistence on being accorded the recognition he believed he was due.[80]

As far as Wilhelm's relationship with his father is concerned, the trouble may in part have been due to the pronounced disparity in their personalities and intellects, for the Crown Prince had little of his son's effervescence or superficial brightness. Wilhelm may have felt inadequate when he contrasted himself not only with his father but also with his grandfather, both of whom were not only physically imposing men but also, for different reasons, national heroes whom millions venerated. Perhaps that is why Wilhelm, who would have no war experience until the summer of 1914, was eager to adopt such strident military airs, as though thereby to equate himself with his Hohenzollern forefathers. It may have been the generational difference that introduced a fatal ingredient into the relationship between Wilhelm and his father. Hinzpeter had noted in 1879 that the old Kaiser's generation had sunk into a pessimistic and embittered patriarchialism, the Crown Prince's complained that it was powerless, while the excitable youths who were Wilhelm's age were unable to differentiate between the sober realities of history and the heady world of legend.[81] In any case, Wilhelm found much to criticize in his father, whom he reproached with being too proud, too artistically inclined, too eager for popularity, and without character or ability.[82]

Throughout the 1880s, Wilhelm complained that his father ignored him, and indeed the Crown Prince noted wearily that he and his son had fallen into the same antagonistic pattern that characterized his own relations with the aged Kaiser.[83] He would not discuss political affairs with Wilhelm, much as the Kaiser declined to initiate his own son into such matters. When father and son encountered one another, the Crown Prince, according to Wilhelm, "always treated me like a dumb kid *(dummer Junge)* and with the most deliberate rudeness."[84] Wilhelm could hardly have failed to note the difference between this treatment and the adulation he received from his soldiers in Potsdam or the respectful attention Herbert Bismarck, Waldersee, Eulenburg, and other conservatives accorded him.

Wilhelm held that his mother, more than anyone else, was to blame for the trouble he had with his father, whom he rightly felt had become her creature. Although Wilhelm resented the way the Crown Prince often treated him, their quarrels, unlike those with his mother, were sometimes short-lived. Along with his older siblings, Wilhelm was more attached to his father than to his mother.[85] He found that in affairs of state he and the Crown Prince could sometimes work out an understanding; on occasion they even discovered themselves in agreement. Father and son shared a pride in the annals of Prussian history and a conventional evangelical piety, both so at variance with the Crown Princess's Anglophilia and unorthodox religious views. The trouble, Wilhelm maintained, was that the Crown Princess would not leave him alone with his father for more than five minutes and worked constantly to create difficulties between the two of them. The moment she entered the room the Crown Prince's benign demeanor turned into one of cold, sullen suspicion.[86] This Wilhelm much regretted—"I am his for the asking," he assured Herbert Bismarck—and he hoped that he and his father might compose their differences.[87] But a reconciliation never occurred, and by about 1884 the Crown Prince and his son were barely on speaking terms.

Wilhelm's difficulties with his mother are easier to understand, for while he found the Crown Prince merely annoying or pitiable, she exasperated him. There was no point on which the Crown Princess exhibited less sensitivity than in her insistence, so pronounced as to have seemed perverse even to those who liked her, that England should be the standard by which all things German be judged.[88] Sir Edward Malet, the British ambassador in Berlin for many years and a man who had a high regard for the Crown Princess, deplored the hatred she had sown among the Prussian elite. "She has shoved English institutions down their throats," he wrote in 1888, "and that they very naturally resent."[89] Her zeal to be English contributed to her impolitic forthrightness, an attribute that often intensified into dogmatism and intolerance. Hans Delbrück, a tutor of one of the Crown Princess's younger children, once asked an English boy named Fox, who was a friend of Wilhelm's, how the German phrase "*ein verrückter Engländer*" (a mad Englishman) should be translated. The child's answer was that it would be "a man who does what he likes and does not care for other people's opinions." Whereupon, Delbrück reported, the Crown Princess let out a resounding "Bravo, Mr. Fox!"[90]

Other than a few women in her retinue and a handful of bluestockings in Berlin, the Crown Princess made no friends in the forty years she lived in Germany. She often complained that she had no intimates; all her emotions were invested in her husband, with Queen Victoria serving as the outlet for her expressions of loneliness and distaste for Prussia. She felt herself superior, as a Hanoverian princess and as an Englishwoman, as an Anglican (she never joined the establishment Evangelical Church of Prussia), as a figure of wealth in a land of impoverished nobles, as a savant at a court that was intellectually lifeless, as a liberal among political antediluvians, and as a woman who insisted on—and secured—a position of domestic equality with her husband. There was some truth in all this, for Wilhelm's mother was a remarkable woman. She might have realized, however, that discretion, and not hauteur, was what was required of a foreign-born princess whose destiny had taken her to a parochial kingdom.

Berlin society, in which she was known as "*Die Engländerin*," fully reciprocated the Crown Princess's dislike. The Prussian aristocracy decried her unconventional religious and social views, her English liberalism and its pernicious influence on her husband.[91] But this criticism did not much concern the Crown Princess, for she had a low regard for Berlin's stiff and inelegant philistinism. From the moment of her arrival in Berlin in 1858, Vicky had found little in Prussia to admire, and long years of residence there only steeped her distaste for the land her husband one day would rule. On returning to the capital in 1885 after a trip to Italy, the Crown Princess poured out her feelings to her Italian-born friend, Countess Marie von Dönhoff. "I cannot tell you," she wrote, "how bitterly I feel the contrast when I come back to the heavy dull stiffness, to the cold ugliness of north Germany and the neighborhood of Berlin! The moral atmosphere of the Court, the political and official world seems to *suffocate* me! The ideas, the tastes and feelings and habits are so totally different from mine, that I feel the gulf between me and them deepen and widen and bitterest and hardest of all is that my son Wilhelm and his wife stand on the other side of this gulf!!"[92] Because of the Crown Princess's forceful and often tactless manner, she was at the center of many of the disputes that beset the Hohenzollern family. She loved politics and she gloried in argument, pursuing both with fixed and doctrinaire views. It did not faze her that she was a woman, a foreigner, and the powerless wife of a man who had no authority so long as his father lived. Ambassador Malet, commenting on the Crown Princess's enthusiasm for political affairs, wrote in 1886 that "it would be a good thing if she were to leave them alone until she can control them—and probably then also."[93] Malet was a good friend, but he had no more influence on her than anyone else. In her pursuit of politics, the Crown Princess had a docile and resigned captive in the Crown Prince, but in Wilhelm she found an obstinate competitor. The Crown Princess belittled her son and insisted on treating him as a youth, constantly interfering in everything and doing so in an emotional manner that sometimes approached hysteria. Wilhelm, who was colder and quieter than his mother, was determined not to yield. Stubbornness, he told Eulenburg, was a maternal inheritance, but it was also a weapon that he fortunately could employ to thwart his mother's machinations on behalf of England.[94] The Crown Princess's irrepressible taste for argument, Wilhelm noted, had the effect of driving him into the opposite point of view.[95] The two men who knew Wilhelm best at this time, Eulenburg and Waldersee, likewise believed that it was his mother's stridency that had turned him into an Anglophobe guards officer.[96]

Wilhelm's obdurate refusal to accept the Crown Princess's ideas persuaded her that although partially English in blood, he was in character thoroughly Prussian. She suggested that her eldest child was more like his mentally incompetent great uncle, King Friedrich Wilhelm IV of Prussia, or the dictatorial Frederick the Great, or the autocratic and psychically imbalanced Tsar Paul of Russia, who was Wilhelm's great-great-grandfather through the Saxe-Weimar line of the Empress Augusta, his paternal grandmother.[97] Like her husband, the Crown Princess viewed with alarm Wilhelm's transformation from an undistinguished student into a swaggering Prussian lieutenant. From the time that her son went to the university at Bonn in 1877 his mother began to reproach him for his rudeness and indifference. She did not like his failure to inquire about her condition when she was ill, or to consult her, or to show the least concern or interest in his three younger sisters. "He is a curious creature!!!" she wrote in 1885 to Queen Victoria. "A little civility and kindness and empressment [would] go a long way but I never get them from him."[98] The Crown Princess does not seem to have worked very arduously at trying to understand her eldest child. She insisted on having him behave as she expected, and when it became clear that Wilhelm was going to chart his own course, her reaction was a mixture of anger and self-pity. She was entirely incapable of understanding that she was in any way to blame for the deterioration in their relationship.[99] The Crown Princess might have labored with more effort to establish a harmonious relationship with her son had she not convinced herself when her children were young that a mother's lot was invariably to be disappointed by her offspring.[100]

As her children matured, the Crown Princess's forebodings were amply fulfilled. The three eldest, Wilhelm, Charlotte, and Heinrich, whom she had neglected in childhood in favor of her younger children, never developed much attachment to their mother and were all conventionally Prussian in outlook. The Crown Princess found them deficient in loving attention and gratitude as well as hopelessly retrograde in their political views. As a result, she clung very possessively to her three younger daughters, who developed into dutiful girls who shared their mother's devotion to England, and she idolized the memory of her son Waldemar, who had died in 1879.[101] The year 1881 seems to have been the point at which the Crown Princess's disappointment in her elder son grew into an open quarrel. Prince Chlodwig zu Hohenlohe-Schillingsfürst, who knew the family well and who was a distant kinsman of Wilhelm's wife, was surprised to hear in May of that year that Wilhelm was having "conflicts" with his parents.[102] With time the gulf between Wilhelm, Charlotte, and Heinrich on one side and their mother on the other widened, and the Crown Princess finally wrote them off altogether. "These are not my children," she forthrightly declared in 1888 to her friend, King Oscar II of Sweden.[103]

It was Wilhelm who most concerned his mother, for Charlotte was a mindless pleasure-seeker and Heinrich a drab naval officer with no great future. Wilhelm, on the other hand, would one day be a ruler, which made his deplorable behavior and his reactionary political opinions intolerable. The Crown Princess made her disapproval unmistakable, and Wilhelm soon found that the best policy was to avoid any discussion of politics with her. She expressed her anguish in long letters to Queen Victoria, in which complaints about Wilhelm abounded. He was arrogant, unloving, headstrong, and full of "rubbishy" political notions. She

Prince Wilhelm as the Great Elector, 1885

attributed all these wayward traits, insofar as they were not due to Wilhelm's generally poisonous Hohenzollern-Weimar heritage, not to her own negative influence but to two other sources. One was the old Kaiser, who had insisted over her objections on keeping his grandson at Potsdam and Berlin rather than allowing him to broaden his perspective through travel. Like the Crown Prince, she resented Wilhelm's attachment to his German grandparents, whose indulgence she held partially responsible for his boorish behavior. She frequently warned Dona that Wilhelm had better watch out for the day when his grandfather would no longer be on the scene, for what she as Crown Princess could not teach him she would order as Kaiserin.[104]

The Crown Princess identified her enemies, Chancellor Bismarck and Herbert, as the other cause of the ruination of her son, whose admiration for the old man she found extravagant and excessively deferential.[105] The Crown Princess watched her son's entrapment with dismay and sadly admitted that with his immature mind and intractable Prussian instincts Wilhelm had become the chancellor's "tool."[106] Herbert Bismarck was even worse, for he was a "young tiger" with all his father's faults. The animosity between the Crown Princess and the two Bismarcks was entirely mutual. In the chancellor's opinion, she always regarded England as her home and used her influence, often in ways that ran counter to his own, to try to have Germany advance England's interests. As for Herbert, he was equally suspicious of the Crown Princess and believed that in order to counteract her influence Wilhelm could not, as he put it, "be stirred up enough against England."[107]

Wilhelm's dislike of his mother proceeded in part from his feeling that she, like his father, treated him like an immature youth.[108] It may be that her increasingly lacrymose state following her son Waldemar's death in 1879 got on his nerves. That, in any case, is about the time that the first reproaches flying between mother and son are to be noted. But to Wilhelm what was singularly obnoxious about the Crown Princess was her dogged devotion to England. He considered her Anglomania intolerable, and he found the antidote at Potsdam, the haven of "joy, happiness, and contentment on earth," where "all that was highest and most holy: Prussia [and] the army" was revered.[109]

It was in his regiment that Wilhelm first learned to despise England. Even had he had a mother of purely Prussian extraction, Wilhelm would very likely have emerged as no admirer of the British, for Prussian aristocratic society, the only world that Wilhelm knew after leaving Cassel, had no enthusiasm for his mother's country and few ties to it. The Hohenzollern army, a preserve of the nobility, naturally reflected this distaste, and nowhere was it more apparent than in Potsdam, where only the most aristocratic regiments were quartered. This antagonism to England seems to have been especially pronounced in Wilhelm's old regiment, the First Foot Guards, in which even the English language was hated.[110] This, it should be noted, was to some extent due to the unpopularity of the Crown Princess, not only because she was English but also because she dominated her husband. "Nothing appears to an officer more degrading than the tyranny of women," wrote one of Wilhelm's junior officers who shared the army's general dislike of the Crown Princess. "A lash of the whip offends him hardly less than the reproach 'henpecked'! (*Weiberknecht*)."[111] Wilhelm shared this dismay, for he found the Crown Prince's supineness before his wife intolerable. Like the old Kaiser, Wilhelm believed—not without justification—that his mother had made a vassal of his father.[112]

Wilhelm's opposition to his English mother, who had isolated her once heroic husband, and his own conservative and thoroughly martial manner brought him increasing popularity in the army. By the mid-1880s, the young officers in Wilhelm's circle did not hesitate to declare that the Crown Prince should renounce his rights of succession and the court be purged of English influences.[113] Wilhelm never openly advocated his father's abdication, but otherwise his attitude was completely in accordance with his friends' views. He began to reproach his mother with lack of patriotism, declaring that she had failed to become a Prussian and had instead persisted in adhering to the progressive views of her Coburg father, the "sour, anglomaniacal" Prince Albert.[114] In Wilhelm's opinion, the people with whom his mother fraternized were an unworthy collection of extremists and leftist intellectuals. She was, he declared, not liberal but in fact radical and even traitorous in her political ideas, a sort of foreign agent (so Wilhelm assured Herbert Bismarck), always passing on what she learned from her husband to the Queen of England.[115] She had also succeeded in making Anglophiles out of her three younger daughters, Victoria, Sophie, and Margaret. He wrote off these siblings as the "English colony" and for the rest of his life had little to do with them. Germany could never tolerate a foreigner such as his mother on the throne, and Wilhelm even speculated that his father would have to be "separated" from her once he became Kaiser.[116]

It cannot be a coincidence that in the early 1880s the five people who were closest to Wilhelm—Captain von Bülow, Captain Gustav von Kessel, General von Waldersee, Philipp Eulenburg, and Dona—were all anti-

English in sentiment. Bülow, like Waldersee, was a firm conservative and an outspoken opponent of the Crown Princess, who in turn considered Bülow's influence on her son to be especially dangerous. Her anxiety was justified, for Bülow had Wilhelm well in tow. In 1885 Bülow declared, with what seems to have been complete accuracy, that he did not believe that anyone enjoyed Wilhelm's confidence in political affairs as much as he did and that consequently "the balance of the scales is in my hands." If Bülow had a competitor within the junior ranks of the army, it was his successor in 1884 as Wilhelm's adjutant, Captain von Kessel. A cousin of the Eulenburgs and Bismarcks, Kessel was rabidly Anglophobe and eager to spoil Wilhelm's relations with his parents. His influence on Wilhelm was very great, for Wilhelm relished not only Kessel's attacks on England but also his prodigious fund of vulgar anecdotes. As she would with Bülow, the Crown Princess correctly identified Kessel as a very malign enemy.[117] Waldersee conspired with Wilhelm against his parents' liberal ideas and noted with pleasure in 1882 that the efforts by the Crown Princess and her husband to instill notions of English kingship in their son had failed. "He seems to have much of his [Prussian] grandfather in him," the general wrote approvingly. "If his parents had the aim of raising him to be a constitutional king who obediently bows before the will of a parliamentary majority they have had a misfortune. To all appearances he is emerging just the opposite."[118]

Eulenburg watched Wilhelm's increasing dislike for England with concern, not because he had any attachment to the British, but because he was afraid that Wilhelm's Anglophobia was drawing him too close to Russia. Eulenburg (by his own account) attempted, unsuccessfully as it turned out, to make Wilhelm more moderate, but he shared his aversion for England. Eulenburg, who went there only once, regretted that there were many Germans who took pleasure in aping what they saw across the North Sea.[119] Dona agreed entirely with her friend Eulenburg. She had had an English governess and spoke and wrote English better than her husband. But Dona developed an intense and inflexible dislike of England, believing that Englishmen were immoral, untrustworthy hypocrites who held dangerously liberal ideas.[120] The Crown Princess initially had formed a good opinion of her son's fiancée, but not long after the wedding in 1881 she began to feel disenchanted with Dona, whose docility—a characteristic with which no one could reproach the Crown Princess—struck her as quite odd. Vicky had nothing in common with her thoroughly domesticated daughter-in-law, whom she found uncommunicative and whose eager and indiscriminate support of Wilhelm she resented.[121] It appears that Dona, rebuffed in her efforts to establish a good relationship with her mother-in-law, consequently treated the Crown Princess with a cold formality that revealed hardly any traces of affection. The "Hallelujah Aunts," like the men in Dona's retinue, shared the abiding hostility for England of their royal mistress and did not like the Crown Princess, who in turn referred to her daughter-in-law's ladies as a "blessed set of donkeys."[122]

It is hard to say who should bear the blame for the unfortunate relationship between Wilhelm and his mother. One of the few people who knew them well and liked them both, Sir Edward Malet, the British envoy, declared that he was unable to determine where the fault lay.[123] Certainly much of the responsibility rested with the Crown Princess because of her insensitivity to the fact, however unpalatable it may have been to her, that her children were dynastically Prussian and not English. As Wilhelm grew up, she did not concentrate her attention so much on nurturing his positive qualities as continually seizing upon what she found deficient in him. In her letters to the Crown Princess, Queen Victoria almost always took her daughter's side, but she conveyed the impression that she believed that the blame for the feud was not entirely Wilhelm's.[124] Wilhelm was of course not innocent, for he was cold and sometimes mean to his mother, almost perversely adopting mannerisms, ideas, and friends calculated to dismay the Crown Princess. But he certainly should not bear all, or perhaps even most, of the blame. It may be that Wilhelm was right, and the tempest within his family best accounted for, when he declared that he and his mother were too much alike to have got along.[125] She proclaimed her alien English views with stridency and determination, oblivious to the consequences, and he replied in kind in his aggressively Prussian manner. The Crown Prince, regretting the hostile division within his family, occasionally tried to intervene, but his efforts were entirely fruitless. When he urged his son to pay more attention to his mother, Wilhelm imperiously replied, "I don't want to hear that kind of talk."[126]

What had begun as a family feud soon acquired a wider audience, for by the end of 1882 Wilhelm's outrage at England had become quite unrestrained, due to the cumulative effect of his quarrels with his mother and the pervasive influence of his friends. An additional factor that may explain why Wilhelm's attacks on England became so much more inflamed at this time was his resentment at the imperial ascendancy in Egypt that the Liberal government of William Ewart Gladstone had established in 1882. Wilhelm, like the Bismarcks, believed that the aim of

Gladstone's policy was not only to prevent any conquests by Germany in Africa but also to break up Wilhelm I's solidarity with the Habsburg Emperor and the Tsar.[127] In any case, a conservative acquaintance reported with approbation in December 1882 that Wilhelm "stressed at every opportunity his antipathy to everything English and his sympathy for strong, robust, conservative qualities."[128]

Even Queen Victoria, with whom Wilhelm had always had the most affectionate relations, fell victim to her grandson's wrath. He claimed alternately that the Queen was the captive of his mother, or the reverse.[129] Queen Victoria meanwhile had begun to form a negative impression of her oldest grandchild. For years the Queen had shared the concern of her late consort, Prince Albert, that Wilhelm might develop into a "conceited Prussian." From the time that Wilhelm was a small child she had feared that there was cause for worry. Like the mother, the grandmother found Wilhelm inclined to be headstrong and prideful, but she was nevertheless quite fond of him and enjoyed his visits to England. The Queen had hoped—in vain, as she eventually realized—that when Wilhelm entered the university at Bonn he would retain the virtues his parents and Hinzpeter had tried to instill in him. But before Wilhelm had completed his first semester, Queen Victoria declared that her grandson's "affectation of independence and of 'mystery' is quite intolerable and not at all right or kind."[130] The admirable boy who had gone off to Bonn with such promise had swiftly degenerated into an inconsiderate and pretentious Prussian. Finally, in 1883, she declared that Wilhelm had turned against England. The Queen, who could be quite peevish, was annoyed because her grandson had failed to express the appropriate congratulations when in the course of 1882 her armies reduced Egypt to a British sphere of influence, a triumph that Wilhelm much resented.[131]

In the midst of this discord, two new and related issues arose that subjected Wilhelm's relations with his family to further strain. One was his diplomatic mission to Tsar Alexander III in May 1884. The other, which was connected to the first but far more important, was the engagement at the end of 1883 of his sister Victoria to Alexander Battenberg, the ruling Prince of Bulgaria, a backward Balkan principality over which Russia had a commanding influence. Wilhelm was furiously opposed to the Hohenzollern-Battenberg marriage, while his mother and eventually his father favored the match.

In the spring of 1884, over the objections of the Crown Prince and Princess, the Kaiser decided to send his grandson to St. Petersburg as his representative at the coming-of-age ceremonies for the Tsarevitch, the future ill-fated Nicholas II. The Crown Prince, who had expected to be his father's deputy, was very offended. The decision to deputize Wilhelm originated with Chancellor Bismarck, who hoped that entrusting the mission to the conservative young Prince rather than his Anglophile father would make a favorable impression on the dour and reactionary Tsar. The chancellor was anxious to bring about an improvement in Russo-German relations, which had seriously deteriorated as a result of the unfavorable terms meted out to Russia at the Congress of Berlin in 1878, over which Bismarck had presided. The assassination in 1881 of Tsar Alexander II, the nephew and admirer of the old Kaiser, had loosened the bonds between the two great empires still more, for Alexander III, the newly crowned Tsar, was suspicious that Germany had designs in the Balkans that could be realized only at Russia's expense.

Wilhelm entirely shared Bismarck's aspiration to tighten Germany's connection with Russia, especially because it was the best safeguard against Britain's ambitions, and he therefore took up his mission with enthusiasm. Accompanied by General Waldersee and his adjutant Bülow, now promoted to major, he arrived in St. Petersburg in May 1884. While Wilhelm's opposition to the Battenberg marriage recommended him to Alexander III, the Tsar, who had always been very reverential toward his parents, considered the reports of Wilhelm's quarrels with his mother and father to be an alarming indictment of his character. The Tsar's concern dissipated, however, when Herbert assured him that it was the Crown Princess, and not Wilhelm, who was responsible for the difficulties within the Hohenzollern family. Wilhelm succeeded in pleasing his difficult host, and after the visit had been concluded Alexander assured the German ambassador that "everything the Prince told me pleased me enormously. He grasps things exactly right and understands everything. I was very gratified by our conversation."[132] Wilhelm I was delighted with his grandson's performance on his first exercise in diplomacy.[133]

Wilhelm enjoyed his trip to Russia immensely, for while his parents had always treated him like a boy, the Russians had paid proper court to an heir to the throne.[134] As soon as Wilhelm left St. Petersburg he began to write to the Tsar. In his first letter, written from Moscow on 25 May 1884, he warned Alexander of English duplicity and boldly urged him not to be alarmed by what he heard concerning the anti-Russian inclinations of the Prussian Crown Prince. "He loves being contrary," Wilhelm informed the Tsar, "and is in the hands of my mother, who is directed in turn by the Queen of England and makes him see everything through 'English spectacles.' I assure you that the Emperor, Prince Bismarck, and

I are in agreement, and I will never cease to regard as my very highest duty the consolidation and maintenance of the Three Emperors League. The triangular bastion must defend monarchies and Europe against the waves of anarchy, and it is precisely that which England fears more than anything else in the world."[135] Wilhelm was no sooner back in Berlin than Bismarck sent him out again, this time to Vienna, where he discussed Balkan affairs with the Emperor Franz Josef and King Milan of Serbia. Wilhelm's parents found their son's diplomatic missions galling, for they underlined his closeness to Kaiser Wilhelm I as well as the old ruler's preference for his grandson. Wilhelm's activity abroad in the chancellor's service also made it obvious that he was now firmly enmeshed in Bismarck's conservative, Russophile web.[136]

In the mid-1880s, the greatest stumbling block jeopardizing Bismarck's attempt to improve Russo-German relations was the uncertain condition of the Balkans, where Russia rivaled Austria-Hungary, Germany's ally, in eagerness to appropriate the European territories of the decaying Ottoman Empire. A potentially dangerous area was the nominally independent principality of Bulgaria, which the Great Powers had taken from the Ottoman sultan in 1878 and then awarded to Russia as a sphere of influence. In the following year, the Bulgarian national assembly had elected Alexander Battenberg to be the country's ruling prince. Tsar Alexander II immediately ratified the choice, since he was the Prince's uncle by marriage and expected him to be a loyal vassal. The new ruler, however, soon indicated that he did not intend to be a puppet sovereign, and as a result he and Alexander III, who succeeded to the Russian throne in 1881, became bitter opponents.

The young and handsome Battenberg was well connected to many European courts. His father was a member of the grand ducal house of Hesse-Darmstadt, which had many genealogical connections with the Prussian Hohenzollerns. Alexander's cousin, the Grand Duke, had been married to Princess Alice, a sister of the Crown Princess of Prussia. Alexander, however, had no wife, and he appealed to his cousin and friend, the Crown Princess, to help him find a suitable bride with whom he could share his lonely existence in primitive Sofia. The Crown Princess liked Alexander very much, as did her husband, and she readily agreed to serve as matchmaker. She proposed a number of royal candidates, including one of Dona's younger sisters, but for one reason or another all proved unsuitable or uninterested. A few years later, in the summer of 1883, Alexander paid a visit to Berlin, where he met and instantly fell in love with Princess Victoria, the seventeen-year-old daughter of the Crown Prince and Princess. They became engaged without informing anyone of their intentions.

Wilhelm I and Bismarck found this romantic development, which was not long in being revealed, very undesirable, since they were convinced that the presence of a Prussian princess alongside the Russophobe Battenberg on the Bulgarian throne would impair the restoration of cordial relations between Berlin and St. Petersburg. Bismarck even threatened to resign should the match succeed.[137] The Crown Princess, however, believed that even among royalty love should prevail in marriage, and with typical imprudence she refused to consider the political ramifications of the match. The Crown Prince, who was usually susceptible to his wife's importunities, on this occasion refused to consent to the marriage. Fritz had to take into account his father's objections, but the real reason for his opposition was that Alexander, as the descendant of a morganatic marriage, was an unsuitable candidate for the hand of a Prussian princess. "He is a parvenu," the Crown Prince haughtily declared. "Any Prussian noble of an old family is more distinguished."[138]

Like his father, Wilhelm considered the Battenbergs to be pretentious upstarts, and he shared Bismarck's concern about the damaging effect that such a marriage would have on Russo-German relations.[139] He did not like Alexander and was completely unconcerned about his sister's happiness, for she was a member of the Crown Princess's "English colony" and therefore of no interest to him. Wilhelm argued that the surest way to kill the romance would be to have Alexander toppled from his princely throne, making him incontrovertibly unsuitable for a Hohenzollern bride. Alexander could then be given a cavalry regiment somewhere in southern Germany and fade into celibate obscurity.[140] The Tsar, for different reasons, had the same intention.

In contrast to her Prussian son-in-law and grandson, the Queen of England was not in the least troubled by the morganatic cloud that obscured Battenberg's ancestry, and she was happy to have him marry her granddaughter. Alexander, moreover, possessed an irresistible asset: in his dignified, modest manner and darkly handsome appearance he reminded the Queen of her beloved, long-dead husband, Prince Albert.[141] In April 1884 Queen Victoria had given her consent to Alexander's brother Ludwig to marry one of her Hessian granddaughters. The Battenberg connection with England was further solidified when, early in January 1885, Queen Victoria's youngest child, Princess Beatrice, became engaged to the third Battenberg brother, Heinrich, a guards officer in Potsdam. Wilhelm was aghast and regarded his Aunt Beatrice's engagement as an English maneuver to prepare the ground for Victoria's marriage to Alexander Battenberg.[142]

Queen Victoria did not gladly countenance any opposition in family matters. King Carol of Rumania, whose nephew and heir had just become engaged to a granddaughter of the British monarch, declared in 1892 of the Queen that "in politics she may be liberal but in her house she is the greatest autocrat I have ever encountered. She expects to be treated by her children like a supernatural being."[143] The Queen became enraged when she learned from the Crown Princess that not only Wilhelm but also Dona were opposed to Victoria's engagement to Alexander because of the nonroyal ancestry of Alexander's mother. This was too much. Dona herself, "a poor little insignificant princess," the Queen pointedly reminded her daughter, had a grandmother who was "*only a countess*."[144] "As for Willie," Queen Victoria wrote again a few weeks later, "that very foolish, undutiful and I must add unfeeling boy, I have no patience with, and I wish he could get a good 'skelp'g' as the Scotch say and seriously a good setting down."[145] Because of her annoyance, the Queen declined to allow her grandson to pay a visit to England later in 1885. Queen Victoria's refusal to receive Wilhelm irked him, but it was a rebuff that he could use to advantage at home. The behavior of his grandmother—"the old hag" (*alte Reff*)—at least would provide him an effective retort to his mother's reproaches that it was *he* who was hostile to the Queen.[146]

In September 1886, a mutiny of the Bulgarian army inspired by Russia deposed Alexander, and after a brief return to Sofia he abdicated. Almost a year later the Bulgars elected a Coburger to assume the throne in Sofia. Although Alexander's removal from Sofia defused the possibility of a Russo-German collision over Bulgaria, Kaiser Wilhelm I and Bismarck continued to oppose any nuptial connection between the Hohenzollerns and the lowly, unsuitable Battenbergs. Wilhelm's prediction that the collapse of Alexander's fortunes would quash the Battenberg marriage project proved incorrect, for Alexander's misfortune did nothing to lessen his fiancée's love or deter the Crown Princess from continuing to press for the wedding. She had meanwhile won her impressionable husband over to the marriage, and Fritz came to the conclusion that Alexander Battenberg's statesmanlike qualities made him worthy of being granted some high position in the German government or army. Perhaps the Crown Prince shared his wife's belief that Alexander might even eventually become chief of the General Staff or even, ne plus ultra, imperial chancellor.[147] Wilhelm did not know of his parents' extravagant ambitions for Alexander, but he believed that the Crown Prince intended, when he became Kaiser, to appoint his future son-in-law viceroy of Alsace-Lorraine. Wilhelm rhetorically declared that rather than allow this he would kill Battenberg. "No one," he vowed, "will be named to Strasbourg other than myself." Warming to this sanguinary prospect, Wilhelm assured Herbert Bismarck that "if all else fails I will shoot the Battenberger dead."[148] The real hope for the enemies of the marriage lay not in Wilhelm's imaginary revolver but in the old Kaiser, who could force the Crown Prince to promise that when he became sovereign he would not allow the marriage. Meanwhile the Crown Princess went on with her plans.

The Battenberg crisis facilitated Wilhelm's emergence as a diplomat, since he was prominently identified as opposing a marriage that Tsar Alexander also disapproved. In the summer of 1886, Wilhelm I, having first taken his grandson to Bad Gastein to confer with the Habsburg Emperor Franz Josef, decided, apparently at Bismarck's suggestion, to send Wilhelm to Russia once more. The Crown Prince was disqualified because his partisanship of Battenberg made him persona non grata in St. Petersburg. The Crown Princess predicted that no good would come of Wilhelm's trip, for he was, she assured Queen Victoria, "as blind and green, wrong-headed and violent on politics *as can be*!"[149] In spite of her objections, Wilhelm went to Russia, where he discussed the Battenberg marriage and other Balkan affairs with the Tsar.[150]

The chancellor and Herbert observed Wilhelm's behavior on these diplomatic assignments with interest and approbation, and shortly after his return from Russia in 1886 Herbert, now state secretary at the Foreign Office, suggested that Wilhelm be given a temporary appointment there so that he could learn something about the formulation as well as the execution of diplomacy. Wilhelm himself had brought up with his grandfather the matter of such an assignment, but the Kaiser was reluctant to agree, for he knew that the Crown Prince would be resentful. Eventually, however, the Kaiser consented, instructing Herbert to begin his grandson's training at the Wilhelmstrasse, "in order that his young soul be protected from error."[151] The Crown Prince, already aggravated because he had repeatedly been rejected for service as the Kaiser's emissary, expressed his outrage to his son in such a forceful way that Wilhelm told Herbert Bismarck that he had never seen his father so beside himself with anger. The Crown Princess was equally furious, and Wilhelm was convinced that his parents' opposition stemmed in part from their fear that he would use his entrée in the Foreign Office to wreck the Battenberg marriage.[152] Perhaps they also detected the danger to Wilhelm's already well-developed ego that Franz von Roggenbach, one of their closest confidants in the anti-Bismarck camp, perceived. Roggenbach was alarmed that Wilhelm's posting to the Foreign Office was yet another sign of the great chancellor's favor for the Prince. "It would be a misfortune for the young man," Roggenbach wrote to a friend, "if his self-esteem became still more inflated by thinking that he now possessed some special inspiration because he was the acolyte of the High Priest."[153]

Perhaps as a sop to the Crown Prince, Wilhelm went briefly to the Prussian Finance Ministry to learn something of fiscal affairs, but his attention concentrated on diplomacy. In spite of his parents' objections, in the fall of 1886 and on into the spring of the following year Wilhelm went once or twice a week to the Wilhelmstrasse 76, where he was shown selected diplomatic documents. Ordinarily, Friedrich von Holstein, the most influential counsellor in the Foreign Office, would have guided Wilhelm, but Holstein had opposed the Prince's being introduced into diplomatic affairs because such an assignment would only increase the influence on Wilhelm exercised by Holstein's opponent Herbert Bismarck. Herbert's hold on Wilhelm, Holstein felt, was already great enough. Moreover, Holstein had reservations about Wilhelm's discretion and believed it impolitic to disregard the Crown Prince's objections to his son's involvement in diplomacy. Besides, Holstein would be unable to conceal from Wilhelm the fact that he did not favor the conception of a Russo-German alliance to which the Prince was attached.[154]

With Holstein unavailable, it fell to Herbert to try to dispense instruction in European politics. He found, however, that after an initial burst of enthusiasm Wilhelm showed little interest in the dispatches assembled for his inspection.[155] Ludwig Raschdau, a young official in the trade section, took charge of familiarizing Wilhelm with colonial and non-European matters. The Prince had considerable difficulty in finding time for his work, since he continued to have to fulfill all of his military responsibilities in Potsdam. In spite of the shuttling back and forth, Wilhelm liked his exposure to the Wilhelmstrasse, where, he boasted to Queen Victoria, he had learned "how to do politics and how to manage to steer the ship of state between the shoals and intricate channels of treaties, foreign susceptibilities etc. It is vastly interesting and gives one a much broader horizon for judging people or nations in their actions."[156] If Wilhelm enjoyed his introduction to foreign affairs, the personnel of the Foreign Office generally did not like having him underfoot. As a student of diplomacy in Berlin, Wilhelm displayed the same superficiality that had characterized his university career in Berlin. He was neither faithful in attendance nor serious about his work.[157] Perhaps the Foreign Office staff failed to counter Wilhelm's resistance to concentration by interspersing their instruction with jokes and banter, a ploy Wilhelm's adjutant Major von Bülow vainly advised diplomats to adopt if they wanted to snare their royal pupil.[158]

While Wilhelm was desultorily leafing through the diplomatic archives, on 22 March 1887 his grandfather celebrated his ninetieth birthday, the occasion of a great outpouring of national thanksgiving. The remarkable physical vitality of the Kaiser was a bitter reminder to the Crown Prince that he himself was now entering his late fifties, a fact that doubtless fed his morbid preoccupation that his father's longevity might rob him of the throne. The aging Kaiser clearly believed that after his death what he had stood for would be defended not by his Anglophile son but by his staunchly Prussian grandson, to whom in the twilight of life he drew increasingly close.[159] In April 1887, the Crown Princess wrote to her mother of the impasse in the relations of the three generations of Hohenzollerns. Wilhelm was indulged by his grandfather, while the Bismarcks pandered to his ego. "He is *so* headstrong, *so* impatient of any control, except the Emperor's, and *so suspicious* of everyone who *might* be only a half-hearted admirer of Bismarck's that it is quite *useless* to attempt to enlighten him, discuss with him, or persuade him to listen to other people, or other opinions! . . . Fritz takes it profoundly *au tragique*, whilst I try to be patient and do not lose courage!"[160]

The animosity and rivalry between Wilhelm and his parents augured poorly for the inevitable day when the Crown Prince would come to the throne. Wilhelm I's health was exceptionally strong for a man of his age, and the British ambassador, writing at the end of 1886, not long before the Kaiser's ninetieth birthday, declared that the old sovereign was in "marvellous health, full of life and eating his dinner like a man of 20."[161] But for a year or so Wilhelm I had begun to have brief periods during which he lost consciousness, and he became easily confused, often referring to Wilhelm rather than the Crown Prince as his son. Although the Kaiser recovered quickly and resumed his insistent attention to affairs of state, there was increasing concern in Berlin that the end could not be far off and that the long deferred reign of the Crown Prince and his English wife would at last begin.

Four

THE END OF A REIGN

THE FESTIVITIES in March 1887 marking the ninetieth birthday of Kaiser Wilhelm I were to be followed in June by Queen Victoria's far more elaborate Golden Jubilee celebration, which many of her fellow sovereigns planned to attend. The Kaiser's great age and uncertain physical condition would not permit him to undertake a journey to England. Under ordinary circumstances, the Crown Prince would have represented his father, but in the spring of 1887 it seemed as though illness might prevent his being present in London to pay tribute to the mother-in-law he greatly admired.

Throughout the fall of 1886 the Crown Prince suffered from a persistent hoarseness, and by Christmas he was frequently unable to speak. In March 1887 a throat specialist discovered a growth on the left vocal cord, which when cauterized quickly reappeared. This disturbing development led to a further consultation in May with six prominent German laryngologists, who unanimously declared that the polypous growth was a malignant epithelioma that should be removed immediately, even though the necessary operation, which held some danger for the patient's life, would render him permanently speechless.[1] Confronted by this grave verdict, the Crown Prince bravely agreed to submit to the operation, and a room was prepared in the palace where it would be performed.

The German physicians, whose spokesman was Berlin's leading surgeon, Ernst von Bergmann, decided that before undertaking the operation, which might have serious political as well as medical consequences, they should consult the leading European authority. The doctors agreed that Dr. Morell Mackenzie of Harley Street in London, with whose magisterial text on disorders of the larynx they were familiar, should be called from England. In choosing Mackenzie, Bergmann was partly influenced by his knowledge that the Crown Princess would be sure to prefer an English specialist, and she did indeed wish to have Mackenzie examine her husband. But the Crown Princess, aware of her unpopularity in Berlin, was afraid that if *she* summoned a London specialist, it would be interpreted as yet another proof of her British prejudices. She therefore proposed that Queen Victoria request that the doctor go to Germany. Although the Queen's investigation of Mackenzie indicated that his ambition for fees and honors was at least as great as his medical reputation, she agreed. Mackenzie readily submitted to his sovereign's request and arrived in Berlin on 20 May.

On examining the patient, Mackenzie insisted on a biopsy, which revealed no traces of malignancy. The surgery was deferred and a subsequent and more extensive biopsy, which seemed to him to reveal no traces of malignancy, once again indicated that there was no cause for alarm. Mackenzie was very gratified that his positive verdict had been sustained. The Crown Prince had only to rest for six months in a warm climate and he would be healed.[2] The German physicians who were involved in the case were not persuaded by their British colleague and continued to insist that the lesion was malignant. The Crown Prince's position was more difficult at this juncture than it had been a few weeks earlier, when all his German doctors had agreed that a laryngotomy was imperative if his life was to be saved. Now there was a division of opinion, and while the great majority insisted that surgery be performed without delay, the most eminent specialist assured him that the growth was benign and that there was no need to operate. In making up his mind what course to follow, it seems likely that the Crown Prince was guided less by weighing the rival opinions of his physicians than he was by the political factors involved. As he reflected on what lay before him, the Crown Prince came to the conclusion that a man who could not speak would be incapable of assuming the crown. If he submitted to the laryngotomy and survived, he might live for years, but only to be forced to surrender his rights of succession to Wilhelm. To live, however briefly, with a voice was the only way he could hope to mount the throne he and his wife had so long dreamed of occupying. There was, besides, the chance that time might prove Mackenzie right.

The Crown Prince therefore declined to undergo the laryngotomy and declared that a change of climate, as well as sparing his throat by avoiding all but the most necessary conversation, would soon restore him to health. In his heart, however, the Crown Prince was characteristically pessimistic about the outlook and continued to brood about the likelihood that he would die before his nonagenarian father.[3] He accepted his illness, as he had resigned himself to every other misfortune, with an apathy not devoid of self-pity. "What does it matter if I die," the Crown Prince said to a friend at the time the suspicion of cancer had not yet been confirmed. "It is agreeable to me."[4] His wife, on the other hand, was the very picture of confidence. Mackenzie's opinion was all she required, and she dismissed the forebodings of the German physicians. She was convinced that her husband's life was not in any danger and that he would soon be well. "She swims in optimism," a friend wrote at the end of May, for Mackenzie's assurances meant that there was now no reason that the Crown Prince must submit to a dangerous operation and thereby miss being present in London for the Jubilee celebration.[5]

The Crown Prince's serious illness became common knowledge by the middle of May 1887, and the disagreement between Mackenzie's favorable prognosis and the much gloomier opinion of the German doctors was at the center of the discussion of his condition. With few exceptions, the Prussian court and public opinion at large were convinced that the Crown Prince was mortally ill with cancer and that his life was being jeopardized by his wife's insistence on following the advice of a single British physician. The Crown Prince would soon be dead, as inevitably would the old sovereign. By an unexpected turn of events it was quite suddenly conceivable that within months Prince Wilhelm might ascend the throne, a prospect which pleased hardly any statesmen in Berlin. Friedrich von Holstein, an official at the Foreign Office who had observed Wilhelm during his assignment there in 1886, thought that he was immature and potentially dangerous. All that could be said for his ascension was that it would present new opportunities. With economy both of language and feeling he wrote to Herbert Bismarck that the Crown Prince's illness "means a turning point in world history. God's ways are wonderful. Your father is old and Wilhelm II is young."[6]

Chancellor Bismarck and his son, who had no reason to look forward to the Crown Prince's becoming Kaiser, were alarmed at the thought of Wilhelm on the throne. The news of the Crown Prince's illness—the chancellor was sure from the outset that the malady would prove fatal—brought on a neuralgic attack and reduced him to tears, for Bismarck recognized that, little as he liked the Crown Prince's English affinities, Wilhelm was too inexperienced to succeed his grandfather as Kaiser. "No," he declared, "the Crown Prince is necessary for us. May God spare him until my dear Prince Wilhelm [becomes] mature."[7] Herbert took an equally pessimistic view, since he was convinced that the Prince was a frivolous but cold-hearted martinet. Both father and son believed that if Wilhelm came to the throne in his present inexperienced state, the results, especially in diplomacy, could be disastrous.[8]

Unpalatable as the thought of Wilhelm clothed in imperial purple might be, the young Prince had now to be courted, for it seemed likely that the Crown Prince's reign, if he managed to outlive his aged father, would be quite brief. Those, such as the Bismarcks, who had been concerned about the continuation of their power under the future rule of the Crown Prince now shifted their attention to Wilhelm. One of the few figures in Berlin who was eager to see Wilhelm become Kaiser was General von Waldersee, who was as interested in the improvement of his own political fortunes as the Bismarcks were in the retention of their power. Waldersee noted that he was not the only one in Berlin who was watching the Prince with a new degree of expectation. On 21 May 1887, only a few days after the dire nature of the Crown Prince's illness had become known, Waldersee reported in his diary, "it is interesting to see how certain clever people have instantly changed their evaluation of Prince Wilhelm. If yesterday they complained about him, finding him heartless, inconsiderate and I know not what else, today he is said to have a firm character and to promise much for the future."[9]

Wilhelm received the news of his father's illness with the same lack of feeling for which his mother had so often reproached him. Philipp Eulenburg noted that when Wilhelm informed him of the seriousness of the Crown Prince's ailment, he did so "with earnestness but without any warmth."[10] Wilhelm, unlike his mother, was convinced that the growth on his father's larynx was cancerous. He dismissed Mackenzie, with whom he refused to have any contact whatsoever, as a fraud whose bland assurances that the lesion was benign were false.[11] When Wilhelm first encountered his mother after learning how dangerously ill his father was, his behavior could not have surprised her. He informed her that it would have been better for his father to have fallen on the battlefield against the French almost two decades earlier than now to have to face a long, dehumanizing illness. The Crown Princess was horrified at her son's frigidity and reminded him, to no effect, that the Crown Prince's safe return from the Franco-Prussian war had provided the two of them almost twenty years of abundant married happiness.[12]

Once Mackenzie had overruled the laryngotomy proposed by the German physicians, his prescription for the Crown Prince was a sojourn in a favorable climate that would free him from excessive use of his voice and thus enable Mackenzie's promised "healing" to occur. The Kaiser agreed that his son might recuperate abroad, but this meant that Wilhelm would have to assume his father's public functions. Even before the onset of his illness, the Crown Prince felt resentment at the official role that Wilhelm I had frequently deputized his grandson to perform. Now for the sake of his health he would have to surrender some of his own representational duties. This was a prospect that did not please the Crown Prince, who enjoyed the ritual occasions over which he was asked to preside.

The first confrontation between Wilhelm and his father because of the Kaiser's insistence that Wilhelm replace the Crown Prince occurred over the question of who would represent the Kaiser at Queen Victoria's Jubilee on 20 June 1887. The Crown Prince was determined to take part in the festivities. Mackenzie had no objections, since this official trip could be combined with a vacation in the cool highlands of Scotland. The Kaiser, unaware of Mackenzie's opinion and anxious to spare his son any unnecessary exertion, decided that Wilhelm should be the Hohenzollern representative. Unfortunately, before the Kaiser's decision had reached the Crown Prince, Wilhelm informed his mother and father of this development with what seemed to them to be ill-concealed self-satisfaction and entirely too much officiousness. The Crown Prince, who had every intention of being in London, was very annoyed by his son's behavior and by the fact that the Kaiser had not consulted him in the matter. He succeeded in persuading Wilhelm I to change his mind and appoint him as the Prussian representative, and the question now became one of whether Wilhelm, who was insistent on being included in the German deputation, would accompany his parents. The Crown Princess, who would have preferred to punish her son by having him remain in Berlin, advised Queen Victoria that even though Wilhelm's conduct toward his parents and his grandmother had of late left much to be desired, it would be expedient to invite him, since otherwise he would surely fall into a rage.[13] The Queen had no wish to receive her grandson after his opposition to her wishes in the Battenberg marriage affair, and she fumed to the Crown Princess about his "impertinence." "I am furious with his behavior," she declared, but since the Crown Princess believed that in the long run it would be less unpleasant if Wilhelm were invited, the Queen did not expressly strike him from the list of guests.[14] On 13 June the Crown Prince took leave of his father, whom he would never see again, and departed from Berlin, which he would next reenter nine months later, on 11 March 1888, as Kaiser Friedrich III.

Even before his arrival in England, Wilhelm provided an intimation of what a difficult guest he would be. He insisted, to Queen Victoria's irritation, on bringing a larger suite than she felt his position as a second-in-line to the throne warranted. Wilhelm responded to his grandmother's objections by telling his friend Eulenburg a few days before his departure for England that it was "high time the old woman died." On the next day

Wilhelm gave further proof of his nasty frame of mind in his remark to Eulenburg that "one cannot have enough hatred for England."[15] Wilhelm's attitude was hardly a propitious beginning, and his conduct on the trip did nothing to ingratiate him with the English. According to Herbert Bismarck, Wilhelm aspired to make a conquest of official London, thereby reminding his mother that he did not need to depend on her to make himself popular in England.[16] Once across the North Sea, however, Wilhelm failed to make the impact on the haut monde that he had hoped for. Wilhelm's behavior in England only worsened his already ragged relations with his mother, with whom he quarreled and whom he annoyed by his ostentation and effervescence.[17] Queen Victoria restricted her contact with Wilhelm to formalities, which led him to the resentful conclusion that his grandmother was the senile captive of her Germanophobe children.[18] The visit ended as it had begun—on a sour note—inasmuch as Wilhelm and Dona both acutely resented the fact that at court ceremonies they were not accorded what they believed to be the proper honors, the most egregious insult being the precedence before Dona awarded to the dusky Queen of Hawaii.[19]

After the Jubilee, the Crown Prince remained in Britain, to enjoy first the warm breezes of the Isle of Wight and then, in August, the cooler air of Scotland. This prolonged sojourn led to objections in Germany that he should be being treated at home. While his condition did not perceptibly decline, it also gave no evidence of the improvement that Mackenzie had assured his patient that he could effect. The Crown Prince and his wife continued nonetheless to place their confidence in the English doctor. The ailment was harmless, she assured a friend, and Mackenzie was "confident and happy" about the Crown Prince's health.[20] A week or so after the Crown Princess wrote this reassuring word, she and her husband, together with their three younger daughters, moved on to Toblach, a resort in the Austrian Tirol the Crown Prince had always especially liked. Here, however, he encountered cold, rainy weather and had increasing difficulty with his throat. On Mackenzie's advice, the royal party now departed for Italy, in the hope that a warmer climate might prove efficacious. Venice was the first stop, followed by Baveno on Lake Maggiore, but the weather there proved to be unseasonably cold, and the change of scene did the Crown Prince no good. The Crown Princess, who was delving into the medical texts dealing with disorders of the throat, hastily summoned Mackenzie to Baveno, and he now reversed his original diagnosis, declaring that the growth was in fact malignant.[21] On 3 November 1887, the royal household decamped to San Remo on the

Italian riviera, where a lease had been taken on a newly constructed house, the Villa Zirio. Here the Crown Prince would spend the next four months, walking in the garden and reading Thomas à Kempis's *Imitation of Christ*.

Mackenzie had by now become thoroughly alarmed. Although the Crown Prince felt well and could speak, sometimes quite normally if he elected not to spare his voice, the tumor, almost certainly malignant, appeared to be spreading. This meant that at some point, and possibly in the near future, the Crown Prince might begin to experience difficulty in swallowing and breathing. In light of this foreseeable complication, on 9 November Mackenzie gathered all of the German physicians for an examination of the patient's throat. Wilhelm had secured his grandfather's permission to go to San Remo and to take along a laryngologist from Frankfurt, Dr. Moritz Schmidt.[22] Wilhelm's motives in traveling to Italy were not entirely clinical, however. Except for a brief visit to Baveno to celebrate the Crown Prince's fifty-sixth birthday in mid-October, Wilhelm had not seen his father since their trip to Queen Victoria's Jubilee the previous June. His sister Charlotte and brother Heinrich had both made visits to Italy, and Wilhelm feared that he would seem to the public to be unconcerned if he failed to make an appearance in San Remo.[23] Wilhelm and Schmidt arrived in San Remo just as the joint consultation of all the Crown Prince's doctors was getting underway, an arrival that the Crown Princess complained was "unannounced and unasked."[24] The examination resulted in a unanimous diagnosis of incurable carcinoma, and this devastating opinion appeared in Berlin's semiofficial *Reichs-Anzeiger* on 12 November.

Wilhelm was present two days later when the doctors informed his father of their verdict. The Crown Prince, according to his son's account in a letter to Queen Victoria, received the grim report "like a Hohenzollern and a soldier. He knows that he is irretrievably lost and doomed. . . . It is quite horrible, this confounded word 'hopeless.' "[25] The Crown Prince initially was hurt that Wilhelm acted as though he had already become the heir to the throne and wished his father out of the way. When Wilhelm had the temerity to bring up the question of abdication, his father's indignation knew no bounds.[26] He spoke so harshly of his son's imperious behavior that even the Crown Princess cried out in dismay: "Fritz, you shouldn't think things like that. After all he's our child."[27] By the end of Wilhelm's four-day visit, however, he and his father managed to part amicably. As Wilhelm remarked to Count Hugo von Radolinski, the marshal of the Crown Prince's court, the tragic circumstances dictated an armistice in the war long waged between them.[28]

The Crown Princess, however, proved to be more difficult. She had not wanted either Wilhelm or Dr. Schmidt to come to Italy, fearing that they would try to force her husband to return to Berlin for a laryngotomy.[29] Wilhelm did in fact agree with the majority of his father's doctors that the operation should be attempted. It would be dangerous and offered only a slender chance of saving the Crown Prince's life, but in Wilhelm's opinion death was preferable to a protracted agony.[30] This difference of opinion between Wilhelm and his mother as to how the Crown Prince's malady should be treated led to a titanic storm, and the Crown Princess became so enraged that she threatened to have her son thrown out of the villa. Wilhelm eventually apologized—presumably for having taken too forceful a hand in interrogating his father's doctors—and thereafter his mother had to admit that her son's visit had gone off agreeably. She told Queen Victoria that she found that Wilhelm could be quite nice "when he has not had his head stuffed with rubbish at Berlin." But, she added, "I *will not* have him dictate to me."[31] Although Wilhelm acknowledged that the last part of his stay in San Remo had been calm, his trip to Italy did nothing to heal the breach between him and his mother. He came back to Berlin full of admiration for his father's heroism but very angry at the Crown Princess. "She treated me like a dog," he told Waldersee on his return.[32]

The Crown Prince calmly accepted the verdict that he was a dying man, once again declining to submit to a laryngotomy. Better, he reasoned, to yield to the will of Providence and to hope for the best.[33] In spite of the Crown Prince's qualified optimism, his wife, so dogged in her faith in Mackenzie, was forced to admit that her husband was lost.[34] But rather than concede defeat, the Crown Princess now launched upon the role she would play until only days before her husband's death seven months later. Except with her family and a few intimates, she assumed a resolutely optimistic attitude, insisting that the Crown Prince's condition would stabilize so that he would live for years and airily dismissing any ominous portents as transitory or insignificant. "We are *not justified* in saying that is *not* a cancer . . . but . . . it is *not* proved [that it is] beyond all possibility of doubt!" she equivocated to her friend the former Countess Dönhoff and now the wife of Bernhard von Bülow. It was a brave, though fraudulent, part, but the Crown Princess, with that fierce intensity that so marked her character, played it grandly.[35]

The fatal announcement from San Remo threw all of Europe into consternation, for now the Crown Prince had to be written off as a man already dead. A sense of doom lay heavily on Berlin, where in almost all quarters the news from Italy was received with dismay. Dona noted that the end could come at any time and that she and Wilhelm lived "under a shadow." "It would have been so good," she lamented, "had we not so prematurely succeeded to this responsible position."[36] Those who, like the chancellor, had from the onset of the Crown Prince's illness feared the consequences for the succession, were reduced to despair. The only consolation that Bismarck could unearth was that Wilhelm, although immature for his age, was at twenty-eight exactly as old as Frederick the Great had been when he had become King of Prussia in 1740.[37] But Bismarck very likely shared the opinion expressed two months earlier by General Leo von Caprivi, who in 1890 would succeed him as chancellor and who found Wilhelm disagreeably obstinate. "Good Heavens," Caprivi had declared late in September 1887, "whatever will happen if Prince Wilhelm becomes Kaiser as early as this?"[38] Herbert Bismarck, however, judged the sudden turn in events with his accustomed brutality. Herbert admitted the selfishness of his reaction at first learning of the Crown Prince's serious illness. Now, Herbert believed, he was assured of holding his position as head of the Foreign Office for life, if not of eventually obtaining the chancellorship. And when, in November, the verdict of an incurable malignancy was confirmed, the chancellor's son had only the laconic comment: "consummatum est!"[39]

The mortal nature of the Crown Prince's illness meant that Wilhelm's position suddenly became crucial. The old Kaiser took the verdict calmly that his son was incurably afflicted, but he was shaken.[40] Wilhelm I was ninety but hardly feeble—he even went hunting at the end of October 1887—but his health was uncertain, and he could no longer perform all of his ceremonial tasks. Ever since the Crown Prince had gone abroad the previous June there had been considerable feeling that Wilhelm should be allowed to shoulder some of his grandfather's burden. Such an authorization would be sure to upset the Crown Prince and Princess, who would regard it as an attempt by their son to encroach on their own position. But there was the more alarming possibility that the Kaiser, who fainted from time to time, might some morning be discovered dead in his bed. In such an event, the Crown Prince could be incapable of making the journey to Berlin to assume his crown, or, even if that effort did not kill him, he might be too debilitated to perform any of his royal offices. One means of averting the constitutional dilemmas that Wilhelm

I's decline or death would pose was for his grandson to become regent in either eventuality. A more extreme solution, one to which Bismarck gave some consideration, was that the dying Crown Prince should abdicate his rights of succession in favor of his son and heir.[41] Wilhelm was himself susceptible to such speculation and declared to his friend Eulenburg that it was "very questionable whether a king who cannot speak can indeed really be King of Prussia."[42] The Crown Princess was outraged and declared that even though her husband was sick he would nevertheless make a better ruler than their healthy but immature son.[43]

The Kaiser evaded making any decision on the regency question until the medical examination on 9 November revealed that his son's condition was hopeless. He then decided that the wisest procedure would be not to establish a regency but instead to assign Wilhelm certain limited rights of representing the crown. This would spare the aged monarch's strength, yet, it was hoped, give no cause for offense to the Crown Prince. Without consulting his son, on 17 November the Kaiser issued an order granting Wilhelm general authority to serve as a surrogate at the sovereign's pleasure.[44] The order did not produce the desired reaction in San Remo. The Crown Princess declined to show her husband the official communication transmitting the Kaiser's order, out of fear that it might undermine his condition, but she failed to intercept a letter from Wilhelm to his father, informing him of the new powers Wilhelm I had granted his grandson. When the Crown Prince read his son's letter he broke into tears and denounced both Wilhelm and Bismarck for having secretly plotted his exclusion from affairs of state. The Crown Princess had to restrain her husband from going at once to Berlin to protest.[45]

Wilhelm's execution of his new representative commission would not provide him with any systematic opportunity to increase his very limited knowledge of the working of the Prussian or imperial governments, for his duties would be essentially ceremonial. The Kaiser therefore decided that his grandson would have to be introduced quickly into such matters. Over the objections anticipated from San Remo, in late November 1887 Wilhelm I decreed that Wilhelm would recommence the training initiated in 1886 in the Foreign Office and also expand his indoctrination to include other branches of the government.[46]

The supervision of Wilhelm's instruction in foreign affairs fell to Chancellor Bismarck, a task that he was anxious to undertake. Bismarck had not displayed more than a polite interest in Wilhelm until the onset of the Crown Prince's fatal illness, a development that meant that, contrary to all former expectations, he had to contemplate a future in which the Prince would be his master. During the early 1880s, while Wilhelm served with his regiment in Potsdam, the chancellor invited him frequently to dine with the Bismarck household, where, in contrast to his parents' home, he found himself treated as an adult worthy of attention.[47] The chancellor also occasionally wrote to Wilhelm about political and military affairs of mutual interest. Bismarck liked the Prince's alert and spirited manner—"a nice young man," he declared in 1885, "a very nice young man." The chancellor's only complaint was that Wilhelm talked too much.[48] Bismarck admitted that although Wilhelm was too immature for the throne that stood so imminently before him, there was material in the man from which a sovereign could perhaps be made. That would depend on Wilhelm's being willing to follow his lead, which Bismarck was confident would be the case.[49]

Wilhelm responded to the chancellor's attentions with unreserved admiration and treated him with the utmost deference.[50] As early as 1883 Wilhelm was reported to be for Bismarck *sans phrase*, and over the next few years the chancellor found that Wilhelm's homage to him was, if anything, excessive. Herbert Bismarck declared in 1886 that his father was the surest channel for handling the Prince, inasmuch as Wilhelm's reverence for Bismarck was so great that he believed every word the chancellor uttered.[51] Both the Bismarcks would gradually learn, however, that the Prince, for all his dutifulness, liked to be his own man. Once the prospect emerged that he might soon become Kaiser, Wilhelm had to consider whether, in spite of his admiration of Bismarck, he would follow his grandfather's example in allowing the chancellor to wield the dominant authority in Germany. In the fall of 1887, a rumor spread through Berlin that the chancellor had suddenly died. Wilhelm's reaction to the news, which reveals the coldness with which he often dismissed other people's misfortunes, was to observe that "no man was irreplaceable, even Prince Bismarck. There are other excellent men who would be suitable to succeed him." When it was pointed out to Wilhelm that the highest office in the land required a man who could combine excellent judgment with a firm hand, his retort was that such attributes were indeed not necessary for a chancellor but rather for a ruler.[52] By the end of 1887 Wilhelm had come to the conclusion that while Bismarck's continuation in office for a few years was certainly absolutely essential, eventually many of the functions the chancellor performed would have to be assumed by the crown.[53] The great contest of wills that led to Bismarck's resignation in 1890 was thus prefigured even before Wilhelm came to the throne.

Wilhelm certainly did not share Chancellor Bismarck's assumption that one day his son Herbert would succeed to the chancellorship and to his father's role as the unchallenged arbiter of German policy. Although Wilhelm had initially derived a vicarious thrill from observing Herbert's bacchanalia and relished listening to his piquant conversation, by the time of the crisis brought about by his father's illness he had become disenchanted with Herbert's crudeness and familiarity.[54] This change in Wilhelm's attitude was undoubtedly due in part to Dona, whose rectitude clashed with Herbert's earthiness. She believed that Herbert's enemy, the sanctimonious Waldersee, with whose Christian welfare efforts she was closely involved, was instead the person on whom Wilhelm should rely. She was therefore quite concerned at the influence that Herbert, so unlike Waldersee and so opposed to him, seemed to have on her husband.[55] Like the chancellor, Herbert was unflagging in his courtesies to Wilhelm, but these polished efforts were only a mask for what was a basic dislike. Although Herbert frequently assured Eulenburg, who was sure to repeat what he heard, that he respected Wilhelm, in fact he thought the Prince narrow-minded and "cold as a hound's nose."[56]

The attentions that the chancellor and Herbert paid to Wilhelm—such as the elder Bismarck's urging Wilhelm to assert himself forcefully—were undoubtedly in part responsible for the Prince's growing self-importance.[57] The chancellor's intent, never openly revealed but suspected by many who watched his relationship with Wilhelm, was to strengthen the young man's autocratic, conservative views so that he might serve as a counterweight to the parliamentary notions imported from England by his mother.[58] It apparently did not occur to Bismarck that Wilhelm, with his willfulness intensified by such encouragement, might one day turn this trait of character against him. For several years the chancellor had believed that Wilhelm's development would be channeled into the right direction if he moved from Potsdam to Berlin. In the capital he could learn something of how the civil government worked, and the influence of the young officers in his regiment, of whom Bismarck disapproved, would be correspondingly reduced.[59] Now that it appeared that Wilhelm might soon become Kaiser, such a move was all the more imperative. This would also enable the chancellor to keep a closer watch on a young man who was lately showing disquieting signs of wanting to have his own way.

In seeking to bring Wilhelm to Berlin late in 1887, the chancellor had a number of allies. The Crown Prince and Princess, who for years had been alarmed by the military tone that prevailed in Potsdam and their son's susceptibility to its allure, agreed to the move. In the Foreign Office, Herbert Bismarck, Wilhelm's friend Bernhard von Bülow, and the influential counsellor, Friedrich von Holstein, had for some time been trying to bring Wilhelm to Berlin in order to liberate him from the "lieutenant's viewpoint" that had been ingrained in him by his narrow-minded military companions.[60] A number of highly placed figures in the Prussian army also wanted to have Wilhelm in the capital, for in the absence of the Kaiser because of age and of the Crown Prince because of illness there was no longer any royal figure to stand in public view at the head of the troops. In light of the widespread belief in 1887 in German military circles that war with France (if not with Russia, or both) was imminent, this seemed particularly desirable. Field Marshal Helmuth von Moltke, the chief of the General Staff, as well as General Emil von Albedyll, the chief of the Prussian Military Cabinet, argued that Wilhelm should be given the command of an army in Berlin. Such a promotion would have the desirable effect of separating him from his cronies in Potsdam while at the same time investing him with a more responsible military role.[61]

General von Waldersee, who was at the center of the opposition to the Bismarcks, also favored having Wilhelm in Berlin, where Waldersee was stationed as quartermaster-general. The general had no doubt that he, rather than the chancellor and his son, would triumph in the contest for Wilhelm's allegiance. Now that the Crown Prince's life expectancy was so limited, the chancellor would have to ingratiate himself with Wilhelm, a task, Waldersee noted with satisfaction, that would be impossible because of their differences in age and temperament.[62] In 1887, Bismarck turned seventy-two, while Wilhelm was only twenty-eight, and Waldersee a comfortable fifty-five. The general's prognosis would prove quite correct, although Bismarck's failure to maintain his grasp on Wilhelm did not, as Waldersee had confidently expected, work in the general's favor.

The Kaiser hesitated to bring his grandson to Berlin, first because he felt Wilhelm was not ready for promotion to the high rank that would be required for an army command and also because with his habitual parsimony he did not want to disburse the appropriate salary. He was also worried about the effect that such an appointment would have on the Crown Prince. Wilhelm I did agree, however, that three advisors, whose responsibilities would be to carry out a scheme of instruction devised by Bismarck, were to be attached to his grandson. The chancellor's first nominee was Ludwig Herrfurth, an official in the Prussian Interior Ministry, who was learned but somewhat doctrinaire in his views. Wilhelm complained that Herrfurth was too old and too boring for them ever to be able to establish a sympathetic relationship.[63] Wilhelm's objections must have made the septuagenarian Bismarck wonder how he and the Prince would one day manage to get on as ruler and servant, for Herrfurth, at fifty-seven, was fifteen years younger than the chancellor. Herrfurth, who did not relish the thought of working with Herbert, quickly asked to be withdrawn from consideration.[64] The chancellor then turned to the distinguished legal scholar, Professor Rudolf von Gneist of the university in Berlin, who was over seventy. According to Bismarck's plan, Gneist would restrict his efforts to explaining to Wilhelm the general lines of government policy.[65] A second advisor would be a younger man more to Wilhelm's taste who could serve as a daily companion and a sort of "living lexicon" on the details of how Germany and Prussia were ruled. The chancellor nominated Hans von Brandenstein, a thirty-eight-year-old Prussian provincial official who was conspicuous for his snobbery and political conservatism. It seems likely that Wilhelm, who had recently met Brandenstein while on a hunt, suggested his name.[66] A third advisor, Maj. Gen. Adolf von Wittich, also joined Wilhelm's retinue to instruct him in military affairs. By the end of 1887 all three were ready to begin their work, and in mid-January 1888 Wilhelm joined his preceptors in the capital. Finally, two weeks later, on the occasion of Wilhelm's twenty-ninth birthday, the Kaiser advanced his grandson to major general with the command of an infantry brigade in Berlin.

Herbert Bismarck expressed his satisfaction that Wilhelm was now liberated from Potsdam, but he noted pessimistically that "a precious time has been irretrievably lost."[67] The instruction began at once, with Brandenstein in daily attendance and Gneist and Wittich meeting with the Prince for a few hours every week. To the Bismarcks, Brandenstein was the critical appointment, and Herbert called him to the Foreign Office for a long talk in order to "set things straight."[68] In spite of the chancellor's efforts and those of his son, Wilhelm's move to Berlin did not effectively detach him from the military influences that had predominated in his life, for he continued to spend a good deal of time in his old haunts in Potsdam. Even had this not been the case, Wilhelm's undistinguished career at Bonn and his cavalier behavior during his earlier training at the Foreign Office made it unlikely that he would absorb much from his tutors, except perhaps for the military intelligence communicated by General von Wittich. Wilhelm must quickly have formed a favorable opinion of Wittich, for immediately after becoming Kaiser in

1888 he made the general an adjutant. The British military attaché in Berlin reported late in 1887 that while Wilhelm was strongly opinionated, he would listen with special attention to arguments propounded by army officers.[69] Both Brandenstein and Gneist, in contrast to General von Wittich, got short shrift from their pupil, and as a result Bismarck complained a few months after their appointment that Wilhelm had taken no interest in the material presented by his civilian tutors and consequently had learned nothing about internal affairs.[70] The problem, Gneist informed the French ambassador in Berlin, was that the Prince, convinced that he knew a great deal, disdained any instruction designed to expand his narrow horizons.[71]

Although the Bismarcks had encouraged Wilhelm to assert his independence from his mother and father, they became alarmed when his self-confidence threatened their own authority or interests. The instructional program had accomplished little except to indicate that Wilhelm was not inclined to pay attention to civilian advisors, no matter how experienced they might be. The taste Wilhelm had had of diplomacy encouraged him to think that he possessed a particular talent in this area of statecraft.[72] Throughout the winter of 1887–88 both the chancellor and Herbert discovered alarming signs that the Prince was not inclined to listen to them any more than he was to Gneist and Brandenstein. It was as though he were already on the throne, and the Bismarcks found this attitude intimidating. When Wilhelm I remarked to the chancellor that he wondered what would become of his grandson when he had no Bismarck on whom to rely, the answer had been "Your Majesty, he does not need one."[73] The ailing Crown Prince, always inclined to be jealous of his son, complained that Wilhelm strutted about with such airs that one might think he imagined that *he* were the Crown Prince. Clearly his son could hardly wait until he was dead.[74]

Although neither the Crown Prince nor the Bismarcks were aware of it, Wilhelm was in perfect readiness in the event that both his father and the Kaiser should suddenly expire and he should become sovereign. He assured his military friends that he had made provision for a change in the throne, with orders for what to do written down and placed in his desk drawer. Eulenburg, in whom Wilhelm also confided his plans, noted in his diary on 22 November 1887 that "the Prince has pondered and weighed everything down to the tiniest detail in order to be prepared at any moment. No one can reproach him with lack of energy."[75] Bismarck knew of only one of Wilhelm's plans for the succession and found it deplorable. This was an address formulated in the winter of 1887–88, as the health of both his father and grandfather was becoming increasingly fragile, that he intended to deliver to the sovereigns of the German states immediately on his ascent to the Prussian-imperial throne.[76] The German rulers, according to Wilhelm's analysis, were for the most part men of his father's generation and were likely to protest being presided over by such a youthful Hohenzollern. He would therefore adopt a policy of consideration mixed with kindness, and he would soon have his German colleagues in hand. But Wilhelm warned Bismarck that he did not intend to tolerate any obstruction on the part of his fellow sovereigns.

The chancellor, who waited for over a month to answer, argued against Wilhelm's proposed proclamation for two reasons.[77] First, the fact that Wilhelm had composed such a document before either his grandfather's or his father's death would make him appear to have an unseemly haste to assume the crown. Moreover, Bismarck did not share Wilhelm's estimation of the efficacy of his charm and believed that the German rulers would be sure to resent being lectured by an inexperienced sovereign. This would be very unfortunate, since these sovereigns, in their unified allegiance to the Prussian King-Emperor, were the strength of the empire. If princely solidarity were to be destroyed, the imperial parliament, always Bismarck's bête noire, would inevitably be the victor. The chancellor's advice, which Wilhelm accepted, was that the address should be burned and forgotten.

Even more alarming to Bismarck than the sort of impolitic arrogance revealed in Wilhelm's proposed proclamation to the German princes was his association with General von Waldersee. The chancellor had never liked the pious Waldersee and perceptively viewed him with suspicion as a contender for the chancellorship. But now that Wilhelm's early ascent to the throne was a foregone conclusion, his close friendship with Waldersee added a potentially dangerous ingredient to the rivalry between Bismarck and the general. Waldersee's domestic schemes were equally offensive to Bismarck, for the general was the most prominent supporter of the Christian Socialist movement of the court chaplain, Adolf Stoecker, whose personality and program the chancellor disliked intensely. Stoecker had become a court chaplain in 1874 and later served in both the Prussian House of Deputies and the Reichstag as a member of the Conservative party. Stoecker was a plump, smooth courtier with a rich wife, considerable homiletic gifts, and a deep-seated aversion to Jews.[78] He exercised a charismatic attractiveness on some people but thoroughly repelled others. Stoecker was the founder and leader of the City Mission, a group largely composed of fervent aristocrats, such as Count and Countess Waldersee, who hoped by a series of social welfare programs to wean the working class of the capital away from socialism. In 1884, on the eve of the Reichstag elections, Stoecker became involved in a venomous defamation suit against a Jewish journalist. The trial, which attracted widespread notice, resulted in a judgment for Stoecker, but its unsavory revelations in fact greatly undermined the preacher's stature.

Although Stoecker was reelected to the Reichstag not long after the verdict was returned, the proceedings had considerably weakened his position at the Kaiser's court. The publicity that attended the affair greatly displeased Wilhelm I, who had only grudgingly approved Stoecker's earlier political activity. He feared that the chaplain, who in his orations often made pointed reference to his position in the entourage, had now involved the crown in an unseemly dispute. Since Stoecker showed no signs of being willing to give up his political career, Wilhelm I decided that he would have to forfeit his post. The Crown Prince and Princess, who had many friends among the Jewish intelligentsia in Berlin, found Stoecker's anti-Semitism repellent and were delighted by the Kaiser's decision. For years they refused to worship in the royal chapel if Stoecker was to preach, and the Crown Princess declared to Queen Victoria that it was a disgrace that he was allowed to hold a chaplaincy. She made her hostility to Stoecker's "Potsdam set" unmistakable.[79]

Wilhelm and Dona, however, were firmly in Stoecker's camp. Dona had known and approved of Stoecker since 1882, and her high chamberlain, Baron Ernest von Mirbach, was a prominent figure in the City Mission.[80] Probably even more influential in their association with Stoecker were Waldersee and his wife, both ardent supporters of the chaplain. Wilhelm and Dona found Stoecker impressive and invited him, to the Crown Princess's disgust, to participate in the christenings of their children. Wilhelm took an increasingly lively interest in the City Mission and described Stoecker to his great-uncle, the Grand Duke Friedrich of Baden, as "one of our strongest pillars of monarchical loyalty and patriotism." He even liked to refer to the chaplain as a "second Luther."[81] Wilhelm sympathized with Stoecker's plight in his libel trial and was determined that he was not to be deprived of his post in the royal entourage. He assured his grandfather that Stoecker was one of the warmest supporters of the throne and responsible for converting no fewer than 60,000 workers from socialism to political respectability.[82] As a result of his grandson's appeal, the Kaiser agreed to reconsider the matter, and he eventually decided that Stoecker might remain in office provided he curbed his political activity.

In spite of his difficulties with the Kaiser, Stoecker did not retreat from politics but in fact identified himself and his movement still more closely with the extreme right wing of the Conservative party. Although Bismarck approved of Stoecker's conservatism and had his own prejudices against Jews, he felt that the chaplain's anti-Semitism verged on demagoguery and that the privately funded City Mission was in competition with the chancellor's own governmental welfare programs designed to win over the working class. As long as Stoecker behaved in a restrained fashion, Bismarck was prepared to enlist him as an ally, but the libel trial had revealed that the chaplain was a political liability rather than an asset. By the beginning of 1887 the chancellor and Stoecker found themselves in a sharp conflict. The chaplain, whose urge for publicity was insatiable, finally went so far as to attack Bismarck openly. "Prince Bismarck is a master in foreign policy," Stoecker declared in a speech delivered in mid-January. "He should not be reproached too much that he does not possess the same virtuosity in internal affairs, for a man cannot excel in everything."[83] The chancellor's rage was boundless.

It was not until the end of November 1887 that Wilhelm's connection with Stoecker became a matter of public attention. On 28 November 1887, the Prince organized a reception for the chaplain, which was held in Waldersee's official residence in the general staff building on the Königsplatz.[84] The guests, whom Wilhelm chose, included Stoecker himself; Count Otto zu Stolberg, the lord high chamberlain to the Kaiser; Robert von Puttkamer and Gustav von Gossler, both conservative Prussian ministers whom the chancellor did not like; Baron Wilhelm von Hammerstein, the anti-Semitic editor of the Conservative party organ, the *Kreuzzeitung*; and an assortment of wealthy aristocrats who were Bismarck's enemies. After a few introductory remarks by Stoecker, Wilhelm addressed the gathering.[85] He declared that religion was the most effective force in combating the attacks on throne and altar being made by the godless. Stoecker's Christian-social movement was especially suited to promote religion—and thus civic obedience—in the working class, and Wilhelm therefore insisted that every effort to be made to promote the City Mission, not only in Berlin but throughout Germany. He concluded by declaring, quite falsely, that he had the permission of both his father and his grandfather to support Stoecker's cause. A fund-raising committee was established, and at Wilhelm's insistence Putt-kamer assumed the chairmanship.

The reaction to Wilhelm's association with Stoecker was for the most part quite unfavorable. The liberal press, in which German Jews had a large interest, condemned his connection with such a notorious anti-Semite. This criticism, the first recorded in the press against Wilhelm, stung him, but even more annoying was an article in the semiofficial *Norddeutsche Allgemeine Zeitung,* known to be a mouthpiece of Bismarck, expressing disapproval of his appearance at the meeting at Waldersee's residence. Waldersee at once urged Wilhelm to write in protest to the chancellor, and on 21 December 1887 the Prince sent Bismarck a long letter insistently defending his support of the court chaplain.[86] Wilhelm began somewhat petulantly by noting that before launching the attack in the *NDAZ* the chancellor might have sought him out for a clarification of the matter. The purpose of the meeting had not been to hold a political rally for Stoecker's City Mission but rather, he assured Bismarck, to create throughout the empire a broad Christian-social front in which Stoecker would have only a secondary role. Wilhelm denounced the press attacks on the chaplain as scandalous, for Stoecker and the men and women Wilhelm had assembled at Waldersee's were devoted to the monarchy and to the church. He had addressed the meeting because he had hoped that his support for the chaplain would quell the intemperate attacks on Stoecker in the socialist and radical press.

In Bismarck's opinion, Wilhelm's association with Stoecker was more than a transitory indiscretion. The bond between the Prince and the chaplain represented a danger to the throne, and the chancellor believed that Waldersee's patronage of the friendship between Wilhelm and Stoecker threatened his continuation as chancellor. Wilhelm's letter of 29 November seemed to him to be a deliberate move—engineered by the chancellor's enemy, Interior Minister Puttkamer—to provide a warning that when Wilhelm ascended he intended to rule as he pleased.[87] Bismarck therefore yielded no quarter in replying to Wilhelm's missive.[88] He tartly informed the Prince that the people he had invited to the November meeting at Waldersee's were sycophantic careerists whom Wilhelm would do well to avoid, advice which also applied to Stoecker, whose Christian-social movement would do nothing to strengthen the cause of conservatism. "I have nothing against Stoecker," Bismarck declared. "He has for me only one failure as a politician and that is that he is a priest, and as a priest [his drawback is that] he involves himself in politics." Herbert von Bismarck, who had even less use for Stoecker than did his father, hoped that the chancellor's letter would become Wilhelm's "constant bedside reading." He was skeptical, however, fearing that it might take the Prince ten years to grasp the importance of keeping the crown out of the mire of party politics.[89] One effect of the Stoecker affair was to increase Wilhelm's exasperation with Herbert, and he attributed the attacks in the semiofficial press on his participation in the Waldersee meeting to Herbert rather than to the chancellor.[90]

The rift in Wilhelm's heretofore close relations with the chancellor and his son alarmed Philipp Eulenburg, who was on good terms with both the Bismarcks. Eulenburg was indifferent to Stoecker personally, but, like the chancellor, he was concerned that Wilhelm's connection with the City Mission was drawing him more tightly into Waldersee's archreactionary web, for which Eulenburg had no sympathy. The Bismarcks' attacks on Stoecker, according to Eulenburg, were really designed as assaults on Waldersee.[91] Throughout December 1887 Eulenburg used his very considerable influence with Wilhelm to persuade him that there was no personal animosity on the part of the Bismarcks against him and that the chancellor and his son were in fact animated only by a desire to protect the crown from the contamination of party politics. Early in January Eulenburg succeeded in effecting a reconciliation between Wilhelm and Herbert, and on the last day of the month Wilhelm had a conference with the chancellor about the Stoecker affair. At its conclusion Herbert noted that the Prince had completely accepted the elder Bismarck's viewpoint. "The matter is thus laid to rest," Herbert concluded.[92] But at the Foreign Office, Holstein, who was party to the conflict through the reports that various informants had sent him, was convinced that the differences between Wilhelm and the Bismarcks had by no means been composed. He reported that there was feeling in Berlin that Wilhelm's displeasure with the chancellor had not dissipated, because Bismarck had failed to realize who was the sovereign-to-be and who was merely the subject.[93]

The year 1888 thus opened gloomily for the Bismarcks, for it appeared that a man on whose support they could not be certain would soon be on the throne. In late February, Wilhelm had to interrupt his duties in Berlin to go to Karlsruhe for the funeral of his first cousin, Prince Ludwig Wilhelm of Baden. Once in Karlsruhe he would be almost halfway to San Remo, so Wilhelm I instructed his grandson to proceed on Italy to visit the Crown Prince, whom he was to urge to return at once to Germany. The Crown Princess was very opposed to Wilhelm's coming to see his father, but he nonetheless proceeded south and arrived in San Remo on 2 March, where he received a cordial welcome from his father. The Crown Prince had had to submit to a tracheotomy on 9 February, in order to be able to breathe, and therefore could no longer speak. Wilhelm was aghast at the condition in which he found his father, who in spite of all the Crown Princess's optimistic assurances was now considerably emaciated, jaundiced, and wracked with coughing. His mother, Wilhelm had written after his trip to San Remo in November 1887, was apparently determined to treat her husband like a modern-day Cid and eventually bring his corpse to Berlin sitting upright on a throne.[94] He was enraged at Dr. Krause, whom he dismissed as a "Jewish boor" (*Judenlümmel*) and Sir Morell Mackenzie (whom Queen Victoria had recently knighted) for having prevented Dr. Bramann, a surgeon who had accompanied Wilhelm to San Remo, from examining his father.[95] Wilhelm as usual refused to have anything to do with Mackenzie, and on seeing him one day on the street declared to a companion that he regretted that he had no cane with which to thrash the English doctor.[96] The Crown Princess adamantly dismissed any thought of taking her husband to Berlin, and Wilhelm concurred only because of the exceptional severity of the winter of 1888 in Germany. He and his mother agreed that the move would not be undertaken until warmer weather prevailed—to the Crown Princess that meant May at the earliest—and that in the interim daily medical reports would be relayed to Berlin.[97]

Wilhelm left San Remo on 5 March—full of regal airs and incapable of uttering "one word of sympathetic affection," his mother declared—and arrived back in Berlin two days later, only to learn that during the journey his grandfather's heart had begun to fail and that his death was expected momentarily. Wilhlem went directly from the train station to the palace, where he found the Kaiser conscious but very weak. On 8 March Wilhelm I lapsed into a coma from which he only spasmodically rallied. The dying Kaiser's consolation was his confidence in his grandson. "Prince Wilhelm will do well," he declared not long before he died. "If only I could be there to see it."[98] Once the Kaiser, thinking that Chancellor Bismarck bending low over his bed was his grandson, said to him: "I have always been pleased with you, for you have done everything right."[99] Wilhelm hardly left his grandfather's bedside, and he was holding his hand as the Kaiser expired early on the morning of 9 March 1888.

The news of the Kaiser's death reached the Crown Prince as he sat in the garden of his villa in San Remo. He almost fainted but then quickly recovered his composure. There was no question in his mind that, voiceless or not, he would rule. The first act of the new sovereign, Kaiser Friedrich III, was to invest his wife with the insignia of the Black Eagle, the highest Hohenzollern decoration, after which he scribbled a note to his assembled doctors. "Thank you," the Kaiser wrote, "for having let me live long enough to recompense the valiant courage of my wife."[100] Later that day, the new Empress wrote to Queen Victoria about the reign that she and her husband now began, but she did so in a tone that was already elegaic. "To think of my poor Fritz succeeding his father as a sick and stricken man is *so* hard. How *much* good he might have done! Will time be given him? I pray that it may and he may be spared to be a blessing to his people and to Europe."[101] Early on 10 March, a windy, rainy day, the new Kaiser and his consort left San Remo and arrived just before midnight of the following day in Berlin, which mourned its dead sovereign in the midst of a devastating blizzard. Wilhelm first welcomed his father affectionately and then his mother. His greeting to the Kaiserin Friedrich, as she would always be known, must have been perfunctory, for she complained that Wilhelm pushed her aside.[102] So the brief and unhappy reign of Kaiser Friedrich III began.

Five

THE NINETY-NINE DAYS

OF KAISER FRIEDRICH III

THE DEATH of the old sovereign made the mortality of his successor all the more apparent. Friedrich III was unable to greet the royal dignitaries who came to Berlin for his father's funeral, and he had to watch the somber procession, moving between towering banks of snow piled on the sidewalks, from a window in the Charlottenburg Palace. Those who had not seen their new ruler since his departure for England in June 1887 were relieved that his physical appearance belied somewhat the fatal nature of the malady that was devouring him. The Kaiser strove hard to seem well, but he had no illusions about the hopelessness of his condition. It was obvious that there would be no time for fundamental revisions in personnel or policies. The most that Friedrich III could hope for was to award the faithful for their devotion to his cause during the long years through which he had had to stand in his father's shadow.

The stricken Kaiser consequently left the conduct of government entirely in Bismarck's hands, and the chancellor now had even more complete authority than he had enjoyed under Wilhelm I. After Friedrich's brief reign had ended, Bismarck declared, "In fact for those three months I was an absolute *dictator*," a situation entirely to the chancellor's autocratic tastes. "In my entire ministerial career," he wrote afterwards, "the conduct of business was never so pleasant or so lacking in friction as it was during the ninety-nine days of the Emperor Friedrich."[1] Even the Kaiserin Friedrich, who for years had been Bismarck's most remorseless enemy, recognized that her husband's illness made the chancellor's retention imperative and that as long as Bismarck held office it would be dangerous to provoke him.[2] The chancellor was well aware of his strength vis à vis the Empress, for what little influence she possessed with Wilhelm would vanish the moment her consort died, although the chancellor's would continue. On the day Wilhelm I expired, Bismarck called in Dr. von Bergmann to ascertain how long Friedrich III could be expected to survive. Bergmann replied, with what proved to be remarkable prescience, that the chancellor could reckon on a reign of only three months' duration.[3]

The Kaiser realized that because of his enfeebled condition it would be necessary, if distasteful, to permit his son to gain wider exposure to affairs of state. It was one thing to allow Wilhelm to receive useful training by attending meetings and reading documents, but quite another to yield to him any of the prerogatives of the crown. Friedrich III would not consider creating a regency in favor of his son or even granting him the right of representing the sovereign on certain ceremonial occasions, for he had no confidence that Wilhelm could be relied upon. As the new Kaiser traveled from San Remo to Berlin in March 1888 to assume his crown, he felt compelled to send his son, now Crown Prince, an admonitory telegram noting that he expected him to be a model of loyalty and obedience.[4]

There was little in Wilhelm's behavior during his father's brief reign to indicate that he took this injunction to heart. Wilhelm had for some time been secretly in contact with Major von Kessel, who was adjutant to both Wilhelm and his father. Kessel, an avowed enemy of the Kaiser and the Kaiserin, had secured access to Friedrich III's code book and passed on to Wilhelm his parents' private communications with one another.[5] The Kaiser, unlike his wife, refused to believe that Kessel and Wilhelm had conspired against him, but only a few weeks after assuming the throne, Friedrich III was forced to call his son to account. On 1 April 1888, Wilhelm made a speech on the occasion of Bismarck's seventy-third birthday in which he characterized the German Empire as an army that had lost its leader and whose second-in-command was badly wounded. But the Fatherland was fortunate in that the great chancellor had been able to step in and fill the breach caused by Wilhelm I's death and the new Kaiser's illness. All of this was true enough, but also typical of Wilhelm's unfortunate insensitivity. Friedrich III, always very punctilious about his dignity, was offended, and he issued a sharp reproof to his heir. "You probably have not adequately reflected," he wrote to Wilhelm on 3 April, "how little loyal it sounds to describe the monarch as inferior to his minister as the actual driving force in the government, to say nothing of whether it was your business to say anything whatsoever about the matter."[6] The Kaiser was perhaps unduly touchy about what seems to have been an unfeeling but not malicious indiscretion, but the incident had indicated, once more, that Wilhelm's want of tact was part of a more serious problem. What really concerned the dying Kaiser was that his son, so obviously the captive of a reactionary clique, was woefully unsuited in character and also in preparation for the high destiny that stood imminently before him.[7]

The Kaiser could do nothing to improve his son's behavior other than chastise him for his lapses, but Friedrich III did little to prepare Wilhelm for the day when he would rule. The ailing ruler did begin to see his son more frequently and allowed him to attend meetings of the Prussian ministry, but he resisted making Wilhelm party to many affairs of state or granting him rights of ceremonial representation, a privilege Wilhelm was anxious to possess.[8] On 13 April Bismarck eventually succeeded in persuading the Kaiser to issue a decree enabling the Crown Prince to serve in his father's stead. But Friedrich III, to his son's disappointment, never specified exactly what functions Wilhelm was to perform under the order, and Wilhelm therefore played a negligible public role while his father was Kaiser. It seems almost certain that the Empress Friedrich was responsible for preventing her son from coming to the fore. That was certainly Wilhelm's suspicion.[9]

During the ninety-nine days of Friedrich III's reign, it was Wilhelm's mother who kept the Hohenzollern family in turmoil. Victoria had no gift whatsoever for disguising her feelings, and, after decades of frustration and embittered waiting to ascend the throne, she was not prepared to accept or even to admit that the reign of her beloved husband would be fleeting. One unpopular manifestation of her optimism was the engagement of a team of interior decorators, imported from London with quantities of English goods, to refurbish the Charlottenburg Palace, in which she and the Kaiser took up residence. Only in her letters to Queen Victoria and to a few intimates did the Empress give vent to her despair at the ominous fate which was gathering around the Kaiser. "*Yes*, we are our own masters now," she wrote to her mother on the day of Wilhelm I's funeral. "But shall we not have to leave all the work undone which we have so long and so carefully been preparing?"[10] In public, the Empress continued to maintain the resolutely cheerful demeanor she had adopted in San Remo, going about her nursing and household duties in a bright mood that seemed to be in disconcerting contrast to the Kaiser's deteriorating condition. While Victoria's optimism was due in part to her understandable determination not to offer her husband any cause for discouragement, her forcedly exuberant behavior was abnormal and created an unfortunate impression. The Empress's enemies in Berlin declared that her manner indicated that she was on the brink of hysteria or madness, and even friends and admirers thought her conduct regrettable.[11]

From the moment that Friedrich III ascended the throne, Victoria viewed Wilhelm with suspicion and resented his youth and energy, which so contrasted with the Kaiser's debility. While Wilhelm I had still been alive, the Crown Princess had declared that should any attempt be made to appoint Wilhelm regent without his father's consent she would make a public appeal to the German nation.[12] Once her husband became the ruler, Victoria wanted him to give her the same rights of representing the crown the old Kaiser had granted to Wilhelm in the fall of 1887. With her accustomed lack of tact, she based her argument on an invidious comparison between England and Germany. If, the Kaiserin declared, her mother could rule an empire across the seas, she herself surely could attend to the affairs of what was merely a European state.[13] The Empress's plan, which was without precedent because it involved a woman, provoked determined resistance from Bismarck, and she elected not to pursue it. Even so, Victoria was determined to brook no impertinence from her son, whose officious behavior particularly irked her. She complained that he pranced about everywhere as though he were already the ruler. "William fancies himself completely the Emperor and an absolute and autocratic one!" she wrote in disgust to Queen Victoria in May 1888.[14]

This was no invention by the Empress, for the Austro-Hungarian ambassador in Berlin had noted a few weeks earlier that Wilhelm's regal airs had become so pronounced that even the army, which ordinarily regarded him with favor, was becoming alarmed.[15] One of Vicky's recurrent complaints during her husband's reign was that she and Friedrich III were being deserted by courtiers and statesmen alike, who were shamelessly going over to the side of their future ruler. "They regard Crown Prince William as the actual Kaiser," she cried. "Kaiser Frederick is only a shadow."[16] However unseemly such behavior might have been, considering the Kaiser's irreversible illness, it was certainly politic. Victoria never mentioned her son's confederates by name, probably because she lived in fear that Bismarck was subjecting her mail to surveillance, but she meant the chancellor himself, Herbert Bismarck, most of the Prussian ministry, and General von Waldersee. Their intent, she believed, was to deprive her and the Kaiser of any influence whatsoever. The Empress even believed, quite falsely, that there was a conspiracy against her and Friedrich III within the Hohenzollern family led by the domineering old

Kaiserin Augusta.[17] Moreover, Wilhelm was flagrant in his attentions to Dr. von Bergmann, who among the Kaiser's physicians had always been the most persistent in arguing that his disease was cancer. Bergmann was anathema to Victoria, and as Friedrich III's strength waned, his presence in the sickroom was a grim indictment of the Empress's foolish attachment to the false diagnosis and warrantless optimism of Sir Morell Mackenzie.

Victoria's hostility to her son, together with her awareness of the necessity to avoid gratuitously annoying him, led her to avoid Wilhelm as much as possible. When they met, she attempted to turn the conversation from controversial issues, but she still provided Wilhelm sufficient grounds for resentment, continuing to treat him as though he were a youth and successfully encouraging the Kaiser to do the same.[18] To Wilhelm, his mother was unfit to serve as Friedrich III's surrogate, for she insisted on running everything yet was governed not by rational considerations but rather by her prejudices. Even in these she was inconstant, and orders given were often countermanded or left unfulfilled. The result, Wilhelm declared, was chaos.[19] The Crown Prince's behavior during his father's short reign intensified the dislike he had long since felt for her, and he claimed, probably with justification, that she and her confederates at court were doing everything in their power to keep him from seeing the Kaiser. His mother, Wilhelm assured Chancellor Bismarck, hated him "more than anything in the world."[20] By the end of Friedrich III's brief reign the antagonism between mother and son had become so intense that there was no possibility of reconciliation. Both admitted that there were troublemakers at work to separate them, but they could not agree as to who these noxious figures were. Wilhelm's allies were his mother's enemies, and hers were his.[21]

Bismarck regarded the increasing estrangement between the Empress and her son with favor, for he had never liked her nor approved of her liberal, Anglophile views. Once the chancellor realized that if the Crown Prince managed to succeed Wilhelm I, his reign would be brief, he concentrated his attention on Wilhelm, in whom he had previously taken only desultory interest. Bismarck wanted to have his future sovereign well in hand before he came to the throne. But he and Herbert knew from experience that this would require some effort, for Wilhelm had long since indicated that he intended to be his own man. Throughout his long career Bismarck had always been exceedingly jealous of anyone he suspected of being less than totally obedient to his autocratic will, and he was ruthless in eliminating competitors for royal favor. In 1887–88, as the prospect of swift changes on the throne became imminent, the chancellor's touchiness increased. Herbert, the heir-apparent and presently state secretary of the Foreign Office, was the only person to whom the chancellor gave his entire trust, and Herbert was as determined as his father to deal firmly with anyone who might be inclined to challenge the Bismarck hegemony. The suspicions of both Bismarcks concentrated on General von Waldersee, who wanted to become chancellor and who saw in Wilhelm the means of realizing his goal. Neither the chancellor nor Herbert, both notable for their brusqueness, their love of drink, and their indifference to formal religion, had any liking for the pious and straightlaced Waldersee or his views, and they were alarmed by his close friendship with Wilhelm and his wife. They could hardly have failed to note Wilhelm's almost daily visits to the general's residence or the intimate social footing between the general and his countess and the young royal couple.[22] Dona was easily conquered, for she thought Herbert's crudeness unpalatable, and she was therefore delighted to find that once Wilhelm became Crown Prince he spent less and less time with the chancellor's son.[23]

Bismarck had reason to be alarmed by Wilhelm's friendship with Waldersee quite apart from the general's ambition for the chancellorship and his attachment to the reactionary court chaplain, Adolf Stoecker. Waldersee was also the leading exponent of preventive war against Russia, which he believed was bent on an aggressive policy toward Germany and Austria-Hungary. Although Bismarck was ready to acknowledge that Russia's behavior often left much to be desired, he resolutely argued that the cultivation of closer ties to St. Petersburg rather than Waldersee's prescription of preventive war was the proper solution.

Wilhelm, unlike either his grandfather or father, was firmly in Waldersee's camp. His conception of Russia, initially formed in the course of his visit to St. Petersburg in 1884, had been very favorable. The Prince had been immediately attracted to the dour Alexander III, and he returned home a convinced proponent of Bismarck's policy of a solid attachment between Germany, Austria-Hungary, and Russia. A second trip to Russia in 1886, however, brought about a change in Wilhelm's attitude.[24] He by no means lost his admiration for the Tsar, declaring that when he talked to Alexander he felt as though he were conversing with a fellow German.[25] Nevertheless, Wilhelm could not help suspecting that in Alexander there resided a fatal combination of sluggishness and fanaticism and that as a result he was very likely headed for the fate that Louis XVI had suffered in 1792 at the hands of his revolutionary subjects.[26] In the course of his conversations with Alexander in 1886, Wilhelm also noted a menacing tone that had been absent at their first meeting two years earlier.[27] Moreover, the coolly arrogant behavior of a number of Russian officers annoyed Wilhelm, who found this a disturbing change from the pro-German attitude he had noted in the Russian army on his first trip to St. Petersburg in 1884.

After his second trip to Russia in 1886, Wilhelm became increasingly exasperated by the virulence of anti-German feeling in Russia, most of which was occasioned by Bismarck's support of Austria, to Russia's disadvantage, in Balkan matters. Although Wilhelm did not yet advocate a preventive war against the Tsar, he became convinced early in 1887, to Waldersee's delight, that Russia and France had formed an alliance for the purpose of preparing for a forthcoming war against Germany and its Habsburg ally.[28] The prospect that the Crown Prince's illness would lead to Wilhelm's swift succession was to Waldersee an entirely favorable development. With Wilhelm on the throne, the general declared, Germany would have a "strong, proud, and fearless Kaiser who assuredly would have no desire to wait until it suited our enemies to begin the war."[29] Some months before, Waldersee had reported with satisfaction that Wilhelm was positively "eager for war" (*kriegslüstig*), and he was anxious to have him inflame Bismarck in that direction. The battle, Wilhelm declared, had to be fought while the chancellor was still in office, for his diplomatic skill was worth a good three corps of German soldiers. Bismarck's reservations about unleashing war against Russia had to be overcome. "Your father," Wilhelm informed Herbert Bismarck, "must not forget that the best defense lies in attack."[30] Wilhelm himself would produce the victory on the western front. "Like Julius Caesar, I think I have a mission to destroy Gaul," he told the chancellor's son on another occasion.[31]

Bismarck, however, would have nothing to do with such a war. He recognized that the internal situation in Russia *might* propel the Tsar into a war against Germany, but this was not yet inevitable.[32] The chancellor observed Wilhelm's drift into Waldersee's anti-Russian party with alarm, and in February 1888 he launched an assault on the general in a series of inspired articles in the press. The death in early March of Wilhelm I, to whom his nephew the Tsar had always been very deferential, made the Russian situation still more threatening, for Alexander III did not like Friedrich III and found Wilhelm's showy bravura and rudeness to his parents thoroughly distasteful.[33] More alarming to Bismarck was the fact that Wilhelm had begun to express the sharpest criticism of the chancellor's conduct of foreign affairs. Six weeks after his grandfather's death, Wilhelm made a marginal comment on a diplomatic document that questioned the advisability of Bismarck's accommodating policy toward Austria and Russia. Wilhelm's strictures soon came to the chancellor's attention, and Bismarck replied on 9 May with a long analysis of the senselessness of Germany's provoking war with Russia.[34]

Wilhelm, in consultation with Waldersee, composed a reply that revealed the extent to which he had by now fallen under the general's influence.[35] He expressed concern that Bismarck did not fully appreciate the hostility that Russia felt for Germany and the dedication with which both St. Petersburg and Paris were planning a joint attack on Germany. Only Alexander III's restraining hand had thus far prevented the war's outbreak. But meanwhile Russia was doing all she could to undermine Germany's relations with Austria-Hungary, whose stability unfortunately could not in the long run be counted on. That being the case, it would be better immediately to begin a preventive war with Russia, which would undoubtedly be supported by France. Confronted by such a situation, the military had every right to argue in favor of the employment of whatever tactics might enable Germany most successfully to wage war on two fronts. Wilhelm urged the chancellor to accept the opinion of the military authorities as one that, far from competing with Bismarck, was in fact designed to promote his understanding of the perilous situation into which Germany had been forced by her powerful neighbors.

Bismarck dismissed Wilhelm's letter as nothing more than a regurgitation of his mistaken Russophobe views. He declared to a friend that "that young man wants war with Russia and would like to draw his sword straight away if he could. I shall not be a party to it."[36] The chancellor decided, however, that the most prudent course would be to indicate to his future sovereign that he was willing to admit that a war with Russia and France was at least a possibility for which some degree of contingency planning might be entered into. If Wilhelm meant to have his way, resistance was pointless and an appearance of accommodation would strengthen the chancellor's position.[37] Bismarck had reason to be careful, for there were indications to which he could not have been blind that his grasp on Wilhelm was slipping. Berlin abounded in speculation during Friedrich III's short reign that the old chancellor and the young Crown Prince were drifting away from one another. Sir Edward Malet, the British ambassador, wrote to the prime minister, Lord Salisbury, on

21 April 1888, that "there have not been wanting signs that Prince William listens to others besides the Chancellor and recently it was feared that the Junker party had got hold of him."[38]

Although Wilhelm and Bismarck took opposing views of the advantages of war with Russia, they were very much in agreement in 1887–88 about one issue that was closely related to Russo-German relations. To both men, the attempt by Wilhelm's mother to marry her daughter Victoria to Alexander Battenberg had at all costs to be prevented, for although no longer ruler in Sofia, he continued to be persona non grata to the Tsar. Immediately on her husband's ascension to the throne in March 1888, the Kaiserin Friedrich recommenced her efforts to bring about the marriage. Alexander, however, was no longer eager to have Victoria's hand, for he had fallen in love with an ingenue at the Grand Ducal theater in Darmstadt, whom he found that he much preferred to his royal love in Berlin. To Bismarck, the marriage could not, as the Empress insisted, be regarded as a personal rather than a political affair. *Any* attention paid to Alexander, to say nothing of letting him marry the German Kaiser's daughter, would be regarded in St. Petersburg as a hostile act. It therefore did not surprise the chancellor that Queen Victoria and Wilhelm's mother supported the match, for in his opinion they were anxious to create friction between Germany and Russia, since that would work to Britain's advantage. Besides, to Bismarck Alexander was a pushy sort who would use his association with the Hohenzollerns to advance his own ambitions. The marriage was clearly impossible, and the chancellor repeatedly declared that he would resign if Wilhelm's mother persisted in her plans.[39]

Wilhelm's opposition to the marriage was based both on Bismarck's diplomatic considerations as well as on his firm opinion that Alexander, the offspring of a morganatic marriage, was genealogically unworthy of claiming the hand of a daughter of the King of Prussia and German Emperor. "The worst thing," he wrote to his friend Philipp Eulenburg on 12 April 1888, "is the feeling of deep shame for the sunken prestige of my house, which always stood so gleaming and unassailable! But yet more intolerable is that our family escutcheon should be bespotted and the Reich brought to the brink of ruin by the English princess who is my mother!"[40] Wilhelm wrote to Battenberg on 3 April 1888 that his first act as Kaiser would be to banish him and his sister from Germany should they marry, and he informed the Prince that "anyone who promotes this union will be regarded as an enemy of my house and of my Fatherland and treated as such."[41]

Friedrich III agreed with Wilhelm that Battenberg's lineage was insufficiently exalted, but he no longer had the strength to resist his wife's importuning. Early in April, after a monumental scene with her that sent him to bed for two days, he invited Battenberg to come to Berlin in order to invest him with a decoration and to make him commanding officer of the Garde du Corps, the most elite regiment in the Prussian army. The Kaiser anticipated that in the course of the visit the young couple would become formally engaged. On the last day of March he so informed Bismarck, who declared in return that he would resign rather than countenance the marriage. It was manifest that Bismarck meant what he said. The ailing Kaiser had no wish to precipitate a crisis with the chancellor, especially since a number of ruling German princes had made their opposition to the betrothal very clear. So over his wife's hysterical pleas Friedrich III reversed himself and rescinded the invitation to Battenberg.[42]

The Kaiserin, however, was not to be crossed, even by her husband. She proceeded with plans for the couple's engagement, scheduling it for 12 April, the bride's twenty-second birthday. Battenberg, whose infatuation with his actress remained a secret to Victoria and her mother, desperately wanted to have his freedom. He wrote to Victoria on 10 April, telling her that she should feel no commitment to him and that she might bring the quarrel within her family to an end by releasing him. On the day previous, Alexander's cousin, the Grand Duke of Hesse, wrote as head of his house to Friedrich III formally renouncing Alexander's suit for the Princess's hand.[43] At about the same time, Bismarck informed the Empress of Battenberg's liaison with his actress, but she dismissed his report as malicious gossip and continued with her matchmaking. For the moment, however, nothing could be done because of Friedrich III's unwillingness to permit the engagement, even were the Grand Duke of Hesse to rescind his renunciation. Victoria blamed Wilhelm, whom she believed was determined to see to it that "out of hate, revenge, and pride, a non-political, private matter [be] made into a cause célèbre in order to destroy me."[44]

Late in April, Queen Victoria, along with her daughter, Princess Beatrice, and her son-in-law, Prince Henry Battenberg, Alexander's brother, paid a visit to Berlin. The Queen wished to see the Kaiser, for whom she had a great affection, before he died. The Queen's appearance in the German capital occasioned considerable interest in Russia, where it was regarded as a sign of British approval of a marriage between Vicky and Alexander. Queen Victoria did not share Bismarck's exaggerated fear of the Russian reaction to the marriage, but she had reluctantly come to the conclusion that it was pointless to persist in the plan over Wilhelm's strong objections, especially since it was clear Alexander was no longer in love with Princess Victoria.[45] She was infuriated at her grandson because of his "outrageous behavior" to his mother and his heartless insensitivity to his father's grave condition.[46] In spite of the fact that the Queen had now withdrawn her support for the marriage project, on the eve of her visit there was considerable apprehension in both Berlin and London that it would only intensify the Queen's already strained relations with Wilhelm. Count Paul von Hatzfeldt-Wildenburg, the German envoy in London, expressed the misgivings felt in Berlin to Lord Salisbury, who forwarded the gist of the ambassador's remarks to Queen Victoria. "It appears," Salisbury wrote to the Queen concerning her grandson, "that his head is turned by his position, and the hope evidently was that Your Majesty might be induced to have special consideration for his position."[47] Salisbury also informed the Duke of Rutland, who was to be in Berlin during Queen Victoria's visit, of the Queen's low opinion of her grandson. The prime minister wrote, "She thinks very badly of him, resents his conduct to his mother, and has more than once shown her resentment very plainly. He is intensely irritated at this treatment, being quite conscious of his own position. It is feared the Queen will repeat the process when she comes to Berlin with results most disastrous to the interest of the two countries. Do what you can to warn and restrain her. The matter will require much tact, but you can do it if anyone can. She is very unmanageable about her conduct to her own relations; she will persist in considering William only as her grandson. But the matter has become political and very grave, and she must listen to advice."[48]

Queen Victoria heeded Lord Salisbury's advice and managed to keep her irritation at Wilhelm hidden beneath a surface cordiality. Wilhelm was annoyed because he heard that before coming to Germany his grandmother had described him to the Emperor Franz-Josef as a great friend of Russia, but he admitted that the Queen's visit itself passed off smoothly.[49] While in Berlin the Queen had a lengthy audience with Bismarck, in the course of which the Battenberg marriage was deliberately avoided. Both agreed that the Queen's grandson was lamentably inexperienced for the imperial role he would soon assume, but the chancellor expressed confidence that should Wilhelm "be thrown into the water he would be able to swim."[50]

Just a few days before Queen Victoria was due to arrive in Berlin, Friedrich III suddenly took a turn for the worse, and it was feared that he would die at any moment. He recovered, however, and was able to greet his mother-in-law. The improvement in the Kaiser's condition was illusory, and by early May he was hardly able to move. With superhuman effort Friedrich managed to be present at the marriage on 24 May of his son Heinrich to his first cousin, Princess Irene of Hesse. Five days later the Kaiser made his last public appearance, reviewing troops from a carriage in the park behind the Charlottenburg Palace. Friedrich III had long expressed a wish that when death approached he be moved to the New Palace (which he rechristened Friedrichskron) in Potsdam, where he had been born in 1831. On 1 June, after visiting his father's mausoleum, the Kaiser made the ominous departure from Berlin. At Potsdam the Empress continued to maintain a resolutely cheerful face to the world, but she admitted that her husband's death could not be far off. From his bedroom Friedrich III scribbled barely legible notes to Bismarck and other officials, but the only significant act of the last weeks of his life was the dismissal on 8 June of the reactionary Prussian minister of the interior, Robert von Puttkamer, the longtime ally of court chaplain Stoecker. Wilhelm and Dona were close to Puttkamer, and both wrote him letters of condolence. Wilhelm blamed his mother for Puttkamer's fall and let Bismarck know that as soon as he ascended the throne he would restore the minister to his post.[51]

Throughout Friedrich III's reign Victoria had tried to arrange several matters that she believed would be impossible to resolve once Wilhelm came to the throne. Most of her energy was directed at the Battenberg marriage, in which she ultimately failed, but in her other projects the Empress was more successful. She managed, thanks largely to Bismarck's intervention, to provide modest dowries for her three younger daughters, Victoria, Sophie, and Margaret, whose devoted attachment to their mother and father had compromised their relationship with Wilhelm. She also arranged for the protection of her own property. In early June 1887, shortly after the seriousness of her husband's condition had become known, Victoria decided it would be wise to provide for the safekeeping of her papers, which contained many critical observations about Wilhelm and other members of the Hohenzollern family, as well as the Bismarcks, father and son. She therefore proposed to her mother that when she and the Crown Prince came to the Jubilee celebration later that month she bring her papers. Queen Victoria at once agreed, but for some reason—perhaps because Victoria had become convinced that her husband's illness would not prove fatal—she brought only a few documents to London.[52] Before setting out for the Jubilee, the Crown Prince burned a number of his papers. While in England Victoria disposed of some letters, and still others were put in the flames in San Remo and in Berlin after Friedrich III's return as Kaiser in March 1888.[53] In June 1888, when the Kaiser's death was imminent, Victoria was anxious that the bulk of her papers and those of her husband that had not been burned should be sent to England for safekeeping, for Wilhelm had warned his mother that as soon as his father died soldiers would be ordered to surround the palace and make a search for documents belonging to the royal couple.[54] On 13 June, two days before her husband's death, she entrusted a trunk to Dr. Mark Hovell, one of Sir Morell Mackenzie's assistants on duty in Potsdam, which he delivered in turn to Sir Edward Malet, the British ambassador, who was scheduled to depart for London that night. The Kaiserin informed Malet that the trunk contained her jewels, and the envoy added it to the other pieces of his diplomatic baggage.[55]

In some way—probably through Maj. Gustav von Kessel, an adjutant of the Kaiser's—Wilhelm had been informed of his mother's intention to have her papers spirited out of the country. He therefore ordered a detachment of troops to be on the lookout at the palace and at the Potsdam railroad station for a wagon transporting these effects.[56] On the evening of 14 June, almost twenty-four hours after Malet had received the Empress's trunk and left for London, Wilhelm had a cordon of troops drawn around the palace, and on his father's death the next morning had the death chamber sealed. No one was allowed on the grounds, and an especially close watch was kept on the English doctors and correspondents still at Potsdam. Wilhelm intended to have the palace thoroughly ransacked, but Heinrich von Friedberg, the Prussian minister of justice, dissuaded him from doing so by pointing out that although Wilhelm certainly had the right to conduct a search, such a move would create a poor impression with which to begin his reign. Wilhelm relented and also called off the surveillance of the palace.[57] No papers were ever found, and the documents taken away by Malet were delivered to Queen Victoria and stored at Windsor.

The last few days of Friedrich's III's life were clouded by his wife's final resurrection of her hitherto frustrated attempts to secure Princess Victoria's marriage to Alexander Battenberg, even though Alexander plainly had no intention of being party to such an arrangement. On the eve of his death the Kaiser reversed his earlier refusal and once again gave the marriage his blessing. At her husband's command, the Kaiserin informed Battenberg of this development and also wrote to Tsar Alexander III, in an attempt to reassure him that the marriage was not a political but a private matter. On the morning of the thirteenth, two days before he died, Friedrich III summoned Wilhelm in order to give him a letter written earlier in the year enjoining his son to allow the wedding to take place once he became sovereign. Wilhelm did not open the letter but placed it without comment in his pocket. The Kaiserin, with misplaced confidence, now felt assured that her daughter's future was guaranteed, although she, as well as the Kaiser, was displeased that Wilhelm did not deign to reply to his father's letter.[58]

On Thursday, 14 June, Friedrich III's death agony began. Five days earlier, the cancerous growth had perforated the Kaiser's throat, and although this meant he could thereafter no longer eat, he refused any intravenous nourishment. On the evening of the fourteenth, Herbert Bismarck, dining with friends, declared with heartless satisfaction that "our day will soon begin again."[59] Shortly before noon on the following day the Kaiser died. When the end came, Victoria, who for so many months had shown a dauntless face to the world, collapsed in paroxysms of weeping. Quickly regaining her composure, she wrote to Bismarck to remind him that her husband's last act had been to agree to their daughter's marriage to Alexander Battenberg. "All is now over," she wrote. "Now that he is no more, you will certainly keep clearly in mind the wish he expressed yesterday. He died as a hero and his soul dwells now with the angels."[60] Bismarck did not reply, nor did Wilhelm pay any attention to his parents' injunction that he permit the marriage. It never took place. Battenberg married his actress, and Victoria was left to find another husband. She eventually became the bride of the pleasant and inconsequential Prince Adolf of Schaumburg-Lippe, with whom she lived for many years in reasonable happiness.

The widowed Kaiserin's son, now Wilhelm II, German Emperor and King of Prussia, could at last do as he pleased. He ignored his mother's plea and ordered an autopsy to be performed on his father, confident that it would prove (as indeed it did) that he had died from the malignancy that his mother and her English doctor had too long denied existed. The new Kaiser then set out at once for Berlin to confer with Bismarck and to issue an address to his army and to his new subjects.

BISMARCK IN TROUBLE

THE FIRST ACT of the new sovereign was to issue an address to the Prussian army in which he extolled its "stout, unbreakable allegiance to the commander-in-chief." "The army and I," Wilhelm II declared, "were born for one another and will stick together forever, be it, by God's will, through peace or war."[1] The Kaiser's choice of the army as the recipient of his first royal proclamation was a portent of the role that military affairs would play in his reign. In the winter of 1887–88, as he realized that his ascension could not be long deferred, Wilhelm had begun to plan a number of alterations in the military establishment.[2] Some were merely decorative, such as changes in uniforms or retitling army headquarters, formerly known as the "*Maison Militaire*," as the "*Hauptquartier Seiner Majestät*." The young Kaiser's first substantive reform affected military society, which for some years had found relief from duty in the sybaritic luxury of various clubs in Berlin. Wilhelm had conducted a campaign several years earlier against the Union Club, which he considered particularly objectionable because of its members' extravagant drinking and gambling. Only a few weeks after becoming Kaiser, Wilhelm II issued an order to all army commanders that no Prussian officer was to belong to clubs such as the Union.[3] While the royal edict may have offended a number of pleasure-seeking officers, the new Kaiser enjoyed solid popularity with his troops. A young dragoon lieutenant in the capital wrote that he and his comrades were delighted to see a man on the throne who was determined to maintain old Prussian traditions and not introduce unpalatable novelties.[4]

Wilhelm next undertook to make a number of personnel changes in the Prussian army, for he was determined to force into retirement those officers who appeared to be too old to discharge their responsibilities. The Prussian generalship, in Wilhelm's opinion, had become superannuated and needed a thorough weeding. In the summer of 1888, he began to cull the ranks with a ferocity that alarmed some of his officers, even though they realized this step was necessary and was one which Friedrich

III had intended to implement during his brief reign.[5] Rather than leave military assignments to the General Staff and the Military Cabinet, which traditionally had supervised such matters and tended to prefer older generals, the Kaiser himself began to decide who would get what posts.[6] Although many generals who were now pensioned off or shunted to lesser commands were in fact too advanced in age to serve with the requisite vigor, the failing which Wilhelm detected in others was their opposition to him before he came to the throne.[7] Wilhelm was swift to reward those who had stood by him while he waited in the shade of his father and grandfather. Not long after becoming Kaiser, he had an opportunity to make an appointment at the pinnacle of the army. Field Marshal Count Helmuth von Moltke, the legendary architect of victory in the wars of unification twenty years earlier, voluntarily decided in August 1888 to surrender his position as chief of the General Staff. Moltke was almost eighty-eight and physically weak, but he was also prompted to resign because Wilhelm, whom he dismissed as a hard-headed "*Husarenoffizier*," paid no attention to him.[8] No one was surprised that the Kaiser immediately chose his longtime confidant, General Count von Waldersee, as Moltke's successor.

General Waldersee, now securely settled at the head of the army, had been one of Wilhelm's closest friends since 1882, and their relationship became even more intimate once Wilhelm ascended the throne. Waldersee had rushed to Potsdam on hearing of Friedrich III's death on 15 June 1888 and was admitted at once into the new Kaiser's presence. After receiving Waldersee's condolences, Wilhelm II discussed with the general the numerous changes in military positions he wished to effect. On this occasion, and in the months ahead, Waldersee would always prove forthcoming with suggestions concerning reassignments or retirements of the Kaiser's generals. During the first year of his reign, Wilhelm saw Waldersee on an almost daily basis, often taking extended walks with him in the Tiergarten. Waldersee treated him to a strongly conservative, Christian-social, and Russophobe train of thought, all of which the young ruler found appealing. The general, who had a pronounced tendency to self-satisfaction, was very gratified to learn from the Kaiser's old tutor, Hinzpeter, that he was the only person in whom Wilhelm had full confidence.[9]

The military figures who enjoyed the most constant access to the Kaiser were not necessarily those who, like Waldersee, held the highest ranks. Wilhelm's intimates in the army were his adjutants, some of whom were generals. At any given time, the Kaiser had six or eight adjutants, who rotated the taxing duty of being in the presence of the monarch from breakfast through dinner for several days at a stretch. One adjutant described their service as being Wilhelm II's "shadow."[10] Originally, the adjutants represented the various branches of the army, and after a year or two of service at court they were frequently reassigned to the field. From the beginning of his reign, Wilhelm II was determined to have his retinue correspond to his tastes rather than reflect the army's composition. Rather than distributing posts throughout the army, the Kaiser drew his military retinue largely from the guards cavalry and infantry regiments, and these elegantly caparisoned officers endeavored to insure that future recruits to the entourage would come from the same crack units. He appointed naval officers as adjutants, thereby destroying the army's traditionally exclusive claim to such positions. Once an adjutant was installed, Wilhelm was reluctant to see him depart, and a few remained in service from early in the reign until the Kaiser's abdication in November 1918. Wilhelm, who kept the selection of adjutants in his own hands, chose aristocratic men who were often handsome, full of martial brusqueness, possessed of only modest—and usually military—education, and suspicious of those who were more learned.[11] They were overwhelmingly Protestant and Prussian, and in all these qualities they were perfect reflections of the elite regiments in which they had served.

The Kaiser's military retinue, almost without exception, was composed of men whose company he liked not because they were clever or professionally talented but because they were always accommodating and unquestionably loyal. "He must have creatures whom he does not really respect but whom he finds pleasing," one adjutant-general wrote with exasperation when Wilhelm had been on the throne for only three years.[12] Among Wilhelm II's first appointments as adjutants were Generals Wilhelm von Hahnke, Adolf von Wittich, and Maximilian von Versen. An immense man of impressive appearance, Hahnke had been Wilhelm's commanding officer in the First Foot Guards and was a brother-in-law of Adolf von Bülow, who had served as Wilhelm's adjutant while he was still Prince of Prussia. Hahnke, who became chief of the Military Cabinet in 1888, was a soldier pure and simple, with a horizon that never rose above army affairs; he was prosaic, conservative, and intensely loyal to the crown. As Wilhelm's daughter aptly described him, he was "a piece of old Prussia."[13] Wittich's friendship with Wilhelm was a more recent development, for he had joined the retinue as a military advisor as recently as January 1888. Wittich was an expert in the history of war, and the Kaiser paid close attention as they studied the battles of Napoleon one by one.[14] Wilhelm had served under Versen in the hussars, but now their roles were reversed. Versen was a shameless sycophant who rushed to compare the young Kaiser with Frederick the Great. Wilhelm, who admitted that Versen's flattery was sometimes excessive, described him as "an old Prussian officer of the traditional type," and he often turned to him as a source of advice for other appointments to the royal entourage.[15]

Versen and his colleagues reaped handsome rewards from their long years of duty. Standing so close to the throne was not only glamorous but quite satisfying, for Wilhelm, according to his friend Philipp Eulenburg, tended to deify his assembly of adjutants as a sort of "heavenly body" (*Heiligthum*).[16] The adjutants were more lofty even than those who were their superiors in rank, and they acted accordingly. An adjutant might instruct a senior general entering Wilhelm's presence not to argue with him, and many a high-ranking officer took the advice to heart out of fear of being cast from favor.[17] Those who dared to criticize Wilhelm soon found themselves transferred to distant commands. But adjutants themselves could also earn the Kaiser's wrath, and General von Wittich was a case in point. For three years he lived at court, becoming increasingly restive and less and less impressed by his imperial master. Wittich was both malicious and indiscreet, a fatal combination in a courtier. He did not hesitate to describe the Kaiser as "that nitwit" (*Narr*) or as a "stuck-up idiot" (*eitel Thor*). When Wilhelm learned the substance, if not the vocabulary, of Wittich's criticism, the general was sent packing.[18]

Wilhelm II treated the military attachés serving in diplomatic missions abroad with the same favor, and they were often officers who had served as adjutants or who would later do so, or who indeed were simultaneously both adjutants *and* attachés. The attachés were encouraged to act independently of envoys and enjoyed the Kaiser's protection in the squabbles that resulted between these military figures and the German diplomatic corps. To Wilhelm, the attachés were his "comrades," who in his opinion knew more than the diplomats alongside whom they worked.[19]

The entourage of aristocratic soldiers from elegant units, chosen exclusively on the basis of the Kaiser's inclination for their personalities or appearance, did much to insulate Wilhelm from his other subjects. The longer these officers served at court, the more they too became shut off from society at large, and the less realistic their opinions and their advice. What a later chancellor, Prince Hohenlohe, would call the "Chinese wall" gradually descended around the young Kaiser. Intensely jealous of all competitors, including men from less socially preferred army units, the military retinue cut Wilhelm off from those whom he had once sought out for advice.[20] The leaders of the government, including chancellors and high diplomatic officials, found that Wilhelm II listened to soldiers more gladly than civilians, precisely the experience Bismarck had had with Wilhelm when he was only an heir to the throne.

With Waldersee, the adjutants, and attachés serving as his shield, Wilhelm II proceeded to introduce still other reforms in the Prussian army. Additional officers were reshuffled, decorations redesigned, and elaborate dress regulations issued. Following a plan left unfulfilled by Friedrich III, Wilhelm made a much-needed revision of the infantry training manual, the first in more than forty years, but the Kaiser's insistence on maintaining formal rituals of loading and discharging, for which there would have been no time in actual combat situations, nullified many of his improvements. One unimpressed older officer was bold enough to say: "If you please, Your Majesty, the new regulation is very handsome, but we won battles with the old one."[21] Even Waldersee, whose admiration for the young Kaiser ordinarily was boundless, admitted that Wilhelm's passion for military detail was extravagant, and he was also concerned that Wilhelm's personnel changes were excessive in number and insensitive in execution.[22]

In the first years of his reign, Wilhelm's existence centered exclusively on the army, so much so that Dona complained that their family life had been destroyed.[23] Wilhelm was at Potsdam two or three times a week in order to participate in regimental exercises, in which he took great delight. The Kaiser wrote to Philipp Eulenburg on 4 September 1888, after the first massive review had passed before him three days earlier: "The great day has come and gone! My entire guards, 30,000 strong, stood under my command for the first time. And what a magnificent parade! . . . What a feeling it is to call these troops *my own*."[24] Wilhelm studied military history, he paid lively attention to military (though not to civilian) reports, issued innumerable orders, and attended regimental dinners with steady regularity. If anyone tried to talk to him of anything other than military subjects, he quickly lost interest or became distracted.[25] All of the Kaiser's activity occurred in the company of his adjutants and old acquaintances in Potsdam, men—such as Hahnke and Wittich—who were good soldiers but who for the most part knew little of other matters. This *Adjutantenpolitik* soon produced critics. Wilhelm II had not been on the throne for more than a month or so before court circles were apprehensive that he was becoming so bedazzled by military affairs that he would eventually become incapable of reaching an informed judgment of anything else.[26] There was also increasing criticism of Wilhelm's peripatetic existence, the frequent trips aboard, the endless journeys to hunts in Silesia and East Prussia, and his constant appearance at regimental headquarters throughout Germany. This led to many barbs, including the joke current in 1889: "What is the leading firm in Germany?" "*Bismarck und Sohn*, because they have an Emperor as a traveling salesman."[27]

Wilhelm's determination to be the real commander of his troops became especially intense during the annual maneuvers of the Prussian army. The Kaiser had an enormous enthusiasm for these exercises and reserved for himself the command of one of the competing forces. He had a high opinion of his own military ability and was always eager to give advice, countermand orders, and generally assume the role of a military genius. Wilhelm warned that there were officers who thought that *they* ran the army but who would do well to remember that he alone was the supreme commander.[28] Few officers shared their sovereign's olympian estimation of his military ability. Even Waldersee—rarely one to criticize the Kaiser—believed that Wilhelm was basically surefooted both in tactics and leadership but had a tendency to pay too little attention to his staff.[29] The Kaiser's partisans as well as his detractors were all agreed that, leaving aside the question of imperial talent, the maneuvers were fraudulent exercises designed to give Wilhelm the exhilaration of perpetual victory.[30] The army was prepared to do virtually anything to insure the continuation of the Kaiser's martial enthusiasm. At an exercise held at Neuenhagen, just east of Berlin, in the fall of 1889, Wilhelm for the first time assumed the command of one of the rival armies, and any movements by the opposition that would have endangered the Kaiser's success were called off. At the conclusion of this contrived victory, the elated Kaiser declared that in the future he would always assume a command, and that indeed in the event of war he proposed to stand at the head of his troops.[31] At another maneuver that occurred about the same time, Wilhelm's adjutants brazenly spied on the opposing forces, who were ordered to remove their enemy insignia and join the Kaiser's force so that a royal victory could be assured.[32]

At the conclusion of maneuvers, Prussian custom required that Waldersee, as chief of the General Staff, present a critique. However indifferent the Kaiser's performance might have been, few if any of his generals were prepared to criticize his handling of troops, a reticence that only increased the young ruler's already inflated self-esteem. After the exercise at Neuenhagen in 1889, Waldersee, who was responsible for the arrangements that had resulted in the Kaiser's triumph, produced an analysis in which he suggested certain improvements that might have been made in Wilhelm's movements, but he did so in such an innocuous manner that the Kaiser took no umbrage. Waldersee, who was apprehensive at voicing even the slightest criticism of his royal master, noted with relief afterwards that he had "got himself out of it very well." Philip Eulenburg, who was also present, found Waldersee's flattery alarming. Not only had Wilhelm been allowed to win, but he had been led to believe that his performance had been virtually perfect. The effect, Eulenburg declared, was not only to mislead the Prussian troops who had participated but to reveal to the foreign military attachés present that the maneuver had been little more than a charade served up to flatter the sovereign's ego. When Eulenburg protested to Waldersee, the general denied that his critique had spared Wilhelm and airily informed Eulenburg that the ruler's pleasure was not to be trifled with. "The maneuvers amuse him," Waldersee declared, "and why shouldn't he have his fun?"[33] Waldersee's successor in 1891 as chief of the General Staff, General Count Alfred von Schlieffen, believed that letting the Kaiser prevail at maneuvers was a means of sustaining his enthusiasm for military duty and that that was justification enough for delivering him victories.[34]

Wilhelm II's ardor for the Prussian army presented Bismarck with a problem. The chancellor, who was proud of his own military past and almost always wore the rumpled uniform of a major general, knew that the Kaiser's martial attachment might promote solid conservative virtues, but it also gave his Potsdam cronies excessive influence. Even before Wilhelm's ascension, Bismarck had expressed alarm that this group had no knowledge of anything other than military affairs.[35] The Kaiser's devotion to the army was especially troubling to the chancellor, because his closest military associate was the chief of the General Staff, General Waldersee. Since the military attachés in foreign capitals reported directly to him and not to the German envoys to whose legations they belonged, Waldersee had been able to intrude himself into diplomacy, a field in which the chancellor had always insisted on being unchallenged and into which the general's predecessor, Field Marshal von Moltke, had rarely ventured. Waldersee had a low opinion of Bismarck's diplomats and wanted the network of military intelligence to be independent of the chancellor.

Waldersee's challenges in the area of diplomacy were especially annoying to Bismarck. The general, certain of Russo-German conflict and therefore insistent on a preventive war against the Tsar, had won over

Wilhelm to this view, but the chancellor was determined to maintain peace with Alexander III.[36] Germany, the Kaiser believed, must cleave to its Austrian ally, and in 1889 he assured his Habsburg colleague, Emperor Franz Josef, that should Austria become involved in a war with Russia, he could count on Germany's help. It did not matter, the Kaiser added, whether Bismarck approved or not.[37] Furthermore, three months earlier Wilhelm had advised a circle of friends that if it came to war with Russia and the chancellor would not go along, then he and Bismarck would have to part company.[38]

The Kaiser had some confidence that the personal ties between the Hohenzollern and Romanov dynasties could save the situation. Even before coming to the throne, he had crowed to a German diplomat à propos a problem that had arisen between Germany and Russia: "Just send me to St. Petersburg. I know the Tsar and within twenty-four hours I'll have things in order."[39] But the Tsar in question, the churlish Alexander III, found Wilhelm's showy manner and close association with the Russophobe Waldersee repugnant. The German consul general in Warsaw reported in May 1888 that there was widespread regret in Russia that Friedrich III had been fatally stricken with cancer and that with respect to Crown Prince Wilhelm it was "unbelievable what plans and ideas of the most far-reaching offensives [*Übergriffe*] are attributed to him."[40] In order to dispell these rumors, once he became Kaiser, Wilhelm decided, at Bismarck's prodding, to make St. Petersburg the object of his first state visit.[41]

The trip, undertaken in July 1888, went smoothly, and Alexander III declared to the German ambassador that the young Kaiser's frank and open manner had pleased him greatly. This was little more than diplomatic froth, for the Tsar did not find much that was appealing in his guest, and the Kaiser soon realized that his visit to St. Petersburg, intended as a gracious sign of good will, had instead been interpreted there as a manifestation of weakness. Wilhelm became incensed when, after a suitable interval had elapsed, Alexander III showed no inclination to make a reciprocal visit.[42] The Tsar finally came to Berlin in October 1889, fifteen months after Wilhelm's trip to St. Petersburg. Although the encounter went surprisingly well, Wilhelm warned Waldersee that there could be no certainty that the improved state of affairs introduced by the Tsar's visit would be lasting. He was quite right, for Alexander's visit to Wilhelm failed to alter significantly the mistrustful relationship between the two sovereigns.[43] The Kaiser continued to believe that Russia was plotting against Germany and that a war between the two powers was probably inevitable. That being the case, the forthcoming conflict had to be anticipated by keeping the Prussian army in the highest state of fitness. As for the Tsar, his superficial politeness toward Wilhelm merely disguised a deep-seated suspicion. "I certainly have full trust in you," Alexander III informed Chancellor Bismarck in 1889, "but unfortunately your Kaiser gives others his ear, especially General Waldersee, who wants war. That we are very certain of."[44]

Although Bismarck had urged Wilhelm to go to St. Petersburg in 1888, he had not reckoned on the intensity with which the Kaiser would involve himself in dynastic affairs there. The Kaiser, Bismarck regretted, was too inclined to allow momentary impulses and personal feelings to govern his actions. Although the Tsar's hostile behavior made Wilhelm's irritation understandable, this pique had been allowed to become the decisive factor in the Kaiser's calculation of Russo-German relations. Bismarck confessed that it was very difficult to make Wilhelm realize the danger of such an attitude.[45] Since in the chancellor's opinion it was the Tsar, and not his ministers, who charted the course of Russian diplomacy, every caution had to be exercised to avoid driving Alexander into the Germanophobe war party in St. Petersburg.[46] Wilhelm, on the other hand, believed that it was Bismarck who misunderstood the situation: the chancellor erroneously thought that Alexander III was basically a well-intentioned man whom he therefore could influence, when in fact the Tsar was malicious and should only be dealt treatment in kind. Wilhelm declared, quite incorrectly, that it had not been easy to bring Bismarck around but that the chancellor was beginning to realize the error in his judgment.[47]

Germany's relations with Russia, perhaps the most vital element in Bismarck's conception of European diplomacy, was thus an area in which the chancellor encountered a basic disagreement with Wilhelm. They did not concur on how St. Petersburg was to be handled or on the extent to which the Kaiser should be personally involved in this delicate exercise of diplomacy. Russia represented a potential point of collision between Bismarck and Wilhelm, but other problems between the two strong-willed men were even more difficult and overshadowed their differences of opinion in foreign affairs.

Wilhelm II's enthusiasm for the aristocratic army gratified the Prussian elite, but the young sovereign made it clear from the outset of his reign that he intended to be the ruler of all his subjects. Even the noble officer corps, he argued, needed to be opened to middle-class candidates.[48] The Kaiser's appointment of several notable progressives to high posts in the Prussian administration, especially the National Liberal leader Rudolf Bennigsen as president of the Prussian province of Hanover, and his appearance at dinners hosted by Bismarck to honor leaders of friendly Reichstag factions seemed to be indications that Wilhelm intended to broaden the base of the crown's support. In inaugural addresses made in the summer of 1888 to both the Prussian people and to the Reichstag, the Kaiser laid stress on his Christian duty to help the oppressed, and Wilhelm's subjects took him at his word. His ascension was seen as a new beginning, with the result that during the first year or so of his reign Wilhelm enjoyed considerable popularity with the working class. One officer noted that when the Kaiser rode through the more destitute quarters of Berlin, nine out of every ten men removed their caps. Frequently on these expeditions the cheer went up: "Hail to the workers' King!"[49]

Wilhelm II believed that socialism could best be combated by generous reforms from above and by religion, but humanitarian instincts, which were absent from his character, did not form the base of his concern for the laboring poor. Even in youth there was a coldness about Wilhelm's character, one frequently noted by those who knew him well, and it appeared with particular brutality in the utter lack of feeling with which he disposed of those who had once been his friends or servants.[50] It is hard to imagine that a man so notoriously callous in his emotions about individuals he knew well would have had a more compassionate feeling about his subjects at large. The Empress Friedrich, whose charity to the downtrodden was broad and genuine, doubted that her son had ever been really troubled about the poor and their problems.[51] Wilhelm's motives in adopting the poor were mixed. He admitted that in part his charity was a tactical response to the inevitable, for it was better, the Kaiser declared, to take the initiative than eventually to have to yield to pressure from below. The growing belligerence of the Social Democratic party and its alliance with the Catholic Center in the Reichstag forced him to intervene in the social question.[52] If expediency, combined perhaps with some small trace of Christian responsibility, impelled Wilhelm to help the poor, so did an acute desire to achieve popularity.[53] This was natural enough, for both his father and grandfather had won a widespread following among their subjects. Wilhelm II intended to have the same.

The interest the Kaiser showed in the working class in the early years of his reign was due in part to the influence of his former tutor, Hinzpeter, who from his retirement home in Bielefeld, near the great socialist centers in the Rhineland, continued to forward to his former student lengthy analyses of the labor problem and also corresponded with Wilhelm's wife on the social question. To Hinzpeter, working class reforms were to be regarded as a policy, not an obligation. He believed that the repressive measures formulated by Bismarck were mistaken and could lead only to further disturbances and increased socialist victories at the polls. Germany could achieve stability, and the Kaiser win popularity, only if the government granted moderate but timely concessions to the poor.[54]

Two other men with whom the Kaiser had only recently become acquainted but who had quickly won his favor provided him with similar advice. One was a middle-aged painter, August von Heyden, whose lackluster canvasses of German mythological episodes Wilhelm much admired. He was an inconsequential figure in Berlin society, in which no one other than the Kaiser paid him any attention. As a young man Heyden had been a mining official and had retained an interest in labor affairs after turning to a career in art. More impressive was Hugo Douglas, the son of druggist who had made an immense fortune from potash and from salt mining. Douglas had ingratiated himself with Wilhelm I, who in 1886 had made him a baron. Friedrich III had also liked the polished and amiable entrepreneur, but not the Empress Friedrich, who described him as a "great donkey."[55] Wilhelm had first become acquainted with Douglas in 1887, when Douglas had been instrumental in smoothing his relations with Bismarck in the aftermath of the Stoecker affair. One of the first acts of favor of Wilhelm's reign was to elevate his friend to the dignity of count. Douglas reciprocated by making a panegyrical address, published in 1888 as a brochure entitled "What We May Expect from Our Kaiser" (*Was Wir von unserem Kaiser Hoffen Dürfen*) that swiftly went through ten editions, extolling the young sovereign as a ruler of the poor as well as the rich.

Wilhelm was soon to be put to the test as to the genuineness of his sentiments. Less than a year after he became Kaiser, a serious labor disturbance in the coal industry broke out in the Rhineland and in Silesia, in the course of which Prussian troops were called out to protect the mines. In the Kaiser's opinion the strikes, which began early in May 1889, had been fomented by a number of Polish immigrant workers, who were criminals and Catholic fanatics. They bore, however, only part of the blame. The problem with the entire Rhineland, according to

Wilhelm's analysis, was that industrialists deserted it as soon as they had made their fortunes in its mines and foundries. Their enterprises, dedicated solely to maximizing profits, exhibited none of the concern for the condition of the working class that the Prussian government had shown in its state factories in Silesia.[56] Among the Rhenish exploiters, only the Krupps in Essen (as well as the Stumms to the west in the Saar) had succeeded in establishing what the Kaiser believed to be the proper, mutually advantageous relationship between employer and worker.[57] Wilhelm was convinced that if management did not make timely concessions, violence would result, and he was determined that his reign would not begin with bloodshed. The crown would therefore have to intervene to protect workers against unscrupulous employers, for otherwise the incidence of labor trouble would increase, socialism would win ever more adherents and the final consequence would be revolution.[58]

If the crown were thus to behave benevolently, it also expected that labor would abide by the law. Breaking all precedent, the Kaiser allowed a deputation of strikers to come to the palace to present their demands for an eight-hour day. But he warned them that he would greet their entreaties with sympathy only if they strictly abided by the law and purged any socialist elements within the labor movement.[59] Two days later the Kaiser met with a group of mine owners, informing them that the workers' delegation had made a good impression on him and that he expected in the future that the employers would stay in the "closest possible contact" with their employees. The mining companies had an obligation to look after the welfare of their workers, who in turn had a right to share in the profits of their labor.[60] In response to the Kaiser's urging, the strikers and the mine owners entered into negotiations that resulted in a settlement two weeks later. Wilhelm believed that he had been responsible for the agreement, and he now declared, as had Friedrich the Great many years earlier, that in the future he would rule as "the king of beggars" (*roi des gueux*) and secure recognition for the legitimate demands of labor.[61]

Bismarck was appalled. First there had been Russia, and now a domestic issue of the greatest importance threatened to separate him from the Kaiser. To Bismarck, the working class, whose greediness no government could ever satisfy, was to be handled with a mixture of paternalism and coercion, in which the government and employers would dictate the terms of employment. The chancellor dismissed the Kaiser's plans for ameliorating the condition of the working class, which would allow labor to participate in the process, as "humanitarian dizziness" (*Humani-*

tätsdusel) and correctly attributed Wilhelm's interest in such matters to Hinzpeter.[62] Bismarck agreed with the Kaiser that the government had a responsibility, for moral and financial reasons as well as for considerations of preserving order, to keep the poor from acute distress. In Wilhelm I's reign, the chancellor had had welfare legislation implemented to benefit workers in the event of sickness, accident, and other calamities, protection that was unique in Europe at the time. Where Wilhelm II and his premier statesman differed acutely was on the question of how the working class was to be treated when it struck or perpetrated other acts of rebellion. Wilhelm had shown a sympathetic attitude to the plight of the Rhineland strikers, and he insisted on regarding them as loyal subjects who, if treated properly, would at worst be "honest socialists" but not republicans or anarchists. He was convinced that no amount of reform would ever appease a worker who belonged to the Social Democrat party.[63]

Bismarck's misanthropic and even paranoid view of the human condition led him, however, to assume that every working man was a bona fide socialist who had to be hounded and held at bay. In light of the increasing strength of the socialists in Germany, one revealed in its electoral victories, the state, far from accommodating labor, should in fact tighten its repressive grip on the working class. Force, not charity, was what was required, for the Kaiser's subjects had repeatedly made it clear that they were no longer loyal to the Hohenzollern monarchy. The entire authority of the government had to be put at the ready for an internal preventive war against such dangerous subversives.[64] Existing measures designed to secure the traditional order of society would no longer suffice. In 1878 Bismarck had persuaded the Reichstag to pass an anti-socialist law, which ran for a term of three years and thereafter had been periodically renewed. The law, which subjected the Social Democratic party to severe restraints, was due to expire again on 1 October 1890, another reason for the chancellor's concern to deal emphatically with the labor question. In anticipation of the approaching expiration, Bismarck had been at work throughout 1889 drafting a new bill. He proposed to augment the existing legislation by adding a clause that would enable the government with little effort to deport agitators in industrial cities to rural areas that would be more resistant to socialist propaganda, a step which under the 1878 law could be undertaken only under tightly specified conditions.

The initial confrontation between Bismarck and Wilhelm took place on 12 May 1889 at a meeting of the Prussian ministers, all of whom at that point were ostensibly in agreement with the chancellor. Bismarck expressed his opinion that the strikes in the Rhineland, then ten days old, should be allowed to run their course without government intervention except to protect property. The result would be a steadily worsening situation, which would eventually enable the chancellor to take drastic measures against the strikers. The Kaiser, however, advanced an entirely different line, arguing that the Empire's ability to defend itself would be impaired if the strikes continued, and he hinted that Russia might take military advantage of Germany's weakness. If he were the Tsar, war would be declared at once! He certainly did not intend to see Prussian soldiers used to protect the villas and rose gardens of the rapacious mine owners.[65] The chancellor's reaction, expressed only after the Kaiser had left, was to point out to his ministerial colleagues that Wilhelm was showing the unfortunate autocratic tendencies of an earlier Hohenzollern, Friedrich Wilhelm I, the dictatorial father of Frederick the Great. The ministers supported Bismarck, affirming that the dispute should be allowed to grow worse. Wilhelm eventually agreed not to intervene, but the strike soon ended when both sides agreed on a compromise, and the differences between the Kaiser and Bismarck on the labor question were temporarily eliminated.

While Wilhelm had treated Bismarck with great deference when they disagreed during the strike crisis, he was growing impatient at the authoritarian behavior of both the chancellor and his son. The Kaiser complained to Philipp Eulenburg that the Bismarcks were trying to assert a sort of domination that was reminiscent of the forefathers of Charlemagne, who, although merely majordomos of the Frankish kings, had deposed them and seized their throne.[66] This demeaned the crown's position, and Wilhelm was annoyed that the chancellor did not make it sufficiently clear to his subordinates that it was the Kaiser and no one else from whom everything proceeded.[67] From the beginning of his reign, Wilhelm II exhibited unmistakable signs of doing things his own way. This was especially true in diplomacy, which Wilhelm had long believed could best be managed by himself and his "colleagues" among Europe's rulers, and which Bismarck was not conducting entirely to his satisfaction.[68]

The disagreement he and the chancellor had over Russian policy only intensified the Kaiser's belief that *he* had to act as Germany's representative. Since Russia appeared to be Germany's prospective enemy, Wilhelm needed to cultivate allies for the forthcoming struggle. The Kaiser therefore proposed to help Turkey arm against Russia, a policy to which

Bismarck was very opposed, since he was anxious to do nothing to give St. Petersburg offense. The prelude to Turko-German collaboration would be an imperial visit to the Sultan in Constantinople, which the Kaiser, not the chancellor, arranged to take place in June 1889. On the eve of his departure, Wilhelm declared that the bid for friendship with the Turks represented by his journey was one which rested personally with him. He informed his confidant, Prince Radolin (né Count Radolinski but elevated by Friedrich III), that Bismarck should not be told anything about the trip and that he did not care whether the chancellor approved or not.[69] As matters turned out, Wilhelm's mission to Constantinople proved a success and helped pave the way for the military cooperation that existed between Germany and the Ottoman Empire for the ensuing quarter of a century. But, as Bismarck had warned, Wilhelm's fruitful trip only increased the mistrust Tsar Alexander III had for Germany and its ruler.

Bismarck apparently did not take Wilhelm's contrariness in either diplomacy or internal affairs as seriously as might have been prudent. After almost thirty years of wielding near dictatorial power, the Iron Chancellor had grown complacent and believed that he could hold the chancellorship for life, or until he was ready to hand it over to his son Herbert. At the end of May 1889, some two weeks after Wilhelm had first challenged his scheme for dealing with the miners' strikes, the chancellor assured one of his diplomats that he was entirely satisfied with the Kaiser's deportment and that he had no real difficulties with him.[70] Bismarck, however, made no secret of his displeasure that the Kaiser sought advice on any and all matters from a small group of advisors outside the government—the chancellor singled out Hinzpeter, Heyden, Douglas, and the Grand Duke of Baden—just as in the reactionary aftermath of the revolution of 1848 King Friedrich Wilhelm IV of Prussia had had his "camarilla," as the crown's unofficial circle of advisors was known.[71] Although Bismarck himself was optimistic about his ability to handle Wilhelm, from the outset of the reign there were numerous reports that their relations were deteriorating, and by the beginning of 1889 speculation abounded that the chancellor would eventually find himself sacked.[72] Even before coming to the throne, Wilhelm had more than once declared that Bismarck, like any other servant of the crown, was replaceable. Now as Kaiser he realized, as he informed the Austro-Hungarian ambassador, Count Ladislaus von Szögyényi-Marich, that a monarch's greatest misfortune was to become too tied to a person without having a clear awareness as to who, if necessary, might replace him. He assured Szögyényi that he had a substitute for *every* one of his officials, civil and military.[73]

Bismarck, as well as his son Herbert at the Foreign Office, believed that there were a number of figures who were actively conspiring to create a rupture between them and the sovereign. In the opinion of both father and son, their principal enemy was General Waldersee, whose ambition and whose intimate relationship with the Kaiser made him appear to be the coming man, destined one day to replace Bismarck as chancellor. Wilhelm had not been on the throne a week before there were rumors in various Berlin newspapers that he and the chancellor were at odds over Waldersee. The Kaiser quickly had one of his adjutants write to Bismarck to ask him to issue a denial in the semiofficial press and to inform the chancellor that while he highly valued Waldersee's abilities he had no intention of allowing the general to have an "unwarranted influence" on foreign policy. The chancellor was also told that there was no court camarilla at work against him.[74] But the Bismarcks had to reconcile these assurances with the obvious marks of favor Waldersee received from Wilhelm. The general's appointment in August 1888 as chief of the General Staff had been followed five months later, on the occasion of the Kaiser's thirtieth birthday, by his elevation to a seat in the Prussian House of Lords, a step Wilhelm designed to enable Waldersee to widen his influence into civil affairs.

In Bismarck's opinion, Waldersee's hold on the Kaiser was attributable to his unctuousness, a trait which had also helped advance the general's military career. Waldersee did indeed possess a gift for flattery, to which Wilhelm was very susceptible. Through his constant adulation, Waldersee provided the Kaiser's vanity with replenishment it hardly needed. According to the chancellor, one device Waldersee, as well as the Kaiser's "chief flatterer," General von Versen, used was to remind Wilhelm that Frederick the Great would never have been known by his cognomen had he let himself be manipulated by a minister as powerful as Bismarck.[75] Whether or not either of these polished generals was responsible for implanting the idea in Wilhelm's head, he was soon making much the same observation.[76] Herbert took an even more hostile view of the jowly and rotund Waldersee, whose sanctimony he despised. He had always felt that the general's military talents were modest and his diplomatic ability nil. This was frightening enough in a man serving at the head of the army, but Waldersee's political ambitions made him even more dangerous.[77] Herbert was sure that the reason Waldersee worked to provoke trouble between Wilhelm and the chancellor was his hope that eventually

Bismarck would become so irritated that he would resign in a fit of pique. In Herbert's opinion, the result would be an immediate war with Russia, which without Bismarck at the helm would be catastrophic. The best thing to do was to tread very carefully with Wilhelm and try to minimize the sway exerted by the "blubber brat" (*Blubbermatz*) Waldersee.[78]

Waldersee always steadfastly denied that he sought the chancellorship or that he tried to undermine Bismarck's standing with the Kaiser, but the record of his activities from Wilhelm's ascension in June 1888 until Bismarck's fall almost two years later plainly shows that he lost few opportunities to point out to the Kaiser what he considered to be the chancellor's deficiencies. It is equally apparent that the general had no person other than himself in mind to succeed Bismarck. There was hardly an area of foreign or domestic policy on which Waldersee failed to disagree with the Bismarcks. He had sided with Wilhelm in the Stoecker affair, in the Kaiser's argument with Bismarck as to how the Rhenish strikers were to be dealt with, and he wanted war rather than amicable relations with Russia. Waldersee argued that not only was Bismarckian diplomacy toward Russia mistaken but that it was also deliberately alienating Austria-Hungary by mixing in that Empire's internal affairs and also by gratuitously stirring up trouble with Switzerland. Moreover, Waldersee informed the Kaiser that the chancellor's colonial policy was needlessly embroiling Germany in difficulties with other European powers. In Waldersee's opinion, the chancellor acted not in the Fatherland's interest but out of determination to preserve his hegemony and to guarantee the succession to Herbert, for whom Waldersee had little use. The Bismarcks reduced everyone to minions; all bowed before the will of father and son, and only sycophants survived.[79]

By the middle of 1889, it was clear that in the battle for influence over the Kaiser, Waldersee was gaining ground at the Bismarcks' expense. The general had previously been circumspect in his criticism of the chancellor, but now he hinted to the Prussian minister of war, Julius von Verdy du Vernois, that he might in the future have to tell the Kaiser some unpleasant truths.[80] He began to recruit allies for the struggle and noted with satisfaction that Philipp Eulenburg and Karl Heinrich von Boetticher, state secretary of the imperial Interior Office and Prussian minister without portfolio, shared his alarm about the Bismarcks. Wilhelm's uncle, the Grand Duke of Baden, was a good friend of Waldersee's and a valuable ally in the campaign against Bismarck. The Grand Duke resented Bismarck's desire to control everything and described the difference between his nephew and the chancellor as a quarrel over which dynasty should rule Germany, the Hohenzollerns or the Bismarcks. He therefore urged Wilhelm to regard the chancellor and his son as competitors rather than as vassals.[81] Waldersee had reason to be pleased with the progress he had made in undermining the chancellor's position. On all sides, Bismarck's influence was described as being on the wane, while Waldersee took salutes as the man of the future. The Kaiser had lavished the highest offices on him, visited him regularly, and all the while seemed to share Waldersee's misgivings about the Bismarcks' diplomacy. Waldersee viewed his ascending position with customary smugness, recording in his diary in November 1889 that Wilhelm was always "very correct and considerate, never of a contrary opinion. A more favorable relationship is thus hardly conceivable."[82]

The Waldersee coterie was not the only cause of Bismarck's diminished standing with Wilhelm II. The close association the chancellor had with the leading Berlin banker, Gerson von Bleichröder, also compromised him. In the early 1860s Bleichröder had assumed the role of Bismarck's personal banker and had performed this function greatly to the chancellor's financial advantage. Bleichröder had innumerable contacts in high places almost everywhere in Europe and was therefore in a position to give the chancellor information of political as well as economic utility. For thirty years, the relationship between Bismarck, scion of an ancient Prussian noble house, and his banker, a Jew of modest antecedents, became increasingly close.[83] Bleichröder's financial investments and his political liaisons more and more concentrated on Russia, where military and industrial ambitions necessitated the assumption of an increasing level of indebtedness in Western Europe. The Russian loans arranged by Bleichröder and other Berlin bankers fortified Bismarck's diplomatic cultivation of St. Petersburg, and on occasion the Prussian state bank joined Bleichröder's firm in underwriting the Russian debentures. The grateful Tsars invested Bleichröder with orders and decorations, and Bismarck saw to it that Wilhelm I awarded him the predicate of nobility.

Wilhelm did not share Bismarck's need for Bleichröder's services and apparently never met the banker. The chancellor's attachment to Bleichröder damaged his standing at court, for not only was there a pronounced streak of anti-Semitism in the young Kaiser himself, but his retinue was strongly prejudiced against Jews. The root of Wilhelm II's anti-Semitism lay in the aristocratic, military culture in which he lived, to which was added his negative reaction to the cordial relations his mother and father enjoyed with the Jewish intelligentsia in Berlin, a group which had nothing to do with Bleichröder. The military society with which Wilhelm surrounded himself in Potsdam and Berlin was infected with anti-Semitism, as was the social world composed of soldiers and diplomats that played a prominent role in the court circles Wilhelm frequented while a young prince. Bleichröder's pretentious airs and social ambitions made the impoverished Prussian aristocracy regard him with particular distaste.[84]

The Kaiser's intimates shared the prejudices of their class. Philipp Eulenburg found Jews revolting, as did his friend Herbert Bismarck, who had a particular hatred for the "villain" Bleichröder, even though he was his father's friend.[85] General von Waldersee endorsed the anti-Semitism of the Stoecker movement, into which he had drawn the Kaiser, and he especially loathed Bleichröder.[86] Wilhelm was prepared to dislike Bleichröder merely because he was a Jew, but he also had a special grievance against the banker because of his activity in making loans to Russia, which in the Kaiser's opinion served only to enable the Tsar to arm against Germany. The showdown came in the summer of 1889, when Bleichröder and the chancellor were arranging a large loan to St. Petersburg. Wilhelm berated Herbert about his father's truck with the Jewish banker and ordered that the conversion be prevented.[87] It was soon abandoned but the Kaiser did not forget the matter. Waldersee, who was with Wilhelm constantly, believed that the Kaiser's countermanding of the loan was the decisive factor in setting the stage for Bismarck's dismissal eight months later.[88]

The chancellor had another associate for whom the Kaiser had little use. This was Eduard von Liebenau, who also enjoyed good relations with Herbert Bismarck. Liebenau had been Wilhelm's adjutant during his university days at Bonn and, on the Prince's ascension, had by imperial order become chief marshal of the court and household (*Oberhof- und Hausmarschall*). The choice of such an insensitive boor was highly inappropriate, and he soon had among his enemies the three people closest to Wilhelm: the Kaiserin, General Waldersee, and Philipp Eulenburg.[89] As marshal, Liebenau had daily access to the Kaiser, who was beginning to tire of his overbearing manner but who nevertheless incautiously confided all manner of things to him. Liebenau was highly ambitious, and he considered his present position only an interlude en route to an ambassadorship, a post for which by personality and training he was totally unsuitable. Liebenau realized that a diplomatic appointment would depend on ingratiating himself with the Bismarcks, and this he proceeded to do by supplying the chancellor and his son with a continuing narrative of the Kaiser's remarks.[90] Although the Bismarcks did not like Liebenau and had no intention of promoting him to an envoyship, they found his information highly valuable and therefore sedulously encouraged his frequent visits. Liebenau thus became prominently identified as a Bismarck protégé, a fact which eventually undermined his standing with Wilhelm.[91] Eulenburg, who was a close observer of Bismarck and the Kaiser during this period, believed that Liebenau, more than any other person, contributed to the poisoning of relations between Wilhelm and the chancellor.[92]

Herbert's association with Liebenau, which was no less close than his father's, was only one reason for his increasing unpopularity with Wilhelm II. Part of Herbert's problem was that he saw more of the Kaiser than did the chancellor, who deliberately left to his son the daily negotiation of business, mistakenly believing that in spite of his dictatorial manner Herbert had a greater facility for dealing with Wilhelm.[93] There was never any question of the Kaiser's appreciation for Herbert's talents as a diplomat, and some observers thought that in their strident personalities Wilhelm and the chancellor's son were not unalike.[94] But gradually Wilhelm began to take a less indulgent view of Herbert's coarseness and pronounced cynicism, and by the time he had become Kaiser his disenchantment was complete.[95]

Ever since the two men became acquainted in 1884, Herbert had enjoyed excellent relations with Wilhelm, who he assured his father in October 1888 was "tractable, reasonable, and easy to lead."[96] This was wishful thinking, however, and long before Wilhelm became Kaiser his friendship with Herbert had begun to unravel. Count Radolinski, an intimate of Wilhelm's parents who had an unrivaled assortment of friends at court, reported at the very beginning of 1888 that Herbert seemed "to have lost his enthusiasm for the young man. Someone among those who are well informed told me that young B[ismarck] had lost his influence with the young master by his fraternity-boy manners and by the fact that he made himself thick as thieves with him. The other one [Wilhelm] has lost all respect for him and does not listen to him any longer."[97] Herbert certainly was not without grounds for having very strong reservations about Wilhelm's conception of domestic and diplomatic affairs. He found the Kaiser's anti-Russian views dangerous, as was his truckling after the working class, all of whom in Herbert's opinion were "social democratic, republican, materialistic, and covetous."[98] Herbert also resented Wilhelm's interference in diplomatic appointments, especially the intention he had announced of replacing Herbert's brother-in-law, Count Kuno von Rantzau, as Prussian minister to Bavaria. Wilhelm disliked Rantzau and wanted to remove him so that the post in Munich could be made available for his friend Eulenburg, presently accredited to the insignificant Grand Duke of Oldenburg.[99]

Like the chancellor, Herbert was used to having his way, and he therefore tended to take a rather peremptory tone with Wilhelm, as though what he and his father had decided was not to be questioned. Before Wilhelm became Kaiser, Herbert was asked how he would get on with the Prince once he came to the throne. His nonchalant reply was that "we will take him in hand and make of him what we want."[100] The best way to deal with the Kaiser, Herbert advised Rantzau, was to avoid written documents, which he did not like to read and which sometimes produced intemperate marginalia, but to approach him in person, for in conversation Wilhelm could be won over.[101] Wilhelm proved not to be so malleable, however, and even the chancellor felt compelled to urge his son to be more careful.[102]

On the surface, Wilhelm kept up his good relations with Herbert, but they were no longer intimate. The Kaiser was certainly not willing to accord to him the right of succession to the chancellorship, an ascent that Herbert's father took for granted. Wilhelm decided that when Bismarck retired Herbert might retain the Foreign Office but would not replace his father. In Wilhelm's opinion, Herbert had no understanding of the danger Germany faced from the East and indeed had become "half Russian."[103] Dona undoubtedly intensified the Kaiser's feelings, for she was an avowed enemy of both of the Bismarcks and all their circle. The chancellor's great enemy Waldersee was her confidant, she disliked Jews such as Bleichröder, and Bismarck's informant Liebenau was anathema to her. The Kaiserin, who had for years resented the fact that in the 1860s the chancellor had deprived her now long-dead father of his claim to the Danish duchies of Schleswig and Holstein, could not bear Bismarck's domination of her husband. But she particularly detested Herbert because she, like Waldersee, feared that his corrupt morals and licentiousness might rub off on the easily impressionable Kaiser. She treated the chancellor's son cooly, as did her entourage, who also disliked him. Herbert indeed had no friends at court.[104]

Wilhelm thus was surrounded by a group of relatives and friends who were hostile to the chancellor, his son Herbert, and their satellites. The potential conflict between the Kaiser and his chancellor was obvious to those who worked alongside them, but neither Otto Bismarck nor his son was inclined to pay much attention to the frequent rumors that their position was deteriorating, nor did they seem to be at all alarmed by what in retrospect appears to have been a very discernible decline in their hold on Wilhelm. It did not occur to either that the Kaiser would dare to dismiss them.[105] Bismarck believed that he himself would choose the moment of his departure from the chancellor's palace, and Herbert was certain that he was enthroned in Berlin for life.[106] Throughout 1888 and 1889 the chancellor therefore blandly assured his associates that his relations with the Kaiser were excellent and that Wilhelm was getting on very well with Herbert.[107] The reign began with Wilhelm II being, if anything, too deferential for the chancellor's tastes.[108]

That did not mean that Bismarck did not detect some problems. From the outset of Wilhelm's reign, the aging chancellor was aware that the young Kaiser would have to be handled carefully but was confident that it could be done.[109] He clearly wanted to be the dominant force in Germany, and, that being the case, the chancellor decided that he would have to be accommodating on everyday affairs, especially those—such as Wilhelm's determination to spend millions of marks on a royal yacht—that would not contribute to the ruler's popularity. Confrontations could be saved for major issues.[110] But such issues, on both foreign and domestic fronts, were not long arising, and on these Bismarck was not prepared to give any quarter.

Wilhelm, on the other hand, had no intention of letting the Bismarcks frustrate his desire to play the commanding role in imperial Germany. No servant of the crown, he made clear, was indispensable, not even the Iron Chancellor and certainly not his son.[111] Wilhelm was happy to have Bismarck stand at his side on the steps of the throne, but there was to be no question as to who was the greater figure. "I ask nothing other," as the Kaiser explained his position to his friend Eulenburg, "than that he examine those wishes that I consider justified, and if I find myself unable to agree to his reservations (which up to now I have always done) I expect him at the least to give in. But he won't do it! His will is his highest command. He can't bear it that I also sometimes want and desire something."[112]

No one relished the Bismarcks' difficulties more than Waldersee. He assured a friend in May 1889 that the chancellor was in fact faltering in asserting his will against that of the Kaiser.[113] In Waldersee's opinion, Wilhelm was behaving with masterful skill, maintaining the most cordial relations with the chancellor, following his advice in some things but in others doing exactly as he pleased.[114] But in the Foreign Office, Friedrich von Holstein, who was well informed about both sides of the rivalry,

believed that it had a blunter edge. In November 1889, Holstein characterized the chancellor's relationship with the Kaiser as one of "strong
antagonism." If Wilhelm took a position, Bismarck insisted on the opposite.[115] The chancellor nevertheless gave no sign that Wilhelm's opposition to his Russian policy or attitude on the labor question troubled him
seriously. Bismarck believed that the Kaiser could be won over by trivial
concessions or intimidated by threats and cajolery, the means through
which he had for years successfully handled Wilhelm I. Waldersee and
other rivals could be eliminated should they ever prove really dangerous,
for even the most resourceful of them could not approach the extraordinary stature enjoyed by the creator of imperial Germany. As 1889 drew
to an end, no one in Berlin was as sure as Bismarck and his son that the
new year—indeed the forthcoming decade—would perpetuate the autocratic and highly personal regime that the Iron Chancellor had carefully
promoted ever since coming to power almost three decades earlier.

Seven

1890

A FEW DAYS before Christmas 1889, the British ambassador in Berlin reported that "the Emperor is off again shooting. It seems impossible for him to remain quiet for more than two or three days at a time."[1] As soon as 1890 opened, Wilhelm II resumed the chase. Immediately following his traditional New Year's Day reception, the Kaiser left Berlin for a hunt arranged by his friend, Count Guido Henckel at his princely estate at Neudeck in Silesia. Next to Friedrich Alfried Krupp, Henckel was the Kaiser's wealthiest subject, and he lived in splendor befitting royalty, sparing no effort to fulfill the family motto "Live for the moment." Caviar as well as brandy were de rigueur even at the breakfast table, and the peasants on Neudeck's thousands of acres kissed the hem of Countess Henckel's gown as she passed by. Wilhelm delighted in such sumptuousness, and on this trip he derived great pleasure from exterminating no fewer than 550 pheasants in a single day's shooting on a neighboring estate.

In spite of the festive atmosphere, the Kaiser could not conceal his concern at the steadily worsening crisis with Bismarck. Karl Heinrich von Boetticher, the state secretary of the imperial Interior Office as well as a Prussian minister without portfolio, was also Henckel's guest and brought to Neudeck the draft approved by Bismarck of the royal address for the opening of the Prussian parliament on 15 January. After scrutinizing the document, Wilhelm declared that it was unacceptable because it contained no announcement of the government's intention to introduce a bill for the protection of labor (*Arbeiterschutzgesetz*). This was a subject on which the Kaiser had laid particular stress in recent pronouncements, and in December 1889 he had circulated to the Prussian ministry a memorandum that he, in consultation with his old tutor Hinzpeter, had composed on the state's responsibility for accommodating the legitimate demands of labor. Shortly thereafter Wilhelm had reminded the chancellor that improving the welfare of working people was a goal very close to his heart.[2] The strikes in the Rhineland and the collusion of the Social Democrats in the Reichstag with their Catholic Center allies, which created a formidable parliamentary coalition poised against the government, demanded that the crown take action from above before it was forced from below.[3] The Kaiser informed Boetticher that unless the address was amended and assurances given for the formulation of a law for the protection of the working class he would decline to open the parliament in person.[4]

The chancellor's testy response was that he would resign rather than do so, for he was convinced that the working class deserved not concessions but coercion. Bismarck's recalcitrance was annoying, but it also made Wilhelm cautious. He was not inclined to make an issue of the matter at the moment, for the Reichstag elections, due at the end of February, made it imperative for the crown and the government to present a solid front against socialism. The military budget, a critical item of legislation that would come before the parliament in the late spring, would require Bismarck's adroit hand to insure passage. It was hardly the time for a crisis with the chancellor. Wilhelm was very annoyed, however, and he attributed Bismarck's truculence to alcohol and morphine.[5] The Kaiser returned to Berlin on 6 January because of the fatal illness of his grandmother, the Kaiserin Augusta, who died on the following day. For the next few weeks, he was constantly in touch with Hinzpeter, who had come to the capital to advise his former pupil on the labor question. Philipp Eulenberg also hastened to Berlin from his diplomatic post in nearby Oldenburg, and on 13 January he and the Kaiser took a long walk in the snow-covered Tiergarten, during which Wilhelm unburdened himself about his problems with the chancellor, who, he declared, had become a constant trial.[6]

A policy favoring labor that Wilhelm II was determined to introduce would have to be squared with the existing antisocialist law, due to expire on 1 October 1890, that shackled the Social Democratic party, the parliamentary voice of much of the German working class. The Kaiser's uncle, the Grand Duke of Baden, as well as the Grand Duke's envoy in Berlin, Baron Adolf Marschall von Bieberstein, argued with Wilhelm that he could not with one hand insist on a new law protecting labor and with the other renew the legislation against the socialists.[7] The Kaiser's problem was Bismarck, who opposed any new overtures to the working class and was also insistent that the antisocialist law be renewed and even made more stringent. In Wilhelm's opinion, the question was not only a disagreement about policy but a contest of wills, for he believed that Bismarck was using the issue to intimidate the Prussian ministers into taking his side, should they be forced to choose between their loyalty to the chancellor or to the sovereign.[8] Either the Kaiser would back down in the face of collective ministerial opposition or he would have to dismiss the entire Prussian government, both of which would be equally unprecedented steps. On the other hand, as Wilhelm admitted to Eulenburg, to acquiesce in Bismarck's efforts to strengthen the antisocialist law would lead ultimately to a situation bordering on revolution. A strong antisocialist law might in itself be desirable, but the Kaiser could not bring himself to begin his reign with the violence that he believed such a measure would inevitably produce.[9] And since a law along the lines Bismarck contemplated could never pass the Reichstag, the chancellor would have to resort to a coup d'état in order to implement his persecution of the socialists. That Wilhelm could also not countenance.

Although the Kaiser was wrong in claiming that Bismarck was fatally addicted to morphine, the chancellor was indeed in a cranky and petulant mood as 1890 opened. One of Bismarck's closest associates, Baron Robert Lucius von Ballhausen, Prussian minister of agriculture and forestry, noted that the chancellor's stubbornness made him impossibly difficult even for those who sided with him and that he was particularly contrary toward Wihelm II and the Prussian ministry.[10] The chancellor's relations with Wilhelm had been without open friction throughout 1889, but this was because Bismarck spent most of the year on his estates, entrusting the day-to-day conduct of business with the Kaiser to his son Herbert. The chancellor was not prepared to accommodate himself to Wilhelm's progressive views on the labor question, and he left it to Herbert, whom he believed to be more to the Kaiser's liking, to induce Wilhelm to abandon the visionary notions he had borrowed from Hinzpeter.[11] Herbert, long since out of favor with the ruler, did not succeed, however, and it therefore fell to the chancellor to resist Wilhelm's demand that he insert into the speech from the throne some mention of a forthcoming law for the protection of labor. Bismarck would agree to no more than a passage expressing the crown's satisfaction that mine owners in the Rhineland had at last begun to acknowledge the rightful demands of their workers and assuring Prussian laborers that in the future they would have a protector in the government. Wilhelm kept his promise to boycott the opening of parliament on 15 January, a public acknowledgment that there was a rift between the Kaiser and his chancellor.

As far as the Kaiser was concerned, his collision with Bismarck over the contents of his speech to open the Prussian parliament had only temporarily deflected his intention of effecting some sort of reform for the working class that would eliminate any future outbreaks of labor violence. Bismarck, however, was prepared to allow the situation to deteriorate to the point that it would become necessary to impose martial law, a path Wilhelm rejected out of hand. Kaiser Wilhelm I, he argued, could have taken such a step and retained the respect of his subjects, but for a young, untried ruler to do so would be "disastrous."[12] The Kaiser therefore asked Bismarck to come to Berlin on 24 January for a meeting of the council of state (*Staatsrat*), an advisory body that the sovereign periodically convened.[13] Wilhelm selected the twenty-fourth because it was the birthday of Frederick the Great, for he was persuaded that the adoption by the crown of a program benefiting the lower classes would prove no less a milestone in Prussian history than the birth, almost two hundred years earlier, of Prussia's greatest king.

Bismarck arrived in Berlin uncertain of his ability to master the situation. The Kaiser's opposition was disturbing, but much more troublesome to the chancellor was a development in the Reichstag. For several weeks, a commission of deputies had been considering a bill recommended to it by the Federal Council (*Bundesrat*) that would replace the existing antisocialist law when it expired on 1 October 1890. The council's bill provided that the new antisocialist law, unlike the earlier enactments that ran for three-year periods, would have an indefinite term and included an "expulsion" paragraph, enabling the government to exile urban socialist agitators to the countryside. The constitution provided that council proposals be referred to a commission formed of Reichstag deputies, who might then forward the proposal, together with any amendments that they made, to the lower house.

Deputies of the National Liberal party dominated the Reichstag commission examining the Federal Council's proposed antisocialist bill, and they succeeded in having the expulsion paragraph stricken. When the amended measure arrived on the floor of the Reichstag on 23 January 1890, the Conservatives and Free Conservatives, who together with the National Liberals formed the parliamentary majority or "cartel" (*Kartell*) on which Bismarck's majority depended, denounced its weakened provisions. They had no confidence that a mutilated bill would have sufficient strength to quell disturbances among the working class. If this was the sort of measure the Reichstag was likely to accept, the Conservatives wanted the responsibility for its passsage to rest squarely with the chancellor. He would have to assume this by requesting their support. If Bismarck refused to do so, then the Conservatives would have no choice but to form an unholy alliance with the Social Democrats and defeat the bill.

From the chancellor's perspective that would be just as well. The situation would grow worse, violence would erupt, but there would be no law on the books through which to combat socialism. At that point his enemies would have to capitulate and agree to stringent legislation against the socialists. Bismarck had no intention of acceding to the pressure the Conservative group was trying to put on him, and he refused to be intimidated by the Kaiser's reluctance to support a strong antisocialist bill. To ask for the cartel's support for a watered-down bill would be an irreparable humiliation at the hands of the parliamentary factions, for which the chancellor had always had contempt. He intended to insist on a strong bill, leaving the Reichstag to discover that there were not enough votes on the right to pass a weaker measure. The blame for leaving the government without a legal means of curbing socialist insurrection would then be borne by the Kaiser and the Reichstag but not by the chancellor.[14]

Bismarck's first task was to insure that his firm resistance to the weakened bill had the support of the Prussian ministry. Immediately on arriving in the capital he assembled the Prussian ministers, who were thoroughly initimidated by the chancellor's obvious ire.[15] Bismarck quickly secured their unanimous consent that at the forthcoming council, scheduled to take place at 6 P.M. on 24 January, the ministry would present a united front to inform the Kaiser that the question was too complicated for precipitate decision and that additional time was therefore required to consider the question. The ministers did have the temerity to point out to Bismarck that it was neither possible nor advisable for them to drag out a matter on which Wilhelm II's opinion as well as the majority of the Reichstag had already been made clear. This suggestion of ministerial independence of mind annoyed Bismarck, and he concluded the meeting by warning his colleagues against speaking in public without his authorization.

The Kaiser opened the council on 24 January with a lengthy exposition of his views on the labor question, by all accounts outlining his ideas with force and clarity.[16] In Wilhelm II's opinion, the miners' strikes of 1889 in the Rhineland had left a residue of ill-feeling that had to be eliminated. Owing to the rapid development of German industry, thousands of workers—"squeezed like lemons," as he put it—had been forced by exploitative joint stock companies into the ranks of the proletariat. In this debased state they had been enticed by socialist propaganda. All revolutions, according to the Kaiser, came about because governments failed to make timely reforms. He did not wish to commit such an error. While the government would be sympathetic to workingmen, it would not countenance exorbitant wage demands or other economic adjustments that would reduce Germany's ability to compete in international trade. But that still left a wide range of possibilities such as reducing Sunday and night work and limiting the employment of women and children.

In concluding his remarks before the council, the Kaiser delivered two memoranda to the members that he had adapted from material composed by Paul Kayser, a privy counsellor (*Vortragender Rat*) in the Foreign Office, who very probably had sought the help of Wilhelm's old tutor Hinzpeter.[17] These rejected the 50 percent increase in wages and the working day of eight hours demanded by miners in the Rhineland. Such a raise in pay would price German products out of the market, and shortened work hours would lead only to moral disintegration, for laboring men would spend the time won in taverns, there imbibing both alcohol and incendiary ideas. What Wilhelm instead favored was an abolition of Sunday work save where absolutely necessary, no night employment for women and children, no work by women in the last three weeks of pregnancy and for an approximately equal period after giving birth, a pause in the workday for women to accomplish their domestic chores, their elimination from especially dangerous jobs, and limitation of labor by children under fourteen. Finally the government would support worker-employer committees that would cooperate with government inspectors to discuss discipline in factories and mines and the establishment of savings banks, churches, schools, hospitals, and orphanages for the benefit of the laboring class. The Kaiser declared in conclusion that his memoranda were to form the basis of a forthcoming labor program for the kingdom of Prussia, and Bismarck was to have them cast into proclamations that the crown would then issue.

The chancellor's response was predictably negative. He declared that so complicated a question could not be settled at once and that to raise it on the eve of the Reichstag elections set for 20 February was a tactical mistake, for the Kaiser's ideas, which Wilhelm wanted to have announced on his birthday three days following, would alarm the propertied class but embolden the socialists, whose greed was boundless. Bismarck also questioned whether the working class could afford the loss in wages, and German industry the drop in productivity, that would result from abandoning Sunday work. The Kaiser replied that he did not expect the matter to be settled at once but that because new strikes were threatening to break out in the Rhineland at any moment, the working class had to be given a unmistakable indication of the crown's benevolent interest in its welfare. In his response to the chancellor, Wilhelm was careful to declare that in the event of labor unrest he would use every available means to curb it. In the meanwhile the throne must do something for the working class so that it would realize that its aims could be more readily obtained by legal means than by violence.

In the course of his remarks to the council, Wilhelm also declared that he favored the perpetuation of the antisocialist law that had been in existence in the Empire since 1878. The paragraph providing for expulsion from labor centers of socialist agitators, which Bismarck desired but which the Reichstag commission had deleted, was to Wilhelm desirable but not of critical importance, and insistence on its inclusion should not jeopardize the passage of the antisocialist law. Bismarck therefore should inform the Conservatives that he wanted them to support the amended bill. But to the chancellor, the socialist menace was too dangerous to be dealt with by less than draconian means. In an intense voice, Bismarck declared to the council that the bill, even with the exclusion paragraph and the provision that the measure have a permanent duration, would be barely enough to guarantee stability in the country. He therefore insisted on the exclusion paragraph and declared that he would not ask the Conservatives to support the weakened version.

The chancellor realized that his refusal to enlist the Conservatives behind the amended bill would assure its defeat, but the Reichstag, not Bismarck, would be responsible for the "vacuum" that would occur in the absence of any antisocialist legislation on the books. Bismarck ominously warned Wilhelm that in the event of trouble with the working class one would have to protect oneself as best one could. The waves would rise higher and higher and a violent conflict might well come to pass. Wilhelm then reiterated that he could not countenance the deliberate creation of a situation that could easily lead to bloodshed. In response, Bismarck pointed out that it was he who since taking office as minister-president of Prussia twenty-eight years earlier had raised the power and prestige of the Hohenzollern crown to unsurpassed heights. To capitulate now to the Reichstag would be a regressive step that would increase the parliament's power at the cost of the monarchy.[18] The chancellor declared that he would resign if his position were not heeded, to which the Kaiser declared somewhat equivocally that such a step would place him in a difficult position.

The ministers had listened in silence and stupefaction to the debate between the Kaiser and Bismarck, the first that had ever occurred in the open. When Wilhelm asked for their opinions, they were reluctant to speak, for they could not please both Bismarck, who had earlier obtained their unanimous agreement to defer any decision on the question, and the Kaiser, who clearly wanted to hear ministerial approbation for his position. Three of the eight ministers expressed approval of the expulsion and resettlement provision, one other spoke ambiguously, and the remainder did not open their mouths. The state council of 24 January 1890, which concluded without any resolution of the matter, was an important development in the deterioration of the Kaiser's relations with Bismarck. Baron Lucius von Ballhausen, one of the chancellor's staunchest allies, declared that at the end of the meeting "we departed with unresolved differences, with the shattering feeling that an irreparable breach had occurred between chancellor and sovereign."[19] Not only had Bismarck persisted in his opinion about the labor issue in the face of Wilhelm's opposition, but he had done so in language that was singularly uncompromising. Bismarck clearly hoped that the mixture of bravado and threat which for years he had employed so effectively with Wilhelm I would also work with the old Kaiser's grandson. The chancellor had concluded his remarks in the crown council by expressing his displeasure at the Kaiser's unwillingness to acknowledge his superior wisdom. But Wilhelm also had conclusions to draw from the meeting. The ministers' obsequious deference to the chancellor made even plainer what had already become apparent to him: as long as Bismarck was in office, the chancellor rather than the crown would be the superior force in Prussian affairs. "The ministers," the Kaiser informed his uncle, the Grand Duke of Baden, "are not my ministers. They are Prince Bismarck's."[20] The chancellor's implacable opposition to the crown, Wilhelm believed, would inevitably create a crisis of conscience not only among the ministers but throughout the entire ranks of the Prussian bureaucracy. How could these men be loyal subjects of the Kaiser but also remain the intimidated servants of the great chancellor?[21]

The antisocialist law became a dead letter on 25 January, when the Reichstag rejected the weakened version before it by a substantial margin. Since Bismarck, supported by the Prussian ministry, refused to give the signal to the Conservatives and their supporters to drop their opposition to the bill, they had joined with the socialists to kill the measure. There was now no protection on the law books against the socialist menace, leaving Bismarck to await the trouble that he was certain would result. Meanwhile the chancellor had to deal with the framing of proclamations based on the Kaiser's two memoranda presented to the state council on the previous day. While the chancellor had no sympathy for Wilhelm's ideas, having succeeded in torpedoing the antisocialist law the Kaiser had favored, he was reluctant to cross Wilhelm again. "The moods of monarchs are like good and bad weather," Bismarck observed. "They cannot be evaded. You bring an umbrella but you get wet anyway. I think we'll go along with him."[22]

Bismarck's willingness to proceed with the Kaiser's program arrested, at least for the moment, the decline in their relations, and at Wilhelm's thirty-first birthday celebration on 27 January, courtiers noted the chancellor's marked cordiality toward his sovereign. Wilhelm was overheard assuring Bismarck that he hoped that he could reckon on his cooperation for a long time to come.[23] Bismarck was annoyed, despite his pleasant demeanor. At the birthday fête he petulently grumbled to the Austro-Hungarian envoy that he was too old to perform his multitudinous functions and that he would give up his supervision of internal politics and restrict himself to his métier, diplomacy.[24] On the last day of January, the chancellor did in fact surrender the Prussian Ministry of Trade and Industry, but he held on to the minister-presidency and the Prussian Ministry of Foreign Affairs. The chancellor, however, changed his mind about cooperating with Wilhelm on the task of framing the proclamations that would advertise the crown's desire to protect the laboring class. At a meeting of the ministry on 31 January, Bismarck persuaded his colleagues to reject the draft of a proclamation presented by Interior Minister Boetticher, a document he found entirely too conciliatory and too infused with idealistic and impractical language.[25] Boetticher returned to his office to rethink the problem.

On 28 January, the day after Wilhelm's birthday celebration, a new cause for contention between the Kaiser and Bismarck arose. Count Wilhelm von Hohenthal und Bergen, the representative of the kingdom of Saxony to the Federal Council, informed Boetticher that the Saxon government, which had already introduced wide-ranging programs for the benefit of King Albert's working-class subjects, intended in the near future to present to the council a proposal for the protection of labor throughout the Empire. Boetticher immediately informed Bismarck, who declared in return that if Saxony attempted to force the issue in this way, he would resign as chancellor and minister-president.[26] As far as Bismarck was concerned, the King of Saxony wanted an Empire-wide abolition of Sunday work so that paper mills in Saxony, where Sabbath rest was obligatory, would be protected from competitors who operated seven days a week. The only limitation of labor Bismarck was prepared to accept would affect women and children who worked underground.[27]

Hohenthal did not tell Bismarck that the initiative taken by his government in the matter had in fact been at the behest of the Kaiser. Since Wilhelm knew that Bismarck would oppose the abolition of Sunday work and would therefore prevent Prussia's introducing such a measure in the Federal Council, he had asked King Albert to initiate such a bill. On 31 January Hohenthal had an audience with the Kaiser and told him of Bismarck's outburst against the Saxon plan. According to Hohenthal's account, Wilhelm became "exceedingly indignant" and asked the envoy to tell the King that he should pay no attention to the chancellor's opposition. When Hohenthal observed that it would be very painful to the King should Bismarck's resignation occur because of a measure sponsored by the Saxon government, Wilhelm replied with asperity. "Prince Bismarck," he declared, "will not resign over a question in which public opinion is arrayed against him, but in the event that he should do so I will immediately see to it that Europe learns that I let him go because of insubordination."[28] The Kaiser then launched into a long exposition of how difficult the chancellor's behavior had been. He assured Hohenthal that he would not fail to be firm in the event of revolutionary disturbances by the working class, but that before resorting to extreme measures he wanted to make sure that he had first done everything possible to avoid bloodshed. Wilhelm noted that Bismarck, supported by the dutiful Prussian ministers, had wrecked the passage of the antisocialist law, but that on the program for the protection of labor the Kaiser intended to get what he wanted. The most that he would agree to was that Bismarck could use Prussia's dominating position in the Federal Council to delay consideration of the Saxon proposals until after the elections on 20 February.

In his address before the state council of 24 January, Wilhelm had brought up yet another aspect of his labor policy that Bismarck would oppose. In the Kaiser's opinion, the labor question was one of international dimensions, and he therefore decided that Germany should convoke a European conference to study the entire matter of relations between employees and employers. In the summer of 1888 the Swiss government had proposed an international conference to treat the general discontent of European labor, but it had foundered for lack of interest. To Wilhelm this was no misfortune, for republican Switzerland was too radical to give the appropriate tone to such a momentous undertaking. If, however, the German Kaiser sponsored an international meeting on the labor question, it might be expected to proceed to a suitable conclusion.[29] Wilhelm anticipated that the conference would demonstrate to European labor the genuine solicitude felt by the various governments and would deflate the socialist movement by separating "the large mass of honest socialists from those who merely use the name as a cloak to their republican or anarchical designs."[30] Prompted by vanity and in a mood of heady optimism, Wilhelm II ordered Bismarck to announce the convening in Berlin on 15 March 1890 of an international labor conference. The chancellor moved quickly to undermine the Kaiser's fulsome scheme. He proposed that invitations be issued to the great powers to send representatives to Berlin not to discuss labor but rather more nebulously to examine the full range of the consequences of industrialization. A separate commission could be appointed that would study the situation of German mine workers.[31] Such an international conference would prove a harmless affair, and Bismarck believed that he could effectively fend off any unfortunate conclusions the commission reached.

By the end of January 1890 Wilhelm was under no illusions about Bismarck, whose attempt to make the labor conference innocuous he rejected. He recognized that the rivalry between the crown and the chancellor, one that now seemed almost unbridgeable, could not continue indefinitely. He had to be prepared for the worst, and that meant having a successor for Bismarck at hand. Wilhelm knew whom he wanted. On 1 February the Kaiser summoned to Berlin General Leo von Caprivi, the commanding general of the Tenth Army Corps stationed at Hanover and until 1888 head of the imperial Admiralty, and informed him that should a rupture with the chancellor occur, Caprivi was to succeed him. The general's modest reply was that Bismarck, like the Cid of Spanish mythology, was worth more dead than he, Caprivi, alive.[32] Wilhelm II's choice of Caprivi, with whom he had dealt frequently but not always harmoniously on naval affairs, may have been promoted by a number of influential figures. General von Waldersee, who desired the post for himself but perhaps not immediately in the shadow of the great Bismarck, and Col. Adolf von Bülow, the two military intimates of the young Kaiser, both thought the general would make an admirable chancellor, an opinion Friedrich III had in his day endorsed. Even Bismarck considered Caprivi a suitable successor, although he did not let Wilhelm know that he felt so until shortly before his dismissal.[33] Wilhelm's decision to name Caprivi the heir was apparently made without formally consulting anyone, including Philipp Eulenburg, the Kaiser's closest friend.[34]

On 3 February Bismarck had an audience for the purpose of present-
ing the revised proclamation Boetticher had drawn up on the basis of the
memoranda Wilhelm had presented at the 24 January state council. Bismarck also had a second proclamation in hand, this one composed by his
son Herbert, which would convene the international labor conference
the Kaiser had ordered.[35] After handing over the documents, the chancellor informed Wilhelm that he was opposed to the publication of either
of them. When the Kaiser did not reply, Bismarck asked if his continuation in office was desired. Wilhelm persisted in being silent, whereupon
the chancellor declared that he would resign as minister-president of
Prussia on 20 February, election day for the Reichstag. Bismarck added
that at some later time, which he did not specify, he would give up the
chancellorship and become a private citizen. Wilhelm now spoke for the
first time. He did not protest Bismarck's declaration that he intended to
retire, a threat which the chancellor had made many times before. Instead the Kaiser inquired whether Bismarck intended to remain in office
long enough to supervise the passage through the Reichstag in May and
June of the army appropriation bill, always a controversial piece of legislation. The chancellor declared that he would and, in the absence of any
response, assumed that the Kaiser agreed. During the next few days,
arrangements for the transfer of the minister-presidency were completed,
with 20 February set as the day for Bismarck's resignation.

In spite of Bismarck's opposition, the proclamation of the two decrees
in the Kaiser's name occurred on 5 February. In one, addressed to Bismarck, Wilhelm II ordered the chancellor to invite interested nations to
participate in an international labor conference to examine the demands
of the working class. The other went to Albert von Maybach and Baron
Hans Hermann von Berlepsch, respectively Prussian ministers for public
works and for trade and industry. The Kaiser called for the investigation
of labor's demands in order that the state fulfill its obligation to regu-
late the conditions of work and to preserve peace between employers
and employees. To facilitate good relations, arbitration boards com-
prised of employers as well as workers were to be created. Neither decree
bore Bismarck's countersignature, an unprecedented omission and one
counter to both the imperial and Prussian constitutions. The absence of
the chancellor's endorsement was widely, and correctly, interpreted as a
sign of Bismarck's displeasure with the two decrees.[36] Wilhelm, however,
declared that Bismarck's signature was "immaterial" (*unwesentlich*) and
was clearly elated that now, at last, the working class knew that it had a
patron on high.[37] On the evening that the two decrees became public he

dined with Bismarck, the last occasion on which they would meet socially as sovereign and chancellor. In spite of the day's events, Bismarck was ostensibly in a good humor, but after dinner he did not join the Kaiser's circle, sitting instead with friends in a separate room. "The Kaiser loves me," he told one of the assembled confederates. "He really loves me but I cannot impress him."[38]

By mid-February, the chancellor was considering seriously the possibility of a coup d'état to set aside the imperial constitution of 1871.[39] In Bismarck's opinion, the Reichstag's persistent antagonism to the regime, reflected in his inability to secure majority support for many of the measures he proposed, was on the verge of making Germany ungovernable. It was a repetition of the crisis of 1862 between the legislature and the executive that had brought him to power. But the problem was now far worse because the peril of socialism and the hostility of France and Russia threatened the very life of the Fatherland. In such a situation, the crown had to assert itself against the parliament, as it had almost thirty years earlier, for the defense of the nation. Since, in the chancellor's opinion, the German princes and not the German people had made the constitution, they could rescind it. According to the scheme engineered by Bismarck, the Kaiser would abdicate his imperial dignity, and the Empire (and thus the Reichstag) would be dissolved. The sovereigns would then draw up a new imperial constitution, refashioning the electoral procedures to insure that in the reconstituted Empire the socialists and others who refused to support the government would be disfranchised.

If a coup was eventually to be attempted, the minister-president of Prussia, as the representative in a federal assembly of the most powerful German ruler, would be an office of extraordinary importance. As Bismarck thought ever more deeply about a coup, he decided to rescind his offer of 3 February to resign the minister-presidency on the twentieth. He made no further mention of his intention to retire to the Kaiser, who did not insist that the chancellor fulfill his original intention. The result of the elections only heightened the chancellor's resolve to cling to all his positions. Bismarck's cartel of Conservatives, Free Conservatives, and National Liberals suffered a sound defeat at the hands of the electorate, while the Catholic Center, the left-leaning Progressives, and the Social Democrats, all in opposition to the chancellor, scored impressive victories. Unless or until there was a coup, Bismarck would in the future require obtaining the help of the large Catholic Center faction to achieve the slender parliamentary majorities necessary for the conduct of government.

Although Wilhelm II shared the chancellor's alarm at the results of the election, their mutual concern was not enough to draw them back together, and they continued to complain about one another. "The Kaiser is very cordial towards me," Bismarck informed the British ambassador in mid-February 1890, "but he wishes himself to govern. He has not realized the utility of having a screen between himself and his subjects on which the blows of unpopularity may fall without injuring him. He has no doubts. . . . He thinks he can do all things and he wishes to have the entire credit all to himself."[40] The overconfident Kaiser, according to Bismarck, had no respect for his years of experience and treated him like an "elderly nuisance," preferring instead the advice of such amateurs as Hinzpeter, Douglas, and Heyden.[41] At the end of January, the chancellor called Hinzpeter to his office to berate him for mixing in government affairs. Wilhelm's entire unfortunate development, the chancellor believed, was to be attributed to the tutor's mistaken educational program.[42]

Wilhelm was no less critical of the chancellor, whom he found difficult if not impossible to deal with, for what he agreed to one moment he would countermand on the next.[43] Bismarck withdrew to his estates for weeks at a time, refusing to come to Berlin to take care of important business or even to answer his letters and telegrams. The Kaiser resented Bismarck's dictatorial control of the Prussian ministers and was becoming weary of the chancellor's periodic blustering that he would resign if he did not get his way. The Kaiser confided to Eulenburg that no matter how hard he tried to please Bismarck the imperious chancellor acted as though Wilhelm had no right to a will of his own.[44] "Have you noticed how often he [Bismarck] has said 'I'?" the Kaiser inquired of the secretary to the Council of State, Robert Bosse. "At least about 100. He speaks to us from his olympian standpoint as though we were plebians unworthy of attention."[45]

Besides, Wilhelm believed that Bismarck was guilty of treachery, for he knew that although the chancellor appeared to be cooperating on the labor question, he was in fact working against his wishes. Wilhelm's charges were quite accurate, for from the moment that the decree announcing the forthcoming labor conference appeared, Bismarck had worked to sabotage it. The chancellor admitted to Wilhelm's mother that he was trying to render the meeting harmless, and he astonished the French ambassador by urging him to have his government boycott it.[46] The Kaiser, aware of all of Bismarck's maneuvers, regarded them (so he said some years later) as an open "rebellion" (*Auflehnung*) against the

Prussian crown. It was at this moment, Wilhelm declared long after Bismarck's fall from office, that he resolved that Bismarck had to be dismissed.[47] In spite of the chancellor's obstructionary efforts, the conference opened on 15 March and consisted of representatives of the major European nations with the exception of Russia. The deputies, whose deliberations Bismarck tried to foil by withholding adequate secretarial help and even writing paper, discussed the labor question until 29 March, when they submitted a number of recommendations to the Kaiser. By then Bismarck was out of office.

In addition to the labor conference, there was also the unresolved problem of what to do about the antisocialist law when it expired on 1 October. The watered-down version with its expulsion provision had been defeated in the Reichstag, which would surely have been the fate of the draconian measure on which Bismarck insisted. Since the parliament could not agree on an antisocialist law and since Wilhelm would not entertain Bismarck's notion of a coup, there was no course open to the Kaiser but to try to govern without such a measure, a step certain to win working class approval. The government, Wilhelm felt, should for the present keep a watchful eye out, introducing an antisocialist bill only if events should make such a step necessary.[48]

The differences between Wilhelm and the chancellor on the way labor was to be treated seriously troubled their relationship, as did their clash over the antisocialist law. In addition, there was their profound disagreement over whether Russia was a dependable ally or an imminent enemy. All of these were serious disputes, any one of which might have precipitated a resignation crisis. All of them, however, left room for negotiation. Both the Kaiser and Bismarck were prepared to compromise, if only slightly, and as long as the two men were not intransigent, a showdown could perhaps be avoided. If, however, a difference of principle arose that both felt could not be compromised, either Bismarck would have to go or the Kaiser accept the humiliation that came with surrender. At the beginning of March 1890 precisely this sort of issue emerged, and at its root lay what was really the essential issue between the two men: who would rule Germany, Bismarck or Wilhelm II.

The Kaiser clearly meant to be the primary force in his Empire, and a number of his intimates—including the Grand Duke of Baden, Hinzpeter, Eulenburg, and Waldersee—were at work to effect his liberation from what they felt was Bismarck's demeaning grasp.[49] But the chancellor was no less determined to preserve the hegemony he had so long enjoyed. This depended not only on a compliant Kaiser but also on a loyal Prussian ministry. Bismarck knew that he could no longer rely on Wilhelm's docility, and the February elections had made it clear that the Reichstag would in the future be equally intractable. Bismarck was therefore more than ever determined to maintain an iron hold on his Prussian ministerial colleagues. The ministry had indeed supported him on the labor question, but Bismarck believed that the loyalty of some of the cabinet members, especially Karl Heinrich von Boetticher, minister of the interior, and Johannes Miquel, who presided over the Finance Ministry, was in doubt. The chancellor's suspicions of Boetticher were paranoic, but Miquel, who was not adverse to considering himself a suitable successor to Bismarck, in fact opposed the chancellor's coercive labor policy. Bismarck wanted to make sure that none of his ministers would be able to act behind his back in collusion with the Kaiser.

On 2 March Bismarck therefore reminded his colleagues in the Prussian ministry that a cabinet order issued on 8 September 1852 by King Friedrich Wilhelm IV, though seldom used, was still in force. It prescribed that no Prussian minister, with the exception of the minister of war, could have an audience with the sovereign or forward reports to him without having first secured permission of the minister-president.[50] The decree, designed to prevent an alliance between the ministers and the king to the detriment of the minister-president, had been neglected for decades. Inasmuch as Bismarck had throughout the 1880s been accustomed to spend several months every year on his estates, Wilhelm II, as well as his father and grandfather, had customarily dealt directly with the various Prussian ministers. But now the chancellor insisted that none of his colleagues save the war minister see or write to the Kaiser without Bismarck's permission.

If Bismarck was nervous that the Kaiser and some of his ministers might be organizing an opposition group, Wilhelm was no less concerned that the chancellor himself was covertly engaged in an attempt to forge an alliance with the Catholic Center party. Although the Center was a moderate, if not conservative, faction, the Kaiser regarded it as a traitorous, Jesuit-dominated agency of an Italian pope, as well as the tool of the Guelf dynasty of Hanover, dethroned by Prussia in 1866. He was convinced that the Center was attempting to form an alliance with the reactionary wing of the Conservative party, which Wilhelm II despised because it opposed his conciliatory labor policy. He especially detested the Center's Hanoverian leader, Ludwig Windthorst, falsely believing that Windthorst was a socialist and an atheist.[51] Wilhelm's suspicions of Bismarck's intrigue with the Catholics were based on a meeting the chancellor had had on 12 March with Windthorst, who for years had been one of the government's most resourceful enemies in the Reichstag. Although Bismarck was anti-Catholic and loathed Windthorst, the collapse of the chancellor's cartel of Conservative and National Liberal deputies in the February elections meant that he could no longer command a parliamentary majority without drawing the Center into his camp. In the Kaiser's opinion, Bismarck's overtures to Windthorst were not merely a solicitation for votes but in fact presaged a fundamental redirection of the government's policy, for the Center would be sure to make a number of reforms benefiting the Roman Catholic church the price of its cooperation with the chancellor, a course that Wilhelm found intolerable. Such a major reorientation of policy required his consent, and the chancellor therefore should have consulted him *before* making overtures to Windthorst.[52] Bismarck might be prepared to enlist Windthorst out of political expediency but the Kaiser was not.

On 15 March, three days after Bismarck had seen Windthorst, Wilhelm went to the chancellor's residence, where the two men had an acrimonious discussion of the Catholic problem.[53] The Kaiser complained that the chancellor should not have dealt with Windthorst without the sovereign's prior approval. Bismarck replied by defending his right to talk to any Reichstag deputy, and indeed constitutionally he had every right to do so. The chancellor pointed out that his purpose in meeting with Windthorst was not the formation of a political alliance with the Center but only a tactical investigation of the demands the party would make in the forthcoming session. The chancellor's arguments did not persuade Wilhelm, who demanded to know if Bismarck intended to continue to consult Windthorst. The chancellor boldly replied that even if the Kaiser were explicitly to prohibit such consultations, he would not hesitate to persist in them.

Bismarck could have hardly made a more explicit challenge to his sovereign, but it was not over Windthorst that Wilhelm elected to confront the chancellor. The Kaiser turned the audience with Bismarck to the 1852 cabinet order, which he felt constituted an encroachment on the crown's proper prerogative of consulting ministers whenever the ruler wished. The Kaiser announced that he therefore intended to rescind it and asked Bismarck to surrender the document to him, receipt of which would have the effect of nullifying the decree. This was a point as vital to Bismarck as to the Kaiser. The chancellor had lost command of the Reichstag and could no longer control the Kaiser. All that was left was his ascendancy over the Prussian ministry, and to surrender the 1852 order would therefore rob him of his last shred of authority. The chancellor responded to Wilhelm's request for the return of the 1852 order by neither agreeing nor refusing; instead he launched into a digression on the long and hitherto untroubled existence of the document. The conversation became very heated, and, according to Wilhelm's account, the chancellor at one point became so excited that he slammed a folder of letters down on a table next to which the Kaiser was sitting with such force that it upset an inkwell. Finally, as the audience was nearing its end, the chancellor asked the Kaiser if he categorically demanded the delivery of the 1852 order, to which Wilhelm curtly replied in the affirmative.

Bismarck, however, made no move to surrender the order, preferring to wait for a written demand from the Kaiser to do so. "I was quite convinced," the chancellor wrote later about his decision, "that I should have neither the initiative nor the resulting responsibility for my departure from office."[54] The labor question, like the antisocialist law connected with it, or the question of Russian diplomacy, were matters about which a difference of opinion between the Kaiser and the chancellor might be tolerated, for there were always compromises that either side could effect. Even the Windthorst problem concluded short of the Kaiser's confronting Bismarck with an order to stop his negotiations with the Catholic Center. But Bismarck's refusal to surrender the 1852 order was a direct challenge to an explicit command by the sovereign and also one that did not admit of any opportunities for compromise. Either the chancellor had to obey, or he had to put himself incontrovertibly in open defiance of his sovereign. Bismarck without hesitation elected the latter course. With that move, the fate of monarchical prerogative, and the maintenance of the Kaiser's amour propre, now rested unavoidably on whether or not Wilhelm or his chancellor would capitulate. The battle between the Kaiser and Bismarck had now suddenly become not a field for parrying but a confrontation from which there could be but two outcomes: either the chancellor's resignation or Wilhelm II's surrender of Hohenzollern prerogative. This contest of will, long in the making and now crystallized around an ancient scrap of paper, rather than any specific issue, was what led to Bismarck's downfall.[55]

The Kaiser was determined not to give in, and those closest to him strengthened his resolve. Philipp Eulenburg, who during January and February had urged Bismarck to adopt a more conciliatory tone, now abandoned the chancellor altogether. Eulenburg's desertion of Bismarck was due to the fact that he, like the Kaiser, felt that what was now at stake was not policies or ideology but the very dignity of the Prussian crown.[56] Eulenburg's defection was significant, for no one was closer to Wilhelm. Next to Eulenburg, the Kaiser's closest advisor during the crisis was General Waldersee, who for months had been undermining the chancellor's standing with Wilhelm. Now, in the heat of the quarrel over the 1852 cabinet order, Waldersee advised the Kaiser that if Bismarck refused to send in his resignation it should be demanded at once.[57]

Waldersee was also responsible for bringing to the Kaiser's attention another example of the chancellor's challenge to the prerogative of the crown. This was Bismarck's failure to present to the Kaiser diplomatic intelligence revealing that the Russians were moving troops near the German frontier, a development that seemed to confirm Waldersee's assessment of Russia's determination to provoke Germany.[58] Wilhelm demanded the reports in question and became infuriated when he discovered that the chancellor, always anxious to dispell any rumors of war with Russia, had withheld many dispatches from him that confirmed the Russian menace. The Kaiser made public his annoyance with Bismarck by returning the documents to the Foreign Office on 17 March together with an open note in which he expressed his displeasure that the chancellor had not kept him fully informed about a state of affairs that was so potentially dangerous.[59] Bismarck's not entirely persuasive defense was that he had in fact forwarded four of the reports to the Kaiser and that another ten, containing strictly military information that he considered outdated and therefore innocuous, he had sent to the minister of war and to the chief of the General Staff, who were to determine whether the dispatches should be sent on to the palace. The chancellor had in his opinion executed his responsibilities faultlessly, and if the Kaiser had not been given the reports, it was a shortcoming of the military. Wilhelm's complaints, Bismarck declared, were "unwarranted, insulting suspicions" (*unverdiente kränkenden Misstrauen*).[60]

In spite of Waldersee's advice that he should demand the chancellor's resignation, Wilhelm was reluctant to do so. What would be the reaction of public opinion and how, without the chancellor's guidance, could the army appropriation bill safely make its difficult way through a hostile Reichstag in the early summer?[61] But Bismarck, wanting whatever happened to rest with the Kaiser, made not a move, and that forced Wilhelm's hand. Even so, Wilhelm gave the chancellor every opportunity to save himself. After waiting two days for Bismarck to comply with his demand to hand over the cabinet order, the Kaiser summoned one of his adjutants, General von Wittich, on 17 March and ordered him to go to Bismarck and ask the whereabouts of the document. This yielded only an evasive answer, so later in the day the Kaiser instructed another adjutant, General von Hahnke, who firmly believed that the chancellor should be removed from office, to inform Bismarck that he was either to hand over the cabinet order or submit a letter of resignation. Bismarck declined to do either.[62]

The chancellor meanwhile had summoned the Prussian ministers and informed them that he was going to resign all of his offices because he realized that he enjoyed neither the sovereign's confidence nor even the loyalty of his ministerial colleagues.[63] But Bismarck in fact made no move either to send in his letter of resignation or to forward the 1852 order. On the following day, 18 March, Wilhelm therefore sent Hermann von Lucanus, the chief of the Prussian Civil Cabinet, to extract one or the other. Bismarck had already written his letter of resignation, but he did not give it or the 1852 order to Lucanus, and it was not until the following day, 19 March, that the chancellor, convinced that further delay was pointless, sent in his resignation.[64] In his letter, Bismarck wrote that Wilhelm's insistence on abrogating the 1852 cabinet order rendered his continuation in office as minister-president of Prussia impossible. Furthermore, the Kaiser's disapproval of his conversation with Windthorst and his outburst over the diplomatic dispatches dealing with Russia made his serving as chancellor out of the question. He must be both minister-president and imperial chancellor, unquestionably in charge of domestic and foreign affairs, or nothing.

Bismarck's letter struck his close friend Baron Lucius von Ballhausen as being composed in such a way as to create the impression that the chancellor might be willing to stay in office.[65] But the Kaiser now had what he wanted. Bismarck had delivered not the 1852 cabinet order but his resignation, and more was not required. His successor could forward to Wilhelm this document that had provoked such contention. The Kaiser called all the commanding generals to Berlin to explain the crisis with the chancellor and declared that in order to preserve the authority of the crown he had had to confront Bismarck with an ultimatum.[66] "God," he declared a little later to his guards officers, "had shown him the proper course."[67] When Interior Minister Boetticher pointed out that Bismarck might still be persuaded to remain in office, Wilhelm declared that this was "impossible." The Kaiser wrote in pencil across the face of the chancellor's letter "Consented to. W."[68] The deed was done.

The Kaiser's acceptance of his letter of resignation took Bismarck by surprise, for he believed that Wilhelm would not do anything to jeopardize the passage of the military budget later in the year. When an old friend called to express his surprise at the chancellor's resignation, Bismarck laconically replied: "Me too."[69] Yet Bismarck must have intended by his obdurate behavior to bait the Kaiser, deliberately precipitating the final crisis that resulted in his resignation. Everything about the chancellor's behavior was gratuitously provocative, and perhaps this was because he knew that the contest was one from which he would not emerge the victor. Three days after his dismissal, the chancellor told the Prince of Wales, who happened to be in Berlin during the resignation crisis, that he had always said it would take Wilhelm three years to sack him. He had erred, he noted, only by a year, for it had required just over twenty-one months.[70] Like many another discharged official in succeeding years, Bismarck felt that he had been handled with little dignity by a young sovereign who clearly had "no heart."[71] Bismarck declared to those who offered sympathy that his mistake had been in sending forward a letter of resignation; he should instead have done nothing and then waited to see if the Kaiser would have dared to dismiss him.[72]

Bismarck had his last audience as chancellor on 19 March.[73] He had intended it to be a brief meeting, but the Kaiser kept him for an hour, speaking only in commonplaces but doing so in such a way that the chancellor later described as "raising psychiatric questions." On 20 March Wilhelm II formally accepted Bismarck's resignation in two letters addressed to the chancellor—one as Kaiser, the other as supreme commander of the Prussian army—in which he gracefully expressed gratitude for the fallen chancellor's "incomparable success."[74] The Kaiser informed Bismarck that he wished to create him Duke of Lauenburg, the part of Prussia in which Bismarck's favorite estate at Friedrichsruh lay, and that he intended to send him a life-sized portrait. Bismarck accepted the Kaiser's likeness but begged in vain to be spared the ducal dignity, preferring to retain the family name in his existing title as Prince von Bismarck-Schönhausen. General von Caprivi became chancellor and minister-president.

Wilhelm was now at last finished with the Iron Chancellor, but he had no intention of being separated from Herbert Bismarck. The relationship between the Kaiser and Herbert had long since cooled, and there had never been any thought on the Kaiser's part of advancing the younger Bismarck to the chancellorship. But Wilhelm realized that without the old chancellor to superintend German diplomacy, it would be imperative to continue to have an experienced figure in charge at the Foreign Office. In February 1890, before the crisis had become acute, the Kaiser decided that in the event of the chancellor's resignation he wanted Herbert to remain.[75] Once Wilhelm had come to the conclusion that he was going to relieve the chancellor of his position, he energetically attempted to persuade Herbert to retain his office.[76]

There was little that could induce Herbert to stay on. He loved power, to be sure, and had for years been groomed to succeed his father. It was clear, however, that Wilhelm had no intention of appointing him chancellor, and that all he therefore could expect would be to continue in the secondary position as head of the Foreign Office. Herbert was physically exhausted and badly in need of a vacation of several months' duration. Wilhelm's autocratic pretensions were a constant trial to him no less than to his father, as was the meddling in politics by General Waldersee that he had had to endure.[77] But the real problem for Herbert was that he could not envision serving as state secretary under anyone other than his father, and certainly not under General Caprivi, for whose diplomatic ability he had a low regard. Bismarck had for years barely kept the hated Reichstag at bay, but even his fragile cartel could no longer furnish a majority. Now, with a weaker chancellor at the helm, the parliamentary deputies would try to intrude into every diplomatic issue.[78] Herbert's love of having his own way was as marked as his father's, and for him subservience to any man other than the Iron Chancellor was exceedingly distasteful and probably would have been impossible. During the entire crisis between Bismarck and the Kaiser, it was Herbert who had urged his father to take a strong line and to resist Wilhelm's attempts to undermine the chancellor's position.[79] Moreover, Bismarck's dismissal implied that Germany's existing pro-Russian foreign policy, which Herbert approved and had carried out, would likely change. For him to stay in office would therefore be tantamount to rejecting his father. And Herbert had a profound suspicion of the Kaiser's overtures to the working class, for like the chancellor he regarded every laboring man as socialist.[80]

The fallen chancellor did nothing to encourage his son to stay in office, and he refused the Kaiser's urging that he do so. "I know very well," Bismarck declared to the Prussian finance minister, Adolf von Scholz, "that Abraham was prepared on God's direct order to sacrifice his son Isaac, but no such heavenly command exists in this case."[81] On 21 March Herbert asked the Kaiser to relieve him of office. Wilhelm agreed but was nonetheless insistent that after Herbert had recovered his health he should return to his post as state secretary. In a move that surprised Berlin, Baron Marschall von Bieberstein, the envoy from Baden to the Federal Council, was named to Herbert's position at the Foreign Office.

In the nine days that ensued between the acceptance of the chancellor's resignation on 20 March and his departure from Berlin, both Bismarck and the Kaiser were busy circulating their versions of what had led to the rupture. The fallen chancellor gave various accounts of his dismissal to those to whom he talked, but he acknowledged that it had been a clash of wills, and not a specific issue, that had led to his downfall. Bismarck explicitly denied that the cause could have been his health, which he falsely declared to be exemplary.[82] The Kaiser was mindful of the consternation that the chancellor's resignation had caused in Germany and the misgivings it very likely would occasion in foreign capitals. He therefore had to attempt to create the impression that there had not been any insoluble difficulties separating him from Bismarck, but that in fact the dangerous condition of the seventy-five year old chancellor's health—grounds that seemed plausible enough—had alone been the cause of the break. This was the explanation that the Kaiser gave to his fellow sovereigns immediately after Bismarck's resignation, in the hope that his assurances would dissipate any suspicions that Germany's foreign policy would now take a new direction.[83] He informed the representative of the King of Saxony that he would continue to rely on Bismarck's rich store of experience and to use him, even though in retirement, for the good of the Fatherland. Bismarck would be a sort of living Cid, to be brought forth when needed to reduce the Kaiser's enemies to fear and consternation.[84]

This was all prevarication and empty rhetoric. Wilhelm's real reasons for shedding Bismarck were not long in being divulged, and they show how acutely he had resented the Iron Chancellor's domineering behavior. In the final analysis, it was Bismarck's manner, more than his policies, that cost him his great post. Even before coming to the throne, Wilhelm had revealed a certain restiveness at the prospect of having to rule, as had his predecessors, under Bismarck's magisterial thumb. Once Kaiser, his impatience to govern Germany according to his own prescription was apparent well before the divisive internal and diplomatic issues of March 1890 came to the fore. Wilhelm explained to the British envoy, Sir Edward Malet, that the chancellor had disregarded his views on the labor question and tried to sabotage the international labor conference. But worse, as the Kaiser moved on to reveal the root of his objection, Bismarck "treated me like a schoolboy."

Malet's explication of the Kaiser's motives came as no surprise to his chief, the Conservative prime minister, Lord Salisbury, who had for years observed Wilhelm with a mixture of disdain and alarm and who was hardly startled by the dramatic events that had just taken place in Berlin. Salisbury reminded Queen Victoria that Bismarck had dug his own grave, for he had encouraged the Caesarian streak in Wilhelm in order that he might more effectively resist his liberal parents. But in fact the old chancellor himself had become the young Kaiser's victim.[85] Wilhelm reiterated his resentment at Bismarck's high-handedness in a letter to the Austro-Hungarian Emperor Franz Josef, written two weeks after his conversation with Ambassador Malet.[86] It was, Wilhelm declared in English, merely a question of who was to be the "top dog." For years, he complained, he had followed the chancellor with blind devotion, even to the point of allowing Bismarck to alienate him from his mother and father. But once Wilhelm had mounted the throne, the chancellor had been unwilling to show him reciprocal allegiance. Bismarck's recalcitrance in refusing to deliver the 1852 cabinet order was the last straw. The chancellor treated everyone with contempt but he sealed his fate, the Kaiser noted pointedly, "when he took his master for a nobody and tried to degrade him to a retainer." Wilhelm felt that for too long he had had to stand in the great man's shadow, not only being treated by Bismarck in a way that ignored his royal prerogative but having to endure a public mood that interpreted every German achievement as the work of the chancellor. It was time for Wilhelm himself and the Hohenzollern crown to receive the credit, and the attention, they were due.[87]

On 29 March, amid thundering cries of "Return!" as well as "Farewell!" Prince and Princess Bismarck drove to the Lehrter railway station in Berlin, where thousands of admirers and the entire diplomatic corps had assembled to say goodbye to the former chancellor, who was retiring to his estate at Friedrichsruh near Hamburg. Wilhelm ordered a military honor guard to line the platform, and two arrangements of flowers, personally designed by the absent sovereign, were presented to the couple. As Bismarck later observed, it was "a first class funeral."[88] With the former chancellor waving from an open window, the train pulled out and began the journey northwest to Friedrichsruh, where Bismarck would live in self-imposed exile for the remaining eight years of his long life. Wilhelm II, however, had not heard the last of his first and greatest chancellor.

CAPRIVI, EULENBURG, AND

THE FALL OF WALDERSEE

HANCELLOR VON CAPRIVI, a massive man with white hair and mustaches, was in appearance not unlike his great predecessor. Although he was of Italo-Slavic descent, the family, ennobled in the seventeenth century, had been resident in Prussia for several generations, and Caprivi himself was a firm Hohenzollern loyalist. In 1883, Caprivi, then a lieutenant general, had been commissioned a vice admiral and made the commanding officer of the German navy, where he acquired a reputation as an able administrator. Generally modest in bearing and celebrated for his discretion, Caprivi also possessed a determined will and a proud sense of honor. He was also thoroughly realistic and knew that his qualifications for the chancellorship were limited. His sense of duty to the crown, Caprivi declared, dictated his accepting the unwelcome office, one for which he had never shown the least ambition. Caprivi's distaste at becoming chancellor was offset by his expectation that he would not serve for long, inasmuch as the Kaiser had indicated when appointing him that the post would be his only for the interim. It seemed to some observers that the general would serve only until Wilhelm II was ready to call Waldersee.[1]

While the new chancellor's military experience was singularly broad, he had very little knowledge of internal Prussian affairs and almost none of diplomacy. Caprivi was an outsider at the Berlin court, which regarded him as a parvenu, and the pillars of the Hohenzollern bureaucracy resented the fact that a general, rather than some high government official or diplomat, had been awarded the chancellorship.[2] Estrangement from the court did not trouble Caprivi, who had no taste whatsoever for society. Nor did he have any interest in foreign affairs, admitting that he had not the least gift for the contrived arts of diplomatic ingratiation.[3] Caprivi's shortcomings in diplomacy were particularly disturbing because at the time he took office Germany's relationship with the other European powers, and especially with Russia, were in an unsettled state. Bismarck's fall inevitably created suspicions throughout Europe that, in spite of the Kaiser's assurances, Germany could no longer be depended on to follow the former chancellor's policies. Wilhelm, however, did not anticipate any problems with his new chancellor, for he was convinced that Caprivi would very quickly master his new responsibilities.[4]

Unfortunately, Caprivi was wary about seeking guidance in diplomatic affairs, and he never established a satisfactory footing in the Foreign Office.[5] The chancellor's only real confidant there was Friedrich von Holstein, the senior counsellor, who was enormously influential but also quite eccentric. A reclusive bachelor, Holstein was by nature mistrustful and easily offended. To his favorites, he was a source of privileged information as well as malicious tittle-tattle, for he delighted in innuendo and perversely sowed many a suspicion among his diplomatic colleagues. It was Holstein, more than anyone else, who reduced the Wilhelmstrasse 76 to a "poisonous den" (*Giftbude*), as Philipp Eulenburg, with whom Holstein was first an intimate but later an implacable enemy, once described it.[6] Moreover, immediately after Caprivi took office, the state secretaryship of the Foreign Office fell vacant when, on 21 March, Herbert Bismarck resigned and a few days later followed his father into exile, yielding his position to Baron Adolf Marschall von Bieberstein, the representative of the grand duchy of Baden to the Federal Council. Marschall was not the chancellor's choice, for Caprivi had argued that an experienced Prussian diplomat should be appointed. He persuaded the Kaiser to offer the post to Count Friedrich von Alvensleben, the Prussian envoy at Brussels, but Alvensleben declined. Wilhelm thereupon decided on Marschall, and Caprivi acquiesced in this choice. He was not acquainted with Marschall, but after their first conversation Caprivi admitted that while his new state secretary "knows nothing he will do nicely, for he has pluck [*Schneid*]."[7]

Marschall was a curious choice. He was not a Prussian, such familiarity as he had in foreign policy lay in the affairs between the German states rather than in the larger sphere of international relations, and he had a gruff personality that seemed inappropriate in one whose function was diplomacy. Bismarck expressed contempt for his son's successor by archly observing that the inexperienced Marschall's new title should properly be "ministre étranger aux affaires," a clever pun but one perhaps lost on the new state secretary, whose knowledge of French was minimal.[8] Wilhelm II seems to have settled on Marschall in part as a result of advice both he and Caprivi received from Philipp Eulenburg, who was careful to exaggerate Marschall's experience but who also correctly predicted that he would swiftly master the complexities of European diplomacy.[9] Eulenburg also made sure that the Kaiser learned that Marschall had sympathized with the crown in the recent contest with Bismarck.[10] Marschall impressed the Kaiser as a man who possessed a broad understanding of affairs and a gift for public speaking, and he therefore accepted Eulenburg's non-Prussian nominee without demur but also without any show of enthusiasm.[11] To Wilhelm, Marschall's appointment was not a matter of transcendant significance, since it would be, like Caprivi's, only a temporary arrangement of six or eight months' duration. He felt sure that by then Herbert could be coaxed into reassuming his old office.[12]

Caprivi was under no illusions about the difficulties he would face as chancellor, but in his opinion the most formidable would proceed not from the lack of experience under which he and Marschall would labor but rather from the Kaiser, whose erratic temperament was so unlike his own decorous but preceptorial manner. Even before assuming office, Caprivi expressed misgivings about entering upon such a thankless post. He observed to a friend that there was much talk in Berlin of "the gravity of my heritage, of the difficulties of my situation, of those at home and abroad. But the problem of which one speaks the least and the one which is most fearful—not to say one which is unsurmountable—is that which comes from On High."[13] He quickly discovered that Wilhelm did as he pleased and on public occasions had an alarming habit of saying whatever happened to come spontaneously into his head. During the four years of his chancellorship, Caprivi found the Kaiser a constant problem, and he left office admitting that his prediction had been all too true, for Wilhelm II had proved to be his sharpest thorn.[14]

An additional shadow that fell on Caprivi was the fact that he had succeeded the titan Bismarck, of whom all Europe stood in awe. No amount of courage, Caprivi declared, could help him overcome this burden, but he did not intend to try to imitate the Iron Chancellor. While Caprivi shared the general admiration for Bismarck's diplomatic genius, he had never approved of the chancellor's autocratic style and intense sensitivity to criticism. The result in Caprivi's opinion had been the enslavement of the bureaucracy and the abdication of the public's sense of responsibility. The remedy, he believed, was to create a judicious and unified ministry and persuade the Kaiser to allow it real responsibility.[15]

Fortified by a collegial ministry, the crown would rule ably and win the respect of the nation's citizens. In such a scenario, the imperial parliament would be relegated to a secondary role. Caprivi had no great opinion of democracy in the abstract or of the German Reichstag in particular. Its approval of legislation might be constitutionally necessary, but this did not mean that his government had to become dependent on one or another of the various factions. "We will take our advantage where and through whom it may come," was the way the chancellor defined his policy of parliamentary expediency.[16]

The essential difficulty that bedevilled the relationship between the Kaiser and Caprivi from the beginning and that was eventually to become the cause of his losing Wilhelm's favor, was that Caprivi, no less than Bismarck, had a firm will that would inexorably bring him into conflict with his equally pertinacious sovereign. Caprivi struck those who knew him as being needlessly hardheaded and inclined to invest his views with an obdurate self-righteousness. "His sense of honor was often exaggerated, even otherworldly," a friend regretted. "He regarded his position [as chancellor] like a general to whom the leadership of a campaign is entrusted and who says to himself: I cannot change the plan but must conduct it according to the book."[17] A number of observers, many of whom were admirers of Caprivi's, reckoned that the chancellor's well-advertised obstinacy would inevitably clash with Wilhelm II's imperious nature.[18] While head of the navy from 1883 to 1888, Caprivi had had enough contact with Prince Wilhelm to recognize, as had Bismarck, that his future ruler was a man more likely to follow the advice of his friends than those to whom office had been entrusted. Wilhelm was, as Caprivi described him in 1887, "as obstinate as a mule," and he had got along poorly with the Prince in the late 1880s. While Caprivi was prepared to admit that Wilhelm was remarkably well informed about naval matters, the problem was, as he confided to a colleague, that he "thinks he knows *everything.*"[19] The day following Wilhelm's ascension to the throne, Caprivi, annoyed that the new Kaiser had gone over his head to consult an inferior naval official, asked to be relieved of his position as head of the navy and to be allowed to return to an army command. Wilhelm II granted the request.

Although Caprivi seemed by temperament and experience a questionable choice, Wilhelm believed that for a number of reasons his appointment was warranted. He knew from experience that the general was a good administrator, and he had a very high regard for his military abilities.[20] Caprivi was as suspicious of Russia as the Kaiser, while Eulenburg, whose support of the general was invaluable, was full of assurances that Caprivi shared Wilhelm's position that the antisocialist law should not be renewed on its expiration in October 1890.[21] The Kaiser was aware that whoever succeeded Bismarck would be subjected to nothing but invidious comparisons. That being the case, an older candidate who had both military and civilian experience would best be able to withstand such a barrage of criticism. Among the Prussian generals, the fifty-nine-year-old Caprivi stood out as the logical choice.

Wilhelm II was swift to assure his "colleagues" on Europe's thrones that the appointment of Caprivi and Marschall did not signify a change in the direction of Germany's future. On 22 March, two days after Bismarck's resignation, the Kaiser sent a telegram, a melange of insincerity and bombast, to his great uncle, the Grand Duke of Saxe-Weimar, proclaiming his determination to preserve the Bismarckian heritage. The chancellor's resignation, Wilhelm declared, "was as painful as though I had lost my own grandfather, but God's will is to be borne even if one should thereby be brought to dust. The duty of watch officer on the ship of state has fallen to me. The course remains the same. Full steam ahead!"[22]

In spite of Wilhelm's protestation, he was determined that Caprivi's chancellorship would not resemble Bismarck's. From now on, it would be the Kaiser rather than his chief servant who would govern Germany. Insofar as diplomacy was concerned, there was considerable expectation in Berlin that the Kaiser, not Marschall, would set the tone for Germany's foreign policy.[23] Even while his grandfather ruled, Wilhelm had announced that when he became sovereign he intended to shift some of the prerogatives of the imperial chancellor to the throne. He did nothing to implement this as long as Bismarck was in office, but on appointing Caprivi, Wilhelm's response to Caprivi's confession of his inexperience for the chancellorship was to declare: "Don't worry, one cannot expect the impossible. I will assume the responsibility for the conduct of affairs."[24] Youth would replace age, a development Wilhelm had indicated on coming to the throne by retiring many of his elderly generals. "The older generation says 'Yes, if we must,'" the Kaiser declared a few months after Bismarck's fall, "while the younger declares, 'Yes, but of course.'"[25] From the moment that Bismarck resigned, Wilhelm II did in fact intrude himself more and more into diplomatic affairs. With his indefatigable self-assurance, Wilhelm never reflected that he was not only young but also, like his new chancellor, without much in the way of experience. There was nothing of which he did not think himself capable, a confidence that produced misgivings in Berlin. Caprivi's colleague, the state secretary of the imperial Post Office, Heinrich von Stephan, remarked in some bewilderment not long after Caprivi became chancellor, "God knows everything, but the Kaiser knows it even better."[26]

Although Caprivi was very obstinate, as a Prussian army officer whose oath of loyalty was to the ruler and not the state, he was reluctant to challenge the crown. Caprivi knew that he was not Bismarck, and he had no desire to try to duplicate the Iron Chancellor's autocratic rule. It was proper that the Kaiser lead the German people, and Caprivi anticipated that Wilhelm II, now free of Bismarck, would assert a wider claim to power.[27] Duty had impelled Caprivi to assume a position he had not sought, and his responsibility as chancellor, exactly as it had been as a general, would require his fulfilling the Kaiser's orders. One observer who was not well disposed to the chancellor described Caprivi's relationship to Wilhelm as "like a chief of staff under a general."[28] Such a spirit of accommodation delighted Wilhelm II, and he came to respect the chancellor's dignified bearing and his determined but unobtrusive conduct of affairs. Caprivi found to his satisfaction that as time went on the Kaiser consulted him more and more.[29] The honeymoon would be brief, but while it lasted, it was ardent. The Kaiser wrote in high spirits to Queen Victoria on Christmas Day 1890, "We are getting on very well with Caprivi, who is already adored by friends and revered by his opposition. I think he is one of the finest characters Germany ever produced."[30] Working with the new chancellor and Marschall was, Wilhelm II rhapsodized, like being "in paradise."[31] Any thoughts he had of Caprivi as being merely an interim chancellor swiftly evaporated.

Caprivi, on the other hand, became rapidly disillusioned. Before becoming chancellor, he had had a taste of the Kaiser's dictatorial manner, and, once in Bismarck's place, he soon acquired a broad exposure to Wilhelm II's vagaries, the instant judgment, contradictions, bombast, and the sovereign's boundless and diffuse energy. The chancellor gradually realized the danger of permitting such a monarch to go unchallenged, and so rather than continuing to be submissive, he began to argue against some of Wilhelm II's schemes and to threaten to resign if Wilhelm persisted in them. Caprivi did not hesitate to speak up when he was convinced that Wilhelm was wrong, and once that combative attitude had set in, the initial harmony between the chancellor and the ruler was destroyed.

It was not only against Wilhelm II that Caprivi would have to do battle. In assuming the chancellorship, Caprivi inherited a situation that had aggravated Bismarck, but against which even the Iron Chancellor had been powerless. This was Wilhelm's inclination to surround himself with a small group of advisors, a camarilla indifferent to the chancellor's opinion as long as they commanded imperial favor. Bismarck had seen his influence undermined by a clique composed of Waldersee, Eulenburg, Hinzpeter, and their confederates, and he correctly predicted that his successor would suffer the same fate.[32] From the outset of his chancellorship, Caprivi found that his was only one voice, and by no means always the most persuasive, that commanded the sovereign's ear. The military were closer to the throne than anyone else, but it did not help Caprivi that he was a general, for once he became chancellor, most of his fellow generals regarded him as a rival rather than an ally. The Kaiser's military adjutants—and especially General von Wittich, who never left Wilhelm's side—were a potential threat, as was the unctuous flattery of some younger officers.[33] Waldersee, once Caprivi's supporter, had become suspicious that the chancellor wanted to have him removed as chief of the General Staff and therefore became his resolute opponent.[34]

Philipp Eulenburg was a more redoubtable competitor for Caprivi, since he enjoyed the Kaiser's confidence more than any other person. Eulenburg had disapproved of Caprivi's selection as chancellor and never developed any enthusiasm for him.[35] Before coming to the throne, Wilhelm had accorded Eulenburg the privilege of writing to him privately and assured his friend that he might also speak out openly. A few years later the Kaiser invited Eulenburg to address him with the intimate *du,* a privilege ordinarily restricted to relatives and reigning princes, and referred to him as "my best friend." Although Eulenburg had numerous opportunities to discuss affairs with Wilhelm, he often preferred to approach his sovereign in writing, because, as he noted, in conversation the Kaiser could argue, but ink was not so liable to contradiction.[36] The word, as crafted by Eulenburg for his royal patron, was a lush mixture of unctuousness and platitudinous sentimentality. "How happy it makes me," he wrote to Wilhelm in May 1888 in a characteristically truckling vein, "to be able to write so frankly to you. You understand everything that concerns me—serious matters, raillery, duty, learning, art, each neatly separated from the others yet each entirely comprehended. Thus you are and so I hope also to remain, and God will give us His blessing so to be if we in all our affairs are convinced that we can reach the highest only through Him."[37]

Eulenburg's friendship with Wilhelm had begun in the mid-1880s with their common enthusiasm for the arts, and it was Eulenburg's creative side, which embraced music, art, drama, philosophy, and religion—without, to be sure, much rigor or distinction in any except perhaps music—that appealed to Wilhelm. The military nexus in which the Kaiser had spent most of his time was singularly devoid of artistic, intellectual, or spiritual interests, and Eulenburg, who had served unhappily for years a guards officer, chafed at the philistine atmosphere of barracks life. For all his love of the army, so did Wilhelm. Although Eulenburg was aware that his elite army career gave him a cachet that attracted the Kaiser, it was his dilettantism, which was not unlike the Kaiser's superficial and inconstant interest in letters and the arts, together with his sycophantic adulation that won Wilhelm over.[38] Eulenburg was an amusing raconteur, he could play the piano and sing with ability, and he had a gift, which he exercised with many friends besides Wilhelm, for ingratiating himself. Even at moments of acute difficulty, Eulenburg knew how to distract the Kaiser from his worries: in the very midst of the Bismarck resignation crisis Wilhelm had insisted that his friend come and sing his songs.[39] Eulenburg was aware that he possessed a talent for combining lightness of touch with seriousness of purpose. Wilhelm, he declared, "lets me say anything to him about politics *because* I play tennis with him and between flying balls and in little periods of rest have a well-disposed imperial ear within reach. That makes it possible to use his good humor to obtain consent to difficult matters. To sport for country and king! Crazy world."[40]

From Eulenburg's perspective, Wilhelm was a distinctive personality whose cultural enthusiasm, if amateurish and seldom persistently applied, was a welcome departure from the intellectual sterility of the Prussian army and the Hohenzollern court. The Kaiser's patronage enabled Eulenburg to advance his own reputation as a musician, but also to secure royal favor for other artistic projects he favored. Eulenburg, for example, was the channel through whom Cosima Wagner tried, not entirely with success, to promote Wilhelm's interest in the Wagner festival at Bayreuth.[41] Eulenburg also knew how to cultivate Wilhelm's spiritual feelings. The young Kaiser, raised by Hinzpeter to observe a strict attendance at divine worship, had developed a genuine Calvinist piety, and Eulenburg reported that when Wilhelm talked of faith, his eyes reflected a sort of childish fervor.[42] To Wilhelm, Calvinism proclaimed not only the redemption of mankind through Christ but also the special trust given to magistrates, such as the house of Hohenzollern, to be the instruments of God's will on earth. Eulenburg was not a man attracted to institutional religion, but he had no objection to Wilhelm's association of faith and authority. In his letters Eulenburg did not fail to testify to the efficacy of divine guidance, but his religious interests lay more in spiritualism. In 1887 he introduced Wilhelm to the spectral world.[43] Eulenburg advised the Prince to keep this unorthodox experience to himself, but for several years thereafter he and Wilhelm exchanged ideas about extrasensory phenomena. Once Wilhelm became Kaiser in 1888, Eulenburg decided it would be better if the sovereign avoided any sort of séances, perhaps because Wilhelm's physician, Rudolf von Leuthold, had warned Eulenburg that spiritualist activity might result in Wilhelm's becoming undesirably "inwardly directed."[44] As in most matters, however, Wilhelm's enthusiasm for mysticism proved fleeting. By the early 1890s he had ceased to be seriously interested in it, although he continued for another decade to relish tales of the supernatural.[45]

Eulenburg's swift ascent in the diplomatic service, once Wilhelm came to the throne, reflected his intimate footing with the new monarch. Entering the foreign service in 1877 as a Bismarck protégé, Eulenburg had been given a number of choice secretarial posts when Wilhelm II, four months after becoming Kaiser, named him minister to Oldenburg, a grand duchy in northwest Germany that was somnolent but conveniently close to Berlin. In March 1890, the Kaiser promoted his friend to Stuttgart, the capital of the more important kingdom of Württemberg. Eulenburg's nomination only a year later to be envoy to Bavaria, the premier Prussian diplomatic post, satisfied his desire for office. To Eulenburg, the Bavarian position was especially agreeable because it was closer than other vacancies to his estate at Liebenburg, in the mark of Brandenburg, and to Berlin. For this reason Eulenburg resisted the Kaiser's inclination to promote him from Munich to ambassadorial dignity in a foreign capital. In 1894, he finally consented to being named envoy in Vienna, but only because the Habsburg capital was closer to Berlin and Liebenburg than was London, the other post for which Wilhelm had him under consideration.[46]

From the Prussian legation in Munich and later from the Viennese embassy, Eulenburg exerted a profound influence on politics and diplomacy in Berlin. His well-known friendship with the Kaiser insured Eulenburg a special position in the Wilhelmstrasse 76. He had for many years been on intimate terms with Holstein, who controlled appointments and promotions. Eulenburg had gradually accumulated a group of young diplomats—among whom the future chancellor, Bernhard von Bülow, was the most prominent—who proved valuable sources of information. Eulenburg repeatedly denied that he sought a "position of power," but in fact he savored the sway he came to possess and left nothing undone to ensure that it remained in his hands. Eulenburg's denials were nothing more than a reflection of his false modesty, and he was assiduous in cultivating those who could support him in realizing his ambitions.[47] At the center of Eulenburg's conception of power was the Kaiser, and the value Eulenburg set on men was in proportion to their usefulness in his campaign for influence with the throne.

In cultivating Wilhelm II, Eulenburg proved that in a large family celebrated for its diplomatic suavity, he was the model courtier. If he did not flatter the Kaiser quite as shamelessly as some did, he shrewdly calculated what approaches and opinions would find the surest welcome with his royal patron. He was careful not to commit himself until he had ascertained what Wilhelm's own inclinations were. Ever ready with diversion or with a word of dutiful encouragement, Eulenburg proved himself to be not only agreeable but also useful. He could expertly manage delicate situations, such as the marriage of one of the Kaiser's plain and none-too-well-endowed sisters. Eulenburg also had a facility for making Dona, whom Wilhelm rarely included in his numerous trips, feel less rejected by writing her, at the Kaiser's request, long letters full of details on the royal progress. The grateful Kaiserin liked Eulenburg and his music no less than did her consort.[48]

As a result of unremitting efforts, by the time that Wilhelm had come to the throne, Eulenburg had established himself as the leading intimate of the young sovereign. The Kaiser appeared frequently at Liebenburg for hunts, and Eulenburg regularly absented himself from his diplomatic posts in order to wait upon Wilhelm in Berlin. When apart they could exchange messages in the secret cipher Wilhelm entrusted to his friend in 1889. Not long after coming to the throne, Wilhelm told Hinzpeter that Eulenburg was his only intimate friend (*Busenfreund*). This was not one of the Kaiser's rhetorical flourishes, for Eulenburg had in fact no successful rival for Wilhelm's friendship. This intimacy with the sovereign was full of advantages for Eulenburg—advancement in his diplomatic career, offers (not accepted) of money, the performance of his plays at the royal theater—but it also was not without its pitfalls.[49] Wilhelm's energy was extraordinary, and his courtiers had to accommodate themselves as best they could to his restlessness and caprice. Moreover, Eulenburg was well aware that his closeness to Wilhelm could only fuel the jealousy of others who sought to capture the ruler for their own ends.[50] At the same time, the close relationship that Eulenburg formed with the Kaiser reinforced his position in Berlin, for officials and diplomats, both German and foreign, recognized that the surest path to imperial favor lay through Eulenburg.

While Eulenburg rarely ventured to point out to Wilhelm II his numerous lapses of judgment, in observations made to friends he was often critical of the Kaiser's maladroit behavior.[51] Eulenburg regretted that Wilhelm, always very susceptible to the headiest *Klatsch* but rarely interested in serious matters, often let his annoyance at other people or his prejudices impair his judgment.[52] The Kaiser's hardness of heart, so long deplored by Hinzpeter and the Empress Friedrich and a trait that Eulenburg himself would one day painfully experience, further obscured his ability to see things clearly. A courtier could depend on the Kaiser's favor only so long as Wilhelm needed him and their views coincided. Eulenburg knew that his own position would end if he ceased to please. "He loves my music and my conversation," he wrote with prescience in 1887, "but he also likes to criticize me openly. But *everything* in life is just a phase, and my phase too will pass by."[53]

As far as Eulenburg was concerned, the Kaiser's entourage intensified his unfortunate characteristics, for it was composed of dimwits, flatterers, adventurers, and narrow-minded militarists, all without political judgment or culture. The intellectual aridity of the Kaiserin's retinue was equally disturbing, and Wilhelm's constant exposure to such deplorable company would only increase his conviction that he was, at least by this meager standard, a personality of unusual stature.[54] Eulenburg hoped that he might constitute a beneficial influence in this stultifying court. Although he repeatedly used his contacts to secure favors for friends or to advocate political or diplomatic notions promoted by Holstein and his other confederates, Eulenburg considered that his proper role as imperial confidant was to make the Kaiser more moderate in his opinions and actions and to be less frenetic in the pace he set for himself.[55] "The Kaiser," he told his friend Holstein, "has an impulsive nature, which is characterized with extraordinary accuracy in the South German epithet 'Wilhelm the Sudden.' "[56]

Eulenburg did not at all disapprove of the Kaiser's pronounced authoritarian instincts, for he had as profound a loathing for parliamentary institutions and as great a veneration for Hohenzollern absolutism as did Wilhelm himself. But Eulenburg recognized, quite rightly, that the crown's extraordinary power had been disguised for decades by Bismarck's domination of events. With the Iron Chancellor gone, the Kaiser would now be perceived to be the master of Germany's fortunes. Naked to his enemies, Wilhelm II would have to wield his authority carefully and be circumspect in behavior, a prospect for which his conduct to date offered faint expectation. Eulenburg speculated whether the Kaiser's reign would resemble that of Antoninus Pius or of either Hadrian or Nero, a bright flame in the first case, a scourge in the other two. Only Wilhelm's Christian faith might serve to curb his enormous appetite for power.[57] If the Kaiser did not act with greater moderation, he would become increasingly unpopular. If, on the other hand, he listened to Eulenburg's counsel, he could become an effective and even revered sovereign, and Eulenburg himself could be the power behind the throne. It was this perception of his role, and his reward, that informed Eulenburg's every act throughout the 1890s.

Eulenburg's only rival for a position of intimacy with Wilhelm II was General Waldersee, whose friendship with the Kaiser was of somewhat longer duration but whose influence by 1890 seemed to be fading. From their initial acquaintance in the early 1880s, the friendship between the two men had grown increasingly confidential over the next seven or eight years. The Kaiser enjoyed Eulenburg, only a dozen years his senior, but he looked up to Waldersee, who was of his father's generation. Wilhelm treated the general as an elder, and Waldersee in turn dispensed avuncular advice to his young patron. In January 1889, Hinzpeter, who was a frequent guest of the Kaiser, assured Waldersee that he was the only person in whom Wilhelm had complete confidence and whose opinions he regarded as authoritative.[58] The Kaiser found Waldersee's geniality ingratiating and was impressed by his acknowledged military ability. The general, ever intrepid in proclaiming his readiness to do battle with the Fatherland's enemies, seemed to be the very eponym of the stalwart, aristocratic Prussian officer in whom the Kaiser put such great store. The sisterly affection that prevailed between their sanctimonious wives strongly reinforced the bond between Wilhelm and Waldersee, and the Kaiser himself was an admirer of the prim, but disarmingly outspoken, Countess Waldersee. She and Dona, with Wilhelm's protection, organized a "Men's League for the Struggle against Immorality," and it was probably due to the countess's pious influence that, shortly after becoming Kaiser, Wilhelm decreed that the Lord's day not be defiled by horse racing, public dancing, or any other irreverent amusement.[59]

In spite of his high opinion of Waldersee and their close friendship, by the time Bismarck fell, Waldersee's influence was on the wane, one telltale indication being Wilhelm's unwillingness to name him to the chancellorship. The Kaiser discovered that he and Waldersee had basic disagreements on foreign and domestic policy, and that Waldersee, like

Bismarck, was aggravatingly didactic in expressing his views. After Bismarck's departure the general continued to argue that since war with Russia was imminent, Germany had to respond with preventive aggression. Although Wilhelm had once shared this view, by the time Caprivi had succeeded Bismarck he had come to believe that Russia's diplomatic isolation and grave financial problems had diminished its will, and its ability, to attack Germany.[60] There was also a domestic disagreement that separated Wilhelm and Waldersee. Both the general and his countess kept up their close relations with Court Chaplain Stoecker after the Kaiser broke with him in 1890. The dissolution of Wilhelm II's earlier association with Stoecker came about in part because of the preacher's increasing prominence as a political agitator, activity that the Kaiser, but not Waldersee, eventually realized was incompatible with Stoecker's position as a court chaplain.[61] Under Hinzpeter's tutelage, Wilhelm had come to the conclusion that the working class could more effectively be won over by state-sponsored welfare programs and other proofs of concern and good will, rather than by Stoecker's private Christian-social movement with its patronizing aristocratic leadership. Waldersee did not approve of Hinzpeter's ideas and insisted that Stoecker's prescription was in fact the only one that would work.[62] Hinzpeter was a dogmatic and vengeful personality, and he quickly conceived a dislike for Waldersee, who reciprocated in kind.[63] Both tried to use their considerable influence to undermine the other's standing with the Kaiser.

Hinzpeter was by no means Waldersee's only enemy. The general's silky manners and unquenchable taste for intrigue advertised his ambition, at first for high military office but ultimately for the chancellorship. While many contemporaries admitted Waldersee's social amiability and military talent, few felt any affection for such a wily courtier, and many prominent figures were openly hostile to him. Even in the army, in which since 1888 Waldersee had served as chief of the General Staff, the highest position in the service, he was not universally popular.[64] Much of the officer corps had sympathized with Bismarck in the 1890 crisis, in which Waldersee had figured as the chancellor's foe. To the Bismarcks, father and son, Waldersee had been their leading rival, eager to supplant them in influence as well as office. After 1890, those who were for Bismarck were against Waldersee.[65] In the Foreign Office the general had a formidable, if secretive, enemy in Holstein, who considered him to be an intellectual lightweight and also a flatterer and gossip. Eulenburg was in complete agreement with his friend Holstein, for he saw in Waldersee a dangerous intriguer and a military "daredevil" (*Draufgänger*).[66]

Although these were powerful foes, they did not give Waldersee much concern, for he was confident of the Kaiser's grace and favor and believed that he had no cause to fear being toppled from his position. For a long time he did not suspect, anymore than had the Bismarcks in their day, that Wilhelm was beginning to tire of him. But early in 1890 Waldersee, somewhat incredulous at the discovery, came to the realization that his enemy Eulenburg was in fact the only person in whom the Kaiser now confided.[67] Waldersee's fears were entirely justified. Wilhelm could find no fault whatsoever with the artistic and ever agreeable Eulenburg, whose loyalty appeared completely untainted by ambition. But underneath Waldersee's equally genial facade Wilhelm believed that he could detect an unwelcome inclination on the general's part to use his relationship with the crown for the advantages it conveyed.[68] What particularly irked the Kaiser was Waldersee's pedagogical manner and his constant intriguing to assert for himself a political as well as a military role, an ambition which Field Marshal von Moltke, his predecessor as chief of the General Staff, had managed to suppress.[69]

It was Waldersee's attempt to discredit Chancellor Caprivi that completed Wilhelm's disenchantment and led in 1891 to the general's fall from power. Waldersee had long considered Caprivi a rival within the army, and on Bismarck's fall, also for the chancellor's post.[70] Caprivi, although himself a general, wished as chancellor to keep the army firmly restricted to military matters, and he was particularly concerned to reduce the power wielded by the chief of the General Staff. Waldersee indignantly declared to a fellow general that Caprivi lacked the requisite determination and independence to be a great leader.[71] From the moment that Caprivi took office, Waldersee began to snipe at him, much to the Kaiser's irritation. When Waldersee was so bold as to criticize Caprivi in front of the sovereign, Wilhelm told him to mind his own business and stay out of politics.[72] In May 1890, the Kaiser confided to Eulenburg, "Ever since Bismarck's resignation Waldersee has become self-important and talks about politics whenever he can. That's none of his business. He should stick to his own affairs."[73] But Waldersee persisted in competing with diplomats, men whom he scorned as "professional liars." Waldersee was discreet in expressing himself about the Kaiser's failings, but he privately decried Wilhelm's preference for the navy, his willingness to admit men of common birth to the ranks of the Prussian army officer corps, and his failure to listen to seasoned military professionals such as Waldersee himself.[74]

The maneuvers of the Prussian army in the spring and again in the fall of 1890 brought the deterioration of the general's relations with Wilhelm into the open. In March, at the conclusion of the exercises, the Kaiser criticized the strategy Waldersee had employed. The general, always prideful of his standing, was mortified that Wilhelm had challenged his judgment in public. The Kaiser later mollified Waldersee by assuring him that he had meant no harm, but he also coolly informed his adjutant Hahnke that, in finding fault with the general, "I only wanted to show him that I could live without him."[75] Waldersee had his revenge in the September maneuvers in Silesia. The Kaiser mishandled his command of one of the participating corps, and on the return to headquarters Waldersee criticized Wilhelm's tactics. Count Carl von Wedel, a favorite adjutant of the Kaiser's who was an enemy of Waldersee's, described the general's tactful critique of his sovereign as "a masterpiece."[76] But the Kaiser had never been able to accept censure no matter how gracefully it was put, and Waldersee's deft suggestion of error was especially distasteful to Wilhelm, since a few weeks earlier Eulenburg had confessed to him that Prussian generals tended to arrange maneuvers so that Wilhelm's corps always emerged victorious.[77] The Kaiser responded to Waldersee's remarks by blaming others for what had admittedly gone awry.[78] At dinner that evening, Count Friedrich Beck, the chief of staff of the Austrian army, expressed the hope to Wilhelm that he had not resented Waldersee's criticism. The Kaiser answered that he had not, but later General von Wittich, Wilhelm II's adjutant, told Beck, "If I know my Kaiser, he will never forgive him for this."[79] And he did not.

Waldersee's reproaches, however tactfully presented, were more than the Kaiser was prepared to tolerate, and before leaving Silesia he decided that the general would be relieved of his post at the General Staff and reassigned to the command of the thirteenth army corps at Stuttgart. Caprivi, who was anxious for the troublesome general to be removed from Berlin, seconded the Kaiser's plan. Although Waldersee by now recognized that his relationship with Wilhelm was in a state of serious deterioration, he was not prepared to accept such a command, for it was clearly a demotion.[80] Wilhelm did nothing for the moment to implement this change, probably because, like Eulenburg, he was concerned that Waldersee's resignation, although ultimately desirable, might create an unwelcome appearance of governmental instability if it followed too close on the heels of Bismarck's fall.[81]

Although Waldersee remained for the moment in possession of his post at the General Staff, his numerous enemies continued to work against him. It was the general himself, however, who ultimately provided the cause of his removal. The occasion was his attempt to secure virtually independent positions for the military attachés accredited to the major German diplomatic missions. The attachés were not official members of legations and their reports could be scrutinized but not altered by the envoys. The reports, destined for Waldersee, were presumed to contain only military information, but there was suspicion by the chancellor and in the Foreign Office that the attachés, like their chief, were dabbling in political affairs.[82] The Kaiser, resentful of Waldersee's overweening political ambitions, sided with his civil advisors. "Count Waldersee," he informed the British ambassador in the fall of 1890, "is endeavoring to thrust himself between me and the chancellor."[83] On 11 December 1890, Caprivi, with the sovereign's approval, issued an order that required the military attachés to refrain from any "independent political activity" and to consult with the envoys should their duties force them to trespass into nonmilitary matters. A week later, in the course of a hunt with the Kaiser, Waldersee made an outspoken attack on Caprivi and his order regarding the attachés. Wilhelm rebuked him, reminding him that the chancellor's order had royal approval.[84]

Waldersee's assault on Caprivi, according to the Kaiser, was but one more piece of evidence that the general had not abandoned his aspiration to become chancellor.[85] Wilhelm was now resolved that, no matter what impression Waldersee's dismissal might make on public opinion, he had to be sacked. At the gala celebration of the Kaiser's thirty-second birthday on 27 January 1891, Wilhelm informed Waldersee that he would shortly be entrusted with the command of the ninth army corps at Altona, the Prussian suburb of Hamburg, from which point he could keep an eye on the strong socialist movement in Hamburg and on the Bismarck establishment at Friedrichsruh, not far distant to the east.[86]

In a number of encounters during the next week, Waldersee remonstrated to Wilhelm that the post at Altona was an ill-disguised demotion. In spite of the general's protests, the Kaiser, forcefully shored up by Caprivi, was obdurate. In their final audience, Wilhelm dismissed Waldersee after only a few minutes, with a brusqueness that belied their years of close friendship. It was, as several observers noted, yet another disturbing example of the lack of feeling with which the Kaiser treated even his friends.[87] To some of Waldersee's fellow officers his curt dismissal portended the Kaiser's determination to arrogate to himself a greater share of military affairs, more perhaps than he would be able successfully to handle.[88] Waldersee departed for Altona, where he would remain for seven years. He never forgave Caprivi for having toppled him, and he never overcame his ambition to become chancellor. Waldersee's successor was General Count Alfred von Schlieffen, who would serve as chief of the General Staff until 1905 and who was careful to avoid political intrigues.

The ultimate victor in Waldersee's elimination was Philipp Eulenburg, who, after the general's removal from Berlin, had no effective competition as Wilhelm II's most intimate confidant. Eulenburg's part in Waldersee's fall from grace was covert. Like his friend Holstein, Eulenburg specialized in innuendo, and he realized that too concerted an attack on the general might make the Kaiser suspicious and cause him to protect Waldersee.[89] Eulenburg was anxious to get rid of a dangerous rival, for he wanted Wilhelm entirely to himself. As a diplomat, he shared Holstein's alarm at Waldersee's attempt to politicize the military attachés, and he had no taste for the general's reactionary domestic policies and desire for a military confrontation with Russia. Waldersee was notoriously lacking in the very sort of moderation and restraint that Eulenburg believed it was his duty to instill in the Kaiser. The general's departure was therefore good riddance. With Waldersee's relocation to Altona in February 1891, Eulenburg's position of favor was secure from challenge. Now he alone would be the voice that influenced Wilhelm II, while Chancellor Caprivi would serve as the obedient instrument of the Kaiser's pleasure.

Nine

CAPRIVI AND THE
"NEW COURSE"

APRIVI REALIZED that the Kaiser's personality would make his position as chancellor very difficult, but there was consolation in the fact that insofar as Caprivi's "New Course"—as his program came to be called—was concerned, he and Wilhelm II could draw on a substantial measure of agreement. Caprivi's loyalty to the Prussian monarchy was absolute, and he believed that no intrusion on the constitutional exercise of Hohenzollern authority should be allowed. Caprivi made no effort to enforce the 1852 cabinet order, the source of the conflict over prerogatives between Bismarck and Wilhelm II. It was repealed and replaced three weeks after Bismarck's resignation by a new document that essentially revived the old order, requiring all Prussian ministers except the war minister to secure the chancellor's agreement before having an audience with the Kaiser.[1] Caprivi, unlike Bismarck, was always faithful in keeping Wilhelm II informed, and he was alarmed to discover that his predecessor had deliberately secreted various diplomatic documents that should have come to the Kaiser's attention.[2] Because of his inexperience in foreign affairs, Caprivi made no strenuous challenge to the highly personalized diplomacy in which the Kaiser indulged with relish, and when they clashed it was usually over internal matters.[3]

The principal field of Wilhelm II's diplomatic initiatives during Caprivi's chancellorship, as it had been in the Bismarck era, was Russia. The Kaiser continued to regard Tsar Alexander III with hostility and suspicion, even though he believed that Russia was too weak, at least for the moment, to attack Germany.[4] At the time Wilhelm became Kaiser, Russia and Germany were partners in a highly secret alliance, the so-called "Reinsurance Treaty," designed in 1887 by Bismarck. Eight years earlier Bismarck had promulgated a defensive alliance with Austria-Hungary that provided for Germany to come to the Dual Monarchy's aid in the event of an attack by Russia. The Reinsurance Treaty, which had a duration of three years, stipulated mutual assistance in the event that Austria-Hungary should attack Russia, or France attack Germany. The Kaiser alleged, probably truthfully, that he had not known of the treaty until the spring of 1890, when Bismarck had informed him of its existence. In Wilhelm's opinion, Bismarck had hoped that the revelation of so complex a web of treaties would lead to the recognition that only the chancellor could juggle the participants, and he would therefore have to be kept in office. Years later, the Kaiser declared that learning of these intricate secrets instead made him resolve to be rid of Bismarck.[5]

The Russo-German pact would expire on 18 June 1890, and even though Wilhelm was pessimistic about the future of Germany's relations with Russia, he was prepared to renew the Reinsurance Treaty. Caprivi, however, believed that Germany should adhere as closely as possible to the 1879 alliance with Austria-Hungary. To Caprivi and to his staff in the Foreign Office, the Reinsurance Treaty was incompatible in spirit (though perhaps not with the letter) with the Austro-German treaty and would compromise Germany's relationship with Vienna.[6] As an inexperienced diplomat, the new chancellor felt that although Bismarck might have been capable of rationalizing and then upholding such a tortuous policy, he certainly was not. "A man such as yourself," Caprivi informed Bismarck, "can juggle five balls at the same time, while other people do well to limit themselves to *one* or two balls."[7] Caprivi also had to keep in mind the fact that the ex-chancellor, ever spiteful when crossed, could not be relied on to keep the Reinsurance Treaty secret, and its revelation would greatly embarrass Germany's relations with Austria-Hungary. The chancellor feared that should the contents of Germany's treaties with Russia and the Habsburgs become known, German public opinion, to which he unlike Bismarck was highly sensitive, would take a hostile view of such an ambiguous, even duplicitous, system of alliances.[8]

Within a week of Bismarck's fall, Wilhelm changed his mind about the wisdom of renewing the Reinsurance Treaty. The unanimously negative reaction of the Foreign Office to the renewal was influential, as were the efforts of Philipp Eulenburg, who for years had been working to undermine the Kaiser's faith in Alexander III.[9] Especially persuasive was the advice Wilhelm received from General Lothar v. Schweinitz, who since 1876 had been the German envoy in St. Petersburg. Schweinitz saw the Kaiser on 27 March and urged him not to renew the treaty because of the effect it would have on Germany's relations with Austria.[10] Wilhelm believed that he could hardly afford, on the heels of the crisis with Bismarck, to reject the counsel of his chancellor, the Foreign Office, and the Russian experts among Germany's diplomats. "So," he declared to Caprivi and Schweinitz, "it won't work, much as that disappoints me."[11]

Wilhelm realized that Germany's withdrawal would require considerable delicacy, since he had earlier assured the Tsar that he intended to renew the alliance. He instructed Schweinitz to return to St. Petersburg and inform Alexander III that although Germany continued to place the highest value on good relations with Russia, given the recent changes in the chancellorship and at the Foreign Office, a less complex diplomatic policy was necessary.[12] He also disingenuously assured the Russian ambassador that Bismarck's dismissal had been occasioned by the aged chancellor's failing health and not because of any objection to Bismarck's long-standing, if sometimes stormy, attachment to Russia.[13] The Kaiser was confident that Alexander would accept these mollifying explanations, and that Russia, which had neither allies nor an adequate war treasury, would see the wisdom of remaining at peace with Germany.[14]

On all accounts, the Kaiser's confidence in the efficacy of his personal diplomacy with the Tsar proved ill-founded. Alexander had no trust in Wilhelm's explanations about the collapse of the Reinsurance Treaty, to the continuation of which he was in fact indifferent, nor did he believe the Kaiser's assurances that Bismarck's dismissal did not portend danger for Russia. "Wilhelm is as good a liar as his manners are bad," the Tsar more than once told his brother, the Grand Duke Paul, for Alexander believed that with Bismarck's fall he had lost his only friend in Germany.[15] Caprivi could not be trusted.[16] From 1890 until Alexander III's death late in 1894, Russo-German dynastic relations were rarely harmonious. The "barbarian" Tsar, as Wilhelm described his "colleague," deliberately snubbed the Kaiser and rejoiced at his every difficulty, spitefully declaring in 1891 that "the more problems Germany has so much the better for us."[17] From 1891 to 1894, Alexander and Wilhelm avoided one another, but when they did meet, the Tsar behaved with evident *froideur*.[18]

In May 1891, with considerable diplomatic fanfare, the Triple Alliance of Germany, Austria-Hungary, and Italy was renewed, even though it did not expire until the following year, and the Kaiser's state visit to London in July raised suspicions in St. Petersburg that Germany hoped for England's inclusion in the pact. Alexander was thoroughly alarmed at the prospect of Russia's isolation, and his response was to invite a French naval squadron to call in July at Kronstadt, the port that served St. Petersburg, treating its officers with conspicuous courtesy. If the Tsar was perturbed that Germany and Great Britain seemed to be drawing together, Wilhelm was quite alarmed that Russia and France had apparently discovered a community of interest. The Kronstadt incident upset him considerably.[19] While the Kaiser was willing to admit, as did all German diplomats in Russia, that in an empire swarming with violent nationalists Alexander III was the most dependable advocate of peace, he believed that the Tsar was no longer capable of resisting either the tide of Pan-Slavic fervor in his own Empire or the warmongering mobs in Paris.[20] If the Tsar and the Kaiser drew swords, would not Paris gladly come to Russia's aid?[21] Whether the French urge for revenge could long be contained was, in Wilhelm's opinion, very questionable. "The peace of Europe," he declared a few days after the French ships had left Kronstadt, "is like a victim of heart disease. He can live a long, a very long time, but he can also die suddenly and at the most unexpected moment."[22] Russia's friendship would only increase France's lust for war against Germany, and the Fatherland therefore had no choice but to prepare for the worst.[23] Caprivi viewed the Kaiser's excitement with alarm and reminded Wilhelm that his subjects would not go to war against France except for good reason. France's hostility, while a matter for grave concern, had not yet provided such a pretext.[24]

In spite of Wilhelm's dark vision of Russia, he did not abandon his attempts to win over Alexander III to Germany's side, and he continued to believe that his personal diplomacy with the Tsar was useful. A trade treaty with Russia, for which Caprivi was working and which had the Tsar's support, served Wilhelm as a useful object of appeasement. The Kaiser had only a rudimentary understanding of economic matters, but the treaty, apart from the positive effect it might have on Alexander III, appealed to him as a means of reducing food costs in Germany and thereby winning support among his working-class subjects. Ever since 1890, there had been a sharp increase in the price of German bread, the principal ingredient of which was rye. Grain imports were protected by a tariff designed to insure that profitable price levels for domestic rye were maintained, an arrangement that led many political liberals motivated by free trade principles and a number of industrialists concerned by the effect of high bread prices on wages to join together to demand downward tariff revision. Prussian landholders, who were for the most part noblemen and who formed the backbone of the Conservative party, were vehemently in favor of the existing tariff, but they had fallen afoul of the Kaiser because of their rejection of the antisocialist bill in January 1890.

Caprivi was reluctant to offend the aristocratic agrarians, for he recognized that Germany needed food and soldiers, both of which their Prussian estates could supply in abundance. At the same time, the chancellor was dismayed that noble landlords seemed inclined to make their loyalty contingent on protection for their crops.[25] Their interests would have to be subordinated to the need to encourage industry and keep bread prices reasonable. Caprivi therefore decided in 1891 to devise a system of trade treaties whereby Germany would modestly reduce its tariffs on grain in return for reciprocal measures affecting the sale of German manufactured goods abroad. On 18 December 1891, in spite of the violent opposition of most of the Conservatives, the Reichstag approved the trade treaties the chancellor had drawn up with Austria-Hungary, Italy, and Belgium. Wilhelm was delighted with the chancellor's parliamentary victory and made him a count. The Conservatives were furious, however, and from this moment on they were determined to hound Caprivi—"a completely false, unreliable, and cloddish (*büffelhaften*) old soldier," as one of the party stalwarts denounced him—from office.[26]

By early 1894, Caprivi, who the previous year had obtained Reichstag approval for a trade treaty with Rumania, was ready to present a similar measure affecting Russia. His motivation in pressing for the trade treaty with Russia was diplomatic as well as economic. The chancellor had not lost his suspicion of Russia's aggressiveness, but by 1894 he had good reason to reconsider whether a renewed attempt to neutralize that hostility should not be attempted. Germany's two allies, Austria-Hungary and Italy, were neither especially potent in arms nor entirely dependable as diplomatic partners. Among the remaining great powers, France was an implacable enemy, while the Liberal government in Britain, which came to office in 1892, was unresponsive to any idea of associating with Germany in a diplomatic constellation. That left only Russia, which seemed to be drifting into France's camp. Neither Caprivi nor the Kaiser knew, though both may have suspected, that in 1892 Paris and St. Petersburg had arranged a secret military convention that provided for mutual consultation in the event either party felt threatened. Caprivi believed that a trade treaty, quite apart from the benefits that would accrue to the urban working class and to German industry, might promote better Russo-German relations and thus undermine the connection between Russia and France.

Wilhelm II had played little part in the trade treaties with Austria-Hungary, Italy, Belgium, and Rumania, though he had been uniformly supportive of Caprivi and repeatedly denounced the Conservatives for their opposition.[27] In the case of the Russian treaty, however, he took a prominent role, insisting from the beginning of the negotiations that Germany hold out for major concessions.[28] If the Russians had to be worked over, so did the Reichstag, from whom Wilhelm declared he would brook no contradiction. "The trade treaty must be passed," he ordered. "I have given Tsar Alexander *my word*."[29] The Kaiser concentrated his fire on the Conservatives, not only because they were the most fiercely opposed, but because he feared that if the party of aristocrats, officers, and courtiers failed to support the treaty, the Russians would hold him personally responsible. "I have no desire to fight a war with Russia because of a hundred stupid Junkers," he declared at a dinner for a group of Reichstag deputies, an entertainment that was part of Wilhelm's heavy-handed effort to gather votes in favor of Caprivi's forthcoming tariff treaty.[30]

Wilhelm II, with some justification, believed that when the Reichstag adopted the bill on 10 March 1894 by a comfortable majority he had been responsible for the victory. Not only had he browbeaten recalcitrant deputies and ministers, but he was certain that it had been his long, assiduous cultivation of Alexander III that alone had induced the Tsar to grant the concessions necessary to bring the negotiations to a successful conclusion. The economic bonds now established between Russia and Germany might in time mature into a diplomatic rapprochement, drawing the two eastern empires closer together.[31] The Tsar indeed recognized Wilhelm's critical role in securing the adoption of the treaty and in gratitude bestowed on him the rank of admiral in the Russian navy.

The Russian trade treaty, while a parliamentary victory of considerable magnitude for Caprivi, increased the hatred of the Conservatives, who with their allies in the newly founded agrarian interest group, the Agrarian League (*Bund der Landwirte*), would now redouble their efforts to drive the chancellor from office. While important in its economic significance, the tariff arrangement did nothing to lessen Germany's diplomatic isolation, for Russia and France remained tied together, not only by the 1892 military convention but, from January 1894, by a secret, full-fledged defensive alliance. Under Caprivi's guidance, Germany's security seemed to be in jeopardy and the Fatherland in real danger to both the east and the west. The old Bismarckian genius for maintaining Germany's predominance in European diplomacy had, so it appeared, disintegrated.

The Kaiser, however, was certain that the trade treaty he and Caprivi had brought into being had saved the day. In spite of considerable evidence to the contrary, he refused to believe that an alliance had been forged between Russia and France; at the most, he declared, there might be some sort of military convention.[32] Even were that the case, a development late in 1894 put the Franco-Russian connection in jeopardy. Eight months after the Russian treaty had been concluded, Alexander III was stricken with an incurable kidney disorder. The Kaiser responded to the news with the cool prediction that this fatal turn of events would result in an improvement in Russo-German relations.[33] The Tsar died at the beginning of November 1894, and Wilhelm now began what would become a twenty-year campaign to win the friendship of his successor, the young and timorous Nicholas II. The Kaiser's blandishments in Nicholas's direction would prove even less successful than the overtures he once had made to Alexander III. Bismarck's diplomatic "wire" to St. Petersburg had been cut forever, and none of the Kaiser's overtures to his new Russian "colleague" ever succeeded in effecting the necessary repairs.

In domestic affairs, Caprivi agreed with Wilhelm II, as Bismarck never had, that the new regime should try to win over the working class by a series of timely reforms that would wean it away from socialism. The chancellor, like the Kaiser, believed that socialism was the "greatest danger" that Germany faced.[34] To Wilhelm, domestic reform was to be the work of the crown, freely given as a gift to a dutiful people. Caprivi, however, took a fundamentally different view. The chancellor, for all his attachment to the monarchy, believed that the Kaiser's public esteem could not depend upon royal largesse dispensed from on high. It had instead to rest on the establishment of a capable and independent *government* that would design legislation benefiting all of Wilhelm II's subjects and thereby weaken the socialist threat to law and order.[35] Caprivi had hoped to effect this by securing the support of the old Bismarckian cartel, composed of the Conservative, Free Conservative, and National Liberal factions in the Reichstag. The chancellor's trade treaties had alienated the Conservatives, though they had won him considerable following in the other two factions. Without the Conservatives, the cartel could not provide a parliamentary majority, and Caprivi knew that he, like Bismarck in 1890 when he found himself required to negotiate with the Center leader Ludwig Windthorst, would therefore have to enlist the hitherto oppositional Catholic Centrists. With this conciliatory task in mind, early in his administration Caprivi had attempted to placate the Center by freeing certain funds held by the government since Bismarck's anti-Catholic *Kulturkampf* of the 1870s, by allowing the antisocialist law to lapse on its expiration in 1890, by eliminating the "reptile funds" through which Bismarck had long subverted the German press, and by moderating the increases to be made in the army budget.

The chancellor's notion of erecting a strong government of loyal Prussian ministers and imperial state secretaries did not please Wilhelm, who believed that bureaucrats belonged to him and not to the chancellor. The Kaiser was even more apprehensive that in such a system the Reichstag might try to capture the royal prerogative. His distaste for parliament was of long standing, and he often expressed his contempt for its members. Shortly after coming to the throne, Wilhelm undiplomatically informed the Italian ambassador that "after the French, the people I hate most are diplomats and deputies."[36] He denounced the Reichstag as a "chatter chamber" (*Schwatzbude*) and singled out for special abuse the Social Democrat and Catholic Center deputies, who, he assured the doubtless exhilarated Tsar, ought to be hanged.[37] Wilhelm was very resentful of intrusions on his authority and was prepared to tolerate the Reichstag only so long as it obediently passed bills in which he had an interest (such as the Russian trade treaty) and gave him the money he wanted, no matter how extravagant his demands.[38] When, in November 1890, Caprivi tendered a dinner to the Reichstag, the Kaiser behaved rudely, accusing the deputies of knowing nothing of the issues they debated.[39] Wilhelm's eccentric and offensive behavior made the chancellor's aim of assembling a loyal parliamentary following quite difficult.

The Kaiser's first plan for domestic reform had been to make the crown the protector of the working class, one of the many issues over which he and Bismarck had clashed. In the first years of his reign, Wilhelm, to Bismarck's horror, had intervened in labor disputes, issued compassionate proclamations, and assembled an international conference in Berlin to examine the plight of the working class. This activity had attracted great attention, and not a little criticism, but it had done nothing to realize the Kaiser's aim of luring German labor away from socialism and into the orbit of Hohenzollern benevolence. Although Wilhelm gradually became less and less hopeful of gathering the masses under his banner by any means other than force, until almost the end of Caprivi's chancellorship he continued to attempt to find an orderly antidote to the expansion of German socialism. For a long time Wilhelm believed that education might supply the needed corrective, and in 1889, while Bismarck was still in office, he had issued an order to the Prussian ministry that it should examine the ways in which secondary education could be reformed in order to combat the increasing influence of socialism.[40] Instruction in the schools, he informed his ministers, should make clear to young Germans that socialist dogmas were not only incompatible with Christian ethics but also impractical in execution and ruinous to both individuals and society. The history of the Fatherland, if properly taught, would show clearly that socialism was only bondage. In contrast, the paternal, Christian concern of the Hohenzollern monarchs for working class people had brought great material prosperity in the past and was the guarantor for continued improvement in the future.

In February 1890 the Kaiser announced that he intended to assemble a conference that would consider an alteration of civil education along the lines he had prescribed a month earlier for the cadet schools that provided officers for the army.[41] In the Kaiser's opinion, religion was properly the basis of instruction, and he was therefore sympathetic with a plan Caprivi later developed to grant Protestant and Catholic clergy an increased measure of control over education. The Kaiser believed that although some teachers advocated the most incendiary ideas, a reliably conservative instructor, if not overburdened with too many students, constituted the most effective barrier to socialist propaganda.[42] The curriculum, as well as the instructional staff, had to be carefully monitored, for a subject could be as poisonous as the person who taught it. The intense study of the classics that prevailed in the German *Gymnasia* was potentially dangerous, for students might drift into imitating the republicanism of the Greek and Roman heroes about whom they read. The purpose of education was to train young Germans, not would-be Athenians or Romans.[43]

On 4 December 1890, the Kaiser opened the school conference, whose members included his old tutor, Hinzpeter; Rudolf Virchow, the eminent pathologist who had performed the biopsy on Friedrich III's cancerous tumor and was a leader of the National Liberal party; and Friedrich von Bodelschwingh, a pioneer in public charity programs. Wilhelm began by noting his displeasure that the subject matter of the conference had been Frenchified as a "Schulenquête," rather than the more solidly Germanic "Schulfrage."[44] Prussia's secondary schools had lost sight of their responsibility to train good citizens and had failed to safeguard the Empire from destructive movements, especially socialism. Instead, the schools had become the preserve of dessicated philologues with an obsession for academic minutiae. As a result, Germany suffered from an overproduction of intellectuals whose health was undermined by too much work and whose minds were devoid of practical notions of civic responsibility and patriotism. The schools must therefore be reformed in order to mold German students into "young, national Germans." What they needed was modern history, modern languages, German literature, more physical exercise, and less tedious homework. As it was, German students did not understand the world in which they lived, and with their mole-like eyes, strained by hours at their desks, they were of no use to the Prussian army. The Kaiser's emotional address, which disregarded the laborious preparations of the conference delegates, produced what one witness described as "the most painful impression."[45] The assembled educators had little choice, however, but to tailor their deliberations to Wilhelm's notions, and they eventually reported in favor of an increase in instruction in German, a more extensive program of physical exercise, and the elimination of Latin as a prerequisite for graduation from a *Gymnasium*. Over the next few years the curriculum of the schools was altered to conform with these recommendations.

Caprivi, who had little interest in pedagogical questions and believed in the traditional system of German education, went along with the Kaiser's plans for school reform, but his concern, unlike Wilhelm's, was essentially tactical rather than moral or educational.[46] He wanted to invest the German clergy with wider responsibilities in education, but his motivation for doing so was to offer the Catholic Center a further inducement to affiliate with the *Kartell* supporting the government. Such a concession would also appeal to the Conservatives, who believed that the involvement of Protestant pastors in education would reinforce the traditional values to which they were so attached. The Center let Caprivi know that its parliamentary allegiance in the future would be conditional on the introduction of a new school bill that would grant both Catholic and Protestant clerics virtually unfettered control over religious instruction in the primary schools.

Caprivi entrusted to Count Robert Zedlitz-Trützschler, the able and determined Prussian minister of public worship and education, the task of framing such a measure. The draft that emerged provided for confessional instruction in separate Catholic and Protestant elementary schools, supervised by clerical officials and backed by teachers and school boards drawn exclusively from the same religious background as their students. Zedlitz's bill essentially met the Center's demands, but it annoyed the Kaiser, who complained that he had not been consulted in the drafting of the measure. In his opinion, Zedlitz had been too generous to the religious authorities and thereby played into the hands of the Center and the extreme Conservatives, both of which groups he disliked.

A surrender by the government to these two parties on the Zedlitz bill transcended the issue at hand, for it would in fact represent a complete, and to Wilhelm unacceptable, reorientation of parliamentary strategy. The result would be the alienation of southern Germany, which, although largely Catholic, was also heavily progressive and anticlerical. Neither Caprivi nor the crown could afford this.[47]

When the measure was presented before the lower house (*Landtag*) of the Prussian legislature on 15 January 1892, there were protests by political and academic liberals. Although the Kaiserin tried to persuade her husband of the bill's value, Philipp Eulenburg offset these warnings by confirming Wilhelm's view of the dangers inherent in reposing on a Conservative-Catholic Center coalition. He reminded the Kaiser that the South German progressive elements were ardent supporters of the Prussian-led Empire, and to offend them would only weaken the Empire and consequently the crown. Eulenburg recommended that the bill be altered to make it more palatable to the liberals or else be buried in committee.[48] Wilhelm agreed and instructed Zedlitz to revise the measure along the lines Eulenburg had suggested.

At a meeting of the crown council on 17 March 1892, the Kaiser reiterated his view that the Zedlitz bill should be amended in such a way that it would be acceptable to the liberal parties. Meanwhile it should be withdrawn from parliamentary consideration.[49] Zedlitz immediately resigned his ministerial portfolio, and Caprivi, whose sense of collegial loyalty was strong and whom Marschall von Bieberstein described as "linked to Zedlitz with an iron chain as though hypnotized by him," followed suit. He wrote to the Kaiser asking to be relieved both as minister-president of Prussia and as imperial chancellor.[50] Caprivi's allies received the news with incredulity, for the bill had not yet even been reported out of committee, and Caprivi would therefore have ample opportunity to seek some sort of compromise that would preserve the essentials of Zedlitz's measure while appeasing the Kaiser. The chancellor's abrupt resignation, not the first he had sent to Wilhelm II, was an illustration of his tendency to regard every issue as a principle that admitted of no compromise. That was how Wilhelm interpreted the chancellor's move—an "*excès de vertu*" by a "touchy hardhead" (*empfindlichen Dickkopf*) was his characterization of Caprivi's behavior.[51]

Caprivi's resignation threw Wilhelm, ailing from a chronic ear infection, into a highly excited state and provoked the first of the many nervous collapses he would suffer in the wake of political or diplomatic reverses. On the order of the royal physician, Dr. Rudolf von Leuthold, the Kaiser secluded himself in the palace for about two weeks. Wilhelm II's condition was regarded seriously enough in Berlin for there to be mention of the possible need for establishing a regency.[52] In Caprivi's opinion, the Kaiser had given his assent to Zedlitz's bill but then had withdrawn it. That was desertion, and it had to be firmly countered. In his letter of resignation the chancellor declared that he wished to give up his office because he no longer possessed the Kaiser's "inestimable confidence to such a degree as to be able personally to rely on it."[53] Not only had Wilhelm abandoned him, but so had the Prussian ministry. Caprivi was stung by the failure of several of his colleagues, especially Finance Minister Miquel, to give him their unanimous support in his confrontation with the Kaiser over the Zedlitz bill.[54] Wilhelm eventually persuaded the chancellor to reconsider his letter of resignation, with the result that, while Caprivi did quit as minister-president, he continued to serve as Prussian foreign minister and as imperial chancellor. This would insure that his old enemy Waldersee, who seemed to be regaining the Kaiser's favor, would not succeed to these posts.[55]

Caprivi recommended to the Kaiser that he appoint as minister-president Count Botho zu Eulenburg, a man of wide administrative experience who was then governor of the Prussian province of Hesse. The Kaiser agreed because he believed that Eulenburg, a notable reactionary, would be able to curb the contentious opposition of the Conservatives and shape them, as he put it, into a line batallion on which the government could rely.[56] Eulenburg's appointment, which was announced on 24 March, would prove to be an unfortunate development for Caprivi. While the new minister-president was an able bureaucrat, he was, unlike the chancellor, profoundly hostile to the working class and favored a repressive policy toward socialists. He and Caprivi would soon be at odds over who had the right to determine how Prussia voted in the Federal Council. Eulenburg aimed to go far and he was prepared to unseat Caprivi as chancellor should the opportunity arise. The result was a division in the government that would make Caprivi's position much more difficult, especially since the chancellor's resignation as minister-president had dismayed some of the Prussian ministers, who thereafter tended to let themselves be directed by the strong-willed Eulenburg.

The Zedlitz school bill affair, which Caprivi's stubborn behavior had blown up into a major crisis, exasperated the Kaiser. The chancellor had provoked the crisis by proposing such a heavily clerical measure and he, not the Kaiser, would have to be responsible for solving it. "My ministers are old and I am young," Wilhelm complained to the Austro-Hungarian envoy, noting how tiresomely prolix and cautious his senior bureaucrats tended to be. "I have frankly told Count Caprivi, whose dismissal is an impossibility, what I think about his pigheadedness."[57] With Zedlitz out of office and Caprivi no longer minister-president, the way was clear for the withdrawal of the school reform bill. On 28 March 1892, Botho Eulenburg formally tabled the proposed legislation, much to the displeasure of the extreme Conservatives and the Catholic Center, whose support for Caprivi's parliamentary maneuvers in the future would be very problematical.

Wilhelm II's plans for the reform of Prussian primary education followed very closely the prescription he had earlier drawn up for the cadet academies, whose graduates provided the Prussian army with most of its new lieutenants. Military education, the Kaiser declared, was more than academic instruction. Its purpose was also to build character and to provide young officers with a "spiritual armament" that would make them exemplary citizens. Learning should be valued for its usefulness, and to that end he ordered that in the cadet schools history should deal with contemporary affairs, the languages mastered be modern tongues, and that instruction in geography concentrate on the Fatherland.[58]

The revision of cadet education was only one of a series of military reforms Wilhelm II had implemented since coming to the throne in 1888. The Kaiser was insistent on forcing into retirement most of the superannuated generals to whom his grandfather had been much attached, but he accomplished this essential pruning of the ranks with unnecessary ruthlessness. Generals who remained on active service found that Wilhelm II often treated them rudely, criticizing their performance on maneuvers and declining to receive them when they appeared in Berlin.[59] He preferred his younger Potsdam cronies, who offered no contradiction and provided amusement and flattery.[60] The Kaiser also instituted the first of an endless series of uniform regulations, changing army dress no fewer than thirty-seven times in the first sixteen years of his reign. He devised a sumptuary code prescribing in detail the number of courses and the amount of wine that could be served in the messes of the aristocratic army officers, whose taste for gambling and luxury he had condemned while his grandfather was still on the throne. In keeping with his conception of a popular monarchy, Wilhelm in March 1890 ordered that officer recruits were to be drawn from the bourgeoisie as well as the nobility. He assured one of his generals that the middle class feared the socialists more than the throne, and increasing the military participation of the bourgeoisie would bring them more securely into the royal camp.[61]

While Wilhelm could determine promotions in the army, the way his soldiers ate or dressed, what they were taught or how they were moved about on maneuvers, he could not add to the size of the army, or increase its budget, or alter the term of active service without the consent of the Reichstag. During the four and a half years of Caprivi's chancellorship, no issue involved Caprivi's attention, and that of the Kaiser, more than fixing the size, and thus the cost, of the army. It was a question on which both the chancellor and Wilhelm had strong feelings and one over which they repeatedly clashed. Caprivi, although a general, was no less determined than Bismarck that the army be kept subservient to the civil government. He believed that military increases should be moderate in order to placate Reichstag deputies, who were suspicious of army expenditures, and thus to insure that the army budget would not lead to a constitutional crisis pitting the crown against the legislature. He was very opposed to a grandiose enterprise concocted in 1890 by Waldersee and General Julius von Verdy du Vernois, the Prussian minister of War, to make substantial increases in the number of men under service. Caprivi, in contrast, wanted only a small addition to the ranks and a reduction of the active service term from three to two years. Wilhelm's sympathies were with Waldersee and Verdy, but the chancellor persuaded him to accept a compromise whereby three-year service was formally retained, but about half the army's strength was transferred to the reserves after two years' service.[62] On 28 June 1890, this so-called "little army bill" passed the Reichstag. Verdy, who had also had difficulties with the Kaiser on armament questions, resigned in October and was succeeded by General Hans von Kaltenborn-Stachau, who was bland and agreeable.

Caprivi's support for a bill providing only moderate increases in the army was tactical: it was the most that could be pushed through the Reichstag. Given Germany's unenviable position between France and Russia, both of whom seemed to Caprivi dangerously anti-German, in June 1891 the chancellor proposed to the Kaiser that the number of troops again be increased but the term of active service reduced from three to two years. Although Wilhelm had earlier indicated that he might eventually be willing to move to a two-year term, he now responded that it was his "holy decision" not to agree on the reduction because such a provision would lessen discipline in the ranks and, more importantly, because he believed that the demand for a reduced term was a radical plot to erode the power of the crown.[63] Wilhelm informed Caprivi that he himself, without consulting anyone else, had drawn up a plan for the reorganization of the army that would entail an increase in troop strength, three-year service, and an additional annual expenditure of forty million marks.[64] In the great constitutional crisis of 1862–66, when the Prussian parliament had refused his grandfather's plan for army reform, Bismarck had stood up to this legislative assault on royal prerogative, and the Kaiser intended for the chancellor to do the same. Caprivi, he implied, would be *his* Bismarck.

The chancellor promptly replied that the Kaiser's costly plan had no possibility of winning Reichstag approval and that to implement it would therefore require a coup d'état.[65] This was the antithesis of the popular monarchy Caprivi hoped to establish and would endanger the very existence of the Empire. He declared that he would have nothing to do with a plan that might provoke such a disaster and offered his resignation, expressing displeasure that Wilhelm had devised such a scheme without consulting him. The Kaiser thereupon withdrew his proposed reorganization measure, but he warned Caprivi that he was only delaying. Eventually he meant to have an army that reflected *his* views, and he expected Caprivi to help him. Wilhelm informed the chancellor that he had arrived at his decision by examining the matter "before God and my ancestors."[66] When the Kaiser expressed his annoyance at Caprivi's resistance, the chancellor gave no ground. "I will always write in such a way to Your Majesty," Caprivi forthrightly declared of his letter of resignation, "when I perceive that you wish to do something that will harm you or the Empire."[67]

Confronted by the Kaiser's obstinate refusal to agree to two-year service, Caprivi decided in the summer of 1891 not to pursue the matter of army reform for the moment but to concentrate instead on Zedlitz's school bill. This issue occupied him for the rest of 1891 and on into the next year. But with the withdrawal of the school measure at the end of March 1892, the chancellor was free to return to the question of reorganizing the army. Caprivi's position, however, was now considerably weaker because of the displeasure of the Catholic Center and many of the Conservatives over the failure of the government to stand behind Zedlitz and his bill. Caprivi was determined that any legislation affecting the army would be designed by the government and not by the Kaiser, but he recognized that it would be fruitless to proceed with a measure that did not enjoy royal approval. Wilhelm II, however, had not abandoned his determination to have both troop increases and three-year service, even if it required the dissolution of the Reichstag. The former, he declared, was the necessary response to the continuing increase in the French and Russian armies, and the latter was a Hohenzollern tradition that could not be abandoned.[68] The question was one for the military to decide, and the army, in the Kaiser's opinion, was solidly behind three-year service. "The matter *must* be settled," one way or another, he ordered.[69] Eventually, Wilhelm proposed to compromise by a reduction of the term to two and one-half years, but Caprivi refused. The Kaiser thereupon threatened to go before the Reichstag and declare that rejection of three-year service would bring the certainty of defeat in the event of war.[70]

Neither Wilhelm nor the chancellor wanted to precipitate a crisis. Wilhelm recognized that the support of the Catholic Center was critical and that it would be prudent to give it time to forget the withdrawal of Zedlitz's school bill.[71] The chancellor also favored a tactical delay, not only to bring the Center around but also to wear down the Kaiser's resistance to two-year service. Wilhelm, on the other hand, continued to expect that Caprivi would support him. "Only *trust in my leadership* and fight bravely where I point the way," he wrote to the chancellor on 20 July 1892, "and we will have no trouble in managing the *canaille*."[72] Throughout the summer of 1892 Caprivi and the Kaiser struggled over the reduction of service to two years, but the chancellor finally persuaded Wilhelm that there was a way out of the dilemma. Caprivi pointed out that the two-year service on which he insisted in fact corresponded closely to the actual procedure employed in the infantry brigades of transferring troops to the reserves after only two and a quarter years' service.[73] He succeeded in convincing Wilhelm that the two-year term was less a concession than it was an essential confirmation of existing practice.

When Wilhelm indicated he would yield on the term of service, the chancellor made his own concession. The Kaiser had always insisted on a larger army budget, and Caprivi now proposed even more substantial troop increases than Wilhelm himself had planned, at a cost of sixty million marks per annum compared to the Kaiser's projected expenditure of forty. A bill incorporating this agreement was introduced in the Reichstag on 23 November 1892. The chancellor defended the proposed increases, greater than all that had been made since 1871 combined, by pointing to French revanchism and the widespread Germanophobia in Russia. Offsetting the consternation these increases produced was the government's plan to reduce active service to two years and to decrease the term of the military budget from seven to five years.

The bill immediately encountered difficulties, for as a compromise it suited no one. The Conservatives, already arrayed against Caprivi because of his trade treaties and his abandonment of Zedlitz's school bill, felt an aristocratic revulsion at any capitulation to liberal demands for two-year service. While some of the Catholic Center were prepared to accept the bill, the Bavarian wing, composed largely of peasants, shared the Conservatives' anger at the chancellor's agrarian policies and refused their support. Since all the other parties were against the bill, Caprivi agreed to reduce the increases. Here, however, he ran up against Wilhelm II. The Kaiser assured the commanding generals of the Prussian army that he would not countenance any reductions in the bill. "I will get the bill, whatever it costs," he declared. "What does this passel of civilians know about military matters? I will give up neither a man nor a mark and *I will chase this half-crazy Reichstag to the devil if it opposes me.*"[74] The position of the divided Catholic Center, the largest faction in the Reichstag, was critical, and Caprivi succeeded in persuading Georg Cardinal von Kopp, the archbishop of Breslau, to unify the party behind the bill. The chancellor then arranged for Kopp to meet with Wilhelm II. In the course of a conversation that lasted almost three hours, the prelate promised that the Center would support the bill as amended by Caprivi provided that the laws that excluded the Jesuits from Prussia were lifted. In spite of his earlier bluster, Wilhelm agreed in order to insure that the measure passed through the Reichstag.[75]

The help of the Catholic Center, although very useful, did not prove sufficient to obtain a majority in the Reichstag for the army bill. As this became clear, the Kaiser declared to his entourage that rejection of the bill would constitute a revolution from below. He would answer with one from above.[76] On 6 May 1893 the Reichstag defeated the bill, and Wilhelm at once dissolved it and called for elections. The time had come, he declared, to show the deputies he meant business. If the electorate returned a hostile majority, one including a large block of Social Democrats, the result would be such public apprehension that his subjects would demand, and promptly receive, an alteration in the constitution that would eradicate this radical threat.[77] A few days later, in an impromptu speech at a troop parade in Berlin, the Kaiser declared that he expected the new parliament to behave with more patriotism than its unworthy predecessor. But should it also decline the military bill, he was prepared to alter the constitution in order to obtain an amenable Reichstag. "I feel myself one with the federal Princes, the people and the army," he told his soldiers.[78] The elections, held on 15 June, resulted in an increase in the government factions barely sufficient to obtain a majority. With Wilhelm II present in the gallery, on 15 July 1893 the Reichstag passed the army bill by a narrow vote, 201 to 185. The Kaiser telegraphed to Queen Victoria that he had achieved a "great victory."[79] He also addressed a congratulatory letter to Caprivi and then left for a long cruise along the Norwegian coast.

Caprivi had got the army bill he wanted, but the difficulties he had experienced with both the Reichstag and the Kaiser revealed the essential weakness of his position. He had alienated the conservative agrarians by his trade treaties and given the Prussians among them further cause for alarm by his reduction of the army term of service. In the school bill crisis, Caprivi had managed to offend the liberals by initially supporting Zedlitz's bill and then the Conservatives by resigning as minister-president and thus sacrificing Zedlitz in the face of Wilhelm II's opposition to the measure. The Conservatives had innumerable connections at court, and here Caprivi found himself an outcast not only because of his policies but also because he was not descended from an ancient Prussian family. Philipp Eulenburg, who was certainly in a position to know, declared that the chancellor had not a single friend among the entourage.[80] The Catholic Center had no enthusiasm for a chancellor who, by abandoning Zedlitz, had scuttled their hopes of a greater role in education for the clergy. To the Progressives and Social Democrats, Caprivi, as a Prussian aristocrat and a general, was a representative of the old order and in their opinion his reforms had done nothing to erode the privileged station of Germany's ruling elite. In the legislature the chancellor, as he was the first to acknowledge, was without allies, and the best he could do was to patch together feeble and transient majorities for some, but not all, of the reforms he hoped to effect.[81]

The many voices raised against Caprivi would have been ineffective had he continued to enjoy the Kaiser's good will. Wilhelm appreciated the chancellor's formidable industry and his loyalty, but the numerous differences that had arisen between them on matters of policy had gradually lowered his estimation. Caprivi's stubborn, schoolmasterish personality, as Wilhelm himself admitted, inevitably conflicted with the Kaiser's hardheadedness.[82] The chancellor, Waldersee reported (undoubtedly with delight) in 1894, was beginning to bore his master, and Caprivi himself conceded that the Kaiser found their conferences tiresome.[83] When the chancellor ran into resistance from the Kaiser, his invariable reaction was to offer his resignation, a ritual which Wilhelm found very exasperating. On such occasions, the Kaiser would say to him: "Caprivi, you are getting frightfully on my nerves," to which the invariable response was: "Your Majesty, I have always been a very troublesome subject."[84] In the summer of 1892, Wilhelm confided to Eulenburg that the trouble with Caprivi—exactly as it had been with Bismarck—was that he treated him like a mere youth. The chancellor, Wilhelm claimed, failed to appreciate the rich experience of statecraft his sovereign had garnered from years of association with Bismarck. "I'm too young to impress him," the Kaiser complained.[85] Where Wilhelm wanted action, Caprivi insisted on reflection, examination, and discussion, a trait the Kaiser found deplorable in *all* of his ministers.[86] Hinzpeter had trained him to reach judgments instantaneously, and the Kaiser expected others to follow his example. Caprivi had hardly been in office a year and a half when Wilhelm began to ponder the question of who might eventually replace him.[87] As far as the chancellor was concerned, he deplored Wilhelm's impulsiveness and indifference to work, as well as the fact that the Kaiser inclined more and more to make important decisions without consulting him.[88]

In the summer of 1894 a serious conflict broke out anew between the ruler and his chancellor that eventually resulted in Caprivi's retirement. In June, an anarchist assassinated the president of the French republic, Sadi Carnot. The Kaiser's response was to denounce the outrage in a telegram of sympathy to the widow and to make an inflamed speech at Königsberg in which he exhorted an audience composed largely of aristocrats "to the battle for religion, for morality and order against the parties of revolution," a thinly veiled allusion to the Social Democrats and their alleged anarchist confederates.[89] Carnot's murder was the last in a series of events that convinced the Kaiser that the conciliatory policy toward labor with which he had begun his reign six years earlier had been an error.[90] The abolition of the antisocialist law in 1890 and the introduction of a policy of social welfare had failed to win the allegiance of the German working class. Wilhelm II's educational reforms, on which he had placed much store, had proved equally ineffectual in this respect. Socialists continued to multiply at the polls, a fact especially apparent in the Reichstag elections of 1890 and 1893, which resulted in a substantial increase in the number of socialist deputies. Industrial violence had not abated but had reemerged in 1892–93 in prolonged and bitter strikes in Berlin, the Saar, and once again in the Rhenish coalfields.

The disturbances in the Saar, although the most remote from the capital, were probably the most significant for the Kaiser's views on labor, for they brought him into close contact with the great Saarland plutocrat, Baron Carl Ferdinand von Stumm-Halberg.[91] Stumm, whose enormous wealth was derived from coal mining, had a profoundly conservative mistrust of socialism, one that bordered on obsession. Like the court preacher, Adolf Stoecker, he believed that the movement could be combated only by a combination of charity and rigid coercion. He utterly disapproved of the broader protective social concern that Wilhelm II had endorsed early in his reign. Stumm regarded socialists as enemies of the regime and felt that they should be deprived of the franchise if they went out on strike. Stumm had first met Wilhelm in the early 1880s, and by about 1892–93 he had come to enjoy considerable influence with him. So great in fact was Stumm's sway that by 1894 contemporaries described Germany as entering, as indeed it was, into a reactionary "Stumm era."[92]

The Kaiser regarded all signs of public disaffection as deliberate and intolerable affronts to his person. He could not grasp that they were the expression of legitimate dissatisfaction on the part of the working class not only with his leadership but with the entire character of the regime. Just as Wilhelm's sense of rejection by his mother had led him to turn against England and just as later the same feeling would be a major factor in his resolution to build a navy, so here it was rejection that prompted the Kaiser to abandon the conciliatory policy toward labor with which he had so optimistically begun his reign. It was a critical turn in his reign, one from which he would never retreat. By the summer of 1894, Wilhelm II, faced by incontrovertible evidence of his subjects' ingratitude, had come to the conclusion that German labor was unworthy of his benevolence.[93] His subjects had mistreated him, and he would exact his revenge. Wilhelm now realized that Bismarck had been right in 1890, when he had argued so vehemently that the working class deserved not kindness but coercion. "The voice of the people, the voice of the blockheads," the Kaiser declared.[94] So, in July 1894, Wilhelm instructed Caprivi to prepare a new socialist law that, like the measure Bismarck had wanted in 1890, would include a provision for exiling socialist troublemakers to the countryside. In addition, Wilhelm ordered the chancellor to draft a bill that would provide punishment for any person who in speech or writing criticized him or his house.

The Kaiser's attack on the socialists had the full support of the arch-conservative minister-president of Prussia, Count Botho zu Eulenburg, who favored altering the franchise in order to secure the return of a

Reichstag that would enact a law against socialist revolution (*Umsturz-vorlage*) containing an expulsion paragraph. Botho Eulenburg entirely disapproved of the wait-and-see attitude Wilhelm and Caprivi had adopted in 1890, when they declined to badger the Reichstag for a new antisocialist law. The Kaiser, but not the chancellor, had by now come to the conclusion that Botho was right, for the six years of conciliatory policy toward the working class he had instituted on becoming Kaiser in 1888 had yielded nothing. Although Wilhelm realized that a stiff measure directed against the socialists had little hope of being adopted by the Reichstag, he declared that the deputies would not be allowed to stand in the way of action, threatening that in the event of rejection he would dissolve the chamber and call for elections. If, as Botho Eulenburg had argued, that failed to produce the desired majority, he would prorogue it a second time and once again send the voters to the polls. If the Reichstag still held out there would then be no alternative but to execute a coup d'état. In the Kaiser's opinion, it was the German princes, and not their subjects, who had made the imperial constitution in 1871, and consequently they had the right to set it aside. In such an event, the princes would design a new constitution with a franchise provision that would guarantee the return of a more patriotic Reichstag.[95] This had been the plan, advanced by Bismarck in 1890, to which Wilhelm II had been very opposed. Now, four years later, he appeared as the advocate of precisely such a procedure.

Caprivi would have nothing to do with the Kaiser's notions of a coup and early in October 1894 told him so. The government, and the crown, would have to work within the constitution and formulate an antisocialist law moderate enough for the Reichstag to accept.[96] He would resign rather than be a party to a violation of the constitution. The Kaiser resented Caprivi's obstinance and appealed in vain to the chancellor's sense of soldierly loyalty. Defeated by Caprivi's opposition, Wilhelm finally agreed to let the chancellor attempt to frame a law that might be acceptable to the Reichstag. Caprivi returned to Berlin and in the next few days drafted a bill similar to the legislation directed against socialists that had existed from 1878 to 1890, in which there was only a very qualified expulsion provision for banishing agitators to rural areas.[97]

Although Marschall and a few other ministers supported Caprivi, most agreed with Botho Eulenburg, who was unwavering in his insistence on a strong measure with a severe expulsion paragraph. The chancellor realized that there was no possibility of a compromise between his position and Eulenburg's. The failure of many of his ministers to offer their support, the weakness of a government in which the minister-president and the chancellor represented sharply opposing viewpoints, and the fact that Wilhelm sided with Eulenburg forced Caprivi once again to the conclusion that he must resign.[98] To the chancellor, the struggle with Botho Eulenburg was the final indignity he was prepared to suffer at the Kaiser's hands. Wilhelm II, in Eulenburg's presence but without bothering to consult Caprivi, had recently granted an audience to the chancellor's most determined enemies, the conservative leaders of the Agrarian League, who despised Caprivi because of his trade treaties. The deputation, which came to assure the Kaiser of their support in his battle against radicalism of all sorts, avoided the chancellor, who first learned of the meeting from newspaper accounts.[99] Then, on 18 October, Wilhelm had publicly complained that the substantial troop additions provided for in the army bill which Caprivi had got through the Reichstag with such difficulty were insufficient and, later that day at a dinner, pointedly reiterated his dissatisfaction in his toast to the chancellor.[100] The Kaiser's irresponsibility, his errant judgment, and his rudeness were more than the beleaguered chancellor could tolerate. On 23 October 1894 he once again asked to be relieved of office.

Caprivi's resignation stunned Wilhelm, who was hunting on Philipp Eulenburg's estate at Liebenberg. The Kaiser, who apparently had no understanding of the offense his behavior had given Caprivi, had quite unrealistically assumed that the chancellor and Botho Eulenburg would be able to compose their differences and present a mutually acceptable antisocialist bill. Only two days earlier he had assured Philipp Eulenburg that insofar as he and the chancellor were concerned "everything was in the best order."[101] Wilhelm was not eager to part company with Caprivi, difficult as he could be, and Philipp Eulenburg had warned him only a week earlier that the effect on public opinion of the chancellor's resignation would be disastrous. Everyone would know that the cause of the break had been the antisocialist law issue, and the Kaiser would be branded a reactionary tyrant for supporting Botho Eulenburg's draconian views on how the socialist threat should be handled.[102] There was, besides, the question of a successor for Caprivi. If Caprivi resigned in refusal to promote a stiff antisocialist law then must not Botho Eulenburg, recognized as the chancellor's rival and the figure who had the Kaiser's support, succeed? This gave Wilhelm pause, for he did not like the prospect of having a chancellor such as Eulenburg, whose excessively bureaucratic manner got on his nerves.[103] Furthermore, Botho as chancellor was impossible because of his pronounced reactionism, which would arouse such widespread opposition that he would be unable to govern.

The Kaiser therefore resolved to work out a solution whereby both Caprivi and Botho could remain in the government. On his return to Berlin, Wilhelm called on the chancellor and succeeded in persuading him that he, and not the minister-president, enjoyed his favor.[104] Caprivi thereupon yielded to the Kaiser's pleas and agreed to remain at his post. The Kaiser, wanting to make sure that Botho was under no illusions that it was the chancellor's position rather than his own that had royal approval, instructed Caprivi privately to send a copy of his letter of resignation, which persistently criticized Botho's views, to the minister-president. Wilhelm's rejection of Caprivi's resignation would thus plainly indicate to Botho that he sided with the chancellor. When Botho received the letter, he immediately resigned his office.

On 25 October various Berlin newspapers carried accounts of the Kaiser's conversation with Caprivi in which he extended his support to the chancellor and criticized Botho Eulenburg's reactionary antisocialist views. This leak in the press could have come only from Caprivi or someone close to him, since Wilhelm had said nothing to anyone about his talk with the chancellor.[105] The revelation put the Kaiser in a very difficult situation, for it was one thing for him to have rebuked Botho in private, but quite another for the public at large to know that he had done so. If his rejection of Botho in favor of Caprivi, as reported in the newspapers, was left uncorrected, he would alienate the conservative interest, which was dominant in Prussia, and force the monarch in the future to depend not on Prussia but on the Empire. This was a development that could only enhance the authority of the Reichstag and weaken the Kaiser's position. If, on the other hand, Wilhelm let Caprivi go but retained Botho Eulenburg or promoted him to the chancellorship, he would, as Philipp Eulenburg had argued, be condemned by public opinion as a reactionary despot. The problem was greater than the immediate issue of the antisocialist bill. Botho Eulenburg, who had many allies (and many relatives) among the Prussian agrarians and in the army, represented the traditional conservatism of Prussian society, the cornerstone of the Hohenzollern monarchy. Caprivi, on the other hand, drew his following from more moderate, often non-Prussian elements. The support of both were necessary for stable government. Wilhelm had somehow to avoid choosing between Botho Eulenburg and Caprivi and find a way to retain both men. If that were to prove impossible, then both would have to go, and a figure identified neither with Caprivi nor with

Eulenburg appointed to replace them by reuniting in one man the chancellorship and the Prussian minister-presidency.[106]

The Kaiser decided that the best course was for him to decline Eulenburg's offer to resign and to have Caprivi deny the press reports that the crown had sided with the chancellor. The chancellor was to declare that he wanted Eulenburg to remain as minister-president. "It is the minimum that a gentleman would certainly do," Wilhelm declared, "if it mattered to him to serve and to help me and the Fatherland."[107] If Caprivi would agree to the denial, Wilhelm would be able to keep both the chancellor and the minister-president; if he would not, then both would have to be sacked. "Now, whatever happens," the Kaiser told Philipp Eulenburg on 25 October, "better an end with dread than dread without end."[108]

Caprivi, however, refused to fulfill the Kaiser's request. He understandably had no intention of denying to the public that Wilhelm had taken his side in the question of the antisocialist law, for indeed the Kaiser had privately given him precisely that assurance. It was the chancellor's right to let the German people know that he had the ruler's support.[109] And Caprivi had no intention of asking his foe Eulenburg to remain in office. When the chancellor therefore refused the Kaiser's request, on 26 October Wilhelm accepted the letters of resignation both Caprivi and Eulenburg had already tendered. Caprivi came to the palace for a brief farewell, in the course of which the Kaiser declared, "I have come to see more and more that we are not suitable for one another," to which the fallen chancellor replied: "I have myself noted that for a long time."[110] Wilhelm then summoned Prince Chlodwig zu Hohenlohe-Schillingsfürst, a Bavarian grandee serving as viceroy of Alsace-Lorraine, to Berlin to take office both as imperial chancellor and minister-president of Prussia.

Ten

UNCLE CHLODWIG

THE KAISER'S SELECTION of Hohenlohe was one of his disconcerting gestures, for the new chancellor and minister-president of Prussia was neither Prussian nor even Protestant, but a Catholic Bavarian, one of whose brothers was a prominent cardinal. The new chancellor, moreover, was seventy-five, a few weeks older than Wilhelm's grandmother, Queen Victoria, and indeed more aged at his appointment as the Kaiser's principal servant than Bismarck had been when he left office in 1890. No one was more surprised at the appointment than Hohenlohe himself.[1] The prevailing assumption in political circles in Berlin was that the Kaiser intended Hohenlohe only as a caretaker, who after a brief interval would be retired in favor of Philipp Eulenburg or some other royal favorite. Whatever the term of his administration, the frail and reticent Prince was expected to be a weak figure, for he was known to possess neither Bismarck's irascibility nor Caprivi's stubbornness.[2]

Although Hohenlohe was unusually old to be assuming the highest position in the land, his many years of public service provided him with qualifications in no way inferior to those Bismarck himself had possessed. Hohenlohe had proved a capable leader of a liberal Bavarian government in the late 1860s and early 1870s, when he had been the primary exponent of Bavaria's joining in the war against France and supporting Bismarck in the creation of a German Empire dominated by Prussia. The chancellor rewarded Hohenlohe for his support by appointing him ambassador in Paris, a delicate position because of France's recent defeat in the Franco-Prussian war but one that Hohenlohe filled with éclat. After eleven years in Paris, Kaiser Wilhelm I approved Hohenlohe's promotion to viceroy of Alsace-Lorraine, an even more difficult assignment but one in which the grand seigneur displayed toward the French the same conciliatory spirit that had characterized his successful envoyship in Paris. Hohenlohe's exalted status as a mediatized prince and his tangled kinship with many German royal and noble houses enhanced his diplomatic virtues. He was an uncle of Wilhelm II's consort, the Kaiserin Augusta Victoria, but made nothing out of his connection with the Hohenzollerns and refused the Kaiser's invitation to address him with the familiar *du*, reminding his sovereign that "kings have no relatives."[3]

Hohenlohe had served in the Reichstag in the early 1870s as a member of the National Liberal party, but as chancellor he would not be identified with any political faction. The argument for appointing Hohenlohe chancellor made by the Kaiser's uncle, Grand Duke Friedrich I of Baden, was that he, unlike anyone else who might be designated, stood above politics.[4] The Conservatives could find no fault with the new chancellor, who was both an aristocrat and a landed proprietor. Hohenlohe, moreover, had never been intimate with Caprivi and therefore had succeeded in maintaining friendly relations with Bismarck after his fall from office. It was a pity, Bismarck observed, that Hohenlohe had not been *his* heir.[5] In spite of Hohenlohe's Catholic piety, he was vigorously opposed to the Jesuits and the ultramontane movement in southern Germany. He was therefore acceptable to German liberals but at the same time had productive ties with the powerful Catholic Center. Hohenlohe thus would not suffer from the parliamentary alienation that had made Caprivi's position so difficult.

Although Hohenlohe had a rapport with the parliamentary factions that had eluded Caprivi, the new chancellor, like his predecessor, held the Reichstag in low regard. Hohenlohe went so far as to predict that some day the German people would call for its abolition.[6] As long as it existed, however, the parliament would have to be treated exactly as one should treat the Kaiser—with caution and forebearance, not by assault but by skirmish. To Hohenlohe, the art of governing, whether in dealing with the crown or the Reichstag, was learning to be satisfied with incremental victories and basing action on tactical considerations rather than on principles. While Caprivi, whose "New Course" had some sense of positive direction, would make an issue out of the least difficulty he had with the Kaiser, Hohenlohe had a limited concept of what general character his administration should attempt to embody and tended to be inert except when provoked or in full pursuit of a plan he was determined to implement. With such an attitude, the new chancellor seemed likely to place few barriers in the way of the Kaiser's autocratic pretensions.

The difference in the degree of resolution with which Caprivi and Hohenlohe treated the Kaiser was due not only to a difference in temperament. Caprivi's forthrightness, which had so annoyed Wilhelm, reflected the fact that he had neither sought nor later wished to retain his position as chancellor. Caprivi was without ambition and, as a bachelor long inured to an austere military existence, had no need of the office's salary or other emoluments. Hohenlohe, on the other hand, had good reason to want to remain chancellor as long as possible, for the pay and the perquisites were imperative in order to stem the financial decline in which he and Princess Hohenlohe found themselves in the late 1890s.[7] The chancellor and his large family lived in an elegant, costly style for which the Hohenlohe estates in Bavaria no longer provided adequate revenues, while the Princess's vast Russian holdings were threatened with sequestration. In being submissive to Wilhelm II, Hohenlohe was not only following his instincts but also his financial interests.

Hohenlohe was under no illusions about his imperial master, and at the beginning of his chancellorship he, like Caprivi four years earlier, recognized that his role would be difficult. Bismarck warned Hohenlohe that his problem as chancellor would be the Kaiser's interference in affairs of state. Hohenlohe knew from past experience that Wilhelm II was assertive and volatile and may even have entertained a suspicion that he was temperamentally unstable.[8] In the early 1890s, Hohenlohe had often told Chancellor Caprivi that he was relieved not to be in his position. Dumbfounded by his selection as chancellor, Hohenlohe reluctantly agreed to the Kaiser's summons to come to Berlin and declared that only his sense of duty compelled him to accept the post. "Let us hope," he wrote to his wife on the day of his appointment, "that the lucky star which has never deserted me will remain faithful."[9]

Hohenlohe did not expect much from the Kaiser in the way of gratitude, and he knew that he would not have the sort of confidential, and dominating, relationship that Bismarck had enjoyed with Wilhelm II's grandfather, but he nevertheless believed that he could be effective in guiding the sovereign. At the outset of his chancellorship, Hohenlohe decided that at least for the time being the most fruitful way to deal with Wilhelm, one which also suited the chancellor's unobtrusive manner, would be to avoid confrontation or even criticism. Challenging the Kaiser, Hohenlohe believed, would only lead to a perpetual crisis between crown and chancellor and serve to undermine the monarchical principle. It was better, he reasoned, to tolerate the foolish things Wilhelm occasionally did and said rather than to criticize him and thereby diminish Germany's prestige abroad. "I have been called to office to create calm, not to further a politics of conflict," the new chancellor declared.[10] After he had established himself in office, Hohenlohe thought that he might be able to grapple more forcefully with Wilhelm,[11] but in fact the chancellor never developed any taste for contradiction, and a sort of quiescent deference became the fundamental ingredient of his relationship with the ruler. Hohenlohe did not deluge Wilhelm with letters of resignation, as Caprivi had when unable to get his way, nor did he bluster and rage like the vulcanian Bismarck. The chancellor's submissive behavior, added to his wispy physical appearance, belied his inner tenacity. Although Hohenlohe's manner seemed to betray a weakness of will, for which he was reproached, his calm and retiring demeanor was often effective in securing from the Kaiser what he wanted. In the long run, Hohenlohe's patience was considerably more productive than Caprivi's recalcitrance or the Iron Chancellor's imperiousness.

The Kaiser did not always enjoy Hohenlohe's deft manner. He irritably complained to Philipp Eulenburg that the ever-agreeable Hohenlohe airily misinterpreted what were intended as orders as mere "agreements" (*Abmachungen*), declaring that they were unfeasible and had to be dropped.[12] But Wilhelm found that it was a relief to have an unassuming chancellor after the hardheaded and didactic Caprivi, even though he found "the old imperial fool" (*alte Reichsschaute*) Hohenlohe, who was habitually taciturn and slightly deaf, an unfortunate draw as a dinner partner. "I am so delighted with old Hohenlohe and everything goes so beautifully and nicely," Wilhelm wrote to Eulenburg a few months after the new chancellor took office. "We have no secrets from one another and I feel as though I were in paradise."[13] The Kaiser had earlier used the same celestial metaphor to describe his infatuation with Caprivi. As with Caprivi, Wilhelm would eventually come down to earth with Hohenlohe, but for the moment Hohenlohe himself had to admit that insofar as the Kaiser was concerned "*tout est couleur de rose.*"[14] The honeymoon was brief, and the chancellor soon found that like his predecessor he had to deal with an erratic sovereign who preferred his military retinue to his civilian advisors. Although Caprivi had succeeded in reducing the independence of the military attachés and helped to get rid of the chief of the General Staff, General von Waldersee, the Kaiser's adjutants and high military officials continued to have easy access to Wilhelm, who was very susceptible to their influence. Hohenlohe had been in office less than a year and a half when he declared to his wife that "the occult government of the aides-de-camp is a calamity."[15] Almost from the start, the chancellor had to struggle to win the Kaiser's ear, much less his approval.

Hohenlohe's second-in-command was the state secretary of the Foreign Office, Baron Adolf Marschall von Bieberstein. Like the chancellor, Marschall was a South German (although from Baden and a Protestant) but in every other respect he was quite unlike his chief. Marschall, who had been trained as a lawyer rather than a diplomat, had little experience in European diplomacy and none of the courtly grace and polish that Hohenlohe possessed in abundance, being instead notable for his pugnacity and rudeness. Hohenlohe, however, valued Marschall highly for his knowledgeability in economic affairs, for which the chancellor had little interest or understanding. Even more useful to Hohenlohe was Marschall's rhetorical skill in representing the government before the Reichstag, for Hohenlohe had a thin voice and often experienced difficulty finding his place as he read his prepared texts.

Marschall, unlike the chancellor, relished confrontation, his litigious personality showing to advantage on the floor of the Reichstag, where his long association with the Catholic faction in Baden won him much support among the Catholic Center's numerous deputies. For all his parliamentary talents, Marschall nevertheless labored under a great difficulty, because the Kaiser, who in 1890 had not been eager to appoint him state secretary, never developed any liking for him. As a South German and a lawyer, Marschall was doubly suspect to Wilhelm II, who found his bad manners and philistine tastes offensive.[16] The Kaiser did not like to be outshone, and he was jealous of Marschall's bravura before the Reichstag.[17] Marschall reciprocated in full Wilhelm's lack of enthusiasm, admitting that while the Kaiser possessed intellectual powers, his ideas were anachronistic and his manner superficial and affected.[18] What was worse, in Marschall's opinion, was Wilhelm's inclination to regard himself as an accomplished diplomat, ever ready to interfere in the Foreign Office's conduct of Germany's relations with other powers and too inclined to use extravagant language in the audiences he granted to foreign diplomats. "A monarch must have the final word," Marschall admitted, "but H[is] M[ajesty] always wants to have the first one as well. That is a cardinal error."[19]

As a result of Hohenlohe's passivity and Marschall's preference for parliamentary rather than diplomatic affairs, Friedrich von Holstein, the senior counsellor in the Foreign Office, had ample opportunity to increase his already great influence. Holstein and Hohenlohe were old friends, for Holstein had served under the chancellor in Paris in the early 1870s and had kept up a steady correspondence with him ever since.[20] The pursuit of two goals dominated Holstein's activity under Hohenlohe. First, the exile of the Bismarcks, father and son, had to be perpetuated, since both considered Holstein to be their premier enemy, responsible for their fall from power in 1890. To Holstein, the Bismarcks' return to favor would endanger his influential position in the Foreign Office and would, besides, result in a reorientation of German diplomacy in favor of Russia, a policy to which Holstein was opposed. Holstein's second aim was to limit the Kaiser's authority and especially his interference in diplomacy, for he considered Wilhelm's personality very unsuited to such a role. Shelving the Bismarcks and the Kaiser would mean that Holstein himself would emerge as the hidden arbiter of German diplomacy. His friend Hohenlohe represented no threat, nor did Marschall, since his interests were essentially parliamentary. Holstein had every confidence that he could trust the state secretary to carry out his directives and indeed threatened to resign his position if Marschall were to be replaced.

Holstein misjudged Wilhelm II, however, and the Kaiser's resistance to any limitation of his prerogative jeopardized and eventually ruined Holstein's ambitious plan. The Kaiser was not without influential allies in his determination to assert the crown's prerogative. Philipp Eulenburg steadily encouraged Wilhelm to uphold, and indeed to expand, monarchical authority, and Holstein's efforts to convince Eulenburg that the Kaiser's intrusion in diplomacy was dangerous made no headway. Within the Prussian ministry there was a faction headed by the interior minister, Ernst von Köller, whose twin principles were that nothing should be allowed to infringe on the crown's power or on the political and economic hegemony of Prussia's agrarian aristocracy. Köller had a supporter in his ambitious colleague, Finance Minister Johannes Miquel, one of the leaders of the National Liberal party. Although Miquel had vainly hoped that he might succeed Caprivi, he continued to regard himself as a future chancellor who would create a union (*Sammlung*) embracing both agriculture and business—indeed all the responsible elements in the Empire who abhorred socialism. Like Köller and Philipp Eulenburg, Miquel looked to Wilhelm II to provide Germany with the leadership it needed.[21]

Hohenlohe had little sympathy with this viewpoint. Like his predecessor Caprivi, he wished to preside over a government that would allow moderate reforms within a constitutional framework, adroitly restraining Wilhelm II from a too prominent role in German diplomacy and relegating the Reichstag to a role of secondary importance. In these aims, the chancellor's views coincided with those of Holstein, Marschall, and Karl Heinrich von Boetticher, the state secretary of the Imperial

Interior Office and a Prussian minister without portfolio, the three bureaucrats who had embodied the cautious progressivism of Caprivi's
"New Course." Hohenlohe considered Boetticher, who was an excellent
administrator and a trustworthy colleague, to be as indispensable as
Marschall. The aged chancellor's intense determination to retain these
two figures provoked periodic crises with the Kaiser from 1894 until
1897, when Marschall finally resigned to become ambassador in Constantinople and Boetticher was transferred to a position in the provincial
administration.

Hohenlohe, who as minister-president directed the Prussian ministry,
regarded the factional quarrels between his reactionary colleagues and
his own more moderate allies with the greatest distaste, telling his wife
that he felt as though he were a doctor in the midst of imbeciles engaged
in all sorts of stupidities.[22] But Hohenlohe raised hardly a finger against
the intrigues conducted by Miquel and his other rivals, much to the
annoyance of those ministers who hoped that he would take a firmer
lead in creating a Prussian ministry with a uniform outlook.[23] Instead
the chancellor usually took little initiative, declining to become involved
in factional disputes and hoping that his benign calm would eventually
make all the unpleasantness surrounding him go away. Only under severe pressure did Hohenlohe bestir himself and assert a position of leadership. On such occasions he proved surprisingly effective.

In addition to finding a strategy that would enable him to survive
the quarrels of his subordinates, Hohenlohe had also to deal with the
omnipresent spectre of Bismarck, who in his self-imposed exile on his
estate at Friedrichsruh near Hamburg broadcast his opinions through the
press.[24] In many inspired articles (and in multitudinous interviews) Bismarck gave vent to his outrage at his dismissal, and while he did not
criticize the Kaiser openly, he heaped criticism on his successor, General
Caprivi. "I once had a high opinion of Caprivi," the former chancellor
told a Bavarian newspaper editor in a typical indulgence of malice. "But
I have been very much disappointed. In many ways he has no greater
intelligence than a rather old major who suddenly has been promoted to
head a school for noncommissioned officers."[25]

Hohenlohe never questioned Bismarck's great ability, but as viceroy of
Alsace-Lorraine he had stubbornly resisted the Iron Chancellor's puni-
tive notions about dealing with French troublemakers in the captured
provinces. After 1890, he had sympathized with Caprivi in the assaults
Bismarck had openly made on his successor and, by implication, on the
Kaiser. Hohenlohe had no wish to see his own regime crippled by this

sort of animosity, and he refused to associate himself with the anti-Bismarck fronde which centered around Holstein. The chancellor had a number of friends, drawn largely from conservative circles, who urged him to effect a reconciliation between Wilhelm II and Bismarck. On the other hand, Holstein argued adamantly against any rapprochement, and he had confederates, including Philipp Eulenburg, who saw in Bismarck's return to favor a threat to their own influence on the Kaiser.

From the moment of his departure from Berlin on 29 March 1890, the fallen chancellor made it clear that he felt he had been ill-served by Wilhelm II, who, he declared, had "flung" (*herausgeschmissen*) him out of office.[26] Wilhelm declared that he was indifferent to Bismarck's claim that he had been summarily dismissed, but he was determined to prevent the former chancellor from using the press to stir up public opinion against the crown and the government. Wilhelm privately declared that Bismarck might have to be jailed if he continued to make remarks that were not only lèse majesté but in fact treasonous; he believed Herbert Bismarck also to be guilty.[27] On reflection, the Kaiser decided that a martyred Bismarck would be even more dangerous, but nevertheless he continued to speculate on the charges he could bring against his former chancellor.[28] In a plain reference to Bismarck, Wilhelm declared in a speech in Düsseldorf in May 1891, a month after Bismarck had been elected to the Reichstag as a National Liberal, that "there is only one ruler in this Empire and I am he. I will tolerate no one else."[29]

The boast was easier proclaimed than upheld, however, and the Kaiser had to admit that Bismarck's opposition placed him in a difficult position.[30] Once Moltke had been laid in his grave in 1891, the Iron Chancellor was the only surviving national hero and an object of enormous popular veneration. Even out of office, Bismarck had powerful friends among the East Elbian aristocracy, in industrial circles in Silesia and the Rhineland, as well as a wide following in South Germany. The government, the court, and the military establishment all contained men known to be strongly attached to him, while in the Reichstag the former chancellor had a number of allies in the Conservative and National Liberal parties. The Kaiser knew quite well that Bismarck's archives, securely deposited at Friedrichsruh, constituted a further weapon in the former chancellor's arsenal, for they held letters from Wilhelm II which contained indelicate criticisms of statesmen and rulers both in Germany and abroad.[31] And Bismarck was of course in possession of countless diplomatic secrets, revelation of which could cause the Kaiser and his chancellor the greatest embarrassment. From a distance, the former chancellor therefore continued to exercise his old suzerainty in Berlin, where he was handled with great deference and no little trepidation. "Fear of Bismarck is the reigning epidemic in Berlin," Hohenlohe noted not long after becoming chancellor. "It's disgusting."[32]

The disaffection between Wilhelm II and Bismarck was thus more than a personal feud, for it threatened the orderly progress of the government by dividing imperial Germany between its heroic founder and the ruler. Anyone with an interest in the status quo could only regret the increasing polarization of the two camps, since the socialists, who had little use either for the Bismarckian legacy or for the Kaiser, would inevitably profit by a breakdown in the traditional alliance between crown and bureaucracy. A reconciliation was therefore imperative, and as the duel between Wilhelm and Bismarck became more and more intense, a number of figures worked to repair the breach. The former chancellor's great age and precarious health made it essential that the rapprochement not be delayed, since, as Wilhelm well realized, if Bismarck should die unpardoned, his adherents would never forgive the Kaiser.[33]

The problem lay in arranging to bring the two men together in a way that would be mutually satisfactory. Bismarck's resentment at the events of March 1890 did not diminish with time, and he was determined that a reconciliation would have to be staged in such a way as to assuage his injured pride. Since, in the chancellor's opinion, his dismissal had been a sign of imperial disfavor, Wilhelm II alone could indicate that he had returned to grace.[34] Consequently he insisted that the initiative would have to come from the Kaiser. When the question of a reconciliation was broached to Wilhelm II, he agreed to consider such a move, for his animosity centered less on the former chancellor than on Herbert Bismarck, who he believed was responsible for encouraging his father's intransigence. But the Kaiser was as insistent as Bismarck that the first step had to come from the other party. "He must [come] on his knees, on his knees," the Kaiser reportedly decreed.[35] Wilhelm furthermore insisted that any overture by Bismarck would have to be made according to his directions. "He must in a completely *unequivocal way write directly to me* to formulate his request or wish to be allowed to approach me," the Kaiser told General Waldersee, one of the leading exponents of reconciliation, in June 1892.[36] Waldersee had an abiding hatred for Chancellor Caprivi, whom he held responsible for his dismissal as chief of the General Staff, and hoped that a return of the Bismarcks to favor would topple his enemy.[37]

The deteriorating relationship between the Kaiser and his former chancellor reached a crisis in the summer of 1892, on the occasion of Herbert Bismarck's marriage to Countess Marguerite von Hoyos on 22 June. Her wealthy parents lived in Fiume, but the Hoyos decided to have the wedding solemnized in Vienna, where the count had numerous connections in the high aristocracy. This arrangement may have been intended to spare the groom's aged mother and father the long trip to the Adriatic, but the impression in Vienna was that the Bismarcks chose the Habsburg capital in order to maximize the political overtones of the event.[38] Given the prominence of both the bride and the groom, the nuptials would be a notable event of the summer season in Vienna. Caprivi saw the wedding as an opportunity to take his revenge against the fallen chancellor, who, he noted, had done all he could to make his life unpleasant. The chancellor's sense of honor, probably reinforced by his desire to settle old scores, decreed that Bismarck, who had so persistently criticized his own sovereign and refused to make any conciliatory gestures, should not be accorded any honors by other rulers.[39] Holstein, anxious to diminish the Bismarcks' standing in any possible way, concurred and persuaded Eulenburg to exert his influence in this direction with the Kaiser.[40]

Wilhelm agreed that Bismarck was trying to use his visit to Vienna to create a political demonstration. This would be regarded as an attack on the Kaiser, and Wilhelm was therefore concerned to deprive the wedding of any political significance. The Kaiser also wished to punish the former chancellor for his behavior since his fall from office and for the hostile tone Bismarck had adopted in his recent conversations and press interviews toward Germany's ally Austria-Hungary.[41] He therefore agreed to Caprivi's suggestion that the chancellor inform the German ambassador in Vienna, Prince Heinrich VII Reuss, for many years one of Bismarck's closest associates, that neither the envoy nor any member of his staff was to attend the ceremony.[42] Furthermore, Wilhelm wrote what Bismarck later castigated as "Uriah letter" to the Emperor Franz Josef, who had already signified to Reuss his willingness to grant Bismarck an audience, asking him not to receive the former chancellor. In his letter to his Austrian colleague, the Kaiser described Bismarck as an enemy of the Habsburg Empire who intended his son's wedding to be a political sensation. "In my own interests and those of my government may I ask you as a true friend not to complicate my position here by receiving a *disobedient servant* before he has approached me and confessed his sins."[43] Although Wilhelm's request caused Franz Josef considerable embarrassment, he had no choice but to cancel his agreement to receive Bismarck.

In revenge, Bismarck, who had not originally intended his trip to and from the wedding as a political foray, now with rancor turned it into exactly that. Leaving Friedrichsruh on 18 June 1892, and making his way to tumultuous ovations wherever he stopped, the former chancellor's "*grossdeutsche Rundfahrt*" ceased only with his return to his estate at Varzin in Pomerania in early August. In his stopovers in Dresden, Munich, Kissingen, and Jena, and at dozens of places en route where his train did not even halt, an extraordinary outpouring of devotion and sympathy inundated the ex-chancellor. Since Wilhelm II was his manifest enemy, the demonstrations for Bismarck could only be considered expressions of disapproval of the Kaiser. Bismarck's frequent public addresses and newspaper interviews while on his trip were rich in veiled references to the Kaiser, but they quite openly denounced Caprivi.

Wilhelm II was enraged at this assault by the "rebel" Bismarck, and he declared that if the former chancellor persisted in attacking him, he would have him thrown into the royal prison at Spandau in northern Berlin or have him restricted to his estates. "I will not hesitate to take these measures," he warned Eulenburg.[44] In spite of his threats, the Kaiser did not move against his old chancellor, perhaps out of fear that Bismarck might retaliate by publishing the intemperate letters Wilhelm had written years earlier to Tsar Alexander III, in which he had belittled his parents as well as the Prince of Wales, publication of which would be singularly embarrassing.[45]

The battle dragged on without much change through the rest of 1892 and into 1893, when, in August, Bismarck fell seriously ill and fear spread that he might not recover. Wilhelm felt that he could not allow the great man to die without having achieved some sort of rapprochement, so he now made the first tentative move toward a restoration of good relations. The Kaiser offered his former chancellor the use of one of his castles as a place of recuperation, but Bismarck politely declined. The ice nevertheless was broken. In January 1894 Wilhelm heard once again that Bismarck was ailing (although this time only with a cold) and sent him a letter expressing his hope for an early recovery as well as a fine bottle of Steinberg Kabinett Trockenbeerenauslese, vintage 1862, the year Bismarck had become minister-president of Prussia. In deciding to make these gestures, Wilhelm had not consulted Chancellor Caprivi, whose great antipathy to Bismarck made him an opponent of reconciliation. Berlin wits, Herbert Bismarck informed his father, called the Kaiser's offering the "Lacrimae Caprivi."[46]

Bismarck, now satisfied that the initiative in a reconciliation had come from the Kaiser, wrote Wilhelm a letter in which he expressed a wish to come to Berlin to thank him personally for his consideration.[47] On 26 January the former chancellor arrived in the capital to the frenzied greeting of a crowd of between 300,000 and 400,000 Berliners. Wilhelm tendered his old chancellor a formal dinner, during which he studiously avoided any mention of politics, and then accompanied Bismarck to the railroad station.[48] The Kaiser went aboard the old statesman's car and was observed several times clasping him cheek to cheek. Three weeks later, Wilhelm paid Bismarck a reciprocal visit at Friedrichsruh and the reconciliation was complete, if somewhat fragile. In private, Bismarck continued to criticize the Kaiser, who never learned that the chancellor had shared his bottle of Steinberger with one of Wilhelm's most outspoken adversaries, Maximilian Harden, the editor of the irreverent journal, *Die Zukunft*.[49]

Caprivi's fall from office nine months later, at the end of October 1894, removed a redoubtable opponent standing in the way of a complete restoration of Bismarck to favor. Hohenlohe and the former chancellor had no grievances against one another, and many years later in exile in Holland Wilhelm went so far as to claim, perhaps with some truth, that he had chosen Hohenlohe in order to minimize Bismarck's damaging criticism of the government.[50] Hohenlohe was certainly anxious to begin his administration on the right foot and therefore in February 1895 paid a courtesy visit to Friedrichsruh.

Bismarck would celebrate his eightieth birthday on 1 April 1895, an event which occupied the attention of the German public during the winter of 1894–95. As the day approached, cities and organizations framed fulsome resolutions honoring the former chancellor, presents were sent to Friedrichsruh, and legislatures throughout Germany prepared congratulatory addresses. What might have become an occasion of national consolidation proved, however, to be a divisive event. It was in fact the first crisis of Hohenlohe's chancellorship, and his behavior revealed the advantages that this apparently weak and vacillating aristocrat actually brought to the post. On 23 March the Conservative faction in the Reichstag, supported by a number of National Liberal deputies, introduced a motion calling for the parliament officially to convey birthday congratulations to Bismarck. The Catholic Center, which had generally supported Caprivi and which Bismarck had repeatedly attacked in the press and in his speeches during the wedding journey of 1892, would have no part in felicitating its enemy on his longevity. After a lengthy debate, a coalition of Centrists, Socialists, Progressives, anti-Semites, and national minority parties (Poles, Danes, Alsatians, and Hanoverians, all of whom had old grudges against the former chancellor) defeated the Conservative-Liberal resolution. The result was a widespread wave of sympathy for Bismarck.

Wilhelm II had for years been contemptuous of the Reichstag and only recently had referred to it as the "imperial monkey house" (*Reichsaffenhaus*). He at once expressed his "deepest irritation" at the Reichstag's decision.[51] The former chancellor's birthday celebration now emerged as the occasion of a battle between crown and parliament as well as one between Bismarck's friends and enemies. On 26 March Wilhelm went to Friedrichsruh and with ostentatious military pomp greeted the former chancellor. It was a clever performance, for the martial panoply as well as the Kaiser's speech honoring Bismarck the faithful soldier accentuated his determination that the old chancellor, an honorary field marshal in the Prussian army, was in the future to consider himself an obedient officer rather than a refractory statesman.

As for the Reichstag, the Kaiser proposed to Hohenlohe that it be punished by dissolution, his expectation undoubtedly being that the resulting elections would produce a defeat for the parties that had insulted Bismarck. Hohenlohe had no wish to encourage the Kaiser in such a move, for it would result only in an intensification of the conflict between crown and parliament.[52] Moreover, if an election called specifically over the Bismarck birthday resolution had the successful result that Wilhelm anticipated, the government would thereafter be committed to the former chancellor's conservative, agrarian, protectionist ideas. Hohenlohe had little sympathy for such notions and was unwilling to lead a government that advocated them, even though he was candid enough to admit that he himself had no program that could be marshaled to serve as a banner for an election campaign. If, in the wake of an election that vindicated the old chancellor, Hohenlohe resigned rather than agree to carry out a Bismarckian program, the Kaiser would have little choice other than to ask the Iron Chancellor to resume his old office. Two chancellors would thus have resigned within a period of six months, a development that would reveal an unmistakable weakness in Wilhelm II's ability to lead his country. If, on the other hand, the Bismarck clique lost the election, the Kaiser's reputation would suffer, and Hohenlohe would be left to confront a hostile legislature.

Hohenlohe pointed out all these considerations to the Kaiser, advising him that the best course would be to wait to see if the public outcry against the Reichstag's treatment of Bismarck continued. If the protest kept up its momentum, which Hohenlohe doubted that it would, then a dissolution might eventually be ordered, but in such a way as to make it appear that it had occurred not by the Kaiser's will but by the irresistible tide of public opinion. The chancellor succeeded in persuading Wilhelm that this was the correct approach, and, as Hohenlohe had predicted, the excitement surrounding the birthday resolution abated and was eventually forgotten. Delay had dissipated a crisis, a tactic that Hohenlohe would repeatedly employ during his chancellorship.

One reason for Hohenlohe's reluctance to press forward with an attack on the anti-Bismarck parties was his awareness of how transitory the attachment of various factions in the Reichstag was to the causes they adopted. Positions ardently defended one day might be casually abandoned the next. In making his argument to the Kaiser for proceeding cautiously with the Reichstag, Hohenlohe referred specifically to another difficulty the government had experienced with the legislature. This was the controversy surrounding a proposed bill treating the "modification and extension of the civil and military punishment codes and the press law," known in abbreviated form as the "anti-revolution" (*Umsturz*) bill.

The electoral victories by socialist candidates in the Reichstag elections of 1890 and 1893, the virulent attacks by the socialists and left liberals on the whole monarchical-aristocratic structure of Prussia, and the terrorism conducted elsewhere in Europe by anarchists (whose most recent assassination victim had been President Carnot of France, stabbed to death in June 1894) persuaded the right and middle parties in the Reichstag that some alteration in the existing laws against sedition were necessary. This seemed all the more imperative by the mid-1890s because protests against the Kaiser's caesarian personality had even seeped into the "responsible" upper classes. University faculties, the army officer corps, and its noble kinsmen in society, once the principle bastion of Hohenzollern loyalty, were now riddled with critics.[53] The boldest expression of dissatisfaction was Ludwig Quidde's *Caligula* (1894), in which Wilhelm II was implicitly compared to the insanely irresponsible Roman emperor, who had died the victim of assassination. Many conservative Prussians, including those who had no use for Wilhelm personally, found these attacks on the Hohenzollern crown intolerable.

The Kaiser, who was both offended and enraged by this hostility, agreed that something needed to be done to fortify the position of the crown and the responsible elements of society. The entire edifice of German society, Wilhelm argued, had been dangerously undermined on one side by socialism and on the other by Bismarck, whose opposition to the Kaiser had diminished the respect loyal citizens should accord the monarch. Even his bureaucrats, Wilhelm complained with particular reference to Finance Minister Johannes Miquel, failed to understand how important the maintenance of royal supremacy was. In the Kaiser's opinion, the only antidote to these dangers was to insist the more strongly on Hohenzollern authority, to stand firm with other rulers against the insidious influence of France, and at home to deal more firmly with troublemakers. "The French axiom that 'the King rules but does not govern' is basically false and indeed revolutionary. I do not wish to rule in a merely nominal way and I will not do so, but instead intend to be the actual sovereign in the interest of my people."[54]

Meanwhile, the Kaiser had to silence his critics. In July 1894, just after Carnot's assassination, Wilhelm had ordered Caprivi to draft a bill that would introduce stiffer penalties for incitement to breaches of law and order than those provided in existing legislation. By the time the chancellor was dismissed from office the following October, he had prepared such an "antirevolution" bill, which Hohenlohe eventually adopted as his own. The measure specified draconian punishment for any subversive remarks about religion, the monarchy, marriage, the family, or property. Early in 1895 the bill came before the Reichstag, where it was defeated by a coalition of socialists, whose behavior made them the putative if unnamed objects of the proposed law, and National Liberals, who believed that Hohenlohe's ulterior purpose was to repress freedom of expression not only by socialists and anarchists but also by the educated bourgeoisie. The Kaiser was enormously displeased, and he imprudently sent an open telegram to the chancellor advising him that in the future the government, deprived by the Reichstag of a strong law against insurrection, would have no alternative but to combat disorder with fire hoses, or, in extreme cases, with grapeshot.[55]

The Kaiser's insistence on curbing the socialists was reactivated a few months later when *Vorwärts* and other socialist newspapers used the laying of the foundation stone of a massive monument in Berlin to Wilhelm I to attack the old Emperor, the founder of the German Empire. The Kaiser was enraged that the socialists had made such a slur on his much-beloved grandfather, one that had occurred only because the existing "liberal, Jew-inspired law" provided absolutely no punishment for such offenses. Wilhelm insisted that the public outrage, which was enormous, be used to instigate a press campaign against the socialists. This barrage would prepare the ground for a strong antisocialist law that would export agitators to the provinces as well as for a bill providing imprisonment for anyone making a verbal slur on a deceased German ruler.

Once again, Hohenlohe's response was typically cautious.[56] Past experience had shown that the Social Democratic party could operate successfully even when deprived of its right of assembly. An antisocialist measure such as Wilhelm wanted would only drive the socialists into more intense opposition and strengthen the conviction of the politically reliable elements in Germany that the government's attack on the party was in fact a ruse designed to promote an increase in the authority of the crown. The German electorate feared despotism even more than socialism, and therefore it would not approve an antisocialist law. Besides, Hohenlohe believed that the outrage against the socialists' treatment of Wilhelm I would eventually dissipate, leaving the government with no swell of public opinion on which to rest either an antisocialist bill or one against slandering a dead sovereign. What the Kaiser should do, in Hohenlohe's opinion, was to behave with moderation and restraint even under provocation (such as the socialists had provided in abundance on this occasion), in order to show that he was a responsible ruler bent on the national good rather than obtaining his own satisfaction. "Only when the people are convinced, as they are in England, that their progress toward freedom will not be shaken," Hohenlohe counseled, "will it decide to vote conservatively."[57] The chancellor's prescription was to let the matter drag on without attempting to introduce any bills whatsoever, and he eventually managed to convince the reluctant Kaiser that this was the best policy, at least for the moment.

Wilhelm II's willingness to let the antisocialist and slander laws lie in abeyance was due in part to the fact that by the fall of 1895 he had become involved in an issue that concerned him even more than the threat represented by socialism. This was a military matter related to the socialist issue, in that in the absence of a law against sedition, the Kaiser considered the army to be the sole guardian of order. In 1892, with great misgivings, Wilhelm had agreed to a reduction in the term of service in the Prussian army from three to two years, a reform that Chancellor Caprivi had promoted as a popular political measure but to which much of the officer corps had been opposed. Caprivi intended to make further reforms, and for this purpose he had secured the appointment of General Walter Bronsart von Schellendorf as war minister in 1893; to Bronsart would fall the responsibility of representing the government's proposed legislation before the Reichstag. Bronsart, although a Prussian and a man of conservative inclinations, was determined to press on with the task of modernizing the Hohenzollern army. As far as he was concerned, the Kaiser was an impediment to such progress, for he interfered constantly, and in an irresponsible fashion, in military affairs, preferring the advice of courtiers who, Bronsart declared, should be led to the scaffold.[58] Bronsart had a didactic manner that got on Wilhelm's nerves and a will that was quite as pronounced as the Kaiser's. The two men soon fell out with one another.[59]

As part of his reform, Bronsart wished to introduce into Prussia a revision of the military code of 1845 in order to provide for public access to military trials except those in which military secrets might be revealed. In this way, the army was to become less liable to the frequently leveled accusation that it put itself above the law. In the early 1880s the army had planned an alteration of the regulations that would have admitted spectators to all trials except in cases where to do so might endanger national security or public morals.[60] Wilhelm I's opposition had quashed the proposal, but a number of Prussian generals persisted in arguing for a change of the court-martial proceedings. The Reichstag had repeatedly framed resolutions calling for such a reform, which was widely supported in public opinion. Most European nations had introduced such a practice, and it applied as well in several of the German states. Hohenlohe, as minister-president of Bavaria in 1869, had reformed Bavarian military trials in this way, and he therefore sided with Bronsart in his intention of extending the system to Prussia.

In the spring of 1895 Bronsart formulated such a bill. It immediately encountered sharp resistance from Wilhelm II, whose opposition was stiffened by a number of generals. Among these were Bronsart's enemy and the Kaiser's closest military advisor, General Wilhelm von Hahnke, the chief of the Military Cabinet, and Wilhelm's old friend, General Adolf von Bülow, now an adjutant. The Kaiser shared Hahnke's view that the Prussian army was a law unto itself, inviolate from any external scrutiny, especially that exercised by the Reichstag. "The army," Wilhelm II advised the Prussian ministry in 1895, "is an institution within the state that is contained in itself and which, according to the constitution, in both war and peace is subject exclusively to my orders and my action. It is to remain just so."[61] The Kaiser informed both Hohenlohe and Bronsart that he would never approve such a change in army regulations, and this declaration, as far as Wilhelm was concerned, was the end of the matter.[62] To Bronsart, however, admitting the public to courts-martial was a military matter of urgency that he intended to pursue even against the Kaiser's wishes. In October 1895 he presented to the Prussian ministry the draft of a bill allowing public trials, hoping to secure its consent before approaching the House of Deputies (*Landtag*), the lower chamber of the Prussian parliament. The ministry, with the exception of the archconservative and prickly Ernst von Köller, interior minister, supported Bronsart and, in doing so, openly challenged the Kaiser.

Köller's opposition to Bronsart's determination to make military trials open to the public matured into the so-called "Köller crisis," which eventually was to have a decisive impact on Wilhelm II and many of his advisors. A long-established tradition decreed that the proceedings of the Prussian ministry were to be kept confidential. Only the minister-president had the authority to communicate to the crown what transpired in its meetings until a bill based on the deliberations emerged in the House of Deputies. Contrary to this procedure, details of a ministry sitting dealing with courts-martial reform appeared in the press, and the source was easily determined to be a talk Köller had had with two of the Kaiser's adjutants, one of whom admitted that the minister had been his informant.[63] Furthermore, Köller had recently been on a hunt with Wilhelm and had revealed to him details of the discussions. At a meeting of the ministry on 18 November, Bronsart accused Köller of being the leak through whom its deliberations had become public. Köller reluctantly admitted the charge, whereupon Bronsart declared that he could no longer attend meetings of the ministry if Köller were present.[64] Köller's purpose, he claimed, was to make himself the angel of the military and at the same time undermine Wilhelm II's confidence in the war minister.[65] Köller on the other hand took the position that his discussion with the Kaiser's adjutants had been "completely harmless" and concerned merely the contents of Bronsart's bill. He declared that he had made no mention of the ministry's discussion of the measure.[66]

The other ministers, some more readily than others, all eventually sided with Bronsart and believed that what was involved was not a personal difference between the general and Köller but an issue of principle that separated the interior minister from the rest of his colleagues.[67] Köller had an abrasive personality, and his fiercely reactionary speeches before the Reichstag had more than once embarrassed the other ministers, who also resented the dissension he caused by his pedantic exposition of these views. They found Köller's breach of confidentiality appalling and suspected that he was trying to curry favor with the Kaiser by identifying himself as the solitary opponent of Bronsart's proposed reform.[68] Hohenlohe shared the general dislike of Köller and reminded him that only the minister-president had the right to inform the Kaiser about the proceedings in the Prussian ministry.[69] Hohenlohe probably hoped that his admonition would suffice to shelve the matter, but it quickly became apparent that the indignation of his ministerial associates toward Köller was so great that failure to take action would undoubtedly result in a number of resignations. Meanwhile both Holstein and Marschall, who had considerable influence on Hohenlohe, advised him to take a strong stand. The minister-president, fortified by this support, decided to act, for in his opinion Köller's retention would destroy both the ministry's independence and his ability to lead it.[70] In a move without antecedent in living memory, Hohenlohe informed the Kaiser that the entire ministry insisted on Köller's resignation, and that if it were not forthcoming he and every one of the ministers would resign.

The collective remonstrance of the ministry enraged Wilhelm II, who regarded it as an unprecedented violation of Prussian royal prerogative.[71] "I," he proclaimed, "dismiss my ministers myself."[72] It was also the rankest ingratitude. What, the Kaiser declared with extraordinary self-deception, could be easier than to serve a sovereign who with one hand gave his ministers their portfolios and with the other his complete confidence and the right to do as they pleased?[73] Köller struck the Kaiser as the only Prussian minister who understood that he was a servant of the Hohenzollern king and not the creature of his ministerial brethren.[74] Unlike the others, Köller was not afraid to take firm measures against civil disturbances. In light of the Reichstag's refusal to pass a law against revolution, the belligerency that had so annoyed Köller's colleagues was to the Kaiser a trait that argued strongly in favor of his retention in the ministry.[75]

Wilhelm was determined to extract a "concession" from the ministers to atone for the humiliation to which they had tried to subject him.[76] He was not entirely sure whom to blame for the Köller crisis. Nominally, of course, Hohenlohe was responsible, but the Kaiser found it hard to believe that "Uncle Chlodwig" should bear the onus. It was the chancellor's great age, the Kaiser imagined, or the pernicious influence of Interior Minister Boetticher that had led him to endorse this extraordinary act by his colleagues. Even so, the Köller affair prompted Wilhelm II to speculate who might be available to replace Hohenlohe as chancellor.[77] If Hohenlohe was not to be saddled with the responsibility, it could be laid on Marschall, whom the Kaiser on occasion declared was the driving force in the affair, determined to topple Köller because he was Wilhelm II's ally. Once again, Marschall had shown that his errant South

German notions of constitutional monarchy were in conflict with the true nature of Prussian kingship.[78] Then, of course, there was Bronsart, who, Wilhelm claimed (when he was not indicting Marschall or Boetticher) was the linchpin of the disgraceful business. The Kaiser would have liked to remove him from office at once, but he found himself in an unfortunate position. If Bronsart were forced to resign, this would be interpreted as an imperial rejection of the military courts bill then being considered by the ministry, which would lead to a strong negative reaction throughout Germany. If, on the other hand, the Kaiser did not accede to the ministry's demand that Köller be forced from office, not only Bronsart but all the other ministers would resign, which would be even worse. Moreover, Hohenlohe made it clear that in that event he too would surrender office, for it would be ridiculous for him to disapprove as chancellor the same military reform he had earlier successfully championed as head of the Bavarian government. For the Kaiser to lose two chancellors in just over a year would constitute an intolerable humiliation for the crown.

Wilhelm therefore tried to persuade Hohenlohe and the ministry to agree that Köller be granted a face-saving leave of absence, but they would have no part of such a compromise.[79] There was consequently nothing for the Kaiser to do but allow Köller to resign, which he did on 8 December 1895. To advertise the esteem he had for the fallen minister, Wilhelm awarded Köller a high decoration, allowed him formally to retain his title as minister, and tried in vain to persuade him to accept the governorship of one or another of the leading Prussian provinces. The Kaiser proposed two candidates to succeed Köller, but Hohenlohe and the ministry declared them unsuitable. In spite of his boast that *he* alone appointed Prussian ministers, Wilhelm knew that to persist might lead to whosesale resignations. He therefore backed down, and finally Baron Eberhard von der Recke von dem Horst, the president of the government of Düsseldorf, whom Hohenlohe and the ministry found palatable, took over Köller's post.

Wilhelm refused to entertain any suggestion that he had not behaved properly in the Köller crisis. He sought to shore up his dignity by informing the ministry in writing on the day following Köller's resignation that its action was by no means to be construed as a precedent for further incursions on the royal prerogative.[80] As had happened before, it was Philipp Eulenburg who came to the Kaiser's rescue. He was alarmed that Wilhelm's excitability over Köller's fall could lead either to some inappropriate act of revenge or to an emotional collapse, which would be even worse.[81] Eulenburg believed that, first of all, it was essential that Köller's dismissal be advertised as a gracious accommodation by the Kaiser to Hohenlohe and *not* a surrender to the collective will of the Prussian ministry.[82] Second, there was the question of what to do with Bronsart, whose insistence on opening the courts-martial to the public had triggered the crisis. Eulenburg's sympathies were entirely with Wilhelm, but he realized that the effect on public opinion of letting Bronsart go would be disastrous. He therefore proposed that the Kaiser solicit the seventeen commanding generals of the Prussian army for their opinions on the question of reform of the military justice system. This would take almost a year to accomplish, by which time the crisis might safely be defused.[83] Wilhelm accepted Eulenburg's plan, but he did not abandon his determination to prevent courts-martial from being made public, and he lay in wait for Bronsart until the right moment might arrive for his dismissal. Marschall would also pay for his sins by being sacked when a convenient opportunity arose.

The Köller crisis, which represented a quite novel challenge by the Prussian ministry to the crown, resulted in yet another humiliation for the Kaiser. In the first years of his reign he had failed completely to stem the tide of socialism, his personal diplomacy had alienated the Tsar, and the spread of criticism of his regime had penetrated to the upper reaches of society. Now even his own chancellor and ministers had engaged in public opposition. Wilhelm II's discomforture delighted German liberals and socialists, but the courtiers and officials who had every interest in preserving the privileged nature of monarchical society recognized that the Köller debacle might prove to be a unwelcome turning point in German dynastic politics.

The Kaiser's plight produced two quite different assessments in Berlin. One, principally advanced by Holstein and his protégés, was that the Prussian ministry, or the Kaiser's imperial officials, with the Köller precedent in mind, must now use collective action to force Wilhelm II to subordinate himself to his government. The result would be the elimination of any vestiges of personal rule and the elevation of the Prussian-imperial administration to the dominating position in Germany. In such a scheme, Holstein's own influence would of course become the commanding factor in diplomacy. The other view, which was forcefully advanced by Philipp Eulenburg, was that the Köller crisis had painfully illustrated how precarious the traditional absolutism of the monarchy was. A concerted effort therefore had to be made to strengthen the crown against all its enemies, be they in the ministry, in parliament, or among the citizenry at large. The Köller crisis late in 1895 thus placed Wilhelm II between two camps, both composed of the same aristocratic elements and both opposed to parliamentary hegemony. They were, however, antagonistic in their aims, for one wished to see the Kaiser's authority diminished in favor of the government, while the other worked for its expansion.[84]

Although Holstein, an eremitic bachelor, cared nothing for the external insignia of power such as titles and decorations, he aggressively countered any one whom he suspected of trying to contest his enormous authority in the Foreign Office.[85] Because of Holstein's reclusiveness, he met Wilhelm II only once, although the Kaiser conferred honors on him and recognized his singular influence, referring to him, as did many others, as the "grey eminence" of the Foreign Office.[86] Not the least of Holstein's virtues, in the Kaiser's opinion, was his identification as Bismarck's most prominent enemy. "Anyone who attacks Holstein," he declared a few months after Bismarck's resignation in 1890, "attacks me. I rely on Holstein and look upon him as a tower of strength even though I do not know him personally."[87] Even after his reconciliation in 1894 with the former chancellor, the Kaiser continued to place a high value on Holstein's diplomatic expertise.

To Holstein, Wilhelm II was the key to German diplomacy, for all decisions were ultimately his. From the very first week of the Kaiser's reign, Holstein had expressed concern about the personality of the new monarch. "I have the feeling," he wrote gloomily to Philipp Eulenburg on 21 June 1888, "that our young ruler has a will of his own that will—I hope not too often—prove decisive."[88] Holstein was prepared to admit that the Kaiser had some ability, although he added that this was all too often obscured by his unfortunate manner.[89] In Holstein's analysis, the Kaiser's drawbacks were his lack of resolution and the streak of fantasy that rendered him incapable of appreciating the consequences of his actions. As a diplomat, Holstein found the Kaiser to be an imperfect representative of Germany, for he was indiscreet and headstrong, incapable of patience or silence, and blind to the ruinous effect of his loquacity.[90] It was not always easy to take such a man seriously. Given these wayward traits, Wilhelm's worst failing consequently was his insistence on ruling Germany himself. "The Kaiser [as] his own imperial chancellor would be questionable in any circumstances," Holstein wrote in 1895, "but especially now under this impulsive and unfortunately very superficial ruler, who has no suspicion of law, of political precedent, of diplomatic history, and of personal relationships."[91] Diplomats accredited to Wilhelm II's court found that Holstein's analysis was entirely correct and that dealing with the Kaiser, in addition to being conversationally quite strenuous, was often very confusing. Count Nicholas von Osten-Sacken, the Russian ambassador in Berlin for many years, who was well disposed to Wilhelm and may serve as a good example, discovered that there was no predicting the Kaiser's ever-changing moods. An audience with Wilhelm II was little more than an imperial monologue, and Osten-Sacken found that Prussian officials were not dependable as sources of information, for they hesitated to express opinions for fear that the Kaiser would contradict tomorrow what he said today.[92]

At the beginning of his reign, Wilhelm II's forceful behavior was regarded as the natural product of an exuberant youth, free as a ruler to give full expression to his will. The new Kaiser began his reign in a burst of popularity. Even Herbert Bismarck, who often complained of the Kaiser's shortcomings, admitted in October 1888 that Wilhelm's conduct had been exemplary.[93] But by the following year, although many Germans continued to admire their young sovereign, disenchantment was gradually setting in. Wilhelm II's promise of being energetic and serious seemed, even to his admirer General Waldersee, actually to be an excess of restlessness and self-indulgence.[94] With Bismarck's dismissal in 1890, the Kaiser swiftly forfeited much of his popularity among the general public and alienated a good part of the army. The great statesman had been unceremoniously cast aside, and in his place now ruled a willful, incautious princeling.[95] Wilhelm II was aware of the decline in public regard, but he airily dismissed it as a necessary consequence of being a truly great ruler. "*What do I care for popularity!?*" he rhetorically asked Chancellor Caprivi in 1892. "For the guiding principles of my actions I have only the dictates of my duty and the responsibility of my clear conscience towards God."[96] But Wilhelm's blather disguised feelings that were in fact acutely wounded by the failure of his subjects to accord him the respect and affection he believed to be his due. Just as his parents had failed to appreciate his nature, so too had his working-class subjects, who had persisted in their unfortunate attachment to socialism in spite of the benevolent policies introduced at the beginning of his reign. The respectable classes, and even his own ministers, now seemed also to have deserted the throne. Sensing that he was alone and abandoned, the Kaiser's inclination was to depend all the more on the handful of aristocratic courtiers whose loyalty was unquestionable.

This dependence on the advice of favorites rather than the counsel of his responsible servants in the government, and especially those in the Foreign Office, profoundly disturbed Holstein.[97] Diplomacy was an especially acute problem, for here the Kaiser's intrusions were most frequent, since foreign relations, along with military affairs, interested him far more than internal politics.[98] Holstein therefore welcomed any effort, such as the united stand of the Prussian ministry against the Kaiser in the Köller crisis, that challenged Wilhelm's authoritarian pretensions. As Holstein mapped out the future, he believed that what had to be done was somehow to make the Kaiser recognize that he could not follow his own inclinations but had instead to heed the counsel of his appointed, but not his elected, officials. In the first instance this meant the chancellor himself. Bismarck had not been altogether successful in asserting himself, and Caprivi, in Holstein's opinion, had been totally deficient in this respect. Holstein hoped that Hohenlohe would prove firmer, and he had lost no time once the new chancellor succeeded Caprivi in urging him to stand up to Wilhelm.[99]

Hohenlohe, however, was not willing to act as forcefully as Holstein would have liked, for he considered his proper role to be the agent of conciliation rather than conflict. "From the day that I took office I made it clear to myself that the Kaiser would not have the same relationship to me as Kaiser Wilhelm I had to Bismarck," Hohenlohe wrote to Holstein in March 1896. "If I did not like that I should absolutely not have assumed the post. But having accepted it, I must take the Kaiser as he is."[100] Since Holstein's entreaties with Hohenlohe were having no effect in stiffening his resistance to the Kaiser, he appealed to Eulenburg to work on the chancellor. "In Hohenlohe's great compliance lies the overwhelming danger for the Kaiser," Holstein wrote to Eulenburg, "for it will actually strengthen his arbitrary tendencies. . . . When you deal with Hohenlohe, *you* must advise him that in certain unavoidable circumstances he must play the *Chancellor of the Reich* in dealing with the Kaiser. In reality the old gentleman now behaves as though he were [merely] the second High Chamberlain to the family."[101] Eulenburg, however, could not exercise much influence on Hohenlohe, who recognized Eulenburg's utility as a channel to the Kaiser but who disliked him and incorrectly suspected that he had ambitions to succeed as chancellor.[102] The chancellor kept Eulenburg at a safe remove, almost never encountering him and keeping their correspondence to a minimum.

As a result, Holstein had to rely on Eulenburg himself as the person through whom Wilhelm might be most effectively managed. Like the chancellor, Holstein hoped that Eulenburg could make the Kaiser's diplomatic activity accord more with the wishes of the Foreign Office, which Wilhelm seemed all too often to ignore. Holstein was so secretive and Eulenburg so disingenuous that, even though the volume of their correspondence was enormous and stretched over many years, it is hard to know what real appreciation they had of one another. It seems unlikely that the mutual esteem between the two diplomats was ever very great, for they were opposites in personality and tastes. In a letter written to Eulenburg on New Year's Day 1895, Holstein commented on their differences. "We are two men of monarchical loyalty," he wrote, "but our aims are not entirely the same. *You* stand close [to the throne] and see the individual peaks; *I* [observe] at a distance, regarding the entire mountain chain as well as the weather that gathers behind it. You think about the Kaiser, but I also think about the dynasty and do not deceive myself that His Majesty lives off of royalist *capital*."[103] Holstein suspected, without warrant, that Eulenburg was ambitious for high office, while Eulenburg eventually found Holstein to be a meddlesome busybody whose only virtue was his long experience in European diplomacy and whose retention in office was therefore essential.[104] However different the principals were in character, the Eulenburg-Holstein partnership was remarkably successful in the Caprivi administration and for the first few years of Hohenlohe's chancellorship. The two did much to discredit their common enemy, General Waldersee, with the Kaiser, they kept Wilhelm's feud with Bismarck percolating as long as possible, and all manner of small matters affecting diplomatic personnel or policy were arranged to their satisfaction. Holstein was thus the secret partner, while Eulenburg, the public representative of the pair, assumed the role of imperial counsellor.

Eulenburg was a man enthralled by social distinctions and niceties, and he never wearied of making meticulous inventories of his own position. He despised the masses for their lack of refinement, the bourgeoisie for their ineluctable philistinism, the bureaucracy (including his own diplomatic colleagues) for their petty quarrelsomeness and careerism. Even his fellow aristocrats did not escape Eulenburg's censure, and he seems to have found most of them indistinguishable, save for their titles, from the lower orders.[105] For democracies, parliaments, or modern ideas he had little interest, and he was immune to appreciating features of other governments, especially those of the British. To Eulenburg only the monarchy, with the best of its noble satellites, epitomized all the traditional virtues of Prussia, and he was consequently prepared to guard its prerogatives against any assault. Even the Prussian ministry, however aristocratic in composition, could not be allowed to interpose itself between crown and people. Eulenburg, unlike Holstein, was therefore unable to draw any satisfaction from the Kaiser's predicament in the Köller crisis. Nor did he have any interest in Holstein's plea that he try to curb Wilhelm II, for Eulenburg in fact wanted the monarchy to assert itself more aggressively.

While Eulenburg was certainly aware of the advantages inherent in his close relationship with the Kaiser, the maintenance of whose authority was therefore essential, he genuinely liked and admired him. Eulenburg knew that his sovereign was not without blemishes. Wilhelm's sudden and spontaneous nature, which to Holstein spelled only danger for Germany, had for Eulenburg a certain boyish charm, a "Slavic" aspect, that admittedly on occasion created difficulties for German statesmen.[106] Eulenburg was also aware of the Kaiser's susceptibility to depression (of which Eulenburg himself was a frequent victim), and there were times when he moved quickly to encourage Wilhelm's already well-developed sense of self-confidence. Eulenburg had few original ideas, diplomatic or otherwise, and he was guided only by his conviction that the crown's supremacy had to be maintained. For this endeavor, appropriate behavior in the sovereign was of utmost importance. Eulenburg's advice generally took the form of moderating the Kaiser's excesses of enthusiasm or temperament by urging delay, more conciliatory language, or gestures that were less brusque. His purpose was to guide, not to force, to insinuate rather than to direct. In that respect he was not unlike Chancellor Hohenlohe, who saw Wilhelm II as an object to deflate rather than to try to lead. To the Kaiser, increasingly beset by socialists, a hostile press, unruly ministers, and (as he characterized them) ungrateful subjects, Eulenburg's loyal, unquestioning devotion must have been very welcome.

The cooperation between Eulenburg and Holstein in political and diplomatic affairs, as well as their personal relations, began to experience a serious strain not long after Hohenlohe became chancellor in October 1894. The issue over which they disagreed and which eventually ended their once close association was the Kaiser's growing inclination to personal rule, which Holstein deplored but which Eulenburg encouraged. Although Holstein was a devoted Prussian monarchist who was never the parliamentary "liberal" Eulenburg imagined him to be, he resented the Kaiser's increasingly frequent intervention in diplomatic affairs, often without any prior consultation with the Foreign Office. This was the antithesis of Holstein's concept of a monarchy that would consult and respect the advisors it had appointed. Given Hohenlohe's passivity and

Eulenburg's encouragement of the Kaiser's autocratic tendencies, Holstein had little reason to have confidence in the future. He knew how great Eulenburg's influence was and how valuable an ally he would be if only his entrée with Wilhelm could be used in the proper way. Holstein warned in the most explicit language that Eulenburg's view that "The King can do no wrong" was likely to have the direst results. "It cannot go on like this or the Kaiser and the Empire will go to pieces," he wrote to Eulenburg at the end of 1895. "I'm warning you now once more. Be careful that history does not someday picture you as the dark horseman who was at the side of the imperial wanderer when he turned into the false path."[107]

Eulenburg agreed with Holstein that the Kaiser's behavior was sometimes regrettable and that he should at least consider the advice tendered by the Foreign Office. But Holstein, he felt, exaggerated the problem, and Eulenburg did not agree that Wilhelm II's unfortunate barging into diplomatic affairs warranted binding him to his servants in the government.[108] To Eulenburg, a stronger assertion of the royal will was in fact desirable for a number of reasons. The liberalizing trend of the Caprivi administration, always distasteful to him, had to be arrested under Hohenlohe, for Eulenburg believed that the appetite of liberals was so excessive that it could never be satisfied, no matter how many concessions Wilhelm made.[109] Having no enthusiasm for progressive ideas, Eulenburg believed that Germany's diplomatic future lay with Russia, not Great Britain. Unlike Holstein, he despised England, whom German liberals seemed determined to imitate.[110] In his opinion, Prussian kingship was an institution that had a future only in cooperation with the conservative elements, but Eulenburg had a very narrow definition of the forces on the right with which Wilhelm should associate. Although by profession successively an army officer and a diplomat, Eulenburg mistrusted both the army and the Foreign Office, nor did he have a good opinion of any of the Kaiser's courtiers except his cousin, Count August zu Eulenburg, the chief marshal of the Court and Household. Proceeding by elimination, Eulenburg concluded that it would be quite satisfactory if the Kaiser would listen only to Hohenlohe, whose cautious manner and many of whose ideas Eulenburg found compatible with his own, and to Eulenburg himself.

What Eulenburg sought was influence, and he rightly believed that it could be most successfully exercised if he were not constantly in Berlin. He therefore preferred to rely on the written word, and no one, Holstein admitted, could wield a pen so skillfully as Eulenburg.[111] To Eulenburg,

Wilhelm II, so singular in his energy and so free of the philistinism of his subjects, was by right the supreme arbiter of Prussia and the Empire, subject to no other man and no institution or popular force. But the possession of such vast authority was one question, its exercise another. In Eulenburg's analysis, a monarchical autocracy without limitations, such as that of Tsarist Russia, was unthinkable in nineteenth-century Germany. A regime of this sort would be unacceptable to the German people and lead eventually to the fall of the dynasty.[112] Eulenburg believed that this was especially true in the post-Bismarck era. Under the Iron Chancellor's long domination of Wilhelm I, the German people had come to expect a strong government and a passive sovereign, one who, like the old Kaiser, was beloved for his presence rather than for his initiative.[113] Once Bismarck fell, it was necessary to restore to the crown its eroded prerogatives. It would be imperative to keep a close watch on Holstein, whom Eulenburg correctly regarded as the mainspring of the movement within the government that was at work to curb the Kaiser's powers.[114] Since the liberal mania for reform could never be satisfied, Wilhelm's rule would have to depend on his conservative subjects, no matter how the fastidious Eulenburg might abhor their personal characteristics. What would result would be an indefinite continuation in office of Hohenlohe, the elimination of Holstein from influence, a well-regulated cooperation between the Kaiser, the chancellor, and Eulenburg, and a gradual reduction of the excessive liberalism of Caprivi's "New Course."

By the end of 1894, both Eulenburg and Holstein had staked out their rival positions on the question of royal prerogative, and the campaign between their forces began.[115] In 1895, the successful attempt by Bronsart and his colleagues in the Prussian ministry to have Köller removed as interior minister had hardened the divisions between the two camps. To Holstein, Wilhelm's defeat by the ministers was a welcome development that he hoped would become a precedent for further effective ministerial challenges to the Kaiser's willfulness. Eulenburg, on the other hand, regarded the Köller crisis as an unwarranted assault on the Prussian crown, one that must never happen again. Throughout 1896 the contest raged between Holstein and Eulenburg over the issue of the Kaiser's prerogative, and only in the following year would the matter be resolved in Eulenburg's favor. With that victory, the changing of the guard would proceed, leaving Wilhelm II and Eulenburg firmly in charge and Holstein, isolated and increasingly less influential, in his office in the Wilhelmstrasse.

Eleven

CLEARING THE DECKS,

1 8 9 5 – 1 8 9 7

THE KÖLLER CRISIS, in which Wilhelm II for the first time in his reign found himself confronted by a solid, and effective, opposition on the part of the Prussian ministry, was in his opinion an insult for which satisfaction had to be required. The only atonement that would suffice would be the resignation of all the refractory ministers who had supported War Minister Bronsart von Schellendorf's attempt to open military courts-martial to the public, the issue which had ignited the crisis. Then, in the plenitude of regal forgiveness, Wilhelm would decline to dismiss his other erring but repentant servants.[1] The Kaiser declared to Chancellor Hohenlohe that the Prussian ministry's opposition to the royal will had "made me the laughing stock of all Europe."[2] Where was now the "*regis voluntas suprema lex*"—the king's pleasure is the supreme law—which Wilhelm II had so proudly, and undiplomatically, inscribed a few years earlier in the ceremonial register of the city of Munich? Not only had his prerogative been challenged, but the ministers had dared to assail the crown on a matter concerning the army, an institution the Kaiser believed that he alone, as supreme commander, should govern. The ministers had forgotten who they were and would have to be reminded that they existed only as servants of the crown.[3]

The Köller crisis had a marked effect on the Kaiser's psyche. Eulenburg, who had been with his royal friend through many a difficult time, declared that the affair had upset and depressed Wilhelm more than he had ever seen him before.[4] Eulenburg feared that his reaction would consequently be extreme, but in fact, apart from a cascade of rhetoric, it proved fairly temperate. The Kaiser did not fire his ministers but warned that what had occurred was not to happen again.[5] Wilhelm's only public show of sympathy for Köller was a visit to Bismarck he made a week after the minister's fall, a journey interpreted as a slap at the ministry, since the former chancellor and his conservative agrarian allies had instituted a press attack in behalf of Köller.[6] But the Kaiser did not forget what had happened, and he was determined never again to be subjected to such a humiliation by his willful and disloyal ministers. New men, who better understood the principles of Hohenzollern loyalty, would eventually have to take their places.

Although on the surface Wilhelm thus appeared to have accepted his defeat by the Prussian ministry with unusual equanimity, the Köller crisis did nothing to change his views either about the military courts-martial issue or about his own prerogative. He was determined not to open military trials to the public and in the future to countenance no ministerial intrusion on the authority of the crown. But the Kaiser, who ordinarily was cavalier about the force of public opinion, recognized that he was in a difficult position. The issue of public access to courts-martial was one which the German people followed with very great interest, and Chancellor Hohenlohe went so far as to declare that no issue since the Franco-Prussian war of 1871 had so riveted the attention of the population.[7] Since the beginning of Wilhelm II's reign, the Reichstag had repeatedly called for a revision of the military code on this point, and the Köller crisis had indicated that the Prussian ministry, under Minister of War Bronsart's leadership, would solidly support such an alteration.

The army, however, was divided on the issue. While some generals supported Bronsart, there was considerable opposition to public trials, and it centered on the chief of the Military Cabinet, General Wilhelm von Hahnke, whose relationship to the Kaiser had become more and more intimate. Ever since Wilhelm II mounted the throne, the chiefs of his three cabinets—military, naval, and civil—had increased their influence with the crown at the expense of the Prussian and imperial governments.[8] The cabinet chiefs, being servants of the king's household, had no formal connection with the rest of officialdom. By the mid-1890s, Hahnke, allied with the chief of the Civil Cabinet, Hermann von Lucanus, had assumed a particularly pervasive role in the royal entourage. The general was fanatically devoted to the Kaiser and intent on the preservation of the status quo, military or otherwise, in Prussia. Hahnke was outraged by the position into which the Prussian ministry had forced Wilhelm in the Köller crisis. He and Bronsart had long been adversaries, for Hahnke believed that the War Ministry, like all other instruments of government, existed solely to fulfill the Kaiser's will. Hahnke and the Kaiser's other military courtiers therefore encouraged Wilhelm to regard the part played by Bronsart and the ministry in the Köller affairs as rank "insubordination."[9] Wilhelm was receptive to such arguments, for he resented the haughty, didactic tone Bronsart habitually adopted toward him.[10]

Although Bronsart's dismissal would have greatly pleased the Kaiser's entourage and the conservative circles to which they were attached, it would also create difficulties for Wilhelm. The general's resignation would be correctly interpreted as having proceeded from the courts-martial issue, on which he represented the popular attitude. Bronsart had the reputation, not unlike that of Baron Marschall von Bieberstein at the Foreign Office, of being one of the few impressive figures in the Prussian ministry. A persuasive debater, he enjoyed considerable esteem in the Reichstag, with which Wilhelm had enough problems as it was.[11] The courts-martial issue was not the only military matter the Reichstag would have to consider, and without Bronsart's leadership the Kaiser could hardly expect to obtain the budgetary increases in the Prussian army that were being debated in the spring of 1896. Dona declared with a mixture of wifely loyalty and good sense that although her husband was the most talented of Europe's rulers he was also young, sensitive to criticism, and in need of experienced advisors such as Bronsart.[12] His resignation would put Hohenlohe in an intolerable position, and Wilhelm was anxious to do nothing that would jeopardize the chancellor's continuation in office.[13] If Bronsart was to be forced from office, it would have to be arranged in such a way as not to be linked to the courts-martial issue, on which the chancellor was his partisan. This would take both time and ingenuity, and meanwhile Wilhelm II would have to put up with a man who was as temperamental as he was.

In deciding to retain Bronsart, the Kaiser followed the advice of both the chancellor and Eulenburg. As far as Hohenlohe was concerned, Bronsart's premature departure would be "disastrous." Although the chancellor was firmly in favor of opening courts-martial to the public, he wanted to defer consideration of the issue until the end of 1896, by which time Bronsart, having secured the army budget, could safely be sacrificed.[14] As for Eulenburg, he disliked Bronsart and cared nothing for the courts-martial question except for its utility in promoting his conception that Germany should be ruled by the Kaiser and not by the ministry, or the Reichstag, or any other agent of public opinion. Eulenburg shared Hohenlohe's belief that the best policy would be to postpone any consideration of the courts-martial matter in the Reichstag until the fall, by which time the furor surrounding the issue would perhaps have died down. There was always the danger that if the matter came before the parliament and revealed an insoluble conflict between the crown and the Reichstag, Hohenlohe might resign. "If anybody wants to bring about Hohenlohe's downfall," Eulenburg reminded Holstein, "he needs only to bring up the question of the reform of the military courts-martial."[15] As well as Eulenburg knew the Kaiser, he had no idea whom Wilhelm might appoint as Hohenlohe's successor. It was better to stick with Hohenlohe until such time as the stage was set for the assumption of the position by Bernhard von Bülow, the advancement of whose career had long been a special concern of Eulenburg's and who, Eulenburg informed Wilhelm in 1895, was "the most valuable official Your Majesty has, the predestined imperial chancellor of the future."[16] Bülow, who had served as ambassador in Rome since 1894, was only forty-seven in 1896 and in Eulenburg's opinion was not yet ripe to become chancellor. Wilhelm, however, was eager to promote Bülow, and Eulenburg therefore had to work hard to persuade him that he should for the moment be content to leave Hohenlohe in office and keep Bülow in reserve.[17]

While Hohenlohe and Eulenburg were thus urging the Kaiser not to take any precipitate action to stir up the courts-martial issue, Bronsart and Holstein, for quite different motives, were insistent that it be revived. Bronsart's interest in the matter was essentially military, and the constitutional issue of royal prerogative, over which Eulenburg and Holstein were so divided, was to him a secondary, although important, consideration. Bronsart resented Wilhelm's involving himself in the army's deliberation of technical matters, which in his opinion had led only to wasteful expenditures and administrative disorder.[18] Himself a nobleman, the war minister appreciated the virtues of the old aristocratic Prussian army, but he believed that it was becoming moribund and needed to acquire a broader popular base.[19] The lifting of the veil of secrecy from the courts-martial, if not entirely, at least in part, would be a welcome step in this direction.

It was one thing to favor a reform of the courts-martial and another to try to set in motion a constitutional crisis by using the issue to humble the Kaiser. This would be Holstein's contribution. By the time of the Köller crisis late in 1895, and especially in the course of 1896, Holstein had become increasingly alarmed by Wilhelm II's behavior. The Kaiser's ever-changing moods, his restlessness, the superficiality with which he dealt with important matters, and his independent conduct of diplomacy troubled Holstein greatly. There was, in his opinion, a real danger that Wilhelm's careless yammerings, based on his prejudices rather than on any comprehension of German national interest, could plunge the Empire into a European war. At the least, the Kaiser's irresponsibility would ensure that no power would want to enter into an alliance with Berlin.[20] "The chief danger in the life of Kaiser Wilhelm II," Holstein wrote to Eulenburg on 5 May 1896, "is that he is and remains absolutely unaware of the effect that his speeches and actions have on Princes, public men, and the masses. The life work of every Government of Wilhelm II must be to counter this danger and as far as is possible to nullify these effects. A task which soon wears one out."[21]

Holstein believed that the Kaiser had lost touch with reality and considered that it was very possible, as he ominously warned Eulenburg in the summer of 1896, that Wilhelm II was the victim of a psychiatric disorder.[22] Instead of behaving in a normal, responsible fashion, seeking and following the advice of his statesmen, the Kaiser had created a sort of ancillary, unofficial personal regime exclusively composed of aristocratic courtiers. In this constellation conservative generals had assumed more and more importance, a development that disturbed Holstein as much as it did Bronsart. Wilhelm II's adjutants were winning more and more influence over him, and one result of this was the resurrection of diplomatic activity by the military attachés. Although Chancellor Caprivi in 1890 had succeeded in preventing the attachés posted in German legations abroad from operating independently of the envoys, their insinuation into diplomacy did not in fact entirely cease. A few years later Wilhelm assigned his adjutants to keep watch on specific European nations, reporting to him what they had discovered. "Why," Ambassador Count Georg zu Münster in Paris asked Holstein with exasperation in the spring of 1896, "is there still a Wilhelmstrasse if official business is to be divided up among the Aides-de-Camp?"[23] As a Foreign Office dignitary, Holstein resented this, for the attachés and now the adjutants often subverted the authority of the Kaiser's envoys and made the conduct of diplomacy very difficult.

In February 1896, two months after Köller's fall, Holstein rekindled his attack on the Kaiser. On the first day of the month Hohenlohe noted in his diary that he had seen Holstein, who "speaks now of the necessity of *forcing* the Kaiser to consent to Bronsart's proposal concerning the military courts-martial bill."[24] The chancellor's reaction to Holstein's overture was not entirely negative. *If* Wilhelm yielded to pressure to accept public trials, the result would be a strengthening of the position of the chancellor and his government vis à vis the crown, precisely the result Holstein anticipated. But the prospect of this admitted advantage was canceled, in Hohenlohe's opinion, by an attendant deficit: it would not work. Subservience was alien to the Kaiser's nature, and his servants were obliged to take the monarch as he was.[25] And even *if* Holstein's scheme were to be successfully realized, Hohenlohe knew that his personal relations with Wilhelm II would be ruined forever. As far as the chancellor was concerned, the introduction of reforms in the army depended squarely on his remaining in office.[26] It was not proper deliberately to try to entrap the sovereign in an embarrassing position. To do so, in any case, was contrary to Hohenlohe's conception of his role as chancellor, which was to prevent Wilhelm from behaving rashly and otherwise to avoid rather than provoke confrontations.[27]

Had the chancellor felt that Germany was faced by a crisis in 1896, he might have been more inclined to go along with Holstein. But Hohenlohe did not share Holstein's view that the Kaiser was a diplomatic disaster. The danger of war with Russia or France, or both, seemed to be receding. Anglo-German relations, strained by disagreements between the two powers in Africa and Asia, were at a low point, but the chancellor did not think that this difficulty was due (as Holstein insisted was the case) to Wilhelm II's maladroit conduct of affairs, but rather to the colonial and economic rivalries that had emerged under Bismarck and to various mistaken policies of the Wilhelmstrasse 76.[28] The military courts-martial issue was in any case not the matter over which a confrontation should be sought, for Hohenlohe was confident that he would eventually be able to secure the Kaiser's approval of *some* degree of public observation of military trials.[29] Because of all these considerations, the chancellor was opposed to entering into Holstein's scheme to use the courts-martial issue to provoke another battle between the government and the crown.

Although Holstein's concern with the courts-martial was purely tactical and tied to his desire to deflate Wilhelm II's authority, to Hohenlohe it was a problem which had to be resolved because of the public controversy it had generated. The Reichstag's insistence on reform could not be fobbed off forever. In the meantime, the chancellor felt he had to provide some indication of the government's intentions. In May 1896 he therefore informed the Kaiser that he proposed to assure the Reichstag that a bill for the revision of the military courts would be introduced in the fall and that it "would be based on the contemporary principles of law."[30] Even before receiving the chancellor's message, Wilhelm had telegraphed him that he would not tolerate any declaration by the Prussian ministry in favor of an opening to the public of military trials or any leaks to the press about the matter.[31] This was a matter for which Hohenlohe, as minister-president of Prussia, and Wilhelm, as supreme commander, alone were responsible. The Kaiser warned Hohenlohe to be on his guard against certain of his "restless" ministers, who were trying to bring about a repetition of the Köller crisis. Such an attempt, Wilhelm declared, would constitute a "severe constitutional attack on the crown" and would be answered by placing any ministers involved under arrest. The Kaiserin underlined her consort's warning to her uncle Hohenlohe, advising him that Wilhelm was "firm as a rock" (*felsenfest*) in his determination not to yield on this point.[32]

On 18 May 1896, a Center deputy, Ernst Lieber, raised the issue of the military courts on the floor of the Reichstag, and the chancellor used his interpellation as the opportunity to reveal the government's intentions. Hohenlohe declared in his carefully worded response that he believed that there was room for improvement in the existing system of military trials and that work was well in progress on framing a revision that would "be based on modern legal conceptions while recognizing the peculiarities of military considerations."[33] The chancellor's declaration satisfied Lieber and the other deputies, who were content to await his legislative proposals, which presumably would be presented when the Reichstag convened in the fall. The Kaiser, however, was very annoyed that Hohenlohe had alluded to the desirability of introducing a reform that would be "modern." Hohenlohe's reaction was to point out to Eulenburg, who was with the Kaiser on a hunt in Silesia, that his statement may have displeased Wilhelm, but it had after all succeeded in deferring further discussion of the matter until the fall. Hohenlohe believed he had done what was required, and the Kaiser had no cause for complaint. "I am not a minor official," he testily reminded Eulenburg, "but chancellor of the Empire and as such have to determine what I must say."[34]

The question of public admission to courts-martial did not resurface for the remainder of the Reichstag session, but no progress was made toward a resolution of the conflicting views of the Kaiser on the one hand and Hohenlohe and the Prussian ministry on the other. In light of Wilhelm II's fixed opposition to public trials, Hohenlohe believed that the only way in which the reform might eventually be accomplished was to avoid putting undue pressure on the sovereign, hoping that he might gradually be persuaded to change his mind. More could be achieved by waiting than by arguing. To Holstein, the chancellor's reluctance to press forward with the courts-martial reform was not a strategic ploy but another manifestation of Hohenlohe's unfortunate deference to the throne. If the chancellor did not in the future assert himself more forcefully, Wilhelm might think he could do as he pleased.[35] Bronsart was also disillusioned with Hohenlohe and told one of his ministerial colleagues that he was "sick of the whole affair" and had had enough. It was intolerable to have the army run not by its responsible head but by the Kaiser's military entourage.[36]

Although Hohenlohe would have liked to keep Bronsart in office until the Reichstag debate in the fall on the army budget, he gradually came to the conclusion that the general could not be retained. The war minister's dogged insistence on a reform of the courts-martial rankled Wilhelm II and worked at cross purposes with Hohenlohe's own plan for a patient and gradual solution of the question. The only problem was the old dilemma that if Bronsart resigned, it would be perceived as the defeat of the cause of military reform. For Hohenlohe not to follow the war minister into retirement would make it appear that he had capitulated to the Kaiser. The chancellor could not allow that to happen, since he had long since publicly committed himself to public military trials, even though he knew it might take years to break down the Kaiser's resistance. It was therefore imperative to make certain that Bronsart's resignation, when it came, could not be construed as the end of any hope of a reform of the courts-martial regulations.

The Kaiser had his own dilemma. He was determined to get rid of Bronsart, but he had to do so in such a way as to insure that the chancellor would not also resign. Early in August 1896 he sent Eulenburg to Hohenlohe to propose a way out of the impasse.[37] Wilhelm II's plan was that Bronsart would resign as war minister only to be at once appointed as one of the Kaiser's senior adjutants, a move that would dispell any rumors of an irreconcilable conflict between Bronsart and the ruler. Moreover, Wilhelm would give Hohenlohe assurances that he would support a reform of the military courts that would include many modern features although *not* the opening of the trials to the public. According to Eulenburg, the Kaiser believed that to permit open trials would be an act incompatible with his honor and responsibility as a sovereign. Two weeks earlier Wilhelm II had wept as he assured Eulenburg that he would never yield on the issue. "I would appear a very unworthy fellow," he declared, "if I surrendered in a matter that my ancestors had recognized both as necessary and correct. How could I stand before them in heaven, where I am certainly not at all worthy even to enter. And what would be made of me in the army, which would see in my action the destruction of all its protective defenses, the army for which I have assumed a heavy responsibility for the twenty years I have served the colors."[38]

Hohenlohe was not impressed by the Kaiser's proposal. Bronsart's appointment as adjutant would hardly disguise the reason for his having been sacked as war minister. If that were so, then would not the chancellor's remaining in office even though he shared Bronsart's reformist ideas indicate that he had given in to the Kaiser in the military courts issue? Bronsart would emerge as the hero of the hour, Hohenlohe as the Kaiser's lackey. "That," the chancellor declared, "is something to which H[is] M[ajesty] and Count Philipp Eulenburg are completely indifferent. They have little concern about what happens to me, if only the Kaiser's caprice and the will of the Military Cabinet is fulfilled."[39] Hohenlohe, however, had no intention of giving up his position unless the Kaiser commanded his resignation or placed him in some impossibly difficult situation. Being Wilhelm II's chancellor was not an easy business, something which Hohenlohe had anticipated before assuming office. The chancellor knew that Wilhelm kept important diplomatic information from him, but he characteristically shrugged this off as a regrettable idiosyncrasy rather than an outrageous affront. Hohenlohe observed to the British envoy in Berlin that such was the Kaiser's love of secrecy that if he wanted to talk politics with anyone he would prefer a midnight conference in the middle of a forest.[40] Wilhelm's lack of consideration had more than once made Hohenlohe feel that he could not continue in office, but then, he confessed, the Kaiser would take him into his confidence and dissipate his mistrust.[41]

Hohenlohe never candidly revealed his motives for clinging to office, but they were clearly a mixture of self-interest and patriotism. The chancellor's salary to be sure had helped repair his finances, but quite apart from the monetary appeal of the chancellorship, Hohenlohe had a genuine, and commendable, fear of what might happen were he to be replaced. Given the Kaiser's increasingly authoritarian manner, the chancellor felt sure that his successor would come from the reactionary circles and promote monarchical autocracy. In such a development, Eulenburg, for whom Hohenlohe had little use, would emerge as the de facto ruler of the Fatherland, and then there would no longer be any possibility of reforming courts-martial or anything else. Such a regime would attempt, through repeated dissolutions and elections, to obtain a Reichstag that would place no barriers in the way of the crown. A docile legislature, however, could never be obtained by such means, and eventually the Kaiser would be forced to engage in a coup d'état against the imperial constitution of 1871. He would then have to rule with the consent not of the German people but by allying with the German princes. This would quickly prove impossible, and inevitably the Empire would disintegrate.

If Hohenlohe therefore had good reasons that led him to hold on to office, he was compelled to tailor his behavior to insure that he did not run afoul of the Kaiser. Since Wilhelm II could not be changed, he had to be accommodated. Bluster or intransigence would cost the chancellor his position, whereas patient cultivation of the monarch might eventually yield the desired results.

Hohenlohe's colleagues often reproached him with weakness or cowardice, but in fact his acquiescent behavior was a stratagem rather than a reflection of physical or moral torpor. The chancellor was very old and often worn out, but he was not the Kaiser flunkey. Indeed, Hohenlohe frequently declared that he would resign when he realized that Wilhelm II had begun to treat him as a mere plaything. The chancellor did exactly that, but not until 1900, after six years in office, by which time he had in fact accomplished a number of important reforms for which there had initially been little prospect of success. However unassertive Hohenlohe may have appeared as a personality, his shrewd assessment of the Kaiser's personality and its ramifications for the conduct of affairs enabled him to achieve more than most of Bismarck's successors.

Given Hohenlohe's perception of the proper course of action, he informed Eulenburg that while he did not think much of Wilhelm's plan to name Bronsart an adjutant general, he was willing to accept the war minister's resignation provided, however, that the Kaiser would allow the chancellor to continue to try to work out a compromise on the courts-martial.[42] In this way Hohenlohe would be able to advertise that Bronsart's departure did not result from the courts-martial issue but presumably because of personal differences with the sovereign. Hohenlohe would also gain time in which to undermine Wilhelm II's objections to public courts-martial. On 14 August 1896 the Kaiser, with "great" regret, accepted the war minister's resignation on grounds of health. Having got what he wanted, Wilhelm now offered the chancellor a sop by indicating that he would agree to public trials *if* a provision were introduced into military regulations that in the case of each and every court-martial it left to the Kaiser's discretion whether or not public admission was to be allowed.[43]

Hohenlohe knew that Wilhelm's concession was only a ruse, which indeed it was, and that there would never be public trials unless they were legally established independent of the crown. In order to prevent Bronsart's departure from appearing to be a grave defeat for the cause of army reform, on 25 August the chancellor issued a statement to the press announcing that in the fall he would introduce a bill affecting the military courts incorporating the "modern" features to which he had referred on 18 May in his response in the Reichstag to Deputy Lieber.[44] This, he hoped, would counterbalance the misgivings about the Kaiser's autocratic tendencies that Bronsart's resignation had produced. As far as Hohenlohe was concerned, the war minister's departure was a further step along the road away from constitutional government to a personal regime by the Kaiser, Eulenburg, and his military entourage. "His Majesty has fearfully hurt himself by Bronsart's dismissal," the chancellor wrote in his diary on 24 August. "It is very sad and I regard the future rather pessimistically."[45] Hohenlohe believed that Eulenburg had constantly encouraged Wilhelm to provoke a crisis in the courts-martial issue, and, in a letter of extraordinary frankness, he accused Eulenburg of having played that role and of wanting to have him replaced as chancellor. With typical caution, however, Hohenlohe decided not to confront Eulenburg and kept the letter in his desk.[46]

The appointment of Lt. Gen. Heinrich von Gossler as war minister did nothing to reassure the chancellor, for Gossler, whose prior record was undistinguished, insisted that military trials be controlled by the sovereign. Wilhelm II took an entirely positive view of his new minister. "My old friend" Gossler, so he assured Eulenburg, "wishes only to be his Kaiser's general."[47] It was in fact Gossler who had proposed to Wilhelm that public trials be allowed, but subject in every case to the crown's approval.[48] Hohenlohe and the ministry would not accept this scheme, however, for it hardly embraced the "modern" provisions the chancellor had promised the Reichstag. Wilhelm II eventually compromised to the extent of agreeing that any officer involved in court-martial proceedings might have present at the proceedings an active officer of the same or higher rank, his relatives and guardian (*Vormund*), as well as the person allegedly injured by his behavior. The Kaiser warned the ministers that this was the extent of the concessions he was prepared to make, but even so it was the sort of incremental progress Hohenlohe had been certain he could achieve. Wilhelm also instructed the ministry to see to it that any new legislation would emphasize the fact that it was the Kaiser who was the army's supreme commander.[49]

If Hohenlohe's reaction to the situation produced by Bronsart's resignation was negative, the Kaiser regarded the future with considerable optimism. When Wilhelm II reviewed the opposition he had encountered throughout 1896 in the ministry over the issue of public courts-martial, he believed that he had been brought dangerously close to a repetition of the Köller crisis that had profoundly shaken him a year earlier.[50] He felt that his forceful resistance to Bronsart and his subsequent dismissal from office had saved the day. But as long as Bronsart's allies among his fellow ministers were still in office, the crown would continue to encounter friction from its own servants. Emboldened by his elimination of Bronsart, Wilhelm decided next to move against the two other officials whom he believed to have been the war minister's closest confederates, Karl Heinrich von Boetticher, Prussian minister without portfolio, vice president of the ministry, and imperial state secretary of the interior, and the state secretary of the Foreign Office, Baron Adolf Marschall von Bieberstein, who also held a portfolio without office in the Prussian ministry. Caution would be necessary, however, because Bronsart's resignation had not only upset Hohenlohe but had also been widely deplored throughout Germany, with the onus for the war minister's fall fixed squarely, and properly, on the monarch.

Shortly after Bronsart's resignation, Eulenburg informed Hohenlohe that while the Kaiser was prepared to spare Marschall for the moment out of consideration for the chancellor's repeated insistence that his retention was essential, he considered Boetticher a suitable "sacrifice."[51] Boetticher was nearing retirement age and, unlike Marschall, did not have the wide following in the Reichstag that would make his resignation unpopular. In Wilhelm II's opinion, Boetticher had played a deplorable role in opposition to the crown in the Köller crisis, and, from that moment on, the Kaiser had been determined to get rid of him.[52] The Kaiser's restoration in 1894 of good relations with Bismarck contributed to his determination to eliminate Boetticher, for the former chancellor despised Boetticher and held him in part responsible for the crisis of March 1890 that resulted in his fall from office.[53] Although Wilhelm admitted that Boetticher, like Marschall, had a gift for parliamentary skirmishing, he also regarded him as a "limp washrag" (*feige Waschlappe*).[54] The Kaiser, in typical fashion, did not inform Hohenlohe of his intention of replacing Boetticher and Marschall but instead confided in the Austro-Hungarian ambassador, Count Ladislaus von Szögyényi-Marich, asking him to keep the information to himself. Szögyényi, of course, immediately advised Vienna of Wilhelm's intention.[55]

Hohenlohe, however, placed the greatest value on Boetticher's bureaucratic expertise and oratorical talent. Although the Kaiser repeatedly declared that Boetticher had to be removed from his post, he left him in office for almost another year and a half because of Hohenlohe's entreaties. But by May 1897 Wilhelm had had enough. The immediate cause was a violent, if indirect, attack on the Kaiser and his increasingly autocratic pretensions made in the Reichstag on the twenty-sixth by Eugen Richter, the leader of the Progressive party. Wilhelm was furious that Boetticher, the senior member and vice president of the Prussian ministry, had not replied with a defense of the crown, and he demanded his resignation. "I would weaken myself and the monarchy," the Kaiser told Eulenburg, "if I did not demand atonement for such an unworthy silence in the face of this shocking attack on my person in the parliament."[56] Boetticher's taciturnity was in fact a tactical move made in order to eliminate any possibility of making the Kaiser the subject of a Reichstag debate, an unprecedented and very undesirable step that would have exposed the crown to considerable embarrassment. Boetticher believed that the throne stood too high to take notice of a parliamentary radical such as Richter.[57] Hohenlohe remonstrated with Wilhelm that it was the responsibility of the chancellor, and not Boetticher, to defend the throne. Boetticher had been right to remain silent, and Hohenlohe declared that in asking for the minister's resignation Wilhelm would get his as well. The chancellor thereupon sent the Kaiser a letter surrendering his office.[58]

Holstein and his intimate subordinate in the Foreign Office, Alfred von Kiderlen-Wächter, as well as the chancellor's son Alexander, an outspoken critic of the Kaiser, all believed that the rift between Hohenlohe and Wilhelm II over Boetticher should be used to provoke a crisis similar to the Köller affair of 1895. The ministry would face the Kaiser obdurately, surrendering Boetticher but then forcing the Kaiser either to capitulate to its wishes or be confronted with their resignation en masse. They urged the chancellor to insist, on threat of resignation, that if Wilhelm wanted Boetticher ousted—Holstein and his friends had no attachment to Boetticher, who was merely to serve as the vehicle for obtaining the Kaiser's humiliation—his replacement was to be Maximilian von Puttkamer, an official in Alsace with whom Hohenlohe had worked closely when viceroy in Strasbourg between 1885 and 1894. Hohenlohe was to demand, as the other and more controversial condition of his remaining in office, that Wilhelm II accept public courts-martial and dismiss Lucanus, the chief of the Civil Cabinet and the man whom Holstein regarded as a leading advocate of the Kaiser's authoritarian regime.[59]

Hohenlohe, once again, was unwilling to place the Kaiser under such extreme pressure, and his resistance was based on the same considerations that had led to his earlier opposition to Holstein's schemes. Confronting the Kaiser was incompatible with the chancellor's monarchical scruples and would make Wilhelm so angry that Hohenlohe would never again have his confidence.[60] Without the Kaiser's trust, the chancellor could not hope to obtain the gradual reforms that justified his remaining in office, and he would have to resign, to be replaced by a reactionary chancellor under whom all prospects for change would vanish. All that Hohenlohe asked was for the Kaiser to meet him halfway. There was no question of *insisting* on Puttkamer, although his name could be proposed. It would be sufficient for Boetticher's successor to be a person with whom both he and the Kaiser could be satisfied. Hohenlohe disliked Lucanus, who was a parvenu as well as a reactionary, but the Kaiser was too attached to his cabinet chief for there to be any realistic prospects for his removal. As for the military courts matter, Hohenlohe had already secured Wilhelm's agreement to limited access by the family and guardian of the accused as well as the accuser. He knew that this was imperfect, but it was at least a beginning. Why should he now demand, as Holstein and his confederates insisted, *full* public scrutiny? To enrage the Kaiser on this issue was unnecessary, for given time and cultivation Wilhelm's opposition might eventually be overcome. Hohenlohe therefore asked for nothing more than that he be allowed to continue searching for further mutually acceptable changes in the system of military justice.

Since the Kaiser was anxious to retain the chancellor, he was willing to accept such a deferential request. Wilhelm agreed that Hohenlohe could investigate the possibility of additional changes in the courts-martial system, and he proposed that rather than firing Boetticher he be placed on indefinite vacation. After a suitable interval, he could resign and in compensation be made governor of one of the Prussian provinces.[61] Although Hohenlohe would have liked to see Puttkamer succeed Boetticher, the Kaiser would not have him but insisted on the Prussian minister of finance, the able but devious Johannes Miquel. Miquel, however, preferred to stay where he was and nominated Count Arthur von Posadowsky-Wehner, a stiff, pedantic bureaucrat, fanatical agrarian, and political conservative then serving as imperial state secretary of the treasury. Both Hohenlohe and the Kaiser concurred, and on 1 July 1897 Boetticher went on leave and later resigned, eventually being named governor of the province of Saxony.

With both Bronsart and Boetticher now out of the way, Wilhelm II turned to deal with Marschall, a man whom he had always disliked and whom in 1890 he had only reluctantly appointed state secretary of the Foreign Office. For years the Kaiser had been anxious to remove Marschall but had hesitated to do so because of Hohenlohe's dependence on his strong position in the Reichstag, where Marschall had emerged as the government's most persuasive spokesman. Marschall was the aged Hohenlohe's alter ego, party to every decision that was taken. "He is really the actual ruler of the German Empire," complained the Kaiser, who could never bear to be overshadowed.[62] The Köller crisis late in 1895 had sealed Marschall's fate, for Wilhelm believed that he had been largely, perhaps even exclusively, responsible. In the Kaiser's opinion, Marschall's interest in the military question was only to use it to enable the ministers rather than the crown to dominate Prussian politics. Marschall was unfortunately "a pure South German constitutional creature who has no appreciation of the *King of Prussia* and not the least understanding of, nor even an interest for, him or his—thank goodness!—special position. In his eyes, it is the task of the *ministry* of state as a body to order and to govern and to him there is no such thing as a royal wish that runs *counter to the ministry*. Any minister who dares to express such a wish in a ministry whose *majority* is of a contrary opinion is a criminal."[63]

Wilhelm II would have liked to sack Marschall immediately in the wake of the Köller crisis, but Hohenlohe had insisted very firmly that he be retained and threatened to resign if left in the lurch. The removal of Bronsart and Boetticher had left Marschall as the only minister on whom Hohenlohe could rely to deal effectively with the Reichstag. He was much the strongest figure in the ministry and a resolute defender of the chancellor against Miquel and other ministers whose loyalty to Hohenlohe was very questionable.[64] The Kaiser tried in vain to break down Hohenlohe's resistance by insinuating, entirely falsely, that Marschall aspired to become chancellor.[65] In his refusal to abandon Marschall, Hohenlohe had an influential ally in Eulenburg, who also believed that Marschall's retention, at least for the moment, was essential. Marschall was of little consequence to Eulenburg, but Bernhard von Bülow was not quite ready to take over the Foreign Office, the penultimate step of a career, as engineered by Eulenburg (and Bülow), that would culminate in Bülow's replacing Hohenlohe as chancellor. "Marschall *must* be protected," Eulenburg wrote to Holstein on 30 December 1895. "That is a main point, and I will do *everything* to facilitate it."[66]

Eulenburg was as good as his word, and on the next day he wrote to the Kaiser to urge him not to let the Köller crisis, which had just been resolved to the chancellor's satisfaction but not at all to Wilhelm's, impair his relationship with Hohenlohe, who "*loves you personally* and *understands* Your Majesty's individuality." Eulenburg warned that the dismissal of Marschall, a prominent enemy of both Chancellor Bismarck and his son Herbert, must be avoided so that Wilhelm II would not appear to have been ensnared by the former chancellor.[67] Wilhelm II grudgingly accepted Eulenburg's advice. The compelling factor in making him decide to retain Marschall was undoubtedly his fear that if he removed the foreign minister, Hohenlohe might also resign, a threat that the chancellor had made more than once to underline his attachment to his favorite minister. Even so, the reserved and taciturn chancellor, so unlike his bluff, abrasive assistant, recognized that Marschall had become something of a liability insofar as his own task of managing the Kaiser was concerned.[68] Marschall had never developed any talent for ingratiating himself with Wilhelm II, which made for immense problems, and he had equally unfortunate relations with the Kaiser's entourage, to whom Wilhelm allowed more and more influence. Marschall did not like the Kaiser's military adjutants, who, he declared, intoned pieties about the crown's holy rights but who had no conception whatsoever of the workings of parliamentary government.[69]

Marschall was also too closely identified with political Catholicism for Wilhelm II's tastes. Just as the Kaiser had suspected Bismarck in 1890 of concocting a secret arrangement with the Catholic Center leader Ludwig Windthorst and later berated Caprivi for allowing the Zedlitz school bill to have too clerical a tone, so now he was certain that some sort of Jesuitical plot existed between Marschall and his Roman Catholic parliamentary allies, whom the Kaiser somehow imagined were conspiratorial brothers of the socialists.[70] As was so often the case with Wilhelm II there was also a personal note of envy in his assessment of Marschall. Marschall's very success in representing the government before the Reichstag, as Wilhelm admitted, made him unlikable.[71] There was something also about Marschall that the Kaiser found disconcertingly reminiscent of the tyrannical Bismarck. He complained to Eulenburg, "What distresses me is that his position is constantly becoming stronger while my dislike is constantly growing greater. What solution is there for such a situation?"[72] The astute French envoy in Berlin, the Marquis de Noailles, pointed out to the Quai d'Orsay that the one thing Wilhelm could not abide was being eclipsed by his ministers and that this jealousy explained Caprivi's fall in 1894 as well as Boetticher's three years later. Noailles predicted that it would eventually also claim Marschall.[73]

By the end of 1896 Hohenlohe had come to the conclusion that the Kaiser disliked Marschall so intensely that he was prepared to dismiss him even if it meant the chancellor's simultaneous departure. Once

Hohenlohe realized that Wilhelm had made up his mind and there was no chance of changing it, he resigned himself to preparing as slowly as possible for Marschall's successor. Hohenlohe had to admit that Marschall's difficult personality had created friction not only between Wilhelm II and the Foreign Office but among the Prussian ministers as well.[74] There was no question in the chancellor's mind, anymore than there was in the Kaiser's, that Bülow should come to Berlin to head the Foreign Office.[75] As early as the end of 1895 the Kaiser had informed Hohenlohe, to the chancellor's surprise, that Bülow would succeed as chancellor should Hohenlohe die or become incapacitated.[76] Bülow's appearance in Berlin would therefore set the stage for the final act of Hohenlohe's chancellorship. There was, however, the question as to whether the time had come for Bülow, for there were still a number of potentially difficult measures that Hohenlohe wished Marschall to get through the Reichstag. Without Marschall, a hundred government votes in the Catholic Center party would probably vanish. Whether the Kaiser liked it or not, the foreign secretary's following among the Catholics was critical.[77]

Keeping Marschall in office proved to be a very difficult task for the chancellor. Wilhelm II often cut the state secretary dead and, in spite of Hohenlohe's entreaties, refused to consult him.[78] The Kaiser was enraged, as were his courtiers, by Marschall's role in the so-called Tausch case, which held the public's attention all through the fall of 1896.[79] In this lengthy legal battle, Marschall had forced into the open the fact that the chief inspector of the Berlin police, Eugen von Tausch, a favorite at court, had circulated false rumors to the press and then attributed them to Marschall. Marschall had Tausch indicted for libel and, as a lawyer, took an active part in the prosecution. The Kaiser liked Tausch, one of whose responsibilities was the personal safety of the sovereign, and he was infuriated by what he considered to be Marschall's breach of loyalty. The fact that Tausch eventually was exonerated further weakened Marschall's position. "It can't go on like this for long," Wilhelm declared in October 1896 during a conversation with Eulenburg in which he expressed his loathing for Marschall. "Something *must* change."[80] Even before the Tausch case broke, Marschall had informed Eulenburg that it was obvious from the treatment to which he was subjected by both the Kaiser and the Kaiserin that he no longer possessed the royal confidence. Wilhelm would not listen to his ministers but only to his narrow-minded military adjutants.[81] "No one can keep on like this," Marschall told General Waldersee in June 1895. "Today one thing and tomorrow another, and after a few days again something else."[82] And yet he stayed, assiduously defended by Hohenlohe against the Kaiser and his other enemies. Eulenburg, anxious that Bülow not become state secretary of the Foreign Office prematurely, helped influence the Kaiser into agreeing that Marschall might continue to hold his post until he could be dispatched abroad somewhere to serve as ambassador.[83]

When, in the spring of 1897, the time the Kaiser had allowed Marschall had expired, Wilhelm II found himself still in a quandary as to how he could safely jettison the foreign secretary. His dilemma was summarized by Alfred von Kiderlen-Wächter, the German envoy in Bucharest who was frequently called to Berlin for temporary duty, in a letter of 25 April 1897 to Holstein: "H[is] M[ajesty] is afraid to drop Marschall without any reason, but is *very* annoyed with him and would gladly make use of any excuse to get rid of him. Yet H.M. will not sack Hohenlohe in the foreseeable future just because he fears the bad impression it would make. Hohenlohe therefore has it in his power to retain Marschall if he declares his solidarity with him, which he can easily do by pointing to the parliamentary situation. H.M. will not make up his mind to replace Marschall by someone else at the cost of Hohenlohe's departure."[84] The solution eventually adopted was the same face-saving device through which both Bronsart and Boetticher in turn had been dismissed. Marschall's health had long been uncertain, and he knew as well as Hohenlohe how untenable his position in Berlin had become. Marschall therefore requested reassignment to an embassy situated in a comfortable climate. In June 1897 the Kaiser instead permitted him to go on a long vacation leave, and Bülow was brought from Rome to serve as acting state secretary of the Foreign Office until, the official announcement declared, Marschall's condition improved. "You must come forward," Wilhelm told Bülow, "for Marschall has betrayed me."[85] Marschall apparently thought that he would return to his post in Berlin, but Wilhelm had no intention of allowing him back in the capital. Four months later, in October 1897, Marschall's resignation was accepted, and he was appointed ambassador to the Porte in Constantinople. The Kaiser then elevated Bülow to state secretary, a post his father had held in the 1870s under Bismarck.

Bülow's appointment was regarded as a triumph for the conservative agrarian interest, which had long opposed both Caprivi and Hohenlohe, and his presence in Berlin considerably strengthened the autocratic ambitions Eulenburg entertained for Wilhelm II. Bülow was Eulenburg's closest friend and had learned much from him. Like Eulenburg,

Bülow regarded his future solely in terms of his association with the Kaiser. Fastidious in deportment, aristocratic in outlook, Bülow privately scorned parliaments and public opinion, although he was inordinately skillful in playing up to both. "The eel," as his diplomatic colleagues called him, rejoiced in the world of court and society. His talents lay in ingratiation, not in thought, and in time he would become, more than any of Wilhelm II's public servants, the perfect foil for his sovereign.

Holstein would be a problem. Bülow had no taste for Holstein's notion of making the government the dominant power in Berlin, but the oracle of the Wilhelmstrasse would have to be tolerated since Hohenlohe liked him. Bülow himself was tied to Holstein by a long friendship which he, unlike Eulenburg, managed to maintain in spite of their diverging political views. As for the Kaiser, over the dimension of whose role Holstein and Eulenburg had parted company, he would have to be taught to restrain his spectacularly undiplomatic impulses. "The monarch," Bülow declared, "must be like the great clock in the Kremlin. It seldom peals, and then only to announce a great joy or a great sorrow."[86] Bülow would eventually find that imperial taciturnity was easier to recommend than to enforce. But from the beginning, he worked smoothly with the Kaiser, who was delighted that Bülow was successfully asserting his command of the Foreign Office.[87]

Boetticher's replacement by Count Posadowsky and Marschall's by Bülow were only two of the cabinet changes effected by Wilhelm II in 1897, all of which indicated a turn in a more conservative direction. Miquel, a right-leaning member of the National Liberal party, had been Boetticher's replacement as vice president of the Prussian ministry, while the Conservative Reichstag deputy, Lieutenant General Viktor von Podbielski, an agrarian eccentric whom both Wilhelm and Hohenlohe liked, assumed the position of state secretary of the imperial Post Office, recently vacated by the death of the incumbent. The imperial treasury went to the German ambassador in Washington, Baron Max von Thielmann, who had no experience in fiscal affairs. In addition to these changes in 1897, the previous year had brought Bronsart's removal as minister of war in favor of the reactionary General von Gossler, as well as the resignation of Baron Hans Hermann von Berlepsch, minister of trade, and a number of lesser officials who were his allies. Berlepsch found that neither Wilhelm II, under the influence of the reactionary industrialist Baron von Stumm-Halberg, nor the Hohenlohe government had any interest in the welfare legislation he was eager to introduce.[88] Berlepsch's successor, who left no mark on Berlin, was an insignificant official from the imperial railroad administration. The Kaiser picked all these officials, and Hohenlohe acquiesced in their appointment, although he knew that they would intensify Wilhelm II's already well-developed autocratic tendencies, either because they sympathized with such pretensions or because they were, like Thielmann, such nonentities that they would offer no resistance. The new officials would be the Kaiser's men, not Hohenlohe's, and this reshuffling consequently would result in a reduction in the chancellor's influence.

None of this greatly troubled Hohenlohe, who continued to believe more was to be achieved with Wilhelm by accommodation than by confrontation. "My mind is absolutely made up not to become upset about anything and just let matters take their course," he had told Waldersee early in 1896. "If I wanted to behave otherwise, I'd have to resign at least once a week.[89] In any case, from Hohenlohe's ever optimistic perspective all had not been lost. Although the chancellor suspected that Eulenburg and the Kaiser's courtiers would gladly have seen him pensioned off, he was still in office with a number of legislative accomplishments to his credit and confident that he would eventually get his way on the courts-martial issue.[90] The three major cabinet revisions—Bronsart's departure in 1896, followed by Boetticher and Marschall in 1897—had been delayed as long as possible and sweetened with rewards of adjutantships, embassies, or gubernatorial dignities. It was true that, except for Podbielski, the least important of the new men of 1896–97, Hohenlohe had little enthusiasm for Wilhelm II's appointments, but he felt that it was his patriotic duty to remain in office since there was no one suitable to succeed him. As was his custom, Hohenlohe conformed to the Kaiser's wishes and then proceeded to develop a strategy to cope with the situation created by the royal will. Indeed, as he told the Austrian ambassador following Podbielski's appointment to the Post Office, giving in to Wilhelm in personnel questions created a mood of imperial gratitude that actually then worked to strengthen the chancellor's position.[91]

With the elimination of refractory ministers such as Marschall and Bronsart and the appointment in 1896–97 of Bülow, Miquel, Gossler, Podbielski, Posadowsky, and Thielmann, most of whom were to serve for a number of years, Wilhelm was now surrounded by men who believed in monarchical power, who were filled with devotion to him personally, and who agreed with their ruler that Germany must play a leading role in world diplomacy while at home maintaining a thoroughly conservative regime. Thus, 1897 is often seen as the beginning of a "*persönliches Regiment*," a highly individual regime, by the last Kaiser. This is a term, used by contemporaries as well as by historians attempting to portray the long-dead Wilhelmine Empire, which has not proved entirely useful, for it is vague and therefore susceptible to a variety of interpretations. In general, the term "*persönliches Regiment*" has come to mean that Wilhelm II succeeded in giving his individual stamp to the era which bears his name by appointing civil and military figures, not only in the government but also at his court, whose independence of action was entirely contingent upon remaining in the Kaiser's good graces.[92]

To speak of a *persönliches Regiment* as having been established in 1897 is misleading, for the manner in which Wilhelm II reigned from his ascension in 1888 to his abdication thirty years later was substantially the same before and after 1897. The Kaiser insisted on officials of whose loyalty he felt certain and who would recognize that he was the ultimate authority in Germany. As a Hohenzollern, he believed that it was his right to advocate domestic and diplomatic policies and that his servants must execute them. That was the attitude against which Bismarck ran fatally afoul in 1890. His successors learned that to survive in office the Iron Chancellor's dictatorial manner had to be abandoned and a more subservient demeanor adopted toward the Kaiser, one which maintained at least the fiction that he alone ruled. Wilhelm II's inability to sustain more than a spasmodic, superficial interest in affairs ensured that his statesmen, however dutiful their behavior might be, would continue to share with the Kaiser the task of imparting direction to German policy.

After 1890, each of Bismarck's successors as chancellor, and all their allies and rivals at court or in the Prussian or imperial governments, tried to devise strategies that would capture the Kaiser for their own purposes. Wilhelm II was so easily influenced, so susceptible to flattery or to threats of resignation, so eclectic and ungovernable in his enthusiasms, that those who served him had only to discover how to approach the throne in a way that would win the ruler over. Caprivi, although insistent on pursuing principles, understood that sometimes he had to succumb to Wilhelm's vagaries in order to proceed with his policies. Hohenlohe believed in tactical delays and incremental progress, a procedure that kept him in office for six years and enabled him to accomplish many reforms to which the Kaiser had initially raised furious objections. Bülow, in becoming head of the Foreign Office in 1897 and chancellor three years later, represented not a new departure but only a variation in style. Devoid of principles (a reproach which cannot be leveled at either Caprivi or Hohenlohe), he was eager to cater shamelessly to the Kaiser in the hope that he might thereby control him and the operations of the government. But Bülow had to be careful, for that which the Kaiser was opposed (France, for example) or to which he was ferociously committed (notably the fleet), and the men who represented the negative and positive poles of his prejudices, were inalterable factors around which courses of action had to be devised and the personnel of the government built.

A *persönliches Regiment* under Wilhelm II existed only in the sense that, both before 1897 and for two decades thereafter, the parameters of movement that any chancellor or official possessed were determined by the Kaiser's likes and dislikes. Wilhelm did not, except rhetorically, issue orders but rather was pleased to allow or to forbid, to appoint or to dismiss, according to his ever-erratic moods. He was never the German autocrat, but rather the one constant, unavoidable, unpredictable factor with which all statesmen in Berlin, for better or worse, had to reckon. Governing therefore became a task of operating within those confines and using ingenuity to alter Wilhelm's opinions. Every chancellor or courtier found his way through this maze, for a time at least, and there were episodes of good will and sometimes heady exultation, but eventually all of them, even the wily Bülow, annoyed the Kaiser and were coolly cast aside. Wilhelm then simply moved on to other victims, and the business of conducting Germany's affairs began again with a new cast of characters. Only that Bülow's arrival was singularly welcome to the Kaiser made 1897 different from the previous years. Bülow was an old friend (which none of the earlier chancellors and few other high officials had been), their association was particularly ardent at first and ultimately longer lived than that of any of Wilhelm's other chancellors, and Bülow's servility made Wilhelm *feel* that he was fully in charge. But the role into which Bülow entered in 1897 does not mark either the establishment of a *persönliches Regiment* or the triumph of some sort of bureaucratic or polycratic hegemony. German politics after 1888, and after 1897, was an exotic and unsettling farrago of *both* royal caprice and bureaucratic adjustment. No one really led and no one, certainly not the Kaiser's luckless subjects, won. In the end, 1897 was only another year, to be sure an important one because of the new figures introduced into the government, in what Friedrich von Holstein once wearily referred to as the "*Operettenregiment*," a rough sea of imperial bluster to which Wilhelm II's chancellors, as well as his lesser servants, had to accommodate themselves as best they could.[93]

There was, finally, one additional revision within the government in 1897 that was destined to outweigh all the others in significance. On 18

June 1897, the Kaiser selected Adm. Alfred Tirpitz to become state secretary of the imperial Naval Office. The other new men of 1896–97 would have their hour and eventually depart, but Tirpitz was destined to inhabit his position almost to the end of the monarchy in 1918. With Tirpitz's appointment the German navy was born, and once the Kaiser decided to build a battle fleet Germany entered into a struggle with England that would endure until Wilhelm II had been driven from his throne.

T w e l v e

OUR ARROGANT COUSIN,

ALBION

O F ALL THE NATIONS of Europe, none exercised so enduring a fascination on the last German Kaiser as Great Britain. From his boyhood trips to England to his embittered old age, in which on his modest estate in Holland he liked to pose as an Edwardian country gentleman, Wilhelm II loved no land so much save his own Germany, from no quarter did he so crave approval, and to him no disappointments were so acute as those sent his way from London. To the Kaiser, as heir to the Hohenzollern throne, as ruler, and finally in exile, England was an obsession, but his eager pursuit of this chimera, alternately adored and hated, always proved ultimately fruitless.

The root of Wilhelm's affection for England lay, of course, in his birth, for he was a son of England as well as of Prussia. His mother, Princess Royal of England, never ceased to love her home country, and she was determined that her children revere it as well. From infancy, Wilhelm received a steady diet of adulation of England, but as a young man he became exposed to other influences that challenged the British precepts his mother had tried to instill. By the time Wilhelm became twenty in 1879, he had begun to turn against his mother and against England, a process which intensified during the following decade. The principal victim of this attitude was his perplexed and wounded mother, but eventually the entire Royal Family became casualties of Wilhelm's hostility. His distaste for England was partly due to family complications but also to more general causes, to the animosity toward England harbored by the Prussian aristocracy, to the fact that in the 1880s the entire atmosphere of Anglo-German relations was changing for the worse because of Chancellor Bismarck's preference for Britain's rival, Russia, and to the increasingly rancorous economic competition between Europe's two leading industrial and commercial powers. None of these difficulties would ever be overcome. Bismarck's disappearance in 1890 brought other chancellors who were equally devoid of any sort of personal attachment to British institutions or ideas. A race in armaments, first on sea and then on land, began in the late 1890s, while the arena of potential conflict between these British and German warriors widened after 1885 as Germany began to acquire a colonial empire that stretched around the world. When Europe went to war in 1914, Germany and England were enemies, even though their sovereigns were first cousins.

Wilhelm II's adult life might therefore be expected to be a long descent into irremediable hostility toward England. But in fact, although his exasperation at London was sometimes great, his outbursts on occasion spectacularly vitriolic, and his behavior often calculated to offend statesmen on the other side of the North Sea, the Kaiser never entirely lost his affection for England. His pride in being descended from Hanoverian kings and queens who had once occupied the British throne did not wane, nor did his envy of Britain's wealth, glamor, and power.

Wilhelm first saw England in 1861, when at two and a half he visited his grandmother Queen Victoria, who liked her little Prussian grandson and showered him with presents. He returned frequently and greatly enjoyed himself. "Dear Grandmama is a dear Duck," he assured his mother on his third birthday in January 1862.[1] England's ships and sailors especially fascinated him, for there were none of either in land-locked Berlin. Her son's enthusiasm for the sea delighted the Crown Princess, who early on encouraged it "as an antidote to the possibility of a *too* engrossing military passion."[2] Queen Victoria promoted this interest by sending Willy a replica of the masts and rigging of a British man-of-war, which was duly erected on the grounds of the New Palace in Potsdam and afforded the little boy much pleasure.

As Wilhelm grew up, his trips to England became less frequent and his criticisms of the British and their institutions began.[3] His mother, with her doctrinaire views of British perfection always strenuously and often tactlessly advanced, was the person primarily responsible, but there was also Wilhelm's wife as well as figures in his entourage—especially General Waldersee, Captain von Bülow, Captain von Kessel, and Philipp Eulenburg—who were effective in turning him away from his childhood love of England. Moreover, in the early 1880s the government officials with whom Wilhelm began to dine and imbibe political ideas shared Bismarck's preference for Russia rather than England, a land these Prussian aristocrats condemned as morally lax, recklessly liberal in politics, and demeaned by a vulgar mammonism. Prussia, in comparison, represented all that was pious and decent, the undefiled guardian of virtues long since abandoned by the wayward British. This sour combination of economic envy and moral superiority exercised an influence on Wilhelm, and he was soon heard to speak venomously of England ("our arrogant cousin, Albion"), his relatives who composed its Royal Family, its statesmen, and the policies they pursued.[4] He did so with an arrogance that confirmed the fear expressed by his mother and father that their son had degenerated into a narrow-minded Prussian lieutenant, devoid of the cosmopolitan, enlightened views that they had so hoped to inspire in him.

At first there were querulous and hasty remarks made to friends, who circulated Wilhelm's barbs. The earliest outburst on record occurred in May 1882, when Lord Frederick Cavendish, the newly arrived first secretary for Ireland, was murdered as he strolled in a Dublin park. Wilhelm did not know Cavendish, but on hearing of the crime he spouted the observation, both puerile and cold-blooded, that it was "the best news that I have received today."[5] With time, Wilhelm became more vituperative. Early in 1885, filled with delight at the prospect that England might soon be faced by a war with Russia that could lead to native uprisings in India, Wilhelm declared, "*Caeterum censeo. Britannia esse delendam*"— "This I propose: Britain must be destroyed."[6] "One cannot have enough hate for England," he informed his friend Eulenburg two years later.[7] Even making allowance for infantile exuberance, Wilhelm's strident comments were both impolitic and inhuman. There was more than bluster and churlishness here. It was hatred that came to the surface and spilled over in the Prince's innumerable silly and unfortunate remarks. No one took him to task for his odious behavior; on the contrary, Wilhelm's conservative friends relished him all the more for his forthright, Anglophobe, Prussian spirit.

Wilhelm's increasing dislike of his English mother inevitably spread to the rest of the Royal Family. No one, not even the aging Queen Victoria, was spared, but Wilhelm's uncle, the Prince of Wales, bore the brunt of his abuse. How and why Wilhelm and his uncle first fell out is mysterious, and even when this break occurred cannot be determined with exactitude, although it seems likely that there was a spat between them as early as 1880 that was never amicably resolved.[8] The antipathy between Wilhelm and his uncle, which grew worse as the years went by, proceeded from their striking differences in personality. The Prince of Wales was much the more attractive, for he had a sizable fund of charm, tact, and discretion, and he unfailingly understood how to ingratiate himself with the most diverse sorts of people, royal, aristocratic, and common, British or foreign. Although, like his nephew—the one thing they had in common other than their squat stature—the Prince of Wales was a stickler about court ceremonial, he wore his crown with an easy grace and moved about Europe with imperturbable aplomb. The Prince was a rather distant patron of the arts and a forceful advocate of improving the lot of the poor, but otherwise he had little taste for any sort of hard work other than the demands that pageantry exacted, and he had hardly any ambition to play an influential role in British politics or European diplomacy. Life was society, and for that gilded world his fabled bonhommie and grace were essential virtues. Even in Berlin, the fast set regarded him as its exemplar, cutting their clothes and modeling their behavior on his elegant but licentious example. No wonder that in Germany and elsewhere on the continent hotel proprietors aspiring to fashionability named their establishments for him.

Wilhelm, by contrast, had none of these qualities, though he vainly fancied that he possessed his uncle's suavity and kingly carriage. He was usually tiresome and humorless, unpossessed of any sense of discretion, tediously moralistic, unconvincingly pretentious in his displays of learning, and awkward and unnatural when regal gestures were required. He would never enjoy the Prince of Wales's welcome in the drawing rooms, or boudoirs, of Europe (nor the popularity his uncle easily commanded from his subjects), and he admitted that they were not at all alike and that it "was scarcely to be expected that anything like a cordial friendship would exist between them."[9] None ever did.

Wilhelm's relationship with his uncle suffered from a further burden in the person of the Princess of Wales, a daughter of the Danish King, Christian IX, who had lost the duchies of Schleswig and Holstein to Prussia in a war fought when Wilhelm was a small child. The King, a realistic sovereign, accepted defeat and for the rest of his long reign tried to foster good relations with the triumphant Hohenzollerns. Not so his wife, Queen Louise, who had been born a princess of Hesse-Cassel, which Prussia had swallowed up in a war fought in 1866. As a result, the Queen had sworn vengeance on the Prussians and refused ever to set foot in Berlin. She bequeathed her surpassing hatred of Prussia to all her children and thrived on intriguing against the Kaiser through them. Her progeny included, in addition to the Princess of Wales, King George I of the Hellenes; the Tsarina Maria Feodorovna, consort of Alexander III; and the Duchess of Cumberland, whose husband was claimant to the throne of Hanover, seized by Prussia in the same war that had added

Hesse-Cassel to the Hohenzollern domains. Wilhelm knew of the Queen's machinations against him and he disliked her, declaring that the "old spider" (*alte Kreuzspinne*) was responsible for many of his troubles, including his difficulties with Tsar Alexander III.[10]

Queen Louise's children inherited her prejudice against Wilhelm II and perpetuated it long after their mother's death in 1898. The Tsarina Maria Feodorovna loathed Wilhelm, who in turn believed that she was bent on revenge for Prussia's seizure of Schleswig-Holstein.[11] Even when the Kaiser made a rare attempt to treat the Duke and Duchess of Cumberland with consideration, they avoided him.[12] The Princess of Wales could seldom muster any enthusiasm for Wilhelm, whom she thought crazy and hopelessly egotistical. He imagined that he was Charlemagne, she declared, but in actual fact he became "more foolish and conceited every day."[13] Moreover, the Princess of Wales, like her mother, took a patronizing and critical attitude toward Wilhelm's wife Dona, who was a distant cousin from a rival branch of the Danish royal house. The Princess of Wales and her husband (as well as Queen Victoria) considered Dona to be insignificant and drab, even though she had a broad pedigree of Hanoverian ancestors. They looked down on her, and both she and the Kaiser acutely resented these slights.[14] Dona had no use either for the philandering Prince or for the Princess, whose family had eclipsed her own. "My wife," Wilhelm II told Bernhard von Bülow after his uncle and aunt had ascended the British throne, "has a fanatical hate for the British majesties."[15]

In light of all these problems, it is hardly surprising that the course of Wilhelm's relations with his uncle were almost invariably unsatisfactory. Wilhelm had been Kaiser only a few days when a major feud broke out between them, the occasion being the Prince and Princess of Wales's appearance in Berlin for Kaiser Friedrich III's funeral in June 1888. Wilhelm heard that while there his uncle had declared that the deceased ruler had intended to make concessions to France in Alsace-Lorraine, to Denmark in Schleswig, and to restore the Prince's brother-in-law and distant cousin, the Duke of Cumberland, to the defunct throne of Hanover.[16] What in fact appears to have happened—this is the Wales version of the incident—was that on arriving in Berlin the Prince heard rumors about Friedrich III's alleged intentions to this effect and inquired of Herbert Bismarck if they were true. The chancellor's son assured him that they were not, and the Prince let the matter drop.

Wilhelm was not amused when he heard what his uncle reportedly had said. Even if true, it was a minor indiscretion that was best disregarded.

But Wilhelm would not allow the incident to pass and instead plotted his revenge, getting even in September 1888 on the occasion of a visit to the Habsburg Emperor Franz Josef. Shortly before the Kaiser was to appear in Vienna, the Austrians were informed from Berlin, probably on Wilhelm's order, that it was not the Kaiser's pleasure for the Prince of Wales, who had proposed to appear simultaneously in the Habsburg capital, to be in Vienna during his visit. Franz Josef, reflecting on the diplomatic complications that might result if he refused Wilhelm's request, gave instructions that the Prince was to be asked to leave Vienna before the Kaiser's arrival. Wilhelm, as Herbert Bismarck advised his father, was "insanely delighted" (*freute sich unsinnig*) that the Prince of Wales had been forced to make way for him.[17] The Habsburg Crown Prince Rudolf, who found Wilhelm narrow-minded, vain, and quite unlikable, at once intervened to offer the Prince of Wales relief from his embarrassment by inviting him to a hunt in Hungary.[18] The Prince's annoyance at his nephew, already inflamed, increased enormously when Wilhelm refused to accept his assurances that the reports of his remarks at Kaiser Friedrich III's funeral were "a positive lie."[19] Queen Victoria, solidly behind her heir, took the position that Wilhelm's rudeness required both an apology and an explanation. To allow Wilhelm to get away with such "reckless, unfeeling" behavior would only make him more objectionable in the future.[20]

The German envoy in London, Count Paul von Hatzfeldt-Wildenburg, in the course of a conversation with the Marquess of Salisbury, the Conservative prime minister, candidly revealed that the Prince of Wales's alleged remarks were in fact only a part of Wilhelm II's anger at his uncle. The Kaiser was enraged that the Prince "treated him as an uncle treats a nephew instead of recognizing that he was an emperor who, though young, had still been of age for some time."[21] Wilhelm's charge was probably true enough, for the Prince and Princess of Wales, according to Herbert Bismarck, did in fact take a condescending attitude toward the Kaiser during their presence in Berlin for Friedrich III's funeral, handling him as an "immature 'bad boy.' "[22] Queen Victoria was equally guilty of trying to reduce her grandson to the role of an obedient descendant to whom punishment was to be meted out if he failed to display the requisite deference. This was an attitude, the British ambassador in Berlin perceptively observed, that was certain to annoy the Kaiser and ultimately create problems in Anglo-German relations.[23] Queen Victoria, however, dismissed Wilhelm's complaints about the way the Prince and Princess of Wales had dealt with him as "too *vulgar* and too absurd, as well as untrue almost *to be believed.*" In public the young monarch had every right to be deferred to as an imperial majesty, but to insist that his private relations with his mother's family were to have the same pomp was "*perfect madness.*" In such a situation, the Queen made the rules, and her progeny were expected to follow them without either deviation or question. As for a story the Queen had heard of the Kaiser that if the Prince of Wales wrote him a "very kind letter he *might perhaps answer it,*" this revealed an insolence that was not to be tolerated.[24] It was the Kaiser who must write to his uncle, not the reverse. That Wilhelm refused to do, while the Prince of Wales continued with equal insistence to demand a written explanation from his nephew, an attitude which the Prince's sister, Wilhelm's mother, entirely approved.[25]

So the matter dragged on through the spring of 1889, until finally Queen Victoria and her son somewhat grudgingly came around to the view that Herbert Bismarck, conspiring with the Anglophobe German ambassador in Vienna, Prince Reuss, had been responsible for the Prince of Wales's having been asked to leave Vienna.[26] That being the case, Salisbury recommended to the Queen that she write a letter (drafted by the prime minister) to her grandson, expressing her satisfaction that the matter should be considered closed. She did so at once.[27] Wilhelm replied initially that the affair had originated in the Prince of Wales's imagination, but he subsequently wrote the Queen a polite letter in which he expressed his gratification that the incident could finally be laid to rest.[28]

Like Wilhelm's uncivil treatment of his mother and father and his intemperate remarks about England in the 1880s, his affront to the Prince of Wales in Vienna became part of the residue of resentments the Royal Family harbored against the Kaiser. Queen Victoria was never entirely satisfied that the Vienna incident had been resolved, for although Wilhelm had denied his complicity—*that* she was prepared to believe—he had never expressed any regret about the matter. As for the Prince of Wales, what had transpired in the Habsburg capital was a slight that was never satisfactorily atoned for, and relations between the Kaiser and his uncle would go from bad to worse for the next twenty years.[29]

The Kaiser was elated when he heard that his verbal assurances about the Vienna incident had removed the barriers to a visit to England he wanted to make in the summer of 1889. Herbert Bismarck, who gave Wilhelm the welcome news, described him as "almost in ecstasy, like a child on Christmas Eve."[30] The Kaiser proceeded in August 1889 to London, where he was accorded every attention. The Prince of Wales's behavior left nothing to be desired, and if he still felt umbrage he managed not to let it show. As Wilhelm correctly observed, the Prince did not rule England, and therefore the disagreement with his uncle should not hamper good relations between London and Berlin.[31] Queen Victoria greeted her grandson cordially, but she could not overcome her belief that Wilhelm, although not without flashes of endearing loyalty, was spoiled, pretentious, often obnoxious, and married to a woman who was simply undeserving of notice. They were both unfit for the destiny that had descended upon then so prematurely. "It is too dreadful to us all," Queen Victoria wrote to one of her Hessian granddaughters just after Friedrich III's death, "to think of Willy and Bismarck and Dona being the supreme head of all now. Two so unfit and one so wicked."[32]

According to Herbert Bismarck (who cannot have rejoiced at the transformation), the Kaiser returned to Berlin a convinced Anglophile. Swift changes in disposition were not unusual in the Kaiser ("Wilhelm the Sudden" was after all a nickname he bore from childhood), and just after a period of acute Anglophobia he now suddenly began to contemplate forming an alliance with Great Britain.[33] The alteration in Wilhelm II's attitude, so nasty at Vienna and now so favorable, appeared to Lord Salisbury to be positively striking, and in October 1889, two months after the Kaiser had returned to Germany, the prime minister wrote to Queen Victoria that Wilhelm II "is a changed man from what he was twelve months ago."[34] Salisbury would gradually realize how superficial Wilhelm's transformation was, but for the moment his attitude to England had indeed become entirely satisfactory.

The Kaiser's increasing cordiality toward England at the very end of the 1880s was probably due to two changes in the situation in Berlin. One was the fact that after her husband's death in June 1888 the Kaiserin Friedrich no longer played any role in German affairs and had only a negligible part in her son's life. The court exacted its revenge for her attachment to England by totally ignoring her, and Wilhelm rarely ever saw his mother, a slight about which she bitterly complained.[35] She eventually left Berlin altogether and built a castle in Hesse, where she lived, little noticed by anyone, until she died of cancer in 1901, full of sorrow tinctured by self-pity. The Empress had decreed that she was to be laid in an English coffin and buried according to the Anglican rite. Wilhelm followed these instructions to the letter but had the English casket placed in a larger one of German manufacture and ordered that the Church of England service be followed by the German evangelical rite.[36] The exit of Wilhelm's mother from the scene meant that the principal cause of the Kaiser's earlier antagonism to England was gone.

The other alteration in Berlin that undoubtedly turned Wilhelm more favorably to Britain was Bismarck's revision in 1888–89 of his diplomatic perspective.[37] The chancellor was traditionally highly suspicious of England and in the 1870s and early 1880s had arranged a constellation of treaties that joined Germany to Russia, Austria-Hungary, and Italy. Britain, like France, was not a friend but a putative rival in Europe and around the world. By 1887, however, the chancellor had become seriously alarmed by the torrent of revanchism sweeping France under General Georges Boulanger, who called for war to retrieve the lost provinces of Alsace and Lorraine. In Russia, Pan-Slav nationalist bellicosity threatened to force Tsar Alexander III into attacking Germany and the Habsburg Empire. In such a war on two fronts, Bismarck would have only the Austrians and the Italians for allies, neither of whom, he feared, would be able to help Germany prevent defeat, much less achieve victory. Faced by such an emergency, in January 1889 Bismarck had proposed to Lord Salisbury that Germany and Great Britain form a defensive alliance. Salisbury, who had no desire to become involved in an entanglement, politely responded that the temper of parliament against diplomatic commitments made the chancellor's invitation "inopportune."

The crisis eventually evaporated when Boulanger fell from power and the Tsar succeeded in calming the agitation for war among his subjects. Bismarck consequently did not press on with his earlier negotiations with Salisbury but instead concentrated on trying to return Russia to its traditional association with Germany and Austria-Hungary. Wilhelm II, however, continued to pursue the possibility of an Anglo-German entente. In the early years of his reign, the Kaiser envisioned an association between Berlin and London that would draw the two nations together in a tight web, sustained by mutual interests, cultural sympathy, and common Russian and French enemies.[38] The end toward which Wilhelm looked was a diplomatic alliance that would give the two kindred peoples a commanding role in Europe and indeed around the world. This was a view that the Kaiser conceived not out of a prudent assessment of the diplomatic realities that affected Anglo-German relations but rather from an emotional fervor which was romantic and fuzzy about mundane, practical considerations.

There was, first of all, a religious element in Wilhelm's affinity for England, for he believed that as Protestant powers (he had no qualms at disregarding the fact that 40 percent of Germany's population was Roman Catholic) England and Germany had a Christian obligation to join hands for the maintenance of peace.[39] But what really bound the Kaiser to England was a sense of cultural identity, one that was very narrow and quite unlike the equally strong attachment his mother had felt for the country of her birth. The Kaiserin Friedrich's devotion to England revolved around ideas of personal freedom, political liberalism, and toleration for intellectual enterprise, religious novelty, and social independence. While Wilhelm's mother was enormously proud of England's wealth and glory, she had no enthusiasm for society, magnificence of display, or pomp of any sort. All this folderol of high living, on the contrary, was exactly that quality of English life that her son loved and admired most. The political practices, intellectual achievements, and eccentric independence of attitude his mother revered he cared nothing about and indeed often condemned. What enthralled the Kaiser was the dazzling splendor of British ceremonial, the huge Royal Navy, the sumptuousness of English country-house life, and the titanic expenditure of money that provided the ballast for aristocratic society. "The England of *wealth*, of water sports, of an impressive navy, of the court and of the present [Conservative] ministry," the widowed Kaiserin complained to a friend in the early 1890s, "please him greatly, but the true, the inner, the serious England, its significance, its struggles, its aims he knows not, just as little as he knows his own Germany and the better side of the German people."[40]

The one thing that Wilhelm II could not abide was to be deprecated—by statesmen, newspaper writers, or other sovereigns—and the thought that he or his court were objects of ridicule or, at best, neglect alarmed him enormously. Very shortly after his ascension, Ambassador Malet had presciently warned Lord Salisbury that nothing would so affect the new monarch's feelings about England as the suspicion that his efforts to be friendly were being spurned.[41] For the English to treat him with the same indifference or ingratitude as had his parents, or his subjects, or his Prussian ministers, was to Wilhelm II intolerable. Sometimes the Kaiser was absurdly petulant about British lack of attention, such as his outburst in December 1896 that the London press had failed to note the pointed attention he had recently paid to his mother on the occasion of her birthday. The British envoy, Sir Frank Lascelles, had indeed reported Wilhelm's flourishes in the Empress's honor, but to have the British government issue a statement noting the fact would, he rightly felt, have exposed the Kaiser only to ridicule.[42]

Wilhelm II was obsessed that Germany did not measure up to England, and the more personal any invidious comparisons were, the more painful he found them. He worried that the British regarded Berlin, in his own words, as a "parvenu court," and he recognized that the German capital lacked glamor and interest, an admission that may have wounded him all the more, since his mother had always found aristocratic Berlin very deficient in elegance.[43] The Kaiser complained that along the Spree it was hard to have the sort of animated conversation that he had found to his delight in England or in Vienna. Berlin, he confessed, was a dowdy wasteland.[44] He had reason for concern, for European royalty and their aristocratic satellites thought the Hohenzollern court, though lavish and superbly managed, deficient in chic and amusement. Jewelry was minimal, clothes were old, food plain, and nothing really impressive except the milling throngs of brilliantly caparisoned guards officers, all of whom had been well trained in the art of antique cotillions, the only form of dancing Wilhelm II and the Kaiserin would permit on their glistening parquet. The Berlin court was not without its eccentric touches, especially when dining in the palace was part of the program. Wilhelm, who was served first, ate quickly, drank very little, and since etiquette prescribed that all plates be removed when he had finished, those who were served last got nothing. They were thus deprived of the delicacies which the menu had advertised to be forthcoming, always described at the Kaiser's order *auf Deutsch*. His guests, if they were fortunate in their precedence and could consume with dispatch, supped on such morsels as *Kleine Fische zum Divan,* never *canapés d'anchois.*

Wilhelm II had a very clear idea as to how his court was to be put on an equal footing with Queen Victoria's. While the Prussian aristocracy defended its lack of luster by explaining that its tiaras had been sold decades earlier in order to pay for the wars of liberation against Napoleon or by arguing defensively that more brilliance would lend the court an undesirably Jewish or American air, the Kaiser believed that a more aggressive effort at elegance was essential. Berlin would have to become more like London. Wilhelm expended enormous energy in making his court more impressive, and he gradually transformed it into a spectacle entirely different from the modest but quite select society over which his grandparents had presided.[45] Footmen on the royal household staff were ordered to draw on silk stockings identical to those worn at Buckingham Palace, and in countless other ways the Kaiser deliberately refashioned the Berlin court into an approximation of the Hanoverian establishment in England. The Kaiser encouraged Prussian courtiers to dress more fashionably and took a personal hand in designing his consort's gowns and jewelry so that she might cease to appear, as he uncharitably put it, "like the parson's wife" (*comme l'as de pique*).[46] Wilhelm II eagerly welcomed British visitors to Berlin in the hope that society might thereby acquire a little welcome leavening. "Ask your smart London friends to come here," he entreated a British diplomat's aristocratic wife. "Let them teach my court ladies how to do their hair and put on their clothes."[47] The result of the Kaiser's efforts was a physically impressive operation but not a pageant of assured dignity or grace. Wilhelm II's own turbulent manner and banal grandiloquence were often somewhat comical; in spite of an endless variety of costumes, uniforms, and poses, he rarely managed to look the part of a great sovereign. The matronly Kaiserin, for all her virtues, often appeared a trifle worn, and she was quite vacant if conversation strayed beyond the confines of domestic obligations or religious devotion.

Like the court, the lives of the Prussian nobility were to be revised in a manner more in keeping with English country-house life. There was nothing in which Wilhelm took more delight than English landed society, and he liked to visit the ancestral houses of Queen Victoria's peers and occasionally rented estates in the home counties. What a pleasure, the Kaiser declared, to be able in such aristocratic havens to lay aside crown and scepter and mix easily as gentleman with gentleman, a word in which he delighted.[48] English country houses, he asserted, possessed an "indefinable something," and somehow the Kaiser managed to find even the cooking excellent. "I feel at home here" (*Es ist mir eine Heimat*), he proclaimed.[49] Wilhelm II's efforts to pose as an English gentleman were, alas, ludicrous. In his checked suit and boater he looked, as one amused British spectator put it, "more of an incongruous cad than most Bank Holiday trippers to Margate," then as now a distinctly middle-class resort.[50]

The Kaiser revived the English practice of the shooting visit, and with fearful regularity he descended on his hapless nobility, inevitably attended by an enormous suite of gentlemen. This was a sort of outing that his ancestors had indulged in only spasmodically, and the Prussian aristocracy regarded it as an unwelcome innovation imported from England.[51] Sailing, a pastime unknown to earlier Hohenzollerns or to the Prussian aristocracy, was yet another of Wilhelm II's imitations of English society. In his innumerable cruises and sailing regattas, the Kaiser showed a predilection for rich English and American yachtsmen that his courtiers found alarmingly vulgar.[52] To be English was thus to Wilhelm II a question of style rather than an ideal, and he self-consciously promoted an image of himself that was unmistakably derived from London examples, in clothes, speech, and social habits.

But Wilhelm II was also a ruler, and he believed that the affinity for England he felt as a "gentleman" was one which could, and should, be translated in a larger sense into an association between London and Berlin that would set the course for the rest of Europe to follow. To Wilhelm, that meant keeping a vigilant eye on France and Russia, Germany's prospective enemies, who were also Britain's leading imperial rivals. In the late 1880s, of the two conspirators Russia had seemed the more aggressive, but after Nicholas II became Tsar late in 1894, Wilhelm believed that the Russian danger could be defused by the careful application of his personal diplomacy with his new "colleague" in St. Petersburg, who seemed far more susceptible to his counsel than his unpleasant father, Alexander III, had ever been. He therefore tried, but without any success whatsoever, to persuade Nicholas II to detach himself from France. The Tsar, who disliked Wilhelm as intensely as his father had and who shared Alexander III's conviction that the Kaiser was "crazy," scrupulously avoided Wilhelm and stuck to his alliance with Paris.[53]

The French Republic, Wilhelm II was sure, lay in wait to take revenge for her humiliating defeat in the Franco-Prussian war of 1870–71. If France moved against Germany, Russia might be unable to resist the temptation to enter the fray, thus confronting Germany with the dreaded prospect of a war on two fronts. Germany's defensive Dual Alliance of 1879 with Austria-Hungary, which committed Vienna to enter such a war, would ensure that all of Russia's forces could not be directed against Germany, while Italy's adherence in 1882 to this pact would divert part of France's forces to the Mediterranean. Russia, which was less expertly armed, might therefore be contained or even defeated, but Germany's ability to secure France's liquidation was more questionable. Nothing was to be feared from Paris, however, if Britain could be persuaded to cooperate with Germany against France. But London had for decades avoided any participation in continental alliances, and there was every indication, most recently in Salisbury's rejection of Bismarck's 1889 overture, that neither the liberal nor conservative governments of the 1880s and early 1890s had any intention of altering that traditional policy. Wilhelm II, ever ready to engage in personal diplomacy, therefore took it to be his task to persuade England that France, abetted by Russia, was determined on war. England, conveniently enough, was then seriously at odds with both Russia and France because of a number of imperial rivalries.

There were two features of republican France in the early 1890s about which the Kaiser felt compelled to warn the British. One was her rampant socialism, which he declared had created an inflammatory mood similar to 1789. France, being feminine in nature, in contrast to the manliness of the Anglo-Saxons and Teutons, was nervy and potentially explosive.[54] This "hateful country," populated by canaille and led by presidents drawn from the depths of the working class, was bent on war against either Germany or England. One day a farmer presided in the Elysée palace, the next a blacksmith, a development as disgusting as it was dangerous. "Nothing remains," Wilhelm advised the British military attaché in Berlin in 1895, "when the next chance presents itself but to break up France and render her harmless for the future."[55] This was imperial swagger, for the Kaiser wanted not war with France in the 1890s but rather her diplomatic isolation. A nation sinking into degeneracy and likely at any moment to hatch a revolutionary socialist government should be accorded no marks of respectability. Princes should not visit Paris, "the greatest whore house in the world," he advised Chancellor Caprivi in 1892, and the powers should be resolute in withholding diplomatic recognition from any incendiary regime that might be established there. Meanwhile it was imperative that Europe's monarchs keep in consultation about the danger represented by France and show a solid front of resistance to their common enemy.[56]

The second danger France posed to European peace was one which only Great Britain could neutralize. This was the large fleet that the French maintained in the Mediterranean, an area in which Wilhelm believed Russia was ambitious to play an expanded role. This vast sea was clearly a tinderbox ready to blow at any moment.[57] Germany, without a navy or any military bases in the area, was powerless to deal with France there, but, if only they could be made aware of the danger and persuaded to act forcefully, the British were in a position to use their fleet to keep the French at bay. Ever since becoming Kaiser, Wilhelm had repeatedly declared that Britain's role was to be mistress of the seas. "A strong and well armed and ably commanded British fleet is an absolute necessity for the welfare of Europe and the maintenance of the peace," he wrote a British acquaintance, Captain Lord Charles Beresford, R.N., at the end of 1888.[58] Furthermore, there was the danger, one which Wilhelm took quite seriously, that France might someday ally with the United States, then in the throes of a massive naval rearmament program. "Your navy," he warned Queen Victoria in 1890, "must be trebled to be able to meet mounseers and Yankees on equal terms!"[59] But instead of showing firmness to Paris, Britain had allowed her ships and crews to decline in quality. The Kaiser warned his grandmother that the French felt only disdain for England's modest Mediterranean squadron. "Fancy!" he exclaimed, "What would Lord Nelson say!"[60]

Wilhelm was gratified to note that by 1893 the British were becoming more perceptive about the Franco-Russian threat in the Mediterranean and making naval increases, although he felt that they should add still more ships to their fleet.[61] With Admiral Nelson's heirs guarding the seas against France, Russia, and the United States, Britain and Germany could enjoy peace and prosperity. This tranquil future could, in the Kaiser's view, be made yet more enduring if London and Berlin converted their cooperation into a diplomatic alliance. Lord Salisbury, it was true, had spurned Bismarck's soundings, but the Kaiser believed that time was on his side. With the proliferation of diplomatic commitments on the continent and the prodigious rearming of all the powers, an England without allies was worth increasingly little in the European balance of power. Sooner or later, he felt certain, London's traditional policy of splendid isolation would have to be abandoned.[62]

The hoped-for accommodation with England never took place, and certainly one significant barrier to good relations between London and Berlin was the Kaiser's difficult personality that so upset the British and their Royal Family. But even had Wilhelm been endowed with a more irenic disposition suitable for ingratiating himself with the British, the accomplishment of this goal would not have been easy because of the Anglophobia that existed in Germany. As Prince of Prussia and later as German Kaiser, he lived in an atmosphere charged with hostility to England, and his efforts to draw closer to England produced very profound suspicion among the aristocracy grouped around the Prussian throne. Once his father died and his mother left for her self-imposed exile in the Hessian mountains, there were hardly any voices at court or in society in Berlin who felt attracted to England. On the contrary, the Prussian nobility with few exceptions had a pronounced distaste for England that grew only stronger as the years went by.[63] Although there was some mimicry of English tastes in Berlin high society, the nobility regarded Britain as the eponym of vulgar ostentation. The Kaiserin and her ladies—the "donkeys" Wilhelm's mother had dismissed with disdain—rejected England, along with the United States, as immoral and philistine in contrast to the steadfast, Christian virtues so exemplified by the simple German home. Since the Prussian aristocracy led the Kaiser's governments, Berlin officialdom always kept England at a distance. The diplomatic service was a particular stronghold of anti-British sentiment, and those who were most ill-disposed to England, such as Bernhard von Bülow and Philipp Eulenburg, were also the very diplomats who in the 1890s were most influential with the Kaiser.

Chancellor Bismarck, whose attitude was for many years decisive, mistrusted England, especially after 1880, when the government fell into the hands of Gladstone and the Liberals. The chancellor was wary of the prime minister, for his intrusion of moral factors in diplomacy (in particular his detestation of the pagan Turks) and his insistence that European affairs be governed by the "concert" of powers were ideas Bismarck found disturbing. To the Iron Chancellor only considerations of realpolitik were admissable in diplomacy, and he believed that a handful of prominent diplomats and statesmen (and himself in particular), rather than an expanded league of powers, should be the manipulators of European affairs. In the long run, Britain's notions of popular government were incompatible with, and indeed dangerous to, a German Empire that Bismarck saw as increasingly imperiled by liberal, anti-Prussian elements. For this reserved and ultimately hostile attitude, the chancellor could reckon on the support of both his son Herbert as well as old Kaiser Wilhelm I.[64]

The triumph in 1886 of Lord Salisbury and the Conservatives, who would rule with only one interruption (1892–95) for almost twenty years, represented something of an improvement from Bismarck's perspective. Bismarck's investigation in 1889 of the possibility of an Anglo-German alliance, prompted only because Germany simultaneously faced the gravest danger from France and Russia, came to nothing because of Salisbury's lack of interest. Both statesmen nevertheless continued to treat one another with forebearance, behavior perpetuated on the German side by General Caprivi after he succeeded as chancellor in March 1890. This agreeableness found expression in an Anglo-German colonial agreement signed on 1 July of that year, whereby Germany surrendered Zanzibar, in south-eastern Africa, for the North Sea island fortress of Heligoland, some twenty-eight miles off the German coast. Caprivi had expected, as had the young Kaiser, that the colonial settlement would lead to further accommodation between London and Berlin, but in fact little or none was forthcoming.

As far as Wilhelm II was concerned, the fault lay in the sort of people who were in command in London. Diplomacy was always to Wilhelm II a matter of personalities, his "colleagues" on Europe's thrones and their leading statesmen constituting the entire roster of those who mattered. From his youth, Wilhelm had detested Gladstone and the Liberals, whose final government lasted only from 1892 to 1894. Such energy as the octogenarian statesman still possessed had then concentrated on his vain attempt to secure Home Rule for Ireland, a project for which the Kaiser had no sympathy whatsoever.[65] When the aged statesman finally died in 1898, Wilhelm begrudged him the honor of burial among the nation's heroes in Westminster Abbey.[66] The Earl of Rosebery, who succeeded Gladstone and served as prime minister in 1894–95, was a man whom the Kaiser "thoroughly distrusted," so the British ambassador in Berlin reported.[67] Wilhelm was miffed because Rosebery treated him not as a sovereign but as the grandson of the Queen of England. To the Kaiser this was a serious gaffe even when committed by his grandmother and one that was unforgivable in one of her servants. Wilhelm, who considered the prime minister's talents as a statesman to be quite meager, believed without justification that Rosebery had treated his efforts to be agreeable in diplomatic matters either with ridicule or neglect.[68] There was, besides, the compromising friendship that Rosebery had long had with Herbert Bismarck, a relationship that undoubtedly drove a further wedge between him and the Liberal prime minister.[69]

Wilhelm anticipated an improvement in Anglo-German relations when in the summer of 1895 Lord Salisbury replaced Rosebery, but this failed to materialize. Although the new government began promisingly enough, Wilhelm II soon discovered that the prime minister was determined to pursue a diplomatic policy that the Kaiser described as "most mysterious and unintelligible." Besides, Wilhelm found the English grandee, a man of extraordinary remoteness and taciturnity, unsympathetic.[70] Salisbury, far more than Gladstone or Rosebery, occupied a central place in Wilhelm's calculations about England. Unlike Gladstone, Salisbury placed European affairs, in which he had much experience, at the forefront of his responsibilities, and for almost all of the period between 1886 and 1902 he served as foreign secretary as well as premier. This decade and a half, which also marked the first years of Wilhelm II's reign, coincided with the emergence of the most difficult problems that had ever clouded Anglo-German relations. By the time Salisbury finally retired in 1902, the relationship between London and Berlin had degenerated into the mutual suspicion that persisted until the two powers went to war with one another in 1914.

At their first meeting at Queen Victoria's jubilee in 1887, Salisbury had formed a negative impression of Prince Wilhelm. The prime minister indicated not long thereafter that England would have cause to regret his premature ascension.[71] Wilhelm was not to be trusted either in speech or action, and Salisbury recognized that his defective character was a destabilizing factor on which both Queen Victoria and her governments would have to reckon in the future. He wrote to the Queen two months before Wilhelm succeeded his father that "it is nevertheless true—most unhappily—that all Prince Wilhelm's impulses, however blamable and unreasonable, will henceforth be political causes of enormous potency and the two nations are so necessary to each other that everything that is said to him must be very carefully weighed."[72]

Salisbury's prophesy that Wilhelm would be troublesome proved entirely correct, for the contretemps at Vienna involving the Prince of Wales occurred almost immediately after his ascension. Once this dispute had been cleaned up, however, the Kaiser did not for the moment cause Salisbury any further difficulty, but the prime minister nevertheless continued to be wary and very disapproving. A friend who encountered Salisbury in 1891, shortly after yet another of the Kaiser's visits to England, reported that he regarded Wilhelm as "the most dangerous enemy" England had on the continent, a man who spoke far too often and then usually with a double tongue.[73] Salisbury, like Tsar Alexander III and his heir Nicholas II, did not care for people who were noisy and petulant, and all three men found that Wilhelm's antic behavior was an indication that he was not quite right in the head. The Kaiser, as Salisbury put it, seemed to be "ultra-human."[74] In 1888, just after Wilhelm I's death, an unnamed German doctor passed on a medical evaluation of Prince Wilhelm that he had made in the 1870s to John Erichsen, one of Queen Victoria's physicians, who sent it to Lord Salisbury. The German physician diagnosed the young Hohenzollern Prince as marginally abnormal, being subject to "sudden accesses of anger" that prevented his "forming a reasonable or temperate judgment." The prime minister found this document highly interesting and did not forget it. In later years whenever Wilhelm II's behavior became frenzied, Salisbury would tap his head and laconically whisper the single word "Erichsen."[75] Such an imbalanced ruler was not one with whom it was safe for Britain to draw too close.

On returning to power in 1895 after a three-year absence, Salisbury discovered that the Kaiser had become increasingly unreasonable. British policy, the prime minister declared, had always been to be friendly to

Germany without wishing to become enmeshed in Berlin's Triple Alliance with Austria-Hungary and Italy or the Three Emperors' League that loosely bound the Hohenzollerns with the Tsar and the Habsburg Emperor. This had made for good Anglo-German relations in his earlier administration, but now it did not seem to be enough for Wilhelm II, who had become inexplicably hostile to England and to the prime minister personally.[76] The "changed man" Salisbury had encountered on Wilhelm's 1889 trip to England had reverted to his old self. There was some truth in the prime minister's complaint, for the Kaiser was indeed exasperated by what he considered to be Salisbury's coldness. Wilhelm II felt that no matter how hard he tried to be friendly, the prime minister appeared to rebuff his overtures. That was certainly not an entirely inaccurate assessment of the prime minister's behavior, but Salisbury's reserve did not proceed from spite. The Kaiser could neither understand nor accept the fact that Salisbury's reluctance, in part based on constitutional restraints on alliances, was also partially a reflection of the prime minister's misgivings about Wilhelm II's character. It did not occur to the Kaiser that the withdrawn but fastidiously correct Salisbury, who on many occasions had labored to smooth Wilhelm's relations with his British relatives, found his blustering, high-handed manner abhorrent. "Your Kaiser," the prime minister complained to a German diplomat in 1895, "seems entirely to forget that I am not a minister of the King of Prussia but premier of England."[77] For that reason, Salisbury, like the two last Romanov Tsars, was reluctant to discuss affairs of state with Wilhelm II.[78]

What the Kaiser liked best to talk about was diplomacy. In 1895 he had a great deal on his mind, especially the so-called "Eastern Question," the problem of what action the various great powers should take in face of the disintegration of the Ottoman Empire. Russia desperately wanted Constantinople in order to have access to the Mediterranean, while Great Britain feared that such an acquisition would threaten her control of Suez and ultimately of India. Austria-Hungary, which entertained a proprietary attitude toward much of the Balkans, was also opposed to a Russian presence on the Bosporus. Wilhelm wished to see the Tsar become engaged not at Constantinople but in combating the "Yellow Peril" in the Far East, where the happy result, he correctly predicted, would be a Russo-Japanese war in which Russia would be defeated.[79] By the end of 1895 Wilhelm had become convinced, for no good reason, that London and St. Petersburg were plotting a division of spoils in the Balkans without consulting him.[80] But Russia, he realized, had long set her sights on Constantinople and had the military capacity to seize the great port any time she wished. Wilhelm did not at all want to see his ally Austria, whose position in the Balkans would be threatened by such a move, go to war over Constantinople, for Germany might be dragged into the conflict. Vienna could always obtain adequate compensation somewhere in the Balkans.

The thought that Great Britain, working covertly with Russia, would try to upstage the Triple Alliance, all of whose members had important diplomatic interests in the future of the Ottoman Empire, infuriated Wilhelm II. Just before Christmas 1895, the Kaiser summoned his friend the British military attaché, Colonel Swaine, and subjected him to a philippic on the subject of British perfidy.[81] London, according to this imperial tirade, was covertly trying to stir up a crisis, although the British knew perfectly well that the Congress of Berlin in 1878 had provided that any alteration of the status quo in the Sultan's possessions could be accomplished only by international agreement of *all* the great powers. Wilhelm warned that the Palmerstonian days in which England could do as she pleased were over. London could no longer with impunity push the other powers around, for neither Germany nor her partners in the Triple Alliance would tolerate it.

At the end of 1895, the dissolution of the Ottoman Empire was unfortunately not the only problem Wilhelm II saw on the horizon. There was also southern Africa, where differences between London and Berlin came to a head late in 1895, at about the same time that Wilhelm was so enraged over Salisbury's behavior in the Near Eastern situation. Germany's involvement in South Africa had initially been in the hands of traders, whose investments had multiplied in the 1870s and who in the 1880s had persuaded Bismarck to claim certain African territories for Germany. A German presence in Africa, Bismarck reasoned, would be an effective reminder to Great Britain that this continent, like the Ottoman Empire, was an area in which London would have to take Germany's interests into account.

German merchants were also active in areas belonging to other European powers and in the South African Republic, usually called the Transvaal, inhabited by Dutch, or Boer, settlers, who early in the nineteenth century had moved north across the Vaal river after their original African settlements at the Cape of Good Hope had passed under British suzerainty. With the discovery of gold in 1886, the Transvaal, already valued for its diamond deposits, became an immensely rich prize. No one coveted this wealth so much as Cecil Rhodes, who was the leading economic and political figure in the Cape Colony. Rhodes encountered a resolute opponent in Paul Kruger, the president of the South African Republic, whose independence Britain had formally acknowledged in a diplomatic convention. German traders in the Transvaal overwhelmingly favored Kruger, as did Wilhelm II, who, however, was against Germany's becoming involved in the increasingly serious situation.[82] Rhodes considered the Transvaal, backed by Germany, an obstacle to his vision of a gigantic South African fiefdom, the establishment of which would require the elimination of Kruger and his allies followed by the absorption of the Transvaal. Germany repeatedly protested Rhodes's ill-concealed ambition to annex the Transvaal and made it plain that its sympathies lay with Kruger and the Boers.

In the late summer of 1895, as Germany's difficulties with England in the Near East and in Africa were becoming increasingly prickly, Wilhelm discovered still another reason for annoyance. On 5 August two articles critical of him and of German policy appeared in the London *Standard*, written by Lord Salisbury's friend Alfred Austin, who was soon to be elevated to poet laureate. The paper, believed in Germany to be an organ of the prime minister's Conservative government, expressed the hope that the Kaiser would learn something of diplomacy from his grandmother and especially the lesson that it was England and not France or Russia on whom Germany should rely.[83] The articles appeared on the very day that the Kaiser had arrived at Cowes on the Isle of Wight to attend the annual sailing regatta. The Kaiser delighted in these occasions, not only because they involved yachting but also because they enabled him to confer with Queen Victoria. A talk between the two sovereigns, Wilhelm II declared, was the only way satisfactorily to clear up any problems that affected the relations of their two countries.[84]

The excursion to Cowes did not prove the pleasure Wilhelm had anticipated, however, not only because of the bleak welcome provided by the *Standard* articles, but also because of Lord Salisbury's failure to present himself for a final audience that had been scheduled.[85] The prime minister had never shown any enthusiasm at the prospect of a meeting with Wilhelm II, but his patrician manners were faultless, and he would never have deliberately given offense to anyone, least of all a sovereign. Salisbury, who had talked to Wilhelm the previous day, seems unavoidably to have been called to London shortly before he was to have seen the Kaiser. Since in Wilhelm's opinion Salisbury's government controlled the press, the *Standard* attacks together with the Cowes incident left the Kaiser doubly angry at the prime minister and resentful at the lack of respect shown him in England. He was therefore in a bad humor in the fall of 1895 and wary of any further evidence of British high-handedness. It was soon forthcoming, this time in the form of a blunder on the part of Sir Edward Malet, the British envoy in Berlin.

Malet, who had served as ambassador since 1884, was by nature cautious and reserved to the point of being somewhat dreary, but in the course of his long tenure in Berlin he had established excellent relations with Wilhelm II. Malet was certainly not one to want to ruffle his German diplomatic contacts or the Kaiser, especially since he was nearing the completion of his tour in Berlin. The ambassador always urged London to take Wilhelm seriously and to be careful that he was not made to feel that his efforts to be friendly were being spurned. Under Wilhelm I, he argued, it had been enough to understand Bismarck, but with his grandson on the throne it would be the Kaiser's attitude that would count "in a considerable measure."[86]

On the occasion of Malet's retirement in October 1895, Wilhelm II, as a mark of favor, invited him, along with Chancellor Hohenlohe and Baron Marschall von Bieberstein, the state secretary of the Foreign Office, to be part of a shooting party at Huburtusstock, the Kaiser's retreat northeast of Berlin. It was here that the envoy committed his faux pas. Following a dinner on 14 October Malet had separate conversations with the two German statesmen in which he noted that although he was leaving his post with Anglo-German relations in satisfactory condition, he felt compelled to warn both of them that Berlin's support of the Boers in the Transvaal had created a "dark spot"—*schwarzer Punkt*, as Marschall translated the ambassador's English—that could lead to the most serious consequences.[87] Malet later claimed that he had mentioned only a "possible danger to friendly relations of the two countries in the future," his purpose having been to make the Germans realize how strongly British public opinion took the Anglo-Boer antagonism that had developed in the Transvaal.[88] Although the ambassador may not specifically have employed the words "ultimatum" or "war," he gave Marschall the impression that he had such eventualities in mind. Marschall replied that if the Boers were unfriendly to England it was not Germany's fault but that of Cecil Rhodes and his expansive ambitions, which had found support in London. Marschall added that it was inconceivable to him that England, without any allies among the powers, would pick a quarrel with Germany.[89]

In spite of assurances quickly sent from London to the contrary, the Kaiser believed that Malet had spoken of both an "ultimatum" and of

"war" and had left Berlin in an atmosphere of "sulphur and gunpow-
der."⁹⁰ This, he felt, was a bold threat to Germany and an insolent
gesture to his person that must be protested. Imagine, Wilhelm berated
the British military attaché, Colonel Swaine, Malet's threatening Queen
Victoria's grandson over "a few square miles of Negroes and palm
trees."⁹¹ As Marschall had reminded Malet, Britain and not Germany
was the power without allies, a fact that Lord Salisbury would have to be
made aware of in the sharpest way. The ambassador's indiscretion, Wilhelm noted on a diplomatic report, was an error that he intended to use
to his advantage, perhaps by forcing the British to take a more accommodating attitude toward Berlin or perhaps by persuading the Reichstag to
appropriate more money for naval construction.⁹² When Salisbury later
let the Kaiser know that whatever Malet had said was without his authority, the Kaiser falsely interpreted this as the prime minister's "asking
for forgiveness" (*peccavi*). Wilhelm believed that what he saw as an
abject British apology was to be attributed to the sharp language he had
used with Colonel Swaine, no doubt leaving the Kaiser with the impression that forcefulness on his part would in the future be effective in
London. Wilhelm declared with satisfaction that the matter was now
closed, but he was still mad at England, and his good friend Philipp
Eulenburg predicted that he would remain so.⁹³

The Malet affair had hardly subsided when, at the very end of December 1895, a new and far more serious crisis in Anglo-German relations
erupted in the form of the Jameson Raid affair in the Transvaal. In order
to seize the Transvaal, Rhodes had assembled a force on the Transvaal
border of 600 mercenaries under the command of Colonel Leander Starr
Jameson, whose mission at the given signal was to invade the Transvaal
and promote an uprising against President Kruger. On 29 December
1895, Jameson, acting without consultation with Rhodes, ordered his
troops to cross the frontier. On the following day, both the British government as well as Rhodes's Cape Colony disavowed any official connection with the raid and ordered Jameson to evacuate his troops from the
Transvaal. But it was too late, for Kruger had swiftly surrounded the
invaders. On 2 January Jameson surrendered.

At the time the Jameson raid occurred, Wilhelm II felt that he had just
weathered a bad year at England's hands, and his disposition was quite
unpleasant. There had been the attacks in the *Standard*, then Salisbury's
affront to his dignity during the visit to Cowes in August 1895, and then
the Malet affair two months later. In addition to this personal pique, the
Kaiser found England's refusal to enter into a closer diplomatic relation-

ship with Germany, an arrangement he had pursued for some years, humiliating. The British seemed to think that they could plunder as they pleased around the world without any consideration of Germany or of the other powers. That had to stop. "After all," Wilhelm wrote to a British yachting friend a month after Jameson's misadventure, "the commandment 'Thou shalt not steal' is also written for Britons as well as for other people?!"[94] To the Kaiser, the Jameson raid was clearly another example of British arrogance, and it could not be tolerated. Malet's threat in October about the Transvaal as the "dark spot" in Anglo-German relations was proof to his satisfaction that Britain had premeditated the raid.[95] That view had to be squared, however, with Lord Salisbury's denial to Ambassador Hatzfeldt that his government had in any way been party to Colonel Jameson's action. As far as the prime minister was concerned, that assurance, which followed immediately in the wake of Jameson's capture, had laid the matter to rest.[96] So, at least it seemed.

The Kaiser, however, was determined to use the Jameson raid to embarrass London. He believed that the British, Lord Salisbury's denials notwithstanding, were in the unenviable position of having supported the secret invasion of an independent nation without regard to sovereign rights and in violation of a treaty they had earlier signed. Using Jameson's resounding defeat for revenge against British arrogance was to the Kaiser an opportunity to be savored. The question remained, however, as to what Germany could do to capitalize on the disadvantageous situation in which Britain found herself.

That was the subject of a meeting that Chancellor Hohenlohe convened on 3 January 1896, the day after Jameson's capitulation. Wilhelm II, State Secretary Marschall, and other officials attended the conference, which after some wrangling among the participants resulted in the infamous "Kruger Dispatch."[97] Marschall was not an Anglophobe but, like the Kaiser, he felt that over the years London had become too used to doing as it pleased. He may have been worried that his position in Berlin had been undermined by reports that he was too compliant to England.[98] The Jameson raid offered Marschall a welcome opportunity to remind the British they could not "play fast and loose with Germany's friendship" and also to bolster his image as a forceful representative of German interests in the Transvaal.[99] "Now we must act," he wrote in his diary on 31 December, as the news of the raid reached Berlin.[100]

To the Kaiser, Kruger was the guarantor of the millions of marks and thousands of German lives involved in South Africa, and he therefore had to be assured of the Fatherland's support. But how was that to be effected? War with Great Britain was out of the question, for the German fleet was too minute to be engaged in combat with the Royal Navy.[101] A safer approach might be to establish, with Kruger's approval, a German protectorate over the Transvaal through the dispatch of troops, presumably those stationed hundreds of miles across the continent in German East Africa.[102] The logistical difficulties made such an expedition utopian, and the Kaiser was therefore forced to acknowledge that he could not counter the British by force, either on land or sea.

As a less provocative and more feasible measure, on 2 January Wilhelm considered sending a congratulatory telegram to President Kruger. What the Kaiser originally intended to say is not known, but the message was electric enough for Chancellor Hohenlohe, whose role in the meeting was otherwise passive, to declare that he would resign if it were sent.[103] At the meeting in the Wilhelmstrasse on the following day, Marschall objected to any sort of German troop deployment in Africa, which he felt would be certain to provoke war with Britain, but proposed that the Kaiser's idea of sending Kruger a telegram be revived. Since Hohenlohe would not agree to the language Wilhelm had originally employed, Paul Kayser, the head of the colonial division of the Foreign Office, drafted a new wire that became the subject of considerable wrangling between Wilhelm and Marschall, the Kaiser wanting a bolder thrust than Kayser had provided and the state secretary insisting on language that was more cautious. Marschall finally prevailed, and the final version, which reflected the tone which he believed correct, was dispatched on 3 January 1896. In the wire Wilhelm II assured Kruger of his "most sincere congratulations that you and your people have been successful, by your own strength and without appealing for the help of friendly powers, against the armed band that broke into your land as destroyers of peace and restored peace and defended the independence of the country against attacks from without. Wilhelm I.R."[104]

The telegram's contents were not remarkable, since Kruger, in repulsing Jameson's attack, had with might and right upheld the sovereignty of the South African Republic that was guaranteed by treaty. What *was* startling was that it was so plainly gratuitous, for the British had already officially disavowed Jameson, whose raid had ended in failure, to Lord Salisbury's satisfaction no less than the Kaiser's. That should have disposed of the unhappy incident. Yet Wilhelm now insisted on keeping the issue alive. That he did so was surely due to the accumulated grievances he felt he had been dealt by the British in 1895. His personal animus against Salisbury, whose denials he did not believe and whose behavior he found so offensive, played a role in the Kaiser's pursuit of the matter. Wilhelm may also have been motivated in sending his telegram to Kruger by the thought that it would give offense to his uncle, the Prince of Wales, against whom his resentment had smouldered for years. Wilhelm incorrectly considered Jameson to be the emissary of the Prince and his two German-Jewish plutocratic friends, Alfred Beit and Sir Ernest Cassel, both of whom had massive investments in the Transvaal.[105] The telegram certainly did nothing to improve the Kaiser's relations with his uncle, who denounced his nephew's telegram as "a most gratuitous act of unfriendliness."[106]

Wilhelm II's dispatch to Kruger, however superfluous it may have been, proved very popular in Germany. The outburst in England against the Kaiser, on the other hand, was instantaneous and extraordinarily bitter. A head less cool than Salisbury's might have found it difficult to resist such a tide of outrage, but the prime minister was determined not to allow the Kruger telegram to develop into a serious crisis with Germany. Hohenlohe was equally anxious to avoid difficulties, and he persuaded Wilhelm to write a conciliatory letter to Queen Victoria, who was very upset by her grandson's "most unwarranted" wire and who informed him of her "deep regret" at his telegram, noting appropriately enough that he would have been wiser never to have sent it.[107]

Wilhelm let Hohenlohe draft his reply, in which he proclaimed that his message had been intended only to show that he was "standing up for law, order [and] obedience to a gracious sovereign who [sic] I revere and adore."[108] Queen Victoria was not impressed by Wilhelm's "lame and illogical" explanations, but she knew that nothing was to be achieved by giving her grandson "a good snub," for he would only become more irritated.[109] Lord Salisbury, who optimistically expressed a hope to the Queen that Wilhelm had acted in a "moment of excitement," was entirely in agreement and advised the Queen "fully to accept all his explanations without enquiring too narrowly into the truth of them."[110] The Queen did so, but in the following year she punished Wilhelm by declining to invite him to the jubilee celebrating the sixtieth anniversary of her ascension.[111]

Although the Kruger telegram affair soon vanished from diplomatic correspondence, it left a most unfortunate residue. The incident did nothing to enhance Wilhelm II's reputation with many of his officials, for in needlessly stirring up trouble, he had only increased Britain's wrath against Germany. The German military attaché in St. Petersburg, on hearing of the telegram, declared that "The Kaiser must be *mad, mad,*

mad!" and other German officials were also alarmed.[112] Moreover, the Kruger incident had a permanently devastating effect on Wilhelm II's relations with England. Although Marschall was confident that the matter would blow over without leaving any serious complications, Queen Victoria accurately informed Wilhelm's mother that "the bad feeling will last some little time."[113] Salisbury, long perplexed by Wilhelm's eccentricities, declared that he would never be able to understand his behavior. As the Kaiser himself admitted later in 1896, the good relations he had had with the prime minister were not the same after the telegram.[114]

The Kruger incident passed into the storehouse of reservations and resentments that many leading British personages felt against the Kaiser and consequently against Germany, and it remained a subject of discussion for years. For public consumption, the Kaiser made a number of exculpations or explanations, declaring, as he had to his grandmother, that his gesture had been innocent, that he could not understand why it had created such outrage in England, and that indeed all British statesmen agreed that what he had done was justified.[115] After many years had gone by, and as the foolishness of the telegram could not be denied or explained away, the Kaiser admitted that it had been an "idiocy" and claimed entirely falsely that he had known nothing of the wire and had not wanted to send it, but that Marschall and Hohenlohe had forced him to do so.[116]

The Kruger affair had a further repercussion, one that would be directly related to the deterioration in Anglo-German relations that the Kaiser's telegram did much to foster. Wilhelm's inability to grasp any weapon other than words to deal with what he perceived to have been British high-handedness in South Africa was a reflection of Germany's military weakness. The Kaiser had wanted to send German troops into the Transvaal, and he declared that had Jameson's raid succeeded he would in fact have done exactly that.[117] Months after the incident he continued to be susceptible to arguments that marine detachments should be sent into the deserts of German South West Africa to be at the ready against the British.[118] But even Wilhelm, whose inclination to fantasy was well developed, realized that such schemes were totally unrealistic, for they would risk war with England and her vast navy. Without a battle fleet, how could Germany have conducted military operations thousands of miles from home, and what protection might be found in Africa or in the North Sea against British retaliation? The Kaiser's boasts of action, as he surely recognized, were only talk, for the truth of the matter was that, lacking a navy, Germany was helpless to assert any effective diplomatic role outside continental Europe. Wilhelm II's inability to put up anything more than a rhetorical front against British expansion in South Africa was a reminder, much more bitter than any he had yet received, that Germany was not a force in world affairs. From the Kruger telegram would spring the Kaiser's determination to possess a great navy, the fleet that would firmly and unquestionably establish Germany's position as a world power and make the British realize that Kaiser Wilhelm II was no longer a sovereign with whom they could trifle as they pleased.

Thirteen

RULE GERMANIA

ROM HIS EARLY CHILDHOOD, the last Kaiser took the greatest delight in ships and the sea, among his first toys being miniature vessels that he set afloat on the many lakes near Berlin. As a boy Willy learned how to sail, and this remained one of his great passions as a man. He read with consuming interest adventure stories set on the oceans and maritime histories, encouraging his young friends to do the same. There was little in Germany's past that could sustain Willy's interest in the sea, for the military glory of Prussia belonged almost exclusively to the army. The Prussian navy had been a tiny affair, designed more to prevent smuggling than to defend the nation from seaborne enemies, and its successor, the imperial German navy, formed in the 1870s, was also insignificant when compared to the navies of France or Britain, both of which were vast in size and proud of illustrious victories. Even so, the Prusso-German navy had had its occasional heroes and successful engagements, and Willy knew them all. When a student in Cassel, his favorite book had been a popular history of the Prussian navy by Admiral Reinhard Werner, a volume that Willy delighted in reading to his friends and that he declared that he knew by heart.[1]

On concluding his university career in Bonn in 1879, the army duties in Potsdam and in the field that Wilhelm pursued so arduously consumed almost all of his time. In the next decade he did not, however, abandon his childhood interest in naval affairs and often was heard to declare that Germany's future lay on the water.[2] He occasionally spoke to his fellow lieutenants about sea warfare, probably basing his remarks on Janes's *Naval History*. This enormous compendium constituted Wilhelm's evening reading, a habit dating from 1886, when a British admiral presented him with a copy. Brassey's *Naval Annual* also claimed a place on Wilhelm's bedside table, and he boasted, apparently with little exaggeration, that he had committed it to memory.[3] His reading resulted in an eclectic knowledge of nautical design and technology, one which often impressed observers. "I am speechless," the managing director of the great Vulkan shipyard in Hamburg declared shortly before Wilhelm became Kaiser. "The Prince knows every bolt and every instrument that are needed in shipbuilding, as though he had done nothing else in his life but build ships."[4] He liked to make elaborate drawings of ships and guns, and as a young man he took drawing lessons from Karl Saltzmann, a prominent Berlin marine artist who eventually became a fast friend.[5]

By the time Wilhelm II ascended the throne in 1888, his enthusiasm for the navy had become quite intense. Even before succeeding his father as sovereign, he had planned the construction of a seagoing yacht, a vessel Prussian royalty had heretofore managed to do without. In 1889, the "Hohenzollern" went to sea, the epitome of luxury but notoriously unstable in heavy seas because of its faulty design—"a monstrosity," according to one of her officers.[6] The Kaiser adored his new ship and felt particularly relaxed and content when on a cruise, although he was frequently seasick when it rolled and tossed. In the stormiest weather he would have himself lashed to a mast so he could watch the waves break over the decks.[7] All this was a new development in the annals of Prussian kingship, for although Wilhelm's mother was a passionate sailor, neither his grandfather nor his father had ever taken any interest in naval affairs. Wilhelm's love for the water, evident in his youth, led the navy to regard his becoming Kaiser with considerable expectation, but General von Caprivi, the head of the navy when Wilhelm ascended the throne, worried that the young sovereign's habitual interference in naval affairs would prove to be a disadvantage.[8] The army, which welcomed Wilhelm II's ascension, was not happy about the new ruler's enthusiasm for its service rival, especially because the navy was clever at capitalizing on the Kaiser's love of the sea. As time went on, what one officer referred to as Wilhelm's maritime "sickness" eroded some of Wilhelm's initial popularity in the army.[9]

As Kaiser, Wilhelm II quickly revealed that he intended to make a number of changes in the navy, a move that paralleled his early alterations in the Prussian army.[10] He reorganized its structure so that administratively it would be more like the army, and he regularly attended naval maneuvers, often delivering critiques at their conclusion. Wilhelm was tireless in forwarding information to the various branches of his navy and in scrutinizing carefully all promotions. One of the early acts of his reign was the appointment of Captain Baron Gustav von Senden und Bibran as an adjutant, a departure from custom, since the adjutants who had served the Hohenzollern crown traditionally had been drawn exclusively from the Prussian army. At social events, the Kaiser, who made himself an admiral (a dignity neither Wilhelm I nor Friedrich III had claimed), sometimes paid conspicuously more attention to his admirals than to his generals.[11] As one observer noted, Wilhelm's preference for the navy was the only constant in a life that otherwise was notable for its vacillation. The navy was, moreover, the one subject on which the Kaiser was inflexible in his opinions.[12]

Basking in imperial favor, the German navy began to assume a grander air, its officers taking a more critical view of candidates from modest backgrounds who wished to obtain commissions. The aristocratic army officer corps nevertheless viewed the navy with disdain, for many nobles considered a career at sea unsuitable for a man of distinguished lineage and found even water sports beneath their dignity.[13] Although Wilhelm felt that German naval officers lacked the esprit de corps present in such exemplary fashion in his British grandmother's Royal Navy, he recognized their technical skills and was convinced that a navy was fundamental for Germany's self-defense. He intended the attentions he paid to the navy to correct the army's condescending attitude.[14] Wilhelm lectured army officers on marine affairs and saw to it that the members of the General Staff and the War Academy, the cream of his military retinue, became familiar with the navy and its operations. There was progress to be made here, for many an officer in the Prussian military could not even recognize from their insignia what rank a naval officer held. General von Caprivi himself, on becoming head of the navy in 1883, had been unable to do so.[15] Wilhelm's effort, though well intentioned, did not succeed, for the prejudices of the Prussian aristocracy against the sea were not to be so facilely overcome.[16]

Wilhelm II's two closest naval advisors as his enthusiasm for a fleet developed in the early 1890s were Admiral Friedrich Hollmann, the state secretary of the imperial Naval Office, and his adjutant Senden, who was soon promoted to admiral. Hollmann was an amiable man but one who, though sometimes reproached for being too subservient to his master, could on occasion be devastatingly frank. Like Philipp Eulenburg, he knew how to tell a story well, a talent that always ingratiated a courtier with the Kaiser, and he also shared the interest that both Wilhelm and Eulenburg had in spiritualism.[17] In naval affairs, Hollmann advocated a fleet composed primarily of cruisers, funded in annual budgets, and built with moderate acceleration.[18]

Hollmann had to work closely with Admiral Senden, who from 1889 to 1906 was the chief of the Naval Cabinet, the office that served as the conduit between the throne and the navy. A snobbish and reactionary bachelor, Senden had few friends among his colleagues.[19] Wilhelm II, however, liked Senden, "an old-Prussian seigneur," who as his adjutant had become a virtual member of the royal household, taking all his meals with the Kaiser and his family. The Kaiser found Senden's technical expertise very helpful, for the admiral was always available to translate his grandiose conceptions into comprehensible form. So close was Senden to Wilhelm that Eulenburg, who found the admiral's mania for increases in the navy quite excessive, warned the Kaiser that anything the cabinet chief—a "confused thickhead" (*dicker verwirrter Kopf*)—said was ascribed to Wilhelm.[20]

Wilhelm II's enthusiasm for the sea did not mean that from the beginning of his reign he wanted an immense fleet. His desire for an array of battleships and cruisers matured very slowly and in its long gestation mirrored the gradual endorsement of navalism by his subjects. At the time Wilhelm ascended the throne in 1888 he was obsessed by the notion that war with France and Russia was inevitable, a conflict that would be fought primarily on land. His attention in the early years of his reign therefore concentrated on the army, to ensure its readiness for action. During those years Wilhelm shared the view of many Germans that the maintenance of European peace as well as the protection of German commerce abroad could be left to the British, whose navy for decades had served as a sort of international maritime police. The Royal Navy, for which the Kaiser always had the most profound admiration, was exempt from the tirades of abuse that he directed against England. His desk, at which his appearances were not as frequent as his chancellors would have liked, was the gift of the British navy and had Nelson's famous signal at Trafalgar—"England expects every man to do his duty"—intarsiated in enamel letters. It was an offering undoubtedly calculated to please the Kaiser, for to him the British admiral was the greatest of heroes. He told Queen Victoria's military attaché in Berlin at the end of 1888 that it was his desire that Britain continue to be the mistress of the seas. Rather than envying Britain's overwhelming superiority, the Kaiser was concerned that the Royal Navy should be still more powerful in order to be able to deal effectively with Germany's enemies, France and Russia.[21]

Wilhelm believed that his elevation in 1889 by Queen Victoria to the rank of a British admiral, a step which gave him inordinate pleasure, invested him with the right to advise the Royal Navy how to carry out the mission he wanted to entrust to it. He therefore wrote and talked tirelessly to the Queen and to British naval officials, urging them to

Kaiser Wilhelm II in the uniform of a British admiral, 1899

spend more money on ships (and to do so at the Krupp works) and to improve marine technology, forwarding plans of his own creation to London to facilitate the desired improvement in the British fleet.[22] Although Wilhelm's intrusions into British naval strategy were based on a genuine concern about the international situation and his determination that the Royal Navy be in a position to deal effectively with it, his efforts did not always result in approval in London. Admiralty officials admitted that the Kaiser's criticism was often on the mark, but they also regarded his advice as gratuitous and therefore annoying, or, more darkly, as a scheme to stir up trouble between England and France.[23] In any case, there were few thanks forthcoming from London other than an occasional perfunctory letter from Lord Salisbury expressing gratitude for Wilhelm's advice.

The Kaiser took great umbrage that almost all of his overtures to England since coming to the throne had met with rebuff.[24] Nothing rankled Wilhelm so much as to see Britain treat Germany as a "quantité négligeable," the phrase he repeatedly employed when vexed.[25] To the Kaiser, Britain's disdain for Germany was due not to his own eccentric and often offensive behavior but to the perversity of Queen Victoria's statesmen and their allies among London's press lords, and to the fact that Germany lacked the naval power necessary to compel London's respect. His plentiful supply of soldiers could make no impact on the insular British, for they responded only to might assembled upon the sea. "All skill of diplomacy," he complained in 1897 to a South German diplomat with reference to Germany's impotence on the water, "is of no avail if it cannot threaten and induce fright through this threatening."[26] Only with a fleet could Germany be able to elicit from the British the esteem Wilhelm II believed to be his due. Once in possession of a navy, he was certain that his "colleagues" on other thrones would pay more attention to what he had to say.[27]

It was this sense of rejection and impotence that led Wilhelm to conclude in the mid-1890s that he had no recourse other than to order Germany to provide for its own defense on the water.[28] A number of incidents in which Germany and Great Britain faced one another during the first five or six years of the last decade of the century led to an acute resentment that he, in a highly personal sense, as well as the Germany he ruled, was powerless before Queen Victoria's naval might. It was the Transvaal crisis late in 1895, culminating in the telegram to President Kruger at the beginning of January of the following year, that decisively fired the Kaiser's resolution to proceed without delay to a program of

Kaiserin Augusta Victoria, 1899

naval construction of unprecedented dimensions. In building a great navy Wilhelm II believed that he would provide a needed corrective to Germany's status as well as his own.

Europe, after all, had listened when Kaiser Wilhelm I had spoken with his sword. To Wilhelm, his grandfather was always the authentic model of a heroic monarch, fearless in battle and in peace unassailable in his royal prerogative. The Kaiser had an acute and romantic sense of dynastic responsibility that encouraged him to appeal to Hohenzollern precedent as the justification for his actions. His grandfather had been the architect of the Prussian army that had united Germany, and now it fell to Wilhelm II to make his own contribution to the Fatherland's glory.[29] "I will not rest," the Kaiser assured his brother Heinrich in 1897, "until I have brought my navy to the same high level that the army possesses."[30] He often told his friend Philipp Eulenburg that the German navy was "an instrument ordained by God through the divinely appointed house of Hohenzollern to bring Germany forth upon the water."[31] Moreover, like the insulation from parliament Wilhelm I had won for the Prussian army in the constitutional crisis of 1862–66, Wilhelm II wanted the navy to be removed from interference by the Reichstag. It was to be *his* navy, just as the army had belonged to the old Kaiser and by inheritance to him. Shortly after ascending the throne, he concluded a talk at Kiel with a number of naval officers by observing that "just as my grandfather of blessed memory once said my last thoughts will be with my army, so I promise you here that my last thoughts will be with my navy."[32]

Wilhelm II's amour propre, which thus combined resentment at England with a devotion to his Hohenzollern ancestry, was not the only factor in leading him to decide to construct a battle fleet. There were also strategic considerations in the 1890s that led him in the same direction. The Kaiser had become worried in the mid-1890s about the rising power of the Americans, "those people without scruples," who were at work building a navy and whom he believed the British were stirring up against Germany. He often warned that the Yankee threat was closer at hand than Europeans realized.[33] But more unsettling to Wilhelm was his continuing fear, one that rose and fell with circumstances but that never entirely vanished from his calculations, that Germany would sooner or later find itself at war with France and Russia. For that eventuality the Prussian army had to be kept perpetually vigilant. But a war on two fronts would also have a maritime dimension. Germany had vanquished France in 1870–71, even though the French navy had succeeded in blockading the coast. In that war, unlike the conflict Wilhelm saw on the horizon, Russia had remained neutral and supplied the Fatherland with grain. If Germany went to war with both France and Russia, not only would there be two theaters of operations, but Germany would have to be sustained by imports of food obtained from America. Britain had the power to prevent this and would perhaps do so, for she had rejected Germany's offers of friendship. Without a navy of its own to protect its lifeline, the Fatherland therefore could not survive.[34]

The Kaiser's view that in event of war a powerful navy would be a necessity if Germany were to survive reiterated the more general argument made by Captain Alfred Thayer Mahan, U.S.N., in his *The Importance of Sea Power in History* (1890), which held that for centuries only the powers that possessed navies had ultimately prevailed. Wilhelm II, who read Mahan in 1894, excitedly wired to his childhood American friend Poultney Bigelow, "I am just now not reading but devouring Captain Mahan's book, and am trying to learn it by heart. It is a first-class book and classical on all points."[35] Wilhelm thoroughly annotated his copy of Mahan, invited him aboard the royal yacht, and ordered that all German naval officers become familiar with the captain's historical analysis. The decisive role of the small but modern Japanese navy in the Sino-Japanese war, which broke out in 1894, seemed to him to confirm Mahan's theory.[36]

There was also Wilhelm's awareness, one that was more rhetorical than substantial, that there a symbiosis between the fleet and Germany's economy. In a famous proclamation of 1901 the Kaiser would declare that his ambition was to ensure that Germany's "place in the sun be undisputed so that its rays can beam productively on trade and commerce abroad, on industry and agriculture at home, . . . for our future lies on the water."[37] But beyond such verbal effusions, Wilhelm's grasp of the economic ramifications of fleet building, whether in foreign trade or the domestic economy, was rudimentary. Nor did he, quite unlike Tirpitz, display much understanding of the political utility of building a navy in order to promote the social integration that would ensue if the conservative elements in society were united around a fleet and socialists and radicals enticed to support not only the navy but (by extension) the status quo.[38] Wilhelm II's mind, never strong in application to details, was not susceptible to complicated strategies, especially if they involved domestic affairs, which to him were always secondary to foreign policy.

Just as diplomacy was to the Kaiser not a science but essentially the arrangement of ceremonious encounters with his crowned "colleagues" at which he believed he could display both his charm and his authority, so the German fleet was to him not so much a calculated ingredient of domestic or foreign policy but a romantic emblem of Hohenzollern glory. Its impressive ships, freighted with imperial iconography, would promote international power, wealth, and prestige in ways the Kaiser imprecisely reckoned but of which he was entirely sure. A navy was to him a gorgeous apparition through which to humble Germany's enemies and create respect and riches for both ruler and people. Typical of Wilhelm's fantasies on this subject was the dream that came upon him in 1893 in which the warships he did not yet possess would one day in combination with the Royal Navy destroy both the French and Russian fleets. The victory would culminate in a great Anglo-German celebration in London at which Queen Victoria would greet her nephew at the foot of Nelson's stone column in Trafalgar Square.[39] But this sublime reverie had to be squared with the fact that the British usually behaved more like enemies than friends. When crossed by his kinsmen over the sea or threatened by other powers, Wilhelm could seize upon nothing more than bombastic threats, such as his meaningless bravado to the British envoy in Berlin, delivered a few months after his dream, that the German navy would blow Rio de Janeiro to pieces if Brazil fired on German ships anchored there.[40] Without a navy the Kaiser knew that he could take no effective action in either the Atlantic or the Pacific and that this impotence would lead ineluctably to a humiliating decline in Germany's prestige as well as his own.[41] He therefore must have a fleet.

The responsibility for converting the Kaiser's vision of a navy, as yet a vague chimera, into an actuality fell to Chancellor Hohenlohe. Although he came from landlocked Bavaria and had never in his long life had any association with, or enthusiasm for, the sea, Hohenlohe favored building a fleet. Out of purely practical considerations, some increase in the navy was necessary to keep the Kaiser in a tolerable humor, for Hohenlohe realized clearly that with Wilhelm ships, as the chancellor put it succinctly, were "trumps." The protection of commerce and Germany's newly acquired colonies also required a navy, without which no nation could command the respect of the great powers.[42] Nevertheless, to Hohenlohe the construction of a large navy was a project that had to be carefully integrated into both the European diplomatic situation as well as the domestic political and economic realities of the 1890s. There could be no question of pursuing naval power monomaniacally, as Wilhelm II seemed eager to do after the Kruger telegram affair, blundering ahead and demanding an immediate and gigantic increase in the navy. Caution in naval affairs, as in every aspect of political life, was the aged

chancellor's watchword. Hohenlohe was convinced that reasonable annual appropriation bills, rather than cyclopean schemes advanced by
some naval officials, that laid down building schedules and expenditures
over as much as a decade, were the best means of obtaining from the
Reichstag the large navy Wilhelm desired.[43]

In this gradualist view Hohenlohe had considerable support. The
Reichstag feared that a German navy putting forth too suddenly on the
seas would only alarm Great Britian. For this reason, as well as because
of the huge costs that would be involved, it was inclined to vote against
great increases, a defeat, the chancellor noted, that would embarrass the
throne.[44] Moreover, the Foreign Office in Berlin was just as opposed.
Holstein, who oversaw the Wilhelmstrasse 76, found the Kaiser's obsession with his navy "tragically serious," sure to endanger Germany's connection with Britain, the well-being of the Prussian army, and the financial stability of the Empire.[45] State Secretary Marschall von Bieberstein,
likewise deplored Wilhelm's obsession for ships—"He has nothing on his
mind but the navy," Marschall wrote early in 1895.[46]

Even the navy, which certainly could furnish admirals whose frenzy
for ships was boundless, was not uniformly enthusiastic about Wilhelm
II's determination to construct a great fleet with all due speed. To be
sure, the chief of the Naval Cabinet, Admiral Senden, widely regarded as
the actual progenitor of the Kaiser's ideas, exceeded even his master in
enthusiasm for building battleships and for employing them aggressively
against England, for which he harbored a great dislike.[47] But Senden
encountered an opponent in Admiral Hollmann, the state secretary of
the imperial Naval Office, who like Chancellor Hohenlohe and other
members of the government favored a cautious, gradual program of
naval expansion, one that would emphasize cruisers and smaller vessels
rather than battleships. Hollmann, like the chancellor, believed in annual, rather than extended, appropriations, for which he approached the
Reichstag year after year in a rather defensive manner.[48] Hohenlohe was
anxious to do nothing that would jeopardize Hollmann's continuation in
office, for as long as the admiral presided over the Naval Office, Hohenlohe felt that he could successfully resist the Kaiser's boundless naval
ambitions. But the chancellor knew that this would not be easy, since
Hollmann's failure to be forceful in pressing for funds for the navy had
annoyed Wilhelm.[49]

Until the middle of the 1890s, all the factions in the Reichstag were
lukewarm, if not hostile, to granting substantial funds for an increased
navy.[50] The grounds for this negative reaction differed from party to

party and were a combination of resistance to the Kaiser's authority, alarm at the tax burdens implicit in more extensive expenditures, and a conviction that a great fleet was not in Germany's diplomatic interest. An additional, and important, factor was the awareness of the parliamentary deputies that Admiral Hollmann, who was the principal spokesman for the navy in the Reichstag, had a deplorably disorganized and quite unpersuasive view of what sort of increases were in fact necessary. For all his personal charm and utility as a skat partner for the Kaiser, Hollmann was clumsy in dealing with the Reichstag, where his turgid and stupefying addresses often produced laughter and then rejection of the naval budget. Hollmann was also impervious to any appreciation of the value of propaganda in capturing public opinion at large or the Reichstag in particular. He opposed the Kaiser's desire to drum up support among the parliamentary deputies, work Wilhelm was most eager to undertake.[51]

Hollmann's inept performance, one which by 1895 had dragged on for five years, irritated more and more of his colleagues in the navy, who regarded the state secretary as the stumbling block that stood in the way of realizing the Kaiser's dream of a great German fleet. Admiral Senden led the opposition together with Admiral Eduard von Knorr, since 1895 chief of the naval High Command (*Oberkommando*) charged with the tactical as opposed to the administrative management of the navy. They had an effective ally in Knorr's chief of staff, Capt. Alfred Tirpitz, like Wilhelm II an admirer of Captain Mahan. As early as 1892, the year he became chief of staff, Tirpitz, along with Senden, Knorr, and other officers, had begun planning the future construction of a battleship fleet, a scheme that far outdistanced the spare annual requests for cruisers and other small vessels Hollmann regularly made to the Reichstag to replace outmoded vessels.

It fell to the Kaiser to serve as referee in this dispute within the imperial navy, and he did so initially by permitting both sides to develop their positions. The arguments within the navy between the battleship advocates such as Tirpitz and Knorr and those who, following Hollmann's lead, favored more reliance on cruisers confused Wilhelm, who vacillated between the two positions but who seemed to side with Hollmann.[52] Given the Kaiser's proclivity to be concerned with appearances rather than substance, cruisers attracted him because they could be beflagged and deployed all over the world to proclaim imperial Germany's might. Huge battleships locked in North Sea ports to counter England, on the other hand, were powerful but unglamorous and had only a limited representattional capacity.[53] Hollmann's ingratiating manner was a great asset in promoting the concept of a cruiser-based navy with Wilhelm II, but in administrative skill and conceptualization he was no match for Tirpitz. Unlike Hollmann, Tirpitz was convinced of the effectiveness of a concerted propaganda campaign to overcome the Reichstag's hostility to naval increases. He was especially fertile in devising arguments that identified the navy with the economic well-being of the Fatherland and as a vital component in Germany's ability to realize her destiny as a world power. The naval budget was consequently something to be presented to a skeptical Reichstag not only as a technical document but also as an appeal to national greatness.

The question of the navy's future, so differently conceived by Hollmann on the one hand and his critics on the other, came to a head in March 1894, when the Reichstag, jeering at the admiral's bumbling performance in defending his budget, rejected part of the appropriation Hollmann requested. Wilhelm II responded by ordering a press campaign against the Reichstag and desisted from intruding himself into the fray only because of Hollmann's objections.[54] It was not until the beginning of 1895 that the Kaiser, disregarding the admiral's qualms, became actively involved in the propaganda for an increased fleet. Early in January he summoned to Potsdam a group of men, most of whom were Reichstag deputies, to hear his views on the naval question.[55] Wilhelm's guests were treated to a confused lecture that called for an armada that would combine Hollmann's cruisers and Tirpitz's battleships. The result was considerable dismay among those present that the Kaiser, like Hollmann, lacked the requisite degree of clarity about the navy he wanted to put upon the water.

A month later, in February 1895, Wilhelm addressed a meeting of military officers at the War Academy and in the course of his remarks argued at some length that Germany needed a fleet to protect its trade and that the money was at hand to pay for the necessary increases.[56] On this occasion, the Kaiser once again altered his naval plans, abandoning Tirpitz's battleships altogether and insisting that the Reichstag be asked to appropriate money for the construction of no fewer than thirty-six cruisers. This would correct what he decried later in 1895 as the German navy's "total inadequacy."[57] Hollmann considered the Kaiser's prescription to be visionary and asked the Reichstag to appropriate money for only four new cruisers, a request which passed through the chamber without serious difficulty. Tirpitz, however, was highly dissatisfied that no provision had been made for battleship construction, and he and other officers in the High Command continued to press Hollmann for such vessels. During the course of 1895 Tirpitz, elaborating his earlier designs, mapped out a plan for the gradual construction of a great German fleet based on battleships, the scheme that eventually matured into the so-called First Naval Bill passed by the Reichstag in 1898.

This was where matters stood when, in January 1896, Anglo-German relations took a serious plunge as a result of the Kruger telegram affair. On 3 January 1896, the very day that Wilhelm II sent his congratulatory telegram to President Kruger, Tirpitz wrote a memorandum for the Kaiser in which he described his battleship plan. Tirpitz's earlier naval strategy had identified France and Russia as Germany's prospective enemies, but he now included England among the powers with whom the Empire might in the future have to contend. Unless Wilhelm II built a fleet of battleships, Tirpitz argued, Germany would lack both the diplomatic and military means to exert any pressure on London. Nor could Germany defend its economic interests around the world without a powerful navy.[58]

Tirpitz was preaching to the converted, for just at the moment he submitted his memorandum Wilhelm II had independently resolved to act. It was when the Jameson raid produced a crisis in the Transvaal at the very end of 1895 that Wilhelm II, long annoyed by British condescension and arrogance and humiliated by his inability to make any effective retort, decided that he had had enough. What had up to now been a vague notion of leviathans bristling with armor to impress the world and deliver great victories over the Fatherland's enemies became instead an elaborate concept of the German navy of the future, as well as a strategy for obtaining the funds to construct it. Immediately after sending his telegram of 3 January 1896 to President Kruger congratulaing him on Jameson's defeat, Wilhelm informed Chancellor Hohenlohe that he intended to take advantage of the excited state of public opinion to ask the Reichstag to authorize the construction over a number of years of a mammoth cruiser fleet that would cost hundreds of millions of marks. No longer would he be satisfied with the modest naval budgets of the past.[59] In a subsequent letter to the chancellor, written five days after the dispatch of the telegram, the Kaiser not once but twice referred to his naval plans as being "occasioned by [events in] the Transvaal."[60] The temerity displayed in South Africa by the British, he reminded those who questioned him, would never have happened had Germany had a navy with which to respond. And only with a powerful navy could Germany guarantee that such an affront to its colonial interests would not occur yet again.[61] Passivity would yield nothing but further embarrassment, and therefore Germany would have to prepare itself to engage, should it become necessary, in an *offensive* action against Great Britain.[62] It would take two years—from 1898 to 1900—for Wilhelm II to obtain Reichstag approval for a greatly expanded navy, and his passionate advocacy was largely responsible for the creation of a German battle fleet. It was not a victory easily achieved, nor was it to be one without the most dangerous consequences.

A few days after sending his telegram to Kruger, Wilhelm summoned Tirpitz to discuss the eventuality of his replacing Hollmann as state secretary of the imperial Naval Office.[63] Tirpitz insisted that, should he take over this post, his authority within the navy be made virtually absolute. This was Wilhelm II's first exposure to the dictatorial streak in Tirpitz, and, apparently alarmed at the prospect of having a second Bismarck on his hands, he decided against replacing Hollmann, at least for the moment. Hollmann, still opposed to the concept of a giant navy endorsed by Tirpitz and Wilhelm II, argued that another modest budget that would provide for a naval force based on cruisers rather than battleships should be drawn up. The Kaiser reluctantly concurred, and Tirpitz, feeling that he had been rejected, resigned as chief of staff of the High Command and assumed the command of a cruiser squadron based in the Far East.

Hollmann, meanwhile, drafted a moderate naval budget for presentation to the Reichstag in the spring of 1896. Unlike the vast increases pushed by Senden and Knorr that were to be carried out over a decade, Hollmann's budget called for the construction in the next year of only one battleship and three cruisers. The Reichstag, mollified by the state secretary's caution, approved his budget, a victory which visibly raised Hollmann's sinking prestige. Wilhelm and Senden agreed that it would be a mistake to remove Hollmann from office at the moment of triumph, for such a move would only make the Reichstag suspicious of future naval requests. But the Kaiser indicated to Tirpitz that Hollmann would not be allowed to remain in office forever, with the clear implication that Tirpitz would be his successor.[64]

It was Tirpitz who, even though absent from Berlin and therefore required to work through Admiral Senden and his other sympathizers in the navy, finally convinced Wilhelm II in the course of 1896 that Germany's future depended on the construction of a specific sort of fleet, for which provision had to be made in a certain way. Following Tirpitz's lead, the Kaiser gradually accepted the view that the navy of the future was to be led by heavy, short-range battleships assisted by swift cruisers, whose construction would be laid down in the form of a parliamentary law that would specify construction of new ships and retirement of obsolete vessels over a period of approximately ten years.[65] Such a fleet would enable Germany to fight simultaneously against its two prospective enemies, France and Russia, and also serve as a deterrent to any combative designs Britain might have. Tirpitz's plan of action appealed to the Kaiser, whose hostility to the Reichstag was long-standing and who wanted the navy, no less than the army, to be as independent of the parliament as possible. Although it was Wilhelm II's annoyance at England in the wake of the Transvaal crisis of 1895–96 that galvanized his determination to have a battle fleet, he agreed that Germany's naval strength was to be measured by the yardstick supplied by France and Russia. Even as late as 1897, more than a year after the Kruger episode, the Kaiser considered that these were the two enemies, allied since 1894, against whom the German fleet would most likely have to be ranged in the future.[66]

Britain, however, was also a dangerous specter. Like Tirpitz, the Kaiser realized that if the Royal Navy should fall upon Germany before its fleet could be built, the result would be catastrophic, for against his grandmother's overwhelming maritime power Germany was "absolutely defenseless." The Kaiser declared to Chancellor Hohenlohe late in 1896 that Germany should never have got involved in colonial adventures, a legacy of Bismarck's chancellorship under Kaiser Wilhelm I, without having provided itself with the fleet necessary to secure its farflung possessions. His existing "handful of peas" hardly constituted such a force.[67] Wilhelm II believed that a number of the disputes in which Germany and England had been engaged in the mid-1890s—in Samoa, Crete, the Transvaal, and Venezuela—would have been settled more to Germany's satisfaction, or indeed Britain might never have dared in the first place to provoke them, had the Fatherland been in a position to respond with a show of force, or even with a threat of action.[68] As matters stood, Germany had to go hat in hand seeking the help of one or another of the great naval powers, a prospect that was hardly attractive, because all these nations were either its diplomatic enemies or economic rivals. To the Kaiser, it was not at all "normal" for Germany to have to exist in a state of diplomatic subservience.[69]

The Reichstag, however, did not seem likely to endorse Wilhelm II's schemes for naval armament, to be enshrined in a law, as Tirpitz prescribed, that would commit the nation to a decade or more of heavy expenditure. Once granted, these funds would no longer be subject to parliamentary review. Quite apart from the diplomatic and strategic implications of building a fleet, the Kaiser's naval ambitions were a political issue that arrayed the advocates of a parliamentary government against those who favored an autocratic-bureaucratic regime in which Wilhelm II would rule through his appointed servants. There was also the problem of winning over the Hohenlohe government, which preferred Hollmann's gradualism to Tirpitz's radical fleet-building notions. The Kaiser realized that he could not risk letting the naval question cost him the chancellor, who had been in office hardly more than a year when the crisis in the Transvaal broke out. If Hohenlohe were to resign because of Wilhelm's insistence on having a gigantic navy—and he would probably take part of the cabinet with him into retirement—the German government and the crown that appointed it would acquire an undesirable reputation for instability. Wilhelm therefore grudgingly agreed in 1896 to defer the implementation of Tirpitz's plans for the navy, but this enforced delay made him unhappy with the chancellor.[70] As for Marschall, a particularly outspoken opponent of a large fleet and a man whom the Kaiser disliked for a variety of personal and political reasons, he would have to be replaced as state secretary at the Foreign Office. Admiral Hollmann, whose enthusiasm for the sort of battleship navy Wilhelm II and Tirpitz insisted on was suspect and who had had little success with the Reichstag, would also have to vanish.

Admiral Senden was conspicuous for arguing that the parliamentary and bureaucratic decks needed to be cleared of those who opposed Tirpitz's plans. As a member of the imperial retinue, Senden saw the Kaiser far more frequently than either Hollmann or the chancellor, and he took an aggressive view of the naval situation. To Senden, never one to quail before parliamentary obstruction, if the Reichstag was the problem, it would have to be circumvented or, better, put out of commission. The admiral proposed that if the legislature refused to appropriate the necessary funds it be dismissed, new elections held, and the process repeated ten times over if necessary until the Kaiser's subjects elected a Reichstag amenable to his wishes.[71] The difficulty in which Germany found itself, Senden never tired of warning Wilhelm II, was due to the ineptitude and apathy of Hohenlohe and his officials.[72] Like the Reichstag, Hohenlohe, Hollmann, and company could also be jettisoned.

Senden's prescription for eliminating Tirpitz's opposition appealed to the Kaiser, who despised the Reichstag and wished to see it reduced to a compliant tool of the Prussian monarchy. Wilhelm recognized, however, that, for all its superficial attractiveness, Senden's reactionary solution was one that would only reinforce the opposition of both the chancellor and the Reichstag. In spite of his heady confidence following the surge of support for the throne in the wake of the Kruger telegram, on reflection the Kaiser knew that public opinion was not ready to make the sacrifices entailed in a great navy and would see to it that the parliament, no matter how many elections were held, reflected its resistance. As Eulenburg observed to Holstein at the end of January 1896, "H.[is] M.[ajesty] wants a lot, but not the impossible."[74]

Wilhelm therefore shelved Senden's recommendation for the time being, but he continued to concoct fanciful naval plans and discussed the construction of his future fleet with a German shipbuilding firm. He also continued to resent the parliament's opposition and was determined not to allow it to frustrate his naval ambitions. The most extreme device for getting around the legislature was to dismantle it through a coup d'état. This would require violating the imperial constitution of 1871, an idea the Kaiser considered more than once.[75] He exclaimed in disgust to Hollmann, who along with Hohenlohe was opposed to any trifling with the constitution, "I acknowledge no constitution. I know only what I want!"[76] But such an imperial fiat would have created more problems than it might have solved, and the Kaiser knew that his fellow German rulers, although not very attached to the constitution, were not prepared to let the construction of a huge navy, which most of them opposed, be the occasion for a constitutional crisis. Without their approval, a coup would be impossible.[77] Rather than attempt to set the Reichstag completely aside, Wilhelm decided to try to persuade it to accept the naval increases he wanted. He began by warning the deputies that he would dissolve the chamber if they did not approve the naval budget presented by the government, thus requiring them to engage in long and expensive elections. He insisted that Hohenlohe make the naval question *the* issue in parliamentary elections in the hope that a majority in favor of a strong navy could be obtained.[78] Chancellor Hohenlohe was put under orders to dramatize the issue before the parliament—an unwelcome assignment for a man who did not believe in the cause and who realized what a drab speaker he was—and Wilhelm threatened that if he did not get what he wanted, not only would the parliament be dismissed but a reshuffling of the government would follow.[79] Hollmann knew that he would be one of the victims, for the Kaiser had bluntly told him that if his naval budget failed to pass he would be sacked.[80]

Hohenlohe responded by displaying an obstructiveness that thoroughly aggravated Wilhelm. The chancellor knew that his opposition might well result in dismissal, but, as he put it in a letter to Wilhelm regarding their disagreement on naval plans, "I consider it a duty of my office as Your Majesty's principal advisor to express my views candidly to Your Majesty."[81] The navy was to Hohenlohe an issue on which he felt he had to make his reservations absolutely clear. He would have nothing to do with any talk of a coup, for he believed that such an act of royal despotism would lead inevitably to civil war. The chancellor was even unwilling to let the naval question be promoted into a vote of confidence so that in the event that the marine appropriation bill was defeated the Reichstag would be dissolved or the government dismissed, or both.[82] In his typically cautious fashion, Hohenlohe insisted that Hollmann present instead the usual annual budget request, one that the parliament would approve as it had earlier appeals of similar modesty.[83] Wilhelm II, sensing that Hohenlohe, with the government solidly behind him, was going to be resolute on the issue, again reluctantly abandoned his hope of obtaining the sort of naval bill on which Senden and Tirpitz had insisted. But the Kaiser did not forget that it was Hohenlohe and his allies who had been responsible for this singular disappointment. From his observation post in the Wilhelmstrasse 76, Holstein described the situation to his friend Bernhard von Bülow, ambassador in Rome. Holstein wrote that

> It is no *boutade* but tragically serious when I say that to-day the value of a person for H.M. depends on his willingness or usefulness to cooperate directly or indirectly in increasing our supply of ships. Whether it be coup d'état, anti-revolutionary law, or a change of the electoral law, it all amounts to the same thing: to get a Reichstag willing to grant appropriations. . . . H.M. has no doubt whatever . . . that it is only due to the ineptitude, ill-will and lack of interest on the part of his Government that the money for the gigantic fleet hasn't yet been granted. . . . Hence the imperial bad mood against the Government. . . . I don't think things can go on much longer this way.[84]

In the Reichstag, the Kaiser could count on some deputies for support, but there were many others who opposed the naval budget not so much in principle as because it was identified with him personally. Wilhelm had driven that point home by setting up charts with texts and drawings in the imperial hand in the hall outside the Reichstag chamber indicating the skeletal nature of Germany's present fleet and the great navy that he intended to build with funds provided by the legislature.[85] Wilhelm II's lobbying the Reichstag on behalf of the navy was a case of too little too late. After a few overtures early in his reign, he ceased to have much to do with members of the various factions, preferring instead roundly to abuse them for failing to do his will.[86] The Kaiser had particularly alienated the Catholic Center, which would have serious consequences, since it was the largest parliamentary faction. The party considered the existing strength of the German navy quite sufficient and Wilhelm's passion for the water, and especially his frequent pleasure voyages to Scandinavia, frivolous.[87] The Center, and especially one of its leaders, Ernst Lieber, took umbrage at a remark the Kaiser had made to the effect that Hohenlohe should form a new parliamentary coalition excluding the Center (which had generally supported the chancellor) because of its opposition to the navy. Lieber informed Hohenlohe that not only his colleagues in the Center but many other deputies were also incensed by a speech the Kaiser had made at the end of February 1897 in which he had dismissed both Chancellor Bismarck and Field Marshal von Moltke, who together had forged the unification of Germany, as mere "tools" of his beloved grandfather, Kaiser Wilhelm I.[88]

There was, moreover, great resentment in the Center, as well as in the other factions, about an incautious revelation the Kaiser had made to his friend, Baron Carl Ferdinand von Stumm-Halberg, the reactionary Saarland industrialist. Wilhelm told Stumm, a Free Conservative deputy who supported a large navy, that if the bill were not passed he would make an enormous scene, firing the government or making an unconstitutional naval appropriation without the approval of parliament. Stumm related this threat in a speech before the Reichstag, much to the consternation of the deputies.[89] Hollmann was aghast at the Kaiser's lack of political finesse, and he told him quite bluntly that his verbal indiscretions and statistical misrepresentation in the charts he had ordered displayed in the Reichstag had significantly reduced whatever chances there had been for the bill's passage. Wilhelm replied with typical imperturbability that what Hollmann had said might be true, but he would act precisely the same if he could do it all over again.[90]

Many Reichstag deputies were consequently ready to put the Kaiser in his place. The navy was Wilhelm's joy, and any member of parliament eager to please him had only to support the naval bill. Conversely, the Reichstag factions realized that to cut the navy down was to strike out at the monarch himself.[91] Hollmann's measure therefore provided a welcome opportunity to the deputies, whose ability openly to criticize the

Kaiser was circumscribed by both law and custom. On 20 March 1897, the Reichstag, accepting a recommendation made by its budget commission, rejected Hollmann's proposed 70 million mark budget and instead ratified one providing only 58 million, a figure which was close to the previous naval budget. Wilhelm II was predictably enraged—General Waldersee described him as "extraordinarily embittered"—and blamed Lieber and the Catholic Center for being responsible. "The whole thing," he proclaimed, "is a battle by the Catholic Church against the evangelical, imperial dignity."[92] The Center, Wilhelm now informed Hohenlohe, had voted against the naval bill in order to annoy and humiliate him, and he promised that he would get even.[93] He went on to fulminate about a coup or a dissolution of parliament in the event that a future naval budget were to be rejected, excitedly informing Hohenlohe that the universal male franchise that applied in imperial elections would have to be changed. Disregarding the chancellor's protests, Wilhelm declared that nothing got accomplished without struggle and that he was prepared to wage a life-and-death campaign to ensure Germany's ability to protect itself. To Waldersee he announced that a way must be found which would stir up the German people against the parliament. If it would not pass such a measure, "then I will dissolve the Reichstag and keep on doing so until people get tired of having one election after another."[94] It was exactly the course Admiral Senden had earlier recommended.

But in fact, the Kaiser did very little other than make good his earlier threat that the parliament's rejection of the naval budget would cost Admiral Hollmann his post. Hardly a week later, on 31 March 1897, Wilhelm appointed Tirpitz, recently promoted to rear admiral, state secretary of the imperial Naval Office, a position he would hold for the next nineteen years. Hohenlohe had not been happy to see Hollmann go, for their ideas about naval developments were similar, and with the admiral's departure the navy would be controlled by Tirpitz, Senden, and other advocates of a gigantic battle fleet. Besides, Hollmann's resignation on the heels of a parliamentary defeat would only create the undesirable impression that it was the Reichstag and not the government that was in control of Germany.[95] But Wilhelm, Hohenlohe calculated, had to be appeased, and if Hollmann were not offered up as a sacrifice, then Marschall would have to be the victim. Of the two, Marschall was less expendable, and the chancellor therefore resigned himself to Tirpitz's joining the government. The prospect did not please Hohenlohe, for he considered his new colleague to be a "hot head" (*Durchgänger*).[96]

Hohenlohe, with his habitual confidence, was sure that he could secure the Reichstag's approval of a fleet bill provided that the Kaiser would be patient enough to let public opinion mature in favor of such a measure.[97] It was problematical to depend on Wilhelm II, for his defeat at the hands of the parliament had annoyed him considerably, and he was confronted with a choice of courses to pursue. There is no indication that the Kaiser's talk about a coup or circumventing the constitution was more than spume, for he had concluded that he would have to work his way around the existing government. Getting rid of Hollmann in favor of Tirpitz had been a good start, but the Kaiser intended to go farther. He probably would have liked to cashier Hohenlohe, but this was a step he hesitated to take, probably because there was no suitable candidate ready to replace the elderly chancellor.[98] Wilhelm, however, was determined that at the least there would be other changes in personnel, and these ensued in 1897 directly in the wake of the defeat of the naval budget. Most of the victims, notably Marschall at the Foreign Office, had shared Hohenlohe's resistance to naval appropriations.

The government, fortified by the appointment of Tirpitz and Bernhard von Bülow's succession of Marschall at the Foreign Office, embarked on reformulating a budgetary request for the navy. This was Tirpitz's responsibility, and he proceeded in 1897–98 not only to flatten all criticism of his conception of the German navy of the future but also in March 1898 to secure the Reichstag's approval for his epochal First Naval Law. As Tirpitz himself later admitted, this success would have been impossible without Wilhelm II's support.[99] The Kaiser's role in the development of the great German navy in the two decades following Tirpitz's appointment, as it had been in the period before 1897, was neither technical nor administrative, though he had a modest ability in the former and wide pretentions in the latter. He had little to do with strategy or planning once he had endorsed Tirpitz's concept of a battleship-based fleet, for to do so would have required the sort of attention to details for which the Kaiser had no taste. Wilhelm's contribution to the German navy was rather to serve—very effectively—as an emblem, thereby making the fleet glamorous, respectable, and truly national. What Tirpitz and his associates proposed Wilhelm II usually accepted, but often not without imposing annoying delays and indulging in provocative questioning of his admirals.

The relationship between Kaiser Wilhelm II and Tirpitz was seldom easy and occasionally quite acrimonious. On becoming state secretary of the imperial Naval Office in 1897, the admiral could look back on an acquaintance with Wilhelm II of more than a decade. The two had first met on a naval maneuver in 1884, and three years later Tirpitz had commanded the flotilla of torpedo boats that had accompanied the Prince across the North Sea to Gravesend on the occasion of Queen Victoria's Golden Jubilee. Like everyone else who knew the Kaiser well, Tirpitz acknowledged that Wilhelm possessed a talent for grasping things quickly, and he readily acknowledged how indispensable his help had been in winning over public opinion to the idea of a great navy. The admiral admitted that the Kaiser had a thorough knowledge of ships, both German and foreign, as well as naval fortifications, and that he could make fetching watercolors.[100] But beyond that—and these were essentially minor talents—Tirpitz had little good to say about the Kaiser. Like many a general who was happy to use Wilhelm II's martial enthusiasms to the army's advantage while dismissing him as a chocolate soldier, Tirpitz considered the Kaiser to be a bothersome and amateurish sailor.

The trouble with Wilhelm II, in Tirpitz's well-founded opinion, was that he was superficial and unrealistic. The drawings he made of ships were handsome, but their technical details sometimes did not work, and he never comprehended how this or that great vessel would fit with other components of the fleet.[101] Wilhelm was too concerned with the theatrical aspects of the navy and especially dense when naval finances emerged as a vital question. Moreover, the Kaiser imagined himself to be totally in charge of the navy's development and wanted everything at once. He therefore worked at cross-purposes with Tirpitz's carefully schematic plans for a naval program that would attain its goal only in the 1920s.[102] Wilhelm had little appreciation how complex would be the task of surviving through this "danger zone," as Tirpitz called it, until the German fleet had achieved its necessary strength relative to England. At the end of the 1890s, Tirpitz insisted that Germany could not fight on the water for years, but the Kaiser foresaw battle far nearer at hand. "We are now disproportionally weak," he confidently informed Bernhard von Bülow in 1898, "but in a year we'll already be stronger, in three really more powerful. I hope we can keep the peace until 1901 in order then to move forward and attack."[103] Another objection Tirpitz registered against Wilhelm was his failure to fulfill a promise made in 1897 on Tirpitz's appointment that the admiral would be granted virtually dictatorial powers within the navy.[104] This resulted in the abolition of the High Command in March 1899 and its replacement by the Admiralty Staff (*Admiralstab*), which was formally subservient to Wilhelm but which was in fact Tirpitz's instrument.[105] Even so, the Kaiser allowed naval administration to remain divided into a number of competing authorities, and as a result, for the almost twenty years he served in Berlin, Tirpitz had to fight hard against his opponents in the navy for what he wanted. This was often exasperating, but the admiral was a convinced monarchist who believed that the navy of which he dreamed was more likely to be realized under Wilhelm II's patronage than through a parliamentary regime.[106] He therefore tolerated the Kaiser without ever becoming intimate with him.

The relationship between the two men, although openly cordial, was always tenuous and potentially volatile. As early as 1891, Wilhelm had discovered in Tirpitz the future leader of Germany's fleet and, like many a naval officer, often hailed him as "the master."[107] What they had in common was their determination to raise Germany to a position of the first rank so that no other power, and especially not England, could trifle with its destiny. The Kaiser recognized Tirpitz's genius as a planner and his skill in persuading public opinion and the Reichstag to support his vision of a great German fleet.[108] But Wilhelm did not always find himself completely in agreement with Tirpitz's armament programs. While Tirpitz had won the Kaiser's consent that battleships would be the foundation of the German navy, Wilhelm II never entirely succumbed to the admiral's fixation with these gigantic vessels and continued to place a greater value on cruisers than Tirpitz was prepared to grant.[109] As for the admiral's personality, Wilhelm had many reservations. Tirpitz, he declared, was a neurasthenic and therefore "an extraordinarily autocratic personality," in fact a "Bismarck character," which, as Wilhelm noted, did not at all recommend him. As with the Iron Chancellor in diplomacy, Wilhelm was perhaps a little jealous that Germany's naval accomplishments would be seen as the work not of the crown but of its servants. Wilhelm might on some occasions be effusively complimentary to Tirpitz, but on others he would abuse him verbally or write acerbic comments on his reports. Tirpitz was extremely sensitive to criticism from any quarter, and he did not intend to tolerate it even from the Kaiser. He found, as had Caprivi in his day, that when a disagreement surfaced, the most effective course of action was to submit his resignation. On such occasions, the Kaiser would arrange a reconciliation, assuring Tirpitz that what he had said should not be taken so seriously.[110] As the admiral himself observed, in the course of his career he managed to experience every stage of both imperial grace and disfavor.[111]

Once installed as state secretary in 1897, Tirpitz single-mindedly concentrated his attention on developing a plan for the construction of a German navy headed by battleships, leaving the other responsibilities of his office to subordinates. With Tirpitz in charge, the German navy assumed a much more Anglophobe character than it had had under Admiral Hollmann. Intensely patriotic, Tirpitz refused to serve his guests anything other than German food and wine. Among Germany's neighbors Tirpitz preferred Russia, for he was profoundly conservative and mistrustful of the "utilitarian-capitalist culture of the masses" that he believed dominated the West. Tirpitz particularly despised England, for he had come from a household full of anti-English sentiment and had later acquired a distaste, if not a hatred, for the British from observing their overbearing lordship of the Chinese coast, where he had served several tours of duty. Although he greatly admired English culture and spoke the language fluently, throughout his long career Tirpitz approached anything that had to do with British political or military affairs with the utmost skepticism and hostility, and it was virtually impossible for any arguments, no matter how rational, to overcome this deep-seated aversion. No one believed more firmly than Tirpitz that the British were jealous of Germany's rising economic position. For that reason, if for no other, the Fatherland would have to be powerfully armed to be assured of its promising future. "Can one really believe," he asked in 1894, "that worldwide industry is possible without world trade, and world trade without world power? But world power is inconceivable without a strong fleet."[112]

In the early summer of 1897, Tirpitz had an audience with the Kaiser at which he produced a lengthy memorandum detailing his views about the navy he intended to see built. His argument had as its basis a statement made baldly in the second paragraph of this "very secret" document: "For Germany, the most dangerous naval enemy at the present time is England."[113] Since the British far outweighed the Germans in overseas bases, a worldwide engagement, focusing on commerce and employing cruisers, was out of the question. Whatever conflict with Great Britain that might come about therefore had to be fought by battleships, "in as great a number as possible," stationed in the North Sea, vessels which could be used if necessary against the French and the Russians as well. Funds for such a fleet would have to take the form of a single Reichstag appropriation that would irrevocably remain fixed until 1905. Among Tirpitz's reasons for insisting on such a measure was that not only would this eliminate the parliament's annual scrutiny of the navy, but it would also prevent Wilhelm II himself from meddling in affairs about which he had too little knowledge.[114]

Wilhelm II, who had no idea that neutralizing him was part of Tirpitz's objective, approved of the admiral's plan. A naval law, like the long-term Prussian army budget, would put the fleet beyond the reach of a meddlesome parliament. The identification of England as a prospective enemy that might launch a sudden attack on Germany conformed to the view Wilhelm gradually adopted after the Kruger affair. The Fatherland must be prepared to deal with the British, offensively if necessary, and also keep itself in position to overcome the Tsar's Baltic fleet while preventing the French navy in the North Sea from rescuing the Russians.[115] Therefore, the size of the German fleet, which, like Tirpitz, he insisted be provided for in a long-term naval law, had to be half as strong as the Franco-Russian fleet combined.[116] The number of ships necessary to obtain this ratio was enormous, but Wilhelm II's estimates were even greater than those made by Tirpitz, who had settled on nineteen battleships and thirty-two cruisers as opposed to the Kaiser's respective figures of twenty-five and fifty-four.[117]

Although the Reichstag had refused early in 1897 to grant Hollmann the seventy million he had requested for the navy, it seemed inclined to entrust a far greater sum, though one spread over seven years, to Tirpitz and in doing so to deprive the chamber of any control over naval expenditures during that period. Long confused by Hollmann's obfuscatory manner, Tirpitz's plain language and systematic presentation of his budgets meant that they would now know precisely what their money was buying.[118] Circumstances favored Tirpitz in his attempt to find votes, for by the end of the 1890s the electorate had a number of reasons, both internal and diplomatic, to regard the construction of a powerful German navy with favor.[119] To vote against the fleet merely because it was Wilhelm II's pet scheme now had to be weighed against a skillfully executed bill that had enormous support in the electorate. To oppose Tirpitz might therefore be seen as peevish. The national sense of outrage against England produced by the Kruger affair, an attitude which Wilhelm was determined to use to get his navy, was a factor no deputy anxious to retain his seat could fail to disregard.

There were other considerations as well. To some the fleet seemed to promise the means of forming a conservative combination based on national pride against socialism and other forms of political radicalism that were on the rise. There were also technical inducements, such as the fact that steam power, now widely in use in navies, increased the ease with which Germany could be blockaded. This convinced some Germans that against this threat a fleet of battleships was the only effective defense. By the beginning of 1897, at almost the moment Tirpitz took over, the long depression which had afflicted all of Europe for almost a quarter of a century began slowly to lift, leading to an increase in exports and a correspondingly greater concern to ensure that German interests abroad would be adequately protected.[120] Tirpitz knew how to encourage his supporters and showed even more dexterity in cutting out the ground from under his parliamentary enemies by unleashing a truly masterful propaganda campaign to win over their constituents. All but the socialists and a few Progressives and Centrists came forward with their support.

The change in heart of the Reichstag deputies had little to do with Wilhelm II—if anything (as Tirpitz well knew) he was a hindrance in dealing with parliament. Even Philipp Eulenburg felt compelled to advise the Kaiser to withdraw from the scene and entrust the passage of the naval law to Tirpitz and his allies. "The opposition," he wrote to Wilhelm on 18 August 1897, "is unfortunately directed against Your Majesty because the German philistines see in the forthcoming naval law more the satisfaction of a sport of Your Majesty than a necessity for Germany."[121] The Kaiser, for once, listened, and as a result played an insignificant role in the parliamentary skirmishing that took up most of the summer and fall of 1897.

The position of the Catholic Center party was critical, but Tirpitz's clever handling of Ernst Lieber as well as the party's revulsion at the murder early in November 1897 of two German missionaries in China ensured the faction's support.[122] On 28 March 1898, the so-called First Naval Law, committing the Reichstag to appropriate 408 million marks over the next seven years for the construction of a battleship-based fleet essentially according to Tirpitz's formula, handily cleared the chamber 272 to 139. To Wilhelm II the event was a personal victory such as he had not experienced in the ten years of his rule. He triumphantly invited Tirpitz to dinner at the palace, where he proclaimed that his guest was forthwith appointed a member of the Prussian ministry, an unusual step since the navy was an imperial not a Prussian institution. Only Hohenlohe, Bülow at the Foreign Office, and Count Posadowsky-Wehner at Interior enjoyed the distinction of being both imperial state secretaries and Prussian ministers. Neither Hohenlohe nor his colleagues in the Prussian ministry were happy about having Tirpitz, as the representative of an office that was imperial in its responsibilities, take a seat in their midst, but the Kaiser was insistent and the chancellor acquiesced.[123] In a matter of less than a year—from his appointment as state secretary in June 1897 to his assuming a place in the Prussian ministry in March

1898—Tirpitz had moved from the sidelines into a position of commanding authority. He would maintain that eminence, though not without frequent trials at the hands of the Kaiser, for almost twenty years. It was only in 1916, midway through the First World War, that Wilhelm II would cast Tirpitz aside, without ceremony and without regret.

Fourteen

GREATNESS AND

ETERNAL GLORY

FROM 1896 TO 1900, the years following the Kruger telegram crisis, during which Wilhelm II worked to promote the construction of a battle fleet, there had been a number of diplomatic crises in which Germany had been able to make little more than a rhetorical contribution, a bitter reminder to the Kaiser that without a navy the Fatherland was virtually a diplomatic cipher. Until Tirpitz's majestic fleet (inaugurated in 1898) came into being—something that would not happen for at least a decade and not be complete to well into the twentieth century—Germany would have to act prudently until this "danger zone" had been safely negotiated.

The first of the crises that Wilhelm II confronted in this period was in China. Germany had considerable economic interests in the Celestial Empire and in the 1860s had stationed a squadron off the coast to protect German merchants and their property. It was this flotilla that Admiral Tirpitz had commanded before being called to Berlin in 1897 to replace Hollmann as state secretary of the imperial Naval Office. The German presence on the central Chinese litoral depended on the goodwill of the British, who administered the great trading ports in the absence of any effective rule by the Manchu dynasty. To the north of these ports, in the gulf of Pechihli, Russia was asserting more and more influence, especially after China's defeat in the Sino-Japanese war of 1894–95. What the Kaiser wanted, and what he felt entitled to, was a port which could serve as a permanent headquarters for the China squadron and as a much-needed coaling station for German ships on duty in the Pacific. This would enhance German prestige and prevent a valuable concession from falling into the hands of another power.[1] Germany would somehow have to insert itself between the Russian and British spheres of influence without giving offense to either power.

Wilhelm had first begun to consider obtaining a Chinese port in 1895 because of his concern that Britain might take advantage of China's defeat in the recent war with Japan to seize extensive areas of that decaying Empire. This would be a blow to Germany's trade with China, the monetary value of which Wilhelm typically exaggerated.[2] To the Kaiser, China was more than a place where economic exploitation by German merchants would be facilitated by a fleet based on a port in Chinese waters. It was, Wilhelm II declared, Germany's initial move in what he believed was emerging as the arena in which the great powers of Europe would rival one another.[3] In surveying the possibilities for a German acquisition in China, the Kaiser first decided on Wei-hai-wei, on the north coast of the Shantung peninsula bordering the part of China that Russia claimed as its zone, or on Formosa, in which the Japanese were interested. By 1897, however, he had fixed his attention on the undeveloped bay of Kiaochow, on the south side of the peninsula, part of its appeal being that it lay far beyond Britain's sphere of influence.[4]

The murder of two German Catholic priests near Kiaochow on 1 November 1897 provided the Kaiser with a "splendid opportunity" for a resolute action in China that would appeal to the Catholic Center party, whose votes would be decisive for the naval budget Admiral Tirpitz intended soon to present to the Reichstag. Wilhelm, who characteristically regarded the crime as a personal affront, reacted immediately and forcefully. He wired Chancellor Hohenlohe that the murders were to be avenged by energetic deployment of the fleet, which would threaten "the most severe reprisals" if the Chinese did not pay an indemnity. "I am now firmly determined," the Kaiser advised Hohenlohe, "to abandon our hypercautious policy in all of Asia . . . and with full strength and, where required, with brutal disregard now finally show the Chinese that the German Kaiser does not let himself be trifled with and that it's a misfortune to have him as an enemy."[5]

Tirpitz was somewhat reluctant to become involved in China, but Admiral von Senden und Bibran, the chief of the Naval Cabinet, was all for action, and his opinion always weighed heavily with Wilhelm II.[6] Kiaochow was close to the part of China that Russia believed vitally affected its interests, but Wilhelm, who had sounded out Tsar Nicholas II, was convinced that Russia would not go to war with Germany over an unimproved harbor and urged the Tsar to cooperate with Germany in maintaining Christian civilization in China. Without consulting Chancellor Hohenlohe, he ordered a German squadron to drop anchor there and claim the area for Germany.[7] This occurred, completely without incident, on 14 November 1897. Early in 1898, Germany secured from the Chinese government a ninety-nine-year lease on the port, a document that was copied from the British lease just obtained on Hong Kong.

Wilhelm II was elated at the conquest of Kiaochow—the first substantial acquisition of colonial property in his reign—and wired Hohenlohe that "it might please God to make this mean a new chapter in the development of [German] trade and be a blessing to our descendants in the ages to come."[8] As far as Wilhelm was concerned, the acquisition of Kiaochow was due to his own initiative, happily ensured of success because Nicholas II had been unwilling to intervene. The British could reflect, he told Queen Victoria's ambassador in Berlin, Sir Frank Lascelles, that he had repeatedly sounded out London about Germany's obtaining a coaling station in China but that the reply had been a demand for inordinate compensation. So, the Kaiser declared, he had been forced to approach Russia instead.[9] Wilhelm's diatribe was not only false—there had been no Anglo-German soundings on coaling stations in China in the early 1890s—but also ungenerous, for Lord Salisbury and his government had put no obstacles in the way of Germany's obtaining Kiaochow. As far as the prime minister was concerned, Germany's presence in northern China would in fact be a useful deterrent to Russia's ambitions in Manchuria.[10] The Kiaochow incident had concluded successfully, but as Wilhelm well knew, with no battle fleet to put into action, he would have had no choice but to abandon his ambitions in China if either Russia or Great Britain had put up opposition.

Not all of Wilhelm II's subsequent projects worked out as well as Kiaochow. At about the same time as his triumph in China, he encountered a painful defeat in the Mediterranean. In February 1896 the Greek subjects of the Ottoman Sultan on Crete rose in rebellion, whereupon Athens proclaimed the union of Crete with Greece and dispatched troops to seize the island. War with Turkey ensued, but the Greeks fared poorly and applied to the powers for help. Wilhelm was from the beginning highly sympathetic with the Turks, probably because he disliked King George I of the Hellenes, who was a brother-in-law of the Prince of Wales and a brother of his enemy, the dowager Tsarina Maria Feodorovna, widow of Alexander III.[11] The Kaiser had also fallen out with the Greek Crown Princess Sophie, his own sister, who had converted to orthodoxy not long after her marriage in 1889 to Prince Constantine. For almost a decade thereafter neither the Kaiser nor the Kaiserin, who were both enraged by Sophie's change of faith, would have anything to do with her or her husband.[12] Without bothering to consult State Secretary Marschall at the Foreign Office, Wilhelm immediately formed a decided view on the Cretan situation: the British were responsible and the Greek King, their kinsman and puppet, would have to be humbled.[13] The Kaiser, according to the British ambassador, was in a "wild state of excitement," dragging the European envoys in Berlin from their beds at ungodly hours to encourage them to blockade the Greek coast.[14] The inspiration behind Wilhelm's frenzied activity in the Cretan question, as had been the case in his determination to take Kiaochow, was probably Admiral Senden, who encouraged him to dispatch warships, presumably those stationed far away in the North Sea, to bombard the Piraeus.[15] Tirpitz would have none of that, and the German navy stayed in port. All Wilhelm could do, and it was excruciating to him to have to admit it, was to proclaim that *if* he had had a squadron in the Aegean he would have blockaded the Piraeus.[16] Nevertheless, the Kaiser's frenetic diplomatic activity had to be smoothed over. State Secretary Marschall, whose task it was to cover Wilhelm's tracks, found the Kaiser's volubility deplorable and in his typically laconic fashion informed Ambassador Lascelles that Wilhelm II "was sometimes in the habit of going somewhat farther than was necessary in his conversations on foreign policy."[17]

Crete was to Wilhelm II painfully reminiscent of his powerlessness only a month earlier in the crisis in the Transvaal following the Jameson raid. It was one thing to storm about Britain's misdeeds and about the need to administer a dose of humility to the King of the Hellenes but quite another when it came to how this could be done. Britain was in control of the Mediterranean because of its great fleet lying off Malta, and she would therefore call the tune. The Kaiser's helplessness in rendering any aid to the Turks was a bitter reminder of the lesson learned earlier in the Kruger telegram affair. England, he raged, had imposed her will "*because she had the strongest fleet*! Thereby our 100,000 grenadiers are of *no* avail."[18] The Cretan crisis was eventually settled by the powers, under Britain's leadership, in a convention that forbade King George to annex the island. Although disappointed that he had been unable to make a forceful gesture against the King, Wilhelm was satisfied with the way the matter concluded.

Once Crete had been put behind him, the focus of Wilhelm's relations with the British reverted to China. The German presence at Kiaochow paled in significance beside the threat to the Manchu Empire that Russia represented, for the Tsar seemed bent on acquiring not only Manchuria but parts of China proper. No one had more to lose from Russian aggrandizement there than Britain, whose economic and political interests along the Chinese coast were paramount. If the Manchus were to fall, Britain would find it imperative to have a partner in arranging the spoils; otherwise she might have to take what the other powers elected to dole out to her. For that reason, the events in China in 1897–98 led to consideration in London of the desirability of an Anglo-German understanding, an arrangement which to Wilhelm II's irritation the British had heretofore carefully avoided.[19] The principal figure behind such reflections was not Prime Minister Salisbury, whose mistrust of German ambitions and dislike of Wilhelm II were profound and who thought Russia a more sympathetic if undependable candidate for diplomatic association, but his colonial secretary, Joseph Chamberlain. So it was that from 1898 to 1901 Chamberlain, to be sure with flagging enthusiasm, pursued the idea of a diplomatic coalition between London and Berlin. His efforts foundered because in both capitals the decisive figures found his plan either unsympathetic or unfeasible.

Marschall's replacement as state secretary of the Foreign Office in October 1897 by Bernhard von Bülow did not augur well for the future of Anglo-German relations. Bülow was descended from a prominent Danish family that had lost its property in the war of 1864 between Prussia and Denmark in which Britain failed, as the Bülows had hoped and expected, to come to Denmark's aid. Through his long and spectacular diplomatic career, Bülow had nursed a suspicion of Britain, one which he never lost and one which was well known in London.[20] In his long life, Bülow made only two brief trips to England and knew little of the nation's history or institutions. The anti-English mood which enveloped Germany in the wake of the Kruger dispatch was therefore entirely congenial to him. Bülow knew that in light of Germany's naval inferiority vis à vis Great Britain he would have to move carefully, "like the caterpillar before it has grown into the butterfly."[21] The aim of German diplomacy should be to ensure that any danger of war with Britain was avoided until Tirpitz's navy was upon the water, an accomplishment that would greatly enhance Berlin's diplomatic maneuverability. Bülow therefore consistently supported Tirpitz, although he seems to have understood little of the admiral's strategic concepts.[22]

Bülow was determined to pursue what he called a "free hand" policy, which depended on balancing Germany between Britain and Russia, the two powers (unlike France) with which Berlin could hope to achieve some measure of diplomatic stability. Such a scheme would allow Germany to develop its fleet while promoting, yet staying clear of, friction between London and St. Petersburg. Bülow's inclinations always favored

Russia, however, and he hoped that Germany might eventually ally with Tsar Nicholas II. Chamberlain's ambition of forging an alliance, which began to develop at almost exactly the same time that Bülow assumed the direction of foreign affairs, was not likely to prosper in the face of such an attitude. The plan had hardly been broached when, in 1899, a difficulty between the two powers arose. The locale was Samoa, which for twenty years had been jointly administered by a condominium of Germany, Great Britain, and the United States.[23] Wilhelm felt that the British took too assertive a role in the islands but in the absence of a navy he regretted that, as in Crete, he was unable to make any effective protest.[24] In the spring of 1899, the Samoan situation suddenly assumed a new and dangerous dimension when the British and their American allies attempted through a naval action at Apia to dethrone the German-supported King. The coup failed, but it caused the destruction of much valuable property belonging to German merchants.

The Kaiser was beside himself, and he regarded the incident as a personal affront inflicted by his old enemy, Lord Salisbury.[25] What made Wilhelm even angrier was the fact that the prime minister, unlike the Americans, refused to express any regret at the damage sustained by the Germans at Apia. Furthermore, Salisbury had delayed the negotiations between the three powers that began after the attack and that resulted at the end of 1899 in the abolition of the Samoan monarchy and the division of the islands between Germany and the United States, Great Britain having elected to withdraw altogether. Wilhelm complained to Queen Victoria with asperity that the prime minister treated Germany as though she were Portugal or Chile or the Patagonias, a blow to the honor of the Fatherland. And all over "a stupid Island which is a hairpin to England compared to the thousands of square miles she is annexing right & left unopposed every year."[26] "Lord Salisbury's conduct is quite Jesuitical, monstrous and insolent!" he had already noted on a Foreign Office document in July 1898 à propos of a dispute with England over the expected disintegration of the Portuguese Empire in Africa. "One can see once again how the noble Lord plays with us and shifts around, merely because he does not fear us since we have no fleet—which has been continually refused me in ten years of government by that fool (*eseldumm*) Reichstag."[27] The day would come, however, when Germany had a real fleet, and he warned Ambassador Lascelles that then the British would have to show Germany the proper respect.[28]

Although the settlement of the Samoan crisis, which resulted in an expansion of German territory in the islands, was to the Kaiser "a great thing," it did not lead him to reassess his highly negative view of the prime minister.[29] For years, the Kaiser had complained that Queen Victoria's successive governments had rejected his efforts at good will, and the Samoa imbroglio illustrated the pointlessness of trying to be friendly. The Kaiser informed the British military attaché, Col. J. M. Grierson, with whom he was on quite good terms, that he had always been Britain's best friend on the continent but that in return he had got nothing but ingratitude. The Samoan affair, Wilhelm declared, had undone all his efforts.[30] A few weeks later, the Kaiser resumed his complaints, this time to the British envoy. He was, he told Lascelles, like Sisyphus trying to push the stone to the top of the hill. He wore himself out trying to get on with England, and every time he thought he had accomplished an understanding, the British provoked an incident, such as the bombing of Apia, that ruined all his efforts.[31] Finally, Wilhelm unburdened himself to Queen Victoria in a long letter of 27 May 1899. "I of course have been silent as to what I have *personally* gone through these last six months," he wrote, "the shame & pain I have suffered, & how my heart has bled when to my despair I had to watch how the arduous work of years was destroyed . . . by one blow by the highhanded or disdainful treatment of ministers who have never come over to stay here & to study our institutions & people. . . . Lord Salisbury's government must learn to respect and treat us as equals."[32] The fault, Wilhelm believed, was fundamentally Salisbury's, but he found Chamberlain, the would-be founder of Anglo-German understanding, almost equally culpable and certainly completely untrustworthy. Chamberlain and his City friends were warmongers who, having failed to involve Britain in a conflict with France, had now transferred their bellicose intentions to Germany. "Mr. Chamberlain's name," Colonel Grierson reported to London early in May 1899, "is like a red rag to a bull to him."[33]

Wilhelm's tirades were often irrational and revealed his incapacity for making a careful analysis of the increasingly unhappy relationship between England and Germany. Salisbury had, after all, pronounced his blessing on the Samoan settlement, and Chamberlain, who contrary to the Kaiser's indictment had no desire to see a war between Britain and France or Germany, had given clear indications that he genuinely wanted to improve Anglo-German relations. But there was certainly truth in Wilhelm's complaint that Britain often behaved condescendingly to Germany and the other powers, and in the Samoan negotiations Salisbury's manner had seemed to the Germans to be needlessly patronizing. Even Holstein, whose pro-British viewpoint made him a counterweight in the

Foreign Office to Bülow's Anglophobia, noted that he was beginning to turn against the British because of the prime minister's high-handed behavior in the Samoan affair.[34] Holstein's disenchantment was nothing compared to the rage Wilhelm II felt toward Salisbury, which had led to what Holstein described as the sovereign's "unconquerable mistrust" of the prime minister. Wilhelm's fury also spoiled the unusually confidential relationship that had prevailed for years between the prime minister and the conciliatory German ambassador in London, Count Paul von Hatzfeldt-Wildenburg.[35]

Salisbury, however, considered that his deportment in the Samoan crisis had been beyond criticism, pointing out to Queen Victoria that he had not treated Germany with disdain but had in fact tried to meet its demands. Wilhelm II's complaints about his behavior to the Queen annoyed him, for it was really something "quite new," Salisbury wrote to his sovereign, "that one ruler should protest to another about his ministers. It is not a desirable innovation," Salisbury noted, "& might produce some confusion."[36] Queen Victoria in turn wrote to her grandson that his strictures about her prime minister were "most irregular" and that she would never have thought of doing such a thing, even when, some years earlier, she had known what an enemy of England Otto von Bismarck had been.[37] Samoa, like the acquisition of Kiaochow and the Cretan affair, had thus led to complications with England not because of insoluble differences but because of the Kaiser's excessive touchiness, which the British were seldom ready to accommodate. As far as the Kaiser and Bülow were concerned, the problem in the Pacific, which threatened to undo Bülow's "free hand" policy, was entirely the fault of the British. Since Salisbury seemed likely to command the government for some time to come, an agreement was hardly realistic, even though Chamberlain might continue to try to arrange one.

On 12 October 1899, three weeks before England, the United States, and Germany signed the treaty ending their dissension in Samoa, Britain went to war with the South African Republic in the Transvaal and its neighbor, the Orange Free State, both led by Boers, as the Dutch settlers in the area were known. The Boer War dragged on until 1902 and contributed to the tinderbox of Anglo-German problems. Although the Kaiser resented the way he had been treated by the British and threatened that he might intervene to preserve the Transvaal's independence, he in fact took no part in the war.[38] Even before the opening of hostilities Wilhelm had decided to observe a policy of strict neutrality.[39] The Kaiser's benevolence toward England in the Boer War had several roots. In the first place, Germany had no more navy in 1899 than she had had at the time of the Kruger affair in 1896, for the first installments of Tirpitz's great fleet were just beginning to be built. Germany's ability to intervene in South Africa was therefore as negligible at the beginning of the Boer War as it had been three years earlier when, to Wilhelm II's mortification, he had realized that he was powerless to intervene to help Kruger. The Kaiser was prepared to cooperate with Britain in building a Cape to Cairo railroad, part of which would be across German territory. Wilhelm reconciled his differences with the mastermind of this scheme, Cecil Rhodes, of whom he had been violently critical a few years earlier at the time of the Jameson raid, but who had emerged, the Kaiser now declared, as South Africa's Napoleon.[40]

Once the war began in October 1899, Wilhelm was astounded that the Boers were able to inflict a series of humiliating defeats on the British. The reverses suffered by Queen Victoria's armies delighted most of the Kaiser's subjects, and there were figures in his entourage who espoused the Boer cause.[41] The Kaiser, however, supported the British even though he thought that the "filthiest money interests" were responsible for the war and, like his wife, was not adverse to seeing the Boers "humble the English for their greed."[42] Nevertheless, it was unfortunate, he advised his uncle, the Prince of Wales, in December 1899, that the war provided the blacks an opportunity to watch white men slaughter one another, for "the simple suspicion that they might find it practical for their prosperity to fall on the whites in general is enough to make one's blood run cold."[43]

Throughout the war, the Kaiser frequently criticized Britain's strategy in fighting the Boers as well as the vast colonial ambitions that had got his grandmother's subjects enmeshed in the conflict in South Africa. The British were trying to turn Africa into a second India, but Wilhelm was confident it would not work.[44] The Boer War, he declared, was not unlike what Britain had experienced in 1776 in America. This time South Africa would desert the crown, and Queen Victoria's other colonies, as well as Ireland, would follow its example. England needed an ally, for the war against the Boers was showing—Captain Mahan's text notwithstanding—that for a colonial power a huge navy was not enough.[45] He offered unsolicited advice to the Prince of Wales, indelicately suggesting that the British army, mired in a bloody contest, was like a football team that "accepts finally its defeat with equanimity."[46] When the Kaiser sensed that this observation had annoyed his uncle, he wrote again, this time with the marginally more mollifying reassurance that "as long as you keep your *fleet* in good fighting trim and as long as it is looked upon as the first and feared as invincible, I don't care a fiddlestick for a few lost fights in Africa."[47] Generally, Wilhelm was careful to congratulate the British after the war began to turn in their favor at the end of 1900, and he did not fail to remind his relatives and acquaintances in London that he had steadfastly endorsed the British cause and indeed, so he claimed, prevented diplomatic intervention by Russia, France, and the Netherlands.[48] As in the case of Samoa, the Kaiser was eager to point out that it was *he* who had bridled the hostile press in Germany and resisted the intrigues of the Anglophobes at his court, but even he could not serve forever as a safety valve.[49]

In spite of—or perhaps because of—the difficulties Germany and the Kaiser had caused Britain, Chamberlain and his supporters continued to work for some sort of formal accommodation between the two nations. But the series of diplomatic crises around the world that imperiled Anglo-German relations, the relentless hostility of Lord Salisbury, the frostiness of the Prince of Wales and occasionally even of Queen Victoria, and what the Kaiser considered the manifest ingratitude of the British for the favors he had steadfastly rendered them during the Boer War made him wary of Chamberlain's approaches for an alliance. Berlin, in any case, was not going to make the opening move. It was proper for such a step to rest with London, for Wilhelm believed that sooner or later the British would have to resolve their differences with Germany, and not the reverse. Britain was the only great power not involved in a diplomatic alignment—Germany, Austria and Italy had been joined in a defensive alliance since 1882, while France and Russia entered into a similar treaty early in 1894—and this isolation could not continue indefinitely.[50]

In 1898, the year in which Chamberlain's overtures to Germany began, Britain's situation seemed to be especially unenviable, for France, eager to expand her domain in equatorial Africa, was mounting a dangerous challenge to Britain's hold on the Sudan. At the same time Russia appeared to be determined to gorge itself on China, an expansion that London felt compelled to resist in order to preserve its own interests there. Chamberlain's speech in Birmingham on 13 May 1898, in which he pointed to Russia as Britain's prospective enemy and called for an alliance with "some great military power," was to the Kaiser and to many others a plain indication that Britain was seeking a partner on the continent.[51] That clearly meant Germany, for France, the only other possibility, was Russia's ally and Britain's imperial rival.

In spite of Britain's isolation and Chamberlain's indication that this policy had to be revised, Lord Salisbury, supported by a majority of his cabinet, showed no inclination to move closer to Germany. The prime minister and his colleagues, long mistrustful of the Kaiser personally and of late annoyed by Bülow's aggressive diplomacy, had no desire to involve themselves with Berlin. By the end of 1898, it had become clear to Wilhelm II that the prospect of an entente between Germany and Great Britain held no possibility of being realized. The blame, he was certain, did not lie with him, and he found it quite simple to single out the persons in England whom he believed responsible for the frustration of his long-pursued ambition of an Anglo-German understanding. First and foremost, there was Salisbury, who to Wilhelm's irritation spent his vacations at his villa on the Riviera and who obviously preferred France to Germany.[52] The prime minister almost certainly would be no more favorable to an accord with Germany than he had been in 1889 when Bismarck had approached him. It was unfortunately Salisbury's opinion that would be decisive, and Wilhelm II, with Bülow's encouragement, believed that the prime minister was duplicitous, proclaiming a desire to have good relations with Germany but in fact conniving with Russia against the Fatherland.[53] And even had the prime minister been more interested, Wilhelm rightly was concerned that *if* the British constitution would allow one government to enter into a binding treaty, its successors would not be obligated to uphold it.[54]

Although the Kaiser assured Ambassador Lascelles that he desired a "thoroughly good understanding with England," he was suspicious of Chamberlain, who trafficked in "theoretical and obscure phantasies." Wilhelm II, who for years had wanted to draw closer to England, at the moment that a rapprochement seemed perhaps possible was full of reservations and wary of responding to the colonial secretary's overtures.[55] There were a number of reasons, apart from Wilhelm's aversion to Salisbury and his doubts about Chamberlain, for the Kaiser's misgivings about the prospect of an accord with Great Britain. The Germanophobe press in London certainly intensified his resistance to Chamberlain. Throughout Wilhelm II's reign nothing annoyed him more about his mother's country than its press, which the Kaiser believed had fatally undermined his attempts to foster Anglo-German amity. The Kaiser read London papers with a care he did not usually give to the news published in his own country.[56] Wilhelm complained frequently about the vicious and unwarranted attacks on Germany and on his person that were standard features of British papers, arguing that the lords of Fleet Street were Jews or propagandists grown fat on bribes delivered from Paris or St.

Petersburg and that all operated with the connivance, if not the encouragement, of the British government.[57] Moreover, Wilhelm believed that Britain suborned the oppositional press in Germany in the hope of breaking up the Austro-German-Italian Triple Alliance and also bribed newspapers in the United States, France, and Belgium to adopt a critical tone toward him.[58] Wilhelm's charges were largely false, but his annoyance at Fleet Street was entirely justified, for in the twenty years preceding the First World War the British press was on a scurrilous rampage against both the Kaiser and his people. As Ramsay MacDonald, a rising politician who would end his career as prime minister, once observed, British newspapers in this period were edited "in such a way as to bring the techniques of journalism to a high pitch of excellence and its honors to the lowest depths of disgrace."[59]

Wilhelm II's disenchantment with the prospect of an alliance with England found considerable encouragement in Berlin. Hohenlohe, never an Anglophile, had become increasingly alarmed by Britain's overbearing behavior. "We should not expose ourselves to the danger of experiencing at England's hands the fate of Spain at North America's," he wrote to his son in the first week of 1900. "And it is clear that England is only waiting to fall upon us."[60] The negative outlook toward England of Bernhard von Bülow was even more decisive, not only because he was state secretary of the Foreign Office, but also because it was certain that he was destined soon to replace the octogenarian Hohenlohe as chancellor. Like Wilhelm II, Bülow had from the beginning been suspicious that Chamberlain's alliance overture in 1898 was a ploy to contain Germany's colonial expansion or to get it in difficulties with other powers. From the time that he served in the German embassy in St. Petersburg in the mid-1880s, Bülow had been convinced that Germany's destiny lay with Russia and not, as he later said, with "the egotistical English."[61] His "free hand" policy, for all its talk of Anglo-Russian parity, tilted noticeably in favor of St. Petersburg. As early as 1892, Bülow had expressed his opinion of Germany's diplomatic future succinctly and entirely without his usual palaver: "Our relationship to Russia is and should remain the nodal point (*Knotenpunkt*) of our foreign policy."[62] Once installed as chancellor, Bülow would often observe that "if we were to ally with England we would conclusively lose Russia's friendship, and Russia is more valuable to us than England."[63]

As far as Bülow was concerned, an Anglo-German combination was incompatible with the "free hand," for the imperial rivalry between England and Russia was so intense that it would inevitably lead to a war that Bülow unrealistically was certain the Tsar would win. In such an event, Germany had no interest in being obliged to help the British. The Fatherland had to be free to assist not England but Russia in the event of war and thus be in readiness when the smoke cleared to claim her share of Queen Victoria's shattered Empire. Bülow therefore was not only not in favor of an Anglo-German alliance, he worked actively against its consummation.[64]

Bülow realized that preventing an accord with England would depend on undermining Wilhelm II's attachment to England. Bülow consequently labored effectively to deepen the Kaiser's mistrust of Salisbury and Chamberlain, eventually persuading him that the colonial secretary's overtures for an Anglo-German alliance, which was restricted in its specific details to the resolution of colonial disagreements, was without value unless it provided for British support for Germany's position in Europe.[65] Bülow's counsel made sense to the Kaiser, who entirely shared the state secretary's dark view of Salisbury and Chamberlain. While the diplomatic checkerboard of Europe might compel Britain to choose an ally, how, Wilhelm wondered, could London's overtures be reconciled with the remorseless attempts being made by the British to get Germany into trouble with the other powers and to drive the Germans (and everyone else) out of Africa?[66] Did it not appear that what London really wanted was for Berlin to do its dirty work, specifically to assist Britain in forcing the Russians to retreat from China? Any value in Anglo-German cooperation would be more than offset by the closer Franco-Russian relationship that would inevitably result.[67] Eventually Germany would become involved in a two-front war with the Tsar and his French confederates in which the British could do little to help the Fatherland.[68] Nevertheless, unsuitable as the British might be as prospective partners, the French and Russians were even more impossible and in a position to strike a blow across land at Berlin itself. Was the best solution not an alliance with England but the employment of Bülow's "free hand," trying to get along with the British but keeping up a guard and meanwhile building a battle fleet as quickly as possible?[69] Although a formal alliance might not be in sight, the British, provided they would not behave so haughtily, and the Germans, whom Wilhelm warned were "touchy," might cooperate to settle various differences.[70]

So, with the Kaiser's approval, the vague soundings between London and Berlin continued on until 1901, with Wilhelm managing to obfuscate the proceedings by making a number of puzzling observations about Anglo-German relations. In August 1898, he went so far as to claim that

Ambassador Lascelles—to the envoy's mystification—had proposed a deal whereby Germany would become Britain's ally in the event that Britain went to war with France and another European power, by which Wilhelm unmistakably meant Russia.[71] This was an entirely fanciful notion of the Kaiser's, as had been his bluster to Tsar Nicholas II earlier in 1898 that England had offered Germany an alliance.[72] Neither the Russians nor the British took these effusions seriously, for they had learned that what the Kaiser said was often either false or, even if true, subject to instant and baffling change.

Both Bülow and the Kaiser believed that the only defense against the situation that would last for the foreseeable future—Germany surrounded except along her Austrian border by Russia, France, and England—was the maintenance of a strong army and the development with all speed of a vast navy. Like the Kaiser and Tirpitz, Bülow was also a disciple of Captain Mahan, whose advocacy of sea power applied, he was certain, to Germany.[73] As Bülow realized clearly, Germany could not realistically seek both a gigantic navy and an accommodation with England, for the British knew that Wilhelm II's projected fleet of massive, short-range battleships was directed against them. Until it was built, Germany would therefore have to pursue a "doubly cautious" policy toward London.[74]

Tirpitz was also under no illusions on this point. "In the creation of our seapower," he baldly admitted, "we never hoped for Britain's applause."[75] The lessons taught by history in what had happened between 1896 and 1900—Samoa; the defeat of Spain by the United States in their war in 1898; France's inability to resist the military power of Britain in the near collision of their troops in the Sudan in the same year, because she knew that the Royal Navy stood behind Queen Victoria's soldiers; Germany's impotence in the Boer War—all had proved to Tirpitz's satisfaction that Germany must be stronger on the sea if it were to be able to hold up its head with pride. Moreover, as Germany's economic strength developed, the potential for conflict with other powers increased.[76] Until Germany's naval power was safely in hand, Berlin would have to behave with utmost circumspection.

With the concurrence of the Kaiser, who agreed with Tirpitz's rationale, Tirpitz therefore began in 1899 to prepare a second Naval Law, which would double the number of battleship squadrons and commit the Reichstag to building new capital ships at the rate of three per year. When Tirpitz approached Wilhelm for his approval, it was immediately forthcoming, for the Kaiser believed that the fleet provided for in the First Naval Law of 1898 had already proved inadequate to sustain Germany's increasing economic and diplomatic role throughout the world, especially because of fleet increases by other powers.[77] Tirpitz's bill would be ready for presentation in 1901 or 1902, and until that time he wanted the matter kept secret from everyone except Bülow, on whose support and discretion he could rely. Tirpitz's foremost concern was to muzzle the Kaiser, and he had Bülow appeal to Wilhelm II to keep the navy's plans to himself, especially on 18 October, when he was to be in Hamburg for the christening of the battleship *Karl der Grosse.*

The Kaiser, however, was rarely disposed to keep quiet. His Hamburg speech, delivered without prior consultation with Hohenlohe, Bülow, or Tirpitz, demanded that the nation make the necessary sacrifice to create a great navy, for "bitter is the need that we have for a strong German fleet."[78] The message was clear: the navy envisioned in the 1898 Naval Law was no longer enough. Once again the Reichstag would have to be asked to spend hundreds of millions of marks for ships. Unlike Tirpitz and Bülow, who, whatever their flaws as diplomats, recognized the incompatibility of increasing the German navy and at the same time seeking an accommodation with Britain, Wilhelm II believed that the two aims could be simultaneously pursued.[79] The Kaiser even imagined— that he could have derived such a misleading impression is astounding— the increases to the German navy foretold by his Hamburg speech in October 1899 would in fact be greeted with approbation not only by Russia but also by the British.[80]

This was the impression Wilhelm mistakenly brought back from a trip to England in November 1899, during which he and Bülow stayed at Windsor as Queen Victoria's guests.[81] The Kaiser declared that he wanted to achieve a good relationship with Britain but warned that the Germans were not to be treated as "beggarly relatives." Bülow also came to England with a certain misgiving, for he, like Wilhelm II, found the affectation of superiority of many of Queen Victoria's statesmen offensive.[82] Salisbury was to Bülow the most odious example of this arrogance, revealed in the prime minister's declaration that Great Britain relied for her protection not on alliances with Germany or anyone else but on her navy and her chalk cliffs along the channel.[83] Chamberlain presented himself at the castle and pressed his view of the desirability of an Anglo-German alliance on Wilhelm, who, under Bülow's influence, would agree to nothing more than the possibility of an "understanding."

Bülow, preferring his "free hand" policy that inclined toward Russia, lost no time on his return to Germany in repudiating Chamberlain's vision of an Anglo-German alliance.

At the end of December 1899, not long after the Kaiser and Bülow had arrived back in Berlin, British warships stopped a German postal steamer off the South African coast. It was suspected, without reason as it turned out, of carrying contraband for the Boers. The Kaiser's reaction, as the Austrian envoy in Berlin described it, was calm but bitter.[84] Several weeks after the incident, Wilhelm reminded Ambassador Lascelles that Germany was a young power and therefore resented being pushed around by an established empire such as Great Britain. He declared that the steamer affair was, like Samoa, yet another illustration of British perversity in undoing all his efforts at good relations.[85] The matter was eventually settled by London's paying compensation, but, as in Samoa, not quickly enough to satisfy the Kaiser.[86] He used the affair to promote support for the Second Naval Law then before the Reichstag, commanding Bülow to see to it that the incident was utilized to stir up public opinion in favor of budgetary increases that Tirpitz was preparing. The law, Wilhelm decreed, was to be produced at once, and not in 1901 or 1902, as the navy's schedule reckoned. Tirpitz did not like the Kaiser's acceleration of his plans, but the timeliness of Britain's piracy toward the innocent German postal steamer was very gratifying. "Now," the admiral declared with satisfaction, "we have the wind we need to blow our ship into port; the Navy Law will pass."[87]

In his defense of a second Naval Law, Tirpitz specifically noted that the power against which Germany was compelled to arm was England, believing that such a declaration (which, although basic to his planning, had been absent in his defense of the First Naval Law two years earlier) was essential to gather sufficient support for his measure.[88] Wilhelm, whose earlier calculations for the desirable strength of the German navy had been in terms of the size of the French and Russian navies, now declared that the purpose of the Second Naval Law was to make Germany "equal in station" (*ebenbürtig*) to Great Britain.[89] The focus of Germany's naval policy was now to be fixed squarely on the British, and here it would remain for the remainder of Wilhelm II's reign. The Kaiser played a minor role in the passage of the Second Naval Law, and this time, unlike the first such measure in 1898, there were no charts and diagrams by the imperial hand erected in the hall of the Reichstag. Wilhelm did appeal to the German princes to promote increases that he believed public opinion would approve, writing for example to the King of land-locked Württemberg just after the British had stopped the German steamer, "I hope that events of last few days will have convinced ever widening circles that not only German interests but also German honor must be protected in distant oceans, and that to this end Germany must be strong and powerful on the seas."[90]

At the Kaiser's command, Hohenlohe informed the governments of the German states that Wilhelm II believed the naval increases were justified because of the acute diplomatic situation, the expansion of Germany's imperial interests, the economic competition of the powers, and the burgeoning expenditures the Fatherland's rivals were devoting to naval construction.[91] The Reichstag, which had supported the initial Naval Law but which seemed reluctant now only two years later to authorize an additional huge expenditure on ships, could not be allowed to frustrate Wilhelm II's ambitions. Germany stood at the crossroads, the Kaiser declared, and parliamentary opposition threatened to create a dangerous constitutional situation not unlike that which his revered grandfather Wilhelm I had faced in 1862, when he and Bismarck had defied the Prussian legislature over its refusal of the army budget. "On this question," he advised Hohenlohe on 29 November 1899, "which for the Reich is one of life or death, all other considerations must be put in the background."[92]

Wilhelm's fears that the Reichstag would reject the Second Naval Law proved groundless. The bill, essentially as Tirpitz had designed it, was accepted on 12 June 1900 on a tide of anti-English, pro-Boer sentiment, by a margin of 201 to 103, with many deputies abstaining. Wilhelm II was ecstatic. Hohenlohe was less so, for he realized that the passage of the Second Naval Law marked the end of his career. In the battle fleet Wilhelm II had got what he most wanted and could now proceed without his loyal chancellor. Even before the law passed, Hohenlohe had begun to prepare for his departure; once the law was an actuality, he rented an apartment in Berlin, to be ready, he said, for his expulsion from the chancellor's palace in the Wilhelmstrasse.[93] The aged man had no regrets but indeed a measure of justifiable satisfaction. The six years he had spent in office had been remarkable for a person of his advanced years and allegedly feeble willpower. Hohenlohe, never much impressed by Wilhelm's storms of rhetoric about his firm if not irrevocable determination, had succeeded many times in persuading the Kaiser to delay or abandon plans that the chancellor found inadvisable. How often had Wilhelm declared insistently that he would have his way against recalcitrant ministers, parliaments, or subjects, only to back down? Although he had eventually lost his ministerial allies Bronsart, Boetticher, and Marschall, Hohenlohe kept them in office for months and months after Wilhelm had emphatically declared that they had to go at once. Coups that Wilhelm threatened within Germany or risky diplomatic maneuvers that he conceived never materialized after encountering Hohenlohe's objections. More positively, the two great Naval Laws had been enacted, measures for which there initially had been little parliamentary enthusiasm, and a fundamental revision of the civil law effected in 1897. Moreover, the courts-martial issue, which had so excited Wilhelm II in the mid-1890s, had finally been resolved in May 1898 to the Kaiser's satisfaction (and to Hohenlohe's) when the Reichstag passed a bill that significantly expanded civilian accessibility to military trials but, as the Kaiser had rigidly insisted, prevented their being open completely without qualification to the general public.[94]

The chancellor acknowledged that his successes had certainly to be balanced by defeats he had suffered at Wilhelm II's hands. Hohenlohe had been unable, as he openly admitted, to instill in the Kaiser a greater sense of responsibility to the government and to public opinion or a more mature judgment and circumspection of action. The Kaiser did as he pleased and seldom bothered to inform the chancellor. The ultimate disillusionment for the old grandee came in September 1900, when Wilhelm, without consulting him, decided to send a German detachment to China as part of an international expedition to rescue the Western diplomatic colony in Peking, beleaguered in their compound by the Boxer rebels. The handling of the Chinese crisis made it clear to Hohenlohe that Wilhelm II and Bülow wished to chart foreign policy by themselves, and that Bülow, the man of the future, was anxious to occupy his place. The chancellor knew, moreover, that the Prussian ministers, especially Miquel, and the imperial state secretaries paid him no mind since they knew that the Kaiser himself did not.[95] In a bureaucratic system in which honors and preferments depended on the throne, it was unwise for men to cling to causes or personalities that no longer enjoyed the ruler's enthusiasm. Once it was clear that Hohenlohe's departure could not be long deferred, prudence dictated deserting the chancellor and raising Bülow's flag. Hohenlohe had often said that he would not be a man of straw, and so on 16 October 1900, he resigned, concluding his journal for that day with elegaic uncertainty—"Let us hope for the best."[96]

Wilhelm II, who more than once had refused to grant Hohenlohe's requests to surrender his office, accepted his resignation with alacrity and appointed Bülow as his successor. The new chancellor, unaffected by the forebodings about the Kaiser that had given both Caprivi and Hohenlohe pause as they assumed the post, accepted his new office with breezy imperturbability. Bülow, Wilhelm had earlier declared, would some day be a second Bismarck, serving him as the Iron Chancellor had his beloved grandfather.[97] There was in fact nothing whatsoever similar about the two men. One striking, and alarming, difference was the flattering, unctuous prose of which Bülow, like his good friend Philipp Eulenburg, was an undoubted master, contrasted with the unadorned, graphic style for which Bismarck was rightly admired. To Bismarck, statecraft was a profession that demanded utter seriousness, but to Bülow, the quintessential poseur, it was only a diversion, trivially pursued for the sake of making a glamorous impression. Bülow was no less devoted to the trappings and insignia of power than was Wilhelm II, in whose imperial majesty the chancellor would be advantageously reflected. Gone, once Bülow succeeded as chancellor, was the obdurate will with which Bismarck had often confronted both Wilhelm I and his young grandson. Nor would Wilhelm II any longer have to endure the inconvenient insistence on principle with which Caprivi had so often faced him, or the irritating vacillations and subtle delays that had been Hohenlohe's speciality. Instead, Bülow would offer only praise and fealty, and whatever restraints earlier chancellors had succeeded in imposing on Wilhelm were now discarded.

From the moment in 1897 that Bülow assumed office as state secretary of the Foreign Office, he and Wilhelm II worked together in remarkable harmony, a partnership assiduously promoted by Bülow's superlative talent for ingratiating himself with his erratic and visionary sovereign. The new chancellor knew, better than any other person among the monarch's friends and advisors, how to cater to Wilhelm II's sense of self-importance, his desire for fame and honor so that he might be enshrined among the most illustrious of his Hohenzollern forefathers. Bülow had no intention of challenging the Kaiser. Several years earlier he had written to his good friend Philipp Eulenburg, "I would be a chancellor different than my predecessors. Bismarck was a power in himself. . . . Caprivi and Hohenlohe considered themselves as representatives of the 'government' and to a certain degree the parliament. I [however] would regard myself as the accomplishing agent of His Majesty, in a way like his chief of staff. With me the personal regime would begin, in a good sense but also in actuality."[98]

The effect on the Kaiser of Bülow's catering to his every whim proved highly unfortunate and did much to replenish his already well-developed vainglory. As a young lieutenant Wilhelm had received much the same adulation from his fellow officers, who had rarely dared to suggest that there was anything amiss about the foolish or incompetent things he said or did. Early on he became certain that if something unfortunate happened, it was no fault of his own. From that start, in the garrison at Potsdam Wilhelm had grown older, but no wiser, his actions proceeding almost without exception from personal considerations rather than judicious reflection, his knowledge, such as it was, derived from a constricted circle of Prussian aristocrats who composed the only society he knew. Wilhelm thought that he acted out his part magnificently, and mistakenly believed that his bristling gestures and grandiloquent phrases impressed not only his subjects but Europeans of all nations. It was all a sham and required ever more rhetoric, and ever more props, to be sustained. Wilhelm rattled on, fulminating about the revenge he would exact against his many enemies, the wars the Fatherland would someday be required to fight, the supernal destiny to which he would lead his millions of subjects. The ferocious grimaces that contorted Wilhelm's public face, the monumental parades in ever-changing uniforms, the court in Berlin that in spite of determined effort failed to impart the desired aura of majesty were all designed to inflate the Kaiser's image. Even the great navy that Wilhelm II felt compelled to build to gain respect was in that sense proof not only of Germany's economic might but of the bankruptcy of the Kaiser's attempt to realize his regal pretensions.

The year before he became chancellor, Bülow had spoken fulsomely of the path leading to "world power, greatness and eternal glory" on which the Kaiser's subjects would gladly follow him.[99] The new century was now at hand in which Wilhelm II, together with his chancellor, would move forward to make imperial Germany respected, and perhaps even feared, never again to suffer the humiliations that had been inflicted on her because of military weakness or pusillanimous leadership. There was little in Wilhelm II's record to date to justify any expectation that the crown possessed the wisdom to serve effectively as the steward of such a proud future. To his soldiers and admirals, his diplomats and statesmen, apart from those who were either blindly loyal or, like Bülow, single-mindedly ambitious, the Kaiser was regarded as an obstruction, or a useless and sometimes dangerous interference, or an embarrassment. Wilhelm II had matured not into a national glory, nor an asset in government, but a serious liability, fruitlessly squandering the fund of goodwill and expectation that had attended his coming to the throne. In the years that remained of his reign nothing occurred that would allow any amendment of the somber judgment that Germany was ruled by a man unequal to his destiny.

The combination of the new chancellor's effusiveness and the Kaiser's theatricality, neither grounded in a serious attitude toward their positions of immense responsibility and authority, proved fatal and produced neither the greatness nor the glory that Bülow had so suavely assured his master would be his future. Wilhelm II and Bülow possessed power in very great measure, in the Prussian army on land and, as Tirpitz's fleet grew, on the sea as well, armaments that were paid for by Germany's enormous wealth. But in the long decade of Bülow's chancellorship, the employment of this might was exercised with a reckless irresponsibility that betrayed the barrenness of both the ruler and his chief servant and that did much to prepare the way for the great war that broke out in 1914. The new century, proclaimed by the Kaiser to introduce an era of majestic accomplishment reminiscent of the age of Bismarck and by Bülow as one that would yield "eternal glory," led instead to military defeat, the fall of the Hohenzollern monarchy, and Kaiser Wilhelm II's flight by night across the Dutch border into ignominious exile.

N o t e s

Manuscript Sources

The Bibliography of Manuscript Sources gives a complete alphabetical list of archives used in this study, with details of location and the nature of the holdings. In the notes, personal papers are cited by name of depositor, e.g., Albedyll Papers. Government documents, including the papers of the English and German royal households, are listed by depository, abbreviated as follows:

BPHA	Brandenburg-Preussisches Haus Archiv
FO	Foreign Office Papers (British)
GFM Papers	German Foreign Ministry Papers
HHStA	Haus-, Hof- und Staatsarchiv
RA	Royal Archives

Published Sources

BD	G. P. Gooch and H. W. V. Temperley, eds. *British Documents on the Origins of the War, 1898–1914*. 11 vols. London, 1925–38.
Berghahn	Volker R. Berghahn. *Der Tirpitz-Plan: Genesis und Verfall einer innenpolitischen Krisenstrategie unter Wilhelm II*. Düsseldorf, 1971.
Bülow	Bernhard von Bülow. *Denkwürdigkeiten*. 4 vols. Berlin, 1930–31.
Bussmann	Walter Bussmann, ed. *Staatssekretär Graf Herbert von Bismarck: Aus seiner politischen Privatkorrespondenz*. Göttingen, 1964.
DDF	*Documents Diplomatiques Français, 1871–1914*. 40 vols. Paris, 1929–59.
Ebel	Gerhard Ebel, ed. *Botschafter Graf Paul von Hatzfeldt: Nachgelassene Papiere, 1838–1901*. 2 vols. Boppard, 1976.
Fuchs	Walther Peter Fuchs, ed. *Grossherzog Friedrich I. von Baden und die Reichspolitik, 1871–1907*. 4 vols. Stuttgart, 1968–80.

GP   Johannes Lepsius, Albrecht Mendelssohn-Bartholdy, and
        Friedrich Thimme, eds. *Die Grosse Politik der Europäischen
        Kabinette.* 40 vols. Berlin, 1922–27.
GuE   Otto von Bismarck, *Gedanken und Erinnerungen.* Vol. 3.
        Berlin, 1923.
GW   Herman von Petersdorff et al., eds. *Bismarck: Die
        gesammelten Werke.* 15 vols. Berlin, 1923–33.
Hohenlohe Friedrich Curtius, ed. *Denkwurdigkeiten des Fürsten
        Chlodwig zu Hohenlohe-Schillingsfürst.* 2 vols. Stuttgart,
        1907. Karl A. von Müller, ed. *Fürst Chlodwig zu
        Hohenlohe-Schillingsfürst: Denkwürdigkeiten der
        Reichskanzlerzeit.* Stuttgart and Berlin, 1931. Curtius's edi-
        tion is cited as Hohenlohe 1 and 2; Müller's edition is cited
        as Hohenlohe 3.
HP   Norman Rich and M. H. Fisher, eds. *The Holstein Papers.* 4
        vols. Cambridge, 1955–63.
Kennedy Paul M. Kennedy. *The Rise of the Anglo-German Antago-
        nism, 1860–1914.* London, 1980.
Röhl   John C. G. Röhl, ed. *Philipp Eulenburgs Politische
        Korrespondenz.* 3 vols. Boppard, 1976–83.
Schulthess *Schulthess' Europäischer Geschichtskalendar.* 79 vols. Mu-
        nich, 1860–1938.
Tirpitz Admiral Alfred von Tirpitz. *Erinnerungen.* Leipzig, 1919.
Waldersee Heinrich O. Meisner, ed. *Denkwürdigkeiten des General-
        Feldmarschalls Alfred Grafen von Waldersee.* 3 vols. Stutt-
        gart and Berlin, 1923–25.
Wedel   Count Erhard von Wedel, ed. *Zwischen Kaiser und Kanzler:
        Aufzeichnungen des General-adjutanten Grafen Carl von
        Wedel aus den Jahren 1890–1914. . . .* Leipzig, 1943.
Winzen Peter Winzen. *Bülows Weltmachtkonzept: Untersuchungen
        zur Frühphase seiner Aussenpolitik, 1897–1901.* Boppard,
        1977.

CHAPTER I

1. Elizabeth Longford, *Queen Victoria: Born to Succeed* (New York, 1964), pp. 172, 226.

2. Richard Kühn, ed., *Kaiserin Augusta. Bekenntnisse an eine Freundin: Aufzeichnungen aus ihrer Freundschaft mit Jenny von Gustedt* (Dresden, 1935), pp. 243, 249.

3. Letter to Sophie, Crown Princess of the Hellenes (26 Aug. 1892), in Arthur G. Lee, ed., *The Empress Writes to Sophie, Her Daughter, Crown Princess and Later Queen of the Hellenes: Letters, 1889–1901* (London, n.d. [1955]), p. 121.

4. Count Egon Corti, *Wenn . . . : Sendung und Schicksal einer Kaiserin* (Graz, 1954), p. 35.

5. Horst Kohl, ed., *Briefe des Generals Leopold von Gerlach an Otto von Bismarck* (Stuttgart, 1912), p. 291; also Wilhelm v. Schweinitz, ed., *Denkwürdigkeiten des Botschafters General v. Schweinitz*, 2 vols. (Berlin, 1927), 2:97.

6. Undated letter (ca. 19 Feb. 1858) in Corti, *Wenn*, pp. 69–70.

7. RA Z1/6 (27 Feb. 1858). This letter is printed on p. 64 of Roger Fulford, ed., *Dearest Child: Letters between Queen Victoria and the Princess Royal, 1858–1861* (New York, 1964), which begins a series of volumes concluding with *Beloved Mama: The Private Correspondence of Queen Victoria and the German Crown Princess, 1878–1885* (London, 1981). Since Fulford has printed only a fraction of the Princess's letters to her mother, I have throughout cited all letters from the Princess by the Royal Archives signature. All RA letters cited without writer are by the Princess Royal and, unless otherwise noted, are addressed to Queen Victoria.

8. Anton von Werner, *Erlebnisse und Eindrücke, 1870–1890* (Berlin, 1913), p. 508.

9. RA Z21/38 (12 May 1868).

10. RA Z3/50 (to Prince Albert, 15 Dec. 1860). See also RA Z4/15, 36 (to Prince Albert, 27 Apr., 16 Nov. 1861); Z10/64 (4 Mar. 1861); and Z14/30 (12 Jan. 1863).

11. For the King's criticism of Vicky and his son, see Herbert Bismarck to Rantzau (18 Dec. 1886) and to Otto Bismarck (9 Nov. 1886) in Bussmann, pp. 414 and 403, respectively; Albert von Mutius to Friedrich Thimme (1 Feb. 1934), Thimme Papers, no. 16; Johannes Haller, ed., *Aus 50 Jahren: Erinnerungen, Tagebücher und Briefe aus dem Nachlass des Fürsten Philipp zu Eulenburg-Hertefeld* (Berlin, 1923), pp. 187–88.

12. Grand Duke to Gelzer (20, 21, 31 Mar. 1872), Fuchs, 1:54–55, 64.

13. RA Z2/19 (to Prince Albert, 3 May 1859), Z21/38 (12 May 1868).

14. Heinrich O. Meisner, ed., *Peter von Meyendorff, ein Russischer Diplomat an den Höfen von Berlin und Wien: Politischer und privater Briefwechsel, 1826–63*, 3 vols. (Berlin and Leipzig, 1923), 3:376. Fritz apparently did not like his mother much even though Vicky encouraged him to regard her with more favor. RA Z21/55 (4 July 1868), RA Z63/42 (Princess Feodora of Hohenlohe-Langenburg to Prince Albert, 9 Mar. 1858); *HP*, 2:171.

15. Marie von Bunsen, *Kaiserin Augusta* (Berlin, 1940), p. 262. Augusta's complaints about Vicky are in RA Z63/42 (Princess Feodora to Prince Albert, 9 Mar. 1858).

16. RA Z7/118 (25 Apr. 1859); Rowland Prothero, Baron Ernle, "The Empress Frederick," *The Nineteenth Century and After* 106 (Sept. 1929): 404–5.

17. RA Z2/19 (to Prince Albert, 3 May 1859).

18. Malet to Lady Malet (22 Mar. 1888), Malet Papers, no. A-33.

19. On her unorthodox religious views, see RA Z 25/49 (30 Jan. 1871); Mutius to Thimme (1 Feb. 1934), Thimme Papers, no. 16; Mary J. Lyschinska, ed., *Henriette Schrader-Breymann: Ihr Leben aus Briefen und Tagebüchern zusammengestellt und erläutert*, 2 vols. (Berlin, 1927), 2:31; Hans Delbrück, "Kaiserin Friedrich," in his *Erinnerungen, Aufsätze und Reden* (Berlin, 1905), pp. 621-22; Ernst von Dryander, *Erinnerungen aus meinem Leben*, 2d rev. ed. (Bielefeld and Leipzig, 1922), p. 227; Franz Ayme, *Kaiser Wilhelm II. und seine*

Erziehung: Aus den Erinnerungen seines französischen Lehrers (Leipzig, 1898), p. 96.

20. Bülow Papers, no. 110:18–19.

21. For her disparaging remarks about the Berlin court, see her letter to Countess Dönhoff (7 Jan. 1885), Bülow Papers, no. 169; RA Z2/31 (to Prince Albert, 6 Aug. 1859), Z5/18 (15 Feb. 1858), Z9/55 (27 Apr. 1860). On the china and food, see Richard Boschau, ed., *Aus Hannover und Preussen: Lebenserinnerungen aus einem halben Jahrhundert von Julie von Albedyll-Alten* (Potsdam, 1914), p. 221.

22. Letter to Countess Dönhoff (7 Jan. 1885), Bülow Papers, no. 169.

23. RA Z9/11 (30 Dec. 1859), Z13/37 (19 July 1862); also Z14/11, 35 (8 Nov. 1862, 31 Jan. 1863).

24. RA Z15/36 (3 July 1863).

25. Diary (23 Sept. 1862), in Heinrich O. Meisner, ed., *Kaiser Friedrich III.: Tagebücher von 1848–1866* (Leipzig, 1929), p. 161.

26. RA Z18/68 (16 July 1866). See also her praise of Prussia in her letters to Gustav Freytag (28 Dec. 1869, 13 Feb. and 21 Aug. 1870), Freytag Papers.

27. RA Z15/2 (16 Mar. 1863). Even the Empress Augusta agreed that although England always remained Vicky's ideal she raised her children as true Hohenzollerns. Kühn, *Kaiserin Augusta*, p. 255.

28. RA Z19/20 (16 Nov. 1866). In old age Wilhelm II himself commented on this trait of his mother's. See his introduction to Sir Frederick Ponsonby, ed., *Letters of the Empress Frederick* (New York, 1928), p. xvii. On her use of "our," see Bunsen, *Kaiserin Augusta*, p. 253.

29. Bunsen, *Kaiserin Augusta*, pp. 253–54; for her love of argument and certainty of triumph, see Sir James Rennell Rodd, *Social and Diplomatic Memories, 1884–1919*, 3 vols. (London, 1922–25), 1:49; and see Ellen von Siemens, ed., *Anna von Helmholtz: Ein Lebensbild in Briefen*, 2 vols. (Berlin, 1929), 2:174, for her sense of intellectual superiority.

30. *My Memories of Six Reigns* (London, 1956), pp. 94–95.

31. Marie von Bunsen, *Die Welt in der ich Lebte: Erinnerungen aus glücklichen Jahren, 1860–1912* (Leipzig, 1929), pp. 183–84. For the dismay of other admirers, see Baron Hugo von Reischach, *Unter Drei Kaisern*, Volksausgabe (Berlin, 1925), pp. 109–10, 157–58; Charles Hardinge, First Baron Hardinge of Penshurst, *Old Diplomacy* (London, 1947), p. 26; Princess Marie zu Erbach-Schönberg, *Erklungenes und Verklungenes* (Darmsdtadt, 1923), p. 43.

32. Robert Dohme, "Erinnerungen an Kaiser Friedrich," *Deutsche Revue* 47, nos. 1–3 (1922): no. 2:120–21.

33. Gen. Emil von Albedyll to his wife (16 Aug. 1878), in Boschau, *Aus Hannover und Preussen*, p. 299.

34. Hans Delbrück, "Kaiserin Friedrich," p. 624.

35. Ponsonby, *Letters of the Empress Frederick*, p. 7.

36. RA Z19/17 (3 Nov. 1866).

37. RA Z12/35 (15 Nov. 1861), RA Add. MS U/32 (20 June, 8 July 1885); Eulenburg Papers, no. 74:48–49, no. 80:65–66; Röhl, 1:141; Waldersee, 2:138, 243; *HP*, 2:37; Hans F. Helmolt, ed., *Gustav Freytags Briefe an Albrecht von Stosch* (Stuttgart and Berlin, 1913), p. 176.

38. James Rennell Rodd, *Friedrich III. als Kronprinz und Kaiser: Ein Lebens-bild* (Berlin, 1888), p. 43, for the Empress's opinion. For the Crown Prince's vanity, see Dohme, "Erinnerungen," p. 6; Gustav Freytag, *Der Kronprinz und die Deutsche Kaiserkrone: Erinnerungsblätter* (Leipzig, 1889), p. 75.

39. Letter to Gustav Freytag (30 Jan. 1878), Freytag Papers.

40. Letter to Stosch (12 Jan. 1870), Helmolt, *Freytags Briefe*, p. 56; similarly the Grand Duke to Gelzer (21, 31 Mar., 1872), Fuchs, 1:55–56, 64. On Vicky's dominance of her husband, see Arthur von Brauer, *Im Dienste Bismarcks: Per-sönliche Erinnerungen* (Berlin, 1936), pp. 245–46; *HP*, 1:139.

41. RA Z14/22 (17 Dec. 1862).

42. RA Z4/15 (to Prince Albert, 27 Apr. 1861), for the King's charge that Fritz was too tied to his mother; for his complaints about Vicky exercising a similar influence, see note 11 above.

43. Grand Duke to Gelzer (31 Mar., 2 Apr. 1872), Fuchs, 1:64; Hans Del-brück, "Persönliche Erinnerungen an den Kaiser Friedrich und sein Haus," *Preussische Jahrbücher* 62 (1888): 73; RA Z63/42 (Princess Feodora to Prince Albert, 9 Mar. 1858); Empress Augusta to Grand Duke of Saxe-Weimar (29 Jan. 1867), Bunsen, *Kaiserin Augusta*, p. 197.

44. Meisner, *Meyendorff Briefwechsel*, 3:366; Lady Walburga Paget, *Embas-sies of Other Days and Further Recollections*, 2 vols. (London, 1923), 1:71; Schweinitz, *Denkwürdigkeiten*, 1:98, 2:134.

45. Paget, *Embassies*, 1:104.

46. Princess Catherine Radziwill, *Memories of Forty Years* (New York and London, 1915), pp. 192–93. For a rare complaint against his wife, see Gelzer diary (13 Jan. 1873), Fuchs, 1:108.

47. On the falls, Vicky to Lady Constance Villiers (31 May 1858), Hobbs/Gathorne-Hardy Papers. On her pregnancy, see RA Z7/121 (2 May 1859); RA Z63/64, 88, 90 (August Wegner, M.D., to Prince Albert, 10 July, 10, 16 Dec. 1858); Z7/121 (2 May 1859).

48. Martin's account of the birth in his diary (9 Feb. 1859) is in BPHA, Rep. 53a, no. 9; also a memo by Martin's son, August Martin, M.D. (28 Apr. 1931), ibid. There is another version by August Martin that differs in details in Del-brück Papers, no. 22. Wegner's description is in his letter to Queen Victoria (28 Jan. 1859), RA Z63/112; Sir James Clark's in his letters to the Queen (27 Jan., 1 Feb. 1859), Z63/107, 118. Other accounts that add details are Georgiana, Bar-oness Bloomfield, *Reminiscences of Court and Diplomatic Life*, 2 vols. (New York, 1883), 2:78–79; Baron Robert Lucius von Ballhausen, *Bismarck-Erinner-ungen* (Stuttgart and Berlin, 1920), p. 74; Paula von Bülow, *Aus Verklungenen Zeiten: Lebenserinnerungen, 1833–1920* (Leipzig, 1925), p. 46. There is no evi-dence in any of these accounts of an excessive use of chloroform that might in turn explain Wilhelm II's psychological peculiarities in adulthood. This is the view advanced by John C. G. Röhl in the *Frankfurter Allgemeine Zeitung*, 22 July 1987, p. 22, who has elsewhere suggested that Wilhelm's brain may have been damaged during birth. There is, however, no evidence that the attending physicians thought that this was the case. See Röhl, *Kaiser, Hof und Staat: Wilhelm II. und die deutsche Politik* (Munich, 1987), p. 33.

49. RA Z63/107 (Clark's letter to the Queen of 27 Jan. 1859).

50. RA Z7/93 (6 Mar. 1859); RA Z8/55 (1 Oct. 1859), Z63/118 (Clark to Queen Victoria, 1 Feb. 1859). Vicky apparently breast-fed most of her other children. See Lyschinska, *Schrader-Breymann*, 2:31. To do so was contrary to Hohenzollern custom. Bunsen, *Kaiserin Augusta*, p. 252.

51. Kühn, *Kaiserin Augusta*, pp. 257–59.

52. Crown Prince to Queen Elizabeth of Prussia (13 Feb. 1859), in Meisner, *Tagebuch Friedrich III.*, p. 59.

53. RA Z15/15 (28 Apr. 1863), which includes a drawing of the "machine."

54. Wilhelm II, *Aus Meinem Leben, 1859–1888* (Berlin and Leipzig, 1927), p. 31; Schweinitz, ed., *Briefwechsel Schweinitz*, p. 7.

55. For Wilhelm's aplomb in dealing with his arm, see Prince Heinrich von Schönburg-Waldenburg, *Erinnerungen aus Kaiserlicher Zeit* (Leipzig, 1929), p. 165; Baron Werner von Rheinbaben, *Kaiser, Kanzler, Präsidenten: Erinnerungen* (Mainz, 1968), p. 24; Anne Topham, *Chronicles of the Prussian Court* (London, 1926), p. 71; Bülow, 2:147–48. Even as a child, Willy accepted his handicap without demur; RA Z24/60 (28 May 1870). The best descriptions of Wilhelm's arm in maturity are Arthur N. Davis, *The Kaiser as I Know Him* (New York, 1918), p. 200; Rodd, *Social and Diplomatic Memories*, 1:50; also Ayme, *Kaiser Wilhelm*, p. 84.

56. In 1889 Wilhelm's widowed mother heard that he was saying that one English doctor had crippled his arm and another had killed his father, a charge obviously directed against her, since she had chosen the physicians in question; RA Z44/33 (27 Apr. 1889). Almost fifty years later, he made a veiled charge against his parents for being responsible for his handicap. John W. Wheeler-Bennett, *Knaves, Fools and Heroes: In Europe between the Wars* (London, 1947), p. 187. But on other occasions in discussing his arm and the treatments he had received to revivify it, Wilhelm made no reference to his parents. See, for example, Joachim von Kürenberg [pseud.], *War Alles Falsch?: Das Leben Kaiser Wilhelms II.* (Bonn, 1951), p. 23. It seems unlikely that the arm played a significant role in Wilhelm's alienation from his mother and father. See also Hinzpeter's observations, as reported in Bülow, 1:107.

57. In his biography, *Wilhelm der Zweite* (Berlin, 1926), Emil Ludwig argued that Wilhelm's defective arm was largely responsible for his strident personality as an adult. Ludwig's amateur psychological approach received considerable criticism, including an objection from Sigmund Freud, who argued that it was Vicky's attitude toward her son's defect that was in fact the significant factor in Wilhelm's psychological development. Freud overlooked Ludwig's argument (evident on p. 16 of the biography) that there was a connection between Vicky's attitude toward her son's arm and his personality. See James Strachey, ed., *The Standard Edition of the Complete Psychological Works of Sigmund Freud*, 24 vols. (London, 1953–74), 22:66. I am indebted to Professor Thomas A. Kohut of Williams College for this reference. The testimony of Wilhelm's childhood friend, Marie von Bunsen, is of interest. She wrote (*Welt in der Ich Lebte*, pp. 198–99): "It is well known that Emil Ludwig puts the strongest weight on the psychological effect [on Wilhelm II] of his crippled arm. This contradicts my memories from infancy and childhood, and I have asked almost all of those still alive who in those days were close to the household of Wilhelm's parents and all of them

consider Ludwig's argument on this point to be both misleading and wrong." For Wilhelm on his mother's role in forming his personality, see Eulenburg diary (26 July 1887), Eulenburg Papers, no. 47:423–26.

58. RA Z17/62 (6 May 1865).

59. RA Z3/1 (27 Jan. 1860). In similar distress, ibid., Z3/35 (to Prince Albert, 18 Aug. 1860); Z10/48, 56 (26 Jan., 15 Feb. 1861); Z16/67 (26 July 1864); Z21/2 (4 Jan. 1868); Z26/46 (31 Jan. 1872).

60. RA Z17/65 (17 May 1865), Z24/60 (28 May 1870), Z26/46 (31 Jan., 1872).

61. RA Z10/10 (2 Nov. 1860); also Z10/19 (27 Nov. 1860).

62. Meisner, *Tagebücher Friedrich III.* (30 June 1861, 27 Jan. 1863), pp. 98, 185.

63. RA Z25/48 (28 Jan. 1871). Willy's tutor, François Ayme, gave Vicky all the credit for the boy's education. Ayme, *Kaiser Wilhelm*, p. 85.

64. RA Z16/61, 74 (8 July, 16 Aug. 1864).

65. RA Z17/25 (11 Jan. 1865).

66. RA Z26/46 (31 Jan. 1872), Z28/80 (25 Jan. 1874).

67. RA Z12/45 (8 Dec. 1861).

68. RA Z8/44 (3 Sept. 1859); also Z15/2 (16 Mar. 1883), Z16/59 (2 July 1864), Z4/9 (to Prince Albert, 2 Mar. 1861).

69. Shane Leslie, *The End of a Chapter* (London, 1917), p. 79; Hector Bolitho, ed., *Letters of Lady Augusta Stanley: A Young Lady at Court, 1849–1863* (New York, 1927), pp. 283–86, 309; Countess Marie Kleinmichel, *Memories of a Shipwrecked World* (New York, 1923), p. 35.

70. RA Z8/7, 44 (8 June, 3 Sept. 1859); Z12/45 (8 Dec. 1861).

71. RA Z16/14 (3 Feb. 1864), Z19/29 (9 Nov. 1866).

72. Rodd, *Friedrich III.*, p. 147; Karl-Heinz Janssen, ed., *Die Graue Exzellenz: Zwischen Staatsräson und Vasallentreue: Aus den Papieren des kaiserlichen Gesandten Karl Georg von Treutler* (Frankfurt, 1971), p. 115, for parental discipline. For pictures of family life from the mid-1870s, see the diary of Gustav zu Putlitz (7 July 1864), in Sidney Whitman, *Life of the Empress Frederick*, 2 vols. (Leipzig, 1901), 1:259; Ayme, *Kaiser Wilhelm*, pp. 91–95.

73. Wilhelm II, *Aus Meinem Leben*, pp. 21–22; "Bemerkungen" by Wilhelm II (Nov. 1934), BPHA, Rep. 192, no. 20, in which the former Kaiser altered a characterization of his governess from "disgruntled" (*mürrisch*) to "strict" (*strenge*).

74. RA Z17/41 (26 Feb. 1865).

75. RA Z20/15 (18 June 1867); Kürenberg, *War Alles Falsch?*, p. 21, for Wilhelm II's recollection of Schrötter.

76. George Campbell, Eighth Duke of Argyll, K.G., *Passages from the Past*, 2 vols. (London, 1907), 2:263.

77. The discussions can be followed in the Morier Papers, in a box marked "1864–7." See also Rosslyn Wemyss, ed., *Memoirs and Letters of the Rt. Hon. Sir Robert Morier, G.C.B.*, 2 vols. (London, 1911), 2:97–98; Bülow, 1:105.

78. Hinzpeter can best be fathomed by reading his voluminous correspondence over almost forty years with Count Görtz, in the Schlitz von Görtz Papers, no. 217, and his letters to the Empress Augusta Victoria, Wilhelm II's consort, in

BPHA, Rep. 53a, no. 21. There is illuminating material in the Morier Papers, as well as in the portrait by a former pupil, Count Anton von Monts, in Karl F. Nowak and Friedrich Thimme, eds., *Erinnerungen und Gedanken des Botschafters Anton Graf Monts* (Berlin, 1932), pp. 137–38. See also Ayme, *Kaiser Wilhelm*, pp. 120–25; Poultney Bigelow, *Prussian Memories, 1864–1914* (New York and London, 1915), pp. 39–53. Wilhelm II's recollection of Hinzpeter is in his *Aus Meinem Leben*, pp. 23–25.

79. Agatha Ramm, *Sir Robert Morier: Envoy and Ambassador in the Age of Imperialism, 1876–1883* (Oxford, 1973), p. 7.

80. Bigelow, *Prussian Memories*, pp. 52–54.

81. Ayme, *Kaiser Wilhelm*, p. 121.

82. Stockmar to Morier (23 Jan. 1866), Morier Papers, box marked "Miscellaneous Letters, 1852–1876," no. 4.

83. Hinzpeter to Count Görtz (15 Nov. 1867), Schlitz von Görtz Papers, no. 217.

84. Stockmar to Morier (12 Feb. 1865), Morier Papers, box marked "Miscellaneous Letters, 1852–1876," no. 4; also Hinzpeter, *Kaiser Wilhelm II.: Eine Skizze nach der Natur gezeichnet* (Bielefeld, 1888), p. 5.

85. Carpenter diary (8 Aug. 1901), Boyd-Carpenter Papers, Add. MS 46742.

86. RA Z64/58 (Wilhelm to Queen Victoria, 2 Sept. 1874). For Vicky's religious views, see note 19 above. On the lack of religion in the children's education, see Lady Burghclere, *A Great Lady's Friendships: Letters to Mary, Marchioness of Salisbury, Countess of Derby, 1862–1890* (London, 1933), p. 451.

87. Wilhelm II, *Aus Meinem Leben*, p. 26; Ayme, *Kaiser Wilhelm*, p. 130.

88. Rijksarchief Papers, no. 594 (1866).

89. Dealtry to Vicky (30 Apr. 1870), in Ponsonby, *Letters of Empress Frederick*, p. 68; Wilhelm II, *Aus Meinem Leben*, p. 65; Lillie de Hegermann-Lindencrone, *The Sunny Side of Diplomatic Life* (London and New York, 1914), p. 332. Forty years later, the Kaiser was still reading American periodicals. Davis, *Kaiser as I Know Him*, p. 228.

90. Hinzpeter to Count Görtz (5 May 1869), Schlitz von Görtz Papers, no. 217.

91. On Hinzpeter, Wilhelm II, *Aus Meinem Leben*, pp. 27, 42–44; for Queen Augusta, see Willy to his Aunt Louise, Grand Duchess of Baden (9 Aug. 1877), BPHA, Rep. 53a, no. 20; also Bunsen, *Welt in der ich Lebte*, pp. 26–27.

92. Ernst Curtius to Georg Curtius (26 Mar. 1873), in Friedrich Curtius, ed., *Ernst Curtius: Ein Lebensbild in Briefen*, 2 vols. (Berlin, 1913), 2:219.

93. Bigelow, *Prussian Memories*, pp. 48–49; see also Wilhelm II, *Aus Meinem Leben*, p. 39; Bigelow, *The German Emperor and His Eastern Neighbors* (New York, 1892), pp. 18–19; Bigelow, "How the German Emperor Took to the Water," *Harper's Weekly* (15 June 1895).

94. Bigelow, *Prussian Memories*, pp. 40–42.

95. Ibid., pp. 39–40.

96. Manfred Krodt, *Ernst Ludwig Grossherzog von Hessen und bei Rhein: Sein Leben und seine Zeit* (Darmstadt, 1978), p. 122; for a similar criticism, see Princess Evelyn Blücher, ed., *Memoirs of Prince Blücher* (London, 1932), p. 73.

97. Viscount Ullswater, *A Speaker's Commentaries*, 2 vols. (London, 1925), 1:3. On Willy's military expertise in childhood, see Schweinitz, *Briefwechsel Schweinitz*, p. 7. For a positive assessment of Willy as a playmate, see Louise, Princess of Coburg, *Throne die ich Stürzen Sah* (Zurich, 1927), p. 175.

98. RA Z19/30 (10 Dec. 1866).

99. Wilhelm II, *Aus Meinem Leben*, p. 67.

100. Lord Strathnairn to Emma, Countess of Derby (31 Oct. 1874), in Burghclere, *Great Lady's Friendships*, pp. 407–8.

101. Bigelow, *Prussian Memories*, p. 40. For Wilhelm II's complaint in 1910 about Hinzpeter's pedanticism, see Leonidas E. Hill, ed., *Die Weizsäcker-Papiere, 1900–1932* (n.p., n.d.), p. 121.

102. RA Z25/48 (28 Jan. 1871); also Z25/72 (3 May 1871), Z26/23 (19 Oct. 1871).

103. For example, RA Z25/53 (11 Feb. 1871), Z28/78 (7 Dec. 1874).

104. RA Z207/47 (30 Jan. 1877).

105. Hinzpeter to Countess Görtz (28 Jan. 1877), Schlitz von Görtz Papers, no. 352; same to Count Carl (28 Jan. 1871, 7 May 1874), ibid., no. 217; Grand Duke to Gelzer (2 Apr. 1872), Fuchs, 1:64.

106. RA Z19/30 (10 Dec. 1866); also Z22/11 (19 Aug. 1868).

107. RA Z25/48 (28 Jan. 1871).

108. Ponsonby, *Letters of the Empress Frederick*, p. 118.

109. Letter of 15 Mar. 1873 in George E. Buckle, ed., *The Letters of Queen Victoria*, 2d ser., 3 vols. (New York, 1926–28), 2:248. This opinion is retrospectively endorsed in a letter by Princess Victoria Battenberg to Queen Victoria (16 June 1888), RA Add. U166/50. The only carping note came from Queen Sophia of the Netherlands, who was from Württemberg. The Queen may have been influenced by the fact that there was then widespread fear in Holland that it would be Bismarck's next conquest. See the Queen's letter to Lady Derby (9 Aug. 1874), in Burghclere, *Great Lady's Friendships*, pp. 399–400.

110. See Lady [Anne] Macdonell, *Reminiscences of a Diplomatic Life* (London, 1913), pp. 131–32; Wilhelm von Bode, *Mein Leben*, 2 vols. (Berlin, 1930), 1:107; Ayme, *Kaiser Wilhelm*, p. 84.

111. Bunsen, *Welt in der ich Lebte*, p. 43.

112. RA Z11/20 (8 June 1861).

113. RA Z23/8 (16 Jan. 1869). A few days later she thought he looked better; Z23/12 (29 Jan. 1869).

114. RA Z23/11 (27 Jan. 1869).

115. Ibid.; RA Z23/44 (15 May 1869).

116. RA Z28/55, 57 (29 Aug., 5 Sept. 1874).

117. Willy to Charlotte (19 July 1874), BPHA, Rep. 53a, no. 414.

118. RA Z78/25 (28 Jan. 1871); also Marie von Bunsen, *Georg von Bunsen: Eine Charakterbild aus dem Lager der Besiegten* (Berlin, 1900), p. 244; Kürenberg, *War Alles Falsch?*, pp. 29–30.

119. See Hinzpeter's letters to Count Görtz (7 May, 30 July, 28 Sept. 4 Oct. 1874; 5 Aug. 1876), Schlitz von Görtz Papers, no. 217; same to Countess Görtz (1 Oct. 1874), ibid., no. 352.

120. Crown Prince to Gustav von Putlitz (4 Nov. 1874), in G. Schuster, ed., *Briefe, Reden und Erlasse des Kaisers und Königs Friedrich III.* (Berlin, 1907), p. 233. He did not specify what these unfortunate traits were.

121. Bigelow, *German Emperor*, p. 20.

122. There are two surviving examples: in Tirpitz Papers, no. 27b, and in Wilhelm II, *Aus Meinem Leben*, pp. 363–65. See also ibid., pp. 94, 99–100.

123. RA Z28/34, 55, 56, 57 (6 June, 29 Aug., 1 Sept., 5 Sept. 1874); Corti, *Wenn*, pp. 321–23.

124. Hinzpeter to Count Görtz (21 Jan. 1877), Schlitz von Görtz Papers, no. 217.

CHAPTER 2

1. Franz Ayme, *Kaiser Wilhelm II. und seine Erziehung: Aus den Erinnerungen seines französischen Lehrers* (Leipzig, 1898), pp. 119–21; Wilhelm II, *Aus Meinem Leben, 1859–1888* (Berlin and Leipzig, 1927), p. 121.

2. Wilhelm II, *Aus Meinem Leben*, p. 126; Friedrich Schmidt-Ott, *Erlebtes und Erstrebtes, 1860–1950* (Wiesbaden, 1952), pp. 10–11. See RA Z31/9 (15 Feb. 1877) for the Crown Princess's favorable opinion. Vogt's papers in the Staatsbibliothek in West Berlin unfortunately contain only his reading and lecture notes.

3. Undated report by Privy Counselor Wiese in Wolf von Schierbrand, ed., *The Kaiser's Speeches: Forming a Character Portrait of Emperor William II* (New York, 1903), p. 206.

4. On the students' reaction to Wilhelm and their relationship with him, see Wilhelm II, *Aus Meinem Leben*, pp. 124–25; Hinzpeter to Countess Görtz (19 Oct. 1874), Schlitz von Görtz Papers, no. 352; same to Count Emil Görtz (12 Feb. 1875), ibid., no. 383/15; Schierbrand, *Kaiser's Speeches*, p. 205; Count Bogdan von Hutten-Czapski, *Sechzig Jahre Politik und Gesellschaft*, 2 vols. (Berlin, 1936), 1:50.

5. Hinzpeter to Countess Schlitz von Görtz (19 Oct. 1874), Schlitz von Görtz Papers, no. 352; Schmidt-Ott, *Erstrebtes*, pp. 10-11; Ayme, *Kaiser Wilhelm*, pp. 84, 88–89. Ayme's opinion is confirmed by an 1875 report by Privy Counselor Wiese in Schierbrand, *Kaiser's Speeches*, p. 153. There is a suggestion of overbearing behavior in Wilhelm's own account of a classroom episode at Cassel in his address to the Doorner Arbeits-Gemeinschaft (28 Oct. 1937), Rijksarchief Papers, no. 296.

6. Three accounts of the program at Cassel, differing slightly in details, are in RA GV AA6/149 (Hermann Sahl to Mr. Dalton, 19 May 1876); Wilhelm II, *Aus Meinem Leben*, pp. 127–28, 136–39; and Hinzpeter to Countess Görtz (19 Oct. 1874), Schlitz von Görtz Papers, no. 352.

7. Bülow, 1:106.

8. RA Z505/22 (Wilhelm to Queen Victoria, 13 Apr. 1875).

9. Hinzpeter to Count Görtz (24, 28 Sept. 1874), Schlitz von Görtz Papers, no. 217; same to Countess Görtz (1 Oct. 1874), ibid., no. 352.

10. Herbert Gladstone, Viscount Gladstone, *After Thirty Years* (London, 1928), p. 30. Very few of Wilhelm's letters before he was twenty have survived. There is a small sample from 1878–79 to Countess Dönhoff, a friend of his mother's, in Bülow Papers, no. 173, and some from 1869 to Queen Victoria in RA Z78 and Z79.

11. Ayme, *Kaiser Wilhelm*, pp. 89–91, 144–47; cf. Schmidt-Ott, *Erstrebtes*, p. 10.

12. Serge Sazonov, *Fateful Years, 1909–1916: The Reminiscences of Serge Sazonov* (New York, 1928), pp. 44–45.

13. RA Z28/78 (7 Dec. 1874), Z23/11 (27 Jan. 1869). She told Bernhard von Bülow that Wilhelm was only fourteen when he turned agains her and Fritz. Tirpitz notes (4 Jan. 1905), Tirpitz Papers, no. 21.

14. RA Z28/78 (7 Dec. 1874), Z29/38, 91 (17 Aug. 1875, 8 July 1876). For Vicky's concern about the effect of Wilhelm's disabled arm on his education, see chapter 1 at n. 58. Cf. Ayme, *Kaiser Wilhelm*, pp. 95–96, for her praise of her son.

15. RA Z28/76, 78 (1, 7 Dec. 1874).

16. Friedrich Curtius, ed., *Ernst Curtius: Ein Lebensbild in Briefen*, 2 vols. (Berlin, 1913), 2:148.

17. Hinzpeter to Count Emil Görtz (12 Feb. 1875), Schlitz von Görtz Papers, no. 383/15; same to Count Görtz (5 Aug. 1876, 31 Jan. 1877), ibid., no. 217. Prince Alexander von Hohenlohe, who thoroughly disliked Wilhelm, claimed to have seen a letter by Hinzpeter to Sir Robert Morier from this period in which the tutor confided that with regard to Wilhelm's character "you cannot imagine into what an abyss I have peered"; Hohenlohe, *Aus Meinem Leben* (Frankfurt/Main, 1925), p. 368. The letter is not to be found among the Morier Papers. See also Ernst Feder, ed., *Bismarcks Grosses Spiel: Die geheimen Tagebücher Ludwig Bambergers* (Frankfurt, 1933), p. 444, in which Baroness von Stockmar in 1890 claimed Hinzpeter "always" had a low estimation of his royal pupil. The weekly reports Hinzpeter sent from Cassel to Wilhelm's parents have not survived. See Ayme, *Kaiser Wilhelm*, p. 125.

18. Hinzpeter to Countess Görtz (4 Feb. 1875), Schlitz von Görtz Papers, no. 352.

19. Joachim von Kürenberg [pseud.], *War Alles Falsch?: Das Leben Kaiser Wilhelms II.* (Bonn, 1951), p. 25.

20. Hinzpeter to Countess Görtz (6 July 1874), Schlitz von Görtz Papers, no. 352; for Hinzpeter on Wilhelm's genealogical inheritance, see Prince Chlodwig zu Hohenlohe-Schillingsfürst diary (21 Jan. 1891), in Helmuth Rogge, ed., *Holstein und Hohenlohe: Neue Beiträge . . . nach Briefen und Aufzeichnungen aus dem Nachlass des Fürsten Chlodwig zu Hohenlohe-Schillingsfürst, 1874–1894* (Stuttgart, 1957), p. 347. For Hinzpeter's duplicity, compare his generally laudatory *Kaiser Wilhelm II.: Eine Skizze nach der Natur gezeichnet* (Bielefeld, 1888) with the pointed criticisms attributed to him in Waldersee, 2:174, 350; Bülow, 1:106; Hutten-Czapski, *Sechzig Jahre*, 1:312; Feder, *Bismarcks Grosses Spiel*, pp. 440, 444; Holstein to Eulenburg (6 Dec. 1890), Eulenburg Papers, no. 13: 692–93; Széchényi to Kálnoky (3 Mar. 1892), HHStA, no. 142(B). After Hinzpeter's death his correspondence with the Kaiser was returned to Wilhelm. Its

subsequent fate is unknown. See John C. G. Röhl, "The Emperor's New Clothes: A Character Sketch of Kaiser Wilhelm II," in Röhl and Nicolaus Sombart, eds., *Kaiser Wilhelm II, New Interpretations: The Corfu Papers* (Cambridge, 1982), p. 27.

21. RA Z78/134 (Wilhelm to Queen Victoria, 30 Dec. 1874); G. Schuster, ed., *Briefe, Reden und Erlasse des Kaisers und Königs Friedrich III.* (Berlin, 1907), pp. 234, 239–40.

22. Eulenburg diary (26 July 1897), Eulenburg Papers, no. 47:423–26, reporting a conversation with the Kaiser.

23. Wilhelm to Judge Emil Hartwich (2 Apr. 1885), in James C. Albisetti, *Secondary School Reform in Imperial Germany* (Princeton, 1983), p. 175.

24. Cabinet order by Wilhelm II (15 Feb. 1890), regarding the cadet academies, in Schulthess (1890), pp. 25–26; also Wilhelm II, *Aus Meinem Leben*, pp. 132–33, Ayme, *Kaiser Wilhelm*, pp. 88–89.

25. Wilhelm to Emil Hartwich (2 Apr. 1885), in Schierbrand, *Kaiser's Speeches*, pp. 208–10. Hartwich's identity, unrevealed by Schierbrand, is established in Albisetti, *Secondary School Reform*, who prints part of the letter on p. 175. A very similar complaint is in the Kaiser's letter to Houston Stewart Chamberlain (31 Dec. 1901), in Chamberlain's *Briefe, 1882–1924, und Briefwechsel mit Kaiser Wilhelm II.*, 2 vols. (Munich, 1928), 2:141–42.

26. Schulthess (1890), pp. 25–26; Eulenburg notes of talk with Wilhelm II (2 July 1896), Eulenburg Papers, no. 42:471. See also Hohenlohe, 2:449; Albisetti, *Secondary School Reform*, pp. 171–76.

27. Hinzpeter to Count Görtz (2 June 1876, 7 Mar. 1877), Schlitz von Görtz Papers, no. 217.

28. RA Z31/36 (25 July 1877).

29. RA Z31/51 (6 Oct. 1877).

30. On Liebenau and his regime, see especially the critical appraisal in Kleine Erwerbung, no. 814; also Rupprecht Leppla, ed., *Carl Justi/Otto Hartwig: Briefwechsel, 1858–1903* (Bonn, 1968), pp. 272–73. There is a brief description of Jacobi in RA Z31/35 (21 July 1877) and in RA, Queen Victoria's Journal (1 Aug. 1877).

31. Wilhelm II, *Aus Meinem Leben*, p. 160.

32. Wilhelm's poem and his correspondence with Kekule are in the Kekule von Stradonitz Papers, no. 18 G1/21; see also Heinrich Göppert to Kekule (9 Jan. 1878), ibid., no. 2. For Kekule's regret when Wilhelm left Bonn, see his letter to Richard Schöne (4 Aug. 1879), Schöne Papers. On the love of classics Wilhelm developed in his youth, see also his "Erinnerungen an Corfu," Rijksarchief Papers, no. 301, which differs from the later printed version of the same title (Berlin and Leipzig, 1924).

33. On the curator, Wilhelm Beseler, see Ottomar von Mohl, *Fünfzig Jahre Reichsdienst: Lebenserinnerungen* (Leipzig, 1921), p. 96, and Beseler's letter to Heinrich von Sybel (21 Jan. 1876), in Paul Wentzcke, ed., *Im Neuen Reich, 1871–1890: Politische Briefe aus dem Nachlass liberaler Parteiführer*, 2 vols. (1926; rpt. Osnabrück, 1967), 2:190–91.

34. Dryander, *Erinnerungen aus Meinem Leben* (Bielefeld, 1922), pp. 129–30.

35. Gelzer diary (8 Aug. 1878), Fuchs, 1:320.

36. Leppla, *Justi/Hartwig Briefwechsel*, pp. 272–73.

37. Wilhelm to Countess Dönhoff (5 Nov. 1878), Bülow Papers, no. 173.

38. Grand Duke to Gelzer (15 Aug. 1878), Fuchs, 1:322.

39. Franz von Roggenbach to Albrecht von Stosch (1 Feb. 1888), in Julius Heyderhoff, ed., *Im Ring der Gegner Bismarcks: Denkschriften und politischer Briefwechsel Franz v. Roggenbachs mit Kaiserin Augusta und Albrecht v. Stosch, 1865–1896* (Leipzig, 1943), p. 282; Hinzpeter to Count Görtz (18 Jan., 14 Feb. 1879), Schlitz von Görtz Papers, no. 217.

40. Leppla, *Justi/Hartwig Briefwechsel*, pp. 272–73.

41. See Count Harry Kessler, *Gesichter und Zeiten: Erinnerungen* (1935; rpt. Berlin, 1962), pp. 201, 215, and Baron Hugo von Reischach, *Unter Drei Kaisern*, Volksausgabe (Berlin, 1925), pp. 29–30, for descriptions of the fraternity by Borussen who were at Bonn at approximately the same time as Wilhelm. See also the depiction by Szögyényi of Wilhelm's "*Bonner Allüren*" in his dispatches to Kálnoky (24 Mar. 1888, 26 Mar. 1889), HHStA, no. 133(B), 135(V).

42. On Herbert Bismarck, see Holstein diary (28 June 1887), *HP*, 2:346–48; also Manfred Krodt, *Ernst Ludwig Grossherzog von Hesse und bei Rhein: Sein Leben und seine Zeit* (Darmstadt, 1978), p. 124; on Wilhelm's martial life, see RA I59/89 (Swaine to Ponsonby, 1 July 1892). For Queen Victoria on his heartlessness, see RA, Add. MS U/32/470 (31 May 1887); ibid., Add MS A15/5073 (same to the Duke of Connaught, 7 Apr. 1888). Wilhelm admitted that he was cold. See Eulenburg diary (26 July 1897), Eulenburg Papers, no. 57:423–26.

43. Wilhelm to Countess Dönhoff (13 Nov. 1878), Bülow Papers, no. 173. Wilhelm lists his friends in his *Aus Meinem Leben*, p. 164. See Karl Rügemer, *Kösener Korpslisten 1789 bis 1904* (Starmberg/Munich, n.d.), for a roll of Wilhelm's fraternity brothers.

44. Speech of 6 May 1891, in Schulthess (1891), p. 83. For the negative reaction of noncorps students in the audience, see Ludwig Raschdau, *Unter Bismarck und Caprivi: Erinnerungen eines deutschen Diplomaten aus den Jahren 1885–1894* (Berlin, 1939), p. 215. For Wilhelm II's appreciation of the fraternities, see also his *Aus Meinem Leben*, pp. 163–64, and a memo by Prince Max von Ratibor und Corvey (4 May 1901), BPHA, Rep. 53a, no. 44.

45. Philipp Zorn, "Lebenserinnerungen," pp. 123–26, Zorn Papers, no. 1.

46. Wilhelm to Countess Dönhoff (5 Nov., 4 Dec. 1878), Bülow Papers, no. 173.

47. Wilhelm to Grand Duchess Louise of Baden (3 Mar. 1879), BPHA, Rep. 53a, no. 20; Wilhelm II, *Aus Meinem Leben*, p. 167.

48. RA Z81/102 (Wilhelm to Queen Victoria, 11 Dec. 1883).

49. Georgina Müller, ed., *Life and Letters of the Right Honourable Friedrich Max Müller*, 2 vols. (New York and London, 1902), 2:62–63.

50. Theodor Lorenz, ed., *Friedrich Paulsen: An Autobiography* (New York, 1938), p. 286.

51. Kleine Erwerbungen, no. 814.

52. Andrew Dickson White, *Autobiography*, 2 vols. (New York, 1905), 2:219; Hajo Holborn, ed., *Aufzeichnungen und Erinnerungen aus dem Leben des Botschafters Joseph Maria von Radowitz*, 2 vols. (Berlin and Leipzig, 1925), 1:75; RA B52/20 (Benjamin Disraeli to Queen Victoria, 6 Aug. 1877); Alfred Ga-

thorne-Hardy, ed., *Gathorne Hardy, First Earl of Cranbrook: A Memoir with Extracts from His Diary and Correspondence*, 2 vols. (London, 1910), 2:99.

53. RA, Queen Victoria's Journal (1 Aug. 1877); Lord George Hamilton, *Parliamentary Reminiscences and Reflections, 1886–1906* (London, 1922), p. 136.

54. RA Add. A15/2925 (letter of 13 Sept. 1878). For an earlier, and more favorable, opinion by the Duke, see his letter to Wilhelm (22 Dec. 1874), BPHA, Rep. 53a, no. 72.

55. RA Z207/47 (30 Jan. 1877).

56. RA Add U/32/273, 275–76 (Queen Victoria to the Crown Princess, 4 July, 25 Sept. 1877), in which the Queen reports her daughter's feelings.

57. RA, Queen Victoria's Journal (27 Jan. 1866) for Prince Albert's fear; RA Z34/40 (5 Aug. 1880) for the Crown Princess's. For reproaches of Wilhelm's lack of interest in anything outside of Germany, see Z33/43 (27 Oct. 1879); Vicky to Countess Dönhoff (1 Jan. 1880), Bülow Papers, no. 167. Wilhelm expresses his indifference to travel in RA Add. U/34/8 (Wilhelm to his mother, 17 July 1879) and Z34/14 (25 Mar. 1880).

58. RA Z32/42 (17 Apr. 1879); also Z65/85 (27 Mar. 1879), and Crown Princess to Lady Constance Villiers (15 Apr. 1879), Hobbs/Derby-Gathorne Hardy Papers.

59. Crown Princess to Countess Dönhoff (24 Dec. 1880), Bülow Papers, no. 167; same to same (3 Aug. 1879), ibid., no. 166.

60. Gelzer diary (23 July 1878), Fuchs, 1:316. On the Crown Prince's favorable estimation of his son in 1877, see his letter to Friedrich Curtius (21 Feb. 1877) in Schuster, *Briefe Friedrich III.*, p. 253.

61. Schweinitz diary (2 Nov. 1880), Wilhelm von Schweinitz, ed., *Denkwürdigkeiten des Botschafters General v. Schweinitz*, 2 vols. (Berlin, 1927), 2:134.

62. Kürenberg, *War Alles Falsch?*, p. 51.

63. RA Z32/42 (17 Apr. 1879); also Vicky to Countess Dönhoff (2 Nov. 1878), Bülow Papers, no. 166.

64. Holstein to Herbert Bismarck (19 Nov. 1879), Bismarck Papers, no. FC2965/879; Rantzau, "Autobiographische und andere Aufzeichnungen, 1903–1909," ibid., no. FC3030/624; Bülow to Loebell (11 Jan. 1923), Loebell Papers, no. 9.

65. Rijksarchief Papers, no. 315.

66. Wilhelm to Countess Dönhoff (11 Dec. 1878), Bülow Papers, no. 173; also RA Add. U/34/4, 8 (Wilhelm to his mother, 20 May and 17 July 1879).

67. Letter of 20 Feb. 1879, Bülow Papers, no. 173.

68. Bülow, 1:263. On the development of the marriage project, see Anna Wagemann, *Prinzessin Feodora: Erinnerungen an den Augustenburger und den preussischen Hof* . . . (Berlin, 1932), p. 103; Sir Robert Morier to Baron Ernst von Stockmar (3 Mar. 1880), Morier Papers, box marked "Stockmar."

69. Wilhelm to Duke Friedrich (29 Apr. 1879), BPHA, Rep. 53a, no. 25; Wilhelm II, *Aus Meinem Leben*, pp. 224–26. See also Viktoria Luise, Grand Duchess of Brunswick-Lüneburg, *Im Glanz der Krone* (Göttingen, 1967), pp. 92–98.

70. Crown Prince to Prince Carol of Rumania (11 Apr. 1880), in Sidney Whit-

man, *Life of the Empress Frederick*, 2 vols. (Leipzig, 1901), 2:215; Wilhelm to Prince Christian of Schleswig-Holstein (28 Apr. 1879), BPHA, Rep. 53, no. 120.

71. For positive evaluations of Dona by the Crown Princess, see RA Z34/4, 13 (18 Jan., 21 Mar. 1880). For her enthusiasm for the marriage, see RA I53/15 (Lady Emily Russell, wife of the British ambassador in Berlin, to Queen Victoria, 27 Dec. 1880); RA Add. MS U/32/632–33 (Queen Victoria to Crown Princess, 19 Mar. 1890), and ibid., Z48/5 (22 Mar. 1890); Wilhelm to Prince Christian of Schleswig-Holstein (28 Apr. 1879), BPHA, Rep. 53, no. 120. On her low estimation of Dona's intellect, see Richard Kühn, ed., *Kaiserin Augusta. Bekenntnisse an eine Freundin: Aufzeichnungen aus ihrer Freundschaft mit Jenny von Gustedt* (Dresden, 1935), pp. 285, 288.

72. For opposition among the Hohenzollerns and court society, see Prince Chlodwig zu Hohenlohe-Schillingsfürst diary (2 June 1880), Hohenlohe Papers, no. C.C.X.8; Waldersee, 1:202–3; RA Z34/9, ll, 13, 14 (13, 21 Feb., 21, 25 Mar. 1880); Lady Emily Russell to Queen Victoria (27 Dec. 1880), George E. Buckle, ed., *The Letters of Queen Victoria*, 2d ser., 3 vols. (New York, 1926–28), 3:168–69; Holborn, *Aufzeichnungen Radowitz*, 2:121–22.

73. Countess Therese zu Eulenburg to Caecile von Below (19 Mar. 1880), BPHA, Rep. 53a, no. 23. Another notation of Wilhelm's immaturity at the time of his marriage is in Waldersee diary (31 Mar. 1880), Waldersee, 1:202–3.

74. See especially Wilhelm I's letters to Duke Friedrich (29 Apr. and 22 May 1879), BPHA, Rep. 53a, no. 25; also RA Add. U/34/4, 6 (Wilhelm to his mother, 20, 27 May 1879). On Augusta's opinion, Kühn, *Kaiserin Augusta*, p. 285.

75. Wilhelm I to Grand Duchess Alexandrine of Mecklenburg-Schwerin (12 Aug. 1881), in Johannes Schultze, ed., *Kaiser Wilhelms I. Briefe an seine Schwester Alexandrine und deren Sohn Grossherzog Ferdinand Franz II.* (Berlin, 1927), p. 176.

76. Wilhelm I to Bismarck (11 Aug. 1879) and Bismarck to the Crown Prince (18 Aug. 1879), Bismarck Papers, no. FC2962/957–59, 967–68; Bismarck to Wilhelm I (18 Aug. 1879), ibid., no. FC2985/1215–21; memo by Bismarck to Wilhelm I (n.d. but ca. 13 July 1879), ibid., no. FC2986/228–30.

77. Kühn, *Kaiserin Augusta*, p. 285; Schultze, *Wilhelms I. Briefe*, p. 162.

78. Kühn, *Kaiserin Augusta*, pp. 285, 288; Wilhelm to Prince Christian of Schleswig-Holstein (28 Apr. 1879), BPHA, Rep. 53, no. 120.

79. RA Add. U/34/4 (Wilhelm to his mother, 20 May 1879). There is interesting correspondence in the Royal Archives (RA Z65/157, 160, 167, 169) on the unsuccessful attempts by both the Crown Prince and Princess to enlist Queen Victoria's aid in persuading Wilhelm I and the Empress Augusta to favor the marriage. The Queen refused, undoubtedly because, for reasons that are not clear, she was opposed to the match. See RA Vic. Add. U143, film 4 (Queen Victoria to Grand Duke Ludwig of Hesse, 11 Feb. 1880); also note 82 below.

80. Letter of 24 May 1880, Sir Frederick Ponsonby, ed., *Letters of the Empress Frederick*, (London, 1928), p. 180.

81. See the testimony of her kinsman, Prince Hohenlohe, in his diary (2 June 1880), Hohenlohe Papers, no. C.C.X.8.

82. At the same time that Wilhelm courted Dona he had become very attached

to his first cousin, Princess Elizabeth (Ella) of Hesse, who was five years his junior. Late in life, Wilhelm II claimed that he had wanted to marry Ella but that his parents had prevented the match. See Wilhelm II to his grandson, Prince Wilhelm of Prussia (30 Mar. 1931), BPHA, Rep. 53, no. 32. A first cousin was of the opinion that Ella "refused" Wilhelm. See Princess Alice, Countess of Athlone, *For My Grandchildren: Some Reminiscences* (London, 1966), p. 18. For his mother's opposition to Wilhelm's interest in Ella, see her letter to Princess Helene of Schleswig-Holstein (8 June 1878), in BPHA, Rep. 53a, no. 25. Hinzpeter noted his pupil's attraction to Ella in a letter to Countess Görtz (24 June 1879), Schlitz von Görtz Papers, no. 352. Queen Victoria later expressed her regret that Wilhelm had not chosen Ella rather than Dona. RA Add. MS U/32/463 (14 Feb. 1887).

83. Wilhelm to Prince Christian of Schleswig-Holstein (7 Aug. 1879 and 28 Apr. 1879), BPHA, Rep. 53, nos. 123, 120.

84. Dona to Caroline Mathilda (12 Mar. 1881), Glücksburg Papers, no. 2.

85. Margaret, Countess of Jersey, *Fifty-One Years of Victorian Life* (London, 1922), p. 104, reporting Wilhelm's opposition in 1887 to the Primrose League, the popular organization of Britain's Conservative Party, because he believed it gave too much prominence to women.

86. The possibility of this factor is discussed in a letter of 27 Feb. 1880 of Franz von Roggenbach, an intimate of the Empress Augusta, to General Albrecht von Stosch, in Heyderhoff, *Im Ring der Gegner Bismarcks*, p. 205. It is also hinted at in Holstein's diary (27 Sept. 1884), Holstein Papers, no. 3860/195944.

87. Wagemann, *Prinzessin Feodora*, p. 147. See Bülow, 1:261–62, for Dona's dislike of foreigners.

88. Kühn, *Kaiserin Augusta*, pp. 285–87.

89. Dona to Caroline Mathilda (21 Aug. 1881 and 20 Mar. 1882), Glücksburg Papers, nos. 2, 3.

90. Letter of 9 Feb. 1881, BPHA, Rep. 53a, no. 20.

91. Victoria, Princess of Prussia, *My Memories* (London, 1929), pp. 47–48.

92. Baron Robert Lucius von Ballhausen, *Bismarck-Erinnerungen* (Stuttgart and Berlin, 1920), p. 203. Cf. Holborn, *Aufzeichnungen Radowitz*, 2:170, who found the military trappings on this occasion a "fresh and healthy symbol." See also Mrs. David Lee to Mrs. Elizabeth Hoppin (12 Mar. 1881), Waldersee-Lee Papers, no. 2, and Countess Mathilde von Keller, *Vierzig Jahre im Dienst der Kaiserin: Ein Kulturbild aus den Jahren 1881–1921* (Leipzig, 1935), pp. 21–28.

93. Dona to Caroline Mathilda (10 Mar. 1881), Glücksburg Papers, no. 2.

CHAPTER 3

1. On Liebenau's difficult personality, see Kleine Erwerbungen, no. 814; Waldersee, 2:2, 22–23; Bülow, 1:75; Prince Heinrich von Schönburg-Waldenburg, *Erinnerungen aus Kaiserlicher Zeit* (Leipzig, 1929), p. 59; *HP*, 3:347; Anna Wagemann, *Prinzessin Feodora: Erinnerungen an den Augustenburger und den preussischen Hof . . .* (Berlin, 1932), p. 59. He died insane in 1900. For Wilhelm

II on Liebenau's manner, Waldersee, 2:80. For Dona and Liebenau, Széchenyi to Kálnoky (5 Apr. 1890), HHStA, no. 138(B); Dona to Caroline Mathilda (30 Mar., 31 Dec. 1881, 21 June 1886), Glücksburg Papers, nos. 2, 7.

2. On Adolf's relations with Herbert Bismarck, see Adolf to Bernhard von Bülow (10 Nov. 1881, 31 May 1884), Bülow Papers, no. 13; Bülow, 1:181–82.

3. Eulenburg's undated notes, Eulenburg Papers, no. 49:641.

4. Dona to Caroline Mathilda (18 June 1885), Glücksburg Papers, no. 6; notes by Eulenburg (3 Dec. 1895), Bülow Papers, no. 75.

5. Kleine Erwerbungen, no. 708/1, p. 54.

6. On the "aunts," see the following: Countess Mathilde von Keller, *Vierzig Jahre im Dienst der Kaiserin: Ein Kulturbild aus den Jahren 1881–1921* (Leipzig, 1935), pp. 17–18, 38–39; Victoria, Princess of Prussia, *My Memories* (London, 1929), pp. 51–53; Count Robert Zedlitz-Trützschler, *Zwölf Jahre am Deutschen Kaiserhof: Aufzeichnungen* (Berlin, 1924), pp. 211, 242–43; Bülow, 1:246–48, 303; Lelia von Meister, *Gathered Yesterdays* (London, 1963), p. 94; Karl-Heinz Janssen, ed., *Die Graue Exzellenz. Zwischen Staatsräson und Vasallentreue: Aus den Papieren des kaiserlichen Gesandten Karl Georg von Treutler* (Frankfurt, 1971), p. 107; Princess Alice, Countess of Athlone, *For My Grandchildren: Some Reminiscences* (London, 1966), p. 93; Anne Topham, *Chronicles of the Prussian Court* (London, 1926), pp. 60–61; Countess Fanny von Wilamowitz-Moellendorff, *Erinnerungen und Begegnungen* (Berlin, 1936), pp. 98–99; Eugen von Jagemann, *Fünfundsiebzig Jahre des Erlebens und Erfahrens (1849–1924)* (Heidelberg, 1925), p. 180; Viktoria Luise, Grand Duchess of Brunswick-Lüneburg, *Ein Leben als Tochter des Kaisers* (Göttingen, 1965), p. 23; Friedrich Schmidt-Ott, *Erlebtes und Erstrebtes, 1860–1950* (Wiesbaden, 1952), pp. 96–97; undated notes by Eulenburg, Eulenburg Papers, no. 1:57; no. 81, pt. 1:273–74; Eulenburg to his wife (4 July 1898), ibid., no. 53:102; Wagemann, *Prinzessin Feodora*, pp. 59–60. There is a good photograph of the retinue in Thomas Krummacher, *Kaiserin Auguste Viktoria* (Bielefeld and Leipzig, n.d.[1913]), p. 37.

7. The letters are in BPHA, Rep. 53a, no. 21. The quote is from a letter of 7 Feb. 1882.

8. Janssen, *Die Graue Exzellenz*, p. 46; Holstein diary (23 Sept. 1884, 1 Sept. 1885), Holstein Papers, no. 3860/H195944, no. 3861/H196091–92. Three descriptions from the 1880s of the marital relations of the royal couple are in Wagemann, *Prinzessin Feodora*, p. 37; Count Paul Vasili [pseud.], *La Société de Berlin* (Paris, 1884), pp. 36–37, and Johannes Kessler, *Ich Schwöre Mir Ewige Jugend* (Munich, 1935), pp. 119–28, 138.

9. Dona to Caroline Mathilda (12 Mar. 1881), Glücksburg Papers, no. 2. On Wilhelm's attentiveness, see same to same (30 Mar., 26 May 1881), ibid.

10. Keller, *Vierzig Jahre*, p. 29.

11. Eulenburg Papers, no. 81, pt. 1:286–87.

12. RA Z66/53 (29 Jan. 1887); Dona to Caroline Mathilda (6 Jan., 2 Feb. 1887), Glücksburg Papers, no. 8.

13. RA Z45/28 (19 July 1889). The influence of Hinzpeter, clearly a misogynist, was probably important. See Hinzpeter to Dona (23, 27 Feb. 1882), BPHA, Rep. 53a, no. 21. On Wilhelm's desire to have women excluded from his company, see Eulenburg Papers, no. 80:15, n. 1; Eulenburg to Holstein (1 Aug.

1890), ibid., no. 12:517–21, which differs on this point from the version in *HP*, 3:353; Eulenburg's notes (28 Oct. 1892), Eulenburg Papers, no. 2:695–96.

A number of prominent historians of Wilhelmine Germany have recently argued that Wilhelm II, though probably not an overt, practising homosexual, had "homoerotic" tendencies that he successfully suppressed. These arguments are based on the Kaiser's preference for good-looking men and on the fact that his closest friend, Philipp Eulenburg, and a number of other men whom he knew well and liked greatly were homosexuals. See John C. G. Röhl, "The Emperor's New Clothes: A Character Sketch of Kaiser Wilhelm II"; Thomas A. Kohut, "Kaiser Wilhelm and His Parents: An Inquiry into the Psychological Roots of German Policy towards England before the First World War"; Isabel V. Hull, "Kaiser Wilhelm II and the 'Liebenburg Circle' "; and Nicolaus Sombart, "The Kaiser in his Epoch: Some Reflexions on Wilhelmine Society, Sexuality and Culture"; all in Röhl and Sombart, eds., *Kaiser Wilhelm II, New Interpretations: The Corfu Papers* (Cambridge, 1982), pp. 47–48, 79, 204–5, 308; Röhl, 1:47; Hull, *The Entourage of Kaiser Wilhelm II, 1888–1918* (Cambridge, 1982), pp. 20–21, 64. The arguments advanced are suggestive but unpersuasive, perhaps inevitably so because of a lack of evidence. Wilhelm certainly liked to be with men—he danced with them at regimental dinners—but there were nonsexual reasons for his tastes. As Röhl and others point out, Wilhelm and his homosexual friends had artistic, spiritualistic, and sporting interests in common, and not a few were, like the Kaiser, burdened with tiresome or difficult wives. Wilhelm's selection of handsome soldiers to grace his retinue was due, as Eulenburg himself admitted, not to homosexual urges but to his anxiety to maintain an impressive court. Eulenburg Papers, no. 75, pt. 1b:228. On Wilhelm's participation in regimental dances, apparently a usual feature of such occasions, see Széchenyi to Kálnoky (14 Dec. 1889), HHStA, no. 38(V).

14. Charles Hardinge, First Baron Hardinge of Penshurst, *Old Diplomacy* (London, 1947), p. 128; Wilhelm II's notes (3 Nov. 1923), Rijksarchief Papers, no. 646.

15. Zedlitz-Trützschler, *Zwölf Jahre*, pp. 44–45, 67–68, 94–96, 211; Ludwig Raschdau, *Unter Bismarck und Caprivi: Erinnerungen eines deutschen Diplomaten aus den Jahren 1885–1894* (Berlin, 1939), pp. 303–4; Eulenburg diary (Nov. 1888), Eulenburg Papers, no. 81, pt. 1:273–74; Janssen, *Die Graue Exzellenz*, p. 107.

16. For Eulenburg's critical estimation of Dona's ability to beguile her husband, see Bülow, 1:617. On Dona as a young married woman, see ibid., 262–63; Louise, Princess of Coburg, *Throne die ich Stürzen Sah* (Zurich, 1927), pp. 185–88; Victor Mallet, ed., *Life with Queen Victoria: Marie Mallet's Letters from Court, 1887–1901* (Boston, 1968), p. 52; Fritz Max Cahèn, *Der Weg nach Versailles: Erinnerungen, 1912–1919* (Boppard, 1963), p. 123; Marie von Bunsen, *Zeitgenossen die ich Erlebte, 1900–1930* (Leipzig, 1932), pp. 192–97; Queen Marie of Rumania, *The Story of My Life*, 2 vols. (London, 1934), 1:220–22, 227–28; Princess Louise of Tuscany, *My Own Story* (New York, 1911), p. 140; Friedrich Curtius, ed., *Ernst Curtius: Ein Lebensbild in Briefen*, 2 vols. (Berlin, 1913), 2:184.

17. Dona to Caroline Mathilda (3 Nov. 1886), Glücksburg Papers, no. 7; also same to same (20 July, 11 Aug., 4 Nov. 1881), ibid., no. 2; (1 June 1883), ibid., no. 4.

18. There are rumors of peccadillos in Waldersee, 1:273; Vasili, *Société de Berlin*, pp. 14–16, and in Herbert Bismarck to Rantzau (19 Nov. 1882), Bismarck Papers, no. FC3014/1065. In his memoirs, Bismarck claimed that Wilhelm lacked the "strong sexual development" of his great-great-grandfather, King Friedrich Wilhelm II, a notorious philanderer. On this passage the Kaiser made the unrevealing marginal comment "that again!" (*auch das noch!*); BPHA Rep. 53a, no. 42/1, p. 125. For Wilhelm's lack of charm as a ladies' man, see Princess Marie Radziwill, *Lettres de la Princesse Radziwill au Général de Robilant, 1889–1914: Une grand dame d'avant guerre*, 4 vols. (Bologna, 1933–34), 1:4; Louise of Coburg, *Throne*, p. 181; Sigmund Münz, *King Edward VII at Marienbad: Political and Social Life at the Bohemian Spas* (London, 1934), p. 233; Marie of Rumania, *Story of My Life*, 2:169, 229. Some women did find the Kaiser attractive. See Princess Marie zu Erbach-Schönberg, *Erklungenes und Verklungenes* (Darmstadst, 1923), p. 99; Lady Walburga Paget, *In My Tower* (New York, n.d.), p. 410; Enfanta Eulalia of Spain, *Memoirs of H.R.H. The Enfanta Eulalia* (London, 1936), p. 73; Princess Ludwig Ferdinand of Bavaria, *Through Four Revolutions, 1862–1933* (London, 1933), pp. 224–25; Lillie de Hegermann-Lindencrone, *The Sunny Side of Diplomatic Life* (London and New York, 1914), p. 313; Wagemann, *Prinzessin Feodora*, pp. 38, 52–53.

19. John C. G. Röhl, *Kaiser, Hof und Staat: Wilhelm II. und die deutsche Politik* (Munich, 1987), pp. 25–27; Röhl, "Emperor's New Clothes," pp. 43–46. In 1883 Wilhelm had secretly to borrow a large sum from the Habsburg Crown Prince Rudolf, which was probably needed to settle some amorous difficulty, since Wilhelm's ordinary expenses seem to have been quite adequately covered by his appanage. See Rudolf to Crown Princess Stephanie (29 Apr. 1883), in her *I Was to Be Empress* (London, 1937), p. 143. For Rudolf's service in putting Wilhelm in touch with a Viennese procuress, see Brigitte Hamann, *Rudolf: Kronprinz und Rebell* (Vienna, 1978), p. 336. For a later affair in Austria in 1887 that resulted in a paternity claim settled in cash by the German ambassador in Vienna, see ibid., pp. 400–402. There was, however, some doubt among contemporaries that Wilhelm indulged in mistresses. See Waldersee, 1:273–74; Bülow, 4:660–61; Princess Daisy of Pless, *What I Left Unsaid* (New York, 1936), p. 5; Janssen, *Die Graue Exzellenz*, pp. 119–20. Wilhelm II disapproved of other rulers who formed liaisons. See *HP*, 2:242; Ludwig Raschdau, *In Weimar als Preussischer Gesandter: Ein Buch der Erinnerungen an deutsche Fürstenhöfe, 1894–1897* (Berlin, 1939), p. 62; Leopold von Schlözer, *Aus der Jugendzeit* (Dresden, 1938), p. 231.

20. Her sensationalist memoir, *Meine Beziehungen zu S.M. Kaiser Wilhelm II.* (Zurich, 1900), should be used with great caution. Two of Wilhelm's letters to the countess (15, 30 Jan. 1885), are in BPHA, Rep. 53a, no. 71. There were other letters, but apparently these were destroyed by Wilhelm at some time after 1896.

21. Janssen, *Die Graue Exzellenz*, p. 46.

22. Baroness Hildegard von Spitzemberg diary (6 Mar. 1891), in Rudolf

Vierhaus, ed., *Das Tagebuch der Baronin Spitzemberg geb. Freiin v. Varnbüler: Aufzeichnungen aus der Hofgesellschaft des Hohenzollernreiches* (Göttingen, 1960), p. 289.

23. Senden notes, Senden Papers, no. 11.

24. Eulenburg Papers, no. 81, pt. 1:165. Count Maximilian von Berchem, a prominent official in the Foreign Office who was acquainted with Wilhelm, argued that he threw himself into military life faute de mieux. The Prussian countryside was sad and offered few pleasures, the nobility poor, and their intellectual life similarly impoverished. Soldiering was a Hohenzollern tradition, but in fact there was in Prussia nothing else for Wilhelm to do. Herbette to Goblet (30 July 1888), *DDF*, 7:201.

25. Wilhelm II, *Aus Meinem Leben, 1859–1888* (Berlin and Leipzig, 1927), p. 191.

26. RA Z66/24 (Swaine to Ponsonby, 24 Jan. 1884).

27. Széchenyi to Kálnoky (28 Jan. 1888), HHStA, no. 133(B); Baron Hugo von Freytag-Loringhoven, *Menschen und Dinge wie ich sie in Meinem Leben Sah* (Berlin, 1923), p. 169. On Wilhelm's identification with a clique of traditionalist guards officers and generals, see Sir Vincent Corbett, *Reminiscences: Autobiographical and Diplomatic . . .* (London, n.d.), pp. 62–64, and Eduard von Wertheimer, "Ein Kaiser- und Königlicher Militärattaché über das politische Leben in Berlin, 1880–1895," *Preussische Jahrbücher* 201 (1925): 278.

28. Johannes Haller, ed., *Aus dem Leben des Fürsten Philipp zu Eulenburg-Hertefeld* (Berlin, 1924), p. 245, which is an expansion of Eulenburg Papers, no. 76, sec. 5:122. See also ibid., no. 80:16

29. See the Emperor Franz Josef's negative impression as recorded in Holstein's diary (3 Sept. 1885), *HP*, 2:242.

30. Loë to Bülow (16 June 1883), and an undated letter (placed among those from 1882), Bülow Papers, no. 100.

31. Herbert Bismarck to Bülow (12 Apr. 1883), ibid., no. 65, omitted by Bussmann, p. 170.

32. Herbert Bismarck's "Tagebuch" (1884), Bismarck Papers, no. FC3018/163–67, recapitulated with some changes in his "Notizen, Herbst 91," ibid., 237–40. Bülow's successor, Karl von Pfuel, had no influence whatsoever.

33. Malet to Queen Victoria (17 Oct. 1885), Malet Papers, FO 343/4.

34. Holstein diary (11 July 1885), *HP*, 2:219; also diary (28 June 1887), ibid., 346–47.

35. Hardinge, *Old Diplomacy*, p. 27. This is confirmed by another contemporary, Adolf von Wilke, in his *Alt-Berliner Erinnerungen* (Berlin, 1930), p. 98; see also Wertheimer, "Militärattaché," p. 278.

36. Eulenburg Papers, no. 81, pt. 1:130–31.

37. Bosse Papers, no. 16:56.

38. Eulenburg Papers, no. 81, pt. 1:166. On their relationship, see Dona to Caroline Mathilda (2 Aug. 1881), Glücksburg Papers, no. 2; Herman von Petersdorff, *Kleist-Retzow: Eine Lebensbild* (Stuttgart and Berlin, 1907), p. 479; Abraham Yarmolinsky, ed. and trans., *The Memoirs of Count Witte* (Garden City and Toronto, 1921), p. 401; Johannes Haller, ed., *Aus 50 Jahren: Erinnerungen, Tagebücher und Briefe aus dem Nachlass des Fürsten Philipp zu Eulenburg-*

Hertefeld (Berlin, 1923), pp. 187–88; Corbett, *Reminiscences*, p. 83; Karl von Normann to Gustav Freytag (1 Jan. 1886), in Paul Wentzcke, ed., *Im Neuen Reich, 1871–1890: Politische Briefe aus dem Nachlass liberaler Parteiführer*, 2 vols. (1926; rpt. Osnabrück, 1967), 2:445; RA Z66/6 (Lady Ampthill, wife of the British envoy in Berlin, to Queen Victoria, 12 May 1883).

39. Waldersee diary (17 Nov. 1885, 12 Feb. 1886), Waldersee, 1:267, 274.

40. Wilhelm v. Schweinitz, ed., *Denkwürdigkeiten des Botschafters General v. Schweinitz*, 2 vols. (Berlin, 1927), 2:134.

41. Baron Robert Lucius von Ballhausen diary (30 May 1882), in Ballhausen, *Bismarck-Erinnerungen* (Stuttgart and Berlin, 1920), p. 230.

42. On Mossner and Chelius, see Count Bogdan von Hutten-Czapski, *Sechzig Jahre Politik und Gesellschaft*, 2 vols. (Berlin, 1936), 1:107–10; Schönburg-Waldenburg, *Erinnerungen*, p. 100.

43. Eulenburg Papers, no. 81, pt. 1:286; Schönburg-Waldenburg, *Erinnerungen*, p. 59; Wertheimer, "Militärattaché," p. 278; Gen. Paul von Lettow-Vorbeck, *Mein Leben* (Biberach an der Riss, 1957), pp. 38.

44. Wilke, *Alt-Berlin Erinnerungen*, p. 64; Gen. Baron Paul von Schoenaich, *Mein Damaskus: Erlebnisse und Bekenntnisse* (Berlin, 1926), p. 80; Arthur Ponsonby, ed., *Henry Ponsonby, Queen Victoria's Secretary: His Life from his Letters* (New York, 1943), p. 290; Prince Albert zu Schleswig-Holstein-Sonderburg-Glücksburg, "Einiges aus Meinem Leben," 1:27, Glücksburg Papers.

45. Müller diary (1 Jan. 1906), Müller Papers, no. 3. There is a copy of Wilhelm's formal address to his grandson in RA I51/50. On Wilhelm's punctiliousness, see Janssen, *Die Graue Exzellenz*, pp. 45–50; Radziwill, *Lettres*, 1:4; Count Otto zu Stolberg Wernigerode, *Die Unentschiedene Generation: Deutschlands konservative Führungsschichten am Abend des ersten Weltkrieges* (Munich, 1968), pp. 56–57; *HP*, 2:346–48; Marie of Rumania, *Story of My Life*, 1:284–85.

46. Swaine memo (20 Nov. 1887), Salisbury Papers, no. 61.

47. Holstein diary (28 Sept. 1887), *HP*, 2:349; for a similar description by another officer, see Eberhard Kessel, ed., *Alfred Grafen von Schlieffen: Briefe* (Göttingen, 1958), p. 275.

48. Joachim von Winterfeldt-Menkin, *Jahreszeiten des Lebens: Das Buch meiner Erinnerungen* (Berlin, 1942), p. 114. On Winterfeldt's speaking openly to Wilhelm, see Janssen, *Die Graue Exzellenz*, p. 47. He once described Wilhelm as a "false and cowardly" *(falsch und feige)* Coburger. See Bülow diary (25 Mar. 1892), Bülow Papers, no. 150. On Wilhelm's susceptibility to flattery, see Count Hugo Lerchenfeld-Koefering, *Erinnerungen und Denkwürdigkeiten* (Berlin, 1935), pp. 344–45; Waldersee, 1:152. An especially notorious toady was General von Versen, for whose relationship with the Kaiser see Baron Hermann von Eckardstein, *Persönliche Erinnerugen an König Eduard aus der Einkreisungszeit* (Dresden, 1927), pp. 63–69; Winterfeldt-Menkin, *Jahreszeiten*, p. 114; Janssen, *Die Graue Exzellenz*, pp. 41, 47–48, 123.

49. Lamar Cecil, "Jew and Junker in Imperial Berlin," Leo Baeck Institute, *Year Book* 20 (1975): 51. On his association with the Union, see Waldersee, 1:294–95; Wilhelm II, *Aus Meinem Leben*, pp. 211–12, 367–68.

50. On Wilhelm I, Sir Frederick Ponsonby, ed., *Letters of the Empress Freder-*

ick (New York, 1928), p. 383; for the Crown Prince's dislike of Waldersee, see Hans Mohs, ed., *General-Feldmarschall Alfred Graf von Waldersee in seinem Militärischen Wirken*, 2 vols. (Berlin, 1929), 1:8–9; Waldersee, 1:325; on both men RA Z45/28 (19 July 1889). For the Crown Princess's hostility, see Hohenlohe, 2:440; RA Z45/28 (19 July 1889); Ponsonby, *Letters of the Empress Frederick*, p. 365.

51. On Countess Waldersee, see her stupefying *Von Klarheit zu Klarheit: Gräfin Marie Esther von Waldersee* (Stuttgart, 1915); Count Axel von Schwering [pseud.], *The Berlin Court under William II* (London, 1915), pp. 184–96, and the wan book by J. Alton Smith, *A View of the Spree* (New York, 1962). The Countess's papers (Waldersee-Lee Papers) contain little of interest. On Dona and the countess, see *DDF*, 7:556 (Waddington to Spuller, 19 Nov. 1889); Kleine Erwerbungen, no. 104.

52. For Herbert's reservations about Wilhelm's personality, see his letter to Rantzau (16 Dec. 1887), Bussmann, p. 492; Holstein diary (28 June 1887), *HP*, 2:346–48. On Herbert, see the useful introduction in Bussmann, pp. 8–67. Louis L. Snyder, *Diplomacy in Iron: The Life of Herbert von Bismarck* (Malabar, Fla., 1983), adds nothing.

53. On Herbert's influence, see Waldersee diary (14 Mar. 1886), 1:281; Holstein diary (18 June 1885), *HP*, 2:207; for his approval of Wilhelm's diplomatic ideas, see his letter to Rantzau (1 Sept. 1885), Bismarck Papers, no. FC3014/805, which contains a passage omitted by Bussmann on pp. 301–2; also Rantzau to Herbert (16 Oct. 1885), ibid., no. FC3028.

54. Eulenburg's correspondence has been expertly edited by John C. G. Röhl, *Philipp Eulenburgs Politische Korrespondenz*, 3 vols. (Boppard, 1976–83), which contains an illuminating biographical essay (1:9–73). See also Hull, "Kaiser Wilhelm II," 193–220, as well as her useful *Entourage of Kaiser Wilhelm II*, esp. pp. 45–76. The old study by Reinhold Muschler, *Philipp zu Eulenburg: Sein Leben und seine Zeit* (Leipzig, 1930), still retains some value, while the recent treatment by Ekkehard-Teja P. W. Wilke, *Political Decadence in Imperial Germany: Personnel-Political Aspects of the German Government Crisis, 1894–97* (Urbana, 1976), is of only marginal interest, although Eulenburg figures heavily in its narrative. Hans Wilhelm Burmeister, *Prince Philipp Eulenburg-Hertefeld (1847–1921): His Influence on Kaiser Wilhelm II and his Role in the German Government, 1888–1902* (Wiesbaden, 1981) should be avoided. There is a vapid discussion of Wilhelm's friendship with Eulenburg in Judith Hughes, *Emotion and High Politics: Personal Relations at the Summit in Late Nineteenth Century Britain and Germany* (Berkeley, 1983), pp. 136–44.

55. Eulenburg Papers, no. 81, pt. 1:130–31. Röhl, 1:155, n. 4, dates their first meeting as on or about 1 Oct. 1885, but this seems to have been a second encounter, for the Grand Duke of Saxe-Coburg, present in 1883, is not recorded among those in Munich in 1885.

56. Eulenburg to Herbert Bismarck (11 May 1886), Röhl, 1:163; Wilhelm to Eulenburg (11 June 1886), ibid., 170; Muschler, *Eulenburg*, p. 152; Wilhelm II, *Aus Meinem Leben*, pp. 227–28.

57. Letter of 11 Aug. 1886 in Eulenburg Papers, no. 1:48, partially printed in Haller, *Aus dem Leben Eulenburg*, pp. 20–21.

58. Dona to Caroline Mathilda (23 June, 31 July 1886), Glücksburg Papers, no. 7. For Wilhelm's attachment to his new friend, see his letter to Eulenburg (11 Aug. 1886), Röhl, 1:191–92.

59. On parliament in 1883, see John C. G. Röhl, "Emperor's New Clothes," 33; on Wilhelm's susceptibility in 1886 to the notion of a coup d'état, see Schweinitz, *Denkwürdigkeiten*, 2:317–18.

60. General Walther von Loë to Bülow (n.d. but ca. 1882), Bülow Papers, no. 100.

61. Letter to Holstein (17 July 1885), *HP*, 3:148; also Bülow, 1:182.

62. Holstein diary (22 Aug. 1885), *HP*, 2:233; also Rantzau, "Autobiographische und Andere Aufzeichnungen, 1903–1909," Bismarck Papers, no. FC3030/624. Hinzpeter, who disliked the Crown Prince's liberalism, may also have influenced Wilhelm against his father. See Waldersee, 1:312.

63. Corbett, *Reminiscences*, pp. 62–64; Schweinitz, *Denkwürdigkeiten*, 2:343–44; *HP*, 2:46–47.

64. Gen. Leopold V. Swaine, *Camp and Chancery in a Soldier's Life* (London, 1926), pp. 150–51.

65. There is speculation on this point in the Hepke diary (4 Oct. 1875), Kleine Erwerbungen, no. 319/2.

66. Gelzer diary (23 July 1878), Fuchs, 1:316; Herbert to Otto Bismarck (8 Oct. 1886), Bussmann, p. 391.

67. Holstein diary (16 Jan. 1883, 6 Jan. 1884), *HP*, 2:29–30, 46–47.

68. Holstein diary (6 Jan. 1884), ibid., 46. Fifty years later, Wilhelm II denied that his father had criticized him; BPHA, Rep. 192, no. 20. For the Crown Prince's hostile treatment of his son, see *HP*, 2:165; Waldersee, 1:243, 250. Georg Hinzpeter, *Kaiser Wilhelm II.: Eine Skizze nach der Natur gezeichnet* (Bielefeld, 1888), p. 13, notes that Wilhelm felt acutely the fact that he had been too young to participate in the wars of unification in which his father had played such a great role.

69. Eulenburg Papers, no. 81, pt. 1:166.

70. Undated remark in ibid., 301. A somewhat similar observation is in Frederic B. M. Hollyday, *Bismarck's Rival: A Political Biography of General and Admiral Albrecht von Stosch* (Durham, N.C., 1960), p. 235. On Wilhelm's finances, see Herbert to Otto Bismarck (4 Oct. 1886), Bismarck Papers, no. FC3004/1066–67.

71. Serge Sazonov, *Fateful Years, 1909–1916: The Reminiscenses of Serge Sazonov* (New York, 1928), p. 44. On his fear of predeceasing Wilhelm I, see RA Z39/23 (17 May 1887).

72. Waldersee, 1:311; Mohs, *Waldersee*, 1:8–9; Eberhard Kessel, "Die Tätigkeit des Grafen Waldersee als General-Quartiermeister und Chef des General Stabes der Armee," *Welt als Geschichte* 14, no. 2 (1954): 209–11. On the plot, see Herbert to Otto Bismarck (4 Oct. 1886), Bussmann, p. 388.

73. Robert Dohme, "Erinnerungen an Kaiser Friedrich," *Deutsche Revue* 47, nos. 1–3 (1922): no. 1: 8 and no. 2: 120–23; Fuchs, 1:54–55, 64, 136, 142, 2:164, 207; Gustav Freytag, *Briefe an Seine Gattin* (Berlin, n.d.), pp. 125–26; Schweinitz, *Denkwürdigkeiten*, 2:134.

74. On medieval pomp, see Julius Heyderhoff, ed., *Im Ring der Gegner Bis-*

marcks: Denkschriften und politischer Briefwechsel Franz v. Roggenbachs mit Kaiserin Augusta und Albrecht v. Stosch, 1865–1896 (Leipzig, 1943), pp. 229–30. On abdication, see Schweinitz, *Denkwürdigkeiten,* 2:343–44; Fuchs, 2:207, 347; Hans Herzfeld, ed., *Johannes von Miquel: Sein Anteil am Ausbau des deutschen Reiches bis zur Jahrhundertwende,* 2 vols. (Detmold, 1938), 1:461; Gustav Freytag, *Der Kronprinz und die Deutsche Kaiserkrone: Erinnerungs-blätter* (Leipzig, 1889), p. 72.

75. The "mollusk" remark is in Roggenbach to Stosch (27 May 1886), in Heyderhoff, *Im Ring der Gegner Bismarcks,* p. 242; the concluding quotation is in Hollyday, *Bismarck's Rival,* p. 237; see also Hollyday, p. 235, and Heyderhoff, pp. 224–25; Hans F. Helmolt, ed., *Gustav Freytags Briefe an Albrecht von Stosch* (Stuttgart and Berlin, 1913), pp. 145, 176; Freytag, *Kronprinz,* pp. 72–73.

76. Dohme, "Erinnerungen," no. 2: 123.

77. See Karl Samwer, *Zur Erinnerungen an Franz von Roggenbach* (Wiesbaden, 1909), p. 179.

78. Dohme, "Erinnerungen," no. 1: 9; Rowland Prothero, Baron Ernle, "The Empress Frederick," *The Nineteenth Century and After* 106 (Sept. 1929): 402. For Wilhelm's charges of improper behavior in this respect by the Crown Princess, see his letter to Herbert Bismarck (18 Aug. 1886), Bussmann, p. 371, and Herbert's letter to his brother Wilhelm (25 Aug. 1884), Bismarck Papers, no. FC3011. The charge made by Andrew Sinclair in his *The Other Victoria: The Princess Royal and the Great Game of Europe* (London, 1981), that Vicky was an English spy in the heart of imperial Germany cannot at all be sustained.

79. Dohme, "Erinnerungen," no. 1: 8; Gelzer diary (17 June 1883, 21 June 1885), Fuchs, 2:207–8, 347; Arthur Ponsonby, *Henry Ponsonby, Queen Victoria's Private Secretary: His Life from His Letters* (New York, 1943), p. 290.

80. On avoidance of the Crown Prince, Schweinitz diary (Apr. 15, 1887), Schweinitz, *Denkwürdigkeiten,* 2:343–44; on his rudeness, Holstein diary (3 Mar. 1885), *HP,* 2:170–71.

81. Hinzpeter to Count Görtz (18 Jan. 1879), Schlitz von Görtz Papers, no. 217.

82. Undated, unaddressed letter by Crown Prince Rudolf in Hamann, *Rudolf,* p. 336.

83. Wilhelm's complaints are in Herbert to Otto Bismarck (8 Oct. 1886), Bussmann, pp. 391–92; same to Rantzau (10 Dec. 1887), Bismarck Papers, no. FC3014/937–38. See *HP* 2:40, 165, for Holstein's similar observations. See also Wilhelm's remarks made late in life on this subject in Sigurd von Ilsemann, *Der Kaiser in Holland: Aufzeichnungen,* 2 vols. (Munich, 1967–68), 1:46.

84. Herbert Bismarck to Rantzau (20 Dec. 1886), Bussmann, pp. 415–16; also Arthur von Brauer, *Im Dienste Bismarcks: Persönliche Erinnerungen* (Berlin, 1936), p. 284. On the Crown Prince's refusal to take Wilhelm into his confidence, see RA Z43/8 (26 Sept. 1888); Hohenlohe diary (26 Oct. 1883), no. C.C.X.11.

85. *HP,* 2:343; Lerchenfeld, *Erinnerungen,* p. 344. Lerchenfeld does not specify that this was the attitude of the older children, but since he had no

contact with the three younger daughters, he undoubtedly was referring to Wilhelm, Charlotte, and Heinrich.

86. Herbert Bismarck, "Notizen, Herbst 91," Bismarck Papers, no. FC3018/244–45; Herbert Bismarck to Otto Bismarck (8 Oct. 1886), Bussmann, p. 391; Waldersee, 1:304; Eulenburg Papers, no. 81, pt. 1:164. See also a report of a conversation with Wilhelm II (14–15 Jan. 1927) by his adjutant, General von Dommes, BPHA, Rep. 53a, no. 33. Chancellor Bismarck also found that he could deal successfully with the Crown Prince until the Princess appeared. Brauer, *Im Dienste Bismarcks*, p. 245.

87. Herbert to Otto Bismarck (4 Oct. 1886), Bussmann, p. 388.

88. Baron Hugo von Reischach, *Unter Drei Kaisern*, Volksausgabe (Berlin, 1925), pp. 109–10; Princess Marie Louise of Schleswig-Holstein, *My Memories of Six Reigns* (London, 1956), pp. 94–95; Count Eberhard zu Solms-Sonnenwald to Herbert Bismarck (19 Apr. 1888), Bismarck Papers, no. FC2980/1100–1102. In this, as in all her views, the Crown Princess was dogmatic. See Ernle, "Empress Frederick," pp. 404–5; Mary J. Lyschinska, ed. *Henriette Schrader-Breymann: Ihr Leben aus Briefen und Tagebüchern zusammengestellt und erläutert*, 2 vols. (Berlin and Leipzig, 1927), 2:132; Ellen von Siemens, ed., *Anna von Helmholtz: Ein Lebensbild in Briefen*, 2 vols. (Berlin, 1929), 2:174; Sir James Rennell Rodd, *Social and Diplomatic Memories, 1884–1919*, 3 vols. (London, 1922–25), 1:49; Anton von Werner, *Erlebnisse und Eindrücke, 1870–1890* (Berlin, 1913), p. 508.

89. Malet to Lady Malet (22 Mar. 1888), Malet Papers, no. A-33.

90. Hans Delbrück, "Kaiserin Friedrich," *Preussische Jahrbücher* (1901), 12.

91. Bosse Papers, no. 16:50–51; Poultney Bigelow, *Prussian Memories, 1864–1914* (New York and London, 1915), p. 47, for the nickname.

92. Letter of 21 October 1885, Bülow Papers, no. 169; also same to same (12 Jan. 1878), ibid., no. 166.

93. Malet to Lady Malet (22 Nov. 1886), Malet Papers, no. A-31.

94. Eulenburg notes (7 June 1887), in Haller, *Aus 50 Jahren*, p. 136.

95. Memo by Wilhelm II (28 Mar. 1927), BPHA, Rep. 53a, no. 33. This was the view of a close observer of the Crown Princess's entourage, Karl von Normann. See Normann to Freytag (11 July 1888), in Wentzcke, *Im Neuen Reich*, 2:445.

96. Haller, *Aus 50 Jahren*, p. 174; Waldersee, 1:247.

97. Marie von Bunsen, *Die Welt in der ich Lebte: Erinnerungen aus glücklichen Jahren, 1860–1912* (Leipzig, 1929), p. 165. Bodo von dem Knesebeck, for many years an official in the Kaiserin's suite, also pointed out Wilhelm's descent from the mad Tsar. See Vierhaus, *Tagebuch Spitzemberg*, p. 543.

98. RA Z38/21 (25 May 1885); in a similar tone Z35/55, 58 (12, 21 Nov. 1881), Z36/62 (21 Nov. 1882); Z37/21 (3 Mar. 1884), Z38/67 (22 Sept. 1887); Holstein diary (17 Mar. 1882), *HP*, 2:15. On Wilhelm's hostility to his mother, see RA Add. A15/3463 (Duke of Connaught to Queen Victoria, 6 Nov. 1881); Lady Susan Townley, *'Indiscretions,'* (New York, 1922), p. 40; Waldersee, 1:267.

99. This was the opinion of her admirer, Baron Hugo von Reischach, in his *Unter Drei Kaisern*, p. 194.

100. RA Z28/52 (23 Aug. 1874); also Z26/74, 77 (22 May, 2 June 1872), Z39/19 (22 Apr. 1887).

101. RA Z32/42 (17 Apr. 1879). Waldemar was apparently an exceptional child. Franz von Roggenbach, who knew the Crown Princess's three surviving sons as children, expected Waldemar to accomplish more than Wilhelm or Heinrich. See Fuchs, 1:257. According to Holstein, Wilhelm showed little grief when Waldemar died, a reaction which, if true, must have contributed heavily to his mother's disenchantment with her oldest son. Holstein diary (5 Mar. 1884), *HP*, 2:97. See also Wilhelm's rather cool letter of 30 Mar. 1879 to Prince George of Wales about his brother's death in RA GV AA 43/7. Cf. Lord Odo Russell (British ambassador in Berlin) to Salisbury (29 Mar. 1879), describing Wilhelm as "brokenhearted"; Salisbury Papers, no. 9.

102. Hohenlohe diary (20 May 1881), Hohenlohe Papers, no. C.C.X.9. See also RA Add. A15/3463 (Duke of Connaught to Queen Victoria, 6 Nov. 1881), in which the French governess of the Crown Princess's younger children reported that relations between Wilhelm and his mother were "not at all smooth," an impasse Mlle. Perpignan felt was entirely Wilhelm's fault. See also Vicky's letter to Countess Dönhoff (8 Dec. 1881), Bülow Papers, no. 167.

103. Solms to Herbert Bismarck (19 Apr. 1888), Bismarck Papers, no. FC2980/1100–1102.

104. Radziwill diary (6 June 1889), Radziwill, *Lettres*, 1:9. For the Crown Princess on Kaiserin Augusta's deleterious influence on her grandson, see RA Z37/84 (2 July 1885), Z42/29 (13 Aug. 1888); for Wilhelm I's equally harmful effect RA Z39/5, 19 (7 Mar., 22 Apr. 1887).

105. RA Z36/5 (18 Jan. 1882), Z37/53 (21 Dec. 1884).

106. RA Z37/53 (21 Dec. 1884) Z66/6 (Lady Ampthill to Queen Victoria, 12 May 1883); Waldersee diary (20 Sept. 1886), Waldersee, 1:297. For Bismarck's relations with Wilhelm at this time, see Helmuth Rogge, ed., *Holstein und Hohenlohe: Neue Beiträge . . . nach Briefen und Aufzeichnungen aus dem Nachlass des Fürsten Chlodwig zu Hohenlohe-Schillingsfürst, 1874–1894* (Stuttgart, 1957), p. 205; Lerchenfeld, *Erinnerungen*, pp. 344–45; *GW*, 8:532; Brauer, *Im Dienste Bismarcks*, p. 109; Ponsonby, *Henry Ponsonby*, p. 290.

107. Eulenburg Papers, no. 81, pt. 1:180; also Haller, *Aus 50 Jahren*, p. 174; Bülow, 4:456. Chancellor Bismarck's critical summation of the Crown Princess is in *GW*, 15:445.

108. Brauer, *Im Dienste Bismarcks*, p. 284; Herbert Bismarck, "Notizen, Herbst 91," Bismarck Papers, no. FC3018/247. On Wilhelm's relations with his mother, see Kohut, "Kaiser Wilhelm II and His Parents," 63–89, and the much less helpful remarks in Hughes, *Emotion and High Politics*, pp. 122–36.

109. Eulenburg Papers, no. 81, pt. 1:165.

110. Ibid., pt. 2:24–25; Wilke, *Alt-Berlin Erinnerungen*, pp. 103–7, 124, 152. The Prussian nobility's hostility to England warrants close inspection but has been little studied. For a general view, see Fedor von Zobeltitz, *Chronik der Gesellschaft unter dem Letzten Kaiserreich*, 2 vols. (Hamburg, 1922), 1:336–37, and Eckart Kehr, "Das Deutsch-englische Bündnisproblem der Jahrhundertwende," *Die Gesellschaft*, July 1929, 24–31. Count Kuno von Westarp, *Konservative Politik im Letzten Jahrzehnt des Kaiserreiches*, 2 vols. (Berlin, 1935),

2:27–28, provides an interesting revelation of one aristocratic family's hostile view of England.

111. Wilke, *Alt-Berlin Erinnerungen*, p. 107. "Bondage" (*Hörigkeit*) was another word used in the army in this connection. See Marie von Bunsen, *Kaiserin Augusta* (Berlin, 1940), p. 254.

112. For Wilhelm's complaints about his mother's domination of his father, see Eulenburg Papers, no. 81, pt. 1:164; Herbert Bismarck, "Notizen, Herbst 91," Bismarck Papers, no. FC3018/244–45; Wilhelm to Tsar Alexander III (24 May 1884), BPHA, Rep. 53a, no. 5; Herbert to Otto Bismarck (8 Oct. 1886), Bussmann, pp. 391–92.

113. Dohme, "Erinnerungen," no. 1: 8 and no. 2: 127; Herbert Bismarck, "Notizen, Herbst 91," Bismarck Papers, no. FC3018/245–46. On two occasions, once to his father and once to Eulenburg, Wilhelm privately mentioned the question of abdication. See Dohme, "Erinnerungen," no. 1: 10; Haller, *Aus 50 Jahren*, p. 147.

114. Herbert to Otto Bismarck (4 Oct. 1886), Bussmann, p. 388; Bosse Papers, no. 16:51.

115. Wilhelm to Herbert Bismarck (18 Aug. 1886), Bussmann, pp. 370–71. Herbert had already reached the same conclusion. See his letter to Wilhelm Bismarck (25 Aug. 1884), ibid., 252–53. For Wilhelm's accusation of radicalism, see Eulenburg diary (30 June 1892), Eulenburg Papers, no. 20:477–78; Moritz Busch, *Tagebücher*, 3 vols. (Leipzig, 1899), 3:92; also Ballhausen, *Bismarck-Erinnerungen*, p. 307.

116. Holstein diary (6 June 1884), *HP*, 2:154–55.

117. Adolf von Bülow to Bülow (22 Aug. 1885), Bülow Papers, no. 13; for Adolf's influence on Wilhelm, see Bülow, 1:182; Rantzau, "Autobiographische u. Andere Aufzeichnungen, 1903–1909," Bismarck Papers, no. FC3030/624. For the Crown Princess on Adolf, RA Z49/5 (13 Aug. 1890).

118. Diary (6 Dec. 1882), Waldersee, 1:233; also ibid., 238–39.

119. For Eulenburg's attempts to lessen Wilhelm's Anglophobia, see his letter to Herbert Bismarck (5 Aug. 1886), Bismarck Papers, no. FC2962/108. For the dislike of London and much of England that surfaced after Eulenburg's trip there in 1891, see Eulenburg, *Mit dem Kaiser als Staatsmann und Freund auf Nordlandsreisen*, 2 vols. (Dresden, 1931), 1:119–20, 145–48; 2:67–68, 77.

120. Eulenburg diary (8 June 1887), in Haller, *Aus 50 Jahren*, pp. 136–37; Bülow, 1:262, 338; 2:128; 3:198–99; Topham, *Chronicles*, p. 227; also Ethel Howard, *Potsdam Princess* (New York, n.d. [1915]), pp. 3, 11.

121. RA Add. A15/4374 (Crown Princess to Princess Louise of Connaught, 2 Jan. 1885); also Z37/53 (21 Dec. 1884).

122. Arthur G. Lee, ed., *The Empress Writes to Sophie, Her Daughter, Crown Princess and Later Queen of the Hellenes: Letters, 1889–1901* (London, n.d. [1955]), p. 129; Swaine to Ponsonby (16 May 1885), Ponsonby, *Henry Ponsonby*, p. 360; also Bülow, 1:248, 339; Topham, *Chronicles*, pp. 36, 187–88, 197.

123. Malet to Lady Malet (22 Apr. 1888), Malet Papers, no. A-33. Waldersee believed that most of the fault lay with the Crown Princess and her husband; Waldersee diary (17 Nov. 1885, Waldersee, 1:267).

124. Reischach, *Unter Drei Kaisern*, p. 194.

125. For Wilhelm on his similarity to his mother, see Malet to Salisbury (30 Mar. 1889), Salisbury Papers, no. 62; Herbert to Otto Bismarck (4 Oct. 1886), Bussmann, pp. 388. For others who agreed, see Rodd, *Social and Diplomatic Memories*, 1:50; Eulenburg Papers, no. 1:55–56, no. 80:30; Lerchenfeld, *Erinnerungen*, p. 365; Radziwill, *Lettres*, 1:3–4, 28; Wedel, pp. 104, 130; *HP*, 1: 169, 2:97, 165.

126. Holstein diary (17 Mar. 1882), Holstein Papers, no. 3860/H195667, which differs from the version in *HP*, 2:15.

127. Ballhausen diary (16 Dec. 1882), *Bismarck-Erinnerungen*, pp. 243–44; Wilhelm to Tsar Alexander III (25 May 1884, 4 May 1885), BPHA, Rep. 53a, no. 5.

128. Ballhausen, *Bismarck-Erinnerungen*, pp. 243–44. See also Rodd, *Social and Diplomatic Memories*, 3:195, in which Wilhelm's attitude toward England is ambivalent. The British military attaché, Major Swaine, reported in 1884 that he could not detect any anti-English sentiments in the Prince; RA Z66/31 (Swaine to Ponsonby, 10 Apr. 1884).

129. Eulenburg diary (8 Aug. 1887), Eulenburg Papers, no. 81, pt. 1:205; Herbert Bismarck memo (28 Nov. 1887), Bismarck Papers, no. FC3004/1085.

130. It is striking how quickly the Queen, undoubtedly on the basis of information from her daughter, changed her once favorable view of her grandson. Cf. the critical remarks in RA Add. MS U/32 (4 July, 25 Sept. 1877) with ibid. (14 Feb. 1877), which is complimentary about Wilhelm.

131. RA Z81/62 (Wilhelm to Queen Victoria, 28 Jan. 1883); same to Herbert Bismarck (10 Feb. 1885), Bussmann, p. 271; also Z81/116 (same to Queen Victoria, 15 Feb. 1884), in which Wilhelm represents Gladstone's attacks on the "Bulgarian atrocities" as having been made with "crocodile tears." Wilhelm provided his grandmother with a "plan" for relieving General Gordon at Khartoum, which he later claimed that the British appropriated. See Wilhelm to Herbert Bismarck (19 Feb. 1885), Bismarck Papers, no. FC2986/485–87; also RA Z81/116 (same to Queen Victoria, 15 Feb. 1884).

132. Otto Bismarck to Wilhelm (23 May 1884), BPHA, Rep. 53a, no. 31; Herbert to Wilhelm Bismarck (13 May 1884), Bussmann, p. 236. Details of the trip are in Herbert Bismarck, "Tagebuch," Bismarck Papers, no. FC3018/163–67; Bismarck "Notizen, Herbst 91," ibid., 234–36, 256.

133. Hohenlohe diary (2 Nov. 1884), Hohenlohe Papers, no. C.C.X.12.

134. Herbert Bismarck, "Notizen, Herbst 91," Bismarck Papers, no. FC3018/237.

135. BPHA, Rep. 53a, no. 5. The Three Emperors' League was a nonbinding, ideological association of Germany, Austria-Hungary, and Russia that had been in force since the early 1870s.

136. *HP*, 2:153–55; Waldersee, 1:242; Wilhelm to Alexander III (19 June 1884), BPHA, Rep. 53a, no. 5.

137. Otto to Herbert Bismarck (14 May 1884), Bussmann, p. 238; Count Egon Corti, *Alexander von Battenberg* (London, 1954), pp. 122–23; Brauer, *Im Dienste Bismarcks*, p. 250. For Wilhelm I's opposition, see his letter to the Prussian state ministry (n.d.), Reichskanzlei Papers, "Akten betr. persönliche Angelegenheiten S.M.des Kaisers sowie Mitglieder des Königlichen und Kaiserlichen

Hauses," 2:1–11. For Herbert Bismarck's opposition, see his "Tagebuch," Bismarck Papers, no. FC3018/161.

138. Herbert Bismarck to Otto Bismarck (9, 10 Sept. 1885), Bussmann, pp. 310–12, 314; Count Egon Corti, *Wenn . . . : Sendung und Schicksal einer Kaiserin* (Graz, 1954), p. 365.

139. Wilhelm to Otto Bismarck (10 May 1888), Bismarck Papers, no. FC2986/391; same to Eulenburg (12 Apr. 1888), Röhl, 1:284; also Waldersee, 1:240; Wilhelm II, *Aus Meinem Leben*, pp. 317–18. Some years earlier, Wilhelm had favored a match between Alexander and one of Dona's sisters; RA Z39/19 (22 Apr. 1887).

140. Wilhelm to Herbert Bismarck (10 Feb., 25 Oct. 1885), Bussmann, pp. 271, 323; Rantzau to Herbert Bismarck (Nov. 13, 1885), Bismarck Papers, no. FC3028; same to Bülow (14 Feb. 1885), Bülow Papers, no. 65.

141. RA Add. MS U/32 (15 Dec. 1886).

142. Herbert Bismarck to Bülow (9 Jan. 1885), Bülow Papers, no. 65. For the negative reaction in Berlin, see Crown Princess to Countess Dönhoff (7 Jan., 2 Feb. 1885), ibid., no. 169.

143. Bülow to Eulenburg (27 Sept. 1892), Eulenburg Papers, no. 21:637.

144. RA Add. U/32 (10 Jan., 3 Sept. 1885).

145. Ibid., 395 (same to same, 13 Feb. 1885).

146. *HP*, 2:254.

147. Herbert Bismarck to Otto Bismarck (23 Sept. 1886) and to Rantzau (31 Oct. 1886), Bussmann, pp. 377–78, 400; Ernle, "Empress Frederick," p. 404.

148. Herbert to Otto Bismarck (23 Sept., 4 Oct. 1886), Bussmann, pp. 377–78, 388. See also *GW*, 6c:318, for Gen. Emil von Albedyll's interesting reflections on Wilhelm's likely intemperance in the event that he should become viceroy.

149. RA Z38/34 (11 Aug. 1886). On the Crown Prince's objections, see Wilhelm to Herbert Bismarck (17 Aug. 1886), Bismarck Papers, no. FC2986/504–8.

150. On this trip, see Wilhelm's notes (11 Sept. 1886), Bismarck Papers, no. FC2986/342–45; Wilhelm II, *Ereignisse und Gestalten aus den Jahren 1878–1918* (Leipzig, 1922), pp. 12–13; Count Richard von Pfeil, *Neun Jahre in Russischen Diensten unter Kaiser Alexander III.* (Leipzig, 1911), pp. 148–50; also *GP*, 5:63–65.

151. RA Z43/36 (10 Nov. 1888); Herbert Bismarck to Rantzau (13, 16, Dec. 1886), Bismarck Papers, no. FC3014/930, 933. In a letter to Albrecht von Stosch (11 Jan. 1882), Gustav Freytag reported that one Eduard von Möller was giving Wilhelm lectures on social and economic policy. Möller, an official in the administration of Alsace-Lorraine, had died in 1880, and Freytag probably confused him with Ernst von Möller, an under secretary in the Prussian Ministry for Trade and Industry. See Helmolt, *Freytags Briefe*, p. 139.

152. For the reaction of both parents, see Herbert Bismarck to Rantzau (20 Dec. 1886), Bussmann, pp. 415–16.

153. Roggenbach to Stosch (9 Dec. 1886), in Heyderhoff, *Im Ring der Gegner Bismarcks*, p. 252.

154. Holstein diary (18 Sept., 1 Dec. 1886), *HP*, 2:303, 315; Holstein to Harden (5 Aug. 1906), Harden Papers, no. 62/52.

155. Bismarck, "Notizen, Herbst 91," Bismarck Papers, no. FC3018/244.
156. RA Z500/1 (Wilhelm to Queen Victoria, 28 Dec. 1886).
157. Bismarck, "Notizen, Herbst 91," Bismarck Papers, no. FC3018/244; Herbert Bismarck to Rantzau (23 Dec. 1886), ibid., no. FC3014/941; Raschdau, *Unter Bismarck und Caprivi*, pp. 15–17; Ebel, 1:615; Holstein diary (5 Nov. 1887), *HP*, 2:355.
158. Holstein diary (11 July 1885), *HP*, 2:219. Holstein later gave diplomats the same advice; ibid., 4:241–42.
159. Karl von Normann to Gustav Freytag (1 Jan. 1886), in Wentzcke, *Im Neuen Reich*, 2:424. Cf. Herbert Bismarck to Rantzau (18 Dec. 1886), Bussmann, p. 414.
160. RA Z39/19 (22 Apr. 1887).
161. Malet to Lady Malet (29 Dec. 1886), Malet Papers, no. A-31.

CHAPTER 4

1. Count Egon Corti, *Wenn . . . : Sendung und Schicksal einer Kaiserin* (Graz, 1954), pp. 399, 405. The most recent treatment of the Crown Prince's illness and brief reign is J. Alden Nichols, *The Year of the Three Kaisers: Bismarck and the German Succession, 1887–88* (Urbana and Chicago, 1987), which is especially detailed on party politics and the press. See also Michael Freund, *Der Drama der 99 Tage: Krankheit und Tod Friedrichs III.* (Cologne, 1967) and H.-J. Wolf, *Die Krankheit Kaiser Friedrichs III. und ihre Wirkung auf die Deutsche und Englische Öffentlichkeit* (Berlin, 1958). The physicians' reports are in Gustav von Bergmann, *Rückschau: Geschehen und Erleben auf meiner Lebensbühne* (Munich, 1953), and Sir Morell Mackenzie, *The Fatal Illness of Frederick the Noble* (London, 1888). For the Crown Princess's version, see James Rennell Rodd, *Friedrich III. als Kronprinz und Kaiser: Ein Lebensbild* (Berlin, 1888).
2. Crown Princess to Marie von Bülow (15 Aug. 1887), Bülow Papers, no. 170. Mackenzie's notes and the Crown Princess's informative letters to Queen Victoria are respectively in RA Z39/37 and Z39/23, 25, 26, 29.
3. RA Z39/23 (17 May 1887); also Malet to Lady Malet (20 May 1887), Malet Papers, no. A-32.
4. Albrecht von Stosch to Karl von Normann (16 May 1887), in Frederic B. M. Hollyday, *Bismarck's Rival: A Political Biography of General and Admiral Albrecht von Stosch* (Durham, N.C., 1960), p. 237.
5. Roggenbach to Stosch (30 May 1887), in Julius Heyderhoff, ed., *Im Ring der Gegner Bismarcks: Denkschriften und politischer Briefwechsel Franz v. Roggenbachs mit Kaiserin Augusta und Albrecht v. Stosch, 1865–1896* (Leipzig, 1943), p. 261. See also RA Z39/29 (27 May 1887).
6. Letter of 17 May 1887, Bussmann, p. 443.
7. Eulenburg notes (11 June 1887), Eulenburg Papers, no. 2:31–32; Roggenbach to Stosch (8 Jan. 1888), Heyderhoff, *Im Ring der Gegner Bismarcks*, p. 280; Malet to Lady Malet (25 May 1887), Malet Papers, no. A-32.
8. Holstein diary (28 June 1887), *HP*, 2:346–48.

9. Waldersee, 1:327; also diary (3 Mar. 1888), ibid., 365. For Waldersee's fine calculation of his own position in the event of Wilhelm's succession, see ibid., 371.

10. Eulenburg diary (7 June 1887), Eulenburg papers, no. 81, pt. 1:195; *HP*, 2:347–48. Count Radolinski, a confidant of the Crown Prince and Princess, noted that Wilhelm had nothing whatsoever to say about his father's illness. General Emil von Albedyll to his wife (7 July 1887), in Richard Boschau, ed., *Aus Hannover und Preussen: Lebenserinnerungen aus einem halben Jahrhundert von Julie von Albedyll-Alten* (Potsdam, 1914), p. 326.

11. Roggenbach to Stosch (30 May 1887), in Heyderhoff, *Im Ring der Gegner Bismarcks*, p. 261.

12. Freund, *Drama der 99 Tage*, p. 90.

13. RA Z39/13 (26 Mar. 1887).

14. RA Add. U/32 (4 June 1887); also RA Z39/30, 34 (30 May, 3 June 1887).

15. Both observations are in Eulenburg notes (9 June 1887), Eulenburg Papers, no. 2:28–31.

16. Bismarck, "Notizen, Herbst 91," Bismarck Papers, no. FC3018/248.

17. Infanta Eulalia of Spain, *Memoirs of H.R.H. the Infanta Eulalia* (London, 1936), pp. 70–71; Hatzfeldt to Holstein (11 June 1887), Ebel, 1:614.

18. Eulenburg notes (8 Aug. 1887), Eulenburg Papers, no. 2:47–48.

19. *HP*, 3:219. The Crown Prince was also annoyed that the Queen outranked him. Princess Alice, Countess of Athlone, *For My Grandchildren: Some Reminiscences* (London, 1966), p. 148.

20. Crown Princess to Marie von Bülow (15 Aug. 1887), Bülow Papers, no. 170.

21. Same to same (3 Dec. 1887), ibid.; Anton von Werner, *Erlebnisse und Eindrücke, 1870–1890* (Berlin, 1913), p. 502.

22. Corti, *Wenn*, p. 420; Waldersee diary (7 Nov. 1887), Waldersee, 1:331–32.

23. Wilhelm to General von Albedyll (11 Oct. 1887), Albedyll Papers.

24. Crown Princess to Marie von Bülow (3 Dec. 1887), Bülow Papers, no. 170; same to Baroness von Stockmar (17 Nov. 1887), Ernst Feder, ed., *Bismarcks Grosses Spiel: Die geheimen Tagebücher Ludwig Bambergers* (Frankfurt, 1933), p. 369.

25. RA Z66/109 (Wilhelm to Queen Victoria, 11 Nov. 1887); same to Hinzpeter (11 Nov. 1887), Wilhelm II, *Aus Meinem Leben, 1859–1888* (Berlin and Leipzig, 1927), pp. 388–39; same to the Grand Duke (9 Nov. 1887), Fuchs, 2:487.

26. Robert Dohme, "Erinnerungen an Kaiser Friedrich," *Deutsche Revue* 47, no. 1–3 (1922): no. 1: 10; also *HP*, 3:227.

27. Dohme, "Erinnerungen," no. 3: 249.

28. Eulenburg notes (14 Nov. 1887), Johannes Haller, ed., *Aus 50 Jahren: Erinnerungen, Tagebücher und Briefe aus dem Nachlass des Fürsten Philipp zu Eulenburg-Hertefeld* (Berlin, 1923), p. 147; Radolinski to Hatzfeldt (12 Nov. 1887), Ebel, 1:635.

29. Crown Princess to Marie von Bülow (3 Dec. 1887), Bülow Papers, no. 170; RA Z38/87 (14 Nov. 1887).

30. Radolinski to Hatzfeldt (21 Nov. 1887), Ebel, 1:642; Arthur von Brauer,

Im Dienste Bismarcks: Persönliche Erinnerungen (Berlin, 1936), p. 259.

31. RA Z38/87 (15 Nov. 1887).

32. Waldersee diary (14 Nov. 1887), Waldersee, 1:333; also Roggenbach to Stosch (14 Nov. 1887), Heyderhoff, *Im Ring der Gegner Bismarcks*, p. 272; RA Z38/87 (15 Nov. 1887).

33. Corti, *Wenn*, pp. 421–22; also Ebel, 1:634–35; Radolinski to Bismarck (23 Nov. 1887), Reichskanzlei, "Akten betr. persönliche Angelegenheiten S.M. des Kaisers sowie Mitglieder des Königlichen und Kaiserlichen Hauses," 2:5–11.

34. RA Z38/84 (9 Nov. 1887).

35. Letter (3 Dec. 1887), Bülow Papers, no. 170. On the Crown Princess's warrantless optimism after her husband's death sentence in November 1887, see Werner, *Erlebnisse*, p. 507; *HP*, 3:231, 257–60, 266, 270; Ebel, 1:614–15, 642. See also *HP*, 2:344, 348.

36. Dona to Caroline Mathilda (10, 19 Nov. 1887), Glücksburg Papers, no. 8; Anna Wagemann, *Prinzessin Feodora: Erinnerungen an den Augustenburger und den preussischen Hof* . . . (Berlin, 1932), p. 102; Eulenburg notes (14 Nov. 1887), Eulenburg Papers, no. 2:70–72.

37. Baron Robert Lucius von Ballhausen diary (19 Nov. 1887), Ballhausen, *Bismarck-Erinnerungen* (Stuttgart and Berlin, 1920), p. 405.

38. Holstein diary (28 Sept. 1887), *HP*, 2:349.

39. Herbert to Wilhelm Bismarck (11 Nov. 1887), Bussmann, pp. 478–79; Holstein diary (11 Jan. 1888), *HP*, 2:360–61 and 356.

40. Széchenyi to Kálnoky (12 Nov. 1887), HHStA, no. 131(B).

41. Radolinski to Hatzfeldt (21 Nov. 1887), Ebel, 1:642. For similar opinions, see Crown Princess to Baroness von Stockmar (17 Nov. 1887), Feder, *Bismarcks Grosses Spiel*, p. 369. The Prussian ministry discussed the question without coming to a conclusion on 18 November; Bosse diary (18 Nov. 1887), Bosse Papers, no. 8.

42. Eulenburg notes (14 Nov. 1887), Haller, *Aus 50 Jahren*, p. 147.

43. Feder, *Bismarcks Grosses Spiel*, p. 369; RA Z38/88 (16 Nov. 1887).

44. Order printed in Wilhelm II, *Aus Meinem Leben*, pp. 338–39; drafts in Reichskanzlei, "Akten betr. persönliche Angelegenheiten S.M. des Kaisers sowie Mitglieder des Königlichen und Kaiserlichen Hauses," 2:3–11.

45. RA Z38/92 (21 Nov. 1887); Fuchs, 2:495–96; Waldersee, 1:338; Wilhelm II, *Aus Meinem Leben*, pp. 339–40; Ballhausen, *Bismarck-Erinnerungen*, pp. 407, 416–17; Ebel, 1:641–42.

46. Moritz Busch, *Bismarck: Some Secret Pages of His History*, 3 vols. (London, 1898), 3:293–95, 333–34. In October 1887 Wilhelm had worked briefly in the Prussian Finance Ministry, where he was found to be eager but ill-prepared. Wilhelm von Scholz, ed., *Staatsminister Adolf von Scholz: Erlebnisse und Gespräche mit Bismarck* (Stuttgart and Berlin, 1922), pp. 80–81; Ballhausen diary (27 Dec. 1887), Ballhausen, *Bismarck-Erinnerungen*, p. 411.

47. Brauer, *Im Dienste Bismarcks*, p. 190; Count Hugo Lerchenfeld-Koefering, *Erinnerungen und Denkwürdigkeiten* (Berlin, 1935), p. 344.

48. *GW*, 8:532 for the compliment. The complaint is in Giles St. Aubyn, *The Royal George, 1819–1904: The Life of H.R.H. Prince George, Duke of Cam-*

bridge (London, 1963), p. 236. Wilhelm's letters to Bismarck are in Bismarck Papers, nos. FC2986/328–65.

49. Lothar v. Schweinitz diary (16 Apr. 1886), Wilhelm v. Schweinitz, ed., *Denkwürdigkeiten des Botschafters General v. Schweinitz*, 2 vols. (Berlin, 1927), 2:317–18.

50. Lerchenfeld, *Erinnerungen*, pp. 344–45; Brauer, *Im Dienste Bismarcks*, p. 190; Malet to Lady Malet (22 Apr. 1888), Malet Papers, no. A-33.

51. Herbert Bismarck to Bülow (5 Sept. 1886), Bussmann, p. 372; also Holstein diary (28 June 1887), *HP*, 2:347; Hohenlohe diary (26 Oct. 1883), Helmuth Rogge, ed., *Holstein und Hohenlohe: Neue Beiträge . . . nach Briefen und Aufzeichnungen aus dem Nachlass des Fürsten Chlodwig zu Hohenlohe-Schillingsfürst, 1874–1894* (Stuttgart, 1957), p. 205; Moritz Busch diary (27 Sept. 1888), Busch, *Tagebuchblätter*, 3 vols. (Leipzig, 1899), 3:249.

52. Scholz, *Staatsminister von Scholz*, pp. 81–83; also Prince Alexander von Hohenlohe, *Aus Meinem Leben* (Frankfurt/Main, 1925), p. 307.

53. Ballhausen diary (31 Dec. 1887), Ballhausen, *Bismarck-Erinnerungen*, p. 413.

54. On the deterioration of Wilhelm's friendship with Herbert, see Holstein to Hatzfeldt (13 June 1887, 14 Jan. 1888), Radolinski to same (15 Jan. 1888), Ebel, 1:615, 658, 660; Holstein diary (11 Jan. 1888), *HP*, 2:360–61; Eulenburg to same (6 Jan. 1888), ibid., 3:251; Waldersee diary (2 Feb. 1888), Waldersee, 1:357; Sir James Rennell Rodd, *Social and Diplomatic Memories, 1884–1919*, 3 vols. (London, 1922–25), 1:110.

55. Waldersee diary (8, 22 Feb., 27 Apr. 1888), Waldersee, 1:358, 361, 393.

56. His assurances to Eulenburg in Eulenburg to Herbert Bismarck (30 Apr. 1888), Eulenburg Papers, no. 3:94; same to same (19 May 1888), Bismarck Papers, no. FC2962/156–57; criticism in Herbert Bismarck to Rantzau (16 Dec. 1887), Bismarck Papers, no. FC3014/1011; Holstein diary (28 June 1887), *HP*, 2:346–47.

57. Lerchenfeld, *Erinnerungen*, pp. 345–46.

58. Baron Robert Lucius von Ballhausen, *Die Entlassung des Fürsten Bismarck, März 1890* (Stuttgart, 1922), pp. 27–28; *HP*, 2:306.

59. Otto Bismarck to the Crown Prince (2 Oct. 1886), Bismarck Papers, no. FC3014/917–18; *GuE*, 3:3; Lerchenfeld, *Erinnerungen*, p. 344.

60. On Holstein, Bülow to Adolf von Bülow (n.d. but in sequence between letters of 22 Aug. and 29 Oct. 1885), Bülow Papers, no. 13; on Bülow, same to same (1 Aug. 1885), ibid.; on Bismarck, Holstein diary (28 June 1887), *HP*, 2:347.

61. For Moltke, Eulenburg Papers, no. 81, pt. 1:229–30 and pt. 2:108–10; on Albedyll, Herbert to Otto Bismarck (14 Nov. 1887), Bussmann, p. 481; also Waldersee, 1:333; Széchenyi to Kálnoky (28 Jan. 1888), HHStA, no. 133(B).

62. Waldersee diary (23 May 1887), Waldersee, 1:327.

63. Ballhausen diary (23 Feb. 1888), Ballhausen, *Bismarck-Erinnerungen*, p. 421.

64. Bosse Papers, no. 16, pp. 58–59.

65. Gneist to Otto Bismarck (1 Mar. 1888), Reichskanzlei, "Akten betr. per-

sönliche Angelegenheiten S.M. des Kaisers sowie Mitglieder des Königlichen und Kaiserlichen Hauses," 2:5–11.

66. Otto Bismarck notes (22 Feb. 1888) and his letter to Radolinski (Feb. 23, 1888), ibid.; Bülow, 1:61–62. On Wilhelm's choosing Brandenstein, see Holstein to Eulenburg (24 Feb. 1888), Röhl, 1:271–72; Ballhausen, *Bismarck-Erinnerungen*, p. 421.

67. Herbert to Wilhelm Bismarck (29 Jan. 1888), Bussmann, p. 505.

68. Same to same (25 Feb. 1888), Bismarck Papers, no. FC3011/561.

69. Swaine memo (20 Nov. 1887), Salisbury Papers, no. 61.

70. RA Z500/2 (memo by Queen Victoria, 25 Apr. 1888).

71. Herbette to Foreign Minister Léopold Flourens (7 Mar. 1888), *DDF*, 7:80.

72. See, for example, Ludwig Raschdau, *Unter Bismarck und Caprivi: Erinnerungen eines deutschen Diplomaten aus den Jahren 1885–1894* (Berlin, 1939), p. 17.

73. Wagemann, *Prinzessin Feodora*, pp. 55–56; also *HP*, 2:356.

74. Radolinski to Holstein (10 Nov. 1887), *HP*, 3:227.

75. Eulenburg Papers, no. 2:77.

76. *GuE*, 3:12–14. On the contents, Eulenburg diary (25 Nov. 1887), Haller, *Aus 50 Jahren*, p. 149; Eulenburg to Wilhelm (17 Apr. 1888), ibid., p. 283.

77. Letter of 6 Jan. 1888, *GuE*, 3:14–17.

78. On Stöcker, see Walter Frank, *Hofprediger Adolf Stoecker und die christlich-soziale Bewegung*, 2d rev. ed. (Hamburg, 1935), and more recently Hans Engelmann, *Kirche am Abgrund: Adolf Stöcker und seine anti-Jüdische Bewegung* (Berlin, 1984). There is an acute portrait in Hellmut von Gerlach, *Erinnerungen eines Junkers* (Berlin, n.d.), pp. 68–77. See also Max Braun, *Adolf Stoecker* (Berlin, 1929).

79. Werner, *Erlebnisse*, p. 508; RA I54/31 (Crown Princess to Queen Victoria, 16 Nov. 1883).

80. Dona to Caroline Mathilda (17 Dec. 1882), Glücksburg Papers, no. 3.

81. Letter of 24 Mar. 1888 to the Grand Duke, in Fuchs, 2:521, n. 1; Herbert Bismarck, "Notizen, Herbst 91," Bismarck Papers, no. FC3018/252, and his "Notizen V," ibid., no. FC3018/449.

82. Wilhelm to Wilhelm I (5 Aug. 1885), as summarized in Frank, *Stoecker*, pp. 145–46.

83. Speech (14 Jan. 1887), ibid., p. 161.

84. Accounts of the meeting in *GuE*, 3:8; Frank, *Stoecker*, pp. 166–67; Herman von Petersdorff, *Kleist-Retzow: Ein Lebensbild* (Stuttgart and Berlin, 1907), pp. 516–17; Albert von Puttkamer, *Staatsminister von Puttkamer: Ein Stück preussischer Vergangenheit, 1828–1900* (Leipzig, n.d. [1928]), pp. 176–80; see also Eulenburg Papers, no. 81, pt. 1:224–25. For Wilhelm's connection with Stoecker's movement earlier in 1887, see Waldersee diary (2 Mar. 1887), Waldersee, 1:318.

85. Speech in *Kreuzzeitung* (2 Dec. 1887), partly printed in Frank, *Stoecker*, p. 167, and Petersdorff, *Kleist-Retzow*, pp. 516–17.

86. *GuE*, 3:7–12, prints the letter; on Waldersee's role, Waldersee, 1:346.

87. Rantzau, "Autobiographische und andere Aufzeichnungen," Bismarck Papers, no. FC3030/701–3.

88. The letter is printed in *GuE*, 3:17–22.

89. Herbert Bismarck to Rantzau (7 Jan. 1888), Bussmann, p. 497; for Herbert's low opinion of Stoecker, see his "Notizen V," Bismarck Papers, no. FC3018/449.

90. Eulenburg notes (27 Dec. 1887), Eulenburg Papers, no. 2:106–8. The version in Haller, *Aus 50 Jahren*, pp. 153–56, has been altered. See also Eulenburg's undated notes, Eulenburg Papers, no. 2:110.

91. Eulenburg notes (27 Dec. 1887), ibid., pp. 106–8.

92. Herbert to Wilhelm Bismarck (1 Feb. 1888), Bismarck Papers, no. FC3011/558. See also Eulenburg notes (29, 31 Dec. 1887), Eulenburg Papers, no. 2:110, 113; Eulenburg to Holstein (6 Jan. 1888), Röhl, 1:259. On the apparent termination of the conflict, see Waldersee, 1:356, 359; 2:46.

93. Holstein diary (4 Feb. 1888), *HP*, 2:362–63.

94. Eulenburg diary (27 Dec. 1887), Eulenburg Papers, no. 81, pt. 1:228.

95. Wilhelm to Eulenburg (19 Feb. 1888), Röhl, 1:269; same to Prince Albrecht of Prussia (29 Feb. 1888), BPHA, Rep. 53a, no. 74; Wilhelm II, *Aus Meinem Leben*, pp. 335–36. For Wilhelm's sympathy for Bergmann and Bramann in the doctors' battle, see Wied Papers.

96. Brauer, *Im Dienste Bismarcks*, p. 259.

97. Mary J. Lyschinska, ed., *Henriette Schrader-Breymann: Ihr Leben aus Briefen und Tagebüchern zusammengestellt und erläutert*, 2 vols. (Berlin and Leipzig, 1927), 2:40–41.

98. Richard Kühn, ed., *Kaiserin Augusta. Bekenntnisse an eine Freundin: Aufzeichnungen aus ihrer Freundschaft mit Jenny von Gustedt* (Dresden, 1935), pp. 293–94.

99. Ballhausen diary (8 Mar. 1888), Ballhausen, *Bismarck-Erinnerungen*, p. 425.

100. Victoria, Princess of Prussia, *My Memories* (London, 1929), p. 88.

101. RA Z40/29 (9 Mar. 1888).

102. Gustav von Kessel diary (11 Mar. 1888), BPHA, Rep. 53a, no. 29.

CHAPTER 5

1. Herbette to Goblet (25 Jan. 1889), *DDF*, 7:317; Hermann Hoffmann, *Fürst Bismarck, 1890–1898 . . .*, 3 vols. (Stuttgart, 1913–14), 1:185; also *GW*, 15:446, 635. Arthur von Brauer, *Im Dienste Bismarcks: Persönliche Erinnerungen* (Berlin, 1936), pp. 242–46, pictures a more contentious situation between the chancellor and the royal couple.

2. RA Z41/59 (8 June 1888). On the Empress Friedrich's desire to be rid of Bismarck, see Hohenlohe, 2:435, and Waldersee, 1:380.

3. Gustav von Bergmann, *Rückschau: Geschehen und Erleben auf meiner Lebensbühne* (Munich, 1953), pp. 70–71.

4. Waldersee diary (11 Mar. 1888), Waldersee, 1:370.

5. Eulenburg Papers, no. 81, pt. 2:28–36.

6. Count Egon Corti, *Wenn . . . : Sendung und Schicksal einer Kaiserin* (Graz,

1954), p. 460; speech partly printed in Schulthess (1888), p. 72.

7. Corti, *Wenn*, pp. 468–69.

8. Waldersee diary (11 Mar. 1888), Waldersee, 1:370–71; Waldersee to Consul General Baron Julius von Rechenberg (1 Apr. 1888), in Heinrich Meisner, ed., *Aus dem Briefwechsel des Generalfeldmarschalls Alfred Grafen von Waldersee: Die Berliner Jahre, 1886–1891* (Berlin and Leipzig, 1928), p. 168.

9. On the Empress Friedrich's role, see Waldersee, 1:373, 375; Baron Robert Lucius von Ballhausen, *Bismarck-Erinnerungen* (Stuttgart and Berlin, 1920), p. 438. See also Wilhelm's letter to his great-uncle, Grand Duke Ernst II of Coburg (24 Mar. 1888), Fuchs, 2:521, n. 1.

10. RA Z41/27 (16 Mar. 1888).

11. Suggestions of insanity by Rantzau in Eulenburg's notes (5 June 1888), Eulenburg Papers, no. 4:113; Waldersee diary (3 Mar., 22 Apr. 1888), Waldersee, 1:365, 391. See also Radolinski's more restrained criticism in his letters to Holstein (12, 28 Feb., 6 Mar. 1888), *HP*, 3:257–60, 266, 270; Gen. Emil von Albedyll diary (10 Apr. 1888), in Richard Boschau, ed., *Aus Hannover und Preussen: Lebenserinnerungen aus einem halben Jahrhundert von Julie von Albedyll-Alten* (Potsdam, 1914), p. 270; Baroness Hildegard von Spitzemberg diary (Mar. 13, 1888), in Rudolf Vierhaus, ed., *Das Tagebuch der Baronin Spitzemberg, geb. Freiin v. Varnbüler: Aufzeichnungen aus der Hofgesellschaft des Hohenzollernreiches* (Göttingen, 1960), p. 243. For an affecting picture of the Empress's ministrations as a nurse, see Bergmann, *Rückschau*, pp. 67–68. For her admirers' concern, see Hohenlohe, 2:429; Ebel, 1:665.

12. Radolinski to Holstein (6 Mar. 1888), *HP*, 3:270.

13. Széchenyi to Kálnoky (21 Mar. 1888), HHStA, no. 133(B).

14. RA Z41/47 (12 May 1888); an earlier complaint is in Z40/27 (6 Mar. 1888). The Empress may not have known it, but at the time she wrote, Wilhelm was ordering a naval sailing ship made ready for the voyage he intended to take, as monarch, in the coming summer. Herbert Bismarck to Rantzau (17, 20 May 1888), Bismarck Papers, no. FC3014/1167, 1169.

15. Széchenyi to Kálnoky (24 Mar. 1888), HHStA, no. 133(B).

16. Empress Frederick to Baroness von Stockmar (16 May 1888), in Ernst Feder, ed., *Bismarcks Grosses Spiel: Die geheimen Tagebücher Ludwig Bambergers* (Frankfurt, 1933), p. 358; RA Z40/16 (2 Feb. 1888), Z41/32 (23 Mar. 1888); Herbert Bismarck, "Notizen, Herbst 91," Bismarck Papers, no. FC3018/251–52.

17. RA Z41/44 (7 May 1888). She mentions only Heinrich and Charlotte by name, but the implication is clear that Wilhelm belonged to this group of her children. See also ibid., Z43/32, 36 (2, 10 Nov. 1888). For Augusta's favorable opinion of Wilhelm and Dona, see Waldersee, 1:351.

18. Brauer, *Im Dienste Bismarcks*, p. 284, Swaine to Ponsonby (ca. 18 Nov. 1888), in Sir Frederick Ponsonby, ed., *Letters of the Empress Frederick* (New York, 1928), p. 365; also Arthur Ponsonby, *Henry Ponsonby, Queen Victoria's Private Secretary: His Life from His Letters* (New York, 1943), p. 296.

19. Wilhelm to the Grand Duke (29 May 1888), Fuchs, 2:546–47.

20. Brauer, *Im Dienste Bismarcks* p. 284. For Wilhelm's complaints about his mother, see his letter to the Grand Duke (29 May 1888), Fuchs, 2:546–47;

Waldersee 1:391–92; Wilhelm II, *Aus Meinem Leben, 1859–1888* (Berlin and Leipzig, 1927), pp. 350–51.

21. Eduard von Liebenau to Holstein (1 June 1888), *HP*, 3:277.

22. On Wilhelm's contacts with Waldersee, Waldersee diary (14 Mar. 1885), Waldersee, 1:253–54; Eduard von Wertheimer, "Ein Kaiser- und Königlicher Militärattaché über das politische Leben in Berlin, 1880–1895," *Preussische Jahrbücher* 201 (1925): 276. On Bismarck's suspicions, Waldersee diary (12 May 1887), Waldersee, 1:325; *HP*, 1:137.

23. Waldersee, 1:393, 358, 361.

24. Lamar Cecil, "William II and his Russian 'Colleagues,'" in Carole Fink, Isabel V. Hull, and MacGregor Knox, eds., *German Nationalism and the European Response, 1890–1945* (Norman, Okla., 1985), pp. 104–5.

25. Swaine memo (20 Nov. 1887), Salisbury Papers, no. 61.

26. Hohenlohe diary (25 Mar. 1888), Hohenlohe, 2:432; also Szögyényi to Kálnoky (18 Feb. 1893), HHStA, no. 143(B).

27. Wilhelm II, *Aus Meinem Leben*, p. 324, and his *Ereignisse und Gestalten aus den Jahren 1878–1918* (Leipzig and Berlin, 1922), p. 13. The Tsar's remarks may be a later fabrication by Wilhelm, for in his notes taken at the time Wilhelm reported nothing of the sort, nor did he say anything critical of Alexander to his confidant Waldersee. Wilhelm's notes (11 Sept. 1886), in Bismarck Papers, no. FC2986/342–45; Waldersee diary (20 Sept. 1888), Waldersee, 1:297–98.

28. For the change in Wilhelm's view of Russia, see Swaine memo, "Prince William of Prussia" (20 Nov. 1887), Salisbury papers, no. 61; Malet to Salisbury (19 Nov. 1887), ibid.; Holstein diary (1 Dec. 1886), *HP*, 2:316; Count Hugo Lerchenfeld-Koefering, *Erinnerungen und Denkwürdigkeiten* (Berlin, 1935), p. 321. The Franco-Russian pact was signed only in 1894.

29. Waldersee to Col. Count Yorck von Wartenburg (17 Nov. 1887), in Heinrich O. Meisner, "Briefwechsel zwischen dem Chef des Generalstabes Grafen Waldersee und dem Militärattaché in Petersburg Grafen Yorck von Wartenburg, 1885–1894," *Historische-Politisches Archiv zur Deutschen Geschichte des 19. und 20. Jahrhunderts* 1 (1930): 151.

30. Herbert Bismarck to Rantzau (27 Jan. 1888), Bussmann, p. 504; Waldersee diary (15 Feb. 1887), Waldersee, 1:316; Lerchenfeld, *Erinnerungen*, p. 321. See also Holstein diary (11 Jan. 1888), *HP*, 2:361; Holstein to Hatzfeldt (14 Jan. 1888), Ebel, 1:658.

31. Holstein diary (1 Nov. 1888), *HP*, 2:381.

32. Notes by Szögyényi of his talk in August 1889 with Bismarck, in Helmut Krausnick, ed., *Neue Bismarck-Gespräche* . . . (Hamburg, 1940–43), pp. 59–60.

33. Ian Vorres, *The Last Grand Duchess: Her Imperial Highness Grand Duchess Olga Alexandrovich, 1882–1960* (New York, 1964), p. 40; Abraham Yarmolinsky, ed. and trans., *The Memoirs of Count Witte* (Garden City and Toronto, 1921), pp. 404–5; Gleb Botkin, *The Real Romanovs: As Revealed by the Late Czar's Physician and His Son* (New York, 1931) pp. 102–3; Alexander, Grand Duke of Russia, *Once a Grand Duke* (New York, 1932), p. 174; Herbert Bismarck, "IV Notizen," Bismarck Papers, no. FC3018/425.

34. *GP*, 6:304–7. For Bismarck's alarm at Wilhelm's intrusion in diplomacy, see Holstein to Hatzfeldt (14 Jan. 1888), Ebel, 1:658.

35. Versions of the letter, differing slightly in details, appear in Bismarck, *GuE*, 3:136–41, Waldersee, 1:395–98; *GP*, 6:307n. On Waldersee's role in the composition of the letter, see *HP*, 2:374. For Wilhelm's attitude on preventive war with Russia, see Herbert Bismarck to Franz von Rottenburg (4 Dec. 1888), Rottenburg Papers, no. 3. On his initial resistance to the idea and the dismay this caused in the army, see Anna Wagemann, *Prinzessin Feodora: Erinnerungen an den Augustenburger and den preussischen Hof . . .* (Berlin, 1932), p. 55.

36. Holstein diary (13 May 1888), *HP*, 2:374.

37. This, in any case, was Waldersee's reasoning; Waldersee diary (16 May 1888), Waldersee, 1:399.

38. Salisbury Papers, no. 61. Holstein thought that Bismarck was in dread of running afoul of Wilhelm. See Holstein diary (27 Mar., 3, 11 Apr., 13 May 1888), *HP*, 2:365, 367, 369, 375.

39. Holstein diary (4 May 1884, 3 Apr. 1888), *HP*, 2:138, 367; Malet to Salisbury (15 Apr. 1888), Salisbury Papers, no. 61; Moritz Busch, *Tagebuchblätter*, 3 vols. (Leipzig, 1899), 3:227–28.

40. Röhl, 2:284.

41. The full text of the letter is missing, but part is printed in Count Egon Corti, *Alexander von Battenberg* (London, 1954), pp. 287–88. Its composition is described in Kleine Erwerbungen, no. 271. The quote is from a letter of Baron Marschall (to whom Wilhelm showed the letter) to Turban (9 Apr. 1888), Fuchs, 2:531.

42. Kleine Erwerbungen, no. 271; Holstein diary (31 Mar. 1888), *HP*, 2:366. On the princes' opposition, see Fuchs, 2:527, 532–37.

43. Corti, *Battenberg*, p. 290; Corti, *Wenn*, p. 472; Grand Duke to Turban (12 Apr. 1888), Fuchs, 2:535.

44. Empress Friedrich to Ludwig Bamberger (21 May 1888), Feder, *Bismarcks Grosses Spiel*, p. 371; also Corti, *Wenn*, p. 503. For her long letter on the matter to Wilhelm's old tutor Hinzpeter, see Wilhelm to the Grand Duke of Saxe-Coburg and Gotha (3 Apr. 1888), Fuchs, 2:526.

45. RA Add. MS U/32 (21 Mar., 10 Apr. 1888); Corti, *Wenn*, p. 466; Corti, *Battenberg*, pp. 294–95; Hohenlohe diary (17 May 1888), Hohenlohe, 2:435; Marschall diary (27 Apr. 1888), Fuchs, 2:542.

46. RA Add. MS A/12/1565 (Queen Victoria to Ponsonby, 9 Apr. 1888); RA Add. MS A/15/5073 (same to Duke of Connaught, 7 Apr. 1888).

47. Letter of 21 Apr. 1888, in George E. Buckle, ed., *The Letters of Queen Victoria, 1886–1901*, 3d ser., 3 vols. (London, 1930), 1:398–99. For concern in Berlin about the Queen's visit, see Holstein diary (25 Apr. 1888), *HP*, 2:373.

48. Undated letter in Charles Whibley, *Lord John Manners and His Friends*, 2 vols. (Edinburgh and London, 1925), 2:267–68; also Salisbury to Queen Victoria (21 Apr. 1888), in Lady Gwendolen Cecil, *Life of Robert, Marquis of Salisbury*, 4 vols. (London, 1921–32), 4:101–2.

49. Wedel diary (29 Apr. 1888), Wedel, pp. 29–30; Holstein diary (25 Apr. 1888), *HP*, 2:373.

50. RA Z500/2 (Queen Victoria memo, 25 Apr. 1888); RA Queen Victoria's Journal (25 Apr. 1888).

51. Wilhelm to the Grand Duke (10 June 1888), Fuchs, 2:554.

52. RA Add. MS U/32 (7 June 1887).

53. On leaving England in Sept. 1887, the Crown Princess gave her old friend Rowland Prothero a packet of letters with orders to burn it on her death, a request which Prothero followed. See Rowland Prothero, Baron Ernle, "The Empress Frederick," *The Nineteenth Century and After* 106 (Sept. 1929): 403. On the San Remo and Berlin conflagrations, see RA Z41/66 (20 June 1888).

54. Malet to Salisbury (14 June 1888), Salisbury Papers, no. 61.

55. Ibid; RA Z41/62 (13 June 1888); RA Queen Victoria's Journal (17 June 1888); Queen Victoria to the Empress Friedrich (22 June 1888), RA Add. MS U/32. See also Kessel diary (15 June 1888), BPHA, Rep. 53a, no. 29; Holstein diary (17 Apr. 1888), *HP*, 2:371. In July 1888, Queen Victoria returned some of the letters to the Empress. RA Add. MS U/32 (17 July 1888); Herbert to Otto Bismarck (4 Aug. 1888), Bussmann, p. 519. Shortly before her death in August 1901, the Empress returned the letters to Windsor; RA GV/AA 68/79 (Ponsonby to the Duchess of Argyll, 17 July 1924).

56. Eulenburg Papers, no. 81, pt. 2:39–41.

57. Malet to Salisbury (16 June 1888), Salisbury Papers, no. 61; Kessel diary (15 June 1888), BPHA, Rep. 53a, no. 29; Count Philipp Konrad zu Eulenburg to Eulenburg (17 June 1888), Röhl, 1:299.

58. Corti, *Wenn*, pp. 528–33. Friedrich III's will also expressed such a wish; ibid., p. 467.

59. Széchenyi to Szögyényi (26 June 1888), HHStA, no. 135(V).

60. Letter of 15 June 1888, Bismarck Papers, no. FC2962/1178.

CHAPTER 6

1. Wilhelm's address to the army as well as two that followed to his people and to the Reichstag are in Schulthess (1888), pp. 94–100.

2. Kessel diary (29 Nov. 1887), BPHA, Rep. 53a, no. 29; also Hans Mohs, ed., *General-Feldmarschall Alfred Graf von Waldersee in Seinem Militärischen Wirken*, 2 vols. (Berlin, 1929), 2:11; Ludwig Raschdau, *Unter Bismarck und Caprivi: Erinnerungen eines deutschen Diplomaten aus den Jahren 1885–1894* (Berlin, 1939), p. 14.

3. Wilhelm II to Prussian minister of war, Gen. Julius von Verdy du Vernois (5 July 1888), in "Akten des königlichen Militär-Kabinetts betreffend Bestimmungen gemischten Inhalts," vol. 1, GFM 26/2/00092–94.

4. Gen. Baron Paul von Schoenaich, *Mein Damaskus: Erlebnisse und Bekenntnisse* (Berlin, 1926), p. 80. See also the younger Helmuth von Moltke's letter to his wife (27 June 1888), in Eliza von Moltke, ed., *Helmuth von Moltke. Erinnerungen, Briefe, Dokumente, 1877–1916: Ein Bild vom Kriegsausbruch, erster Kriegsführung und Persönlichkeit des ersten militärischen Führers des Krieges* (Stuttgart, 1922), p. 145.

5. Wilhelm Groener, *Lebenserinnerungen: Jugend-Generalstab-Weltkrieg* (Göt-

tingen, 1957), p. 62; Baron Hugo von Freytag-Loringhoven, *Menschen und Dinge wie Ich sie in Meinem Leben Sah* (Berlin, 1923), p. 63; Waldersee, 2:150–51. On Friedrich III's similar plans, see Ebel, 2:693.

6. Waldersee diary (16 and 23 June, 7 July 1888), Waldersee, 1:405–6, 411–12. While still Crown Prince, Wilhelm had begun deciding which generals would be relieved. Wedel diary (29 Apr. 1888), Wedel, pp. 30–31.

7. For Wilhelm's intense dislike of General Emil von Albedyll, chief of the Military Cabinet, and his determination to be rid of him, see Bülow diary (13 July 1891), Bülow Papers, no. 150; Herbert to Otto Bismarck (4 Oct. 1886), Bussmann, p. 388; Waldersee diary (11 Feb., 20 Sept. 1886; 16 Apr. 1888), Waldersee, 1:274, 298, 389; Eulenburg to Count Philipp Konrad zu Eulenburg (7 May 1888), Röhl, 1:291; Wilhelm II, *Aus Meinem Leben, 1859–1888* (Berlin and Leipzig, 1927), p. 216. Even so, Wilhelm sometimes sought Albedyll's advice or help. See his letter to the general (11 Oct. 1887), Albedyll Papers.

8. For Wilhelm's treatment of Moltke, see Waldersee diary (2 May 1891), Waldersee, 2:205; for Moltke's negative opinion of Wilhelm II, see Herbert Bismarck to Rantzau (16 Dec. 1887), Bismarck Papers, no. FC3014/1011; Széchenyi to Kálnoky (19 Mar. 1892), HHStA, no. 142(B).

9. Waldersee diary (28 Jan. 1889), Waldersee, 2:34; also diary (5 July 1888), ibid., 1:410–11.

10. Isabel V. Hull, *The Entourage of Kaiser Wilhelm II, 1888–1918* (Cambridge, 1982), p. 181.

11. Eulenburg Papers, no. 75:57–60.

12. Wedel diary (9 June 1891), Wedel, p. 185.

13. On Hahnke, see Wilhelm II, *Aus Meinem Leben*, pp. 220, 236–38, and his *Ereignisse und Gestalten aus den Jahren 1878–1918* (Leipzig and Berlin, 1922), p. 20; Viktoria Luise, Grand Duchess of Brunswick-Lüneburg, *Im Glanz der Krone* (Göttingen, 1967), pp. 241–42; Karl von Einem, *Erinnerungen eines Soldaten, 1853–1933* (Leipzig, 1933), p. 53; Waldersee, 2:140–41; Bülow, 1:64–66; Hull, *Entourage*, p. 178.

14. Széchenyi to Vienna (3 Apr. 1888), HHStA, no. 137(B); Princess Marie Radziwill, *Lettres de la Princesse Radziwill au Général de Robilant, 1889–1914: Une grande dame d'avant guerre*, 4 vols. (Bologna, 1933–34), 1:4.

15. On Versen, Karl-Heinz Janssen, ed., *Die Graue Exzellenz. Zwischen Staatsräson und Vasallentreue: Aus den Papieren des kaiserlichen Gesandten Karl Georg von Treutler* (Frankfurt, 1971), pp. 41, 123; Baron Hermann von Eckardstein, *Persönliche Erinnerungen an König Eduard aus der Einkreisungszeit* (Dresden, 1927), pp. 63–69; also Wilhelm II, *Ereignisse und Gestalten*, p. 19; Ballhausen, *Bismarck-Erinnerungen*, p. 475.

16. Johannes Haller, ed. *Aus dem Leben des Fürsten Philipp zu Eulenburg-Hertefeld* (Berlin, 1924), p. 248.

17. Einem, *Erinnerungen* p. 52; Raschdau diary (2 Apr. 1897), Raschdau, *In Weimar als Preussischer Gesandter: Ein Buch der Erinnerungen an deutsche Fürstenhöfe, 1894–1897* (Berlin, 1939), p. 128; Wedel diary (9 June 1891), Wedel, p. 185.

18. Széchenyi to Kálnoky (14 May 1892), HHStA, no. 142(B).

19. Lamar Cecil, *The German Diplomatic Service, 1871–1914* (Princeton, 1976), pp. 129–34; Röhl, 1:680.

20. His grandmother, the Empress Augusta, and his uncle, the Grand Duke of Baden, both lost ground. Radziwill diary (April 1889), Radziwill, *Lettres*, 1:5, on Augusta's waning influence; on the Baden connection, see her diary (1 Feb. 1890), ibid., 29; Eugen von Jagemann, *Fünfundsiebzig Jahre des Erlebens und Erfahrens (1849–1924)* (Heidelberg, 1925), p. 115; Arthur von Brauer, *Im Dienste Bismarcks: Persönliche Erinnerungen* (Berlin, 1936), p. 341; Ludwig Bamberger diary (23 Mar. 1891), in Ernst Feder, ed., *Bismarcks Grosses Spiel: Die geheimen Tagebücher Ludwig Bamberger* (Frankfurt, 1933), p. 467. The Grand Duke's influence never entirely vanished, and Wilhelm continued to consult him until his uncle died in 1907.

21. Gerold von Gleich, *Die Alte Armee und Ihre Verirrungen: Eine kritische Studie* (Leipzig, 1919), pp. 92–93.

22. Waldersee diary (7 July, 26 Aug., 9 Oct. 1888), Waldersee, 1:411–12; 2:1, 4. For other officers critical of Wilhelm at this time, see Schoenaich, *Damaskus*, p. 82; Freytag, *Menschen und Dinge*, p. 63.

23. Eulenburg diary (31 May 1891), Eulenburg Papers, no. 15:171.

24. Röhl, 1:311. The extent to which Wilhelm involved himself in army affairs can be followed in Rijksarchief Papers, no. 595.

25. Radziwill, *Lettres*, 1:4.

26. Széchenyi to Kálnoky (2 Aug. 1888), reporting a conversation with Dr. Rudolf von Leuthold, Wilhelm's physician, and same to same (29 Dec. 1888), HHStA, no. 134(B).

27. Same to same (14 Dec. 1889), ibid., no. 138(V).

28. Memo by Gen. Karl von Einem (30 Sept. 1898), Einem Papers, no. 2:4–5.

29. Waldersee's negative judgment in Waldersee, 2:126–27, 145, 150–51; his positive view in ibid., 1:346; 2:4–5; Mohs, *Waldersee*, 2:12. For other critical observations by army officers on Wilhelm's inability to lead troops, see Caprivi to Tirpitz (19 Dec. 1889), Tirpitz Papers, no. 16; Brauer to Turban (4 June 1892), Fuchs, 3:149; Wedel, pp. 120–21; Schoenaich, *Damaskus*, pp. 82–84; Janssen, *Die Graue Exzellenz*, p. 47; Einem's undated memo, Einem Papers, no. 2:26. See also Count Anton Monts to Bülow (27 Mar. 1896), Bülow Papers, no. 106; Georg Nostitz-Rieneck, ed., *Briefe Kaiser Frans Josephs an Kaiserin Elisabeth, 1859–1898*, 2 vols. (Munich, 1966), 1:331. The few positive evaluations are in Groener, *Lebenserinnerungen*, p. 464, and D. S. Macdiarmid, *The Life of Lieut. General Sir James Moncrief Grierson . . .* (London, 1923), p. 123. The Kaiser did enjoy some reputation for his critiques. See Einem, *Erinnerungen*, p. 139; Waldersee, 2:144; Freytag-Loringhoven, *Menschen und Dinge*, p. 63; Bülow, 1:623–24.

30. Eulenburg to Holstein (4 Nov. 1889), Johannes Haller, ed., *Aus 50 Jahren: Erinnerungen, Tagebücher und Briefe aus dem Nachlass des Fürsten Philipp zu Eulenburg-Hertefeld* (Berlin, 1923), pp. 284–86; Schoenaich, *Damaskus*, pp. 83–84; Moltke, *Moltke, Erinnerungen*, pp. 304–13; Friedrich von Bernhardi, *Denkwürdigkeiten aus meinem Leben: Nach gleichzeitigen Aufzeichnungen und im Lichte der Erinnerungen* (Berlin, 1927), pp. 212, 263; Gen. Karl

Litzmann, *Lebenserinnerungen*, 2 vols. (Berlin, 1927), 1:88–89; Eulenburg Papers, no. 80:46–47; Count Robert Zedlitz-Trützschler, *Zwölf Jahre am Deutschen Kaiserhof: Aufzeichnungen* (Berlin and Leipzig, 1924), pp. 37–38.

31. For this maneuver, see Haller, *Aus 50 Jahren*, pp. 284–86; Waldersee, 2:4–5.

32. Schoenaich, *Damaskus*, pp. 82–83.

33. Waldersee, 2:4–5; Eulenburg to Holstein (4 Nov. 1889), Haller, *Aus 50 Jahren*, pp. 284–86.

34. Bernhardi, *Denkwürdigkeiten*, p. 223; Einem, *Erinnerungen*, pp. 146–47.

35. Otto Bismarck to the Crown Prince (2 Oct. 1886), Bismarck Papers, no. FC3014/917–18.

36. On Waldersee and preventive war, see Konrad Canis, *Bismarck und Waldersee: Die aussenpolitischen Kriesenerscheinungen und das Verhalten des Generalstabs 1882 bis 1890* (East Berlin, 1980), pp. 260, 268; Waldersee diary (Feb. 21, 1887), Mohs, *Waldersee*, 2:9; J. Alden Nichols, *The Year of the Three Kaisers: Bismarck and the German Succession, 1887–88* (Urbana and Chicago, 1987), pp. 67–75; also Karl-Ernst Jeismann, *Das Problem des Präventivkrieges im Europäischen Staatensystem mit besonderem Blick auf die Bismarckzeit* (Munich, 1957).

37. Edmund von Glaise-Horstenau, *Franz Josephs Weggefährte: Das Leben des Generalstabschefs Grafen Beck* . . . (Zurich, 1930), pp. 337–38. See also Ebel, 2:725, n. 11.

38. Radowitz diary (29 May 1889), in Hajo Holborn, ed., *Aufzeichnungen und Erinnerungen aus dem Leben des Botschafters Joseph Maria von Radowitz*, 2 vols. (Berlin and Leipzig, 1925), 2:297.

39. Raschdau, *Unter Bismarck und Caprivi*, p. 17.

40. Baron von Rechenberg to Waldersee (24 May, 16 June 1888), in Heinrich O. Meisner, ed., *Aus dem Briefwechsel des Generalfeldmarschalls Alfred Grafen von Waldersee: Die Berliner Jahre, 1886–1891* (Berlin and Leipzig, 1928), pp. 174, 184; also Col. Karl von Villaume, military plenipotentiary in St. Petersburg, to Herbert Bismarck (24 Apr. 1888), Bismarck Papers, no. FC2983/0791; same to Bülow (Nov. 1889), Bülow Papers, no. 22.

41. Charles Scott (secretary, British embassy, Berlin) to Salisbury (21 July 1888), FO 64/1187.

42. On the trip, see the two letters by Villaume in note 40 above, as well as Lothar v. Schweinitz to Otto Bismarck and Herbert Bismarck's memo (both July 1888), *GP*, 6:326–27; Antoine de Laboulaye (ambassador, St. Petersburg) to Goblet (25 July 1888), *DDF*, 7:193; Széchenyi to Kálnoky (2 Aug. 1888), HHStA, no. 134(B). For details on the impression the Tsar formed of the Kaiser, see Lamar Cecil, "William II and his Russian 'Colleagues,'" in Carole Fink, Isabel V. Hull, and MacGregor Knox, eds., *German Nationalism and the European Response, 1890–1945* (Norman, Okla., 1985), pp. 104–14. On Wilhelm's resentment of the Tsar's failure to return the courtesy, see Malet to Salisbury (22 June 1889), Salisbury Papers, no. 62; Villaume to Bülow (Nov. 1889), Bülow Papers, no. 22; Radowitz diary (29 May 1889), Holborn, *Aufzeichnungen Radowitz*, 2:297.

43. Waldersee diary (15 Oct. 1889), Waldersee, 2:71.

44. Waldersee to Wartenburg (21 Oct. 1889), in Heinrich O. Meisner, ed., "Briefwechsel zwischen dem Chef des Generalstabes Grafen Yorck von Wartenburg, 1885–1894," *Historisch-Politisches Archiv zur Deutschen Geschichte des 19. und 20. Jahrhunderts* 1 (1930): 174.

45. Notes by Szögyényi of a talk with Bismarck (Aug. 1889), in Helmuth Krausnick, ed., *Neue Bismarck Gespräche* . . . (Hamburg, 1940–43), pp. 60–61.

46. Baron Alois von Aehrenthal (Foreign Ministry, Vienna) to Kálnoky (17 May 1888), ibid., pp. 49–50.

47. Szögyényi's notes of a talk with Wilhelm II (Aug. 1889), ibid., pp. 68–70.

48. Order of Wilhelm II to Ministry of War (29 Mar. 1890), in Schulthess (1890), p. 27; Wedel diary (15 Apr. 1890), Wedel, pp. 90–91.

49. Széchenyi to Kálnoky (27 Feb. 1890), HHStA, no. 138(B); Schoenaich, *Damaskus*, p. 82.

50. Among the many examples, see Hinzpeter to Countess Görtz (4 Feb. 1875), Schlitz von Görtz Papers, no. 352; Ebel, 2:763; *HP*, 2:97, 346–48; Széchenyi to Kálnoky (10 Jan. 1890), HHStA, no. 138(B); Eulenburg Papers, no. 80:42; Prince Alexander von Hohenlohe, *Aus Meinem Leben* (Frankfurt/Main, 1925), p. 307.

51. RA Z47/34 (19 Feb. 1890). The genuineness of Wilhelm II's social-political ambitions has been the subject of some historical debate. Willy Real, "Die Sozialpolitik des Neuen Kurses," in Wilhelm Berges and Carl Hinrichs, eds., *Zur Geschichte und Problematik der Demokratie: Festgabe für Hans Herzfeld* (Berlin, 1957), pp. 441–57, argues that Wilhelm was committed to working class reforms but lacked the mettle to implement them. Karl Erich Born, *Staat und Politik seit Bismarcks Sturz* (Wiesbaden, 1957), pp. 20–22, holds that the Kaiser was motivated by tactical advantage and not by real concern. In her important *Wandlungen des deutschen Kaisergedankens, 1871–1918* (Munich and Vienna, 1969), pp. 196–97, Elisabeth Fehrenbach treats the question generally but tends to agree with Real.

52. RA I58/34 (Malet memo, n.d. but ca. 22 Mar. 1890). Some who knew Wilhelm II sensed this as his motive. See Radziwill, *Lettres*, 1:112–13 (5/6 Mar. 1892); Franz Ayme, *Kaiser Wilhelm II. und Seine Erziehung: Aus den Erinnerungen seines französischen Lehrers* (Leipzig, 1898), pp. 89–90.

53. Waldersee diary (11 Aug. 1890), Waldersee, 2:138.

54. Haller, *Aus 50 Jahren*, pp. 226–27; Ballhausen, *Bismarck-Erinnerungen*, pp. 507–8; Bülow, 1:105; Széchenyi to Kálnoky (7 Feb. 1890), HHStA, no. 138(B); RA Z47/32 (15 Feb. 1890). For Hinzpeter's dislike of Bismarck, see Brauer, *Im Dienste Bismarcks*, p. 117.

55. RA Z47/32 (15 Feb. 1890).

56. Boyd Carpenter "Emperor William," Boyd-Carpenter Papers, Add. MS 46765; Boyd Carpenter diary (4 Aug. 1889), ibid., Add. MS 46730. The strikes have been the subject of much attention by historians. See S. H. F. Hickey, *Workers in Imperial Germany: The Miners of the Ruhr* (Oxford, 1985), esp. chap. 5; Klaus Tenfelde, *Sozialgeschichte der Bergarbeiterschaft und der Ruhr im 19. Jahrhundert*, 2d ed. (Bonn, 1981); Wolfgang Köllmann and Albin Gladen, eds., *Der Bergarbeiterstreik von 1889 und die Gründung des 'Alten Verbandes' in Ausgewählten Dokumenten der Zeit* (Bochum, 1969): Paul Grebe, "Bismarcks

Sturz und der Bergarbeiterstreik vom Mai 1889," *Historische Zeitschrift* 157 (1938): 84–97.

57. Ballhausen diary (22/23 Nov. 1889), Ballhausen, *Bismarck-Erinnerungen*, p. 505.

58. Ibid., and diary (24 Jan. 1890), ibid., pp. 507–8; Raschdau, *Unter Bismarck und Caprivi*, p. 99; Baron Hans Hermann von Berlepsch, *Sozialpolitische Erfahrungen und Erinnerungen* (Mönchen-Gladbach, 1925), pp. 27–29; Radziwill, *Lettres*, 1:29–30.

59. Wilhelm II, "Bemerkungen zur Arbeiterfrage," dated 21 Jan. 1890, in Baron Georg von Eppstein, ed., *Fürst Bismarcks Entlassung: Nach den hinterge-lassenen . . . Aufzeichnungen des Staatssekretärs des Innern, Staatsministers Dr. Karl Heinrich von Boetticher und des Chefs der Reichskanzlei unter dem Fürsten Bismarck Dr. Franz Johannes von Rottenburg* (Berlin, 1920), pp. 152–55; Wilhelm's remarks to a deputation of strikers (14 Aug. 1889), in Schulthess (1889), p. 64. See also Hickey, *Workers in Imperial Germany*, pp. 207–8, 211.

60. Wilhelm's remarks to mine owners (16 May 1889), Schulthess (1889), p. 70; also Széchenyi to Vienna (15 May 1889), HHStA, no. 137(B).

61. Ballhausen diary (24 Jan. 1890), Ballhausen, *Bismarck-Erinnerungen*, pp. 507–8; Herbert Bismarck, "Notizen, Friedrichsruh, April 1890," Bismarck Papers, no. FC3018/312. See also Count Paul Vasili [pseud.], *La Société de Berlin* (Paris, 1884), p. 16.

62. For Bismarck's resentment at Hinzpeter's influence, see Eulenburg's "Als Bismarck ging," Eulenburg Papers, no. 76, sec. 2:16; Haller, *Aus 50 Jahren*, pp. 293–94; for "humanitarian dizziness," see Eppstein, *Bismarcks Entlassung*, p. 37. Herbert Bismarck also resented Hinzpeter's influence on Wilhelm on this question; *DDF*, 8:87–88.

63. Waddington to Ribot (21 May 1890), *DDF*, 8:87.

64. Otto Pflanze, *Bismarck and the Development of Germany*, 3 vols. (in press).

65. Ballhausen, *Bismarck-Erinnerungen*, p. 497; *GuE*, 3:58–59.

66. Eulenburg, "Als Bismarck Ging," Eulenburg Papers, no. 76, sec. 2:1, printed in somewhat different form in Haller, *Aus 50 Jahren*, pp. 224–25.

67. Herbert Bismarck, "Notizen, Friedrichsruh, April 1890," Bismarck Papers, no. FC3018/321, reporting a remark by Adjutant-General von Hahnke (ca. 25 Feb. 1890).

68. Marschall diary (30 Jan. 1889), Fuchs, 2:617.

69. Radolin to Hatzfeldt (5 June 1889), Ebel, 2:734–35.

70. Radowitz notes (late May 1889), Holborn, *Aufzeichnungen Radowitz*, 2:295.

71. Franz Fischer (*Kölnische Zeitung*) to Rudolf von Bennigsen (19 Feb. 1890), in Paul Wentzcke, ed., *Im Neuen Reich, 1871–1890: Politische Briefe aus dem Nachlass liberaler Parteiführer*, 2 vols. (1926; rpt. Osnabrück, 1967), 2:454; Ballhausen, *Bismarck-Erinnerungen*, p. 512; Count Hugo Lerchenfeld-Koefering, *Erinnerungen und Denkwürdigkeiten* (Berlin, 1935), pp. 357–58.

72. Holstein to Ida von Stülpnagel (13 Nov. 1889), Helmuth Rogge, ed., *Friedrich von Holstein: Lebensbekenntnis in Briefen an eine Frau* (Berlin, 1932), p. 152; Waldersee diary (5, 13 Nov. 1889), Waldersee, 2:76–77; Radolin to

Hatzfeldt (5 June 1889), Ebel, 2:735; Radowitz diary (29 May 1889), Holborn, *Aufzeichnungen Radowitz*, 2:298; Raschdau, *Unter Bismarck und Caprivi*, p. 72.

73. Szögyényi's notes of a talk with Wilhelm II (Aug. 1889), in Krausnick, *Neue Bismarck Gespräche*, pp. 68–70; Wilhelm von Scholz, ed., *Staatsminister Adolf von Scholz: Erlebnisse und Gespräche mit Bismarck* (Stuttgart and Berlin, 1922), pp. 81–82.

74. Lt. Col. Baron Moritz von Bissing (adjutant to Wilhelm II) to Bismarck (22 June 1888), in *GuE*, 3:172.

75. Spitzemberg diary (6 Mar. 1891), Rudolf Vierhaus, ed., *Das Tagebuch der Baronin Spitzemberg geb. Freiin v. Varnbüler: Aufzeichnungen aus der Hofgesellschaft des Hohenzollernreiches* (Göttingen, 1960), pp. 289–90; *GuE*, 3:35, 48. In the copy annotated by Wilhelm (BPHA Rep. 53a, no. 42/1, p. 48) he denies he was ever so advised.

76. Stosch to Frau von Rosenstiel (17 May 1888), in Frederic B. M. Hollyday, *Bismarck's Rival: A Political Biography of General and Admiral Albrecht von Stosch* (Durham, N.C., 1960), p. 242.

77. Herbert to Holstein (24, 26 Aug. 1888), *HP*, 3:127–29; same to Bülow (27 Aug. 1884), same to Wilhelm Bismarck (11 Feb. 1888), Bussmann, 254–55, 506. Also *HP*, 1:137.

78. Herbert to Wilhelm Bismarck (11 Feb. 1888), same to Rantzau (4 July 1889), Bussmann, pp. 506, 540–41.

79. Waldersee diary (28 Feb. 1889), Waldersee, 2:41–42; see also ibid., 1:282, 299.

80. Waldersee to Verdy (14 Aug. 1889), ibid. 2:66–67.

81. Hohenlohe, 2:466–67; Waldersee diary (18 Jan. 1890), Waldersee, 2:94–95.

82. Diary (13 Nov. 1889), Waldersee, 2:77.

83. See Fritz Stern's important *Gold and Iron: Bismarck, Bleichröder and the Building of the German Empire* (New York, 1977), pp. 342–49, 439–50.

84. Lamar Cecil, "Jew and Junker in Imperial Berlin," Leo Baeck Institute, *Year Book* 20 (1975): 47–58. On the prejudice specifically directed against Bleichröder, see Marie von Bunsen, *Die Welt in der ich Lebte: Erinnerungen aus glücklichen Jahren, 1860–1912* (Leipzig, 1929), p. 49; Vasili, *Société de Berlin*, pp. 155–59; Princess Catherine Radziwill, *Memories of Forty Years* (New York and London, 1915), pp. 68, 150; Count Bogdan von Hutten-Czapski, *Sechzig Jahre Politik und Gesellschaft*, 2 vols. (Berlin, 1936), 1:63; Count Johann-Heinrich Bernstorff, *Memoirs* (New York, 1936), p. 27; Brauer, *Im Dienste Bismarcks*, p. 208; Vierhaus, *Tagebuch Spitzemberg*, pp. 130, 138; Johannes Werner, ed., *Maxe von Arnim, Tochter Bettinas, Gräfin Oriola, 1818–1894 . . .* (Leipzig, 1937), pp. 269–70; *HP*, 2:313; Count Axel von Schwering [pseud.], *The Berlin Court under William II* (London, 1915), p. 211.

85. For Eulenburg's prejudice against Jews, see Cecil, *German Diplomatic Service*, pp. 99–100; for Herbert Bismarck's, see *HP*, 3:104, 107; Herbert to Franz von Rottenburg (Aug. 8, 1882), Rottenburg Papers, no. 2.

86. Waldersee to Wilhelm (21 Nov. 1887), Canis, *Bismarck und Waldersee*, p. 255; same to Verdy (14 Aug. 1889), Waldersee, 2:66–67.

87. Eppstein, *Bismarcks Entlassung*, pp. 108–15; Count Maximilian von Ber-

chem to Herbert Bismarck (27 June 1889), Bismarck Papers, no. FC2954/389–90.

88. Waldersee diary (7 July 1889), Waldersee, 2:55.

89. On the Kaiserin, see her letters to Caroline Mathilda (30 Mar., 31 Dec. 1881, 21 June 1886), Glücksburg Papers, nos. 2 and 7; Waldersee diary (27 Aug. 1888), Waldersee, 2:2; Széchenyi to Kálnoky (5 Apr. 1890), HHStA, no. 138(B); for Waldersee, see his diary (27 Aug. 1889), Waldersee, 2:2; for Eulenburg, Eulenburg Papers, no. 7:206–8; Haller, *Aus 50 Jahren*, pp. 220, 225, 246. On Liebenau's unfortunate personality, see Kleine Erwerbungen, no. 814; Bülow, 1:75; Countess Mathilde von Keller, *Vierzig Jahre im Dienste der Kaiserin: Ein Kulturbild aus den Jahren 1881–1921* (Leipzig, 1935), pp. 131–32; *HP*, 3:347, and Eulenburg Papers, no. 17:206–8.

90. Eulenburg Papers, no. 7:206–8; Haller, *Aus 50 Jahren*, p. 246.

91. Waldersee diary (17, 25 Nov. 1888), Waldersee, 2:78, 80.

92. Eulenburg Papers, no. 7:206–8; Haller, *Aus 50 Jahren*, p. 225; also Eulenburg to Wilhelm II (3 Dec. 1889), Röhl, 1:381.

93. Brauer, *Im Dienste Bismarcks*, p. 126; *GW*, 8:622.

94. *HP*, 2:207, 219.

95. Ibid., 360–61; Eulenburg to Bülow (29 Jan. 1890), Haller, *Aus 50 Jahren*, p. 289.

96. Herbert to Otto Bismarck (5 Oct. 1888), Bussmann, p. 523; same to Holstein (17 Oct. 1888), *HP*, 3:301.

97. Radolinski to Hatzfeldt (15 Jan. 1888), Ebel, 1:661. See also the following for the mutual decline in the relationship: Holstein diary (11 Jan. and 17 Apr. 1888), *HP*, 2:360, 371; Waldersee diary (18 Mar. 1888), 1:375–76; Hohenlohe notes (7 Mar. 1888), Hohenlohe 2:428; Siegfried von Kardorff, *Wilhelm von Kardorff: Ein nationaler Parlamentarier im Zeitalter Bismarcks und Wilhelms II., 1828–1907* (Berlin, 1936), p. 207; *DDF*, 7:555.

98. Herbert to Wilhelm Bismarck (25 Feb. 1890), Bismarck Papers, no. FC3011/601.

99. Eulenburg to his mother (4 Oct., 17 Dec. 1888), Röhl, 1:313–15, 324; Herbert to Otto Bismarck (5 Oct. 1888), Bussmann, p. 523. For another rebuff by Herbert of Wilhelm's attempts to introduce his friends into the diplomatic service, see Wied Papers.

100. Waddington to Léopold Flourens (foreign minister) (12 Mar. 1888), *DDF*, 7:87; Brauer, *Im Dienste Bismarcks*, p. 300; also Waldersee diary 10 (May 1888), Waldersee, 1:398–99.

101. Herbert Bismarck to Rantzau (4 July 1889), Bussmann, pp. 539–40. For the Kaiser's triviality, see Waldersee diary (11 Oct. 1888, 13 Nov. 1889, 4 Oct. 1890), Waldersee, 2:6, 77, 153; Kiderlen to Holstein (16, 25 July 1888; 3 Aug. 1891), Holstein to Radolin (28 Nov. 1889), in *HP*, 3:280, 291, 323, 383.

102. Baron Hermann von Mittnacht, *Erinnerungen an Bismarck: Neue Folge* (Stuttgart, 1905), p. 53.

103. Brauer, *Im Dienste Bismarcks*, p. 118; Eulenburg to Bülow (29 Jan. 1890), Haller, *Aus 50 Jahren*, p. 289.

104. For Dona's resentment of the chancellor and his son, see the following: Dona to Caroline Mathilda (5 Apr. 1890), Glücksburg Papers, no. 11; Bülow,

1:230, 263; Eulenburg's notes (1 Aug. 1898), Eulenburg Papers, no. 51:234–36; Holstein to Eulenburg (9 May 1895), ibid., 64; Haller, *Aus 50 Jahren*, pp. 220, 247; Waldersee diary (8 Feb., 24 Oct. 1888), Waldersee, 1:358–59, 2:11; also Bülow, 1:263; Brauer, *Im Dienste Bismarcks*, pp. 301–2. She also seems to have believed that Bismarck had opposed her marriage; Bülow's notes, Bülow Papers, no. 153:341. The chancellor in fact thought highly of Dona. Brauer, *Im Dienste Bismarcks*, pp. 284–85; Holborn, *Aufzeichnungen Radowitz*, 2:295.

105. Holstein to Karl von Eisendecher (Prussian minister to Baden) (16 Apr. 1890), *HP*, 3:337.

106. Holstein diary (11 Jan. 1888), *HP*, 2:360–61.

107. Radowitz's report of a conversation with the chancellor (late May 1889), Holborn, *Aufzeichnungen Radowitz*, 2:295.

108. Moritz Busch, *Tagebuchblätter*, 3 vols. (Leipzig, 1899), 3:249; also Brauer, *Im Dienste Bismarcks*, p. 265; Holborn, *Aufzeichnungen Radowitz*, 2:295.

109. Herbert Bismarck to Holstein (17 Oct. 1888), *HP*, 3:301; Radolin to Hatzfeldt (5 June 1889), Ebel, 2:735.

110. Bismarck to Adolf von Scholz (2 Aug. 1888), Scholz, *Staatsminister von Scholz*, pp. 84–89; Holstein to Ida von Stülpnagel (Nov. 1889), Rogge, *Holstein: Lebensbekenntnis*, p. 152. See also Lerchenfeld, *Erinnerungen*, p. 346; Waldersee to Baron von Rechenberg (29 May 1889), Heinrich O. Meisner, ed., *Aus dem Briefwechsel des Generalfeldmarschalls Alfred Grafen von Waldersee: Die Berliner Jahre, 1886–1891* (Berlin and Leipzig, 1928), p. 292; Waldersee diary (13 Nov. 1889), Waldersee, 2:76.

111. Ballhausen diary (31 Dec. 1887), Ballhausen, *Bismarck-Erinnerungen*, p. 413; Scholz, *Staatsminister von Scholz*, pp. 81–82.

112. Haller, *Aus 50 Jahren*, pp. 229–30.

113. Waldersee to Rechenberg (29 May 1889), Meisner, *Briefwechsel Waldersee*, p. 292.

114. Waldersee diary (13 Nov. 1889), Waldersee, 2:76.

115. Letter to Ida von Stülpnagel (Nov. 1889), Rogge, *Holstein: Lebensbekenntnis*, p. 152,

CHAPTER 7

1. Malet to Lady Malet (15 Dec. 1889), Malet Papers, no. A-34.

2. Baron Georg von Eppstein, *Fürst Bismarcks Entlassung: Nach den hintergelassenen . . . Aufzeichnungen des Staatssekretärs des Innern, Staatsministers Dr. Karl Heinrich von Boetticher und des Chefs der Reichskanzlei unter dem Fürsten Bismarck Dr. Franz Johannes von Rottenburg* (Berlin, 1920), p. 35, n. 11; the letter to Bismarck is in Schulthess (1890), p. 1. The memorandum has not survived.

3. RA I58/34 (Malet memo, n.d. [21 Mar. 1890]).

4. Boetticher to Bismarck (5 Jan. 1890), Eppstein, *Bismarcks Entlassung*, p. 120.

5. Eppstein, *Bismarcks Entlassung*, pp. 77–78; Johannes Haller, ed., *Aus 50 Jahren: Erinnerungen, Tagebücher und Briefe aus dem Nachlass des Fürsten Philipp zu Eulenburg-Hertefeld* (Berlin, 1923), p. 225.

6. Röhl, 1:406, n. 3, for a 1914 memo by Eulenburg on this conversation; also Eulenburg's undated notes in Eulenburg Papers, no. 8:22–25.

7. Marschall to the Grand Duke (3 Mar. 1890), Fuchs, 2:736–38.

8. Same to same (18 Feb. 1890), ibid., 723.

9. Eulenburg's notes of his talk with Wilhelm II on 13 Jan. 1890, Röhl, 1:406, n. 3.

10. Baron Robert Lucius von Ballhausen, *Die Entlassung des Fürsten Bismarck, März 1890* (Stuttgart, 1922), pp. 28–29. For Bismarck's irritability, see Széchenyi to Kálnoky (19 Feb. 1890), HHStA, no. 138(B); Arthur von Brauer, *Im Dienste Bismarcks: Persönliche Erinnerungen* (Berlin, 1936), p. 302; Count Hugo Lerchenfeld-Koefering, *Erinnerungen und Denkwürdigkeiten* (Berlin, 1935), pp. 242, 349–50; Eppstein, *Bismarcks Entlassung*, p. 90. Herbert Bismarck declared that *he* was also at the end of his rope. Letter to Eulenburg (3 Feb. 1890), in Haller, *Aus 50 Jahren*, p. 291.

11. Brauer, *Im Dienste Bismarcks*, p. 301; Bismarck's conversation (Aug. 1888) with Francesco Crispi, *GW*, 8:622. On the generally satisfactory course of Bismarck's relations with Wilhelm II in 1889 and how suddenly the January 1890 crisis came about, see Brauer, *Im Dienste Bismarcks*, p. 300, Lerchenfeld, *Erinnerungen*, p. 358. Of the twenty-one months that elapsed between Wilhelm II's ascension on 15 June 1888 and Bismarck's dismissal on 21 March 1890, the chancellor apparently spent almost twelve months on his estates. See Otto Pflanze, *Bismarck and the Development of Germany*, 3 vols. (in press).

12. RA I58/34 (Malet memo, n.d., but ca. 22 Mar. 1890).

13. Herbert to Otto Bismarck (23 Jan. 1890), Bussmann, pp. 559–60.

14. See John C. G. Röhl, "The Disintegration of the *Kartell* and the Politics of Bismarck's Fall from Power, 1887–1890," *Historical Journal* 9, no. 1 (1966): 60–89, which carefully examines Bismarck's strategy but which advances an unconvincing claim that it was differences over the *Kartell* that were *singularly* responsible for Bismarck's crisis with the Kaiser in 1890.

15. Undated memo by Boetticher, in Eppstein, *Bismarcks Entlassung*, p. 43, and Lucius von Ballhausen, *Entlassung Bismarck*, pp. 7–8.

16. Protocol of meeting in Eppstein, *Bismarcks Entlassung*, pp. 44–47. Various accounts by participants also by Herbert Bismarck in his "Notizen, Friedrichruh, April 1890," Bismarck Papers, no. FC3018/310; Otto Bismarck in *GuE*, 3:54–56; Lucius von Ballhausen, *Entlassung Bismarck*, pp. 9-11, and his *Bismarck-Erinnerungen* (Stuttgart and Berlin, 1921), pp. 507–10; Wilhelm II to the Grand Duke (24 Jan. 1890), Fuchs, 2:697; Wilhelm II, *Ereignisse und Gestalten aus den Jahren 1878–1918* (Leipzig and Berlin, 1922), pp. 28–29. For Wilhelm's expert conduct of the meeting, see Paul Kayser to Eulenburg (1 Mar. 1890), Holstein to same (7 Mar. 1890), Marschall to same (12 Mar. 1890), in Röhl, 1:460–62, 482, 493. A few minor details of the meeting are in Waldemar Müller, *Dr. August Pflug: Aus Leben und Geheimkanzlei unter Bismarck, 1860–1914* (Berlin, 1942), pp. 188–90.

17. Both memoranda printed in Eppstein, *Bismarcks Entlassung*, pp. 146–55.

The second incorporates verbatim passages in a letter of Kayser to Eulenburg (19 Jan. 1890), Röhl, 1:415–16. For Kayser's association with Hinzpeter, see Holstein to Eulenburg (6 Dec. 1890), Röhl, 1:611.

18. *GuE*, 3:58; Baron Robert Lucius von Ballhausen, *Bismarck-Erinnerungen* (Stuttgart and Berlin, 1920), p. 509.

19. Ballhausen, *Bismarck-Erinnerungen*, p. 509.

20. Undated memo by Boetticher, Eppstein, *Bismarcks Entlassung*, p. 47.

21. Marschall to Grand Duke (18 Feb. 1890), Fuchs, 2:723; Hubert Richter, ed., "Aus Kritischen Tagen: Berichte des königlichen sächsischen Gesandten in Berlin, Grafen Hohenthal und Bergen, aus den Jahren 1889–1892," *Deutsche Rundschau* 190 (1922): 158–59.

22. Undated memo by Boetticher, Eppstein, *Bismarcks Entlassung*, p. 49.

23. Ibid.; Ballhausen diary (29 Jan. 1890), Ballhausen, *Bismarck-Erinnerungen*, pp. 512–13.

24. Széchenyi to Kálnoky (7 Feb. 1890), HHStA, no. 138(B).

25. Kurowsky notes (31 Jan. 1890), Kurowsky Papers, no. 3; undated memo by Boetticher, Eppstein, *Bismarcks Entlassung*, pp. 50–52.

26. Undated memo by Boetticher, in Eppstein, *Bismarcks Entlassung*, p. 50.

27. Herbette to Spuller (11 Feb. 1890), *DDF*, 7:606–7.

28. Hohenthal und Bergen report (31 Jan. 1890), in Richter, "Aus Kritischen Tagen," p. 158.

29. Memo by Wilhelm II (22 Jan. 1890), in Eppstein, *Bismarcks Entlassung*, p. 148.

30. "Secret" memo by Malet for Salisbury, recording a conversation with Wilhelm II on 21 Mar. 1890, Salisbury Papers, no. 63.

31. Kurowsky notes (31 Jan. 1890), Kurowsky Papers, no. 3.

32. Caprivi to Max Schneidewin (28 Dec. 1894), Schneidewin, "Briefe des Toten Reichskanzlers von Caprivi," *Deutsche Revue* 47, no. 5 (1922): 142–43.

33. Bismarck's recommendation of Caprivi is in Eulenburg's notes (n.d. but probably ca. 1903), Eulenburg Papers, no. 59:125–26; see also Haller, *Aus 50 Jahren*, p. 255; Wedel diary (19 Mar. 1890), Wedel, p. 46; Lerchenfeld, *Erinnerungen*, p. 369. Marschall later claimed that Bismarck had in fact *not* nominated Caprivi. Malet to Salisbury (1 July 1892), FO 64/1274. On Waldersee and Bülow, see Waldersee's diary (17 Mar. 1890, 2 Aug. 1891), Waldersee, 2:118, 214; on Friedrich III, Ballhausen, *Entlassung Bismarck*, p. 26.

34. Caprivi's appointment as chancellor in March took Eulenburg by surprise. See his letter to Holstein (18 Mar. 1890), Eulenburg Papers, no. 10:279.

35. Adolf von Scholz (Prussian minister of finance) diary (7 Feb. 1890), in Wilhelm von Scholz, ed., *Staatsminister Adolf von Scholz: Erlebnisse und Gespräche mit Bismarck* (Stuttgart and Berlin, 1922), pp. 102–4; Bismarck to Prince Albrecht of Prussia (23 Mar. 1890), Bismarck Papers, no. FC2952/464.

36. Herbette to Spuller (6 Feb. 1890), *DDF*, 7:601; for the importance public opinion attributed to the two decrees, see Schulthess (1890), pp. 19–20; see also Ballhausen, *Bismarck-Erinnerungen*, p. 515.

37. Ballhausen diary (4 Feb. 1890), Ballhausen, *Bismarck-Erinnerungen*, p. 515.

38. Siegfried von Kardorff, ed., *Wilhelm von Kardorff: Ein nationaler Parla-*

mentarier im Zeitalter Bismarcks und Wilhelms II., *1828–1907* (Berlin, 1936), p. 219. Another account of this dinner is in Max von Eynern, ed., *Ernst von Eynern: Erinnerungen aus seinem Leben* (n.p., 1909), pp. 298–300. See also Bismarck's similar statement a few days later to the French ambassador; Herbette to Spuller (10 Feb. 1890), *DDF*, 7:606.

39. See the useful discussion in Michael Stürmer, "Staatsstreichgedanken im Bismarckreich," *Historische Zeitschrift* 209 (1967): 566–615, and in Egmont Zechlin, *Staatsstreichpläne Bismarcks und Wilhelms II.*, *1890–1894* (Stuttgart and Berlin, 1929), pt. 1. See also John C. G. Röhl, "Bismarcks Politik in der Entlassungskrise," *Historische Zeitschrift* 203 (1966): 610–24.

40. RA I58/16 (Malet to Salisbury, 12 Feb. 1890).

41. Ibid. Malet discussed the age issue in a letter to his mother (13 Feb. 1890), Malet Papers, no. A-35. "I take it he is not pleased at his young master's activity. There is a long difference between 75 and 32 and they can hardly meet on common ground." Bismarck was in fact 74 and Wilhelm 31 at the time.

42. For Bismarck's condemnation of Hinzpeter, see Ballhausen, *Entlassung Bismarck*, p. 15, and Gustav Adolf Rein, Wilhelm Schüssler, Alfred Milatz, et al., eds., *Otto von Bismarck: Werke im Auswahl*, 8 vols. (Stuttgart, 1962–83), 8b:66.

43. Count Friedrich Vitzthum von Eckstädt to Bülow (12 Apr. 1890), Bülow Papers, no. 127. Bismarck's ministerial colleagues made the same complaint. Waldersee diary (13 Nov. 1889), Waldersee, 2:77. See also Haller, *Aus 50 Jahren*, p. 229.

44. Haller, *Aus 50 Jahren*, pp. 229–30; also Marschall to Grand Duke (3 Mar. 1890), Fuchs, 2:736–37.

45. Bosse Papers, no. 15a and no. 16:90–92.

46. RA Z47/34 (19 Feb. 1890); Herbette to Spuller (10, 11 Feb. 1890), *DDF*, 7:603–5.

47. Eulenburg notes of talk with Wilhelm II (12 July 1896), Eulenburg Papers, no. 42:486–87, partially printed in Haller, *Aus 50 Jahren*, p. 269.

48. Marschall to Grand Duke (3, 5 Mar. 1890), Fuchs, 2:736, 744.

49. On the Grand Duke, see his letter to Eulenburg (23 Nov. 1889), Fuchs, 2:683–84; Waldersee diary (18 Jan. 1890), Waldersee, 2:94–95; Hohenlohe diary (21 Apr. 1890), Hohenlohe, 2:466–67; Ernst Feder, ed., *Bismarcks Grosses Spiel: Die geheimen Tagebücher Ludwig Bambergers* (Frankfurt, 1933), p. 467. Bismarck later felt the Grand Duke had been responsible for his fall. Ludwig Raschdau, *In Weimar als Preussischer Gesandter: Ein Buch der Erinnerungen an deutsche Fürstenhöfe, 1894–1897* (Berlin, 1939), p. 48. On Hinzpeter, Holstein to Eulenburg (1 Feb. 1890), Röhl, 1:428. See also Haller, *Aus 50 Jahren*, p. 231. On Waldersee, see his diary (15 Mar. 1890), Waldersee, 2:115–16.

50. The order is printed in Schulthess (1890), p. 47. On the meeting of 2 March, Zechlin, *Staatsstreichpläne*, pp. 178–84; Marschall to Grand Duke (2 Mar. 1890), Fuchs, 2:736–38.

51. For Wilhelm II on Windthorst, see Boyd Carpenter diary (4 Aug. 1889), Boyd-Carpenter Papers, Add. MS 46730; Wedel, pp. 106–7; also Waldersee, 2:114; Wilhelm II, *Ereignisse und Gestalten*, p. 82. On his suspicion of a Center-

Conservative pact, see Herbert to Otto Bismarck (6 Jan. 1890), Bismarck Papers, no. FC3004/1125. On Bismarck's dealings with Windthorst in early March 1890, see Margaret Lavinia Anderson, *Windthorst: A Political Biography* (Oxford, 1981), pp. 385–88.

52. Waldersee diary (15 Mar. 1890), Waldersee, 2:114.

53. Bismarck's accounts of the meeting in *GuE*, 3:81–87; Ballhausen, *Bismarck-Erinnerungen*, pp. 522–23; Wilhelm's account is in Eulenburg Papers, no. 76, pt. 2:21–24; Waldersee diary (15 Mar. 1890), Waldersee, 2:114–16.

54. *GuE*, 3:87.

55. This was Bismarck's view. See Freytag to Stosch (26 Aug. 1890), in Hans F. Helmolt, *Gustav Freytags Briefe an Albrecht von Stosch* (Stuttgart and Bonn, 1913), pp. 236–37. Bismarck's two most recent biographers, Otto Pflanze and Lothar Gall, treat the resignation crisis as prompted by various disagreements on internal policy, regarding the clash over Russian policy as secondary. Both— Pflanze with more detail and clarity—argue that the cause of Bismarck's fall lay in his contest of will with the Kaiser, for which the various internal issues merely provided ammunition. To Pflanze, Bismarck in the course of 1889 turned not only against socialism but against labor at large, blaming it for the continuing unrest. He was therefore determined to reject Wilhelm's conciliatory gestures to the working class. Gall also sees Bismarck as obsessed, but less over issues than power. He was determined to retain his personal authority and incapable of tolerating rivals or of recognizing any considerations other than those that affected his own position. See Pflanze, *Bismarck and the Development of Germany*; Gall, *Bismarck: The White Revolutionary*, trans. J. A. Underwood, 2 vols. (London, 1986), esp. 2:chap. 16.

56. Haller, *Aus 50 Jahren*, pp. 235–36.

57. Waldersee diary (15 Mar. 1890), Waldersee, 2:115.

58. Waldersee diary (17 Mar. 1890), ibid., 117; Haller, *Aus 50 Jahren*, pp. 224–25.

59. Wilhelm's note is printed in *GuE*, 3:88.

60. Notes by Otto Bismarck (ca. 1891), given by Herbert Bismarck to Bülow, Bülow Papers, no. 66; *GuE*, 3:89–90, 92.

61. Wilhelm's concern at Bismarck's getting the military bill through the Reichstag is in Scholz, *Staatsminister von Scholz*, pp. 103–7; Lerchenfeld, *Erinnerungen*, pp. 361–64.

62. Haller, *Aus 50 Jahren*, p. 237; Waldersee diary (17 Mar. 1890), Waldersee, 2:117; Hohenlohe diary (26 Apr. 1890), Hohenlohe, 2:467–69.

63. *GuE*, 3:90–93; also protocol of ministry meeting in Eppstein, *Bismarcks Entlassung*, pp. 179–88.

64. On Lucanus's mission, see Haller, *Aus 50 Jahren*, p. 240. Bismarck's letter of resignation is printed in *GuE*, 3:95–100.

65. Ballhausen diary (19 Mar. 1890), Ballhausen, *Bismarck-Erinnerungen*, p. 524.

66. Gen. Walter Bronsart von Schellendorf diary (19 Mar. 1890), in Eberhard Kessel, "Bismarck und die Halbgötter," *Historische Zeitschrift* 181, no. 2 (1956): 284, n. 1; Waldersee diary (19 Mar. 1890), Waldersee, 2:118–19; Hohenlohe diary (31 Mar. 1890), Hohenlohe, 2:466.

67. Karl-Heinz Janssen, ed., *Die Graue Exzellenz. Zwischen Staatsräson und Vasallentreue: Aus den Papieren des kaiserlichen Gesandten Karl Georg von Treutler* (Frankfurt, 1971), p. 117.

68. Ballhausen diary (19 Mar. 1890), Ballhausen *Bismarck-Erinnerungen*, p. 524.

69. Hohenlohe, 2:465–66; also Count August zu Eulenburg to Eulenburg (22 Mar. 1890), Röhl, 1:509.

70. Kenneth Rose, *King George V* (London, 1983), p. 166.

71. Radowitz diary (25 Mar. 1890), in Hajo Holborn, ed., *Aufzeichnungen und Erinnerungen aus dem Leben des Botschafters Joseph Maria von Radowitz*, 2 vols. (Berlin and Leipzig), 2:321. King Carol of Rumania thought that the way Bismarck had been dismissed augured poorly for the future. Bülow Papers, no. 147: Merkblatt 39.

72. August Eulenburg to Eulenburg (22 Mar. 1890), Röhl, 1:509.

73. The only source is Scholz, *Staatsminister von Scholz*, pp. 118–19.

74. *GuE*, 3:102–4.

75. Waldersee diary (18 Feb. 1890), Waldersee, 2:103.

76. August Eulenburg to Eulenburg (22 Mar. 1890), Röhl, 1:508; Malet to Salisbury (25 Mar. 1890), FO 64/1234; Hohenthal und Bergen report (24 Mar. 1890), in Richter, "Aus Kritischen Tagen," 167; Széchenyi to Kálnoky (23 Mar. 1890), HHStA, no. 138(B).

77. Holstein to Karl von Eisendecher (Prussian envoy in Baden) (26 Mar. 1890), *HP*, 3:332; for an earlier complaint about Wilhelm by Herbert, see Eulenburg to Holstein (21 June 1889), Eulenburg Papers, no. 6:108–9. See also Herbert's letter to Sir Charles Dilke (30 Mar. 1890), Dilke Papers, British Library, Add. MS 43914.

78. Haller, *Aus 50 Jahren*, p. 249; Herbert Bismarck to Archibald Primrose, Fifth Earl of Rosebery (30 Mar. 1890), Bussmann, p. 567; same to Bülow (7 May 1890), Bülow, 4:644; Ludwig Raschdau, *Unter Bismarck und Caprivi: Erinnerungen eines deutschen Diplomaten aus den Jahren 1885–1894* (Berlin, 1939), pp. 134–35.

79. *HP*, 1:157–58; Kardorff, *Wilhelm von Kardorff*, pp. 221–22; notes by Franz von Rottenburg (1905), in Eppstein, *Bismarcks Entlassung*, p. 91.

80. Herbert Bismarck to Wilhelm II (21 Mar. 1890), Bussmann, p. 565; same to Wilhelm Bismarck (25 Feb. 1890), Bismarck Papers, no. FC3011/601, on foreign policy. On socialism, see Bülow to Eulenburg (28 Aug. 1890), Röhl, 1:563–64.

81. Scholz, *Staatsminister von Scholz*, pp. 118–19.

82. On Bismarck's uncertainty as to the cause of his downfall, Lerchenfeld, *Erinnerungen*, p. 361; Bismarck to Prince Albrecht of Prussia (28 Mar. 1890), in Rein et al., *Bismarck: Werke im Auswahl*, 8b:3; Bismarck's conversation with Adolf von Heerwart (27 Mar. 1890), ibid., 8; undated memo by Philipp Zorn, Zorn Papers, no. 26. See also Bismarck's account of the crisis in Széchenyi to Vienna (25 Mar. 1890), HHStA, no. 138(B), in which he argues his health is excellent; *GW*, 9:6–7; RA I58/36 (Malet to Queen Victoria, 29 Mar. 1890).

83. Two telegrams by Széchenyi to Vienna (22 Mar. 1890), HHStA, no.

138(B); RA, Queen Victoria's Journal (29 Mar. 1890); RA I58/32 (Wilhelm to Queen Victoria, 27 Mar. 1890)

84. Report of 24 Mar. 1890, in Richter, "Aus Kritischen Tagen," pp. 167–68.

85. "Secret" memo by Malet, sent to Salisbury on 22 Mar. 1890, Salisbury Papers, no. 62; Salisbury to Queen Victoria (7 Apr. 1890), in George E. Buckle, ed., *The Letters of Queen Victoria*, 3d ser., 3 vols. (London, 1930), 1:591; also Széchenyi to Kálnoky (22 Mar. 1890), HHStA, no. 138(B).

86. RA Add. U/228 (extract of letter of 3 Apr. 1890). There is no copy of this letter in the Kabinetts-Archiv papers. Wilhelm wrote again to Franz Josef on 14 April (Kabinetts-Archiv, Geheim Akten, vol. 2) that Bismarck's insistence on managing Germany's diplomatic affairs had made it impossible for him to know what was going on.

87. For Wilhelm's jealousy, see Waldersee diary (25 Jan. 1890), Waldersee, 1:96–97; his concern at the decline in Hohenzollern prestige is in Kardorff, *Wilhelm von Kardorff*, pp. 221–22.

88. *GuE*, 3:108.

CHAPTER 8

1. For Caprivi's modest appraisal of his suitability as chancellor, see Max Schneidewin, "Briefe des Toten Reichskanzlers von Caprivi," *Deutsche Revue* 47, no. 5 (1922): 142–43; Holstein to Hatzfeldt (20 Mar. 1890), Ebel, 2:766; *GuE*, 3:114; Heinrich O. Meisner, *Der Reichskanzler Caprivi: Eine biographische Skizze* (Darmstadt, 1969), p. 6, n. 7; Karl Alexander von Müller, "Die Entlassung: Nach den bayerischen Gesandtschaftsberichten," *Süddeutsche Monatshefte* 19, no. 1 (1921): 169; Otto Hammann, *Der Neue Kurs: Erinnerungen* (Berlin, 1918), p. 26. On the temporary nature of Caprivi's appointment, Waldersee diary (20, 22 Mar. 1890), Waldersee, 2:119, 121; for suspicion that Caprivi was only a stalking horse for Waldersee, see Gustav Freytag to his wife (22 Mar. 1890), in his *Briefe an Seine Gattin* (Berlin, n.d.), pp. 460–61.

2. Major von Ebmeyer, "Caprivis Entlassung," *Deutsche Revue* 47, no. 12 (1922): 206; Lt. Gen. August Keim, *Erlebtes und Erstrebtes: Lebenserinnerungen* (Hanover, 1925), p. 54.

3. Holstein to Hatzfeldt (22 Mar. 1890), Ebel, 2:766.

4. Hohenthal und Bergen report (24 Mar. 1890), in Hubert Richter, ed., "Aus Kritischen Tagen: Berichte des königlichen sächsischen Gesandten in Berlin, Grafen Hohenthal und Bergen, aus den Jahren 1889–1892," *Deutsche Rundschau* 190 (1922): 168.

5. Bülow to Eulenburg (6 Apr. 1892), Röhl, 2:842–43.

6. Lamar Cecil, *The German Diplomatic Service, 1871–1914* (Princeton, 1976), pp. 245, 264–68.

7. Holstein to Eulenburg (27 Mar. 1890), Röhl, 1:516. On Marschall's appointment, ibid., p. 512, n. 5; Norman Rich, *Friedrich von Holstein: Politics and Diplomacy in the Era of Bismarck and Wilhelm II*, 2 vols. (Cambridge, 1965),

1:289–92; J. Alden Nichols, *Germany after Bismarck: The Caprivi Era, 1890–1894* (Cambridge, Mass., 1958), pp. 51–52; Arthur von Brauer, *Im Dienste Bismarcks: Persönliche Erinnerungen* (Berlin, 1936), pp. 330–31; Wedel diary (27 Mar. 1890), Wedel, pp. 60–62. For the surprise Marschall's appointment occasioned, see Malet to Salisbury (29 Mar. 1890), FO 64/1234, and the references in Cecil, *German Diplomatic Service*, p. 260, n. 14.

8. Bülow, 4:639; Baron Hermann von Eckardstein, *Lebenserinnerungen u. Politische Denkwürdigkeiten*, 3 vols. (Leipzig, 1919–21), 1:131.

9. Eulenburg to Wilhelm II (26 Mar. 1890), Röhl, 1:513. Under State Secretary Count Berchem also recommended Marschall to Caprivi. See RA I58/38 (abstract of letter by Malet to Salisbury, 5 Apr. 1890).

10. Marschall's letter (12 Mar. 1890), in Röhl, 1:493–96; Eulenburg to Wilhelm II (14 Mar. 1890), ibid., 497–98. For Marschall's admiration for the Kaiser at this time, see Eulenburg diary (17 Feb. 1890), Eulenburg Papers, no. 9:135–36.

11. Malet to Salisbury (29 Mar. 1890), FO 64/1234.

12. RA I58/36 (Malet to Queen Victoria, 29 Mar. 1890).

13. Princess Marie Radziwill diary (22 Mar. 1890), in her *Lettres de la Princesse Radziwill au Général de Robilant 1889–1914: Une grande dame d'avant guerre*, 4 vols. (Bologna, 1933–34), 1:31; also Waldersee diary (22 Mar. 1890), Waldersee, 2:121; Baron Hans Hermann von Berlepsch, *Sozialpolitische Erfahrungen und Erinnerungen* (Mönchen-Gladbach, 1925), p. 33.

14. Caprivi to Schneidewin (17 Mar. 1895), in Schneidewin, "Briefe Caprivi," 146; also Hohenlohe diary (13 Dec. 1891), in Helmuth Rogge, ed., *Holstein und Hohenlohe: Neue Beiträge . . . nach Briefen und Aufzeichnungen aus dem Nachlass des Fürsten Chlodwig zu Hohenlohe-Schillingsfürst, 1874–1894* (Stuttgart, 1957), p. 377.

15. Caprivi to Schneidewin (28 Dec. 1894), in Schneidewin, "Briefe Caprivi," 141–42.

16. Georg Gothein, *Reichskanzler Graf Caprivi: Eine kritische Würdigung* (Munich, n.d. [1917]), pp. 18–19; see also Nichols, *Germany after Bismarck*, p. 164.

17. Count Hugo Lerchenfeld-Koefering, *Erinnerungen und Denkwürdigkeiten* (Berlin, 1935), p. 369; also Holstein to Eulenburg (27 Mar. 1890), Röhl, 1:516; Eulenburg diary (17 July 1892), Eulenburg Papers, no. 21:517–19; Wedel diary (19 Mar. 1890), Wedel, p. 46; Hammann, *Neue Kurs*, pp. 26–27.

18. Széchenyi to Kálnoky (19 Mar. 1892), HHStA, no. 142(B); Eulenburg diary (17 July 1892), Eulenburg Papers, no. 21:517–19; Waldersee diary (17 Mar. 1890), Waldersee, 2:118. On Caprivi's willfulness, Waldersee diary (18 Feb. 1890), Waldersee 2:103; Müller, "Die Entlassung," pp. 167, 169; Ebmeyer, "Caprivis Entlassung," 206.

19. Holstein diary (28 Sept. 1887), *HP*, 2:349; also diary (28 June 1887), ibid., 346; Stosch to Gustav Freytag (10 Oct. 1887), in Frederic B. M. Hollyday, *Bismarck's Rival: A Political Biography of General and Admiral Albrecht von Stosch* (Durham, N.C., 1960), p. 234.

20. Wilhelm II to Bismarck (21 Nov. 1887), Bismarck Papers, no. FC2986/354; Eulenburg to Holstein (18 Mar. 1890), Eulenburg Papers, no. 10:279;

Nichols, *Germany after Bismarck*, p. 34; Wilhelm II, *Ereignisse und Gestalten aus den Jahren 1878–1918* (Leipzig and Berlin, 1922), p. 43.

21. Eulenburg to Wilhelm II (7 Mar. 1890), Röhl, 1:479.

22. Schulthess (1890), p. 47; Bülow, 4:637–38. Cf. Wedel, p. 59, n. 5, which gives a slightly different version of the telegram and claims it was addressed to Count Emil Schlitz von Görtz. See also Meisner, *Caprivi*, p. 8, n. 5. Letters to other sovereigns in this vein are in RA I58/32 (Wilhelm II to Queen Victoria, 27 Mar. 1890); same to the Emperor Franz Josef (14 Apr. 1890), Kabinetts-Archiv, Geheime Akten, vol. 2. Also Malet to Salisbury (21 Mar. 1890), FO 64/1234; Széchenyi to Vienna (22, 23 Mar. 1890), HHStA, no. 138(B).

23. Bülow to Karl von Lindenau (1 June 1890), Bülow Papers, no. 99.

24. *GuE*, 3:114; Bülow diary (20 Apr. 1891), Bülow Papers, no. 150. See also Ballhausen diary (31 Dec. 1887), Baron Robert Lucius von Ballhausen, *Bismarck-Erinnerungen* (Stuttgart and Berlin, 1920), p. 413; Waldersee, 2:110, n. 3; Müller, "Die Entlassung," p. 140, n. 3.

25. Max von Eynern, ed., *Ernst von Eynern: Erinnerungen aus seinem Leben* (n.p., 1909), p. 304.

26. Radziwill diary (12/13 Feb. 1891), Radziwill, *Lettres*, 1:65.

27. Caprivi's speech to the Prussian house of deputies (15 Apr. 1890), in Schulthess (1890), pp. 55–56.

28. Stosch to Franz von Roggenbach (9 Feb. 1891), in Hollyday, *Bismarck's Rival*, pp. 268–69. See also *GuE*, 3:114.

29. Lerchenfeld to Baron Christoph Krafft von Crailsheim (Bavarian minister of the royal house and foreign affairs) (29 Oct. 1894), in Egmont Zechlin, *Staatsstreichpläne Bismarcks und Wilhelms II., 1890–1894* (Stuttgart and Berlin, 1929), pp. 222–23; see also Herbette's analysis of Caprivi's increasingly close relationship with the Kaiser in his letter to Ribot (7 Dec. 1891), *DDF*, 9:150, and a similar view in Brauer to Turban (17 Dec. 1890, 17 Nov. 1891), Fuchs, 3:37, 90–91.

30. RA I58/63 (25 Dec. 1890).

31. Wilhelm II to the Grand Duke (10 Apr. 1890), Fuchs, 3:1.

32. Wedel diary (19 Mar. 1890), Wedel, p. 46.

33. Széchenyi to Kálnoky (14 May 1892), HHStA, no. 142(B). Even before becoming chancellor Caprivi had recognized this danger. Caprivi to Tirpitz (19 Dec. 1889), Tirpitz Papers, no. 16.

34. Waldersee to the Grand Duke (28 Jan. 1891), Fuchs, 3:39–40.

35. Eulenburg to Holstein (18 Mar. 1890), Röhl, 1:503, n. 2.

36. Szögyényi to Kálnoky (17 Mar. 1894), HHStA, no. 145(V); Eulenburg to Wilhelm (6 May 1888), Eulenburg Papers, no. 3:95; same to the Grand Duke (13 Mar. 1890), ibid., no. 10:255–58; same to Herbert Bismarck (10 Apr. 1888), in Johannes Haller, ed., *Aus dem Leben des Fürsten Philipp zu Eulenburg-Hertefeld* (Berlin, 1924), p. 44; same to Wilhelm (17 Apr. 1888), Johannes Haller, ed., *Aus 50 Jahren: Erinnerungen und Briefe aus dem Nachlass des Fürsten Philipp zu Eulenburg-Hertefeld* (Berlin, 1923), p. 283.

37. Letter of 6 May 1888, Eulenburg Papers, no. 3:95.

38. Eulenburg diary (10 Oct. 1889), Haller, *Aus 50 Jahren*, p. 222; see also Eulenburg to Marschall (9 Jan. 1891), Röhl, 1:622.

39. Eulenburg notes (17 Mar. 1890), Eulenburg Papers, no. 10:277–78.
40. Eulenburg's notes (ca. 1894), Haller, *Aus dem Leben Eulenburg*, p. 111.
41. Eulenburg to Wilhelm (6 Feb., 5 July 1888), Wilhelm to Eulenburg (28 Aug. 1888), Röhl, 1:265, 301, 310; Eulenburg to Cosima Wagner (18 Nov. 27, 1888), and Cosima to Eulenburg (25 Nov. 1888), Eulenburg Papers, no. 4:175–78, 187–91; Eulenburg to Wilhelm (8 Feb. 1889), ibid., no. 5:32.
42. Eulenburg diary (10 Oct. 1889), Eulenburg Papers, no. 6:153.
43. Eulenburg to Wilhelm (9 Aug. 1887), Röhl, 1:231–34; also ibid., 50–51. Eulenburg declared that Wilhelm had developed an interest in spiritualism before they first met; Eulenburg to his sister, Countess Ada von Kalnein-Kilgis (23 Feb. 1889), ibid., 329. There is no other evidence that this was the case, and it appears likely that Eulenburg was the initiator. Eulenburg had also developed an interest in hypnotism. See Eulenburg Papers, no. 73:16–17. On Eulenburg's spiritualistic tie to Wilhelm, see John C. G. Röhl, *Kaiser, Hof und Staat: Wilhelm II. und die deutsche Politik* (Munich, 1987), pp. 74–76.
44. Eulenburg to Wilhelm (27 Mar., 15 Oct. 1888), Röhl, 1:280–81, 318. See also Eulenburg Papers, no. 75:137–38; Kiderlen to Holstein (19 July 1890), *HP*, 3:346–47.
45. Eulenburg Papers, no. 81, pt. 1:300; on Leuthold, ibid., no. 75:137–38. For the Kaiser's later interest, see Eulenburg to Bülow (27 Sept. 1900), ibid., no. 77; same to same (18 Feb. 1902), Haller, *Aus dem Leben Eulenburg*, pp. 30–31.
46. Röhl, 1:25–26; Eulenburg's undated notes, Eulenburg Papers, no. 25:390, n. 1.
47. See Eulenburg's revealing analysis of his role in a note later added to a letter to Holstein (2 June 1890), Röhl, 1:549, n. 3.
48. See, for example, his letter to Dona (6 Mar. 1888), Eulenburg Papers, no. 3:26, and the letters in Eulenburg's *Mit dem Kaiser als Staatsmann und Freund auf Nordlandsreisen*, 2 vols. (Dresden, 1931), 2:7–118. For her love of Eulenburg's music, see Eulenburg's notes (4/5 Nov. 1888), Eulenburg Papers, no. 3:167–69, and the letter of 6 Mar. 1888 above.
49. For Wilhelm II on Eulenburg's career, see his letter to Eulenburg (31 Oct. 1888), Haller, *Aus 50 Jahren*, p. 197; Herbert to Otto Bismarck (5 Oct. 1888), Bussmann, pp. 523–24; Eulenburg to Holstein (17 Mar. 1888), *HP*, 3:271; Széchenyi to Kálnoky (9 Jan. 1889), HHStA, no. 136(B). For the offer of money, Eulenburg to Hohenlohe (29/31 July 1900), Röhl, 3:1986–87. Wilhelm declined to appoint Eulenburg minister of the household (*Hausminister*) because of his inexperience in handling large sums of money. Count Bogdan von Hutten-Czapski, *Sechzig Jahre Politik und Gesellschaft*, 2 vols. (Berlin, 1936), 1:249–40.
50. Eulenburg to Holstein (4 Feb. 1889), *HP*, 3:307. On the difficulty of serving Wilhelm II, see Eulenburg notes (30 Nov., 1, 2 Dec. 1886), Eulenburg Papers, no. 1:54; Eulenburg to Holstein (8 Nov. 1888), ibid., no. 4:172–73.
51. For an example of a criticism made in writing by Eulenburg to the Kaiser, see his letter (26 Feb., 28 Nov. 1891), Haller, *Aus dem Leben Eulenburg*, pp. 118–19.
52. Eulenburg diary (22 June 1891), ibid., p. 115; Eulenburg to Holstein (4 Feb. 1889), *HP*, 3:307.

53. Eulenburg diary (9 June 1887), Haller, *Aus 50 Jahren*, p. 138.

54. Eulenburg diary (4/5 Nov. 1888), ibid., p. 201; Eulenburg to Holstein (8 Nov. 1888), Eulenburg Papers, no. 4:172–73; Eulenburg notes, "Im Neuen Palais" (11 Oct. 1889), ibid., no. 81, pt.1:286–87. He especially despised the chief marshal of the court, Eduard von Liebenau. See Eulenburg notes (n.d.), in Haller, *Aus 50 Jahren*, pp. 197–98.

55. Eulenburg to the Grand Duke (25 Dec. 1889), Röhl, 1:392–93; Eulenburg's undated notes, Eulenburg Papers, no. 75, pt. 1:30–31.

56. Eulenburg to Holstein (25 Jan. 1890), Röhl, 1:421.

57. Eulenburg diary (10 Oct. 1889), Eulenburg Papers, no. 6:152–54.

58. Waldersee diary (28 Jan. 1889), Waldersee, 2:34. Hinzpeter did not add, however, that only a few days earlier Wilhelm II had described Eulenburg, and not Waldersee, as his only intimate friend. See Eulenburg notes (17 Jan. 1889), Eulenburg Papers, no. 5:16.

59. RA Z45/28 (19 July 1889); Russell to chargé, Berlin (5 Feb. 1891), FO 64/1253; on the League, Széchenyi to Vienna (3 Apr. 1889), HHStA, no. 137(B). See also Count Axel von Schwering [pseud.], *The Berlin Court under William II* (London, 1915), pp. 184–96.

60. RA I59/53 (Wilhelm II to Queen Victoria, 8 Dec. 1891); Malet to Salisbury (22 Nov. 1890), Salisbury Papers, no. 63; also Wilhelm to Bismarck (1 May 1888), *GuE*, 3:138; Münster to Caprivi (4 Jan. 1891), *GP*, 7:193–96, and Wilhelm's II's marginalia in ibid., 207–16, 225 n.

61. Holstein to Radolin (5 Dec. 1889), *HP*, 3:323; Wedel diary (6 Jan., 3 Feb. 1891), Wedel, pp. 128, 142; Johannes Kessler, *Ich Schwöre Mir Ewige Jugend* (Munich, 1935), p. 160.

62. Holstein to Eulenburg (26 Dec. 1889), Röhl, 1:394; Waldersee diary (3 Feb. 1890), Waldersee, 2:99–100.

63. Holstein to Eulenburg (26 Dec. 1889), Röhl, 1:394; Waldersee diary (7 Dec. 1890, 19 Jan. 1891), Waldersee, 2:164, 176; RA Z45/28 (19 July 1889).

64. Eduard von Wertheimer, "Ein Kaiser- und Königlicher Militärattaché über das Politische Leben in Berlin, 1880–1895," *Preussische Jahrbücher* 201 (1925): 278–79; Wedel diary (27 Jan., 3 Feb. 1891), Wedel, pp. 132, 139–40; Eberhard Kessel, "Die Tätigkeit des Grafen Waldersee als Generalquartiermeister und Chef des General Stabes der Armee," *Welt als Geschichte* 14, no. 2 (1954): 209, for a negative opinion in 1888 by Bronsart.

65. Waldersee diary (12 May 1887), Waldersee, 1:325; diary (21 Jan., 9, 13 Feb. 1889), ibid., 2:31–32, 36–37; *HP*, 1:137; Herbert to Rantzau (4 July 1889), Bussmann, pp. 540–41; Herbert Bismarck, "Notizen V," Bismarck Papers, no. FC3018/454. On the officer corps' support of Bismarck in 1890, see Gen. Wilhelm Groener, *Lebenserinnerungen: Jugend—Generalstab—Weltkrieg* (Göttingen, 1957), p. 59.

66. Holstein to Eulenburg (4 July 1890), Eulenburg Papers, no. 12:512–15; same to same (31 Oct. 1890, 2 Jan. 1891), Röhl, 1:587, 620. On Eulenburg, see his notes (1895), Eulenburg Papers, no. 20:455–59; memo by Eulenburg (1890/91), in Haller, *Aus 50 Jahren*, pp. 245–46. The Empress Friedrich also hated Waldersee, blaming him for having alienated Wilhelm from her and his

father. RA Z45/28 (19 July 1889); Swaine to Ponsonby (ca. 18 Nov. 1888), in Sir Frederick Ponsonby, ed., *Letters of the Empress Frederick* (New York, 1928), pp. 363–64; see also Waldersee, 1:325.

67. Waldersee diary (22 Feb. 1890), Waldersee, 2:106. See also Eulenburg notes (17 Jan. 1889), Eulenburg Papers, no. 5:16.

68. Eulenburg to Holstein (1 Aug. 1890), *HP*, 3:353.

69. Széchenyi to Kálnoky (13 Dec. 1890), HHStA, no. 140(V) on Waldersee's manner; Russell to chargé (5 Feb. 1891), FO 64/1253, on his capacity for intrigue.

70. Baron von Eissenstein to Kálnoky (7 Oct. 1890), HHStA, no. 140(V); Kiderlen to Holstein (19 July, 21 Sept. 1890), *HP*, 3:347, 354–56.

71. Waldersee to Gen. Conrad von Bartenwerffer (4 Jan. 1891), Waldersee Papers, no. 17.

72. Eulenburg to Holstein (1 Aug. 1890), *HP*, 3:352; same to same (20 May 1890), Röhl, 1:542; same to Maximilian von Brandt (26 Dec. 1890), ibid., 362; Eissenstein to Kálnoky (7 Oct. 1890), HHStA, no. 140(V).

73. Eulenburg to Holstein (20 May 1890), Röhl, 1:542.

74. Waldersee diary (9 Oct. 1888, 6 May, 19 Aug. 1890), Waldersee, 2:4, 126–27, 140–41. For Waldersee's low opinion of diplomats, see Cecil, *German Diplomatic Service*, pp. 130–31.

75. Kiderlen to Holstein (21 Sept. 1890), *HP*, 3:355; also Count August zu Eulenburg to Eulenburg (22 Mar. 1890), Röhl, 1:508; Wedel diary (27 Jan. 1891), p. 133.

76. Wedel diary (19 Sept. 1890), Wedel, p. 120.

77. Eulenburg to Holstein (1 Aug. 1890), *HP*, 3:352.

78. Wedel diary (19 Sept. 1890), Wedel, pp. 120–21.

79. Edmund von Glaise-Horstenau, *Franz Josephs Weggefährte: Das Leben des Generalstabschefs Grafen Beck* . . . (Zurich, 1930), p. 341. Other accounts in Waldersee diary (21 Sept. 1890), Waldersee, 2:145–47; Kiderlen to Holstein (21 Sept. 1890), *HP*, 3:354–56.

80. Wedel diary (30 Sept. 1890), Wedel, p. 121; Kiderlen to Holstein (21 Sept. 1890), *HP*, 3:355; Waldersee diary (24 Sept. 1890), Waldersee, 2:147–48.

81. Eulenburg to Wilhelm (7 Oct. 1890), Haller, *Aus dem Leben Eulenburg*, p. 116; also Wedel diary (27 Jan., 3 Feb. 1891), Wedel, pp. 133, 139, for other problems connected with Waldersee's reassignment.

82. Holstein to Eulenburg (4 July 1890), Röhl, 1:559; same to Brandt (26 Dec. 1890), *HP*, 3:362; Waldersee diary (10, 13, and 17 Aug. 1890, 22 Dec. 1890), Waldersee, 2:136, 139–40, 169–70.

83. Malet to Salisbury (13 Mar. 1891), FO 64/1253.

84. Holstein to Eulenburg (18 Dec. 1890), Röhl, 1:615; same to Brandt (26 Dec. 1890), *HP*, 3:362; Wedel diary (3 Feb. 1891), Wedel, p. 139. For the order, see Cecil, *German Diplomatic Service*, pp. 131–32.

85. Holstein to Eulenburg (18 Dec. 1890), Röhl, 1:615; same to Maximilian von Brandt (26 Dec. 1890), *HP*, 3:362.

86. Waldersee diary (28 Jan. 1891), Waldersee, 2:177–79.

87. Archduke Albrecht to Beck (4 Feb. 1891), in Glaise-Horstenau, *Franz Jo-*

sephs Weggefährte, p. 343; August zu Eulenburg to Eulenburg (1 Feb. 1891), Eulenburg Papers, no. 14:28–29.

88. Russell to chargé, Berlin (13 Feb. 1891), FO 64/1253.

89. Eulenburg to Holstein (22 Nov. 1890), Röhl, 1:603.

CHAPTER 9

1. J. Alden Nichols, *Germany after Bismarck: The Caprivi Era, 1890–1894* (Cambridge, Mass., 1958), pp. 42–43.

2. Waldersee diary (20 Apr. 1890), Waldersee, 2:124.

3. Ludwig Raschdau, *Unter Bismarck und Caprivi: Erinnerungen eines deutschen Diplomaten aus den Jahren 1885–1894* (Berlin, 1939), p. 137, on the chancellor's passivity.

4. Wilhelm's marginalia on Herbert Bismarck to Wilhelm II (20 Mar. 1890); also memo by Lothar v. Schweinitz (14 May 1890), GP, 7:3, 20–21; Raschdau, *Unter Bismarck und Caprivi*, p. 142; Serge Goriainov, "The End of the Alliance of the Emperors," *American Historical Review* 23 (1918): 343. Alexander III had momentary doubts about the wisdom of continuing the alliance after he heard of Bismarck's resignation, but he soon decided to go ahead.

5. Lascelles to Salisbury (25 Nov. 1896), FO 64/1379; also Szögyényi to Goluchowski (14 Nov. 1896), HHStA, no. 147(B).

6. Szögyényi to Goluchowski (14 Nov. 1896), HHStA, no. 147(B).

7. Julius von Eckardt, *Aus den Tagen von Bismarcks Kampf gegen Caprivi* (Leipzig, 1920), pp. 52–53; also Caprivi's marginalia on an unsigned memo (18 July 1890), GP, 7:348–49, and his address to the Federal Council (27 Mar. 1890), Boetticher Papers, no. 58.

8. Caprivi memo (23 May 1890) and his letter to Schweinitz (29 May 1890), GP, 7:29–30, 33–36.

9. Eulenburg to Bülow (28 Feb. 1887), Röhl, 1:220; Eulenburg's notes (June 11, 1887), in Johannes Haller, ed., *Aus 50 Jahren: Erinnerungen, Tagebücher und Briefe aus dem Nachlass des Fürsten Philipp zu Eulenburg-Hertefeld* (Berlin, 1923), p. 139.

10. Caprivi memo (28 Mar. 1890), GP, 7:10–11.

11. Holstein memo (10 June 1904), ibid., 48–49. See also Hajo Holborn, ed., *Aufzeichnungen und Erinnerungen aus dem Leben des Botschafters Joseph Maria von Radowitz*, 2 vols. (Berlin and Leipzig, 1925), 2:317, for Wilhelm's suspicions of Bismarck's secret negotiations with the Russian ambassador in Berlin. See also Hans Hallmann, *Zur Geschichte und Problematik des Deutsch-Russischen Rückversicherungsvertrages von 1887* (Darmstadt, 1965).

12. Caprivi memo (23 May 1890), GP, 7:29–30.

13. Goriainov, "End of the Alliance," 343–44.

14. Malet to Salisbury (22 Nov. 1890), Salisbury Papers, no. 63, on French republicanism; RA I59/53 (Wilhelm to Queen Victoria, 8 Dec. 1891) on Russia's financial difficulties. See also Wilhelm to Bismarck (1 May 1888), GuE, 3:138;

Wilhelm's marginalia on Münster to Caprivi (4 Jan. 1891), *GP*, 7:195–96.

15. Maurice Paléologue's diary (16 Feb. 1904), in his *Three Critical Years (1904–05–06)* (New York, 1957), p. 19. For the Tsar's dim view of the treaty, see George F. Kennan, *The Decline of Bismarck's European Order: Franco-Russian Relations, 1875–1890* (Princeton, 1979), p. 409; Goriainov, "End of the Alliance," p. 344.

16. Arthur von Brauer, *Im Dienste Bismarcks: Persönliche Erinnerungen* (Berlin, 1936), p. 316.

17. Alexander III's marginalia on a letter of Shuvalov to Count Vladimir Lamsdorff (24 Feb. 1891), in Viktor A. Wroblewski, "Lamsdorff über Deutschland und seine Zukunft," *Berliner Monatshefte* 14, no. 5 (1936): 352. For Wilhelm's unfavorable characterizations of the Tsar, see Princess Marie Radziwill's diary (5/6 Jan. 1891), in her *Lettres de la Princesse Radziwill au Général de Robilant, 1889–1914: Une grande dame d'avant guerre*, 4 vols. (Bologna, 1933–34), 1:57–58; Marschall diary (17 Mar. 1890), Fuchs, 2:750. See also RA I59/53 (Wilhelm to Queen Victoria, 8 Dec. 1891) and Brig. Gen. W. H.-H. Waters, *'Private and Personal': Further Experiences of a Military Attaché* (London, 1928), p. 50, for the animosity between the two rulers.

18. Captain de Beauchamp (military attaché, Copenhagen) to the minister of war (20 Sept. 1893), *DDF*, 10:584, n. 3. At the end of 1891 the Russian ambassador in Berlin declared that as long as Alexander III and Wilhelm II occupied their thrones, the cleft between Russia and Germany would be as profound as that between France and Germany because of Alsace-Lorraine. Herbette to Ribot (10 Dec. 1891), ibid., 9:158–59.

19. Eulenburg's undated notes later added to his diary (30 July 1893), Eulenburg Papers, no. 25:325–28, partially printed in Johannes Haller, ed., *Aus dem Leben des Fürsten Philipp zu Eulenburg-Hertefeld* (Berlin, 1924), pp. 84–85, and in Eulenburg's *Das Ende König Ludwigs II. und andere Erlebnisse* (Leipzig, 1934), pp. 214–15. See also Wilhelm II to Foreign Office (9 May 1891), *GP*, 7:295–96.

20. Alfred von Bülow to Caprivi (30 July 1891), Schweinitz to same (5 Aug. 1891), military attaché (Vienna) Col. Adolf von Deines report (4 Nov. 1891), all with the Kaiser's marginalia, in *GP*, 7:207–15, 225–26.

21. Hohenlohe diary (9 May 1891), Hohenlohe Papers, no. 1455; Wilhelm's marginalia on Captain von Funcke's (military attaché, Paris) report (13 Apr. 1891), *GP*, 7:201.

22. Wilhelm's marginalia on Bülow to Caprivi (4 Aug. 1891), *GP*, 7:215–16; also the Kaiser's marginalia on Alfred von Bülow to same (30 July 1891) and on Schweinitz to same (8 Aug. 1891), ibid., 207–15.

23. Hallmann, *Geschichte des Rückversicherungsvertrages*, pp. 238–39.

24. Hohenlohe diary (22 May 1891), Hohenlohe Papers, no. 1455.

25. Caprivi to Max Schneidewin (17 Mar. 1895), Schneidewin, "Briefe des Toten Reichskanzlers von Caprivi," *Deutsche Revue* 47, no. 5 (1922): 146.

26. Kardorff to his wife (5 May 1892), in Siegfried von Kardorff, ed., *Wilhelm von Kardorff: Ein nationaler Parlamentarier im Zeitalter Bismarcks und Wilhelms II., 1828–1907* (Berlin, 1936), p. 266.

27. Hohenlohe diary (13 Dec. 1891), Hohenlohe Papers, no. 1455; Prince Alexander von Hohenlohe, *Aus Meinem Leben* (Frankfurt/Main, 1925), pp. 357–58; Fritz Hellwig, *Carl Ferdinand Freiherr von Stumm-Halberg, 1836–1901* (Heidelberg and Saarbrücken, 1936), pp. 468–69; Brauer to Turban (8 June 1891), Fuchs, 3:73.

28. Rolf Weitowitz, *Deutsche Politik und Handelspolitik unter Reichskanzler von Caprivi, 1890–1894* (Düsseldorf, n.d. [1978]), p. 284; cf. Waldersee diary (3 Dec. 1893), Waldersee, 2:299.

29. Waldersee diary (12 Mar. 1894), Waldersee, 2:310.

30. Waldersee diary (9 Feb. 1894), ibid., 306; also A. Hohenlohe, *Aus Meinem Leben*, pp. 357–58. For Wilhelm's pressure on the deputies, see Weitowitz, *Politik und Handelspolitik*, p. 239, and Nichols, *Germany after Bismarck*, p. 306.

31. Szögyényi to Kálnoky (17 Mar. 1894), HHStA, no. 144(B); for an assessment of Wilhelm's important role in the Russian treaty, see Jagemann to Brauer (21 Mar. 1894), in Fuchs, 3:294–95; also Weitowitz, *Politik und Handelspolitik*, p. 290.

32. Szögyényi to Goluchowski (14 Nov. 1896), HHStA, no. 147(B).

33. Eulenburg notes (28 Sept. 1894), Eulenburg Papers, no. 31:711.

34. Caprivi's address to the Federal Council (27 Mar. 1890), in the Boetticher Papers, no. 58; also Heinrich O. Meisner, *Der Reichskanzler Caprivi: Eine biographische Skizze* (Darmstadt, 1969), p. 34.

35. There is a useful discussion of Caprivi's attitude to socialism in Georg Gothein, *Reichskanzler Graf Caprivi: Ein kritische Würdigung* (Munich, n.d. [1917]), pp. 163–70.

36. Holstein diary (11 Nov. 1888), *HP*, 2:382.

37. Wilhelm to Nicholas II (7 Feb. 1895), in Walter Goetz, ed., *Briefe Wilhelms II. an den Zaren, 1894–1914* (Berlin, n.d.), p. 290. For the *Schwatzbude* remark, see Cornelius Gurlitt, "Der Platz der Republik und der Wallotbau," *Wasmuths Monatshefte für Baukunst und Städtebau* 14 (1930): 340. For other imperial condemnations of the Reichstag, see Radziwill diary (27 Nov. 1890), Radziwill, *Lettres*, 1:47–48; Holstein to Eulenburg (30 Nov. 1896), *HP*, 3:657–58.

38. See Helmuth Rogge, ed., *Friedrich von Holstein: Lebensbekenntnis in Briefen an eine Frau* (Berlin, 1932), p. 157; Hohenlohe, 3:278–79; *HP*, 3:656–59, for Wilhelm's irritation in the 1890s at Reichstag incursions on his prerogative.

39. Radziwill diary (27 Nov. 1890), Radziwill, *Lettres*, 1:47–48. For Wilhelm's summary and often rude treatment of deputies, see Hermann Pachnicke, *Führende Männer im Alten und im Neuen Reich* (Berlin, 1930), p. 223; Friedrich Payer, *Von Bethmann Hollweg bis Ebert: Erinnerungen und Bilder* (Frankfurt, 1923), pp. 13, 173–74; Eugen Schiffer, *Ein Leben für den Liberalismus* (Berlin, 1951), pp. 58–59; Bülow, 1:479.

40. Order in Schulthess (1889), p. 166; see also James R. Albisetti, *Secondary School Reform in Imperial Germany* (Princeton, 1983), p. 87.

41. Speech by Kultusminister Gustav von Gossler in the Prussian House of Deputies (18 Mar. 1890), Schulthess (1890), p. 43.

42. Baron Robert Lucius von Ballhausen diary (16 Dec. 1888), Ballhausen, *Bismarck-Erinnerungen* (Stuttgart and Berlin, 1920), p. 485; Radziwill diary (5/6 Mar. 1892), Radziwill, *Lettres*, 1:112–13.

43. Hohenlohe diary (22 Feb. 1895, 14 Oct. 1897), Hohenlohe, 3:45, 391; Wilhelm's speech (4 Dec. 1890) opening the school conference, Schulthess (1890), p. 176; Friedrich Schmidt-Ott, *Erlebtes und Erstrebtes, 1860–1950* (Wiesbaden, 1952), pp. 23–24; Ballhausen diary (16 Dec. 1888), Ballhausen, *Bismarck-Erinnerungen*, p. 485.

44. Speech in Schulthess (1890), pp. 174–79. The Kaiser's intemperate language was cleansed before the address was published. See Count August zu Eulenburg to Eulenburg (8 Dec. 1890), Röhl, 1:613; Schmidt-Ott, *Erstrebtes*, pp. 23–24. Waldersee diary (5 Dec. 1890), Waldersee, 2:164, claims that the speech was written by Konrad Schottmüller, secretary of the German Historical Institute in Rome.

45. Theodor Lorenz, ed., *Friedrich Paulsen: An Autobiography* (New York, 1938), pp. 340–42; for evaluations of the speech, see Brauer to Turban (7 Dec. 1890), in Fuchs, 3:34–36; August zu Eulenburg to Eulenburg (8 Dec. 1890), Röhl, 1:613; also, Albisetti, *Secondary School Reform*, p. 214.

46. Caprivi to Schneidewin (28 Dec. 1894), "Briefe des toten Reichskanzlers von Caprivi," *Deutsche Revue* 47:5 (1922), 143; Albisetti, *Secondary School Reform*, p. 235.

47. For Wilhelm's complaints, see RA I59/68 (abstract by Malet of the Kaiser's memo of 2 Apr. 1892) and Count Otto von Helldorff-Bedra (Conservative deputy) to Eulenburg (7 Mar. 1892), Röhl, 2:789. The essential paragraphs of the bill are printed in Schulthess (1892), pp. 8–11.

48. Eulenburg to Wilhelm (21 Jan. 1892), Eulenburg Papers, no. 17:20–21, printed in Haller, *Aus dem Leben Eulenburg*, p. 66, with the incorrect date of 28 January; same to same (10 Mar. 1892), Röhl, 2:796–97.

49. Széchenyi to Kálnoky (25 Mar. 1892), HHStA, no. 142(B).

50. Holstein to Eulenburg (18 Mar. 1892), Röhl, 2:807; Marschall diary (18 Mar. 1892), in David B. King, "Marschall von Bieberstein and the New Course, 1890–1897," Ph.D. diss. (Cornell, 1962), p. 117, n. 38.

51. RA I59/72 (Wilhelm to Queen Victoria, 12 Apr. 1892); Brauer to the Grand Duke (25 Mar. 1892), Fuchs, 3:135–36. Caprivi's associates thought that he had acted rashly. See Marschall diary (19 Mar. 1892), ibid., p. 127, n. 2; also August zu Eulenburg to Eulenburg (19 Mar. 1892), Röhl, 2:812; and Röhl, *Germany without Bismarck: The Crisis of Government in the Second Reich* (Berkeley and Los Angeles, 1967), p. 86.

52. Radziwill diary (22/23 Mar. 1892), Radziwill, *Lettres*, 1:116–17; Wilhelm to Queen Victoria (15 Mar. 1892), in George E. Buckle, ed., *The Letters of Queen Victoria*, 3d ser., 3 vols. (London, 1930), 2:106; Malet to Ponsonby (4 Apr. 1892) and Salisbury to Queen Victoria (14 Apr. 1892), ibid., 106, n. 2, 110.

53. Nichols, *Germany after Bismarck*, pp. 182–83.

54. Ibid., p. 183; Marschall diary (22 Mar. 1892), Fuchs, 3:132–33; Caprivi to Schneidewin (17 Mar. 1895), Schneidewin, "Briefe Caprivi," 146.

55. Nichols, *Germany after Bismarck*, pp. 184–85; Eulenburg to Wilhelm (19

Mar. 1892), Röhl, 2:809–10; August zu Eulenburg to Eulenburg (20 Mar. 1892), ibid., 815–16.

56. Brauer, *Im Dienste Bismarcks*, p. 341.

57. Széchenyi to Kálnoky (27 Mar. 1892), HHStA, no. 142(B).

58. Cabinet order (15 Feb. 1890), in Schulthess (1890), 25–26.

59. On his hostility to older generals: Waldersee diary (13 Mar. 1886, 13 Sept. 1890), Waldersee, 1:280, 2:144; Wedel diary (29 Apr. 1888), Wedel, pp. 30–31; Raschdau, *Unter Bismarck und Caprivi*, p. 14; on Wilhelm's ruthlessness, see Waldersee diary (25 Sept. 1890), Waldersee, 2:150–51; Baron Hugo von Freytag-Loringhoven, *Menschen und Dinge wie Ich sie in Meinem Leben Sah* (Berlin, 1923), p. 63; on his rudeness, Waldersee diary (6 May, 13, 25 Sept. 1890), Waldersee, 2:126–27, 144, 150–51.

60. Eduard von Wertheimer, "Ein Kaiser- und Königlicher Militärattaché über das Politische Leben in Berlin, 1880–1895," *Preussische Jahrbücher* 201 (1925): 278; Waldersee diary (6 May 1890), Waldersee, 2:127; Gen. Paul von Lettow-Vorbeck, *Mein Leben* (Biberach an der Riss, 1957), p. 38.

61. Order to Ministry of War, in Schulthess (1890), 50–51. See also Wedel diary (15 Apr. 1890), Wedel, pp. 90–91, for his discussion of the order with Wilhelm II.

62. On Wilhelm's initial refusal to compromise, see Waldersee diary (8 June, 25 July 1890), Waldersee, 2:130, 133. On his enthusiasm for Verdy, see Waldersee to Gen. Conrad von Bartenwerffer (12 Jan. 1890), Waldersee Papers, no. 17.

63. Wilhelm to Caprivi (15 June 1891), Meisner, *Caprivi*, pp. 73–75; Waldersee diary (13 Aug. 1891), Waldersee, 2:214–15. On the Kaiser's initial agreement to two-year service, see Nichols, *Germany after Bismarck*, pp. 206–7.

64. Wilhelm to Caprivi (15 June 1891), Meisner, *Caprivi*, pp. 73–75.

65. Caprivi to Wilhelm (16 June 1891), ibid., pp. 75–77.

66. Wilhelm to Caprivi (16 June 1891), ibid., pp. 77–78.

67. Holstein to Eulenburg (17 June 1891), Röhl, 1:694–95.

68. Eulenburg to Caprivi (31 July 1891), ibid., 701–3.

69. Ibid., 702.

70. Eulenburg's notes (3 July 1892), ibid., 2:906.

71. Waldersee diary (26 Apr. 1892), Waldersee, 2:240.

72. *HP*, 3:420.

73. Waldersee diary (19 Oct. 1892), Waldersee, 2:266.

74. Waldersee diary (3 Jan. 1893), ibid., 274.

75. Karl Bachem, *Vorgeschichte, Geschichte und Politik der Deutschen Zentrumspartei* . . . , 9 vols. (Cologne, 1928–32), 5:280–81.

76. Szögyényi to Kálnoky (27 May 1893), HHStA, no. 144(V).

77. Brauer to the Grand Duke (7 May 1893), Fuchs, 3:237–38.

78. Speech (9 May 1893), in Schulthess (1893), 54–55.

79. RA I59/101 (14 July 1893). The wire is incorrectly dated one day after being sent.

80. On the chancellor's alienation from the conservative aristocracy, see Szögyényi to Kálnoky (10 Nov. 1894), HHStA, no. 144(V); Lt. Gen. August Keim, *Erlebtes und Erstrebtes: Lebenserinnerungen* (Hanover, 1925), p. 54; Eulen-

burg's judgment is in his letter to Bülow (1 Nov. 1894), Bülow Papers, no. 75.

81. For Caprivi on his parliamentary isolation, see his letter to Schneidewin (28 Dec. 1894), Schneidewin, "Briefe Caprivi," p. 143.

82. Brauer, *Im Dienste Bismarcks*, p. 341; Eulenburg diary (July 17, 1892), Eulenburg Papers, no. 21:517–19.

83. Waldersee to Gen. Friedrich von Bernhardi (n.d. but ca. Oct. 1894), in Bernhardi, *Denkwürdigkeiten aus Meinem Leben: Nach gleichzeitigen Aufzeichnungen und im Lichte der Erinnerungen* (Berlin, 1927), pp. 178–79. Caprivi admitted the Kaiser often acted bored during their conferences. Wertheimer, "Militärattaché," p. 282. See also Raschdau, *Unter Bismarck und Caprivi*, p. 175.

84. Egmont Zechlin, *Staatsstreichpläne Bismarcks und Wilhelms II., 1890–1894* (Stuttgart und Berlin, 1929), p. 224; also Holstein diary (11 Jan. 1909), Holstein Papers, no. 3861/196553–54.

85. Brauer, *Im Dienste Bismarcks*, p. 341.

86. Eulenburg diary (17 July 1892), Eulenburg Papers, no. 21:517–19.

87. Waldersee diary (21 Nov. 1891), Waldersee, 2:223. For speculation on this point by others, see Wilhelm von Kardorff to Baron Carl von Stumm-Halberg (4 May 1892), same to wife (5 May 1892, 5 Feb. 1894), in Kardorff, *Wilhelm von Kardorff*, pp. 266, 289; Wedel diary (6 Dec. 1893), Wedel, p. 193.

88. Caprivi on Wilhelm's tactlessness: Hohenlohe diary (13 Dec. 1891), in Helmuth Rogge, ed., *Holstein und Hohenlohe . . . nach Briefen und Aufzeichnungen aus dem Nachlass des Fürsten Chlodwig zu Hohenlohe-Schillingsfürst, 1874–1894* (Stuttgart, 1957), p. 377; Radziwill diary (5/6 Mar. 1892), Radziwill, *Lettres*, 1:112. On Wilhelm's laziness, Wertheimer, "Militärattaché," 282. On Caprivi's annoyance at the Kaiser's failure to consult him, Caprivi to Wilhelm (ca. 16 June 1891), in Nichols, *Germany after Bismarck*, p. 208; same to same (23 Oct. 1894), Zechlin, *Staatsstreichpläne*, pp. 204–7; Szögyényi to Kálnoky (21 Jan. 1894), HHStA, no. 144(B).

89. Speech of 4 Sept. 1894, Schulthess (1894) p. 140. For Wilhelm's reaction to the assassination, see Zechlin, *Staatsstreichpläne*, pp. 186–88.

90. The murder intensified (but it did not cause) Wilhelm II's determination to curb the socialists. See Baron Axel von Varnbüler (Württemberg representative to the Federal Council) to Eulenburg (16 July 1894); Count Botho zu Eulenburg to same (24 July 1894), Röhl, 2:1328, 1332.

91. On Stumm and his relation with the Kaiser on the social question, see Hellwig, *Stumm-Halberg*, esp. pp. 490–508; for a contemporary evaluation of Stumm's influence, see Fedor von Zobeltitz, *Chronik der Gesellschaft unter dem Letzten Kaiserreich*, 2 vols. (Hamburg, 1922), 1:63–65.

92. For the interesting reaction of a Bavarian socialist whose hopes that Wilhelm II would prove a reformer were dashed by the ruler's attachment to Stumm, see Reinhard Jansen, *Georg von Vollmar: Eine politische Biographie* (Düsseldorf, 1958), p. 44.

93. Wilhelm II's highly personal view of this matter can be seen in his marginalia on Baron Hans Hermann von Berlepsch (minister of Trade and Industry) to Wilhelm (6 June 1895), in Heinrich O. Meisner, "Der Kanzler Hohenlohe und die Mächte seiner Zeit," *Preussische Jahrbücher* 230 (1932): 45–46; also the

testimony of Count Siegfried von Roedern, in Kleine Erwerbungen, no. 317/
2:162, and Hellmut von Gerlach, *Erinnerungen eines Junkers* (Berlin, n.d.),
pp. 86–87.

94. Wilhelm to Hohenlohe (13 Apr. 1895), in Reiner Pommerin, *Der Kaiser
und Amerika: Die USA in der Politik der Reichsleitung, 1890–1917* (Cologne
and Vienna, 1986), p. 19.

95. Wilhelm to Caprivi (9 Sept. 1894), Zechlin, *Staatsstreichpläne*, pp. 191–
92. See also Haller, *Aus dem Leben Eulenburg*, pp. 69–70, for Wilhelm's reflections on the relationship of the Empire and the German princes.

96. Protocol of meeting of Prussian ministry (12 Oct. 1894), Zechlin, *Staatsstreichpläne*, pp. 193–98.

97. Marschall diary (6 Oct. 1894), in Fuchs, 3:328, n. 2.

98. Caprivi to Wilhelm (23 Oct. 1894), in Zechlin, *Staatsstreichpläne*,
pp. 193–98; protocol of meeting of Prussian ministry (12 Oct. 1894), ibid.,
pp. 193–98.

99. Bosse diary (27 Oct. 1894), Bosse Papers, no. 8; Marschall diary (21 Oct.
1894), Fuchs, 3:343, n. 4.

100. Eulenburg's notes (21 Oct. 1894), Haller, *Aus dem Leben Eulenburg*,
pp. 152–53; Marschall diary (21 Oct. 1894), Fuchs, 3:343, n. 4; Ebmeyer, "Caprivis Entlassung," p. 203; Nichols, *Germany after Bismarck*, pp. 348–49.

101. Haller, *Aus dem Leben Eulenburg*, p. 152; also Lerchenfeld to Prince
Luitpold of Bavaria (26 Oct. 1894), in Zechlin, *Staatsstreichpläne*, pp. 208–10.

102. Eulenburg to Bülow (17 Oct. 1894), Röhl, 2:1386.

103. Bülow, 1:373.

104. Marschall diary (23 Oct. 1894), Fuchs, 3:343, n. 4.

105. Nichols, *Germany after Bismarck*, pp. 352–53, attributes the leak to
Holstein; Zechlin, *Staatsstreichpläne*, pp. 211–12, makes it clear the chancellor
was not adverse to having his conversation divulged to the press.

106. Nichols, *Germany after Bismarck*, pp. 353–54.

107. Haller, *Aus dem Leben Eulenburg*, p. 158.

108. Ibid.

109. Zechlin, *Staatsstreichpläne*, pp. 211–12.

110. Boetticher Papers, no. 19.

CHAPTER 10

1. Hohenlohe to Prince Alexander von Hohenlohe (26 Oct. 1894), Hohenlohe
Papers, no. 1596.

2. On Hohenlohe's role as a placeholder for Eulenburg, see Szögyényi to Kálnoky (24 Nov. 1894), HHStA, no. 145(V); Siegfried von Kardorff, ed., *Wilhelm
von Kardorff: Ein nationaler Parlamentarier im Zeitalter Bismarcks und Wilhelms II., 1828–1907* (Berlin, 1936), p. 302. For speculation that Hohenlohe
was holding the post warm for Wilhelm II's former adjutant, Gen. Adolf von
Bülow, see Ludwig Raschdau, *Unter Bismarck und Caprivi: Erinnerungen eines
deutschen Diplomaten aus den Jahren 1885–1894* (Berlin, 1939), p. 365. See

also Raschdau's *In Weimar als Preussischer Gesandter: Ein Buch der Erinnerungen an deutsche Fürstenhöfe, 1894–1897* (Berlin, 1939), p. 8, for similar speculation about Count Botho zu Eulenburg.

3. Count Bogdan von Hutten-Czapski, *Sechzig Jahre Politik und Gesellschaft*, 2 vols. (Berlin, 1936), 1:240. Mediatized nobles were those German houses of princes and counts who had forfeited their sovereignty (though not their land) during the wars against France under the Revolution and Napoleon.

4. Grand Duke to Eulenburg (25 Sept. 1894), Fuchs, 3:320.

5. On Bismarck, see Hohenlohe, 3:17–18.

6. Hohenlohe's notes (17 May 1895), ibid., 66.

7. Eulenburg to Wilhelm (5 Feb. 1895, 24 Aug. 1896), Röhl, 2:1451, 3:1736. For Princess Hohenlohe's urging her husband to remain in office, see Karl von Lindenau to Holstein (31 July 1896), *HP*, 3:640. As chancellor, Hohenlohe received from the Kaiser a secret donation of 120,000 marks annually. See John C. G. Röhl, *Germany without Bismarck: The Crisis of Government in the Second Reich, 1890-1900* (Berkeley and Los Angeles, 1967), p. 176.

8. Bülow, 1:139–40, 179. For Bismarck's warning, see Hohenlohe diary (14 Jan. 1895), Hohenlohe, 2:519.

9. Letter of 1 Nov. 1894, Hohenlohe Papers, no. 1860. See also his letters to her of 28, 30 Oct. 1894, ibid., and Raschdau, *Unter Bismarck und Caprivi*, p. 368; Szögyényi to Vienna (31 Oct. 1894), HHStA, no. 144(B).

10. Hohenlohe's undated notes, Hohenlohe, 3:21–22; Waldersee diary (21 Jan. 1896), Waldersee, 2:365; Prince Alexander von Hohenlohe, *Aus Meinem Leben* (Frankfurt/Main, 1925), pp. 347, 352–54.

11. Hohenlohe diary (31 Dec. 1894), Hohenlohe, 3:27.

12. Wilhelm to Eulenburg (5 Jan. 1897), Röhl, 3:1773.

13. Letter of 21 Feb. 1895, ibid., 1479; also Bülow, 1:10–11.

14. Hohenlohe to his wife (23 Feb. 1895), Hohenlohe Papers, no. 1860.

15. Letter of 9 Mar. 1896, ibid., no. 1861.

16. Raschdau, *In Weimar*, pp. 153–54; Eulenburg to Hohenlohe (16 Feb. 1895), Hohenlohe, 3:40.

17. Notes by Bülow of talk with Hollmann (25 Apr. 1897), Bülow Papers, no. 30.

18. Waldersee, 2:139; Raschdau, *Unter Bismarck und Caprivi*, p. 369; Helmuth Rogge, ed., *Holstein und Hohenlohe: Neue Beiträge . . . nach Briefen und Aufzeichnungen aus dem Nachlass des Fürsten Chlodwig zu Hohenlohe-Schillingsfürst, 1874–1894* (Stuttgart, 1957), p. 347; Rudolf Vierhaus, ed., *Das Tagebuch der Baronin Spitzemberg, geb. Freiin v. Varnbüler: Aufzeichnungen aus der Hofgesellschaft des Hohenzollernreiches* (Göttingen, 1960), pp. 355, 421.

19. Marschall diary (25 Dec. 1895), in David B. King, "Marschall von Bieberstein and the New Course, 1890–1897," Ph.D. diss. (Cornell, 1962), p. 180, n. 1; Lascelles to Salisbury (19 Feb. 1897), FO 64/1409. A similar criticism by Hollmann is in Bülow notes (25 Apr. 1897), Bülow Papers, no. 30.

20. Norman Rich, *Friedrich von Holstein: Politics and Diplomacy in the Era of Bismarck and Wilhelm II*, 2 vols. (Cambridge, 1965), 2:435, on the relationship; Rogge, *Holstein und Hohenlohe*, p. 412, on Holstein's role in Hohenlohe's appointment as chancellor.

21. A quite helpful guide on the dissension between various factions early in Hohenlohe's administration is Röhl, *Germany without Bismarck*; Ekkehard-Teja P. W. Wilke, *Political Decadence in Imperial Germany: Personnel-Political Aspects of the German Government Crisis, 1894–97* (Urbana, 1976), is also of some use. See also Hans Herzfeld, ed., *Johannes von Miquel: Sein Anteil am Ausbau des deutschen Reiches bis zur Jahrhundertwende*, 2 vols. (Detmold, 1938), 2:183–89.

22. Letter of 31 Oct. 1895, Hohenlohe Papers, no. 1857.

23. Bosse diary (16, 18 May 1895), Bosse Papers, no. 8:140–42.

24. Manfred Hank, *Kanzler ohne Amt: Fürst Bismarck nach seiner Entlassung, 1890–1898* (Munich, 1977), pp. 719–20, 723–73, lists Bismarck's interviews and articles.

25. Conversation with A. Memminger of Würzburg (16 Aug. 1890), *GW*, 9:81.

26. Wedel diary (1 Apr. 1890), Wedel, p. 70.

27. Hank, *Kanzler ohne Amt*, p. 287; Brauer to Turban (8 June 1891), Fuchs, 3:73; Eulenburg to Holstein (11 June 1891), Röhl, 1:690; Eduard von Wertheimer, "Ein Kaiser- und Königlicher Militärattaché über das Politische Leben in Berlin, 1880–1895," *Preussische Jahrbücher* 201 (1925): 271–77. On Herbert, see Hohenlohe diary (9 May 1891), in Rogge, *Holstein und Hohenlohe*, pp. 359–60.

28. Eulenburg notes (29 June 1892), Röhl, 2:904–5; Hohenlohe diary (17 Aug. 1892), Hohenlohe, 2:491.

29. Schulthess (1891), p. 81.

30. Szögyényi to Kálnoky (1 Feb. 1895), HHStA, no. 146(V).

31. Hank, *Kanzler ohne Amt*, p. 286; Eulenburg notes for Bülow (8 Nov. 1896), Bülow Papers, no. 75.

32. Hohenlohe to his wife (15 June 1895), Hohenlohe Papers, no. 1860.

33. Brauer to Turban (17 May 1892), Fuchs, 3:144.

34. Bismarck to Baron Robert Lucius von Ballhausen (20 Dec. 1892), Ballhausen, *Bismarck-Erinnerungen* (Stuttgart and Berlin, 1920), pp. 588–89; Waldersee diary (15 June 1892), Waldersee, 2:246. He also insisted Herbert Bismarck be given an ambassadorial post and Marschall fired. See Kiderlen to Eulenburg (13 June 1892), Röhl, 2:894. On the former chancellor's halfheartedness, indeed his objection, to a reconciliation, see Spitzemberg diary (5 Mar. 1891), Vierhaus, *Tagebuch Spitzemberg*, pp. 287–88.

35. Spitzemberg diary (9 Aug. 1904), based on a recollection of Boetticher, Vierhaus, *Tagebuch Spitzemberg*, p. 441; Hohenlohe diary (13 Dec. 1891), Hohenlohe, 2:483.

36. Wilhelm to Waldersee (10 June 1892), Waldersee, 2:244; also Hohenlohe diary (13 Dec. 1891), Hohenlohe, 2:483; Holstein to Eulenburg (7 May 1892), Röhl, 2:859; undated paraphrase by Eulenburg of Wilhelm's remarks, Eulenburg Papers, no. 20:467–71.

37. Gen. Friedrich von Bernhardi, *Denkwürdigkeiten aus meinem Leben: Nach gleichzeitigen Aufzeichnungen und im Lichte der Erinnerungen* (Berlin, 1927), p. 144.

38. Decrais (ambassador in Vienna) to Ribot (24 June 1892), *DDF*, 9:525–28.

On the wedding, see Otto Gradenwitz, *Akten über Bismarcks Grossdeutsche Rundfahrt vom Jahre 1892* (Heidelberg, 1922).

39. Count Hugo Lerchenfeld-Koefering, *Erinnerungen und Denkwürdigkeiten* (Berlin, 1935), pp. 370–71; J. Alden Nichols, *Germany After Bismarck: The Caprivi Era, 1890–1894* (Cambridge, Mass., 1958), p. 197. For Caprivi on the difficulties Bismarck caused him, see Max von Eynern, ed., *Ernst von Eynern: Erinnerungen aus seinem Leben* (n.p., 1909), p. 305.

40. Holstein to Eulenburg (3 June 1892), Röhl, 2:879–80; Eulenburg to Wilhelm II (5 June 1892), ibid., 885–86.

41. Wertheimer, "Militärattaché," 271–72, 281–82.

42. Marschall diary (9 June 1892), Fuchs, 3:152, n. 2. It seems certain that it was Marschall and Kiderlen who urged the chancellor to have Wilhelm write to the Habsburg ruler. Marschall diary (13 June 1892), ibid.; Kiderlen to Eulenburg (10, 15 June 1892), Röhl, 2:890, 895–96; Hank, *Kanzler ohne Amt*, pp. 342, 361, n. 8.

43. Kabinetts Archiv, Geheim Akten, no. 2. The letter (dated 12 June 1892) was first published in the *Osterreiche Rundschau* 58, no. 3 (1919): 107–8; it is printed in Wolfgang Stribrny, *Bismarck und die Deutsche Politik nach seiner Entlassung (1890–1898)* (Paderborn, 1977), p. 126. In 2 Samuel 11:14 David writes a letter to Joab ordering Uriah, a Hittite, to be sent to the forefront in battle so that he would be killed.

44. Eulenburg diary (7 July 1892), Eulenburg Papers, no. 20:502–3.

45. Eulenburg to Holstein (7 Oct. 1893), Röhl, 2:1116–17.

46. On Wilhelm's initiative in the reconciliation, see Marschall's diary (23 Jan. 1894), Röhl, 2:1197, n. 3; Marschall to Eulenburg (23 Jan. 1894), Johannes Haller, ed., *Aus 50 Jahren: Erinnerungen, Tagebücher und Briefe aus dem Nachlass des Fürsten Philipp zu Eulenburg-Hertefeld* (Berlin, 1923), p. 261. For the role of Wilhelm's adjutant, Col. Count Helmuth von Moltke, see his "Die Versöhnung zwischen Kaiser und Kanzler," *Die Woche*, 27 Jan., 3 Feb. 1934; Moltke to Eulenburg (28 Jan. 1894), Röhl, 2:1199. Wilhelm's letter has disappeared, but its contents can be reconstructed from evidence presented in Hank, *Kanzler ohne Amt*, p. 401. For the "Lacrimae Caprivi," see Herbert to Otto Bismarck (10 Feb. 1894), Bismarck Papers, no. FC3004/1173. Caprivi's reaction to the reconciliation is in Marschall's diary (23 Jan. 1894), in Röhl, 2:1197, n. 3; Nichols, *Germany after Bismarck*, p. 300.

47. Printed in Eduard von Wertheimer, "Neues zur Geschichtes des Letzten Jahre Bismarcks (1890–1898)," *Historische Zeitschrift* 133 (1925): 246–47. See also the correspondence about the reconciliation in Haller, *Aus 50 Jahren*, pp. 261–67.

48. Marschall diary (27 Jan. 1894), Fuchs, 3:288, n. 1.

49. Hank, *Kanzler ohne Amt*, p. 412.

50. Wilhelm II, *Ereignisse und Gestalten aus den Jahren 1878–1918* (Leipzig and Berlin, 1922), p. 51.

51. Wilhelm to Hohenlohe (23 Mar. 1895), Hohenlohe, 3:53.

52. Hohenlohe diary (24 Mar. 1895), ibid., 53–54.

53. On the nobility and intelligentsia, see Count Harry Kessler, *Gesichter und*

Zeiten: Erinnerungen (1935; rpt. Berlin, 1962), pp. 250–51; Princess Marie Radziwill, *Lettres de la Princess Radziwill au Général de Robilant, 1889–1914: Une grand dame d'avant guerre,* 4 vols. (Bologna, 1933–34), 1:134; Adolf von Wilke, *Alt-Berliner Erinnerungen* (Berlin, 1930), pp. 233–34; Holstein to Hatzfeldt (6 Apr. 1891), Ebel, 2:824. For the army, see Waldersee, 2:126–27, 136–37, and for public opinion in general, Arthur von Brauer, *Im Dienste Bismarcks: Persönliche Erinnerungen* (Berlin, 1936), p. 344.

54. Szögyényi to Kálnoky (1 Feb. 1895), HHStA, no. 146(V); Holstein to Bülow (23 Jan. 1895), *HP,* 3:491; Wilhelm II to Nicholas II (25 Oct. 1895), in Walter Goetz, ed., *Briefe Wilhelms II. an den Zaren, 1894–1914* (Berlin, n.d.), pp. 297–98.

55. Telegram (11 May 1895), Hohenlohe, 3:63.

56. Wilhelm to Hohenlohe (23 Aug. 1895), Hohenlohe to Wilhelm (n.d. but ca. 31 Aug. 1895), ibid., 92–94.

57. Hohenlohe notes (19 Sept. 1895), ibid., 99.

58. Marschall diary (16 Feb. 1895), Fuchs, 3:394, n. 2.

59. Hutten-Czapski, *Sechzig Jahre,* 1:284–85; Hutten-Czapski to Holstein (15 Nov. 1895), *HP,* 3:560–61; Wertheimer, "Militärattaché," 279, on Bronsart's didacticism.

60. Hutten-Czapski, *Sechzig Jahre,* 1:280–85, provides background on this issue.

61. Wilhelm to the Staatsministerium (1 Sept. 1895), Reichskanzlei, "Akten betr. Militärstrafgerichtsordnung: Militär 11/1 (Militärstrafsachen)," 3, 1312/1–5. On Bülow's influence, see Szögyényi to Goluchowski (20 Nov. 1897), HHStA, no. 148(V); on Hahnke's influence, see notes by Boetticher, "Köller Krisis," Boetticher Papers, no. 19; Hohenlohe diary (2 Nov. 1895), Hohenlohe, 3:116–17; Hutten-Czapski to Holstein (15 Nov. 1895), *HP,* 3:561.

62. Eulenburg to Hohenlohe (29 Oct. 1895); Hohenlohe diary (31 Oct. 1895), Hohenlohe, 3:114–15.

63. Holstein to Hatzfeldt (4 Dec. 1895), Ebel, 2:1061.

64. Marschall diary (16, 17, 26 Nov. 1895), Fuchs, 3:475, n. 2. There is a detailed account of the Köller crisis in Marschall to Eulenburg (20 Dec. 1895), in Röhl, 3:1612–15.

65. Bosse diary (19 Nov. 1895), Bosse Papers, no. 8:150–52.

66. Köller to Hohenlohe (20 Nov. 1895), Hohenlohe Papers, no. 1601.

67. Bosse diary (29 Nov. 1895), Bosse Papers, no. 8:152–53; Marschall diary (26–30 Nov. 1895), Fuchs, 3:475, n. 2.

68. For the dislike various ministers had for Köller well before the crisis of November 1895, see Bosse diary (16, 19 May 1895), Bosse Papers, no. 8:140–41; Hohenlohe notes (3 Mar. 1895), Hohenlohe Papers, no. 1599.

69. Bosse diary (19 Nov. 1895), Bosse Papers, no. 8:150–51; for the chancellor's dislike of Köller, see his letter to Eulenburg (2 Dec. 1895), Hohenlohe, 3:131; same to same (9 Dec. 1895), Eulenburg Papers, no. 71.

70. Marschall diary (29–30 Nov. 1895), Fuchs, 3:475, n. 2; Hohenlohe to Wilhelm II (1 Dec. 1895), Hohenlohe diary (4 Dec. 1895), Hohenlohe, 3:129–30, 135.

71. Marschall diary (2, 3 Dec. 1895), Fuchs, 3:475, n. 2; Hohenlohe diary (2, 4 Dec. 1895), Hohenlohe, 3:130–31; Eulenburg notes (3 Dec. 1895), Bülow Papers, no. 75.

72. Boetticher, "Köller Krisis," Boetticher Papers, no. 19.

73. Marschall diary (15 Dec. 1895), Fuchs, 3:475, n. 2. Years later Wilhelm II was making the same claim. See Eulenburg Papers, no. 74:37.

74. Wilhelm to Eulenburg (25 Dec. 1895), Röhl, 3:1620–21; Hohenlohe diary (14 June 1889), Hohenlohe Papers, no. 1454; Boetticher, "Köller Krisis," Boetticher Papers, no. 19; Eulenburg to Hohenlohe (21 Sept. 1895), Hohenlohe, 3:101.

75. Holstein to Eulenburg (29 Nov. 1895), Röhl, 3:1593.

76. Marschall diary (3, 4 Dec. 1895), Fuchs, 3:475, n. 2.

77. Eulenburg notes (3 Dec. 1895), Bülow Papers, no. 75, omitted from the version printed in Johannes Haller, ed., *Aus dem Leben des Fürsten Philipp zu Eulenburg-Hertefeld* (Berlin, 1924), pp. 160–61; Marschall diary (25 Jan. 1896), Fuchs, 3:496, n. 1.

78. Wilhelm to Eulenburg (25 Dec. 1895), Röhl, 3:1620.

79. Bosse diary (29, 30 Nov., 4 Dec. 1895), Bosse Papers, no. 8:152–54, 156.

80. Wilhelm to the ministry (9 Dec. 1895), Hohenlohe, 3:139; Lucanus to Eulenburg (5 Dec. 1895), Röhl, 3:1604. For Wilhelm's defense of his behavior, see Marschall diary (19 Dec. 1895), Fuchs, 3:486, n. 1.

81. Eulenburg to Hohenlohe (6 Dec. 1895), Hohenlohe, 3:137.

82. Same to Holstein (7 Dec. 1895), *HP*, 3:570.

83. Eulenburg to the Grand Duke (6 Nov. 1895), Fuchs, 3:465–67; also Eulenburg Papers, no. 76, sec. 7:194.

84. On this point, see especially Röhl, *Germany without Bismarck*, chaps. 4, 5; Wilke, *Political Decadence*, chaps. 8–10, is less valuable.

85. Raschdau, *Unter Bismarck und Caprivi*, pp. 138–41; Hutten-Czapski, *Sechzig Jahre*, 1:557–58; Lerchenfeld, *Erinnerungen*, pp. 388–92; Alexander Hohenlohe, *Meinem Leben*, p. 324–26; Otto Hammann, *Der Neue Kurs: Erinnerungen* (Berlin, 1918), pp. 67–68.

86. On this meeting, which occurred only in 1904, see Loebell Papers, no. 27:27; Friedrich Rosen, *Aus einem Diplomatischen Wanderleben*, 4 vols. in 3 (Berlin, 1931–59), 1:86–87; Holstein to Radolin (25 Nov. 1904), *HP*, 4:312–13.

87. Eulenburg to Holstein (1 Aug. 1890), *HP*, 3:354; same to same (20 July 1892, 5 Apr. 1894), ibid., 421, 469; Széchyenyi to Kálnoky (7 Mar. 1892), HHStA, no. 142(B); Bülow, 2:216.

88. Eulenburg Papers, no. 4:124.

89. Holstein to Radolin (28 Nov. 1899), *HP*, 3:323; Karl F. Nowak and Friedrich Thimme, eds., *Erinnerungen und Gedanken des Botschafters Anton Graf Monts* (Berlin, 1932), p. 357.

90. Holstein to Eulenburg (5 May 1896), *HP*, 3:612–13; also same to same (26 Dec. 1895), Haller, *Aus dem Leben Eulenburg*, pp. 184–85; same to same (19 Mar. 1892 and 7 Jan. 1897), Röhl, 2:813, 3:1775; Hutten-Czapski, *Sechzig Jahre*, 1:466.

91. Holstein to Eulenburg (26 Dec. 1895), Haller, *Aus dem Leben Eulenburg*, pp. 184–85.

92. Camille Barrère (chargé, Munich) to Hanotaux (Sept. 30, 1896), *DDF*, 12:763–64.

93. Herbert Bismarck to Holstein (15 Oct. 1888), *HP*, 3:300. Other praise dating from 1888 is in Kardorff, *Wilhelm von Kardorff*, p. 203; Bernhard Schwertfeger, ed., *Kaiser und Kabinettschef: Nach eigenen Aufzeichnungen und dem Briefwechsel des Wirklichen Geheimen Rats Rudolf von Valentini* (Oldenburg i.O., 1931), p. 37; Baron Paul von Schoenaich, *Mein Damaskus: Erlebnisse und Bekenntnisse* (Berlin, 1926), pp. 80, 82; Hajo Holborn, ed., *Aufzeichnungen und Erinnerungen aus dem Leben des Botschafters Joseph Maria von Radowitz*, 2 vols. (Berlin and Leipzig, 1925), 2:288; Kurd von Schlözer, *Letzte Römische Briefe, 1882–1894* (Berlin, 1924), pp. 130–31.

94. Waldersee diary (13 Nov. 1889), Waldersee, 2:76–77; Radziwill diary (31 Dec. 1889), in Radziwill, *Lettres*, 1:22. For continuing admiration in 1889, see Kardorff, *Wilhelm von Kardorff*, p. 206; Ottomar von Mohl, *Fünfzig Jahre Reichsdienst: Lebenserinnerungen* (Leipzig, 1921), p. 238; Ebel, 2:729, 735.

95. Kessler, *Gesichter und Zeiten*, pp. 250–51; Waldersee, 2:136–37; Gen. Karl von Einem, *Erinnerungen eines Soldaten, 1853–1933* (Leipzig, 1933), p. 40; Baron Hugo von Freytag-Loringhoven, *Menchen und Dinge wie ich sie in meinem Leben Sah* (Berlin, 1923), pp. 65–66; Marianne Weber, *Max Weber: Ein Lebensbild* (Heidelberg, 1950), p. 142; Brauer, *Im Dienste Bismarcks*, p. 344; Ebel, 2:824.

96. Letter of 20 July 1892, *HP*, 3:420.

97. Holstein to Eulenburg (5 May 1896), *HP*, 3:612; same to same (28 Feb. 1891), Röhl, 1:647; same to Bülow (12 Nov. 1895), ibid., 3:1588; Bülow to Eulenburg (27 Dec. 1895), ibid., 1625; Eulenburg Papers, no. 40:126a–e; no. 76, pt. 4:6.

98. RA Z500/2 (Queen Victoria's memorandum, 25 Apr. 1888, reporting a talk with Bismarck); Eulenburg to Holstein (4 Feb. 1892), Röhl, 2:758; Dallwitz memoir, p. 8, in Thimme Papers; Bernhard Schwertfeger, ed., *Kaiser und Kabinettschef: Nach eigenen Aufzeichnungen und dem Briefwechsel des wirklichen Geheimen Rats Rudolf von Valentini* (Oldenburg i. O., 1931), p. 73, n. 1.

99. Holstein to Hohenlohe (17 Nov. 1894), Hohenlohe, 3:15.

100. Hohenlohe to Holstein (8 Mar. 1896), Hohenlohe, 3:193; Alexander Hohenlohe, *Meinem Leben*, p. 319.

101. Holstein to Eulenburg (21 Dec. 1895), *HP*, 3:577.

102. Hohenlohe diary (4 Aug. 1896), Hohenlohe, 3:250. Cf. Hohenlohe to Prince Max von Ratibor und Corvey (consul general, Budapest) (5 Nov. 1895), ibid., 117, with same to Alexander Hohenlohe (7 Jan. 1900), ibid., 554, for Hohenlohe's declining opinion of Eulenburg. See also Hutten-Czapski, *Sechzig Jahre*, 1:249–50.

103. Röhl, 2:1440–41.

104. For Holstein's opinion of Eulenburg, see Rich, *Holstein*, 1:231–32, and John C. G. Röhl, "Friedrich von Holstein," *Historical Journal* 9, no. 3 (1966): 379–88; for Eulenburg on Holstein, see his notes (1895), Eulenburg Papers, no. 20:447–55; Eulenburg to Wilhelm (23 Jan. 1894, 14 Feb. 1895), Röhl, 2:1193–94, 1463–64.

105. Eulenburg Papers, no. 75, pt. 1:39–40.

106. Eulenburg to Holstein (25 Jan. 1890), Röhl, 1:421.

107. Holstein to Eulenburg (21 Dec 1895), Bülow Papers, no. 90. The version in *HP*, 3:576–77, omits various passages.

108. Eulenburg to Bülow (29 Dec. 1895), Haller, *Aus dem Leben Eulenburg*, pp. 187–89.

109. Eulenburg to Holstein (2 Dec. 1894), Haller, *Aus dem Leben Eulenburg*, p. 172.

110. Eulenburg diary (9 July 1891), Eulenburg Papers, no. 15:214.

111. Holstein to Bülow (10 June 1896), Bülow Papers, no. 90.

112. Eulenburg to Holstein (2 Dec. 1894), Haller, *Aus dem Leben Eulenburg*, pp. 170–72.

113. Eulenburg to Waldersee (30 Nov. 1891), ibid., pp. 98–99.

114. Ibid., p. 170.

115. For their differences as they moved apart, see especially Holstein to Eulenburg (9 Feb. 1896) and Eulenburg to Holstein (14, 17 Feb. 1896), ibid., pp. 193–96.

CHAPTER 11

1. Eulenburg notes (3 Dec. 1895), in Johannes Haller, ed., *Aus dem Leben des Fürsten Philipp zu Eulenburg-Hertefeld* (Berlin, 1924), p. 161; Wilhelm to Hermann von Lucanus (2 Dec. 1895), in Heinrich O. Meisner, "Der Kanzler Hohenlohe und die Mächte Seiner Zeit," *Preussische Jahrbücher* 230 (1932): 46.

2. Hohenlohe notes (28 Feb. 1896), Hohenlohe, 3:181.

3. Wilhelm to Hohenlohe (6 May 1896), ibid., 218; for the Kaiser's view of his prerogative, especially in military matters, see same to same (16 May 1896), ibid., 225, and his marginalia on a letter to him from the minister for trade and industry, Baron Hans Hermann von Berlepsch (24 May 1896), in Meisner, "Kanzler Hohenlohe," 49–50.

4. Eulenburg to Hohenlohe (6 Dec. 1895), Hohenlohe, 3:137; also same to Holstein (7 Dec. 1895), *HP*, 3:569.

5. Wilhelm to the ministry (9 Dec. 1895), Hohenlohe, 3:139.

6. Marschall to Eulenburg (18 Dec. 1895), Eulenburg Papers, no. 39:913. There is a useful introduction to the courts-martial issue in J. David Fraley, "Government by Procrastination: Chancellor Hohenlohe and Kaiser William II, 1894–1900," *Central European History*, 7:2 (1974), 159–83. See also Wilhelm Deist, "Kaiser Wilhelm II in the Context of His Military and Naval Entourage," in John C. G. Röhl and Nicolaus Sombart, eds., *Kaiser Wilhelm II, New Interpretations: The Corfu Papers* (Cambridge, 1982), pp. 173–74.

7. Hohenlohe diary (4 Aug. 1896), Hohenlohe, 3:250.

8. Hohenlohe diary (2 Nov. 1895), ibid., 116–17. On the cabinet system, see Isabel V. Hull, *The Entourage of Kaiser Wilhelm II, 1888–1918* (Cambridge, 1982), esp. pp. 26–27, 175–80; Heinrich O. Meisner, "Zur Neueren Geschichte des Preussischen Kabinetts," *Forschungen zur Brandenburgischen und Preussischen Geschichte* 36 (1924): 39–66, 180–208; Rudolf Schmidt-Bückeburg, *Das*

Militärkabinett der Preussischen Könige und Deutschen Kaiser: Seine geschicht-liche Entwicklung und staatsrechtliche Stellung, 1787–1918 (Berlin, 1933); Wal-ther Hubatsch, *Der Admiralstab und die Obersten Marinebehörden in Deutsch-land, 1848–1945* (Frankfurt, 1958); Gordon Craig, *The Politics of the Prussian Army, 1640–1945* (Oxford, 1956), pp. 225–32.

9. Waldersee diary (19 Aug. 1890), Waldersee, 2:140–41; Eulenburg notes (3 Dec. 1895), Haller, *Aus dem Leben Eulenburg*, p. 160. See also Count Bogdan von Hutten-Czapski to Holstein (15 Nov. 1895), *HP*, 3:560–61. See Bülow, 1:268, on the Hahnke-Bronsart relationship.

10. Eduard von Wertheimer, "Ein Kaiser- und Königlicher Militärattaché über das politische Leben in Berlin, 1880–1905," *Preussische Jahrbücher* 201 (1925): 278.

11. Count Bogdan von Hutten-Czapski, *Sechzig Jahre Politik und Gesell-schaft*, 2 vols. (Berlin, 1936), 2:285 on his popularity in the Reichstag; on Bron-sart's high standing in the Prussian ministry, see Ludwig Raschdau, *In Weimar als Preussischer Gesandter: Ein Buch der Erinnerungen an Deutsche Fürstenhöfe, 1894–1897* (Berlin, 1939), pp. 51, 89; also Rudolf Vierhaus, ed., *Das Tagebuch der Baronin Spitzemberg geb. Freiin v. Varnbüler: Aufzeichnungen aus der Hof-gesellschaft des Hohenzollernreiches* (Göttingen, 1960), p. 347.

12. Hohenlohe to Augusta Victoria (n.d. but 1896) and Augusta Victoria to Hohenlohe (29 July 1896), Hohenlohe Papers, no. 1673.

13. Eulenburg to Holstein (19 Dec. 1895), *HP*, 3:575; Hutten-Czapski to Prince Alexander von Hohenlohe (16 Mar. 1896), Hutten-Czapski, *Sechzig Jahre*, 2:289.

14. Hohenlohe to Eulenburg (20 May 1896), Hohenlohe, 3:233.

15. Eulenburg to Holstein (29 Feb. 1896), *HP*, 3:595.

16. Eulenburg to Wilhelm (14 Feb. 1895), Haller, *Aus dem Leben Eulenburg*, p. 225.

17. Eulenburg to Bülow (24 May 1896), Röhl, 3:1686–87; Hohenlohe to Holstein (5 Aug. 1896), Hohenlohe, 3:250. For Wilhelm's desire to have Bülow as chancellor, see his letter to Eulenburg (25 Dec. 1895), Röhl, 3:1621.

18. Hutten-Czapski to Holstein (15 Nov. 1895), *HP*, 3:560–61; also Mar-schall diary (16 Feb. 1894), Fuchs, 3:394, n. 2.

19. Hutten-Czapski, *Sechzig Jahre*, 2:244.

20. Holstein to Hatzfeldt (21 Dec. 1895, 27/28 Nov. 1896), Ebel, 2:1063–64, 1099.

21. *HP*, 3:612–13.

22. Holstein to Eulenburg (17 Feb. 1896), Haller, *Aus dem Leben Eulenburg*, pp. 195–96, on the Kaiser's lack of reality. For Holstein's suspicions of the Kaiser's mental problems, see same to Karl von Lindenau (29 July 1896), *HP*, 3:637–38.

23. Münster to Holstein (19 Mar. 1896), *HP*, 3:599. For Holstein's objection to this military presence, see his letters to Radolin (22 Mar. 1896), ibid., 601; to Hohenlohe (6 Mar. 1896), Hohenlohe, 3:193–94; and to Hatzfeldt (21 Mar. 1896), Ebel, 2:1080–81.

24. Hohenlohe diary (1 Feb. 1896), Hohenlohe, 3:164; Hohenlohe notes (28 Feb. 1896), ibid., 181.

25. Hohenlohe notes (28 Feb., 2 Mar. 1896), ibid., 181–82, 186.
26. Hohenlohe probably to Baron Karl von Wilmowski (14 May 1896), ibid., 224.
27. Hohenlohe notes (28 Feb. 1896), diary (7 Mar. 1896), ibid., 181, 191.
28. Hohenlohe diary (7 Mar. 1896), ibid., 191–92; Hohenlohe to Holstein (8 Mar. 1896), ibid., 192–93.
29. Hohenlohe diary (15 June 1896), ibid., 235. Waldersee believed that Wilhelm II had decided to accept a change in the court-martial regulations but did not want to afford Bronsart any satisfaction by doing so while Bronsart was war minister. Waldersee diary (June 8, 1896), Waldersee, 2:370.
30. Hohenlohe to Wilhelm (17 May 1896), Hohenlohe, 3:224.
31. Wilhelm to Hohenlohe (16 May 1896), ibid., 225–26. See also the Kaiser's marginalia on a clipping from the *Münchener Neueste Nachrichten* (4 Nov. 1895) reporting that in a ministerial meeting the chancellor had favored open trials: "How could this have got into the papers? Investigate at once"; Hohenlohe Papers, no. 1601.
32. Augusta Victoria to Hohenlohe (17 May 1896), Hohenlohe, 3:226–27.
33. Hohenlohe to Wilhelm (18 May 1896), ibid., 228–29; the speech is printed in Schulthess (1896), p. 76.
34. Hohenlohe to Eulenburg (19 May 1896), Hohenlohe, 3:231.
35. Hohenlohe diary (15 June 1896), ibid., 235.
36. Raschdau, *In Weimar*, p. 82.
37. Hohenlohe diary (4 Aug. 1896), Hohenlohe, 3:249–50.
38. Conversation of 21 July 1895, Haller, *Aus dem Leben Eulenburg*, p. 202.
39. Hohenlohe diary (4 Aug. 1896), Hohenlohe, 3:250.
40. Lascelles to Salisbury (7 Mar. 1896), Salisbury Papers, no. 120.
41. Hohenlohe to Alexander Hohenlohe (17 Oct. 1896), Hohenlohe, 2:259, and reprinted in ibid., 3:268–69.
42. Hohenlohe diary (8 Aug. 1896), Hohenlohe, 3:251–52; diary (9 Aug. 1896), Hohenlohe Papers, no. 1861.
43. Wilhelm to Eulenburg (14 Aug. 1896), Röhl, 3:1733.
44. Hohenlohe, 3:256.
45. Ibid., 257.
46. Hohenlohe to Eulenburg (n.d. but ca. Aug. 1896), ibid., 253–54.
47. Wilhelm to Eulenburg (13, 14 Aug. 1896), Röhl, 3:1731–33.
48. Same to same (13 Aug. 1896), ibid., 1731–32.
49. Wilhelm to the Prussian ministry (19 Sept. 1896), Reichskanzlei, "Akten betr. Militärstrafsachen," vol. 4; same to Gossler (6 May 1897), ibid., vol. 6.
50. Eulenburg notes (15 May 1896), Eulenburg Papers, no. 41:307; Eulenburg to Hohenlohe (24 Aug. 1896), Hohenlohe, 3:255.
51. Eulenburg to Hohenlohe (24 Aug. 1896), Hohenlohe, 3:255–56; also Hohenlohe diary (1 July 1896), ibid., 240.
52. Eulenburg to Hohenlohe (3 Dec. 1895); Hohenlohe diary (4 Dec. 1895); Wilhelm to Hohenlohe (1 June 1897), ibid., 132, 134, 348.
53. Baron Georg von Eppstein, *Fürst Bismarcks Entlassung: Nach den hinter-gelassenen ... Aufzeichnungen des Staatssekretärs des Innern, Staatsministers Dr. Karl Heinrich von Boetticher und des Chefs der Reichskanzlei unter dem*

Fürsten Bismarck Dr. Franz Johannes von Rottenburg (Berlin, 1920), pp. 75–76; Count Hugo Lerchenfeld-Koefering, *Erinnerungen und Denkwürdigkeiten* (Berlin, 1935), p. 349; Ferdinand Philipp, "Die Erinnerungen von Bismarcks Anwalt," *Süddeutsche Monatshefte*, Jan. 1927, 309.

54. Wilhelm to Eulenburg (25 Dec. 1895), Röhl, 3:1621. On Boetticher, see Hohenlohe diary (3 June 1897), Hohenlohe, 3:350; also Bülow, 1:10; Lerchenfeld, *Erinnerungen*, p. 213.

55. Szögyényi to Goluchowski (10 Apr. 1897), HHStA, no. 148(V).

56. Eulenburg to Bülow (1 June 1897), Haller, *Aus dem Leben Eulenburg*, pp. 233–34; Hohenlohe diary (31 May 1897), Hohenlohe, 3:345–46.

57. Bosse diary (17 June 1897), Bosse Papers, no. 9; Hohenlohe diary (31 May 1897), Hohenlohe, 3:345.

58. Hohenlohe diary (31 May 1897), Hohenlohe, 3:345–46.

59. Hohenlohe diary (1 June 1897), ibid., 347–48. See also Holstein to Eulenburg (9 Feb. 1896), HP, 3:593.

60. Hohenlohe diary (1 June 1897), Hohenlohe, 3:347–48.

61. Wilhelm to Hohenlohe (1 June 1897), ibid., 348; Eulenburg to Bülow (1 June 1897), Haller, *Aus dem Leben Eulenburg*, p. 233.

62. Wilhelm to Eulenburg (7 June 1896), Eulenburg Papers, no. 71:21.

63. Wilhelm to Eulenburg (25 Dec. 1895), Röhl, 3:1620. See also his letter of 21 Feb. 1895 in ibid., 1480; Eulenburg to Bülow (10 Dec. 1896), ibid., 1766; Waldersee diary (6 Jan. 1897), Waldersee, 2:382–83.

64. Holstein to Bülow (6 June 1896), Bülow Papers, no. 90.

65. Wilhelm to Eulenburg (25 Dec. 1895), Röhl, 3:1621.

66. HP, 3:578. Holstein agreed. See his letter to Hatzfeldt (19 Jan. 1895), Ebel, 2:1017.

67. Eulenburg to Wilhelm (31 Dec. 1895), Röhl, 3:1630.

68. Eulenburg to Wilhelm (27 Feb., 16 Mar. 1896), Röhl, 3:1642–43, 1652; Hohenlohe to Eulenburg (16 July 1896), ibid., 1705–6. For Eulenburg's vain effort to persuade Wilhelm to pay more attention to Marschall, see his letter to Holstein (31 Dec. 1895), HP, 3:579. He also worked tirelessly—and with more success—to encourage the Kaiser not to fire Marschall. See, for example, Eulenburg's letters to Wilhelm II (20 Jan., 4, 16 Aug., 8 Dec. 1896), Röhl, 3:1638–39, 1725–26, 1734, 1765.

69. Bosse diary (29, 30 Aug. 1896), Bosse Papers, no. 8:176–77. For the dislike of the entourage for Marschall, see Eulenburg to Holstein (12 July 1896), HP, 3:623.

70. Hohenlohe diary (25 Nov. 1896), Hohenlohe, 3:279; Lascelles to Salisbury (28 Nov. 1896), Salisbury Papers, no. 120.

71. Eulenburg to Bülow (13 Mar. 1896), Röhl, 3:1650.

72. Ibid.; Lascelles to Salisbury (27 Nov. 1896), Salisbury Papers, no. 120.

73. Noailles to Hanotaux (8 Oct. 1897), DDF, 13:489–90.

74. Szögyényi to Goluchowski (15 Jan. 1898), HHStA, no. 150(B); Kiderlen to Holstein (3 July 1897), Bülow Papers, no. 92; Hutten-Czapski, *Sechzig Jahre*, 1:341.

75. Hohenlohe to Eulenburg (16 July 1896), Röhl, 3:1705–6.

76. Wilhelm to Eulenburg (25 Dec. 1895), Röhl, 3:1620–22.

77. Hohenlohe to Eulenburg (16 July 1896), Röhl, 3:1706; Hohenlohe diary (22 May 1897), Hohenlohe, 3:342.

78. On the failure to consult, see Lascelles to Salisbury (20 Feb. 1897), Salisbury Papers, no. 120; on hostility, Marschall diary (9 June 1896), Fuchs, 3:526, n. 2; on the Reichstag, Marschall to Eulenburg (17 Feb. 1895), Röhl, 3:1467–69.

79. Kiderlen to Holstein (3 July 1897), Bülow Papers, no. 92. On the Tausch case, see Dieter Fricke, "Die Affaire Leckert-Lützow-Tausch und die Regierungskrise von 1897 in Deutschland," Zeitschrift für Geschichtswissenschaft 8 (1960): 1579–1603; and Helmuth Rogge, "Affairen im Kaiserreich: Symptome der Staatskrise unter Wilhelm II.," Die Politische Meinung 81 (1963): 58–72; also Hohenlohe to Wilhelm (8 Dec. 1896), Hohenlohe, 2:287–88; Haller, Aus dem Leben Eulenburg, p. 210; Norman Rich, Friedrich von Holstein: Politics and Diplomacy in the Era of Bismarck and Wilhelm II, 2 vols. (Cambridge, 1965), 2:520.

80. Eulenburg's notes of a conversation with Wilhelm (4 Oct. 1896), Röhl, 3:1740.

81. Spitzemberg diary (13 Aug. 1896), Vierhaus, Tagebuch Spitzemberg, p. 345.

82. Waldersee diary (4 Feb. 1896), relating an earlier conversation, Waldersee, 2:367.

83. Eulenburg to Bülow (10 Dec. 1896), Röhl, 3:1766–67.

84. HP, 4:34.

85. Bülow to Loebell (9 May 1912), Loebell Papers, no. 7.

86. Bülow to Eulenburg (27 Dec. 1895), Röhl, 3:1626.

87. Eulenburg to Bülow (13 July 1898), ibid., 1906.

88. Berlepsch, Sozialpolitische Erfahrungen und Erinnerungen (Mönchen-Gladbach, 1925), pp. 32–33, 45–46. See also Fritz Hellwig, Carl Ferdinand Freiherr von Stumm-Halberg, 1836–1901 (Heidelburg and Saarbrücken, 1936), pp. 534–35.

89. Waldersee diary (21 Jan. 1896), Waldersee, 2:365.

90. For Hohenlohe's suspicion of Eulenburg, Hohenlohe diary (4 Aug. 1896), Hohenlohe, 3:250; Hohenlohe to Eulenburg (n.d.), ibid., 253–54; Lindenau to Holstein (5 Aug. 1896), HP, 3:646. For a positive assessment of Hohenlohe's chancellorship up to this point, see Holstein to Hatzfeldt (27 June 1896), Ebel, 2:1088. Hohenlohe had enlisted the Grand Duke's help. Grand Duke to Tirpitz (9 Nov. 1897), Tirpitz Papers, no. 4.

91. Szögyényi to Goluchowski (19 June, 2 July 1897), HHStA, no. 148(V); also Hohenlohe to Baron Otto von Völderndorff-Waradein (Bavarian Staatsrat) (6 July 1897), Hohenlohe, 3:365.

92. The conception of Wilhelm II's reign as a "persönliches Regiment," a term and an idea prevalent during his reign, was first advanced by Erich Eyck in his Das Persönliche Regiment Wilhelms II. (Erlenbach-Zurich, 1948). It has since been subtly refined by John C. G. Röhl in his Germany without Bismarck: The Crisis of Government in the Second Reich, 1890–1900 (Berkeley and Los Angeles, 1967), in which 1897 rather than 1890 (as with Eyck) is taken as the year in which the Kaiser's personal regime was established, and most recently in his essays collected as Kaiser, Hof und Staat: Wilhelm II. und die deutsche Politik

(Munich, 1987). For Röhl, the personal regime is not the dictatorial rule of a sovereign but rather his creation of a court structure amenable to his will that stood above and was independent of the government. Isabel Hull's important *Entourage of Kaiser Wilhelm II* has endorsed and expanded Röhl's views. The *persönliches Regiment* viewpoint has never lacked critics. Initially, the narrow, juridical claim was advanced that inasmuch as the last Kaiser had never violated either the imperial or the Prussian constitutions he could not be reproached with having assumed powers that were not properly his. See Hans Helfritz, *Wilhelm II. als Kaiser und König: Eine historische Studie* (n.p., 1954); Ernst R. Huber, "Das persönliche Regiment Wilhelms II.," *Zeitschrift für Religion und Geistesgeschichte* 3 (1951): 134–48, and an article of the same title by Fritz Hartung in the *Sitzungsberichte der Deutschen Akademie zu Berlin* (1952). Since the 1950s a more imaginative attack on the concept of a *persönliches Regiment* has been advanced by a number of historians who take two quite separate paths. One argues that the Kaiser did not rule but rather that Germany staggered along under a sort of "authoritarian polycracy" compounded of interest groups, political factions, and oligarchies, all representing rival, inanimate forces active in imperial Germany. This is Hans-Ulrich Wehler's view in his *Das Deutsche Kaiserreich, 1871–1918* (Göttingen, 1973), in which he is sharply critical of "personalized history" and in which Wilhelm II plays no role whatsoever. The other faction denies that Wilhelm II established a personal regime and instead argues that Bülow and other officials succeeded in capturing him for their own purposes. See as examples Ekkehard-Teja P. W. Wilke, *Political Decadence in Imperial Germany: Personnel-Political Aspects of the German Government Crisis, 1894–97* (Urbana, 1976), and Terry Cole, "Kaiser Versus Chancellor: The Crisis of Bülow's Chancellorship, 1905–6," in Richard J. Evans, ed., *Society and Politics in Wilhelmine Germany* (London and New York, 1978), pp. 40–70. None of these approaches is entirely convincing, since in Wehler the Kaiser unrealistically disappears as a political force; for Wilke and Cole, he is made to appear more subservient to his officials than was the case; and for Röhl, after 1897 Wilhelm becomes the autocrat that in fact he was not. The most enlightened discussion of the *persönliches Regiment* question can be found in John C. G. Röhl's *Kaiser, Hof und Staat*, esp. chaps. 1 and 4, in his introduction to Röhl and Sombart, *Kaiser Wilhelm II*, in Paul Kennedy's perspicacious, "The Kaiser and German *Weltpolitik*: Reflexions on Wilhelm II's Place in the Making of German Foreign Policy," in ibid., pp. 143–68, and in the suggestive book by Elisabeth Fehrenbach, *Wandlungen des Deutschen Kaisergedankens, 1871–1918* (Munich and Vienna, 1969), esp. pp. 11–13, 89–104. There is a sound discussion of the *persönliches Regiment* and the navy in Berghahn, pp. 354–59.

93. Holstein to Eulenburg (27 Nov. 1894), Röhl, 2:1414.

CHAPTER 12

1. RA Z12/69 (27 Jan. 1862).
2. RA Z16/60 (6 July 1864); also Z16/74 (16 Aug. 1864).

3. The causes of Wilhelm's hostility are treated above in chapter 3 at note 108. On Anglo-German relations in general at this time, see the expert work by Paul M. Kennedy, *The Rise of the Anglo-German Antagonism, 1860–1914* (London, 1980), and more recently on the British side, A. J. Anthony Morris, *The Scaremongers: The Advocacy of War and Rearmament, 1896–1914* (London, 1984).

4. The "Albion" remark is in Wilhelm to Herbert Bismarck (17 Aug. 1884), Bismarck Papers, no. FC2986/328–29.

5. Letter of 17 Aug. 1884, ibid., no. FC2986/328–29; Lucius von Ballhausen diary (28 Apr. 1884), in Baron Robert Lucius von Ballhausen, *Bismarck-Erinnerungen* (Stuttgart and Berlin, 1920), p. 292. In April 1884, Wilhelm denied to the British military attaché in Berlin, who could not detect any signs of Anglophobia in him, that he had made any disparaging remarks about British military institutions. RA Z66/31 (Swaine to Ponsonby, 10 Apr. 1884).

6. Letter of 8 May 1885, Bismarck Papers, no. FC2986/494–96.

7. Eulenburg diary (9 June 1887), Eulenburg Papers, no. 81, pt. 1:201–2. In similar vein, all denunciations dating from the 1880s, see Ballhausen, *Bismarck-Erinnerungen*, pp. 243–44, 292; Sir James Rennell Rodd, *Social and Diplomatic Memories, 1884–1919*, 3 vols. (London, 1922–25), 3:195; Waldersee, 1:247; Wilhelm to Herbert Bismarck (17 Aug. 1884), Bismarck Papers, no. FC2986/328–29.

8. Lamar Cecil, "History as Family Chronicle: Kaiser Wilhelm II and the Dynastic Roots of the Anglo-German Antagonism," in John C. G. Röhl and Nicolaus Sombart, eds., *Kaiser Wilhelm II, New Interpretations: The Corfu Papers* (Cambridge, 1982), p. 114, n. 41.

9. Lascelles to Salisbury (2 Feb. 1898), Salisbury Papers, no. 121. Wilhelm also resented the Prince of Wales's support of the marriage proposed between Wilhelm's sister Victoria and Prince Alexander Battenberg. See Wilhelm to Tsar Alexander III (25 May, 19 June 1884), BPHA, Rep. 53a, no. 5.

10. Lamar Cecil, "William II and His Russian 'Colleagues,'" in Carole Fink, Isabel V. Hull, and MacGregor Knox, eds., *German Nationalism and the European Response, 1890–1945* (Norman, Okla., 1985), 119–20.

11. For Maria Feodorovna's hostility to Wilhelm and to Germany, see Cecil, "William II and his Russian 'Colleagues,'" pp. 119–23. On the influence of the Tsarina on her elder son, see Richard Wortman, "The Russian Empress as Mother," in David L. Ransel, ed., *The Family in Russia* (Urbana, 1978), pp. 60–74.

12. Baron Wilhelm von Schoen, *Erlebtes: Beiträge zur politischen Geschichte der neuesten Zeit* (Stuttgart and Berlin, 1921), pp. 12–13; Princess Marie Radziwill, *Lettres de la Princesse Radziwill au Général de Robilant, 1889–1914: Une grande dame d'avant guerre*, 4 vols. (Bologna, 1933–34), 3:56; Alexander Izvolsky, *Recollections of a Foreign Minister* (Garden City, 1921), p. 61. The feud ended only in 1913 with the marriage of the Kaiser's only daughter to the Cumberlands' oldest son.

13. Paul Cambon (ambassador, London) to Théophile Delcassé (foreign minister) (29 Jan. 1903), *DDF*, 2d ser., 3:67–68; Princess of Wales to Prince George (17 Oct. 1888), in Kenneth Rose, *King George V* (London, 1983), p. 164.

14. Bülow, 1:342; Sigmund Münz, *King Edward VII at Marienbad: Political and Social Life at the Bohemian Spas* (London, 1934), p. 101.

15. Bülow notes (1908), Bülow Papers, no. 153:140; also Bülow, 1:261–62; 2:246–47.

16. On relations at the funeral, see the Prince of Wales to Prince Christian of Schleswig-Holstein (3 Apr. 1889), George E. Buckle, ed., *The Letters of Queen Victoria*, 3d ser., 3 vols. (London, 1930), 1:487–89; on Wilhelm's annoyance, RA T9/110 (Salisbury to Queen Victoria, 13 Oct. 1888); Malet to Salisbury (29 Sept. 1888), Salisbury Papers, no. 61. Both Marschall and Herbert Bismarck later claimed that the Prince *had* in fact initiated the story that Friedrich III intended to restore Alsace-Lorraine to France. See Marschall to Turban (16 Sept. 1888), in Fuchs, 2:573, and Bismarck's "Notizen, Herbst 91," Bismarck Papers, no. FC3018/255–57. He may have done so, for his equerry, General Arthur Ellis, told Ponsonby that the Prince "very likely . . . said more to Herbert Bismarck and the chancellor than was prudent," and repeated things that the Empress Friedrich had told him. Ellis to Ponsonby (19 Apr. 1889), in Arthur Ponsonby, *Henry Ponsonby, Queen Victoria's Private Secretary: His Life from His Letters* (New York, 1943), pp. 110–11.

17. Letter of 16 Sept. 1888, Bismarck Papers, no. FC3004/1098. See also Herbert Bismarck, "Notizen, Herbst 91," ibid., no. FC3018/257; Malet to Salisbury (29 Sept. 1888) and Swaine memo (27 Dec. 1888), Salisbury Papers, no. 61; Hatzfeldt to Salisbury (15 May 1889), ibid., Class G; RA Z281/17 (Malet to Foreign Office, 9 Apr. 1889).

18. For Rudolf's aversion to Wilhelm, see John C. G. Röhl, "The Emperor's New Clothes: A Character Sketch of Kaiser Wilhelm II," in Röhl and Sombart, *Kaiser Wilhelm II*, p. 33; Sidney Lee, *King Edward VII: A Biography*, 2 vols. (London, 1925–27), 1:649–51; Brigitte Hamann, *Rudolf: Kronprinz und Rebell* (Vienna, 1978), pp. 333, 360–61; also Princess Stéphanie of Belgium, *I Was to Be an Empress* (London, 1937), pp. 45, 148; Julius Szeps, ed., *Politische Briefe an einen Freund, 1882–1889* (Vienna, 1922), p. 160; Lady Walburga Paget, *Embassies of Other Days and Further Recollections*, 2 vols. (London, 1923), 2:460, 465; Karl F. Nowak and Friedrich Thimme, eds., *Erinnerungen und Gedanken des Botschafters Anton Graf Monts* (Berlin, 1932), pp. 131–32. Wilhelm reciprocated the dislike, and he disapproved of Rudolf's immorality. See Waldersee, 2:35; *HP*, 3:307.

19. Prince of Wales to Prince Christian of Schleswig-Holstein (3 Apr. 1889), in Buckle, *Letters of Queen Victoria*, 3d ser., 1:487–89. For Wilhelm's refusal to accept his uncle's assurances, see RA Z281/2, 3, 10 (Ellis to Swaine, 12 Sept. 1888; Swaine to the Prince of Wales, 20 Sept. 1888; Sir Augustus Paget, ambassador in Vienna, to Foreign Office, 4 Oct. 1888). One of the Prince's equerries declared that he had never seen him so upset. RA Z281/2 (Ellis to Swaine, 12 Sept. 1888).

20. Queen Victoria to Salisbury (Sept. 1888), Salisbury Papers, no. 122; RA Add. MS A/15/5166 (same to Duke of Connaught, 27 Sept. 1888); RA Z281/7, 8, 10 (Salisbury to Paget, 30 Sept. 1888; Paget to Salisbury, 30 Sept., 4 Oct. 1888).

21. RA T9/110 (Salisbury to Queen Victoria, 13 Oct. 1888). See also RA Z281/34 (memo by Prince Christian of Schleswig-Holstein, 16 Apr. 1889) on Wilhelm's touchiness on this point.

22. "Notizen, Herbst 91," Bismarck Papers, no. FC3018/254.

23. Radziwill diary (6 June 1889), Radziwill, *Lettres*, 1:9.

24. RA T9/111 (Queen Victoria to Salisbury, 15 Oct. 1888).

25. On Wilhelm, RA Z281/26 (Malet to Foreign Office, 12 Apr. 1889); on the Prince of Wales, Z281/37 (Prince of Wales to Prince Christian, 19 Apr. 1889); Z44/33 (27 Apr. 1889).

26. RA Z281/38 (Queen Victoria to Prince of Wales, 21 Apr. 1889); Z280/74 (same to same, 1 June 1889); Z280/75 (Ponsonby to Queen Victoria, 5 June 1889); Z498/49 (Prince of Wales to Queen Victoria, 8 Feb. 1889).

27. Queen Victoria to Wilhelm (25 May 1889), BPHA, Rep. 53a, no. 31; Salisbury memo (n.d.), Queen Victoria memo (21 May 1889), RA Z281/51, 52.

28. RA Z281/88 (Salisbury's draft of a letter by Queen Victoria to Wilhelm, 4 June 1889); RA I57/36 (Wilhelm to Queen Victoria, 23 June 1889).

29. Malet to Salisbury (29 June 1889), Salisbury Papers, Class E (Malet); Ponsonby to Prince Christian (12 May 1889), in Buckle, *Letters of Queen Victoria*, 3d ser., 1:499. On the relationship, see Cecil, "History as Family Chronicle," in Röhl and Sombart, *Kaiser Wilhelm II*, 102–11.

30. "Notizen, Herbst 91," Bismarck Papers, no. FC3018/266–67.

31. Radolin to Hatzfeldt (2 Mar. 1889), Ebel, 2:729.

32. RA Add. U/173/143 (Queen Victoria to Princess Victoria of Hesse, 4 July 1888).

33. Herbert Bismarck, "Notizen, Herbst 91," Bismarck Papers, no. FC3018/269; Radziwill diary (17 Sept. 1889), Radziwill, *Lettres*, 1:14–15.

34. RA I57/66 (Letter of 24 Oct. 1889).

35. Empress Friedrich to Henriette Schrader-Breymann (27 June 1889), in Mary J. Lyschinska, ed., *Henriette Schrader-Breymann: Ihr Leben aus Briefen und Tagebüchern zusammengestellt und erläutert*, 2 vols. (Berlin, 1927), 2:47; same to Ponsonby (8 Mar. 1889), in Magdalen Ponsonby, *Mary Ponsonby: A Memoir, Some Letters and a Journal* (London, 1927), pp. 271–72; Kardorff to his wife (22 Mar. 1890), in Siegfried von Kardorff, ed., *Wilhelm von Kardorff: Ein nationaler Parlamentarier im Zeitalter Bismarcks und Wilhelms II., 1828–1907* (Berlin, 1936), p. 222.

36. Edith Countess of Lytton's diary (13/14 Aug. 1901), in Mary Lutyens, ed., *Lady Lytton's Court Diary, 1895–1899* (London, 1961), pp. 317–18; also Bülow, 1:534–35.

37. See Wilhelm Steglich, "Bismarcks Englische Bündnissondierungen und Bündnisvorschläge, 1887–1889," in Hans Fenske, Wolfgang Reinhard, and Ernst Schulin, eds., *Historia Integra: Festschrift für Erich Hassinger zum 70. Geburtstag* (Berlin, 1977), 283–86; Kennedy, pp. 190–97.

38. For the role of Wilhelm II in the decline of Anglo-German relations, see Kennedy, pp. 405–9, and Paul M. Kennedy, "The Kaiser and German *Weltpolitik*: Reflexions on Wilhelm II's Place in the Making of German Foreign Policy," in Röhl and Sombart, *Kaiser Wilhelm II*, esp. 153–64, both of which assign the Kaiser a central role. Thomas A. Kohut, in an essay on "Kaiser Wil-

helm II and His Parents: An Inquiry into the Psychological Roots of German Policy towards England before the First World War," 63–89 in the same volume, argues that Wilhelm's Anglophobia was a continuation of his psychologically rooted rebellion against his mother. This is a suggestive approach, but it does not take adequately into account the Kaiser's positive feelings about England. There is also a limp and unpersuasive attempt to promote the personal factor in Anglo-German relations in Judith Hughes, *Emotion and High Politics: Personal Relations at the Summit in Late Nineteenth Century Britain and Germany* (Berkeley, 1983).

39. Malet to Lord Kimberley (foreign secretary) (16 Jan. 1895), FO 64/1350; Swaine to Lascelles (20 Dec. 1895), ibid., 1351.

40. Undated letter (ca. 1891–92) to Henriette Schrader-Breymann in Lyschinska, *Schrader-Breymann*, 2:56–57. In an interesting letter to Frau Houston Stewart Chamberlain (7 June 1931), Wilhelm drew exactly such a distinction between the elegance of English "civilization" of manners—sports, fine houses, etc.—and the deplorable state of English "culture"—politics, institutions, morals, religion etc.; Rijksarchief Papers, no. 288.

41. Malet to Salisbury (4 July 1888), FO 64/1187.

42. Lascelles to same (24 Nov., 3 Dec. 1896), ibid., 1379. For another example, see same to same (2 Dec. 1896), ibid.

43. On the "parvenu court," see Waldersee diary (25 Nov. 1889), Waldersee, 2:80; on the Empress Frederick, see RA Z5/18 (15 Feb. 1858), and Z2/31 (to Prince Albert, 6 Aug. 1859). The matter is treated in greater detail in Cecil, "History as Family Chronicle," 105–7.

44. Wilhelm to Houston Stewart Chamberlain (23 Dec. 1907), in Chamberlain's *Briefe, 1882–1924, und Briefwechsel mit Kaiser Wilhelm II.*, 2 vols. (Munich, 1928), 2:227; Prince Philipp zu Eulenburg-Hertefeld, *Erlebnisse an Deutschen und Fremden Höfen* (Leipzig, 1934), pp. 63–64; Bülow, 3:63. See also John C. G. Röhl, *Kaiser, Hof und Staat: Wilhelm II. und die deutsche Politik* (Munich, 1987), p. 104.

45. An exposition of the differences between the two courts is a set piece in the memoir literature of Prussian-imperial court life. For a sampling, see Marie von Bunsen, *Die Welt in der Ich Lebte: Erinnerungen aus glücklichen Jahren, 1860–1912* (Leipzig, 1929), pp. 92–93; Prince Alexander von Hohenlohe, *Aus Meinem Leben* (Frankfurt/Main, 1925), p. 348; Princess Louise of Belgium, *My Own Affairs* (New York, 1921), pp. 161–62; Queen Marie of Rumania, *The Story of My Life*, 2 vols. (London, 1934), 2:225–26; Count Axel von Schwering [pseud.], *The Berlin Court Under William II* (London, 1915), pp. 250–58.

46. Fritz Max Cahèn, *Der Weg nach Versailles: Erinnerungen, 1912–1919* (Boppard, 1963), p. 123; Louise, Princess of Coburg, *Throne die ich Stürzen Sah* (Zurich, 1927), pp. 187–88; also Infanta Eulalia of Spain, *Memoirs of H.R.H. The Infanta Eulalia* (London, 1936), p. 73; Anne Topham, *Memories of the Fatherland* (New York, 1916), pp. 121–22.

47. Lady Susan Townley, *'Indiscretions'* (New York, 1922), pp. 53–54.

48. Wilhelm to Chamberlain (23 Dec. 1907), in Chamberlain, *Briefe, 1882–1924*, 2:226–27.

49. Eulenburg Papers, no. 74, pt. 2:50–51.

50. Alan Clark, ed., *'A Good Innings': The Private Papers of Viscount Lee of Fareham* (London, 1974), p. 116; also Charles à Court Repington, *Vestigia: Reminiscences of Peace and War* (Boston and New York, 1919), p. 86; Bülow, 1:340.

51. Ottomar von Mohl, *Fünfzig Jahre Reichsdienst: Lebenserinnerungen* (Leipzig, 1921), pp. 316–17.

52. Eliza von Moltke, ed., *Helmuth von Moltke. Erinnerungen, Briefe, Dokumente, 1877–1916: Ein Bild vom Kriegsausbruch, erster Kriegsführung und Persönlichkeit des ersten militärischen Führers des Krieges* (Stuttgart, 1922), pp. 296–97; Bülow, 1:575; Alexander Hohenlohe, *Meinem Leben*, pp. 348–49; Ludwig Raschdau, *In Weimar als Preussischer Gesandter: Ein Buch der Erinnerungen an deutsche Fürstenhöfe, 1894–1897* (Berlin, 1939), p. 40; Edith Keen, *Seven Years at the Prussian Court* (New York, 1917), p. 115.

53. For details on Wilhelm's unfortunate relations with the last two Tsars, see Cecil, "William II and His Russian 'Colleagues,' " esp. 106, 126–27.

54. Charles Hardinge, First Baron Hardinge of Penshurst, *Old Diplomacy* (London, 1947), p. 128, and his letter to Sir Edward Grey (16 Aug. 1906), Lascelles Papers, FO 800/13.

55. Swaine to Malet (23 Jan. 1895), FO 64/1350.

56. Wilhelm to Caprivi (20 July 1892), Hohenlohe to Holstein (25 Jan. 1895), *HP*, 3:419–20, 492; Wilhelm to Nicholas II (25 Oct. 1895) in Walter Goetz, ed., *Briefe Wilhelms II. an den Zaren, 1894–1914* (Berlin, n.d.), pp. 297–99.

57. Szögyényi to Kálnoky (28 Oct. 1893), HHStA, no. 144(V); Swaine to Malet (14 Jan. 1892), FO 64/1273.

58. Letter of 20 Dec. 1888, GFM 31/19/00126. See also two letters by Wilhelm to Beresford (26 Dec. 1888 and 13 Feb. 1890), in the Beresford Papers. See also Swaine memo (27 Dec. 1888), Salisbury Papers, no. 61. For Wilhelm's warnings to other British dignitaries, see RA I59/113 (abstract of Malet to Foreign Office, 7 Nov. 1893) as well as a great number of memos and letters by Swaine from 1893–95 in FO 64/1295, 1350f.

59. RA I58/21 (Letter of 24 Feb. 1890). See also Col. Leopold V. Swaine, *Camp and Chancery in a Soldier's Life* (London, 1926), pp. 198–99.

60. RA I57/75 (Letter of 22 Dec. 1889).

61. Szögyényi to Kálnoky (28 Oct. 1893), HHStA, no. 144(V); same to same (19 Aug. 1894), ibid., no. 144(B).

62. Swaine to Lascelles (20 Dec. 1895), FO 64/1351; Baron von Call (chargé, Berlin) to Goluchowski (26 Oct. 1895) and Szögyényi to same (9 Nov. 1895), HHStA, no. 146(B).

63. See chap. 3 at notes 59 and 110.

64. For Bismarck's attitude to England, see Kennedy, esp. pp. 28–29, 144–45; see also ibid., pp. 127–29, for the King, and pp. 140–41, for Herbert Bismarck.

65. RA J42/27 (memo by Baron Vivian, ambassador to Italy, for Queen Victoria, 23 Apr. 1893).

66. Lascelles to Salisbury (27 May 1898), Salisbury Papers, no. 121.

67. Malet to same (6 July 1895), ibid., no. 120.

68. On Rosebery's treating him shabbily, see Holstein to Eulenburg (16 June 1894), Röhl, 2:1323; Call to Goluchowski (2 June 1895), HHStA, no. 146(B);

Wilhelm to the Kaiserin Friedrich (1 June 1898), *HP*, 4:83. For his low estimation of Rosebery and his government, see Malet to Salisbury (6 July 31, 1895), Salisbury Papers, no. 120; Salisbury to Lascelles (10 May 1899), Lascelles Papers, no. 9; for Wilhelm on Gladstone, see RA I58/63 (Wilhelm to Queen Victoria, 25 Dec. 1890).

69. Call to Goluchowski (17 Aug. 1895), HHStA, no. 146(B). Rosebery declared that Wilhelm exercised a "great fascination" on him. See his letter to Herbert Bismarck (24 July 1887), Bismarck Papers, no. FC2977/92, a file that contains the voluminous correspondence between the two statesmen.

70. Wilhelm II to Nicholas II (25 Oct. 1895), Goetz, *Briefe Wilhelms II.*, p. 299.

71. Bismarck to Salisbury (22 Nov. 1887), Salisbury Papers, no. 122; Salisbury to Malet (16 Nov. 1887), ibid., no. 64; Salisbury to Queen Victoria (21 Apr. 1888), RA A66/107.

72. Salisbury to Queen Victoria (21 Apr. 1888), RA A66/107.

73. Lord George Hamilton, *Parliamentary Reminiscences and Reflections, 1886–1906* (London, 1922), p. 137; also Salisbury to Queen Victoria (22 Apr. 1892), RA I59/78.

74. Salisbury to Lascelles (10 May 1899), Lascelles Papers, no. 9.

75. RA GV M688a/1 (Memo of 26 Oct. 1914, by Sir Schomberg McDonnell, Lord Salisbury's private secretary).

76. Salisbury to Lascelles (10 Mar. 1896), Lascelles Papers, no. 9.

77. Baron Hermann von Eckardstein, *Lebenserinnerungen u. Politische Denkwürdigkeiten*, 3 vols. (Leipzig, 1919–21), 1:214.

78. St. John Broderick (under secretary for foreign affairs) to Lascelles (1 Sept. 1899), Lascelles Papers, FO 800/9.

79. Eulenburg notes (28 July 1895), Röhl, 3:1517; Swaine to Malet (30 Aug. 1895), FO 64/1351.

80. Swaine to Lascelles (20 Dec. 1895), FO 64/1351; also Wilhelm to Marschall (25 Oct. 1895), Hohenlohe Papers, no. 1601.

81. Swaine to Lascelles (20 Dec. 1895), FO 64/1351. The Kaiser's version is in his letter to Hohenlohe (20 Dec. 1895), *GP*, 10:251–55. For the reaction this interview produced in Berlin, see *HP*, 3:576–78; Hohenlohe, 3:146.

82. Kiderlen to Joseph von Radowitz (4 Oct. 1888), in Ernst Jäckh, ed., *Kiderlen-Wächter der Staatsmann und Mensch: Briefwechsel und Nachlass*, 2 vols. (Berlin and Leipzig, 1924), 1:109.

83. Extract of the article in Schulthess (1895), p. 170. For Wilhelm's reaction, see Swaine to Lascelles (19 Jan. 1896), FO 64/1376; Lascelles to Salisbury (11 Jan. 1896), Salisbury Papers, no. 120. See also Morris, *Scaremongers*, p. 16.

84. Swaine, *Camp and Chancery*, p. 199.

85. On the misunderstanding, see Kiderlen to Holstein (7 Aug. 1895), Hatzfeldt to same (14 Aug. 1895), *HP*, 3:537–38, 542–43; same to Foreign Office (7 Aug. 1895), *GP*, 10:25–27; Salisbury to Hatzfeldt (8 Aug. 1895), ibid., 27. See also J. A. S. Grenville, *Lord Salisbury and Foreign Policy: The Close of the Nineteenth Century*, 2d rev. ed. (London, 1970), pp. 37–39, as well as Raymond J. Sontag, "The Cowes Interview and the Kruger Telegram," *Political Science Quarterly* 40 (1925): 217–47.

86. Malet to Salisbury (4 July 1888), FO 64/1187.

87. Marschall's notes (15 Oct. 1895), *GP*, 11:5–7; this language was also reported by Holstein in a letter to Hatzfeldt (15 Oct. 1895), Ebel, 2:1057.

88. Martin Gosselin (first secretary, Berlin) to Foreign Office (4 Nov. 1895), Malet to Salisbury (7 Nov. 1895), Salisbury Papers, no. 120.

89. Marschall memo (15 Oct. 1895), *GP*, 11:5–7. The remark about allies appears the account Marschall later gave to Szögyényi of his talk with Malet. Szögyényi to Goluchowski (9 Nov. 1895), HHStA, no. 146(B).

90. Gosselin to Malet (4 Nov. 1895), Malet Papers, no. B-35. Wilhelm later retracted his insistence that the word "ultimatum" had been used. See same to same (22 Nov. 1895), Salisbury Papers, no. 120. See also Wilhelm's marginalia on Marschall's memo (15 Oct. 1895), *GP*, 11:5–7.

91. Wilhelm to Marschall (25 Oct. 1895), *GP*, 11:8–11; for Wilhelm's annoyance, see also Eulenburg to Bülow (12 Nov. 1895), Röhl, 3:1587–88.

92. Wilhelm's marginalia on Hatzfeldt to Foreign Office, Berlin (25 Oct. 1895), *GP*, 11:11–12; Eulenburg probably to Marschall (6 Nov. 1895), Hohenlohe, 3:118; Holstein to Eulenburg (26 Oct. 1895), Röhl, 3:1580. The navy also hoped for more ships as a result of the crisis. See Kiderlen to Holstein (Oct. 28, 1895), Kiderlen-Wächter Papers, box 5, drawer 71.

93. Wilhelm's marginalia on a letter from Marschall (17 Nov. 1895), *GP*, 11:14–15; Eulenburg to Bülow (12 Nov. 1895), Röhl, 3:1588.

94. Wilhelm to Sir Edward Sullivan (3 Feb. 1896), in Repington, *Vestigia*, pp. 191–92. For the Kaiser's bad humor at this time, see Raschdau, *In Weimar*, p. 40.

95. Szögyényi to Goluchowski (18 Jan. 1896), HHStA, no. 147(B).

96. Marschall to Hatzfeldt (31 Dec. 1895), *GP*, 11:19. Hatzfeldt to Foreign Office, Berlin (3 Jan. 1896), ibid., 32–33. On Chamberlain's complicity, see Robert Blake, "The Jameson Raid and 'The Missing Telegrams,'" in Hugh Lloyd-Jones, Valerie Pearl, and Blair Worden, eds., *History & Imagination: Essays in Honor of H. R. Trevor-Roper* (New York, 1982), 326–39; Grenville, *Salisbury and Foreign Policy*, pp. 98–102.

97. The German documents on the Kruger affairs are in *GP*, 11:16–61; see also *Weissbuch vorgelegt dem Reichstage in der 4. Session der 9. Legislatur: Aktenstücke betreffend die Südafrikanische Republik* (Berlin, 1896); David B. King, "Marschall von Bieberstein and the New Course, 1890–1897," Ph.D. diss. (Cornell, 1962), pp. 188–94; Friedrich Thimme, "Die Krüger Depesche: Genesis und historische Bedeutung," *Europäische Gespräche: Hamburger Monatshefte für auswärtige Politik* 3 (1924): 201–44. The best recent account of the episode is in Rich, *Holstein*, 2:466–69.

98. Lascelles to Salisbury (11 Jan. 1896), Salisbury Papers, no. 120; Marschall diary (1 Jan. 1896), in Thimme, "Krüger Depesche," 211.

99. Memo by Valentine Chirol (25 Jan. 1896), Salisbury Papers, no. 120; see also Chirol's recollection of Marschall's attitude in the London *Times* (11 Sept. 1920).

100. Thimme, "Krüger Depesche," 210.

101. Szögyényi to Goluchowski (18 Jan. 1896) HHStA, no. 147(B).

102. Marschall diary (3 Jan. 1896), Thimme, "Krüger Depesche," 212–13.

103. Arnold Oskar Meyer, "Fürst Hohenlohe und die Krüger Depesche," *Archiv für Politik und Geschichte* 2 (1924): 592–93, based on a conversation on 2 Jan. 1896, between Radolin and Wilhelm II.

104. *GP*, 11:31–32.

105. Bülow, 1:473. Bülow is not always reliable, and there is no confirmation of this, but it would not have been out of character for Wilhelm II to have taken this view.

106. Knollys to Bigge (4 Jan. 1896), Buckle, *Letters of Queen Victoria*, 3d ser., 3:7–8.

107. RA O45/169 (Draft, [5] Jan. 1896). Salisbury agreed with the contents. RA O45/168 (Salisbury to Queen Victoria, 16 Jan. 1896).

108. Letter of 8 Jan. 1896 in Hohenlohe, 3:154–56.

109. RA O45/140 (Queen Victoria to the Prince of Wales, 11 Jan. 1896); ibid., Queen Victoria's Journal (10 Jan. 1896).

110. RA A72/46 (Salisbury to Queen Victoria, 12 Jan. 1896).

111. RA Z500/6 (Queen Victoria to Wilhelm II, 15 Jan. 1896).

112. Brig. Gen. W. H.-H. Waters, *Potsdam and Doorn* (London, 1935), pp. 138–39 on General von Lauenstein in Russia. See also Münster to Holstein (13 Jan. 1896), *HP*, 3:585; Holstein to Eulenburg (15 Jan. 1896), Johannes Haller, ed., *Aus dem Leben des Fürsten Philipp zu Eulenburg-Hertefeld* (Berlin, 1924), p. 211; Raschdau, *In Weimar*, p. 60.

113. RA Add. MS U321 (8 Jan. 1896). For outrage by other members of the Royal Family, see RA GV/CC.22 (Duke and Duchess of York to the Grand Duchess Augusta of Mecklenburg-Strelitz, 7, 22 Jan. 1896). On Marschall, see Szögyényi to Goluchowski (6 Jan. 1896), HHStA, no. 147(B).

114. Salisbury to Lascelles (10 Mar. 1896), Lascelles Papers, FO 800/9; Grierson to Lascelles (5 May 1896), FO 64/1377 on relations with Salisbury; Waldersee diary (16 Mar. 1897), Waldersee, 2:394, on Wilhelm's continuing suspicions.

115. Lascelles to Salisbury (4 Mar. 1896, 19 Feb. 1900), FO 64/1376, 1492; Wilhelm to Sir Edward Sullivan (3 Feb. 1896), Repington, *Vestigia*, pp. 191–92.

116. For "idiocy," see Raschdau, *In Weimar*, p. 73; for blaming others, see Wilhelm to Schiemann (6 Feb. 1919), Schiemann Papers, no. 85; Walter Görlitz, ed., *Der Kaiser . . . : Aufzeichnungen des Chefs des Marinekabinetts Admiral Georg Alexander v. Müller über die Ära Wilhelms II.* (Göttingen, 1965), p. 71; Leonidas E. Hill, ed., *Die Weizsäcker-Papiere, 1900–1932* (n.p., n.d.), p. 121; Bülow, 1:473; Alfred Niemann, *Wanderungen mit Kaiser Wilhelm II.* (Leipzig, 1924), p. 56.

117. Wilhelm to Hohenlohe (6 Jan. 1896), *GP*, 11:36–37.

118. Holstein to Eulenburg (5 May 1896), *HP*, 3:610.

CHAPTER 13

1. Wilhelm II, *Aus Meinem Leben, 1859–1888* (Berlin and Leipzig, 1927), pp. 133–35; see also Constance, Baroness Battersea, *Reminiscences* (London, 1922), p. 315.

2. Baron Hermann von Eckardstein, *Persönliche Erinnerungen an König Eduard aus der Einkreisungszeit* (Dresden, 1927), pp. 72–74; Eckardstein, *Lebenserinnerungen u. Politische Denkwürdigkeiten*, 3 vols. (Leipzig, 1919–21), 1:106.

3. Sir Frederic William Fisher, *Naval Reminiscences* (London, 1938), p. 201; Lord George Hamilton, *Parliamentary Reminiscences and Reflections, 1886–1906* (London, 1922), pp. 136–37; Wilhelm II, *Aus Meinem Leben*, p. 140.

4. Anna Wagemann, *Prinzessin Feodora: Erinnerungen an den Augustenburger und den preussischen Hof . . .* (Berlin, 1932), p. 53; memo by Hollmann (27 Aug. 1880), GFM 31/19/000189–91.

5. Wilhelm II, *Aus Meinem Leben*, pp. 270–72; there are some drawings from 1885 in BPHA, Rep. 192, no. 21. For a very favorable opinion of Wilhelm's technical expertise in naval architecture, see Eulenburg Papers, no. 80:46, but cf. Bülow, 1:68–69. The Kaiser was an honorary member of the British Institute of Naval Architects.

6. Adm. Erich Raeder, *Mein Leben*, 2 vols. (Tübingen, 1956–57), 1:62; Capt. L. Persius, *Menschen und Schiffe in der Kaiserlichen Flotte* (Berlin, 1925), p. 43. Between 1891 and 1913 Wilhelm also had built five sailing yachts, all christened *Meteor*, as well as a "Privatyacht," the *Iduna* (1899).

7. Eulenburg Papers, no. 80:43; also Herbert Bismarck to Rantzau (30 July 1889), Bismarck Papers, no. FC3014/1219, and Ludwig Raschdau, *Unter Bismarck und Caprivi: Erinnerungen eines deutschen Diplomaten aus den Jahren 1885–1894* (Berlin, 1939), p. 175.

8. Undated memo by Senden, Senden Papers, no. 11:21; Capt. Georg Müller to Tirpitz (8 Dec. 1899), Tirpitz Papers, no. 207.

9. Wedel diary (9 Apr. 1891), Wedel, p. 166; Waldersee diary (9 Oct. 1888, 6 May 1890), Waldersee, 2:4, 126–27; Capt. Georg Müller to Tirpitz (8 Dec. 1899), Tirpitz Papers, no. 207.

10. On Wilhelm and the navy, see the important study by Ivo N. Lambi, *The Navy and German Power Politics, 1862–1914* (Boston, 1984), esp. pp. 31–37. See also Berghahn, esp. pp. 23–45, and Wilhelm Deist, *Flottenpolitik und Flottenpropaganda: Das Nachrichtenbureau des Reichsmarineamtes, 1897–1914*, (Stuttgart, 1976), esp. pp. 19–69, both excellent books, Deist's being far richer in content that his somewhat technical title indicates. Hans Hallmann, *Der Weg zum Deutschen Schlachtflottenbau* (Stuttgart, 1933), pp. 48–101, is still useful. All show that Wilhelm's significance in German navalism lay in his enthusiasm for the cause rather than in any substantial contribution to technology or strategy.

11. For Wilhelm II's attention to the navy early in his reign, see Lambi, *Navy and Power Politics*, pp. 32–33; undated memo by Senden, Senden Papers, no. 11:21, 40.

12. Baron Werner von Rheinbaben, *Viermal Deutschland: Aus dem Erleben eines Seemanns, Diplomaten, Politikers, 1895–1954* (Berlin, 1954), p. 27; Friedrich Rosen, *Aus einem Diplomatischen Wanderleben*, 4 vols. in 3 (Berlin, 1931–59), 1:11–12, 3/4:14.

13. Gen. Baron Paul von Schoenaich, *Mein Damaskus: Erlebnisse und Bekenntnisse* (Berlin, 1926), p. 29; also Persius, *Menschen und Schiffe*, pp. 7–12, on snobbery within the navy. See also Holger H. Herwig, *The German Naval*

Officer Corps, 1890–1918: A Social and Political History (Oxford, 1973), chaps. 3–4; Jonathan Steinberg, *Yesterday's Deterrent: Tirpitz and the Birth of the German Battle Fleet* (London, 1965), pp. 39–41, and his "The Kaiser's Navy and German Society," *Past and Present* 28 (1964): 102–10. On the disdain for water sports, see Poultney Bigelow, "How the German Emperor Took to the Water," *Harper's Weekly* (June 15, 1895).

14. Georg Hinzpeter, *Kaiser Wilhelm II.: Eine Skizze nach der Natur gezeichnet* (Bielefeld, 1888), p. 7; also Wilhelm II, *Aus Meinem Leben*, pp. 274–75.

15. Senden's undated memo, Senden Papers, no. 11:39–40.

16. For aristocratic hostility, see the memoir by Baron Walter von Keyserlingk in *Das Buch der Keyserlinge: An der Grenze zweier Welten. Lebenserinnerungen aus einem Geschlecht* (Berlin, 1937), p. 352.

17. Prince Heinrich von Schönburg-Waldenburg, *Erinnerungen aus Kaiserlicher Zeit* (Leipzig, 1929), p. 148; Eulenburg to Bülow (25 Sept. 1900), Röhl, 3:1998. There is an interesting letter by Wilhelm II to Hollmann on spiritualism (15 Feb. 1903) in BPHA, Rep. 53a, no. 59. Accusations of toadyism are in Captain Müller to Tirpitz (22 Oct. 1896), Tirpitz Papers, no. 207; Count Robert Zedlitz-Trützschler, *Zwölf Jahre am Deutschen Kaiserhof: Aufzeichnungen* (Berlin and Leipzig, 1924), p. 181, and Bülow, 1:68.

18. Hollmann memo (20 Apr. 1895) on the need for ships, in Senden Papers, no. 9. On his failure to formulate any long-range plans, see Jagemann to Brauer (12 Mar. 1897), Fuchs, 3:618–19.

19. On Senden's unpopularity, see Tirpitz to Hollmann (13 May 1901), Tirpitz Papers, no. 20; Hohenlohe diary (12 Dec. 1896), Hohenlohe, 3:288–89; Eulenburg to Holstein (7 Feb. 1897), *HP*, 4:14; Holstein to Eulenburg (9 Feb. 1896), ibid., 3:593; same to same (15 Feb. and 5 Mar. 1897), Röhl, 3:1787, 1796; Ernst Jäckh, ed., *Kiderlen-Wächter, der Staatsmann und Mensch: Briefwechsel und Nachlass*, 2 vols. (Berlin and Leipzig, 1924), 1:100; Eckardstein, *König Eduard*, p. 81; Marschall diary (15, 19 Mar. 1897), Fuchs, 3:626, nn. 1, 3. There is a hostile sketch in RA I61/35a (Grierson to Bigge, 26 Feb. 1898).

20. Eulenburg to Wilhelm (12 Nov. 1896), Röhl, 3:1754. For Senden's technical assistance, see Hohenlohe diary (12 Dec. 1896), Hohenlohe, 3:288–89; his Prussian character in Tirpitz diary (11 Sept. 1904), Tirpitz Papers, no. 21.

21. Memo by Swaine (27 Dec. 1888), Salisbury Papers, no. 61; Wilhelm to Lord Charles Beresford (26 Dec. 1888), Beresford Papers. There is a letter by Wilhelm's cousin, the Grand Duchess Augusta Caroline of Mecklenburg-Strelitz to Princess Adolphus of Teck (7 Sept. 1888) in which she reports that the young Kaiser's aim is "to out-do *all* other fleets"; RA GV CC50/184. Eckardstein, *Lebenserinnerungen*, 1:106, reports Wilhelm's saying in 1890 that Germany's fleet must be equal to, or at least worthy of (*ebenbürtig*), Great Britain's in size. There is no other evidence that Wilhelm II entertained such ambitions as early as 1888, and these two sources are not entirely reliable, for Wilhelm had no direct contact with the Grand Duchess, and Eckardstein's memoirs are notoriously inaccurate. See chapter 12 at note 57 for Wilhelm II's view in the first years of his reign that the Royal Navy should guard the Mediterranean against France and Russia.

22. Wilhelm to Beresford (13 Feb. 1890), Beresford Papers; Swaine to Malet (14 Jan. 1892), FO 64/1273; Swaine memos (4, 5 Nov. 1893), ibid., 1295; Wilhelm to Salisbury (20 Dec. 1893), GFM 26/40/00548–57; same to Queen Victoria (22 Dec. 1889, 24 Feb. 1890, 16 Feb. 1891), RA I57/75, I58/21, E56/40; Hamilton, *Parliamentary Reminiscences*, p. 138; Lady Gwendolen Cecil, *Life of Robert, Marquis of Salisbury*, 4 vols. (London, 1921–32), 4:367.

23. Lord George Hamilton, First Lord of the Admiralty in 1885–86 and from 1886 to 1892, both appreciated and mistrusted the Kaiser's advice. See his *Parliamentary Reminiscences*, p. 138, and his letter to Salisbury (21 Feb. 1891), GFM 26/69/frame numbers illegible.

24. See his letter to his mother (1 June 1898), *HP*, 4:82–84.

25. Lascelles to Salisbury (11 Mar. 1899), Salisbury Papers, no. 121; same to Knollys (17 Jan. 1902), Lascelles Papers, FO 800/10; Szögyényi to Goluchowski (29 Jan. 1902), HHStA, no. 158(V).

26. Wilhelm II's remarks to Baron Axel von Varnbüler (5 Nov. 1897), in Lambi, *Navy and Power Politics*, p. 35.

27. For example, Lascelles to Salisbury (26 May 1899), FO 64/1470; Bülow, 1:55–56, 2:319.

28. Wilhelm's marginalia on Hatzfeldt to Caprivi (11 Nov. 1894), *GP*, 9:155–56.

29. Treutler Papers, no. 15:2.

30. Berghahn, p. 253.

31. Eulenburg's undated notes, Eulenburg Papers, no. 74, pt. 2:56.

32. *Das Buch der Keyserlinge*, pp. 330–31; Berghahn, pp. 27–28. Tirpitz encouraged Wilhelm II in this view. See Karl F. Nowak and Friedrich Thimme, eds., *Erinnerungen und Gedanken des Botschafters Anton Graf Monts* (Berlin, 1932), p. 195.

33. Camille Barrère (chargé, Munich) to Hanotaux (30 Sept. 1896), Hanotaux notes (2 Oct. 1896), *DDF*, 12:763–64, 781; Wilhelm II's memo (22 Aug. 1898), *GP*, 14(1):333–38; RA I58/21 (Wilhelm to Queen Victoria, 24 Feb. 1890).

34. Speech by Wilhelm II before the Royal War Academy, Berlin, 8 Feb. 1895, in GFM, PG/50658.

35. W. D. Puleston, *Mahan: The Life and Work of Captain Alfred Thayer Mahan, U.S.N.* (New Haven, 1939), p. 159. See also Charles C. Taylor, *The Life of Admiral Mahan, Naval Philosopher* ... (New York, 1920), p. 130. For Wilhelm's enthusiasm for Mahan, see Andrew Dickson White, *Autobiography*, 2 vols. (New York, 1905), 2:224; Richard von Kühlmann, *Erinnerungen* (Heidelberg, 1948), p. 130.

36. Wilhelm II's speech (8 Feb. 1895), to the Royal War Academy, GFM, PG/50658; William L. Langer, *The Diplomacy of Imperialism, 1890–1902*, 2d ed. (1935; rpt. New York, 1956), p. 431.

37. Berghahn, p. 144; also p. 150, n. 157.

38. Wilhelm to Hohenlohe (10 Jan. 1900), Hohenlohe, 3:555–56, urges building a fleet to pander to anti-British sentiment that was then widespread in Germany. This was a momentary reaction and reveals no sense of a more subtle use of the navy as a unifying element in German society. Berghahn, pp. 145–46,

makes a brief and general argument that Wilhelm II did in fact regard the navy as a means of "negative integration" but supplies no supporting evidence.

39. Eulenburg diary (5 Aug. 1893), Eulenburg Papers, no. 25:361.

40. Malet to Lord Rosebery (3 Feb. 1894), FO 64/1325.

41. This was Wilhelm's reaction to a serious crisis in Siam in 1893 that he feared would expand into a war with France and Russia. See Eulenburg notes (30 July 1893), Johannes Haller, ed., *Aus dem Leben des Fürsten Philipp zu Eulenburg-Hertefeld* (Berlin, 1924), pp. 84–85; a less informative version is in Prince Philipp zu Eulenburg-Hertefeld, *Das Ende König Ludwigs II. und andere Erlebnisse* (Leipzig, 1934), pp. 214–15.

42. Count Bogdan von Hutten-Czapski, *Sechzig Jahre Politik und Gesellschaft*, 2 vols. (Berlin, 1936), 2:243; Szögyényi to Goluchowski (13 Mar. 1897), HHStA, no. 149(B); Hohenlohe memo (14 Mar. 1897), Hohenlohe, 3:320 and also 151–52; Deist, *Flottenpolitik*, p. 28.

43. Szögyényi to Goluchowski (13 Mar. 1897), HHStA, no. 149(B).

44. Hohenlohe to Wilhelm (14 Jan. 1896), Hohenlohe, 3:156–58.

45. Holstein to Bülow (17 Feb. 1897), *HP*, 4:19; same to Eulenburg (15 Feb. 1897), Röhl, 3:1787; Vice Adm. Adolf von Trotha, *Grossadmiral von Tirpitz: Flottenbau und Reichsgedanke* (Breslau, 1933), pp. 82–83.

46. Marschall diary (5 Feb. 1895), Fuchs, 3:390, n. 4. Ambassador Hatzfeldt in London also deplored the Kaiser's naval mania. See Eckardstein, *Lebenserinnerungen*, 2:161.

47. For Senden's Anglophobia, see Berghahn, p. 189.

48. Jagemann to Brauer (12 Mar. 1897), Fuchs, 3:618–19; Hohenlohe memo (n.d.), Hohenlohe, 3:152; Szögyényi to Goluchowski (13 Mar. 1897), HHStA, no. 149(B).

49. Walter Görlitz, ed., *Der Kaiser . . . : Aufzeichnungen des Chefs des Marinekabinetts Admiral Georg Alexander v. Müller über die Ära Wilhelms II.* (Berlin, 1965), p. 32.

50. Still unsurpassed on this point is Eckart Kehr, *Battleship Building and Party Politics in Germany, 1894–1901: A Cross-section of the Political, Social and Ideological Preconditions of German Imperialism*, trans. Pauline R. and Eugene N. Anderson, (1930; rpt. Chicago, 1973), esp. chaps. 6, 8.

51. Eugen von Jagemann, *Fünfundsiebzig Jahre des Erlebens und Erfahrens (1849–1924)* (Heidelberg, 1925), p. 131.

52. Tirpitz, p. 49; Szögyényi to Goluchowski (13 Mar. 1897), HHStA, no. 149(B); Hohenlohe memo (n.d. but ca. Jan. 1896), Hohenlohe, 3:152; Jagemann to Brauer (12 Mar. 1897), Fuchs, 3:618–19.

53. Berghahn, p. 189.

54. Deist, *Flottenpolitik*, pp. 28–29, 32. Wilhelm had reduced Hollmann's original budget request in the vain hope that the Reichstag might find a more modest figure palatable; ibid., pp. 25–26.

55. Kehr, *Battleship Building and Party Politics*, p. 47; Tirpitz, pp. 49–50.

56. Speech of 8 Feb. 1895, GFM, PG/50658. Tirpitz probably wrote part of it. See his undated notes in Tirpitz Papers, no. 100.

57. Lambi, *Navy and Power Politics*, p. 33.

58. Ibid., p. 86; Tirpitz to Albrecht von Stosch (13 Feb. 1896), Tirpitz, pp. 50–51.

59. Hohenlohe to Wilhelm (7 Jan. 1896), Hohenlohe, 3:152–53. For Wilhelm's earlier view of the hopelessness of asking the Reichstag to approve a massive naval budget, see Eulenburg to Holstein (7 Oct. 1893), Röhl, 2:1117–18 and Senden to Tirpitz (25 July 1894), Tirpitz Papers, no. 208. At the end of 1895, Wilhelm instructed Hollmann to adopt the plan advanced by Tirpitz of asking the Reichstag to appropriate funds over a period of several years rather than for a single fiscal year. See Berghahn, p. 82.

60. Wilhelm to Hohenlohe (8 Jan. 1896), Hohenlohe, 3:153–54. On Senden's role in using the Transvaal affair to promote the navy with Wilhelm, see Berghahn, pp. 84, 184; Winzen, p. 76, n. 70; and Tirpitz, pp. 79–81, for the Anglophobic effect the crisis had on the German navy in general.

61. Eulenburg notes (9 July 1896), Röhl, 3:1702; Wilhelm to Hohenlohe (25 Oct. 1896), Bülow Papers, no. 112.

62. Winzen, p. 76, n. 70.

63. Lambi, *Navy and Power Politics*, pp. 115–16, on the 28 Jan. 1896 meeting. As early as 1891 Wilhelm had seen Tirpitz as the future head of the navy. See Berghahn, p. 70.

64. Senden to Tirpitz (31 Mar. 1896), in Steinberg, *Yesterday's Deterrent*, p. 96.

65. Tirpitz, p. 79, indicating differences on details but not on the principle of a battleship-based fleet. There is little evidence for why Wilhelm changed his mind. Tirpitz's battleship strategy, which the Kaiser had rejected earlier in favor of a cruiser-based navy, had not changed. Wilhelm's adoption of Tirpitz's idea, which Tirpitz said he adopted in June 1897, seems therefore to have been due to the aggravation he felt at England in the wake of the Transvaal crisis. This led him not only to insist on a fleet but one that was much larger and more powerful than anything Hollmann had thus far proposed. See Tirpitz notes (15 Apr. 1909), Tirpitz Papers, no. 8.

66. Unsigned naval memo (4 Apr. 1897), GFM 26/1, vol. 1/00002; Wilhelm to Senden (9 Apr. 1897), ibid., 00004; Senden to Capt. Wilhelm Büchsel (9 Apr. 1897), ibid., 26/98/00045–46; Hohenlohe diary (3 Feb. 1897), Hohenlohe, 3:295.

67. Wilhelm to Hohenlohe (25 Oct. 1896), Bülow Papers, no. 112; on the French blockade, Hohenlohe diary (7 Mar. 1897), Hohenlohe, 3:311.

68. On the Transvaal, Eulenburg notes (9 July 1896), Röhl, 3:1703; on Crete, Holstein to Eulenburg (15 Feb. 1897), ibid., 1787; on Samoa, Hohenlohe diary (31 Jan. 1895), Hohenlohe, 3:32; on Venezuela, Wilhelm to Hohenlohe (8 Jan. 1896), ibid., 153. On Anglo-German rivalry in Venezuela in 1896, see Holger H. Herwig's important study, *Germany's Vision of Empire in Venezuela, 1871–1914* (Princeton, 1986), esp. pp. 212–13. Some of these disputes are discussed below in chapter 14 at note 11.

69. Holstein to Bülow (16 Nov. 1896), Bülow Papers, no. 90.

70. Szögyényi to Goluchowski (6 Feb. 1896), HHStA, no. 148(V); Waldersee diary (Jan. 21, 1896), Waldersee, 2:365.

71. Eulenburg to Wilhelm (12 Nov. 1896), Röhl, 3:1753; Holstein to Eulenburg (9 Feb. 1896), *HP*, 3:593.

72. Marschall diary (19 Mar. 1897), Fuchs, 3:626, n. 3; Szögyényi to Goluchowski (31 Jan. 1897), HHStA, no. 149(B).

73. Waldersee diary (21 Jan. 1896), Waldersee, 2:365. On Wilhelm's annoyance at the Reichstag, see Ludwig Raschdau diary (14 Jan. 1896) in his *In Weimar als Preussischer Gesandter: Ein Buch der Erinnerungen an deutsche Fürstenhöfe, 1894–1897* (Berlin, 1939), p. 55.

74. Eulenburg to Holstein (31 Jan. 1896), *HP*, 3:589.

75. Hohenlohe diary (7, 30 Mar. 1897), Hohenlohe, 3:311, 327; Holstein to Bülow (17 Feb. 1897), *HP*, 4:19.

76. Holstein to Bülow (5 Mar. 1897), Bülow Papers, no. 90; same to Eulenburg (5 Mar. 1897), Röhl, 3:1796.

77. On *Bundesfürsten* opposition, Hohenlohe diary (24 Mar. 1897), Hohenlohe, 3:321; Hohenlohe to Wilhelm (late Mar. 1897), ibid., 325; Holstein to Hatzfeldt (14 Apr. 1897), *HP*, 4:28.

78. Holstein to Bülow (17 Feb. 1897), *HP*, 4:18–19; same to Eulenburg (15 Feb. 1897), Röhl, 3:1787.

79. Holstein to Eulenburg (15 Feb. 1897), Röhl, 3:1787; Marschall diary (7 Mar. 1897), Fuchs, 3:618, n. 3.

80. Hohenlohe diary (8 Mar. 1897), Hohenlohe, 3:312.

81. Letter of 6 Mar. 1897, ibid., 310.

82. Hohenlohe to Wilhelm (9 Mar. 1897), Hohenlohe, 3:312–13; same to Eulenburg (25 Mar. 1897), ibid., 322; Hohenlohe's undated notes (ca. Mar. 1897), ibid., 325; Holstein to Bülow (17 Feb. 1897), *HP*, 4:19.

83. Szögyényi to Goluchowski (13 Mar. 1897), HHStA, no. 149(B).

84. Holstein to Bülow (17 Feb. 1897), *HP*, 4:19; see also same to Eulenburg (5 Mar. 1897), Röhl, 3:1796, Hohenlohe to same (25 Mar. 1897), Hohenlohe, 3:322.

85. Jagemann to Brauer (15 Feb. 1897), Fuchs, 3:601.

86. Eugen Schiffer, *Ein Leben für den Liberalismus* (Berlin, 1951), p. 58; Friedrich Payer, *Von Bethmann Hollweg bis Ebert: Erinnerungen und Bilder* (Frankfurt, 1923), pp. 16, 173–74.

87. Princess Marie Radziwill diary (30/31 Mar. 1897), in her *Lettres de la Princesse Radziwill au Général de Robilant, 1889–1914: Une grande dame d'avant guerre*, 4 vols. (Bologna, 1933–34), 2:74.

88. Hohenlohe diary (27 Mar. 1897), Hohenlohe, 3:323; Holstein to Bülow (Feb. 17, 1897), *HP*, 4:18; Szögyényi to Goluchowski (Mar. 13, 1897), HHStA, no. 149(B).

89. Hohenlohe to Eulenburg (25 Mar. 1897), Hohenlohe, 3:322–23; Raschdau diary (28, 29 Apr. 1897), Raschdau, *In Weimar*, p. 133.

90. Holstein to Bülow (17 Feb. 1897), *HP*, 4:18–19; Raschdau diary (29 Apr. 1897), Raschdau, *In Weimar*, p. 133.

91. Hellmut von Gerlach, *Von Rechts nach Links* (Zurich, 1937), p. 188; Eulenburg to Wilhelm (18 Aug. 1897), Röhl, 2:1853.

92. Waldersee diary (16 Mar. 1897), Waldersee, 2:393.

93. Hohenlohe diary (30 Mar. 1897), Hohenlohe, 3:327.

94. Waldersee diary (n.d. but 2 Jan. 1898), Waldersee, 2:408; Prince Alexander von Hohenlohe to Eulenburg (30 Mar. 1897), Röhl, 3:1809.

95. Hohenlohe to Wilhelm (28 Mar. 1897), in Heinrich O. Meisner, "Der Kanzler Hohenlohe und die Mächte seiner Zeit," *Preussische Jahrbücher* 230 (1932): 146–47; Hohenlohe's undated notes (Mar. 1897), Hohenlohe, 3:325.

96. Hohenlohe diary (30 Mar. 1897), Hohenlohe, 3:326; Szögyényi to Goluchowski (10 Apr. 1897), HHStA, no. 148(V).

97. Hohenlohe diary (30 Mar. 1897), Hohenlohe, 3:326.

98. Alexander Hohenlohe to Eulenburg (30 Mar. 1897), Röhl, 3:1809; Jagemann to Brauer (8 Apr. 1897), Fuchs, 3:635.

99. Tirpitz to Crown Prince Wilhelm of Prussia (15 Apr. 1909), Tirpitz Papers, no. 8; Tirpitz, p. 134. For a recent assessment of Wilhelm's important role in German navalism, see John C. G. Röhl, *Kaiser, Hof und Staat: Wilhelm II. und die deutsche Politik* (Munich, 1987), p. 129.

100. Tirpitz, pp. 133–34; Ulrich von Hassell, *Tirpitz: Sein Leben und Wirken mit Berücksichtigung seiner Beziehungen zu Albrecht von Stosch* (Stuttgart, 1920), p. 156. Tirpitz's undated notes on his early relationship with Wilhelm, Tirpitz Papers, no. 100.

101. Tirpitz notes (16 June 1897), Tirpitz Papers, no. 4; Tirpitz, pp. 133–34.

102. Tirpitz notes (10 Dec. 1903), Tirpitz Papers, no. 20; Tirpitz notes of a talk with Count August zu Eulenburg (24 Nov. 1916), ibid, no. 203; Berghahn, pp. 207, 351.

103. Winzen, p. 89.

104. Lambi, *Navy and Power Politics*, pp. 165–67.

105. Ibid.; also pp. 191, 197; Berghahn, pp. 92–93. On the Admiralstab, see Walther Hubatsch, *Der Admiralstab und die Obersten Marinebehörden im Deutschland, 1848–1945* (Frankfurt, 1958).

106. Berghahn, p. 456.

107. Caprivi to Tirpitz (28 Mar. 1891), Hassell, *Tirpitz*, p. 65; Gen. Albrecht von Stosch to same (5 Oct. 1894), ibid., p. 102; Trotha, *Tirpitz*, p. 44; Bülow, 1:113.

108. Letter of 29 August 1897, Röhl, 3:1863–64.

109. Deist, *Flottenpolitik*, p. 44.

110. Gen. Karl von Einem, *Erinnerungen eines Soldaten, 1853–1933* (Leipzig, 1933), p. 153; Tirpitz, pp. 85–86, 134–37; Bülow, 1:113 on Wilhelm's treatment of Tirpitz. For Wilhelm on Tirpitz's personality, see Hohenlohe diary (6 Oct. 1893), Hohenlohe 3:463; Müller, *Kaiser*, pp. 62–64; report of a conversation between Wilhelm II and Lt. Col. Alfred Niemann (17 Dec. 1926), Rijksarchief Papers, no. 253. Admiral von Lans once told Hans Delbrück that Tirpitz always had "the greatest anxiety" before Wilhelm II. Delbrück's undated notes, Delbrück Papers, no. 55.

111. Tirpitz, p. 145; Bülow, 1:113.

112. This passage was omitted from the published version in the *National Zeitung* (16 Mar. 1894). See Deist, *Flottenpolitik*, p. 35. For Tirpitz's interest in British economic development, see Tirpitz Papers, no. 114.

113. Steinberg, *Yesterday's Deterrent*, pp. 208–23, prints a memo of June

1897 for an audience of 15 June. On Tirpitz's anti-British orientation from the outset of his service as state secretary, see Deist, *Flottenpolitik*, p. 10.

114. Tirpitz, pp. 85–86.

115. Holstein to Hatzfeldt (31 May 1898), *HP*, 4:81–82; Winzen, p. 76, n. 70.

116. Wilhelm to Senden (9 Apr. 1897), GFM 26/1/00004.

117. Ibid.; Senden to Büchsel (20 May 1897), ibid., 26/97/00045–46.

118. Deputy Fritz Hoenig to Tirpitz (6 Dec. 1897), Tirpitz Papers, no. 4; Berghahn, p. 122.

119. See especially ibid., pp. 13–14, 30, and Deist, *Flottenpolitik*, pp. 26–27.

120. On the economic factor in fleet building, see most recently Berghahn, pp. 129–57; also Eckart Kehr, "Soziale und Finanzielle Grundlagen der Deutschen Flottenpropaganda," in Hans-Ulrich Wehler, ed., *Moderne Deutsche Sozialgeschichte* (Cologne, 1966), 389–403.

121. Röhl, 3:1853.

122. Radziwill diary (19/20 Nov. 1897), Radziwill, *Lettres*, 2:99.

123. Hohenlohe to Wilhelm (23 Mar. 1898) and Wilhelm to Hohenlohe (27 Mar. 1898), Hohenlohe, 3:435–37.

CHAPTER 14

1. Wilhelm to Hohenlohe (31 Aug. 1895), Hohenlohe, 3:95.

2. John E. Schrecker, *Imperialism and Chinese Nationalism: Germany in Shantung* (Cambridge, Mass., 1971), pp. 22–23; see also Reiner Pommerin, *Der Kaiser und Amerika: Die USA in der Politik der Reichsleitung, 1890–1917* (Cologne and Vienna, 1986), pp. 63–70. For Wilhelm on coaling stations, see Hohenlohe diary (2 Nov. 1894), Hohenlohe, 3:8; also Eulenburg notes (19 Sept. 1895), Eulenburg Papers, no. 37:609–10. On his concern at Japan, see Ludwig Raschdau's diary (24 Apr. 1895), in his *In Weimar als Preussischer Gesandter: Ein Buch der Erinnerungen an deutsche Fürstenhöfe, 1894–1897* (Berlin, 1939), pp. 24–26.

3. Szögyényi to Goluchowski (2 Jan. 1898), HHStA, no. 150(B).

4. Holstein to Hatzfeldt (20 Apr. 1895), Ebel, 2:1035; Hohenlohe diary (11 Apr. 1895), Hohenlohe, 3:58; Count Bogdan von Hutten-Czapski, *Sechzig Jahre Politik und Gesellschaft*, 2 vols. (Berlin, 1936), 1:345; Lascelles to Salisbury (30 Dec. 1897), FO 64/1412. Gustav Detring, an official in the German customs service stationed in China who had great influence in the Chinese government, apparently influenced the Kaiser to take Kiaochow. See Holstein to Bülow (23 Nov. 1896), Bülow Papers, no. 90. On Detring, see Schrecker, *Imperialism and Chinese Nationalism*, p. 8.

5. Wilhelm to Hohenlohe (6 Nov. 1897), Hohenlohe Papers, no. 1607; see also Schrecker, *Imperialism and Chinese Nationalism*, pp. 33, 136.

6. Holstein to Eulenburg (23 Nov. 1897), Röhl, 3:1874; same to Hatzfeldt (13 Nov 1897), *HP*, 4:49.

7. Grierson to Viscount Gough (first secretary, Berlin) (18 Dec. 1897), FO 64/1412. For Wilhelm's efforts to gain the Tsar's approval of a German occupa-

tion at Kiaochow, see his letter to Hohenlohe (7 Nov. 1897) informing the chancellor of the message and Nicholas II's response; Hohenlohe 3:409. See also Abraham Yarmolinsky, ed. and trans., *The Memoirs of Count Witte* (Garden City and Toronto, 1921), p. 410, and Bülow's analysis of the Russian interest in Kiaochow in Szögyényi to Goluchowski (20 Aug. 1897), HHStA, no. 149(B). The Kaiser first brought the matter of Russia's helping Germany take an unspecified Chinese port as early as April 1895. See Wilhelm to Nicholas II (20 Apr. 1895), in Walter Goetz, ed., *Briefe Wilhelms II. an den Zaren, 1894–1914* (Berlin, n.d.), p. 291.

8. Wire of 7 Nov. 1897, Hohenlohe, 3:409.

9. Lascelles to Salisbury (26 May 1898), FO 64/1438.

10. William L. Langer, *The Diplomacy of Imperialism, 1890–1902*, 2d ed. (1931; rpt. New York, 1955), p. 453.

11. For the Kaiser's relations with King George and the Tsarina, see Lamar Cecil, "William II and his Russian 'Colleagues,'" in Carole Fink, Isabel V. Hull, and MacGregor Knox, eds., *German Nationalism and the European Response, 1890–1945* (Norman, Okla., 1985), pp. 121–23.

12. This unsavory business can be followed in Arthur G. Lee, ed., *The Empress Writes to Sophie, Her Daughter, Crown Princess and Later Queen of the Hellenes: Letters, 1889–1901* (London, n.d. [1955]), passim. Wilhelm and his sister were not reconciled until 1898.

13. Lascelles to Salisbury (16 Feb. 1897), Salisbury Papers, no. 120; same to same (5 Mar. 1897), FO 64/1409; on humbling the King, same to same (18 Feb. 1897), ibid. For Wilhelm's failure to consult Marschall, see Lascelles to Salisbury (20 Feb. 1897), Ebel, 2:1130, n. 2. See also Wilhelm to Hohenlohe and Hohenlohe to Wilhelm (both 25 Feb. 1897), Hohenlohe Papers, no. 1605.

14. Lascelles to Salisbury (18 Feb. 1897), FO 64/1409; also same to same (20 Feb. 1897), Ebel, 2:1130, n. 2; RA I61/2a (Grierson to Bigge, 20 Feb. 1897).

15. Holstein to Hatzfeldt (15 Feb. 1897), Ebel, 2:1130–31; same to Eulenburg (15 Feb. 1897), Röhl, 3:1787. Eulenburg complained to Wilhelm about Senden's influence. See Eulenburg to Wilhelm (12 Nov. 1896), ibid., 1753–54. William sent Queen Victoria a number of annoying telegrams on the Cretan situation that she correctly described as "grandiloquent": RA Queen Victoria's Journal (8, 13 May 1897).

16. Noailles to Hanotaux (14 Feb. 1897), *DDF*, 13:199.

17. Lascelles to Salisbury (19 Feb. 1897), FO 64/1409.

18. Wilhelm II's marginalia on Baron Ludwig von Plessen (minister at Athens) to Hohenlohe (28 Mar. 1897), *GP*, 12:395–96.

19. The literature is vast, but see esp. H. W. Koch, "The Anglo-German Alliance: Missed Opportunity of Myth?" *History* 14 (1969): 378–92; Winzen, chap. 3; Paul M. Kennedy, "German Weltpolitik and the Alliance Negotiations with England, 1897–1900," *Journal of Modern History* 45 (1973): 605–25; Kennedy, chap. 13; Christopher Howard, *Splendid Isolation: A Study of Ideas Concerning Britain's International Position and Foreign Policy during the Later Years of the Third Marquis of Salisbury* (London, 1967).

20. For Bülow's hostility to England, see Holstein to Ida von Stülpnagel (Nov. 1902), in Helmuth Rogge, ed., *Friedrich von Holstein: Lebensbekenntnis in*

Briefen an eine Frau (Berlin, 1932), p. 214; same to Maximilian von Brandt (23 Dec. 1905), *HP*, 4:376–78; Holstein diary (11 Jan. 1902), ibid., 244–45; Princess Evelyn Blücher, ed., *Memoirs of Prince Blücher* (London, 1932), p. 218; Fairfax Cartwright to Sir Edward Grey, (30 Aug. 1907), *BD*, 7:51–52; Gerhard von Mutius to Friedrich Thimme (11 Feb. 1930), Thimme Papers, no. 17; Loebell Papers, no. 27, 2:30. For British awareness of Bülow's attitude see, in addition to the Cartwright letter above, Edward Goschen (ambassador, Berlin) to Charles Hardinge (under secretary, Foreign Office) (28 Jan. 1910)), *BD*, 7:437; Austen Chamberlain, *Politics from Inside: An Epistolary Chronicle, 1906–1914* (London, n.d. [1936]), p. 95; Marie von Bunsen, *Zeitgenossen die ich Erlebte, 1900–1930* (Leipzig, 1932), p. 80. For the Anglophobe strain in Bülow's diplomacy, see Winzen and also his *Die Frühphase der Bülow'schen Aussenpolitik, 1897–1901* (Boppard, 1976) and Barbara Vogel, *Deutsche Russlandpolitik, 1900–1906* (Düsseldorf, 1973).

21. Bülow to Baron Oswald von Richthofen (26 July 1899), in Paul M. Kennedy, *The Samoan Tangle: A Study in Anglo-German-American Relations, 1878–1900* (New York, 1974), p. 191.

22. Ivo N. Lambi, *The Navy and German Power Politics, 1862–1914* (Boston, 1984), pp. 151–59; also see ibid., p. 164, for Tirpitz's reservations about Bülow.

23. Kennedy, *Samoan Tangle*, esp. chaps. 3–5; Pommerin, *Kaiser und Amerika*, pp. 95–103.

24. Wilhelm's marginalia on Hatzfeldt to Caprivi (11 Nov. 1894), *GP*, 9:153–59; Hohenlohe's notes of a talk with the Kaiser (31 Jan. 1895), Hohenlohe, 3:32.

25. RA I62/10, 10a, 11, 12 (Grierson to Lascelles, 3 May 1899; same to Bigge, 4 May 1899; Lascelles to Salisbury, 5 May 1899; same to Foreign Office, 26 May 1899).

26. RA I62/14 (27 May 1899).

27. Marginalia on Richthofen to Eulenburg (20 July 1898), in Kennedy, *Samoan Tangle*, p. 130.

28. Lascelles to Salisbury (26 May 1899), FO 64/1470.

29. RA Queen Victoria's Journal, (24 Nov. 1899).

30. RA I62/10 (Grierson to Lascelles, 3 May 1899); also same to Gough (6 Nov. 1899), FO 64/1471; see also Lascelles to Salisbury (19 Feb. 1900), FO 64/1492.

31. Lascelles to Salisbury 26 (May 1899), FO 64/1470.

32. RA I62/14.

33. RA I62/10a (Grierson to Bigge, 4 May 1899); RA I62/10 (same to Lascelles, 3 May 1899).

34. Holstein to Hatzfeldt (27 Aug. 1899), Ebel, 2:1257.

35. Baron Hermann von Eckardstein, *Lebenserinnerungen u. Politische Denkwürdigkeiten*, 3 vols. (Leipzig, 1919–21), 2:14–15.

36. RA I62/15 (3 June 1899).

37. RA I62/18 (12 June 1899).

38. Waldersee diary (16 Mar. 1897), Waldersee, 3:394.

39. Holstein to Hatzfeldt (17 Aug. 1899), Ebel, 2:1253.

40. Szögyényi to Goluchowski (15 Mar. 1899), HHStA, no. 151(B); RA I62/6 (Grierson to Bigge, 18 Mar. 1899); Winzen, p. 188.

41. For Wilhelm's surprise, see Grierson to Gough (6 Nov. 1899), FO 64/1471. On general sympathy, see Waldersee diary (14 Oct. 1899), Waldersee, 2:4, 6; Lady Susan Townley, *'Indiscretions'* (New York, 1922), pp. 62–64; Monts to Holstein (2 Nov. 1899), in Karl F. Nowak and Friedrich Thimme, eds., *Erinnerungen und Gedanken des Botschafters Anton Graf Monts* (Berlin, 1932), p. 390. On the figures in the entourage: Szögyényi to Goluchowski (18 Dec. 1900), HHStA, no. 154(V); Lascelles to Salisbury (2 Mar. 1900), FO 64/1492; on the Kaiserin, Bülow, 1:398.

42. Eulenburg papers, no. 74, pt. 2:59–60; Waldersee diary (23, 29 Oct, 1899), Waldersee, 2:436–37. On the Kaiserin, see her letter to Bülow (9 Nov. 1899), Bülow Papers, no. 109.

43. RA W60/26 (Letter of 21 Dec. 1899).

44. For the India comparison, see Lascelles to Salisbury (20 Jan. 1899), FO 64/1439; for the Kaiser's criticism of the British role in South Africa, see Townley, *'Indiscretions,'* pp. 65–67; Lascelles to Salisbury (31 Oct. 1900), FO 64/1495.

45. Szögyényi to Goluchowski (16 Jan. 1900), HHStA, no. 153(B).

46. Wilhelm II memo (4 Feb. 1900), *GP*, 1:554–58; also Wilhelm's "Notes on the War in the Transvaal," in RA W60/26.

47. Letter of 23 Mar. 1900, *GP*, 15:559–60.

48. RA W60/105 (Wilhelm to the Prince of Wales, 3 Mar. 1900); ibid., I62/90, 92 (same to Queen Victoria, 31 Mar. 1900; Salisbury to the Queen, 10 Apr. 1900); Lascelles to Salisbury (2 Mar. 1900), FO 64/1492; same to Foreign Office (3 Mar. 1900), Salisbury Papers, no. 121; memo by Alfred Beit (29 Dec. 1905), Lascelles Papers, FO 800/13; Wilhelm to Queen Wilhelmina (27 Mar. 1900), *GP*, 15:533–39.

49. Lascelles to Salisbury (2 Mar. 1900), FO 64/1492; Szögyényi to Goluchowski (18 Dec. 1900), HHStA, no. 154(V); Wilhelm to Prince of Wales (23 Feb. 1900), *GP*, 15:559–60; Winston S. Churchill, *A Roving Commission: My Early Life* (New York, 1930), p. 303.

50. Swaine to Lascelles (20 Dec. 1895), FO 64/1351; RA I61/32a (Grierson to Bigge, 21 Jan. 1898).

51. Wilhelm's reaction to the speech is in Szögyényi to Goluchowski (26 May 1898), HHStA, no. 151(V); on the speech and its diplomatic repercussions, see Langer, *Diplomacy of Imperialism*, pp. 505–14.

52. RA I62/113 (Swaine to Bigge, 23 Dec. 1900); Lascelles to Salisbury (26 May 1899), Salisbury Papers, Class E (Lascelles).

53. RA I61/52 (Kaiserin Friedrich to Queen Victoria, 15 July 1898). For Bülow's efforts to persuade the Kaiser of Britain's deceit, see Winzen, pp. 173, 326.

54. Bülow to Friedrich von Rosen (16 Aug. 1921), Bülow Papers, no. 117.

55. Lascelles to Salisbury (26 May 1898), *BD*, 1:35. The quotations are Lascelles' paraphrase of the Kaiser's viewpoint. For Wilhelm's reservations about Chamberlain, see his letter to Bülow (8 Apr. 1898), *GP*, 14(1):168–69.

56. Swaine to Lascelles (19 Jan. 1896), FO 64/1376. Cf. Swaine memo (20 Nov. 1887), Salisbury Papers, no. 61, which notes that Wilhelm read only the *St. James Gazette*.

57. For the Kaiser's avidity in following the British press, see Swaine to Lascelles (19 Jan. 1896), FO 64/1376; on Jews, Poultney Bigelow to Wilhelm (28 Feb. 1898), Bülow Papers, no. 112. For Wilhelm's complaints about the way the British press treated him, see, inter alia, RA P21/135 (Cecil Rhodes to Prince of Wales, ca. Mar. 1899); Grierson to Lascelles (3 Mar., 5 May 1896), FO 64/1376–77. See also Szögyényi to Goluchowski (25 Apr. 1896), HHStA no. 147(B) for Chancellor Hohenlohe's concern at the damage the London press was doing to the improvement of Anglo-German relations. On the Kaiser's belief in the complicity of the London government, see Anne Topham, *Chronicles of the Prussian Court* (London, 1926), p. 133; Malet to Salisbury (5 Jan. 1889), Salisbury Papers, no. 62; Wilhelm to Marschall (25 Oct. 1895), Hohenlohe Papers, no. 1601. Queen Victoria worked to dampen press criticism of her grandson. See RA I61/30, 33 (Sir Theodore Martin to the Queen, 13 Jan. 1898; Bigge to same, 26 Jan. 1898). Wilhelm appreciated his grandmother's intervention. See Lascelles to Salisbury (27 May 1898), Salisbury Papers, no. 121; Szögyényi to Goluchowski (26 May 1898), HHStA, no. 151(V).

58. Wilhelm to Eulenburg (8 Jan. 1887), Röhl, 1:207; Maurice V. Brett, ed., *Journals and Letters of Reginald, Viscount Esher*, 4 vols. (London, 1934–38), 2:136–38; Count Robert Zedlitz-Trützschler, *Zwölf Jahre am Deutschen Kaiserhof: Aufzeichnungen* (Berlin and Leipzig, 1924), p. 97.

59. Ludwig Stein, ed., *England & Germany: By Leaders of Public Opinion in Both Countries* (London, 1912), p. 95; also Fedor von Zobeltitz, *Chronik der Gesellschaft unter dem Letzten Kaiserreich*, 2 vols. (Hamburg, 1922), 2:8–9.

60. Hohenlohe to Alexander Hohenlohe (7 Jan. 1900), Hohenlohe, 3:554.

61. Bülow to Eulenburg (8 Feb. 1892), Röhl, 2:763.

62. Ibid., 761.

63. Loebell Papers, no. 27, 2:30.

64. Winzen, passim; also Berghahn, pp. 380–401. See also Bülow's letter to Holstein (24 Nov. 1899), in Holger H. Herwig, *Politics of Frustration: The United States in German Naval Planning, 1889–1914* (Boston, 1976), p. 39.

65. Winzen, pp. 166–68.

66. Szögyényi to Goluchowski (18 Aug. 1898), HHStA, no. 151(V). On Africa, see same to same (3 Dec. 1898), ibid., no. 150(B); Lascelles to Salisbury (20 Jan. 1899), FO 64/1439.

67. Wilhelm to Bülow (10 Apr. 1898), GP, 14(1):217–18; Wilhelm to Nicholas II (18 Aug. 1898), Goetz, *Briefe Wilhelms II.*, p. 312.

68. Lascelles to Salisbury (27 May 1898), Salisbury Papers, no. 121.

69. Wilhelm to Bülow (10 Apr. 1898), GP, 14(1):217–18; Szögyényi to Goluchowski (3 Dec. 1898), HHStA, no. 150(B).

70. Bülow to Holstein (24 Nov. 1899), Bülow Papers, no. 91, partially printed in Bülow, 1:335.

71. Wilhelm's version in his memo (22 Aug. 1898), GP, 14(1):333–38; also Wilhelm to Bülow (8 Apr. 1898), ibid., 168–69, indicating it was Arthur James Balfour and not Chamberlain who seemed to be initiating the offer. Wilhelm describes his relations to England in Szögyényi to Goluchowski (Dec. 3, 1898), HHStA, no. 150(B). Lascelles' version is in his letters to Balfour (Aug. 26, Dec.

10, 1898), Salisbury Papers, no. 121, to Salisbury (21 Dec. 1898), FO 64/1655, and in RA I61/78 (Lascelles to Queen Victoria, Dec. 9, 1898). See also Winzen, pp. 178–81.

72. Wilhelm to Nicholas II (30 May 1898), Goetz, *Briefe Wilhelms II.,* pp. 309–11.

73. Berghahn, p. 145.

74. Kennedy, p. 226; Bülow to Holstein (28 Nov. 1899), *HP,* 4:168.

75. Tirpitz, p. 176; see also his *Politische Dokumente,* 2 vols. (Stuttgart and Berlin, 1924–26), 1:7.

76. Tirpitz notes (28 Sept. 1899), Tirpitz Papers, no. 5; Tirpitz, pp. 103–4.

77. Hohenlohe memo to the Federal governments (29 Nov. 1899), Tirpitz Papers, no. 5. Wilhelm's remarks to Count Axel von Varnbüler (Württenberg representative to the Federal Council) (ca. 2 Nov. 1899), in Lambi, *Navy and Power Politics,* p. 145. Wilhelm also believed there were lessons to be drawn from the Spanish-American war. Captain Büchsel to Tirpitz (19 July 1898), Tirpitz Papers, no. 200. See also Paul M. Kennedy, "Tirpitz, England and the Second Naval Law of 1900," *Militärgeschichtliche Mitteilungen* 2 (1970): 33–57.

78. Schulthess (1899), 151–52. Tirpitz's negative reaction to the speech is in Jagemann to Brauer (20 Dec. 1899), Fuchs, 4:214.

79. Eulenburg Papers, no. 74, pt. 2:51–53.

80. Wilhelm to Hohenlohe (29 Nov. 1899), Hohenlohe, 3:547; Tirpitz, p. 105.

81. The record on this trip is relatively scant. The fullest contemporary account is in Bülow to Holstein (24 Nov. 1899), Bülow Papers, no. 91, partially printed with other materials in Bülow, 1:334–44. See the reconstructions in Winzen, pp. 210–24, and J. A. S. Grenville, *Lord Salisbury and Foreign Policy at the Close of the Nineteenth Century,* 2d rev. ed. (London, 1970), pp. 277–81. See also Eckardstein, *Erinnerungen,* 2:106–7; Ebel, 2:1301–2.

82. Bülow to Holstein (Nov. 24, 1899), Bülow Papers, no. 91.

83. Same to Loebell (15 Nov. 1911), Loebell Papers, no. 7.

84. Szögyényi to Goluchowski (Jan. 16, 1900), HHStA, no. 153(B). Wilhelm II gives an account in his *Ereignisse und Gestalten aus den Jahren 1878–1918* (Leipzig and Berlin, 1922), pp. 196–97. At the same time, the British stopped a second German steamer elsewhere on the African coast.

85. Lascelles to Salisbury (19 Feb. 1900), FO 64/1492.

86. Same to same (20 Apr. 1900), FO 64/1493.

87. Peter Padfield, *The Great Naval Race: The Anglo-German Naval Rivalry, 1900–1914* (New York, 1974), p. 90. For Wilhelm's acceleration of the law, see his message to Hohenlohe (10 Jan. 1900), Hohenlohe, 3:555–56.

88. Tirpitz, p. 105.

89. Szögyényi to Goluchowski (16 Jan. 1900), HHStA, no. 153(B).

90. Letter of 9 Jan. 1900, in Oron J. Hale, *Publicity and Diplomacy: With Special Reference to England and Germany, 1890–1914* (New York, 1940), p. 224. See also Berghahn, p. 218, for Wilhelm's communications to the princes. An example is in his letter to the Grand Duke (2 Nov. 1899), Fuchs, 4:188. See also an unsigned and undated document outlining how Hohenlohe was to deal with the German governments in GFM 26/101/00608.

91. Hohenlohe to the German governments (6 Nov. 1899), Fuchs, 4:191–93.

92. Hohenlohe, 3:547.

93. Jagemann to Baron Karl von Reck (counsellor, Baden Ministry of the Royal House and Foreign Affairs, 17 Sept. 1900), Fuchs, 4:260.

94. For the provisions, see Schulthess (1898), 111–13.

95. Hohenlohe notes (n.d. but ca. Sept. 1900), Hohenlohe, 3:582.

96. Ibid., 592.

97. Eulenburg to Wilhelm (22 Oct. 1900), Röhl, 3:2009.

98. Letter of 23 July 1896, ibid., 3:1714.

99. Bülow's speech (25 Feb. 1899) on the occasion of Germany's acquisition of the Caroline islands, in Fritz Fisher, *Krieg der Illusionen: Die deutsche Politik von 1911 bis 1914* (Düsseldorf, 1969), p. 93. See also Bülow's inaugural speech before the Reichstag as state secretary of the Foreign Office (6 Dec. 1897), in Winzen, p. 68.

The manuscript sources listed below have been used in this volume. The dates given indicate the materials consulted, not the full run of the various collections. After the name of the collection is its location, for which the following abbreviations are used:

AI	Deutsches Archaeologisches Institut, Berlin-Dahlem
BA	Bundesarchiv, Koblenz
BA-MA	Bundesarchiv-Militärarchiv, Freiburg i.B.
GS	Geheimes Staatsarchiv Preussischer Kulturbesitz, Berlin-Dahlem
HHStA	Haus-, Hof- und Staatsarchiv, Vienna
PRO	Public Record Office, London and Kew Gardens
RA	The Royal Archives, Windsor Castle, Berks.

1. Albedyll Papers, GS, Repositur 52. Gen. Emil von Albedyll was the chief of the Prussian Military Cabinet from 1873 to 1888. This is a *Restnachlass*, consisting of only two letters by Albedyll (1887–88).
2. Beresford Papers, Manuscript Division, Duke University Library, Durham, N.C. Capt. Lord Charles Beresford, R.N., was a friend of Wilhelm II's. There are two letters by Wilhelm (1888–90).
3. Bismarck Papers, BA. This is a vast collection of microfilm copies of part of the archive deposited at Friedrichsruh near Hamburg; it contains the papers of the chancellor and his family. The microfilms are described in Lamar Cecil, "The Bismarck Papers," *Journal of Modern History* 47, no. 1 (1975): 505–11. Cited by reel/frame numbers. The following reels, all of which with the exception of no. FC3028 have legible frame numbers, were used.

    Nos. FC2952, 2954, 2962, 2965f, 2980, 2983, 2985–86, 3004, 3011, 3014. Correspondence to and from Prince Otto von Bismarck-Schönhausen and to and from his sons, Counts Herbert and Wilhelm von Bismarck.

    Nos. FC3018/161–669, contains Herbert's valuable memoirs bearing various titles ("Tagebuch," "Herbert Bismarcks Notizen, Herbst [18]91," "IV Notizen," "Notizen V").

    Nos. FC3028, 3030. Correspondence to and from Count Kuno von Rantzau, the chancellor's son-in-law. Nos. FC3030/580–720, contain Rantzau's important memoir entitled "Autobiographische und Andere Aufzeichnungen, 1903–1909."
4. Boetticher Papers, BA. Karl Heinrich von Boetticher was state secretary of the

Imperial Interior Office and a Prussian minister without portfolio from 1880 to 1897. This is a large collection but not of great interest for the Kaiser.

No. 19 Manuscript by Boetticher entitled "Notizen für Erinnerungen.

No. 58 Correspondence with Caprivi (1890).

5. Bosse Papers, GS, Repositur 192. Robert Bosse was an official in the Imperial Interior Office from 1881 to 1891 and later Prussian minister for culture and imperial state secretary of the Justice Office.

No. 8 Diary (1887–96).

No. 15a Notes of meetings of the Prussian ministry (1890).

No. 16 A useful memoir entitled "Zehn Jahre im Reichsamt des Innern, 1881–1891" and another entitled "Ein Jahr im Reichsjustizamt."

6. Boyd-Carpenter Papers, British Library, London. The papers of the Rt. Rev. William Boyd Carpenter, bishop of Ripon, a friend of the Kaiser.

Add. MS 46730 Diary (1889).

Add. MS 46765 Memoir entitled "Emperor William."

7. Brandenburg-Preussisches Haus Archiv (BPHA), GS. This large collection, a surviving fraction of the Hohenzollerns' papers, is briefly described in Hans Branig et al., eds., *Übersicht über die Bestände des Geheimen Staatsarchiv in Berlin-Dahlem*, 2 vols. (Cologne and Berlin, 1967), 2:265–78. This is a very miscellaneous body of material, some of it of the greatest value, some inconsequential.

Cited by Rep[ositur] and file numbers. The following folders, some from the old enumeration in Repositur 53a, others in the more recent renumbering scheme in Reposituren 53 and 192, were used:

Repositur 53a

No. 5 Letters by Wilhelm to Tsar Alexander III (1884–85).

No. 9 Memoirs by Eduard Martin, M.D., and his son August Martin, M.D., on Wilhelm's birth in 1859.

No. 20 Letters by Wilhelm to his aunt, Grand Duchess Louise of Baden (1872–78).

No. 21 Letters by Wilhelm's tutor, Georg Hinzpeter, to Wilhelm's wife Augusta Victoria (1882–87).

No. 23 Countess Eulenburg to Frau von Below (1890).

No. 25 Correspondence between Wilhelm and his future father-in-law, Duke Friedrich of Schleswig-Holstein-Sonderburg-Augustenburg (1879), and a letter by his mother to her sister, Princess Helene of Schleswig-Holstein-Sonderburg-Augustenburg (1879).

No. 29 Fragments of a diary of Wilhelm's adjutant, Maj. Gustav von Kessel (1879, 1888).

No. 31 Letters by Prince Bismarck to Wilhelm (1884–87).

No. 33 Miscellaneous notes by Wilhelm II (1927).

No. 42/1 A copy of volume 3 of Bismarck's *Gedanken und Erinnerungen* with Wilhelm's revealing marginalia.

No. 44   Notes by Prince Maximilian von Ratibor und Corvey (1901).

No. 59   Letter by Wilhelm to Admiral Hollmann (1903).

No. 63   Correspondence to and from Wilhelm, Count Bernhard von Bülow, and Prince Philipp zu Eulenburg (1900).

No. 71   Letters by Wilhelm to Countess Elizabeth von Wedel-Bérard (1885), as printed in the Munich magazine *Quick*, (Nov. 10, 1956).

No. 74   Letter by Wilhelm to his uncle, Prince Albrecht of Prussia (1888).

Repositur 53

No. 32   Letter by Wilhelm II to his grandson, Prince Wilhelm of Prussia (1931).

No. 120   Letters by Wilhelm to his uncle, Prince Christian of Schleswig-Holstein (1879).

No. 132   Wilhelm to Prince Christian of Schleswig-Holstein (1879).

No. 376   Letters by Wilhelm to King Albert of Saxony and to the Prince of Wales (1887–88).

No. 414   Letter by Wilhelm to his sister Charlotte (1874).

Repositur 192

No. 20   Notes by Wilhelm II (1934) concerning Dora von Beseler's translation into German of J. Daniel Chamier's *Fabulous Monster*.

No. 21   Naval Drawings by Wilhelm (1885).

8. Bülow Papers, BA. A sprawling and very valuable collection of papers of Bernhard von Bülow, a leading diplomat who became chancellor in 1900.

No. 13   Correspondence with his brother, Adolf von Bülow (1880–87).

No. 22   Miscellaneous reports (1889–1900).

No. 30   Notes for speeches (1897).

No. 65f   Correspondence with Herbert Bismarck (1883–85).

No. 75f   Correspondence with Philipp Eulenburg (1895–97).

No. 90f   Correspondence with Friedrich von Holstein (1895–97).

No. 92   Letters by Friedrich von Holstein to Philipp Eulenburg and Aldred von Kiderlen-Wächter (1894–97).

No. 99   Correspondence with Karl von Lindenau.

No. 100   Correspondence with Gen. Baron Walter von Löe (1883–84).

No. 106   Correspondence with Count Anton Monts.

No. 109   Correspondence with the Kaiserin Augusta Victoria (1899).

No. 110   Manuscript, undoubtedly by Bülow, entitled "Die Kaiserin Friedrich: Allgemein[e] Charakteristik ihrer

Wesen und ihrer Anschauungen." Cited by file:page number.

No. 112   Miscellaneous correspondence to and from Wilhelm II (1896–98).

No. 117   Correspondence with Friedrich von Rosen.

No. 127   Correspondence with Count Friedrich Vitzthum von Eckstädt (1890).

No. 147   Miscellaneous, undated notes on numbered *Merkblätter.*

No. 150   Merk- und Notizbücher (1892).

No. 153   Numerierte Zettel betr. 1859–1910.

Nos. 165–67,   Correspondence between the Crown Princess and
169–70   Countess Marie von Dönhoff (1885, Marie von Bülow) (1876–89).

No. 173   Letters by Wilhelm to Marie von Bülow (1878–80).

9. Delbrück Papers, BA. Papers of Hans Delbrück, a historian.

No. 22   Notes for a planned but unexecuted biography of Wilhelm II.

No. 55   Correspondence regarding a Reichstag committee (1926).

10. Einem Papers, BA-MA, N[achlass] 324. Col. Gen. Karl von Einem was a prominent military figure from the 1890s.

No. 2   Undated, untitled memoir.

11. Eulenburg Papers, BA. This is an immense collection of the greatest value, for Count Philipp zu Eulenburg (after 1900, Prince zu Eulenburg-Hertefeld) was not only a leading diplomat but also for many years Wilhelm II's most intimate friend. Almost all of the letters here, as well as much additional material, has been fastidiously edited by John C. G. Röhl in *Philipp Eulenburgs Politische Korrespondenz,* 3 vols. (Boppard, 1976–83). Some of Eulenburg's notes and miscellaneous writing have been printed in two collections edited by Johannes Haller, *Aus 50 Jahren: Erinnerungen, Tagebücher und Briefe aus dem Nachlass des Fürsten Philipp zu Eulenburg-Hertefeld* (Berlin, 1923) and *Aus dem Leben des Fürsten Philipp zu Eulenburg-Hertefeld* (Berlin, 1924), which often omit or alter important passages. There is nevertheless much vital information in Eulenburg's papers that has not been printed in any of these sources.

Nos. 1–59   Eulenburg's "Eine Preussische Familiengeschichte," a typescript consisting primarily of letters to and from Eulenburg, interspersed with diary entries and later reflections (1886–1902). Cited by folder:page number.

Nos. 63–64   Correspondence with Bernhard von Bülow (1896).

No. 71   Letters to and from Wilhelm II, Holstein, Hohenlohe, and others (1888–1900).

No. 73   Eulenburg's memoir entitled "Ich Selbst" (1900).

No. 74   Eulenburg's memoir entitled "Die Norlandsreise, 1903," divided into two parts. The second, entitled

"Zur Psyche und Politik Kaiser Wilhelms II." is much the more valuable. Cited by part:page number.

No. 75   Eulenburg's memoir entitled "Aufzeichnungen des Fürsten Philipp zu Eulenburg-Hertefeld," divided into two parts. Cited by part:page number.

No. 76   A continuation of 75, but divided into sections. Cited by section and page number.

No. 80   Eulenburg's memoir entitled "Kaiser Wilhelm II." Cited by page number.

No. 81   Eulenburg's memoir entitled "Hineinregende Persönlichkeiten," divided into two parts. This is the richest of Eulenburg's memoirs. Cited by part:page number.

12. Foreign Office (FO) Papers, PRO. This important correspondence from the British embassy in Berlin with the Foreign Office (1888–1900) is filed in series 64, vols. 1187–1655. Cited as FO/volume number.

13. Freytag Papers, Staatsbibliothek, Berlin. Gustav Freytag, a prominent literary figure, was a good friend of the Crown Prince and Princess. There are a number of letters between them in this collection, which has no file numbers.

14. German Foreign Ministry (GFM) Papers, Naval Historical Branch, Ministry of Defense (Lillie Rd., S.W.6.), London. These are microfilms of the records of the *Marinekabinett*, discovered in 1945 at Schloss Tambach in Bavaria. Of this microfilm, series 26 and 31 (1893–1900) were used. Cited as GFM 26 or 31, followed by reel/frame numbers. The Naval Historical Branch also has a printed copy of a speech by Wilhelm II in 1895 to the *Kriegs-Akademie*, filed as PG/50658.

15. Glücksburg Papers, Schlossarchiv, Glücksburg. Approximately two thousand letters, filed in series 23A, by Wilhelm's wife, Augusta Victoria, to her sister, Princess Caroline Mathilda of Schleswig-Holstein-Sonderburg-Augustenburg. They reveal the writer's unenterprising mind and are therefore disappointing on all subjects other than domestic routine. There is also a valuable memoir in three volumes by Gen. Prince Albert zu Schleswig-Holstein entitled "Einiges aus Meinem Leben," which has material on the Kaiser and German aristocratic society.

16. Harden Papers, BA. Harden was a journalist sharply critical of Wilhelm II and his regime.

No. 62/52   Correspondence with Holstein.

17. Haus-, Hof- und Staatsarchiv Papers (HHStA). The series Preussen III, vols. 131–54, contain the reports from the Austrian embassy in Berlin (1887–1900) to Foreign Ministers Counts Gustav Kálnoky von Köröspatak and Agenor von Goluchowski. There are two series, *Berichte* (B) and *Varia* (V), with a volume for each year in both series. These are very valuable papers, for the Austrian ambassadors in Berlin in this period, Counts Imre Széchenyi and Ladislaus von Szögyényi-Marich, enjoyed close relations with Wilhelm II and his highest officials. Cited by volume number followed by B (*Berichte*) or V (*Varia*).

18. Hobbs/Derby Gathorne-Hardy Papers, Corpus Christi College, Cambridge

University. A few letters of limited interest, without file numbers, by the Crown Princess to her friend Lady Constance Villiers (1858–79).

19. Hohenlohe Papers, BA. A large assortment of the former chancellor's papers, some, but by no means all, of which were published in Friedrich Curtius, ed., *Denkwürdigkeiten des Fürsten Choldwig zu Hohenlohe-Schillingsfürst*, 2 vols. (Stuttgart, 1907) and in Karl Alexander von Müller, ed., *Fürst Chlodwig zu Hohenlohe-Schillingsfürst: Denkwürdigkeiten der Reichskanzlerzeit* (Stuttgart and Berlin, 1931).

No. C.C.X.8, 9, 11–12. Diaries and Letters (1881–84). These are old file numbers, since reordered.

Miscellaneous papers: nos. 1454f, 1596–97, 1599, 1601, 1605, 1607, 1611, 1646, 1673; nos. 1860–61 contain Hohenlohe's letters to his wife (1894–97), which are of great interest.

20. Holstein Papers, National Archives, Washington, DC. This is a microfilm copy of the papers of Friedrich von Holstein, the most important counsellor in the Foreign Office in Berlin from 1888 to 1906. The originals are held in the Politisches Archiv of the Auswärtiges Amt in Bonn. The microfilms are filed in series T–120, reels 3860–61, and include Holstein's important correspondence with many leading figures in the German government. The microfilms contain some material not printed in Norman Rich and M. H. Fisher, *The Holstein Papers*, 4 vols. (Cambridge, 1955–63). Cited by reel/frame numbers.

21. Kabinetts-Archiv, HHStA. File Geheim Akten, vol. 2, contains the correspondence of Wilhelm II with the Habsburg Emperor, Franz Josef (1888–1898). The correspondence is essentially ceremonial in content.

22. Kekule von Stradonitz Papers, DAI. Reinhard Kekule, later ennobled, was a favorite professor of Wilhelm's at Bonn. File no. 18 G1/21 contains correspondence and other material by or concerning Wilhelm (1878).

23. Kiderlen-Wächter Papers, Sterling Library, Yale University. A very large but ill-arranged collection of the papers of a prominent German diplomat, Alfred von Kiderlen-Wächter. Only box 5, drawer 71, has material of value for the period before 1900. Some of the material was published in Ernst Jäckh, ed., *Kiderlen-Wächter, der Staatsmann und Mensch: Briefwechsel und Nachlass*, 2 vols. (Berlin and Leipzig, 1924). Cited by box/drawer/document numbers.

24. Kleine Erwerbungen, BA. These are miscellaneous collections, often consisting of only a single item but sometimes substantial in bulk and very valuable.

No. 104	Letter of Kaiserin Augusta Victoria to the police president of Berlin (1 Jan. 1890).
No. 271	Letter of Wilhelm II to King Albert of Saxony (6 Apr. 1888).
No. 317/2	MS by Count Siegfried von Roedern, "Manuskript über den 1. Weltkrieg."
No. 319	The papers of Robert Hepke, a lower official in the Foreign Office under Bismarck. Folder 2 is Hepke's diary for 1875 and has some useful information.
No. 708/1	"Lebenserinnerungen," by Countess Antonie zu

Eulenburg-Prassen, provides a few details on life at court.

No. 814   Adolf von Oechelhaeuser, "Erinnerungen aus meinem Leben," offers valuable details on Wilhelm's university experience at Bonn.

25. Kurowsky Papers, BA. Friedrich von Kurowsky was an official in the Reichskanzlei who attended and made important reports of meetings of the Prussian ministry.

No. 2   Correspondence between Caprivi and Wilhelm II, protocols of ministerial meetings (1891–98).

No. 3   Protocols of ministerial meetings (1888–95).

26. Lascelles Papers, PRO. Sir Frank Lascelles was ambassador in Berlin from 1896 to 1908 and enjoyed good relations with the Kaiser. Filed in FO (Foreign Office) 800, vols. 9–10, 13 (1896–1905). Cited as FO 800/volume number.

27. Loebell Papers, BA. Friedrich Wilhelm von Loebell was an official in the Reichskanzlei and a close associate of Chancellor Bülow.

Nos. 7, 9   Correspondence with Bülow.

No. 27   Typescript entitled "Erinnerungen," vol. 2. Cited by volume:page number.

28. Malet Papers. Sir Edward Malet was the rather drab British envoy in Berlin from 1884 to 1895. His papers, which are of limited interest, are divided between two collections.

Manuscript Division, Duke University, Durham, N.C.

No. A   Folders 31–35, contains Malet's letters to his mother (1885–90).

B   Folder 35, contains miscellaneous correspondence concerning the circumstances of Malet's departure from Berlin in 1895.

Public Record Office, London and Kew Gardens

FO 343   Vols. 1, 4. Correspondence to and from Malet (1885–89).

29. Morier Papers, Balliol College Library, Oxford University. Morier was a British diplomat stationed in Germany who was a good friend of Wilhelm's parents. The collection is filed in boxes having various titles. The following were used: "1864–7," "Miscellaneous Letters, 1852–1876, no. 4," "Stockmar." Some of this material was published in Mrs. Rosslyn Wemyss, ed., *Memoirs and Letters of the Rt. Hon. Sir Robert Morier, G.C.B.*, 2 vols. (London, 1911), and in Agatha Ramm, *Sir Robert Morier: Envoy and Ambassador in the Age of Imperialism* (Oxford, 1973).

30. Müller Papers, BA-MA, N[achlass] 159. Adm. Georg Alexander von Müller was chief of the Naval Cabinet from 1908 to 1918 and was a particular favorite of the Kaiser's. His papers are difficult to read but informative. Some of the material for the prewar period has been published in Walter Görlitz, ed., *Der Kaiser . . . : Aufzeichnungen des Chefs des Marinekabinetts Admiral Georg v. Müller über die Ära Wilhelms II.* (Berlin, 1965).

No. 3   Diary (1899–1910).

31. Reichskanzlei Papers, BA. A huge collection of microfiche copies of the originals in the Deutsches Zentralarchiv I in Potsdam. The following materials, cited by volume, file, and (where legible) document numbers, were used. "Akten betr. Militärstrafgerichtsordnung: Militärstrafsachen," vols. 2, 3, 6, 7.

"Akten betr. persönliche Angelegenheiten S.M. des Kaisers sowie Mitglieder des Königlichen und Kaiserlichen Hauses," vols. 2, 3, 5.

32. Rijksarchief Papers, Rijksarchief, Utrecht. These are the Kaiser's huge collection of papers at Doorn, seized by the Dutch government in 1945. Almost all the material dates from the post-1918 period but occasionally is of interest for Wilhelm II's reign. There is a very comprehensive guide in D. T. Coen, *Inventaria van het Archief van Ex-Keiser Wilhelm II tidjenszijn Verblift in Nederland, 1918–1941 (1945)* (Utrecht, 1977). Cited by folder.

No. 253   Flottenpolitik (1925).
No. 288   Correspondence with Frau Houston Stewart Chamberlain.
No. 296   Speech by Wilhelm II to Doorner Arbeits-Gemeinschaft (28 Oct. 1937).
No. 301   Wilhelm II's manuscript, "Erinnerungen an Korfu" (1924).
No. 315   Book entitled "Manual-État 1914. Hausmarschall."
No. 594   Wilhelm's school exercise books (1866–69).
No. 595   "Wilhelm II. Tagebuch als Soldaten." This is the engagement book of one of the Kaiser's adjutants and consists only of schedules of events (1888, 1892–94).
No. 646   "Bolshewismus," Wilhelm II's commentary on various press clippings (1923).

33. Rottenburg Papers, BA. Franz von Rottenburg was a friend of Wilhelm's parents.

Nos. 2, 3   Letters of Herbert Bismarck to Rottenburg (1882–88).

34. The Royal Archives (RA), Windsor Castle, Windsor, Berkshire. This is the single richest source for Wilhelm's early life. The materials dealing with him are scattered through the archive's vast holdings. Some of the materials relating to Queen Victoria and to the Crown Princess have been published in various places, notably in the edition of the Queen's letters in three series by Arthur C. Benson, Viscount Esher, and George E. Buckle, eds., *The Letters of Queen Victoria*, 9 vols. (London, 1907–1930), and in Roger Fulford's edition of those of the Crown Princess, which bear differing titles. All materials from the Royal Archives are cited as RA, followed by the folder/document numbers.

A66   A letter by Lord Salisbury to Queen Victoria on Wilhelm (1888).
A68   A letter by Lord Salisbury to the Queen on Wilhelm's treatment of his sister Sophie (1891).
A72   Correspondence to and from the Queen and Salisbury on the Kruger telegram affair (1896).

A75   Letter of Salisbury to the Queen on Anglo-German relations (1898).

Add. MS J   Wilhelm's letter to Sir Edward Sullivan (1896).

Add. MS U/32   Copies of Queen Victoria's letters to Wilhelm's mother (1863–1900).

Add. MS U/34   Correspondence dealing with Wilhelm's birth (1858–59).

Add. MS U/166   Letter of Princess Victoria Battenberg to Queen Victoria (1888).

Add. U/173   Letter by the Queen to her granddaughter, Princess Victoria of Hesse (1888).

Add. U/228   Extract of a letter by Wilhelm II to the Emperor Franz Josef (1890).

Addl. MS A/12   Letter by Sir Francis Knollys to Sir Henry Ponsonby (1889).

Addl. MS A/15   Correspondence between Queen Victoria and her son Arthur, Duke of Connaught (1878–1888) and between Wilhelm and the Prince of Wales (1891–1900).

B52   Letter by Benjamin Disraeli to Queen Victoria on his impression of Wilhelm (1879).

E56   Letters by Wilhelm and Lord George Hamilton to the Queen on the British navy (1891).

GV AA/6   Letter by Hermann Sahl to Mr. Dalton on Wilhelm's education (1876).

GV AA/43/7   Wilhelm's letter to Prince George (1879).

GV AA 68   Correspondence by Sir Henry Ponsonby; Louise, Duchess of Argyll; and others about the transfer of the Empress Friedrich's papers to England in 1901 (1924–26).

GV CC.22   Letter by Prince George of England to his aunt, Grand Duchess Augusta of Meckenburg-Strelitz, about the Kruger telegram (1896).

GV M688a   Memo by Sir Schomberg McDonnell on Wilhelm II (ca. 1914).

I51   Address by Wilhelm I to Wilhelm on his joining the Prussian army (1869).

I53   Miscellaneous correspondence on Wilhelm's marriage (1880–81).

I54   Correspondence by the Crown Prince and Princess with Queen Victoria (1883–84).

I57–59, 61–62   Correspondence to and from Queen Victoria and various British political and diplomatic figures on Wilhelm II and the state of Anglo-German relations (1888–1900). Very important.

J42   Memo for Queen Victoria by Lord Vivian on Wilhelm II (1893).

L4   Letter of Wilhelm II to the Prince of Wales on Anglo-

	German relations (1899).
L7	Salisbury to Queen Victoria on Wilhelm (1895).
O45	Correspondence by Wilhelm II, Queen Victoria, Salisbury, and others on the Kruger telegram (1896).
P5	Letter by Colonel Grierson to Sir Arthur Bigge on the Boer War (1900).
P21	Letter by Cecil Rhodes to an unnamed party on Wilhelm II and England (n.d. but ca. another letter by Cecil Rhodes to an unnamed party, 1899).
Queen Victoria's Journal	Extracts of the Queen's diaries (1859–99), cited by page number.
T9	Correspondence by Queen Victoria, Salisbury, and the Prince of Wales about the Vienna incident (1888–89).
T10	Letter by Wilhelm II to the Prince of Wales about China (1900).
Vic Add. MS A17	Letter by Wilhelm II to Louise, Duchess of Argyll, on Anglo-German relations (1906).
Vic Add. MS U143, film 4	Copies of a letter by Queen Victoria to Grand Duke Ludwig of Hesse und bei Rhein on Wilhelm's marriage (1880).
W60–61	Correspondence between Wilhelm II and the Prince of Wales on the Boer War (1899–1900).
X37	Letters of Wilhelm II to the Prince of Wales (King Edward VII) on Anglo-German relations (1900–01).
Z1–4	Correspondence between Prince Albert, the Prince Consort, and Wilhelm's mother (1858–1861).
Z5–60	The letters of Wilhelm's mother to Queen Victoria (1858–1900). These thousands of letters are the heart of the Royal Archive's materials on Wilhelm.
Z63	Miscellaneous papers concerning Wilhelm's mother's marriage (1858–59).
Z64	Letters between Wilhelm and Queen Victoria and others (1874–77).
Z65	Letters by the Crown Prince and Princess to Queen Victoria on Wilhelm's engagement (1879).
Z66	Letters between Wilhelm and Queen Victoria and others (1883–88).
Z78, 81	Letters by Wilhelm to Queen Victoria (1869–87).
Z207	Letter by the Crown Princess to Queen Victoria on Wilhelm's tutor, Hinzpeter (1877).
Z280–81	Correspondence to and from Queen Victoria, the Empress Friedrich, and the Prince of Wales concerning the Vienna incident (1888–1889).
Z498	Letter by the Prince of Wales to Queen Victoria on the Vienna incident (1889).
Z500	Correspondence between Wilhelm and Queen Victoria (1886–97).

Z505   Letter by Wilhelm to Queen Victoria (1875).

35. Salisbury Papers, Hatfield House, Hertfordshire. These are the valuable papers of Robert Arthur Talbot Gascoyne-Cecil, third marquess of Salisbury, prime minister, 1885–86, 1886–92, and 1895–1902. All papers cited in the notes are filed in Series A unless otherwise indicated. A fraction of the material has been published in Lady Gwendolen Cecil, *Life of Robert, Marquis of Salisbury*, 4 vols. (London, 1921–32).

Series A, vols. 9,
45,   These contain primarily Salisbury's correspondence
61–64, 120–22.   with the British ambassadors and military attachés in Berlin (1879–1900).
Class E.   Special correspondence with Queen Victoria, Sir Edward Malet, and Sir Frank Lascelles (1885–99).
Class G.   Salisbury's miscellaneous correspondence with Bismarck and other German dignitaries (1887–89).

36. Schiemann Papers, GS. Theodor Schiemann was a writer and Russian expert who knew Wilhelm II.
No. 85   Letter by Wilhelm to Schiemann on the Kruger affair (1919).

37. Schlitz von Görtz Papers, Hessisches Staatsarchiv, Darmstadt. This contains the very interesting correspondence of Wilhelm's teacher, Dr. Georg Hinzpeter, with various members of the Schlitz family, whom he also served as tutor. All documents cited are from series F23A.
No. 217   Hinzpeter's letters to Count Carl Schlitz genannt von Görtz (1867–79).
No. 352   Hinzpeter's letters to Countess Anna Schlitz von Görtz (1874–79).
No. 383/15   Hinzpeter's letters to Count Emil Schlitz von Görtz (1875–90).

38. Schöne Papers, DAI. Richard Schöne was an academician at Bonn and friend of Wilhelm's teacher Reinhard Kekule. There are no file numbers, and only a letter by Kekule to Schöne on Wilhelm's education (1879) is of use.

39. Senden Papers, BA-MA N[achlass] 160. Adm. Baron Gustav von Senden und Bibran was chief of the Naval Cabinet from 1889 to 1906, and his large collection of papers is important.
No. 9   Miscellaneous correspondence (1893–95).
No. 11   A memoir entitled "Notizen" (1888).

40. Thimme Papers, BA. Friedrich Thimme was a historian whose research led to correspondence with a number of figures of importance under Wilhelm II.
No. 16   Letters of Lt. Gen. Albert von Mutius on Friedrich III (1934), and a memoir, "Aus den Erinnerungen des verstorbenen Staathalters von Dallwitz."

41. Tirpitz Papers, BA-MA N[achlass] 253. This very large collection of the papers of Grand Adm. Alfred von Tirpitz, state secretary of the Imperial Naval Office from 1897 to 1916, is disappointingly thin on Wilhelm II prior to 1900, indicating the marginal role the Kaiser played in the early stages of naval planning.

No. 4   "Flottengesetz von 1898."

No. 5   "Akten betr. die Novelle von 1900."

No. 8   "Privat, = ganz geheim." Correspondence with Wilhelm II and others (1909).

No. 16   Letter by General von Caprivi to Tirpitz (1889) on Wilhelm II and the army.

No. 20–21   "Entwicklung der Marine" (1901–05).

No. 27b   Report by Prince Wilhelm to his grandfather, Kaiser Wilhelm I, on the naval installations at Portsmouth, England (12 Nov. 1880).

No. 100   "Privatakten, Krieg 1914/15, ganz geheim." This contains an undated memo by Tirpitz on his relations with Wilhelm II before 1897.

No. 114   Letter by Tirpitz's son (20 Feb. 1918) on his father's view of England's economic development.

No. 200   Correspondence with Capt. Wilhelm Büchsel (1898).

No. 203   Correspondence with Count August zu Eulenburg (1916).

No. 207   Correspondence with Capt. Georg von [1900] Müller (1889–96).

No. 208   Correspondence with Adm. Baron Gustav von Senden und Bibran (1892–94).

42. Treutler Papers, in the possession of his granddaughter, Baronin Anne-Katrin von Ledebur, Schwenningdorf, Westphalia. Karl Georg von Treutler was an army friend of Wilhelm's and later a prominent diplomat. His papers consist of a long memoir written between 1922 and 1930, most of which has been published in Karl-Heinz Janssen, ed., *Die Graue Exzellenz. Zwischen Staatsräson und Vassallentreue: Aus den Papieren des kaiserlichen Gesandten Karl Georg von Treutler* (Frankfurt, 1971). Cited by chapter and page numbers.

43. Waldersee Papers, BA-MA N[achlass] 182. These papers of Gen. Count Alfred Waldersee are a small fragment of the much larger collection in the Deutsches Zentralarchiv, Merseburg, to which I was denied access.

No. 17   A letter by Waldersee to General von Bartenwerffer on army affairs (1888).

44. Waldersee-Lee Papers, Houghton Library, Harvard University. A largely unimportant collection of papers of Countess Marie von Waldersee, wife of the general, and her American relatives. Much of the material has been published in J. Alton Smith, *A View of the Spree* (New York, 1962). Folder 2 has some information on Wilhelm's wedding in 1881.

45. Wied Papers, Fürstlich Wiedisches Archiv, Neuwied. A letter by Wilhelm to Prince Wilhelm zu Wied (21 Feb. 1888).

46. Philipp Zorn Papers, BA. Zorn was tutor to several of Wilhelm II's sons and an acquaintance of Bismarck.

No. 1   "Lebenserinnerungen."

No. 26   Miscellaneous correspondence.

Index